Lecture Notes in Computer Science 12762

More information about this subseries at http://www.springer.com/series/7409

Masaaki Kurosu (Ed.)

Human-Computer Interaction

Theory, Methods and Tools

Thematic Area, HCI 2021
Held as Part of the 23rd HCI International Conference, HCII 2021
Virtual Event, July 24–29, 2021
Proceedings, Part I

 Springer

Editor
Masaaki Kurosu
The Open University of Japan
Chiba, Japan

ISSN 0302-9743 ISSN 1611-3349 (electronic)
Lecture Notes in Computer Science
ISBN 978-3-030-78461-4 ISBN 978-3-030-78462-1 (eBook)
https://doi.org/10.1007/978-3-030-78462-1

LNCS Sublibrary: SL3 – Information Systems and Applications, incl. Internet/Web, and HCI

Foreword

Human-Computer Interaction (HCI) is acquiring an ever-increasing scientific and industrial importance, and having more impact on people's everyday life, as an ever-growing number of human activities are progressively moving from the physical to the digital world. This process, which has been ongoing for some time now, has been dramatically accelerated by the COVID-19 pandemic. The HCI International (HCII) conference series, held yearly, aims to respond to the compelling need to advance the exchange of knowledge and research and development efforts on the human aspects of design and use of computing systems.

The 23rd International Conference on Human-Computer Interaction, HCI International 2021 (HCII 2021), was planned to be held at the Washington Hilton Hotel, Washington DC, USA, during July 24–29, 2021. Due to the COVID-19 pandemic and with everyone's health and safety in mind, HCII 2021 was organized and run as a virtual conference. It incorporated the 21 thematic areas and affiliated conferences listed on the following page.

A total of 5222 individuals from academia, research institutes, industry, and governmental agencies from 81 countries submitted contributions, and 1276 papers and 241 posters were included in the proceedings to appear just before the start of the conference. The contributions thoroughly cover the entire field of HCI, addressing major advances in knowledge and effective use of computers in a variety of application areas. These papers provide academics, researchers, engineers, scientists, practitioners, and students with state-of-the-art information on the most recent advances in HCI. The volumes constituting the set of proceedings to appear before the start of the conference are listed in the following pages.

The HCI International (HCII) conference also offers the option of 'Late Breaking Work' which applies both for papers and posters, and the corresponding volume(s) of the proceedings will appear after the conference. Full papers will be included in the 'HCII 2021 - Late Breaking Papers' volumes of the proceedings to be published in the Springer LNCS series, while 'Poster Extended Abstracts' will be included as short research papers in the 'HCII 2021 - Late Breaking Posters' volumes to be published in the Springer CCIS series.

The present volume contains papers submitted and presented in the context of the Human-Computer Interaction (HCI 2021) thematic area of HCII 2021. I would like to thank the Chair, Masaaki Kurosu, for his invaluable contribution to its organization and the preparation of the proceedings, as well as the members of the Program Board for their contributions and support. This year, the HCI thematic area has focused on topics related to theoretical and methodological approaches to HCI, UX evaluation methods and techniques, emotional and persuasive design, psychological and cognitive aspects of interaction, novel interaction techniques, human-robot interaction, UX and technology acceptance studies, and digital wellbeing, as well as the impact of the COVID-19 pandemic and social distancing on interaction, communication, and work.

I would also like to thank the Program Board Chairs and the members of the Program Boards of all thematic areas and affiliated conferences for their contribution towards the highest scientific quality and overall success of the HCI International 2021 conference.

This conference would not have been possible without the continuous and unwavering support and advice of Gavriel Salvendy, founder, General Chair Emeritus, and Scientific Advisor. For his outstanding efforts, I would like to express my appreciation to Abbas Moallem, Communications Chair and Editor of HCI International News.

July 2021   Constantine Stephanidis

HCI International 2021 Thematic Areas and Affiliated Conferences

Thematic Areas

- HCI: Human-Computer Interaction
- HIMI: Human Interface and the Management of Information

Affiliated Conferences

- EPCE: 18th International Conference on Engineering Psychology and Cognitive Ergonomics
- UAHCI: 15th International Conference on Universal Access in Human-Computer Interaction
- VAMR: 13th International Conference on Virtual, Augmented and Mixed Reality
- CCD: 13th International Conference on Cross-Cultural Design
- SCSM: 13th International Conference on Social Computing and Social Media
- AC: 15th International Conference on Augmented Cognition
- DHM: 12th International Conference on Digital Human Modeling and Applications in Health, Safety, Ergonomics and Risk Management
- DUXU: 10th International Conference on Design, User Experience, and Usability
- DAPI: 9th International Conference on Distributed, Ambient and Pervasive Interactions
- HCIBGO: 8th International Conference on HCI in Business, Government and Organizations
- LCT: 8th International Conference on Learning and Collaboration Technologies
- ITAP: 7th International Conference on Human Aspects of IT for the Aged Population
- HCI-CPT: 3rd International Conference on HCI for Cybersecurity, Privacy and Trust
- HCI-Games: 3rd International Conference on HCI in Games
- MobiTAS: 3rd International Conference on HCI in Mobility, Transport and Automotive Systems
- AIS: 3rd International Conference on Adaptive Instructional Systems
- C&C: 9th International Conference on Culture and Computing
- MOBILE: 2nd International Conference on Design, Operation and Evaluation of Mobile Communications
- AI-HCI: 2nd International Conference on Artificial Intelligence in HCI

List of Conference Proceedings Volumes Appearing Before the Conference

1. LNCS 12762, Human-Computer Interaction: Theory, Methods and Tools (Part I), edited by Masaaki Kurosu
2. LNCS 12763, Human-Computer Interaction: Interaction Techniques and Novel Applications (Part II), edited by Masaaki Kurosu
3. LNCS 12764, Human-Computer Interaction: Design and User Experience Case Studies (Part III), edited by Masaaki Kurosu
4. LNCS 12765, Human Interface and the Management of Information: Information Presentation and Visualization (Part I), edited by Sakae Yamamoto and Hirohiko Mori
5. LNCS 12766, Human Interface and the Management of Information: Information-rich and Intelligent Environments (Part II), edited by Sakae Yamamoto and Hirohiko Mori
6. LNAI 12767, Engineering Psychology and Cognitive Ergonomics, edited by Don Harris and Wen-Chin Li
7. LNCS 12768, Universal Access in Human-Computer Interaction: Design Methods and User Experience (Part I), edited by Margherita Antona and Constantine Stephanidis
8. LNCS 12769, Universal Access in Human-Computer Interaction: Access to Media, Learning and Assistive Environments (Part II), edited by Margherita Antona and Constantine Stephanidis
9. LNCS 12770, Virtual, Augmented and Mixed Reality, edited by Jessie Y. C. Chen and Gino Fragomeni
10. LNCS 12771, Cross-Cultural Design: Experience and Product Design Across Cultures (Part I), edited by P. L. Patrick Rau
11. LNCS 12772, Cross-Cultural Design: Applications in Arts, Learning, Well-being, and Social Development (Part II), edited by P. L. Patrick Rau
12. LNCS 12773, Cross-Cultural Design: Applications in Cultural Heritage, Tourism, Autonomous Vehicles, and Intelligent Agents (Part III), edited by P. L. Patrick Rau
13. LNCS 12774, Social Computing and Social Media: Experience Design and Social Network Analysis (Part I), edited by Gabriele Meiselwitz
14. LNCS 12775, Social Computing and Social Media: Applications in Marketing, Learning, and Health (Part II), edited by Gabriele Meiselwitz
15. LNAI 12776, Augmented Cognition, edited by Dylan D. Schmorrow and Cali M. Fidopiastis
16. LNCS 12777, Digital Human Modeling and Applications in Health, Safety, Ergonomics and Risk Management: Human Body, Motion and Behavior (Part I), edited by Vincent G. Duffy
17. LNCS 12778, Digital Human Modeling and Applications in Health, Safety, Ergonomics and Risk Management: AI, Product and Service (Part II), edited by Vincent G. Duffy

38. CCIS 1420, HCI International 2021 Posters - Part II, edited by Constantine Stephanidis, Margherita Antona, and Stavroula Ntoa
39. CCIS 1421, HCI International 2021 Posters - Part III, edited by Constantine Stephanidis, Margherita Antona, and Stavroula Ntoa

http://2021.hci.international/proceedings

Human-Computer Interaction Thematic Area (HCI 2021)

Program Board Chair: **Masaaki Kurosu,** *The Open University of Japan, Japan*

- Salah Ahmed, Norway
- Valdecir Becker, Brazil
- Nimish Biloria, Australia
- Maurizio Caon, Switzerland
- Zhigang Chen, China

- Yu-Hsiu Hung, Taiwan
- Yi Ji, China
- Alexandros Liapis, Greece
- Hiroshi Noborio, Japan
- Vinícius Segura, Brazil

The full list with the Program Board Chairs and the members of the Program Boards of all thematic areas and affiliated conferences is available online at:

http://www.hci.international/board-members-2021.php

HCI International 2022

The 24th International Conference on Human-Computer Interaction, HCI International 2022, will be held jointly with the affiliated conferences at the Gothia Towers Hotel and Swedish Exhibition & Congress Centre, Gothenburg, Sweden, June 26 – July 1, 2022. It will cover a broad spectrum of themes related to Human-Computer Interaction, including theoretical issues, methods, tools, processes, and case studies in HCI design, as well as novel interaction techniques, interfaces, and applications. The proceedings will be published by Springer. More information will be available on the conference website: http://2022.hci.international/:

General Chair
Prof. Constantine Stephanidis
University of Crete and ICS-FORTH
Heraklion, Crete, Greece
Email: general_chair@hcii2022.org

http://2022.hci.international/

Contents – Part I

UX Evaluation Methods, Techniques and Tools

Emotional and Persuasive Design

Contents – Part II

Human-Robot Interaction

Digital Wellbeing

Contents – Part III

User Experience and Technology Acceptance Studies

HCI, Social Distancing, Information, Communication and Work

HCI Theory, Education and Practice

Human-Computer Natural Interaction Design Practice Based on Unconscious Design Concept

Anyuan Wang and Junnan Ye[✉]

East China University of Science and Technology, Shanghai 200237, China

Abstract. Compared with the traditional industrial design, human-computer interaction design is a relatively young field. Throughout its decades of application history, the core of human-computer interaction design is from technology to business, and then from business to users themselves. As a change of human-computer interaction mode, human-computer natural interaction studies the interaction between human and machine —— "let computer adapt to human". There are still some defects in the current human-computer natural interaction. The design practice is based on the research of user's unconscious behavior, combined with the design framework of pervasive computing, to explore a kind of human-computer natural interaction design concept model to adapt to user's behavior habits. The purpose is to realize the cognitive elderly's instinctive interaction with the intelligent voice bracelet, meet the deep emotional and psychological needs of the cognitive elderly, establish a more consistent psychological logic of the cognitive elderly, make the product better serve the cognitive elderly, and bring new inspiration for the future research of human-computer interaction.

Keywords: Unconscious behavior · Human-computer interaction · Cognitive elderly

1 Introduction

1.1 Human-Computer Natural Interaction

In 1983, Stuart K. card, Thomas P. Moran and Allen Newell used the term "human computer interaction" for the first time in "The Psychology of Human-Computer Interaction" [1]. Association for Computing Machinery (ACM) defines human-computer interaction as "focusing on the research, design, evaluation and discipline of interactive computing system for human use, and cooperating with surrounding major phenomena". Professor Alan Dix of Birmingham University defines it as "a discipline that studies people, computers and the way they interact". "The purpose of learning human-computer interaction is to make computer technology better serve human beings" [2]. John M. Carroll of Penn State University thought that "Human computer interaction refers to the study and practice of usability. It is about understanding and building software and technology that users are willing to use, and discovering the effectiveness of products when using them [3]." Generally speaking, the core connotation of these three definitions is consistent - the

© Springer Nature Switzerland AG 2021
M. Kurosu (Ed.): HCII 2021, LNCS 12762, pp. 3–15, 2021.
https://doi.org/10.1007/978-3-030-78462-1_1

relationship between human and computer is the primary concern of human-computer interaction.

The development of human-computer interaction is mainly from the "computer centered" design idea that people adapt to computer to the "user centered" design idea that computers adapt to people. Human computer interaction has experienced TCD (technology centered design), BCD (business centered design), and UCD (user centered design). The concept of natural user interface also leads to a new research direction in the field of human-computer interaction - human-computer natural interaction. Human computer natural interaction design is an interdisciplinary subject of "user centered" Research on natural communication and interaction between system and users. It studies the dialogue between human and machine, endows machine with intelligence, and makes machine become an advanced intelligent tool for human service [4]. The essence of human-computer natural interaction is the study of user's instinctive behavior, and its core design concept is to make the interaction cater to the most basic behavior habits of users, perceive the user situation, and actively adapt to the needs of users.

At present, most of the human-computer interaction practice is still in the GUI stage, and there are still some defects in the application of human-computer natural interaction. For example, the efficiency improvement of AR interaction is limited, and the long-time operation of gesture interface in the air does not conform to ergonomics and behavior habits.

1.2 Unconscious Behavior Design

Japanese industrial design master Naoto Kanazawa first put forward the design concept of "unconscious design", also known as "intuitive design", that is, "turning unconscious actions into visible things" [5]. The essence of unconscious design is that designers observe and explore people's unconscious behaviors in daily life, and transform these unconscious behaviors into visible designs. In other words, "unconscious design" means that the designer realizes the user's unconscious behavior through conscious design.

Jane Fulton Suri, director of human factors engineering at IDEO design company, classifies human unconscious behavior or intuitive behavior. In the design process of the company, she stipulated that the designer must observe and record the original natural state of the design object, so as to help analyze and understand the design object and the unconscious behavior of people who use the design object, and provide the most powerful basis for design [6].

2 Research Summary

2.1 The Theoretical Background of Unconscious Behavior Design

Sigmund Freud's Iceberg Theory of unconsciousness is the definition of unconsciousness. He put forward the famous "Iceberg Theory" in "Studies on hysteria" [7]: "human psychology includes conscious and unconscious phenomena, and unconscious phenomena can be divided into preconsciousness and subconsciousness" (including repressed unconsciousness and latent unconsciousness).

Swiss psychologist Carl Jung put forward the theory of "prototype collective uncon-sciousness" [8]. He thinks that the whole mind has three levels: consciousness, individual unconsciousness and collective unconsciousness. Jung found a general rule that instinc-tive activities bring about self perception, which we later call "intuition". He defined instinct as "the purposive impulse when executing a highly complex action", and intu-ition as "the unconscious and purposive comprehension of a highly complex situation". Jung also found that human beings have some innate archetypes reflecting perception and comprehension, that is, instinctive self portraits, or primitive images. Every instinct has its own prototype, which constitutes the collective unconsciousness.

Jacques Lacan, a French psychologist, creatively interprets Freud's theory of uncon-sciousness with the help of the research results of modern linguistics. He believes that "the unconscious is either condensed by metaphor or transferred by metonymy [9]." Lacan divides unconscious language structure into the relationship among self, others and other things.

In his masterpiece design "psychology: emotional design" [10], Donald Norman expounds the important position and function of emotion in design on the basis of instinct, behavior and reflection. He believes: "In an ideal situation, users' experience of products and goods should be based on behavioral design to realize the harmonious unity of instinctive design and reflective design." Norman divides the process of brain processing information into three levels: (a) the first is the instinct level, which is a part of the most basic protection mechanism of human emotional system, and can make a rapid judgment of the environment; (b) the second is the behavior level, which is the foundation of learning ability, and is triggered in an appropriate mode; (c) the third is the reflection level, which is the foundation of conscious cognition, and develops deep understanding and production Reasoning and conscious decision making.

James J. Gibson, an American psychologist, put forward the concept of "affordabil-ity" [11] in 1977. There are two components of affordability: user's own conditions and product characteristics, which have an impact on user's behavior and stimulate or suppress user's behavior desire.

According to the above theory, a large part of human behavior belongs to unconscious behavior. At present, it is a relatively new research field to guide the design process based on the observed human unconscious behavior.

2.2 Pervasive Computing

In 1991, mark Weiser published the article "the computer for the 21st century" [12] in Scientific American and formally proposed ubiquitous computing. Mark Weiser pointed out: "The most discovered technologies are those that appear. They weave them into the fabric of every day life until they are independent from it."

Paul Dourish thinks about the problem of "how do technologies appear into the background", and analyzes it from two aspects of location and size [13]. The author divides computers into three sizes: inch-scale (the size of a post it note), foot-scale (the size of a piece of paper/book/magazine), yard-scale (The size of a blackboard). Then the author puts forward three basic sizes of pervasive computers: Tab/Badge, Pad and Liveboard. Paul Dourish believes that the most important thing of pervasive computing is to help people overcome the problem of information overload, which means that computers will adapt to the human way of life rather than vice versa.

According to the above research, pervasive computing characterized by unconscious behavior of computing users is an important development direction of computer technology in the future. The goal of pervasive computing is to input the user's behavior and state into a command that the computer can understand and operate through appropriate metaphor, and output the computer's behavior and state into a feedback that people can understand and operate. Its important contents include natural interaction interface, context aware application, automatic capture, record and analysis of user's life experience, etc. [14]. The efficiency and naturalness of human-computer interaction has become one of the core issues in pervasive computing applications. Multi-channel interaction (MCUI), as an interactive way to adapt to the aiot (Artificial Intelligence & Internet of things) era, makes full use of users' different sensory channels to make interaction more natural and efficient, and becomes an important part of pervasive computing human-computer interaction mode.

MIT Oxygen Project (pervasive human centered Computing) [15] combines specific user and system technologies to achieve human centered pervasive computing. Voice and visual technology enables users to communicate with oxygen, thus saving a lot of time and energy. Automation, personalized knowledge access and collaboration technologies can help users perform various tasks in the way they like. Oxygen Project presents many technical challenges (see Fig. 1).

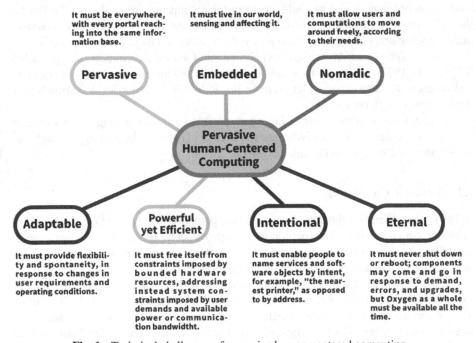

Fig. 1. Technical challenges of pervasive human-centered computing

Professor Dong Shihai [16] analyzed the cognitive characteristics of users in pervasive computing environment from the perspective of cognitive psychology, fully considered that the multi-channel interaction with context participation conforms to the cognitive characteristics of users in pervasive computing environment, and constituted the main structure of pervasive computing human-computer interaction framework (see Fig. 2). He summarized the characteristics of the framework as Multimodal + Context sensitive. In this pervasive computing human-computer interaction framework model, the channel identification module is responsible for calling different sub modules to identify the information input by users through different channels. The context generation module is responsible for perceiving and generating context information. The sources of context mainly include three aspects: (a) Natural environment and device characteristics of user's subjective implicit input; (b) User information input through channel identification module, which is the most concentrated embodiment of user intention and personalized factors, is the main basis of user context learning; (c) The historical information of context recording module is saved after all contexts are formed. Regular information can be extracted from these records to mine meaningful contexts. It is worth noting that the framework model is not a specific architecture, but an abstract description of interaction characteristics, key components and control process. How to implement it depends on the specific situation and user needs.

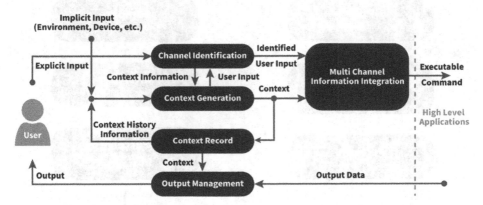

Fig. 2. Human computer interaction framework for pervasive computing

3 Human Computer Natural Interaction Design Framework Based on Unconscious Behavior

Human computer natural interaction design is an interdisciplinary subject which studies the natural interaction between computer and user, including the research of user's instinct level, behavior level and psychological level. The design framework of human-computer natural interaction based on unconscious behavior needs to be built on the user centered design thinking.

Donald Norman put forward the seven stage theory of behavior: goal, plan, confirmation, execution, perception, interpretation and contrast [17] (see Fig. 3). The theory focuses on the process of interaction between user and machine, but lacks the research of user mental model. The cognition and emotion of user in each link may deviate from the system model.

Kenneth Craik, a Scottish psychologist, first proposed Mental Model in 1943. Later, cognitive psychologists did further research. Mental model is people's imagination model of interaction object and inner unconscious cognitive thinking. Susan Carey [18] mentioned that mental model is people's understanding of the surrounding things and environment, which is based on intuitive perception and incomplete facts and past experience. In other words, mental model is the internal cognitive structure of the user, which affects the user's behavior and how to solve the problem.

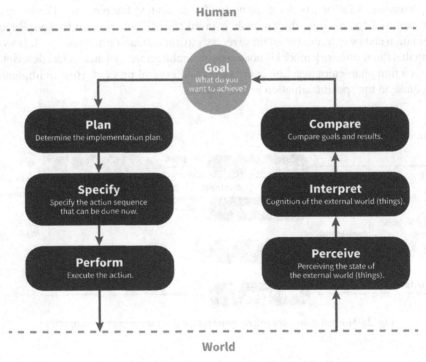

Fig. 3. Donald Norman's seven stage theory of action

According to the five elements of user experience proposed by Jesse James Garrett [19], Metaphor is an important design method for content definition, operation realization and feedback of product function, and its starting layer is mental model. Metaphor Design based on unconscious behavior is based on the research and analysis of user cognitive model and embodied experience to make the conceptual model of design product adapt to and fit the user's mental model, so that users can spontaneously associate and expect the functional results, so as to achieve the goal of behavior guidance and behavior realization of product unconscious design.

The problem of user's unconscious behavior is the problem of user's mental model and behavior design. The construction of design framework needs to analyze the user's instinctive behavior and mental model, introduce the universal computing human-computer interaction framework mentioned above, and get the human-computer natural interaction design framework based on unconscious behavior (see Fig. 4). The application of this design framework must be combined with the user's mental model and actual behavior in a specific scene.

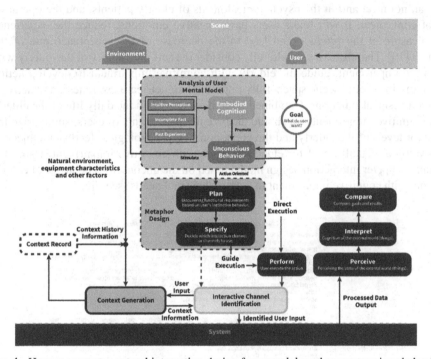

Fig. 4. Human computer natural interaction design framework based on unconscious behavior

4   Design Practice of Intelligent Voice Bracelet for Cognitive Aging

According to the correlation between cognitive elderly mental model and unconscious behavior, this paper studies the physical function and logical function of intelligent voice Bracelet products according to the interaction behavior of user mental model, and constructs the human-computer interaction design model of intelligent voice Bracelet products. As a basis for decision-making, the design practice aims to encourage elderly patients with cognitive impairment to actively participate in daily activities, give them self-care opportunities as much as possible, improve the self-care ability and self-esteem of the elderly with dementia, ensure their independence in life, reduce their depression on cognitive aging, meet their emotional needs, and promote the development of elderly patients with cognitive impairment The aging of the body tends to be healthy.

4.1   Mental Model Analysis of the Elderly with Cognitive Impairment

Cognitive disorder refers to the damage of perception, memory, thinking, reasoning and other cognitive functions caused by local brain tissue lesions or damage. Patients can still take care of themselves, work, study and have normal social interaction with others. Patients in some areas of cognitive decline, belongs to cognitive decline. The elderly with cognitive aging are in a sensitive and vulnerable period in emotion, and their psychological endurance has declined. In the process of human-computer interaction, if it can not meet and fit the psychological needs of elderly patients, and the operation is not convenient, it will make users have negative emotions, reduce the experience and pleasure of the product, and lead to the decrease of the acceptance rate of the product [19]. Therefore, we should fully consider the self-care ability of the elderly with cognitive impairment, guide the elderly with cognitive impairment to develop action autonomy in specific scene space, fully improve their self-care awareness, and actively use their residual functions. Combined with the obstacles in the daily life of the elderly with cognitive impairment, we should analyze the pain points of users, summarize the behavior levels of the elderly and the corresponding psychological feedback Objective to develop a mental model for elderly patients with cognitive impairment. Using the human-computer interaction design model based on the unconscious behavior of elderly patients with cognitive impairment to extract their real needs (see Fig. 5).

	Sence 1 : Home	Sence 2 : Outdoor
Users' Behavior Habits Based on Their Own Cognition	Forgetting how to use household appliances and appliances in daily life and not seeking help for fear of self-esteem damage; Unable to judge the day and night changes, do not sleep at night; Hide what you think is important, and then repeatedly look for what you have forgotten; Forget family and friends, social disconnection; Often anxious, wandering aimlessly, constantly standing up and sitting down, repeating aimless actions.	Forget to bring money or have a vague concept of money when taking transportation or shopping; Lack of space-time positioning ability, lost direction and lost; Tend to turn off voice prompts in public places, and I don't like to attract other people's attention.
Unconscious/Instinctive Behavior	Subconscious actions with independent control over personal living activities (e.g. when to get up, when to fall asleep, personal hygiene, etc.); Looking for and getting close to familiar things; Explore and be curious about new things; Learn how to operate the bracelet; Find the operation key; Control operation key.	Subconsciously use the way of bus card / mobile phone payment to complete the payment operation; Look for familiar roads or buildings.
User Demand	To help the elderly recall the use of household appliances in their daily life and improve their memory skills; Remind of day and night changes and help sleep; Record and remind the old people what they think is important; Record information about family and friends; Emotional interaction with the elderly can relieve anxiety;	Provide the function of intelligent payment; Real time location of the elderly; Call the police when the old man falls down; Provide the elderly as the identity of patients with cognitive impairment, record the information and home address of the elderly, let the police and other personnel pay attention to and give help.
Functions provided by the product that users need	Speech recognition; Voice prompt; Intelligent atmosphere lamp; The music plays regularly; Audio memos; Camera face recognition; Entertainment Interaction (guessing puzzles, playing music drama, etc.).	NFC identifies payment; Positioning service; Alarm prompt; Identification code identification.

Fig. 5.   Mental model of elderly patients with cognitive impairment

According to the mental model of patients with cognitive impairment, the design method of metaphor is used to construct the human-computer natural interaction design model of intelligent voice Bracelet products (see Fig. 6).

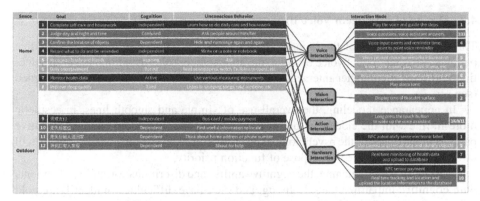

Fig. 6. Human computer natural interaction design model of intelligent voice bracelet

4.2　Human Computer Natural Interaction Mode of Intelligent Voice Bracelet

The physiological and psychological state of elderly patients with cognitive impairment at different times will have a potential impact on their unconscious behavior. As a health care product to help patients with normal daily life and maintain health, combined with the different psychological feedback and user demand levels in users' unconscious behavior, this paper summarizes the multi-channel and multi sensory interaction mode of intelligent voice bracelet.

One of the design cores of human-computer natural interaction is to save energy, not only the physical strength of the user's body movement, but also the mental power of the user's brain. Therefore, in the design process, designers need to pay attention to energy consumption, pay attention to many unconscious human-computer interaction behaviors, establish and screen different levels of user needs according to the pain points of cognitive patients, avoid the interaction complexity caused by unnecessary implicit needs, and simplify and standardize the complex things on the premise of meeting the basic needs of users, the standard process of things and the process of things automation. In the multi-channel interaction technology based on pervasive computing, voice interaction is one of the most important interaction channels in the user interface of pervasive computing system. This is not only because voice interaction is the most natural and in line with human perception, but also because it can solve the problem of channel competition to the maximum extent. Compared with other interactive channels, the feature of voice is strong independence. It does not need to cooperate with hands and eyes, and does not hinder other interactive channels. It can perform interactive tasks, which is in line with the cognitive characteristics of users.

The design practice focuses on the human-computer natural interaction design under the unconscious behavior, establishes the natural interaction mode of intelligent voice Bracelet products through the human-computer interaction design model, distinguishes the function and interaction of intelligent voice bracelet, simplifies and even automates, and forms the active, convenient, safe and reasonable multi-channel and multi sensory interaction experience of cognitive patients in the use process.

4.3 Design of Intelligent Voice Bracelet

Through the analysis of the human-computer natural interaction model of cognitive patients using intelligent voice bracelet, the appearance, color matching, material selection and human-computer interaction mode of intelligent voice bracelet are designed (see Fig. 7).

In appearance modeling, the overall use of simple and smooth lines, in aesthetic more in line with the elderly group, in line with ergonomics, more close to cognitive patients are not used to the psychological needs of complex content, visual elements will be simplified, to achieve the purpose of function priority.

In terms of color matching, the cognitive ability and discrimination ability of patients with cognitive impairment are declining, and they have difficulties in identifying cold light colors such as purple, blue and green. They tend to regard white as yellow and cyan as black [20]. Taking into account the special physiological and psychological needs of patients with cognitive impairment, we use strong contrast warm colors, orange as the main color, yellow and black as the auxiliary color. The effective color matching design can stimulate the psychology of patients with cognitive impairment to a certain extent, so that patients can maintain a happy mood.

In terms of material selection, the watch strap adopts TPU thermoplastic silica gel certified by professional anti-allergy test; the screen adopts TFT display screen, and the front cover plate adopts high-end mold insert injection molding process and anti-fingerprint coating, with glossy surface, anti-fingerprint and scratch resistance; meanwhile, the waterproof and breathable film is used to solve the waterproof performance of intelligent bracelet.

In the aspect of human-computer interaction, the human-computer interaction mode of intelligent voice Bracelet based on human-computer natural interaction model is multi-channel and multi sensory interaction experience, namely voice interaction, visual interaction and tactile interaction, as well as hardware interaction hidden behind the interface.

In the aspect of voice interaction: (a) Family members upload the things or knowledge they need to remember to the database through voice recording on the app on the mobile phone, and paste them on the target objects together with the use of electronic tags. The elderly with cognitive impairment can automatically recognize and play the corresponding recordings through the bracelet close to the electronic tags. This function ensures that the patients with cognitive impairment maintain their life skills and memory, and helps to enhance the independence of independent life. (b) Built in voice assistant database, can consult the weather, memo event reminder, entertainment, hypnosis and so on. (c) Through family recording, we can form positive and good interaction with patients to meet the emotional needs of the elderly.

In terms of visual interaction: the time on the surface of the bracelet is displayed on the screen to enhance the time concept of the elderly with cognitive impairment and remind them of the changes of day and night.

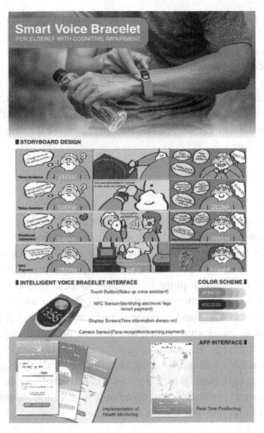

Fig. 7. Design scheme of intelligent voice bracelet for the elderly with cognitive impairment

In terms of tactile interaction: Based on the analysis of unconscious behavior, the elderly have instinctive behavior to touch the strong contrast color button. Therefore, according to the visual stimulation of strong contrast and imitating button shape, set a touch button and press it for 3 s to wake up the voice assistant function with the highest utilization rate.

In the aspect of hardware interaction, the biggest feature is that it is hidden behind the interface and triggered automatically: (a) At the moment of wearing the bracelet, the bracelet automatically senses the skin temperature, automatically starts the machine and starts the Bluetooth connection database to upload data in real time. (b) Through the built-in sensor, the bracelet can monitor and update the elderly's blood pressure, blood oxygen, heart rate, ECG and other health data in real time, and synchronously upload them to the app background for data analysis and conversion into visual reports, which can be viewed by family members remotely. (c) The bracelet has an abnormal alarm function, so that patients can get 24-h health and safety protection. (d) The bracelet has the function of location tracking, real-time monitoring the location information of the elderly, to prevent accidents such as lost. (e) The built-in NFC technology simplifies and automates the online payment process. The characteristics of spontaneity, high efficiency and low learning cost adapt to the internal needs of the elderly with cognitive impairment.

After the preliminary analysis, the product design maximizes to meet the needs of users, reduces unnecessary function points, and increases the way of interactive experience. Through this design practice, it is proved that the human-computer interaction design model of intelligent voice Bracelet product is effective. Through this product, cognitive aging elderly groups can actively, conveniently, safely and reasonably carry out their daily life, at the same time, relieve their psychological pressure, and get a good user experience.

5 Conclusion

The design of human-computer natural interaction based on unconscious behavior makes the product interaction more human and reasonable by studying the user behavior level and mental model. In this paper, starting from the user's unconscious behavior, based on the extracted user behavior level, the pervasive computing design model is cited, and according to the human-computer interaction process and user mental model, a human-computer natural interaction design model based on unconscious behavior is summarized. Then through the specific design practice, taking the elderly patients with cognitive impairment as the design object, through the design of a portable intelligent voice bracelet which can be positioned and monitored, the voice prompt can be realized, and the daily skill memory and daily health monitoring of the patients with cognitive impairment can be strengthened, which verifies the effectiveness of the design model and maximizes the user experience. It provides new research ideas and design methods for the future human-computer interaction design.

References

1. Card, S.K., Moran, T.P., Newell, A.: The Psychology of Human-Computer Interaction. 1st edn. L. Erlbaum Associates Inc., Mahwah (1983)
2. Dix, A., Finlay, J., Abowd, G., et al.: Human-Computer Interaction. 1st edn. Prentice-Hall, Inc., Hoboken (1997)
3. Carroll, J.M.: Human-Computer Interaction: Psychology as a Science of Design. 1st edn. Annual Review of Psychology, USA (1997)
4. Zhang, Y.: Human Computer Natural Interaction, 1st edn. National Defense Industry Press, Beijing (2004)
5. Ding, F., Wu, W.: Naoto Kanazawa and his "unconscious design". J. Hunan Univ. Technol. (Soc. Sci. Ed.) **16**(02), 138–141 (2011)
6. Yu, X.: Product Design Application Research Based on Intuitive Design Method. Shandong University (2011)
7. Breuer, J., Freud, S., Strachey, J.: Studies on Hysteria, 1st edn. Basic Books, New York (1957)
8. Jung, C.G.: Instinct and Unconsciousness, 1st edn. Reform Press, Beijing (1997)
9. Lacan, J., Miller, J.-A., Grigg, R.: The seminar of Jacques Lacan, Book 3: The Psychoses 1955–1956. 1st edn. W. W. Norton & Company, New York (1993)
10. Norman, D.A.: Emotional Design. 1st edn. Association for Computing Machinery, New York (2004)

11. Gibson, J.: The Theory of Affordance. The People, Place, and Space Reader, pp. 56–60 (1979)
12. Mark, W.: The computer for the 21st century. Sci. Am. (09), 91–94 (1991)
13. Dourish, P.: Where the Action Is: The Foundations of Embodied Interaction. 1st edn. MIT, Cambridge (2001)
14. Chen, W., Dong, S., Yue, W., et al.: Research on human computer interaction technology in handheld mobile computing. J. Comput. Appl. (10), 2219–2223 (2005)
15. Rudolph, L.: Project oxygen: pervasive, human-centric computing – an initial experience. In: Dittrich, K.R., Geppert, A., Norrie, M.C. (eds.) CAiSE 2001. LNCS, vol. 2068, pp. 1–12. Springer, Heidelberg (2001). https://doi.org/10.1007/3-540-45341-5_1
16. Dong, S., Wang, Y., Wang, G., et al.: Research on human computer interaction framework of pervasive computing. Chin. J. Comput. (12), 1657–1664 (2004)
17. Norman, D.: The Psychology of Everyday Things. Doubleday, New York (01) (1988)
18. Carey, S.: Cognitive conflict science and science education. Am. Psychol. 41(10), 1123 (1986)
19. Liu, B., Hao, R., Wang, Y., et al.: Research on fault tolerant design of interactive products based on cognitive psychology. Ind. Des. (008), 52–53 (2016)
20. How to design the home environment for the elderly with cognitive impairment. https://www.linkolder.com/article/9218784. Accessed 11 Feb 2021

Implementation of Lean Product Development in a University Course and an Industry Project: Lessons Learned from a Comparative Study

Yu-Hsiu Hung and Chia-Hui Fang[✉]

Department of Industrial Design, National Cheng Kung University, Tainan, Taiwan
idhfhung@mail.ncku.edu.tw

Abstract. The global competition in products and business is becoming intense. Most companies hope to stay ahead of their competitors during global expansion. To stay competitive in the marketplace, Lean Product Development (LPD) has drawn huge attention both from the industry and the academia because (1) enterprises are facing challenges in product development, e.g., long lead time in development, failure in innovation, and poor management in design activities, etc.; (2) most innovations in universities are often impractical and lack economic value. The purpose of the study was to uncover and to compare the processes and the design outcomes of the implementation of LPD among university student groups and among enterprise research and development (R&D) teams. In this study, product development teams were formed among industrial design juniors, as well as among the staff at the R&D department of a hair clipper company. All participants were asked to develop either a hair dryer or an electric hair clipper following the LAMDA (Look, Ask, Model, Discuss, and Act) cycle in LPD under the guidance of the same instructor. The LPD activities and the design outcomes were observed and analyzed by two researchers. Results showed that the student teams generally (1) were more able to think out of box without the constraints of department silos, (2) had more passion towards product and users, (3) had fewer problems in cross-functional collaborations, etc. On the other hand, the R&D teams were generally (self-) restricted psychologically and physically by the organizational culture and structure, and low work motivations, etc., thus resulting in the insufficient innovation momentum. Results of this study provide insight regarding the implementation of LPD especially in industry settings.

Keywords: Lean Product Development (LPD) · Research and Development (R&D) · Design

1 Introduction

These years, Lean Product Development (LPD) has been regarded by many as a key element of maintaining competitiveness in a globalized business environment. The lean system has the ability to reduce costs, improve product quality and increase productivity in the process of product development, which in turn also improves customer satisfaction

M. Kurosu (Ed.): HCII 2021, LNCS 12762, pp. 16–29, 2021.
https://doi.org/10.1007/978-3-030-78462-1_2

(Riezebos et al. 2009). As for Larsson et al. (2014), it is mentioned that Lean Product Development (LPD) is a method that can meet the needs of the organization's growing development goals and meanwhile increase the project success rate. Based on the above, many scholars began to pay attention to the application of lean thinking to product development (Ward et al. 1995; Liker and Morgan 2006; Kennedy and Widener 2008).

LPD has an important influence on enterprises, because lean product development can make a huge contribution to products that can develop rapidly. The concept of Lean Design was first discussed in 1990. At that time, the book "The Machine that Changed the World" compared the performance of product development through case studies, further explaining that Lean Design can reduce product development time and improve product quality (Womack et al. 1990). In terms of research and practice, LPD has the ability to effectively avoid unnecessary waste in the product development process, and maintains customer demand-oriented, the company can make valuable products in a faster and more cost-effective manner. Product (Liker and Morgan 2006; León and Farris 2011; Willumsen et al. 2017).

In recent years, the execution of many companies is worthy of praise. Nevertheless, the life cycle of new products is very short. Studies have pointed out that only a quarter of new product development is successful (Evanschitzky et al. 2012), and about 40% to 50% of product development investment is in product projects with poor results. Even after all development and testing work is performed, it can be estimated that about 40% of new products will fail when they are released. At the same time, in every 7 to 10 new product concepts, only one can create commercial success. What's more, only 13% of companies report that their efforts in new products Fangmi have met their annual profit targets (Cooper et al. 2004; Willumsen et al. 2017). The success of new product development depends on creativity (Scanlon and Jana 2007). Creativity is usually defined as ideas that are original and usable (Smith 1995; Amabile et al. 1996; Runco and Richards 1997; Sternberg and Lubart 1999). Innovation is the process of putting ideas into practice into new products (Sarooghi et al. 2015), so creativity is regarded as the first step in the innovation process. According to previous documents, if the team tends to the status quo during development, and lacks exploration of ideas beyond existing knowledge, it may produce undesirable results for development (Uzzi and Spiro 2005, Fleming et al. 2007). For example, when development members share common attitudes, opinions, and beliefs, they may increase group thinking and accidentally ignore the performance of members' diversity or unique abilities. Although such members will continue to generate ideas, these ideas tend to be more common knowledge than unique ideas, which can easily lead to the simplification of development results (Thomas-Hunt et al. 2003).

Compared with most companies still maintaining a relatively closed environment, the advantage of schools is that they have high-quality R&D manpower, front-end research technology, and the dissemination and diffusion of various innovative ideas. (National Science Board 1983). Over the past 30 years, the scientific and technological innovation and economic growth of the United States have obviously benefited from the research and development and technology transfer of scientific knowledge shared by universities and industry (Hall 2004). Although the results seem to be excellent, there is the problem of separation of academic theory and industrial practice, and the difficulty of integrating the two aspects (Van de Ven 2007). In addition, the inability of the industry or organization to effectively use the academic knowledge of the university (Argyris and Schön 1996; Beer 2001) will also cause the value of the school to fail to be highlighted. At present, there are few studies on this area. Even though schools have their own unique values, they are rarely discovered or used effectively.

In order to maintain market competitiveness, companies need to continuously develop and provide new products. That is, companies need to quickly provide innovative new products to the market while controlling costs (Allocca and Kessler 2006; Goktan and Miles 2011; Farid et al. 2017; Cheng and Yang 2019). Therefore, in addition to LPD, companies need to learn relevant innovative methods and mechanisms from schools to ensure their sustainable survival and development.

As a result, this research is dedicated to exploring the blind spots and advantages of development teams with different backgrounds and environments after practicing LPD, and putting forward reflections after practice. This study hopes that our reflections can be used as a reference for companies to become a key factor in improving development capabilities. The results provided by this research can serve as a reference basis for future academic and industrial circles to practice lean product development methods. First, LPD is an innovative research field. So far, there is still a lack of research focusing on this field. This research can be used to verify the effectiveness of its method. Second, in the past, most researches only explored the changes in a single group of industry and students, and the research comparing the relationship or differences between the two is quite rare. In view of this, this research will conduct in-depth discussion and analysis of the relationship between the two, and strive to provide new research directions for subsequent research.

2 Literature Review

2.1 Insufficient Innovation Capacity of Enterprises

Innovation is a major source of an enterprise's profits (Grant 1991). The enterprise must continue to make innovations in order to maintain its competitive advantages, and the innovation ability is even the key factor in success of innovation (Wang et al. 2008). According to "Harvard Business Review", 84% of top executives worldwide consider innovation "very important" to the company; however, only 6% are satisfied with their company's performance in innovation. The higher innovation ability can clarify the framework of the innovation plan which may develop at a faster development speed,and it also has a higher innovation performance on both quantity and quality (Kessler and Bierly 2002). Compare with less innovative company, Kyläheiko et al. (2011) thinks that the company with strong innovation ability is able to develop and test the concepts of new products more efficiently. The study by Wang et al. (2008) also pointed out that innovation ability is the key to the success of innovation. So it can be concluded that the innovation ability is very important to the enterprise, and the high innovation ability can enhance the enterprise's innovation performance and make the enterprise more competitive. There are a number of reasons that the company lose its ability to innovate, including the absence of senior executives who support and drive an innovation culture, and a lack of appropriate process and mechanism to form an innovation framework, etc.

In many companies, almost all of the current management models oppose the innovations rather than support them, so if there are not proper decision-makers, company culture and processes, any innovative policy may be managed in a consistent and traditional manner, and the company will be moving away further from its innovation goals.

2.2 Potential Problems in Product Development

In order to maintain its competitiveness, the company needs to push new and innovative products to the market rapidly and continuously while keeping good control of costs at the same time (Allocca and Kessler 2006; Evanschitzky et al. 2012; Farid et al. 2017; Cheng and Yang 2019). However, research shows that only a quarter of new products are successful (Evanschitzky et al. 2012), and about 40–50% of product development investments is wasted on eliminating the product projects of poor performance. Faced with complicated new product design and development plans or systematic design work, and when considering numerous and complicated factors, the developers may be trapped in the foggy dilemma, and at a loss in the complex influences in NPD (Cheng and Yang 2019). According to Tortorella et al. (2015), NPD problems are divided into two categories. The first category is related to the results of the development process, that is, the success of the new product's after-market (Hines et al. 2006). Related issues include: lack of consistency between product development strategy and business strategy, excessive unnecessary development activities, and insufficient understanding of customer needs, resulting in a higher failure rate of the final new product (Haque and James-Moore 2004; Graebsch 2005). The second type of problem is related to the efficiency of the development process, including: lack of standardized processes, lack of stable control over the development environment, poor internal communication, lack of common focus (Oppenheim 2004; Riezebos et al. 2009), and inability to improve mistakes or learn and improve from mistakes. In the end, it will lead to too long development time and inability to control costs well.

A study suggests that the traditional company often relies on its internal expertise in the new product development (NPD), which is proved to be effective. However, researchers have found some drawbacks in the NPD process if the company relies on internal expertise only. For example, Katila and Ahuja (2002) pointed out that using the internal knowledge to do NPD to some extent will lead to a decline in production. Furthermore, Kristensson et al. (2004) suggested that the design professionals are constrained by their existing knowledge in the NPD process, resulting in developing the production rather than the innovation. In recent years, it has been pointed out that the team organization also affectes product development greatly. In the process of product development, each department is performing its own work, and poor communication between departments may cause the team members to have no real understanding of the project. Many studies consider that the organization and operation of the project team will have a great influence on the project results (Valle and Avella 2003; Nakata and Im 2010; Cooper 2011; Cooper et al. 2017).

2.3 Lean Product Development

Definition of Lean Product Development. The word "Lean" appeared in the book "The Machine That Changed the World", which originated from Toyota Production System (TPS). Lean production has proved to be very successful in improving the production efficiency (Krafcik 1988; Liker 2004), but the popularity rate of lean tools and methods in product development is low. Therefore, many scholars begin to pay attention to the application of lean thinking on the product development (Ward et al. 1995; Liker and Morgan 2006; Kennedy and Widener 2008). According to the definition of USA Lean Enterprise Institute (LEI), lean product and program development is a powerful system for developing new products. It is not just a strategy for developing a single product, it enables you to use the resources of the enterprise flexibly and to create a sustainable system that can consistently generate a great value flow of products and profits. The purpose is to design products that can enhance the customer lives, to create reusable knowledge and to reduce the risks in the information transmission.

Application of LAMDA to Product Development. The past research has shown that lean product development relies on the LAMDA cycle for knowledge acquisition. The LAMDA cycle requires the presence on-the-spot, that is, the developers shall be present in the user's real work environment and carry out continuous observations and inquires without any presetting positions. And they shall develop several possible scheme sets and make simulated models. After experimenting and discussion, the unsuitable schemes were cancelled and the best scheme was kept for the detailed design at the last stage. The essence of lean product development is to let customer values activate the flow of product development process, so as to avoid unnecessary debates and wastes.

LAMDA cycle are divided into 5 phases, they are Look, Ask, Model, Discussion and Act (Feltrin et al. 2016). It is a upgraded version of the well-known PDCA cycle, that is Plan, Do, Check and Act. The purpose is to improve the deficiencies of PDCA in the "Plan" and "Check" phases. The descriptions of five phase of LAMDA cycle are below:

(1) Look: To create a new product, the first step is to carry out "local and physical" observations. The developer must be on-the-spot to understand the production situations, the suppliers and the related competitors, as well as to observe the users' behavior and interview with them, etc. He shall not rely on second-hand information. He shall be present on the scene to feel the actual situations with his own five senses and to obtain the necessary details and information.

(2) Ask: Asking "who knows about it?" and "what is the root cause of the problem?" and further asking "why" for five times, the developer may find the root causes of the observed events or phenomena, and to look for experts familiar with the problems to provide the available knowledge.

(3) Model: Visualize all concepts and ideas in sketch drawings, physical samples, 3D models, trade-off curves, A3 reports and other "models" which can help people to understand easily and can provide visual sense of the physical presences to help people in communication.

(4) Discuss: Discuss the results from the model phase with the relevant people. The relevant people are those who have the power to make decision (senior officials

and supervisors, etc.), and those who will be affected by this decision (production and technical staff, etc.), and those who have a deep knowledge in this field and can discuss and provide advices from different points of view. This phase will help the developer in re-examining the design, seeking more knowledge and advices, or communicating concepts by more models, and choosing the best solution to solve the problem.

(5) Act: After reaching consensus at the discussion phase, the developer shall draw up a plan based on the information of the previous survey and discussion, and implement the plan accordingly. If the results do not meet expectations, a LAMDA cycle shall be re-conducted to ensure that the final results are satisfactory.

In the book "Lean Practice in China V", the author mentions a lot about the international trends of the lean practice. More and more companies are beginning to pay attention to the lean product development. One of the successful cases is FirstBuild in GE, which has transformed from traditional products into the market by using the concept of lean production. It takes the advantages of the community which is created together by attracting employees, local residents, school professors, students and even entrepreneurs who are interested in co-creating new products. In the talent development and the flow of technology and innovations, FirstBuild plays a key role among GE, the nearby university and the local communities, and finally became a big winner of innovation for three parties. Innovation is an important subject that enterprises must face, and sustainable development is the goal of each enterprise. Lean product development provides a good blueprint for the enterprise to jump out of the competitive red sea market and enter the blue sea market of innovation with higher returns.

The advantage of the LAMDA cycle introduced in the R & D process is that the developer in "Plan" phase is much more careful and can get knowledge of the new product and its applicable principles in person. In the meantime, he uses the obtained data and knowledge to create visual records in trade-off curves or A3 reports that could be shared and discussed by the relevant people. As a result, there are some questions that can not be avoided in design education, and are also crucial to the students, like, how to use visual tools to communicate knowledge? How to design a solution set rather than a single solution?, and so on. The similar questions relating to knowledge gaps can be answered through LAMDA, which has been confirmed in many studies (Feltrin et al. 2016). Kennedy and Widener (2008) said in a Toyota study that a PDCA cycle is equivalent to two LAMDA cycles: one for Plan-Do to solve the problems and the other for Check-Act, which validates and standardizes the solution through LAMDA, and to avoid reoccurrence of the problems.

Summary
In the past, each phase represented the same meanings as the actual operation phase in every design process. Most of the design processes were guided by linear structure mode for linear development which often had problems in design iterations and communications to increase the cost (Summers and Scherpereel 2008). In recent years, product development has evolved from a traditional technology-driven and market-driven model to a more integrated process, with much emphasis on cross-departmental communications and supplier involvement at early phase to shorten product launch time (Yadav et al.

2007). In other words, the enterprise is shifting to a lean thinking of doing the product development from the point of system (Cooper and Edgett 2008). Therefore, this study arranges the implementation of lean product development in two groups with industrial and academic background respectively, and find out whether the results are different.

3 Method

In this study, the lean product development LAMDA method is implemented in university and enterprises respectively. By the comparison of two groups and a comprehensive discussion, we can get to know the changes of different groups in the same development process. Section 3.1 describes the details of the development process in university group and Sect. 3.2 describes the details in the enterprise group.

3.1 LPD in University Course

Participants. This study adopts purposeful sampling by selecting students from the industrial design department of a national university in Taiwan. Because the participants are required to fulfill a complete design process to make a product actually, they shall meet the following conditions: (1) At least two-year experience in product design; (2) Be able to use different design methods/tools to design products. Three students are recruited as a group for the experiment.

Experimental Design. In this study, the "student group" will use "lean product development LAMDA method" for the design of the products "hairdryer for professional hairdresser" and "electric scissors for baby". The purpose is to design a product that can solve the pain points of the customer. The time limit is 18 weeks. There is at least one opportunity to discuss the product with the lean advisor once a week. There is no limit to the design tools/methods.

Procedure

1. In this study, some participants who meet the required conditions are selected from the industrial design department of a national university and the are informed of the purpose and experimental procedure of the study.
2. The design process of the participants is based on "lean product development LAMDA". They will discuss with the lean advisor once every week on the design and implementation. The total time limit is 18 weeks. In the final week they shall provide a complete product design project.
3. The researchers will observe and record the performance of the two groups until the product design project is completed. They will analyze the data and evaluate whether there is any difference in changes and performance between the two groups.

3.2 LPD in Industry Project

Participants. The enterprise group comes from a company which develops and sells hair-care tools. The company is engage in R &D, production and sale of various electric scissors, hairdressers and massagers. It has a successful development in the global hair-care tool industry. The group members include a product manager, a structural engineer and a salesman. The average age of the group is over 30. Each member has experience in product development, and the production manage has even over 10 years of experience in product development. Except for the participants, "enterprise group" performs the same procedure with the "student group".

3.3 Observation and Record

Observation method (observation) is to observe people, things or other phenomena. It is divided into two types: participant observation and non-participant observation, according to whether or not the observer participates in the activities of the object. In this study, non-participant observation is used, that is, there is no participation in the activities of the objects and there is no intervention in their development and changes. The behavior and activity process of the objects are observed and recorded objectively. The following six aspects are observed and filled with details:

- Who: Who are on the spot? What roles are they? What are their positions and titles?
- What: What is going on? What are the behavior of those present? What do they do/say? What tone of voice and body movements do they use when they speak/act? What are the types, nature, and details of the actions as they are created and developed? Do their behavior change during the observation period?
- When: When does the behaviors or event in question occur? How long do these behaviors or events last? How often do an event or behavior occur?
- Where: Where does this behavior or event occur? How does this behavior or event differ from the behavior or event that occurs elsewhere?
- How: How does this behavior happen? What is the relationship between the various aspects of the event? What are the obvious norms or rules?
- Why: Why do these events happen? What are the causes of these events? What do people think differently about the events? What is the purpose, motivation, and attitude of the people who behave like this?

3.4 Data Analysis

The Independent variable of the experiment is the background of team members, and the dependent variables are pain points of the customer, the tool application, the logical context and the team cooperation. This study will analyze the observation and record data by indicating them with the factors and conditions that hinder or facilitate the implementation of the method (Kleinsmann 2006). The problems that two groups encounter are defined in advance as two categories: (1) Cooperation between development teams; (2) Factors that affect the success of product development. The remaining issues that are not suitable to be predefined will be put into other category.

4 Results

In this study, after the two teams practice the lean product development methods respectively, it is known from observation and interview that although the "student team" is not more than the "enterprise team" in product development experience, its performance in product development is not inferior to that of the "enterprise team" in terms of creativity and product practicality. With limited time and experience, the "student team" makes innovative products close to mass production. In the next paragraph of this study, the 2 theme factors shall be analyzed in terms of (1) cooperation between development teams and (2) success factors affecting product development in development between 2 teams, to discuss the learning response of students and industry in implementing lean product development methods and the differences in implementing product development (Fig. 1).

Fig. 1. Experimental status

4.1 Reflection on the Practice of "Student Team"

Team Members Have the Passion to Develop Products. Passion is the power source of product development, and the motivation and working attitude of students participating in research are active and positive. Students will be informed of the workload, goals and uncertain factors before starting to participate in the research, and the unsuitable students will leave on their own, while the students who stay to participate in the research have the passion for developing products. Students who participate in the research want to do a good job, they care about users' ideas and hope to get good results. Because of their passion, they are willing to spend more time discussing problems, and hope to solve all the problems even if they reduce their sleeping time. They don't pay much attention to writing an A3 report and doing an experiment. What they care about is that whether the solution can satisfy users.

Habit for the Unknown Status, the Courage to Explore, Thinking is not Rigid.
The disadvantage of students is that they have no work experience, but because of this, their work scope and content can be adjusted closely around the project theme; in the meantime, the way they do things is relatively simple, and they try to solve problems

when they encounter problems; when they encounter material problems, they try to search for new materials, and then verify whether the new materials can bring new possibilities to products through experiments after understanding the characteristics of the new materials. In this process, the professional knowledge mastered by students can't help them solve most problems. Because of this, they can return to the essence of problems and explore the possibility of solving problems from scratch, thus stimulating innovation.

Without Departmental Barriers, Work can Proceed Smoothly. The product development project of this study does not have to face the barriers of various departments in the company, so the barriers of cross-departmental communication and coordination have disappeared, and the unnecessary problems of "office politics" have also disappeared, including striving for credit, communication waste, subordination, responsibility attribution and other problems. This makes the student team have highly mobility when doing things, so long as they have ideas, they can act quickly.

4.2 Reflection on the Practice of "Enterprise Team"

Lack of Passion and Negative Work Culture. In enterprises, the project members generally lack of passion. In most cases, the project promotion is often simply implemented, and the team members only passively complete the related process of product development, but do not seriously think about how to do things well. For example, it is very important to identify customer value, when implementing the lean product development. However, team members can not only understand the pain spots of customers through long-term observation and interview, but also observe and record the work in a quick way.

In the product development project of enterprise, each team member's motivation and emotion are different. Some people want to do things well, while others are forced to participate under helpless situations; some people are full of confidence in Lean Thinking, while others have doubts. If we ignore the negative motivation and emotion of team members, we can't create positive team interaction and working atmosphere. In addition, many employees are used to the old working style, doing whatever superiors require, doing whatever needed by orders, and looking for ready-made solutions when encountering problems during development. They don't deeply think about how to do a good job, and they don't put customer needs as priority, and they don't challenge the industry convention to make innovations. These are the barriers and challenges that enterprises often encounter when pushing forward lean product development projects. For example, when the project needs to reduce the motor noise (the current noise is 80 dB), the engineer proposed that the noise can be reduced to 78 dB by using a supplier's parts. This proposal seems to be reasonable and better than the current situation. However, the problem is that only 2 dB can be improved, and customers can't feel it at all, and the improvement effect is limited by parts. Adopting this method, it is impossible to design products that satisfy customers, and it is impossible to gain competitive advantage in the market.

Along with The Growth of Enterprises, Organizations are Becoming Increasingly Complex and Rigid in Thinking. Many enterprises are willing to try innovation at the initial stage of starting business, because the organization is small and there are few people, so it is easy to interact with customers and satisfy them. With the increase of business and organization scale, the process management methods, models and tools are applied one by one, which eventually leads the things that were very easy before to become complicated. For example, it needs to fill in many sheets and gain approval from different levels when doing a simple project; putting forward a simple product concept requires filling in many sheets, and the passion of employees for innovation is easy to be smothered. Enterprises often set too many check points in the process of product development, and the development efficiency is low, which seriously hinders the promotion of lean product development.

The Top Management of the Enterprise has Insufficient Support to The Transformation. The lack of top management support of enterprises can directly affect the success or failure of the transformation of lean product development. First of all, the top management of enterprises didn't do it by themselves, but only assigned low management to execute the project, without decentralization, which will inevitably lead to many barriers in the implementation of cross-departmental tasks. Secondly, the low participation of the top management of the enterprise makes the development team slack off easily. In many enterprises, employees are always guessing the supervisors' idea, and the supervisors' attitudes are the weather vane. As long as the leaders' attitudes towards the lean product development are not clear, team members would rather slow down than going forward bravely. For example, because of various reasons, the top management of enterprises can't always pay attention to the progress of lean product development, and can't participate in relevant meetings and give guidance from beginning to end. Therefore, team members think that this project can be done or not, and doing well or not will not have a direct impact on their future. Such an idea can easily lead to the slow progress of the lean product development project.

The Project doesn't Break Down Departmental Barriers. In order to successfully carry out lean product development project, it is necessary to set up an executive team across departments, so that all team members can make efforts to develop the project and realize customer value. When implementing lean product development project, team members should always communicate with each other and provide opinions, feedback and support for the progress at any time. According to the observation of this study, the implementation of lean product development projects is easily challenged by the ethos of personal performance and departmental barriers within enterprises. For example, members of the marketing department may feel that product development and design are not their jobs, so they are passive and not interested, and even find reasons not to participate in relevant meetings and discussions. Design developers feel that understanding customer needs is not their specialty, so they passively wait for market personnel to provide demand information. In this case, even if a cross-departmental team is formed, the implementation of the project is still in its own way, and the product development process is still full of waste. When problems are found or the development direction deviates from customer value seriously, the correction will pay a huge price.

5 Discussion

Product development is an important factor to determine the profit level of the enterprise, and also determines 65%–75% of the product cost. The implementation of the lean product development enables the enterprise to obtain significant economic benefits. The USA Lean Enterprise Institute (LEI), through practical cases in recent years, has proved that the lean product development can help enterprises to make full use of resources to create a sustainable development system, and continuously to create excellent value flow of products and profits. However, there are many kinds of blind spots and pain spots in many enterprises, which prevents the lean product development from being noticed and implemented. In terms of blind spots, many enterprises have formed their own product development system after years of operation, and they are satisfied with the current situation. They do not see their own management dead ends and shortcomings, so will not take the initiatives to contact or implement lean product development. In terms of pain spots, many companies are aware of the benefits of lean product development, but due to their organizational structure and culture, the R & D departments have long been underappreciated, so they are vulnerable to resistance even if they want to change. Therefore, although this study observes that the enterprise group overwhelmed student group in R & D experience, but within the existing enterprise framework, the innovations and changes can not be performed. The lean product development may provide the enterprise with many advantages. The results of this study show the various deficiencies of the implementation of the method in the enterprise, so that the same obstacles can be avoided in the future lean product development.

References

Allocca, M.A., Kessler, E.H.: Innovation speed in small and medium-sized enterprises. Creativity Innov. Manag. **15**(3), 279–295 (2006)

Amabile, T.M., et al.: Assessing the work environment for creativity. Acad. Manag. J. **39**(5), 1154–1184 (1996)

Argyris, C., Schön, D.A.: Organizational Learning II: Theory, Method, and Practice, Addison-Wesley Reading (1996)

Beer, M.: How to develop an organization capable of sustained high performance: Embrace the drive for results-capability development paradox. Organ. Dyn. **29**(4), 233 (2001)

National Science Board. University-industry research relationships: Selected studies, National Science Foundation (1983)

Cheng, C., Yang, M.: Creative process engagement and new product performance: the role of new product development speed and leadership encouragement of creativity. J. Bus. Res. **99**, 215–225 (2019)

Cooper, R.G.: Perspective: the innovation dilemma: How to innovate when the market is mature. J. Prod. Innov. Manag. **28**(s1), 2–27 (2011)

Cooper, R.G., Edgett, S.J.: Maximizing productivity in product innovation. Res. Technol. Manag. **51**(2), 47–58 (2008)

Cooper, R.G., et al.: Benchmarking best NPD practices—I. Res. Technol. Manag. **47**(1), 31–43 (2004)

Cooper, T., et al.: New product development and testing strategies for clothing longevity (2017)

Evanschitzky, H., et al.: Success factors of product innovation: an updated meta-analysis. J. Prod. Innov. Manag. **29**, 21–37 (2012)

Farid, H., et al.: Biotechnology firms-improvement in innovation speed. Int. J. Bus. Innov. Res **13**(2), 167–180 (2017)

Feltrin, C.K., et al.: A Lean Product Development (LPD) approach on education and knowledge management in aircraft design. In: 16th AIAA Aviation Technology, Integration, and Operations Conference (2016)

Fleming, L., et al.: Collaborative brokerage, generative creativity, and creative success. Adm. Sci. Q. **52**(3), 443–475 (2007)

Goktan, A.B., Miles, G.: Innovation speed and radicalness: are they inversely related? Manag. Decis. (2011)

Graebsch, M.: Information and communication in lean product development (2005)

Grant, R.M.: The resource-based theory of competitive advantage: implications for strategy formulation. Calif. Manag. Rev. **33**(3), 114–135 (1991)

Hall, D.T.: The protean career: a quarter-century journey. J. Vocat. Behav. **65**(1), 1–13 (2004)

Haque, B., James-Moore, M.: Applying lean thinking to new product introduction. J. Eng. Des. **15**(1), 1–31 (2004)

Hines, P., Francis, M., Found, P.: Towards lean product lifecycle management: a framework for new product development. J. Manuf. Technol. Manag. **17**(7), 866–887 (2006). https://doi.org/10.1108/17410380610688214

Katila, R., Ahuja, G.: Something old, something new: a longitudinal study of search behavior and new product introduction. Acad. Manag. J. **45**(6), 1183–1194 (2002)

Kennedy, F.A., Widener, S.K.: A control framework: Insights from evidence on lean accounting. Manag. Account. Res. **19**(4), 301–323 (2008)

Kessler, E.H., Bierly, P.E.: Is faster really better? An empirical test of the implications of innovation speed. IEEE Trans. Eng. Manag. **49**(1), 2–12 (2002)

Kleinsmann, M.S.: Understanding collaborative design (2006)

Krafcik, J.F.: Triumph of the lean production system. Sloan Manag. Rev. **30**(1), 41–52 (1988)

Kristensson, P., et al.: Harnessing the creative potential among users. J. Prod. Innov. Manag. **21**(1), 4–14 (2004)

Kyläheiko, K., et al.: Innovation and internationalization as growth strategies: the role of technological capabilities and appropriability. Int. Bus. Rev. **20**(5), 508–520 (2011)

Larsson, J., et al.: Industrialized construction in the Swedish infrastructure sector: core elements and barriers. Constr. Manag. Econ. **32**(1–2), 83–96 (2014)

León, H.C.M., Farris, J.A.: Lean product development research: current state and future directions. Eng. Manag. J. **23**(1), 29–51 (2011)

Liker, J.K.: Toyota Way: 14 Management Principles from the World's Greatest Manufacturer. McGraw-Hill Education (2004)

Liker, J.K., Morgan, J.M.: The Toyota way in services: the case of lean product development. Acad. Manag. Perspect. **20**(2), 5–20 (2006)

Nakata, C., Im, S.: Spurring cross-functional integration for higher new product performance: a group effectiveness perspective. J. Prod. Innov. Manag. **27**(4), 554–571 (2010)

Oppenheim, B.W.: Lean product development flow. Syst. Eng. 7(4) (2004)

Riezebos, J., et al.: Lean production and information technology: connection or contradiction? Comput. Ind. **60**(4), 237–247 (2009)

Runco, M.A., Richards, R.: Eminent Creativity, Everyday Creativity, and Health. Greenwood Publishing Group (1997)

Sarooghi, H., et al.: Examining the relationship between creativity and innovation: a meta-analysis of organizational, cultural, and environmental factors. J. Bus. Ventur. **30**(5), 714–731 (2015)

Scanlon, J., Jana, R.: The state of innovation. BusinessWeek, 19 December 2007. http://www.businessweek.com/innovate/content/dec2007/id20071219_302022.htm. Accessed 29 Apr 2011

Smith, S.M.: Fixation, incubation, and insight in memory and creative thinking. Creative Cogn. Approach **135**, 156 (1995)

Sternberg, R.J., Lubart, T.I.: The concept of creativity: prospects and paradigms. Handb. Creativity **1**, 3–15 (1999)

Summers, G., Scherpereel, C.: Decision making in product development: are you outside-in or inside-out? Manag. Decis. **46**(9), 1299–1312 (2008). https://doi.org/10.1108/00251740810911957

Thomas-Hunt, M.C., et al.: Who's really sharing? Effects of social and expert status on knowledge exchange within groups. Manag. Sci. **49**(4), 464–477 (2003)

Tortorella, G.L., Marodin, G.A., Miorando, R., Seidel, A.: The impact of contextual variables on learning organization in firms that are implementing lean: a study in Southern Brazil. Int. J. Adv. Manuf. Technol. **78**(9–12), 1879–1892 (2015). https://doi.org/10.1007/s00170-015-6791-1

Uzzi, B., Spiro, J.: Collaboration and creativity: the small world problem. Am. J. Sociol. **111**(2), 447–504 (2005)

Valle, S., Avella, L.: Cross-functionality and leadership of the new product development teams. Eur. J. Innov. Manag. **6**(1), 32–47 (2003). https://doi.org/10.1108/14601060310456319

Van de Ven, A.H.: Engaged Scholarship: A Guide for Organizational and Social Research. Oxford University Press on Demand (2007)

Wang, C.-H., et al.: Evaluating firm technological innovation capability under uncertainty. Technovation **28**(6), 349–363 (2008)

Ward, A., et al.: The second Toyota paradox: how delaying decisions can make better cars faster. Sloan Manag. Rev. **36**, 43 (1995)

Willumsen, P., et al.: Applying lean thinking to risk management in product development. In: DS 87-2 Proceedings of the 21st International Conference on Engineering Design (ICED 17): Design Processes, Design Organisation and Management, Vancouver, Canada, 21–25 August 2017, vol. 2 (2017)

Womack, J.P., et al.: The machine that changed the world, Rawson Associates. New York **323**, 273–287 (1990)

Yadav, M.S., et al.: Managing the future: CEO attention and innovation outcomes. J. Mark. **71**(4), 84–101 (2007)

Human Computer Interacting Through a Game Engine: Qualifying Inclusive Design in Architecture

Anders Hermund(✉) [iD]

Royal Danish Academy - Architecture, Design, Conservation, 1435 Copenhagen, Denmark
anders.hermund@kglakademi.dk

Abstract. This paper will discuss quality in interacting in architectural projects through the use of virtual reality and a game engine to achieve better quality of architecture and inclusiveness with universal design. Interacting on architectural projects through digital means has been the focus of the research project Virtual Scenario Responder (VSR) during the last five years. The paper will recapitulate the steps of the studies within the research project in order to elucidate the progress and expose the impact of the findings on a practical level manifested in reports generated using the VSR system as a dialogue tool to extract user feedback for improving the architectural quality. The VSR system is an interface that allows the use of computational digital 3D models in virtual reality to become part of the long tradition of representational models in architectural design. The use of virtual reality can generate a sensation of immersion into the yet unbuild architectural space that cannot be conveyed to future users in the same way through more traditional means of representation. The automatic logging of user behavior and feedback from verbal comments are captured by the VSR and act as the foundation for the feedback reports on actual architectural projects.

Keywords: Virtual reality · Architectural representation · Behavior tracking

1 Introduction

This paper will discuss quality in interacting in architectural projects through the use of Virtual Reality and game engines to achieve better quality of architecture and inclusiveness. Interacting on architectural projects through digital means has been the focus of the research project Virtual Scenario Responder (VSR) during the last five years. The paper will reveal the steps of the research project in order to elucidate the progress and expose the impact of the findings both on a practical level in reports, collecting the feedback from users from the VR experience, and in a suggestion to how this kind of tool could be further investigated in the future to the needs of architectural projects.

2 Starting Point of the Project

Prior to the VSR project, our team at the Royal Danish Academy School of Architecture, had worked with the digitalization of construction in various contexts. Partly through

M. Kurosu (Ed.): HCII 2021, LNCS 12762, pp. 30–49, 2021.
https://doi.org/10.1007/978-3-030-78462-1_3

the PhD project "Applied 3D modeling and parametric design" [1] in 2011 and partly through BVU*net [2] where Digital Construction (Det Digitale Byggeri) was sought to be implemented in educations of construction and architecture in Denmark. Under the auspices of the Royal Danish Academy, this led to projects around the classification system CCS in the architectural education in 2014 and a grant from the Dreyer Foundation in 2015 to the project VR-BIM on the development of intuitive communication between the construction parties. This project introduced Virtual Reality (VR) technology in the work with Building Information Modeling (BIM) with the aim of creating a better, more accurate and more intuitive communication between the architect and the other parties in the construction industry. In this project, we made the first comparisons of the experience of architectural spaces in virtual reality and in reality. The comparison between reality and the virtual model was based on an auditorium at the Royal Danish Academy, as we thus had the real space within reach on a daily basis and could model an accurate digital 3D model of the space for use in the comparison.

2.1 Comparative Studies

One of our first studies of the similarities between the perception of architectural space experienced in physical space conditions and in virtual reality, had the intent to clarify to what extend subjective and objective attributes of architectural space can be conveyed through a direct use of building information models in virtual reality using the simulation engine. The test persons experienced a specific test space as either a physical or a virtual environment, while data from their experiences was collected through a quantitative/qualitative questionnaire. The overall conclusion, from this phase of the study, was that even a simple BIM model through HMD VR can convey rather precise information about both subjective and objective experiences of architectural space [3].

2.2 Selecting of Test Subjects

For all the studies shown in chapter 2 and 3 of this paper a total number of 179 test subjects have been used until now. 30 subjects for the physical reality scenario, 63 subjects for the virtual scenario (33 subjects using eye tracking and 30 without), 32 for the plan & section scenario, and 6 test subjects coming from an architectural studio as a professional benchmark in the plan & section scenario. The EEG pilot study had 8 subjects, and the last behavior tracking had 40 subjects. All the test subjects were students except for the 6 professional architects. The total gender distribution was close to 50/50. The age span among the students ranges from 19 years to 41 years with an average of 22.8 years. The students are primarily in the beginning of their study at the Royal Danish Academy of Fine Arts School of Architecture (KADK)[1] or Aalborg University Sustainable Design (AAU). The age span of the 6 professional architects (JFA arkitekter) ranges from 27 to 52 with an average of 37.2 years. It was an important factor that the test subjects were not familiar with the test space.

---

[1] The name has since officially been changed into "The Royal Danish Academy – Architecture".

2.3 Basic Research in Digital Representation Models

It was an important prerequisite for our future work with virtual realities to establish some starting points for how architecture is experienced in VR in relation to in reality. Therefore, we started with a comparison of reality and VR. This comparison examined the similarities between the perception of architectural space experienced under "normal" physical space conditions in real space and the same space as a digital 3D sketch model experienced using a VR Head Mounted Display (HMD) such as the Oculus Rift.

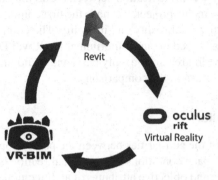

Fig. 1. The workflow from sketching in 3D BIM software through virtual reality to a feedback system that can give information of the user experience.

The purpose of the study was to clarify the extent to which subjective and objective properties of architectural space can be conveyed through a direct use of VR BIM models (Fig. 1).

It was equally important to us that the use of VR in an architectural practice should not burden the time consumption more than absolutely necessary in connection with the preparation of systems and models. Therefore, we set up some criteria for the experiment, such as that the 3D model must be able to be used directly in VR without the need for conversion through more types of software than is absolutely necessary. It was also important that the use of VR in the sketching phase did not require large investments in new equipment and employees who had to spend time modeling special 3D models. We would therefore use the 3D building information models that are already by law required for all public construction in Denmark, and which are also gradually becoming standard in the industry in general, for larger buildings. This meant that we focused on the early sketch phase, where no decision material is yet available regarding detailing, but rather the spatial contexts and processes. A photorealistic VR model, as one can see used in modern computer games or by real estate agents in their presentation material, was thus not what we were aiming for in the early sketching phases of architectural design. We began with a general examination of the visual perception of space in reality and in VR. For this we used eye-tracking of a number of test persons' experience of a space in reality and in VR, respectively.

Fig. 2. The scenarios (A) in real life & (B) in virtual reality respectively.

The experiment was set up using an auditorium at the Royal Danish Academy (Fig. 2) as the physical location (A) and a BIM model of the same auditorium as the virtual location (B). In situation A we define the "normal state" as a situation in which a test person experiences a specified existing physical architectural space, i.e. the auditorium space. In situation B, the test subject is shown the same architectural space presented through the HMD VR technology Oculus Rift, using a 3D digital architectural building information model made for that same purpose. We used initially 60 students for the test. That way, there were 30 persons who experienced the space in reality and 30 others who experienced the space through the VR simulation. It was important that the test subjects did not know about the setup for the study of the space, so therefore we could not use the same persons twice.

Along the way, we used a quantitative/qualitative interview matrix to ask to what extent the perception of space in VR has similarities with the experience of the space under normal or close to normal circumstances. In each scenario, the same two specific locations were used in order to facilitate an easier comparison. Here, the test subjects were asked about their perception of the space they were in. First, they were asked to describe their experience of the atmosphere of the space in three words, and the experience of the height of the room in one word. Then, they were asked seventeen questions that could be answered on a scale of 1 to 7, and three questions about estimating the depth, width, and height of the room. These questions could be categorized into four different architectural areas of perception: the space itself, the lighting, sensation/estimates and materiality (Fig. 3). That Matrix questionnaire was inspired by research in the field, including definitions of corpothetics by architecture researcher Clare Melhuish [4] and neurobiologist Semir Zeki in his work with art and the brain, micro- and macro-consciousnesses [5]. The experiment set up also included eye tracking equipment in both scenarios. That specific eye tracking data was additionally analyzed in a later phase of the study, as I will explain in a forthcoming chapter.

The result of the study showed great similarity between the two scenarios with a difference of less than 1% in 11 of the 20 questions, 1–2% in 4 of the questions, 2–3% in 2 of the questions. Only three questions had a difference over 3%; 3.4%, 4.1% and 5.2%, respectively. The latter, the highest difference, concerned a question of perception of the quality of the materials in the space. This was expected since the material quality is hard to experience provided only through VR vision, in a sketch model without a very high level of detail. The results related to both lighting conditions and feeling good and safe in the space more surprisingly held a difference below 1%, even though the virtual model

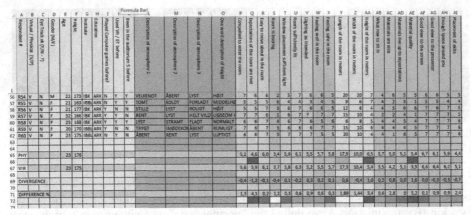

Fig. 3. Example of the matrix questionnaire showing the combined data from virtual (VR) and physical reality (PHY). The color codes show where the divergence was perceived highest (red color). The matrix has been cropped for the sake of this example to show only a few test persons. (Color figure online)

did not provide accurate light or shadows. The results from the open-ended questions about the experience of the atmosphere in space are surprisingly close when compared. Thus, the top three freely chosen words describing the atmosphere in the two scenarios were out of ninety different freely chosen words describing each scenario, rather similar. Bright: 67%, Quiet: 33%, Open: 27% in the physical scenario and Bright: 50%, Open: 30%, Empty: 17% in the virtual scenario. The description 'quiet' makes more sense in the physical environment, while the VR model did not include any auditory stimuli. I will get back to this and revisit this part of the study later on, when comparing the physical and virtual scenarios to a scenario with plan and section drawings of the space.

Overall, we concluded from this phase of the study that even a simple BIM model through HMD with VR can convey fairly accurate information about both subjective and objective experiences of architectural space and architectural atmospheres [3]. These results were motivating for continuing the research and gradually refine a system that could work for architects in VR.

3   The Foundation of the Virtual Scenario Responder

After the findings from the analysis of the questionnaire matrix, we continued analyzing data from the use of the eye tracking that was implicit the study set up for both the physical and the virtual scenario. The further development of the idea of the virtual scenario responder (VSR) took place after receiving additional funding from several places in Denmark, and with the ambition to develop a prototype tool that could be used as a dialogue platform in the designing of architecture. This development included both the use of eye tracking equipment and also the experimental use of an EEG neuro scanner. Eventually the findings from these studies were sought to be included into the prototype tool. The vision was also to include universal design in architectural thinking.

3.1 Eye Tracking

The next phase of the study continued to elaborate on the above-mentioned experiment set up. This time we included eye-tracking data from the two scenarios of the same auditorium at The Royal Danish Academy, and discussed how a skillful application of eye tracking technology can possible contribute to improving on architecture and its quality, before it is actually built. The use of eye tracking in the beginning of the projects continued along the line of the comparative study, in order to determine the validity of the VR model as a representation of a physical space. We had so far analyzed the questionnaire matrix with the answers from all the test persons in both the physical and the virtual space, and could compare the answers in the two scenarios respectively. The test subjects had worn eye tracking glasses both in the physical scenario, and in the virtual HMD with our custom built-in eye tracking equipment. With this additional data-layer of eye tracking, we could suddenly extract another kind of behavior from the two scenarios. While the questionnaire matrix captures a conscious reflection about the test person's perception of the space, we could now combine those answers with the immediate movements of the eyes, i.e. a less consciously controllable behavior. We could combine the answering of questions about the space which involves a conscious reflection on answering with the less conscious eye movement behavior. The immediate perception results from eye tracking at the same time of the verbal reflective perception from the answers to the questions could thus be logged and analyzed. It seemed to be an important consideration to include this diversity in the feedback mechanism, since neuroscience shows [6] that our brains combine input from many different areas to create an experience.

By tracking where the test subjects are actually looking, in a real and a virtual scenario respectively, we can compare the results and estimate how similar the eye movement behavior are in the two scenarios, when answering the same question from the same location. The eye tracking can be visualized in different ways (Fig. 4) and mapped on a common background map of the room, in order to facilitate a comparison.

The eye tracking data from the study can subsequently be converted into heatmaps and it was mapped onto the same 3D BIM model image rendering for comparison between the real scenario and the virtual scenario. To compare the eye tracking from the two scenarios in a quick way, a method was invented in order to speed up the normally tedious and complex process of analyzing these types of data.

Since the resulting data from the eye tracking contains a lot of information, such as Time To First Fixation (TTFF), Time Spent in the different areas of interest, and the number of fixations, it was necessary to choose what is needed in the specific analysis. In the example (Fig. 5), the visualization of our eye tracking data in respectively an aggregated heat map (A) and an opacity map (B) is shown. The Opacity map is converted to grayscale, and through the use of the histogram produced by Adobe Photoshop (C) it is then possible to measure the average intensity in the image to measure the balance between the number of black and white pixels in the converted heatmap.

The comparison made possible by this simple method allowed to take all the eye tracking of the test persons in physical reality and compare them with the map from virtual reality and using the photoshop difference filter to count the difference of pixels in the images (Fig. 6). By measuring the average intensity value in the grayscale pictures

Fig. 4. Eye tracking data visualized on a 360 image of the auditorium space.

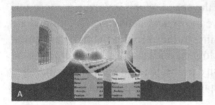 

Fig. 5. The heatmap on a gradient scale from red to green (A) showing eye tracking data related to users answers to a specific question. An opacity map (B) of the same data with a gradient intensity. The Photoshop Histogram (C) used to calculate the average intensity value. (Color figure online)

- the 'Mean' value – it was possible to measure the difference of where the test subjects had been looking while answering the same questions in the two scenarios respectively.

Fig. 6. Eye tracking of physical reality (A) compared to virtual reality (B) combined into the resulting difference map (C).

A comparison of the mean value between the same question in the physical and the virtual reality was calculated, and then the comparison of the mean value between different questions was calculated. These two results could then be compared, with the hypothesis that we should see a better correlation between eye tracking in the same questions in the two scenarios (physical reality and VR), than between eye tracking in non-matching questions.

While the exact method and the obtained results are explained in depth here [7], the general picture of the full comparison showed that there is actually a better correspondence in eye movements between a scenario in physical reality and its counterpart in virtual reality, than between eye movements in general when observing the auditorium space. It showed clearly more consistency between the physical space and the VR model than what can be attributed to coincidence.

Adding the layer of eye tracking to the study substantiated our primary idea that VR representational architectural models can actually be used in architecture and presumably significantly improve the imaginative role of architectural representation.

3.2 Extended Eye Tracking in Areas of Interest

From the findings of analyzing the eye tracking data it was possible to move a bit deeper into the eye tracking data. The heat maps generated in the first round of analyzing the eye tracking, gave us a visual overview of where, and on which elements of the space, it was natural to focus the attention in a next level of comparison.

In the study we had applied, as mentioned, a questionnaire matrix, but we also allowed the test subjects 10 s with no questions upon entering the space, both in the physical space and in the VR model space. These 10 s were also eye tracked, and could then be used for comparisons as well. By looking at the heat maps generated from the eye tracking data, we could divide the space into areas of interest, abbreviated AOIs (Fig. 7), from where measurements and exact data can be calculated.

Usually when eye tracking research is applied in research, it is with the focus on a particular brand or product, often located on a specific place in space e.g. an item on a shelf in a supermarket, or products shown on a homepage. However, our research focus is on the experience of a full architectural space, which requires that we expand the focus from a single particular object to the entire space in question. That is why it was found necessary to divide the architectural space into several AOIs, based on the findings from an analysis of the visual heat maps produced from the eye tracking data in the first place. From the vast amount of data extracted through such AOIs we decided to concentrate on the time spent on fixations (measured in milliseconds) in order to add to the comparison of the correlation between the virtual and the physical scenarios.

The results from that comparison in general again showed a high correlation between the perceived physical and virtual space. The difference of the fixations in the two scenarios span from 0% to a maximum of 6%, with an average of only 1.5% which we considered to be a quite low difference [8]. Examining some of the more striking observations, we found that for instance a large window near the entrance received a lot of attention (fixation time) in the VR model, but almost none in the physical eye tracking measurement. In other words: people were looking out the window in VR but not in real life. Why this difference stands out in such particularity is difficult to know for sure. A qualified guess could be the fact that the test subjects who experienced the physical space had just arrived from the outside a few moments earlier, and were very well aware of the outside and how it looked, while those who experienced the VR scenario did not traverse the same physical distance to the test site. The physical test subjects do not need to check what they find outside, since they feel they already know. In virtual reality, however, the test subjects understand the nature of the simulation, and are perhaps eager

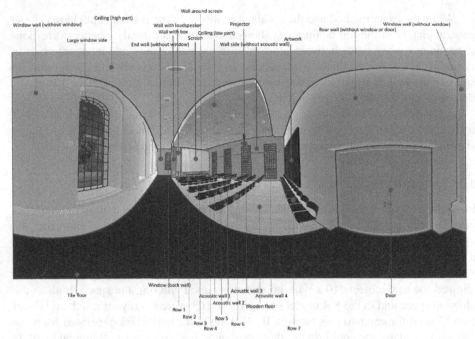

Fig. 7. Heat maps from the first 10 s of observing the space with no exact question used to divide the space into areas of interest.

to check if the outside corresponds to what they would expect and maybe also sustain the experience of being in a specific space.

If we included the arrival situation in the VR model and made the test subjects virtually walk the same way to the test space, we might have had different results in that particular matter. Though these curious findings are interesting in their own respect and give a lot of inspiration to new investigations, they did not interfere with the overall picture of a high correlation between the VR model and the real physical space.

The extended analysis of the eye tracking data from that phase of the research was further consolidating the assumption that the precise use of virtual reality architectural BIM models can improve architectural representation in the interaction between human users and the computational system of the BIM model [8].

3.3 Comparison to a Plan and Section Scenario

With the examinations of physical space versus virtual space we had established a methodology with the use of eye tracking and 3D digital BIM models in VR. The idea occurred that we should try to apply that methodology to one of the archetypal forms of architectural representations, namely the plan and section drawings traditionally used in design of architecture.

In this plan and section scenario, the students were positioned in front of drawings hanging on a wall (Fig. 8 C). We had one architectural plan drawing and one section drawing showing the test space in scale 1:50. In this scenario we had to deal with the

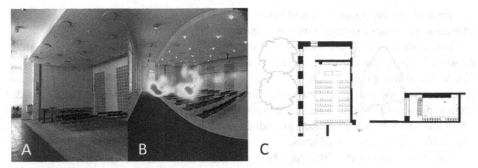

Fig. 8. The physical scenario (A), the virtual reality Scenario with eye tracking heat maps (B), and the plan & section scenario (C).

nature of 2D drawings and let the test subjects overview the entire material from the beginning of the study. Eye tracking equipment collected data of fixations from the test subjects. Especially in this phase of the study no prior knowledge of the space is crucial, since a memory of the actual physical space, invoked from watching the drawings, could disturb the study, if the answers were actually related to memories of the space instead of the space experienced through the drawings.

The findings from this phase of the study is trifold. Like in the previous phases, we collected the data using the same questionnaire matrix and the data from the eye tracking equipment. We also asked the test subjects to describe the architectural atmosphere they sensed in the space by freely choosing three words that came to their mind.

Looking at those freely chosen words in the three scenarios (Fig. 9) makes it obvious that there is a difference in the perception of the architectural atmosphere of the space seen through the three different modes of representation. While physical reality and virtual reality do have slightly different vocabulary – e.g. words such as "sterile" and "clinical" appear in the virtual scenario only - those two scenarios are closer to each other, than to the plan & section scenario. In the plan and section scenario some test subjects could not associate three words with the space, and even with a few words in common, the distribution of words is in general different than in physical reality and VR scenarios.

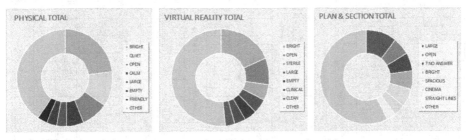

Fig. 9. The hierarchy of words chosen to describe the atmosphere of the space in the physical, virtual, and plan & section scenario respectively.

Though this brief summary will have to suffice here, more thorough schematics and a discussion of these specific findings related to study is available [9].

The answers to the questionnaire matrix from all the test subjects are compared between the physical, the virtual, and the plan & section scenarios, respectively (Fig. 10). The value of the questions ranges from low to high degree (1 to 7) and in the 'Comparisons' part, the divergence has been converted to percent. As mentioned, this plan & section phase of the study includes a cross reference to a small group of professional architects. This serves mainly as an indication of the difference in using students or professionally trained test subjects.

The figure shows the difference between the answers to the questionnaire in the physical and virtual scenario, and between the physical and the plan & section scenario. The intensity of the color shows the more divergent answers related to the specific questions. Looking at the numbers, it is obvious that the overall divergence from the physical scenario is found to be much higher in the plan & section scenario than in the virtual reality scenario. In addition, the room is found more boring in the plan & section scenario. Of course, these questions can be interpreted differently by different test persons, but we are simply searching for indications or trends that could provide information about what to include in a prototype tool concerned with estimation of architectural quality. As previously mentioned in this paper, the questions related to the material quality are hard to answer in the VR model, since the premise for the study is to use a sketch BIM model with very little information of material quality.

	Physical Reality - 30 subjects	Divergence to real measure in m	Virtual Reality - 63 subjects	Divergence to real measure in m	Plan & Section - Students - 32 subjects	Divergence to real measure in m	Plan & Section - Professionals - 6 subjects	Divergence to real measure in m	DIVERGENCE physical and virtual	DIFFERENCE % Physical and Virtual	DIVERGENCE physical and P&S students	DIFFERENCE % Physical and P&S Students	DIVERGENCE physical and P&S professionals	DIFFERENCE % Physical and P&S Professionals	DIVERGENCE P&S students and professionals	DIFFERENCE % P&S Students and Professionals
Compelled to enter the room	5,2		5,4		4,0		5,3		-0,2	2,9	1,2	16,7	-0,1	1,9	-1,3	18,6
Expectations of the room are met	4,6		5,5		4,7		3,5		-0,9	12,7	0,0	0,3	1,1	16,2	1,2	16,5
Easy to move about in the room	6,0		6,2		5,6		6,3		-0,2	2,2	0,5	6,7	-0,3	4,3	-0,8	11,0
Room is booring	3,4		3,8		4,9		2,8		-0,5	6,7	-1,5	21,5	0,5	7,6	2,0	29,2
Window placement sufficient light	5,9		5,9		5,2		6,3		0,0	0,2	0,6	9,3	-0,5	6,7	-1,1	15,9
Room sufficiently lit	6,1		6,4		5,1		4,8		-0,3	4,4	1,0	14,4	1,3	18,1	0,3	3,7
Lighting as intended	5,5		5,2		4,4		3,8		0,3	4,2	1,1	15,6	1,6	23,3	0,5	7,7
Feeling well in the room	5,7		5,4		4,8		5,0		0,2	3,4	0,9	12,6	0,7	9,5	-0,2	3,1
Feeling safe in the room	5,8		5,4		5,2		5,7		0,4	5,6	0,7	9,7	0,2	2,4	-0,5	7,3
What row to sit in	3,7		3,7		2,8		2,7		-0,1	0,8	0,8	11,8	1,0	14,3	0,2	2,5
Materials are nice	5,0		4,2		3,9		4,0		0,8	11,1	1,1	15,2	1,0	14,3	-0,1	0,9
Materials live up to expectations	5,1		5,1		4,2		4,2		0,1	1,2	1,0	14,0	1,0	13,8	0,0	0,1
Material quality	5,4		4,0		3,2		4,2		1,4	20,3	2,2	32,1	1,3	18,1	-1,0	14,0
Good view to the screen	6,7		6,6		4,7		6,2		0,1	1,3	2,0	28,3	0,5	7,1	-1,5	21,1
Good view to the presenter	6,1		6,5		4,5		4,8		-0,4	5,1	1,6	22,9	1,3	18,6	-0,3	4,3
Enough space around you	5,9		6,1		4,6		6,0		-0,2	3,1	1,3	18,2	-0,1	1,4	-1,4	19,6
Good placement of exits	4,4		5,2		4,4		5,0		-0,8	11,5	0,0	0,6	-0,6	9,0	-0,6	8,5
Length of the room in meters (14m)	17,9	3,9	17,6	3,6	25,5	11,5	19,7	5,7	0,2	0,2	-7,6	7,6	-1,8	1,8	5,8	5,8
Width of the room in meters (8,5m)	10,0	1,5	10,7	2,2	14,1	5,6	11,3	2,8	-0,7	0,7	-4,1	4,1	-1,3	1,3	2,8	2,8
Height of the room in meters (5m)	6,5	1,5	5,6	0,6	6,8	1,8	5,2	0,2	0,9	0,9	-0,4	0,4	1,3	1,3	1,7	1,7

Fig. 10. Answers to the questionnaire in the three scenarios.

A more precise comparison can be made from the test subjects estimating the size of the space. There is a high correlation between the perceived length, width, and height of the space between the physical scenario and the VR scenario. Furthermore, the estimations of the length of the space diverge from the actual measure with a maximum of 3.9 m overestimation. That shows that they are not completely right in relation the actual real measures of the space, but it is noteworthy that the divergence between the physical and virtual estimation is similar within a margin of less than 1 m. In comparison the divergence between the plan & section scenario and the actual measures of the length of the space are much higher with a maximum of 11.5 m overestimation. In all the estimations (as an average of the test persons' estimations) of the plan & section scenario, the divergences are higher than between the physical and the virtual scenario.

A final comparison worth briefly mentioning here, is the difference between students and professionals. While the conversion of the eye tracking heat maps from 2D flat drawings into a 3D environment such as used in the physical and virtual scenario is not feasible to a meaningful degree, we can look at the eye tracking data from the plan & section scenario in an investigation of the behavior of students and professionals respectively, while decoding the drawings. The clearest example in the difference of behavior when looking at the drawing is probably seen in the estimation of the height of the space (Fig. 11) where the professional architects are almost exclusively looking at the section drawing and the students are still looking moderately at the plan drawing also, even though very little information about the height of the space can be found there. It is interesting as well, that the professionals are also looking briefly at the scale ratio (showing the 1:50 scale) located at the bottom left corner of each drawing. Perhaps this also assist the professionals in estimating the height of the space closer to its actual height than what is the case for any of the student estimations. Especially the students from the plan & section scenario are far from the actual measurements.

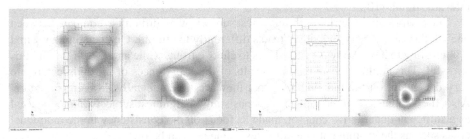

Fig. 11. Heat map showing test subjects estimating the height of the space - students (left) and professional architects (right).

In this study, the architectural virtual reality scenario seems closer to physical reality than the experience of the same space experienced through plan and section drawings. There is an overall higher correlation of both the conscious reflections (the answers to the questionnaire) and the less conscious behavior (the eye tracking) between the real physical architectural space and the virtual reality space, than there is between the real physical space and the space communicated through plan and section drawings. We could in addition note that, for this particular study, the scenario with the best overall size estimations, compared to the actual measures, was the virtual reality scenario [9].

3.4 Neurological EEG Pilot Study

While the VSR was gradually taking shape based on the input from the various findings in the abovementioned studies, the idea of investigating the neurological aspect of an architectural experience resulted in a pilot study involving EEG with the VSR. At the time of this study, the VSR contained several features automatically tracking and logging the position of the test subjects and users. We were also working on a real architectural project case, the sports facility Gaarslevhallen, that was used in the pilot study.

We had initially 12 test subjects, but after a screening only 8 could actually be used. Because the number of test subjects is not sufficient to provide a meaningful quantitative data set, we focused on a qualitative analysis of the consistency of individual test subjects, and constrained ourselves to the cautious considerations that we saw a consistency in the data retrieved on the individual level.

All test subjects were fitted with both the Emotiv Insight 5 channel EEG sensor and Oculus Rift HMD and after a brief tutorial they took a virtual tour through the 3D model of Gaarslevhallen (Fig. 13 left). The matching of the test subjects' location in the model, their field of view, the task, and the neurological activity, showed a possibility to link an architectural experience to specific emotional responses.

The output from the Emotiv Insight is from the EEG signal transformed into graphs providing metrics showing six different areas. We chose to focus on Excitement, Interest and Engagement. Excitement (EXC) is an awareness or feeling of physiological arousal with a positive value. Interest (VAL) is the degree of attraction or aversion to the current stimuli, environment or activity and is commonly referred to as Valence. Engagement (ENG) is experienced as alertness and the conscious direction of attention towards task-relevant stimuli [10].

The performance metrics of the eight test subjects were difficult to compare between one another since every individual reacts differently to stimuli. One person might find it interesting to have many possible doors to choose from, while another might find this stressful. This could indicate that the results of the experiences of the architecture are very dependent on the individual, or that they are fundamentally different in nature. Also, the awareness that the sample size consisting of eight test subjects cannot be used as a sufficient quantitative data set, made us focus on the consistency in the individual cases such as the example of one of the test subjects seen below.

Example of Analysis. An analysis of test subject 2 (Fig. 12) shows a general high Interest throughout the test. The Interest rise from the beginning (A) when receiving the instructions and remain high until the subject reaches a dead end in the basement (between E and F) and the time where the test subject discovers the right door and thus where to go next. When the test subject enters the narrow hallway (C), the Excitement lowers again. When entering the changing room (D) the Excitement rises gradually until the test subject re- enters the foyer (F). In the foyer itself, the Excitement rises again and peaks again when exploring the fitness room (G) and when concluding the test (I). This indicates a test subject who are excited to explore on his own, but also a possible link to

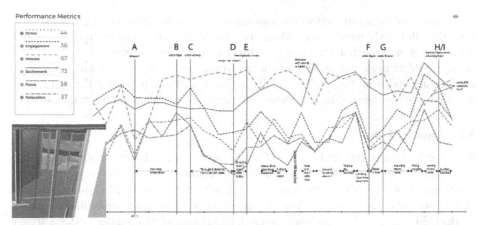

Fig. 12. Performance metrics for test subject 2 showing graphs with markings corresponding to the same specific entry- and exit-points, used for all the test subjects.

the architectural perception of the space. The large foyer with lots of light and spacious qualities seems more exciting than the narrow hallway with only doors. Engagement also corresponds to the activity of opening doors, though on moderate scale. Interest remains mid-range and very steady throughout the test [11].

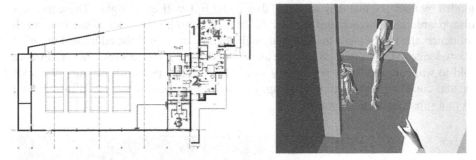

Fig. 13. Plan of the sports facility Gaarslevhallen with zone entry points marked for the analysis (left) and screenshot of the female characters in the locker room (right).

At a certain location in the 3D model, the door sign symbols of the changing rooms had been confused, and caused male test subjects to encounter two female dummy characters in the male changing room (Fig. 13 right). This caused a nonintentional, but apparent, neurological impact in that particular part of the test.

Even though a general comparison between the test subjects made little sense in this study, we could very cautiously qualify the assumptions that the use of interaction, e.g. engaging in opening doors, shows engagement in the test subjects' behavior. A virtual reality scenario incorporating such elements of interaction cannot be provided to the same extent using traditional plan and section drawings or even non-immersive 2D and 3D digital representational tools.

Besides the intriguing individual analysis of the test subjects' behavior, the results from the pilot study were hence addressing a framework for a larger study to find out what sort of neurological data can be retrieved, and if the combination with virtual reality could be made useful. Further studies with expertise from the combined field of architecture and neurology will hopefully in the near future be able to generate more knowledge about the specific application of neurology in architectural perception.

3.5 Tracking Behavior

In a continuation of the pilot study in Gaarslevhallen, we did a larger study using the same architectural case, with 40 new architecture students as test subjects, to test the functionality of the VSR system at that stage. The results from the EEG pilot study had showed us that a general comparison between the test subjects was difficult and instead we decided to change the setup towards the elements that could yield the most qualifying feedback on a slim functionality of the VSR. That study thus focused on the location and the field of view of the test subjects, in combination with a subsequent question matrix. Instead of the expensive (both time wise and equipment wise) pupil eye tracking we had programmed a gaze tracking within the VSR that took the midpoint of the field of view direction of the test subject as an indication for the gaze direction and as the data basis for generating gaze heatmaps.

After a brief tutorial, the first group of 30 test subject (average age 23.6 – 14 male and 16 female) walked one at a time through the 3D digital BIM sketch model in VR. In order to perform a subsequent analysis of the behavior of the test subjects, they were guided by markers, that they were told they could follow (Fig. 14 right). These markers disappeared on approach and showed the next place to go. In order to see how much influence, the use of these markers had on the behavior, we had the additional group of 10 students (average age 24.8 – 4 male and 6 female) using no markers. This group were told to walk around freely where they would like. In this phase of the study the VSR system could log the location tracking, the gaze tracking, and we added information from a subsequent questionnaire.

Fig. 14. The sports facility architectural case as a white sketch model seen from the outside (left) and inside the café area (right) with the marker used in a part the study.

The location tracking is a visual mapping of the movement path of every test subject. That data is visualized as heat maps on a plan drawing. The VSR can combine the paths from all test subjects in one map in order to get the general overview from a study.

This way it becomes quite obvious what part of the building is the busiest, in this case namely the large café and reception area, functioning as distribution space to the fitness and sports facilities (Fig. 15). This methodology of course also allows for isolating individual test subject's heat maps, to combine their time spent at specific locations with their comments about the architectural space.

Fig. 15. The location tracking heat maps on the three floors (basement, 1st, and 2nd floor) of the case building, based on the 30 people test group.

The heat maps from the two groups showed that both took more or less the same route through the building which made the heat maps seem almost similar [12]. That could indicate that the markers had little influence on the flow through the building, in this particular case.

As mentioned above, we had designed a system that would not require a complete setup with eye tracking of the pupil movement, but made a simple logging of the center of view in the VR HMD. That made the system much lighter in respect of both the equipment cost and the data processing. Hence the compromise is between the precision, which is considered acceptable for a building or room scale, and the almost instant visual feedback we can easily obtain using this method.

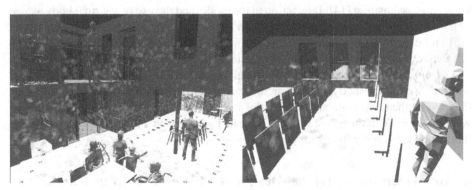

Fig. 16. The gaze heat maps of the café/reception area (left) and from a meeting room (right) where many test subjects looked through on particular window.

The gaze heat maps (Fig. 16) show the areas that requires special attention or interaction. Door handles and an elevator button, are obviously receiving a lot of attention. In addition, the dummy people in the model are also looked at, despite their non-photorealistic appearance. Heat mapping the collected gaze data visually, allows for a general analysis of the points in the architectural models that gets the most attention. We can also see quite accurate details e.g. from which window the test subjects are looking from a small room into the larger hall.

The questionnaire (Fig. 17) was completed after the virtual tour, and shows an example of the data can be cross referenced in VSR to location and gaze tracking.

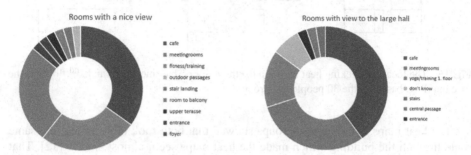

Fig. 17. Example from questionnaire showing perceived architectural atmosphere and visibility

Using a combination of automatic location and gaze tracking with a questionnaire provides feedback on different levels. The memory of previously experienced emotional states used to identify and categorize new architectural experiences are apparently closer linked to surfaces than to geometry [13] which can be difficult to accommodate in an early sketch model without decisions of detailing. The level of detail in the VR model must be sufficient for user-immersion but not creating distractions that could decrease the knowledge acquisition [14]. Interaction in the model and the use of a virtual body avatar or parts of it (in our case: virtual hands) can be an important tool to induce immersion [15] and even to let people experience the world from another point of view, as in a different eye height or in a virtual wheelchair as introduced in the VSR.

To avoid the test subjects to rush through the space like in a game, they were told that they would be asked about the architecture after the virtual tour. We expected that they would then pay more attention to the spaces, however without being told exactly where to look. With this latest study [12] we had approached a functionality in the VSR that seemed to capture the main ideas of our vision.

4 Implementing Universal Design in VSR with a Game Engine

Already in 2017, we began implementing our VSR alpha version into the Unity Game Engine [16] in order to be more flexible with the additions to the tests we would like to perform. Earlier we had borrowed a special BIM viewer platform [17], but needed to be able to program the VSR system with our specific needs. To that purpose we chose the Unity game engine. In the beginning we were assisted by an intern student from the department of game design, but as the task became more time consuming, we hired a skilled Unity game programmer to assist us in developing the VSR tool prototype.

The collaboration with the programmers was in many ways a very interesting time, with a lot of decisions to be made in relation to the user interface and exact functionalities of system. Things we, as architects, took for granted for instance the importance of correct sunlight in relation to the geographical situation of a building in the world, had to be explained, since the gaming perspective usually works with light as an effect to emphasize flow or action in a gaming environment.

In addition to the visual mapping features of position tracking and gaze tracking already mentioned in the descriptions of the studies so far, we improved the VSR through Unity with additional feedback mechanisms in the form of collision maps, and an extended use of materials, simulations of smoke evolution, in case of fire. From the beginning we had the intention to include universal design in architecture and to make sure that the VSR system could be used as a dialogue tool with architects also for the benefit of disabled people. We had included the wheelchair simulation from early on in the design of the prototype, and with the arrival of three real architectural testcases from the universal design project "Fitness for all" [18] we had the possibility of testing these features in real architectural design situations.

4.1   The "Fitness for All" VSR Reports

The VSR was used in the "fitness for all" architectural projects to generate reports that could send easy feedback to the architects about the sensation of the spaces from a wheelchair user, in relation to universal design, and general comments from walking persons. The learnings from all the above-mentioned studies was now implemented into the prototype of the VSR dialogue tool. The tool was now capable of using BIM models in VR and record the experience of the users. The screen and verbal comments are recorded into a movie file along with heat maps on the plan drawings of the house showing both position, collisions. In the 3D environment all the gaze point heat maps are recorded and can be extracted on 360 images or viewed within the 3D or VR model (Fig. 18). The VSR prototype allows to customize materials and backgrounds and insert detailed renders, in areas where the architects would like additional special feedback.

Fig. 18. Plan, position-, collision-, and gaze-tracking heatmaps and a 360 detailed render.

It is also possible to simulate other kinds of scenarios such as fire with smoke accumulation or to have different models in the same viewer i.e. a laser scanning of the existing building to compare e.g. a new restoration project. The reports generated, all inflicted actual change in the architecture in the case projects.

5 Conclusive Remarks

The prototype dialogue VSR tool shows that VR with BIM models can be the foundation for investigations on many levels of architectural quality. The interaction that can be established in the VSR tool in general shows engagement in the behavior of test persons. The visual location tracking and the "slim" version of eye tracking (of an individual or the group or any part of the group) can be cross-referenced to the question matrix and with the general feedback from the users in order to evaluate the behavior of people in an architecture before it is actually built and ready to use. The VSR system tracks both the reflective spoken feedback but also the less conscious actions of where users are stopping and what they are looking at in particular. In this manner there is a potential to determine whether the yet unbuild architectural traits of a sketch project can result in pleasant and emancipatory experiences, or rather frustration and confusion. Catching potential areas of conflict early in the sketching phase makes it a lot cheaper to change spaces of a building, than after the concrete is cast and the beams are welded.

The components of the VSR dialogue tool is now ready for being streamlined into a more broadly used application, and hence become an assisting tool for architects and the building industry and its many users. The VSR dialogue tool can hopefully be a supplementary and virtual factor in improving the quality of inclusiveness, universal design, and the overall architectural quality in our world of real people and real architecture.

References

1. Hermund, A.: Anvendt 3D modellering og parametrisk formgivning, København (2011)
2. BVU*net. webpage of the BVU*net (2012). http://bvunet.dk/
3. Hermund, A., Klint, L.S.: Virtual and physical architectural atmosphere. In: Proceedings of the International Conference on Architecture, Landscape and Built Environment (ICALBE 2016), Kuala Lumpur, Malaysia (2016)
4. Rattenbury, K.: This is Not Architecture: Media Constructions. Routledge (2002)
5. Zeki, S.: Inner Vision: An Exploration of Art and the Brain. Oxford University Press Inc., New York (1999)
6. Mallgrave, H.F.: The Architect's Brain: Neuroscience, Creativity, and Architecture. Wiley (2010)
7. Hermund, A., Bundgaard, T.S., Klint, L.S.: Speculations on the representation of architecture in virtual reality: how can we (continue to) simulate the unseen? In: Back to the Future: The Next 50 Years - 51st International Conference of the Architectural Science Association (ANZAScA), Wellington, New Zealand (2017)
8. Hermund, A., Klint, L.S., Bundgaard, T.S.: BIM with VR for architectural simulations: building information models in virtual reality as an architectural and urban designtool. In: The 6th Annual International Conference on Architecture and Civil Engineering (ACE 2018), Singapore (2018)
9. Hermund, A., Bundgaard, T.S., Klint, L.S.: The perception of architectural space in reality, in virtual reality, and through plan and section drawings. In: Computing for a Better Tomorrow: eCAADe 2018, Poland (2018)
10. Emotiv. Performance metrics. Webpage of Emotiv Pro - Performance metrics. https://emotiv.gitbook.io/emotivpro/data_streams/performance-metrics

11. Hermund, A., Myrup Jensen, M., Klint, L.: The neurological impact of perception of architectural space in virtual reality. In: Virtually Real - 7th eCAADe Regional International Symposium. Aalborg University, Aalborg, Denmark (2019)
12. Hermund, A., Klint, L., Bundgård, T.S.: Neurological feedback from perception of architecture in virtual reality, India (2019)
13. Goldhagen, S.W.: Welcome to Your World: How the Built Environment Shapes Our Lives. 1st edn, xxxiv, 347 p. HarperCollins Publishers, New York (2017)
14. Makransky, G., Terkildsen, T.S., Mayer, R.E.: Adding immersive virtual reality to a science lab simulation causes more presence but less learning. Learn. Instr. **60**, 225–236 (2019)
15. Slater, M., Sanchez-Vives, M.V.: Transcending the self in immersive virtual reality. Computer **47**(7), 24–30 (2014)
16. Unity. Webpage of Unity Game Engine. https://unity.com/
17. Johansson, M., Roupé, M., Bosch-Sijtsema, P.: Real-time visualization of building information models (BIM). Autom. Constr. **54**, 69–82 (2015)
18. Realdania. Fitness skal være for alle: Tre projekter nytænker fitnesscentre (2017). Realdania pressrelease about "Fitness for all". https://realdania.dk/nyheder/2017/11/fitness-skal-v%C3%A6re-for-alle_09nov2017

Human-Computer Interaction in Education: Keyword and Discipline Network in 20 Years

Yongyeon Cho[1]([⊠]), Huiwon Lim[2]([⊠]), and Hye Jeong Park[3]([⊠])

[1] Interior Design Department, Iowa State University, Ames, IA 50011, USA
yongyeon@iastate.edu
[2] Graphic Design Department, Penn State University, State College, PA 16801, USA
hjl5360@psu.edu
[3] Human-Computer Interaction Program, Iowa State University, Ames, IA 50011, USA
hjpark@iastate.edu

Abstract. Human-Computer Interaction (HCI) education covers diverse human-oriented design approaches, which are Human Factors (HF), Human-Centered Design (HCD), User-Centered Design (UCD), and User Experiences (UX) [5]. However, the relationships among those approaches are unclear. To better understand and develop HCI pedagogy, understanding which approach is more involved than another and how it is associated with each other within HCI is significant. Therefore, the purpose of this research is to identify the relationship to the four human-oriented design approaches using the keyword network analysis method to answer the following questions: 1) What descriptors, author-chosen subject headings, related to HCI, HF, HCD, UCD, and UX have been studied in the Education field? 2) How does HCI connect to human-related design approaches? and 3) What discipline in higher education has been studying more about HCI? To find the answers, this research analyzed a total of 684 peer-reviewed journal articles' abstracts published between 2001 and 2020 from the Educational Resource Information Center (ERIC) database. Gephi 0.9.2 was utilized to visualize frequencies and relationships of the keywords. The findings presented that the top five most frequently mentioned descriptors in HCI were "Man Machine Systems," "Educational Technology," "Foreign Countries," "Interaction," and "Teaching Methods." The number of articles with the four human-oriented design approaches have increased over the last 20 years. The top five most identified disciplines in the HCI-related articles were "Educational Technology," "HCI," "Information Science," "Computer and Society," and "Information Systems." The findings of this research would be valuable resources in understanding the current research trend of HCI education, and the relationship among the four human-related design approaches and developing curricula for HCI related subjects.

Keywords: Human-Computer Interaction · Education · Keyword network analysis · Discipline · Gephi · Interdisciplinarity

1 Introduction

Human-Computer Interaction (HCI) has developed as an intertwined discipline including computer graphics, human factors, ergonomics, industrial engineering, operating system,

M. Kurosu (Ed.): HCII 2021, LNCS 12762, pp. 50–65, 2021.
https://doi.org/10.1007/978-3-030-78462-1_4

cognitive psychology, and computer science [9]. HCI's interdisciplinary perspective impacts HCI education to focus on both humans and technology to lead "human-centered technology innovation" [5]. Particularly, investigating the relationship between HCI and human-oriented design approaches such as Human Factors (HF), Human-Centered Design (HCD), User-Centered Design (UCD), and User Experiences (UX) is necessary to develop within the HCI education context since they are the major learning objectives in HCI courses.

Copious research with various methods has been studied in HCI education. However, the keyword network analysis [3] has not been focused much, even though it is vital to understand HCI contents better and unfolds relationships among each subject [4]. Therefore, this research aims to identify HCI research trends and relation to the four human-oriented design approaches (HF, HCD, UCD, and UX) using the keyword network analysis method.

We designed the following three research questions: 1) What descriptors, author-chosen subject headings related to HCI, HF, HCD, UCD, and UX have been studied in the Education field? 2) How does HCI connect to human-related design approaches? and 3) What discipline in higher-education has been studying more about HCI?

The target audience of this article is researchers and educators related to the HCI domain. To support them in future efforts in this discipline, we contain the comprehensive dataset of the keyword network analysis to provide resources for HCI scholars who might expect to see the HCI research trends and developments over two decades.

2 Definitions of HCI and the Four Approaches

Before we moved any further, we defined the terms we had for our research to work with all crystal clear definitions.

HCI is based on an interdisciplinary approach to better understand major phenomena of human surroundings toward the design, evaluation, and implementation of interactive computing systems. Accordingly, HCI might be interpreted in various ways based on the characteristics of disciplines closely related to design and interaction between systems and humans [9].

HF is physiological principles to the discipline of engineering and design of products, processes, and systems. HF could be illustrated by the interactions between humans and environmental systems. Accordingly, the goal of HF is reducing human errors, increasing productivity, and enhancing safety and comfort for human interaction and systems through multiple tools. Thus, HF can be adopted in various disciplines such as psychology, sociology, engineering, industrial design, and interior design [21]. In HCI context, HF plays a vital role in understanding human information processing, communication, and physical characteristics of users [9]. Particularly, multisensory experience in HF has a great potential to improve understanding of human senses and change the existing HCI interaction paradigm [18].

HCD is a design philosophy to emphasize a holistic approach with human-oriented design [17]. More specifically, humans are a center of the design process, which includes an interdisciplinary collaboration to provide useful and usable products and services [22]. Accordingly, HCD allows designers and researchers to use various methods in order to solve complex problems. It highlights the human perspective through the design lifecycle and provides a practice-oriented approach, which naturally fits educators' realities [8].

UCD is a fundamental concept of understanding a user's needs. Like HF and HCD, UCD is involved in various disciplines and impacts on several areas (i.e., user research, cognitive science, and interaction design) [19]. Norman said, "User-centered design emphasizes that the purpose of the system is to swerve the user, not to use a specific technology, not to be an elegant piece of programming [16]." In line with this, good UCD provides users a large room to understand and manage the system in various situations [19].

Over the last decade, UX has become a buzzword in various fields, including HCI. According to the ISO definition, "UX includes all the users' emotions, beliefs, preferences, perceptions, physical and psychological responses, behaviors and accomplishments that occur before, during, and after use" [11]. Accordingly, based on the definition of ISO, UX includes three areas as the user's internal state, designed system, and the context. Hence, UX is a consequence of a user's internal state, the characteristics of the designed system, and the context in the interaction between system and human. This concept of UX creates innumerable design and experience opportunities [15].

Keyword network analysis is described as an investigation of the relation to links and items (e.g., keywords) in a given data set [3]. The findings of network analysis show important information, links between the keywords in the context clearly by its visualization [4, 14]. Visualization of keyword network analysis helps scholars to discover major patterns and trends of domains [6, 10, 13]. Recently, Gephi, an open-source software, provides data visualization [2], it has been used in a wide range of disciplines for visualizing data. For example, Wan et al. [20] generated a keyword map by Gephi for studying recommendation methods based on e-learning systems.

3 Method and Procedure

This study adopted a systematic keyword review and analysis process (see Table 1) to create keyword networks and discipline networks.

In step 1, we searched peer-reviewed journal articles and found a total of 684 articles. We reviewed the articles' abstracts to select appropriate studies, including the five keywords HCI, HF, HCD, UCD, or UX. The collected articles were published between 2001 and 2020 archived by the Education Resources Information Center (ERIC) – a leading international digital library of education research and information for educators, researchers, and policymakers. ERIC is sponsored by the Institute of Education Sciences of the United States Department of Education [7].

In step 2, we collected 8,422 descriptors, author-selected subject headings presented on the ERIC website. Then, we sorted 8,422 collected descriptors by frequency and the number of articles by year to see each five keyword's tendency using Excel.

Step 3 and 4 were for data cleaning processes to visualize the five keyword networks through Gephi 0.9.2. In step 3, we removed duplicated descriptors for creating nodes for Gephi. After this process, a total of 3,240 descriptors remained for the nodes.

In step 4, we created 108,878 edges by 3,240 remaining descriptors that we got from step 3. For example, if an article contains three descriptors such as A, B, and C, they

Table 1. The systematic keywords review process and results

Steps	Process	Keywords	Total number of findings
1. Abstract search	Searched all peer-reviewed journal articles' abstracts including the five keywords in the "Educational Resource Information Center" database from 2001 to 2020. Title, authors, years, and descriptors were recorded on Excel	HCI HF HCD UCD UX	162 articles 172 articles 17 articles 51 articles 282 articles
2. Descriptor search	Searched all author-chosen descriptors from the articles from the step 1 result The frequency of descriptors and the number of articles were measured by years	HCI HF HCD UCD UX	1,983 descriptors 2,061 descriptors 247 descriptors 601 descriptors 3,530 descriptors
3. Descriptor duplication filtering	Removed duplicated descriptors from the list of the step 2 result. Each descriptor was called a Node on Gephi	HCI HF HCD UCD UX	677 nodes 985 nodes 177 nodes 357 nodes 1,044 nodes
4. Descriptor links	For a visualization work through Gephi, descriptors in the same article must be linked to each other in Excel. Each connection was called an Edge on Gephi	HCI HF HCD UCD UX	25,706 edges 25,776 edges 3,815 edges 7,435 edges 46,146 edges
5. Network visualization	Created keyword networks through Gephi from the results of step 3 and 4		5 networks
6. Combined descriptor duplication filtering	Combined HCI nodes with each human-related design approaches' nodes from step 3 and duplicated nodes were removed and categorized, and the nodes were assigned to new IDs	HCI+HF HCI+HCD HCI+UCD HCI+UX	1,254 nodes 737 nodes 819 nodes 1,266 nodes
7. Combined descriptor links	Combined edges from HCI with each human-related design approaches' edges from step 4, and assigned the new IDs from step 6	HCI+HF HCI+HCD HCI+UCD HCI+UX	51,482 edges 29,520 edges 33,741 edges 75,381 edges
8. Network visualization	Created keyword networks through Gephi from the results of step 6 and 7		4 networks
9. Authors disciplines	Collected frequencies of authors' disciplines from ResearchGate		180 authors 123 disciplines
10. Network visualization	Created an author's discipline network through Gephi from the results of step 9		1 network

are three nodes – A, B, and C –, and six edges – A to B, A to C, B to C, B to A, B to C, C to A, and C to B – for the network. We created all possible edges with the 3,240 descriptors through Excel.

In step 5, we created five keyword networks separately for HCI, HF, HCD, UCD, and UX to answer the first research question. We used ForceAtlas 2, a force-directed layout algorithm, on Gephi [12]. We used the default setting to check 'prevent overlap.' We also assigned different colors for each keyword to make a clear distinction between networks and used 'Label Adjust' to avoid overlapping texts.

In steps 6 and 7, we combined the HCI nodes and edges with each human-oriented design approach's (HF, HCD, UCD, and UX) nodes and edges. Then, we created four two-keywords-combined networks as visualization forms in step 8 using Gephi to answer the second research question. We used the same layout, 'ForceAtlas 2' and 'Label Adjust', which we used in step 5.

In step 9, we investigated the author's disciplines from 162 HCI articles that we found in step 1. A total of 357 authors were detected, and we searched their disciplines using the ResearchGate website, a social networking website for 15 million researchers who can self-define the author's disciplines in 2020 [1]. We collected 180 authors' disciplines among 357 authors because only they noted their disciplines on the ResearchGate. We recorded 123 disciplines from the 180 authors on Excel. From the data, we created 303 nodes of the disciplines with pink and the author with blue. Then we created 773 edges. For example, if Author A has multi-discipline such as D1, D2, and D3, the edges are A to D1, A to D2, and A to D3.

In the last step, we created the authors' discipline network as visualization forms using Gephi to answer the third research question. We used 'ForceAtlas 2' and 'Label Adjust' to get consistent visualized data like other results.

4   Results

As a result of steps 1 and 2, this study found the top five descriptors most frequently mentioned in each keyword, HCI, HF, HCD, UCD, and UX (see Table 2).

The top five most frequently mentioned descriptors in each approach are following: in HCI, we found, Man Machine System, Educational Technology, Foreign Countries, Interaction, and Teaching Methods; in HF we obtained, Foreign Countries, Teaching Methods, Human Factors Engineering, Education Technology, and Higher Education; in HCD we noticed, Design, Teaching Methods, Higher Education, Instructional Design, and Interdisciplinary Approach; in UCD we discovered, Design, Usability, Web Sites, Case Studies, and Higher Education; lastly in UX we discovered, Foreign Countries, Educational Technology, Usability, Student Attitudes, and Internet.

We also found six descriptors used repeatedly out of descriptors we had got through the top five of each approach (HCI, HF, HCD, UCD, and UX). The six descriptors are Foreign Countries (from HCI, HF, and UX), Educational Technology (from HCI, HF, and UX), Teaching Method (from HCI, HF, and HCD), Usability (from UCD and UX), Higher Education (from HF, HCD, and UCD), and Design (from HCD and UCD.)

Additionally, we collected the peer-reviewed journal articles' tendencies, focusing on each keyword (HCI, HF, HCD, UCD, and UX) published each year from 2001 to 2020 (see Fig. 1). The number of articles containing each keyword in the abstract has been increased.

As a result of steps 3, 4, and 5, we visualized the data to see and analyze the relationships among descriptors in each keyword (see Figs. 2, 3, 4, 5 and 6). The size of each node (circle) represents the frequencies of descriptors. The thickness of edges (lines) presents how often the two descriptors were mentioned together in an article. The distance of each node and edge represents the relative relationships among some others around in the keyword network.

As a result of steps 6, 7, and 8, we created four two-keywords-combination networks with visualization forms presented in Figs. 7, 8, 9 and 10. Red nodes and red edges on each figure present the descriptors mentioned in both HCI and one of the other four human-oriented design approaches. As shown in Fig. 10, UX is the keyword that is the most common descriptors within HCI than the other three human-oriented approaches.

Table 2. Top 5 descriptors in HCI and human-related design approaches

Rank	Descriptor	Frequency	Percentage
HCI - Total of 677 descriptors			
1	Man Machine Systems	52	2.62
2	Educational Technology	47	2.37
3	Foreign Countries	45	2.27
4	Interaction	38	1.92
5	Teaching Methods	37	1.87
HF - Total of 985 descriptors			
1	Foreign Countries	74	3.59
2	Teaching Methods	30	1.46
3	Human Factors Engineering	26	1.26
4	Educational Technology	23	1.12
5	Higher Education	19	0.92
HCD - Total of 177 descriptors			
1	Design	8	3.24
2	Teaching Methods	7	2.83
3	Higher Education	4	1.62
4	Instructional Design	4	1.62
5	Interdisciplinary Approach	4	1.62
UCD - Total of 357 descriptors			
1	Design	13	2.16
2	Usability	9	1.50
3	Web Sites	9	1.50
4	Case Studies	8	1.33
5	Higher Education	8	1.33
UX - Total of 1044 descriptors			
1	Foreign Countries	108	3.06
2	Educational Technology	50	1.42
3	Usability	49	1.39
4	Student Attitudes	43	1.22
5	Internet	42	1.19

The top five disciplines in the HCI-related articles were "Educational Technology," "HCI," "Information Science," "Computer and Society," and "Information Systems" (see Table 3).

The visualization of the author's discipline network for HCI research in education (see Fig. 11) shows how authors are organically connected to each discipline.

5   Discussion

The findings of this research would be valuable resources in understanding the current research trend of HCI education and its relationship with four human-related design approaches to develop academic curricula regarding HCI subjects.

Search results "HCI" in abstract, Peer-reviewed Journal Articles, a total of 162 articles

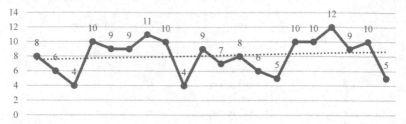

Search results "HF" in abstract, Peer-reviewed Journal Articles, a total of 172 articles

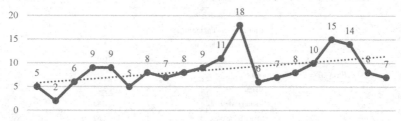

Search results "HCD" in abstract, Peer-reviewed Journal Articles, a total of 17 articles

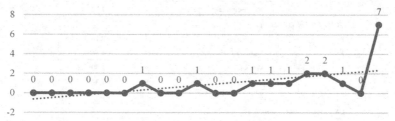

Search results "UCD" in abstract, Peer-reviewed Journal Articles, a total of 51 articles

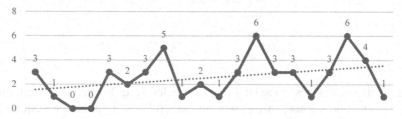

Search results "UX" in abstract, Peer-reviewed Journal Articles, a total of 282 articles

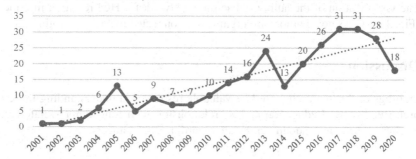

Fig. 1. Number of articles by year from the search results

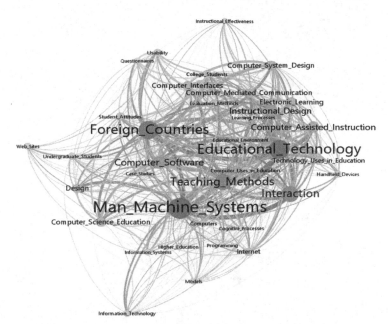

Fig. 2. Descriptors' networks related to HCI in Education. A descriptor network from the 84 peer-reviewed articles that include "Human Computer Interaction" in the abstract nodes = 677 descriptors, edges = 25,706 connections. Descriptors repeated less than 10 times are removed.

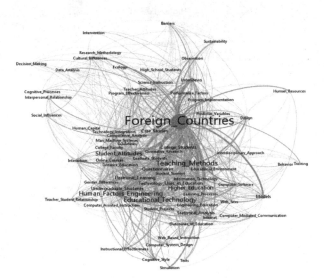

Fig. 3. Descriptors' networks related to HF in Education. A descriptor network from the 172 peer-reviewed articles that include "HF" in the abstract Circles = 985 descriptors, lines = 27,848 connections. Descriptors repeated less than 5 times are removed.

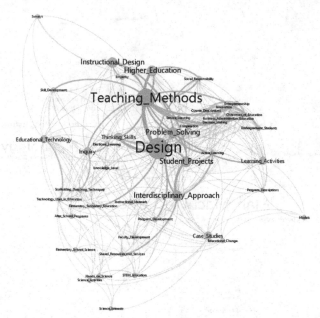

Fig. 4. Descriptors' networks related to HCD in Education. A descriptor network from the 17 peer-reviewed articles that include "HCD" in the abstract Circles = 177 descriptors, lines = 3,814 connections. Descriptors repeated less than 2 times are removed.

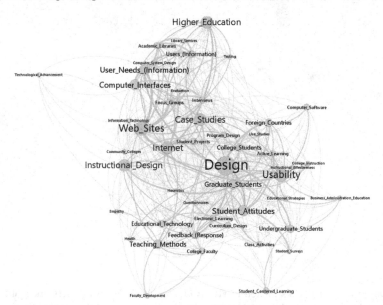

Fig. 5. Descriptors' networks related to UCD in Education. A descriptor network from the 51 peer-reviewed articles that include "UCD" in the abstract Circles = 358 descriptors, lines = 8,035 connections. Descriptors repeated less than 3 times are removed.

Fig. 6. Descriptors' networks related to UX in Education A descriptor network from the 282 peer-reviewed articles that include "UX" in the abstract Circles = 1,044 descriptors, lines = 49,675 connections. Descriptors repeated less than 5 times are removed.

As shown in Table 1, six descriptors, Foreign Countries, Educational Technology, Teaching Method, Usability, Higher Education, and Design, have been repeatedly used out of the 15 descriptors that we got from the top five descriptors in every five keywords (HCI, HF, HCD, UCD, and UX). Based on the result, we confirmed that the research subjects of the five keywords were associated with each other. Nevertheless, there are no five keywords (HCI, HF, HCD, UCD, and UX) that exactly include the same top five descriptors in these five keywords. HCI and HF have the largest number of the same descriptors in the top five descriptors.

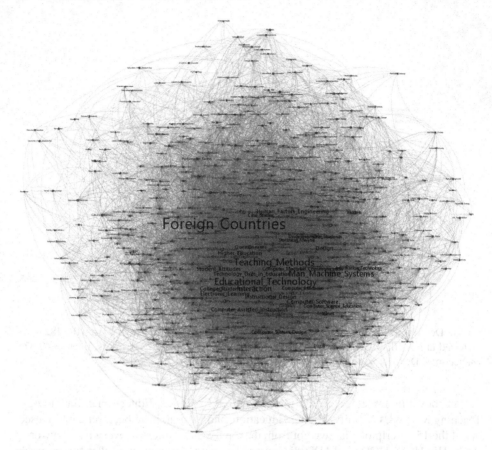

Fig. 7. Two-keywords-combined networks. A comparison descriptor network from the 334 peer-reviewed articles, including "HCI" or "HF" in the abstract, Descriptors repeated less than 2 times are removed. Blue = HCI only, Orange = HF only, Red = Both HCI and HF (Color figure online)

The result in Fig. 1 shows that although there is a difference in increase rates, the five keywords indicate a steadily increasing frequency, and, predictably, it will increase in the future. However, it is difficult to predict the increasing or decreasing tendency of each descriptor in each keyword in this research. Thus, we are looking forward to investigating it in our future research.

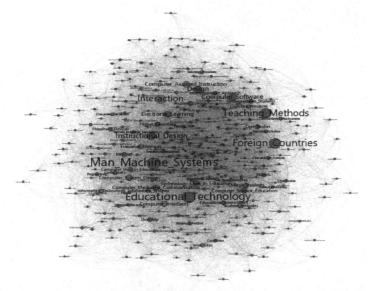

Fig. 8. Two-keywords-combined networks. A comparison descriptor network from the 179 peer-reviewed articles, including "HCI" or "HCD" in the abstract, Descriptors repeated less than 2 times are removed. Blue = HCI only, Yellow = HCD only, Red = Both HCI and HCD (Color figure online)

We found how the descriptors in each keyword are connected to each other using the keyword network analysis using Gephi. For example (Fig. 2), "Foreign Countries," "Educational Technology," and "Man Machine Systems" are the top three descriptors that are most frequently mentioned in HCI. They were located in the center of the visualization, and other descriptors were almost evenly distributed around these three descriptors. For another example, in the HCI network, a descriptor, "Interaction," is more related to "Educational Technology" and "Man Machine Systems" but less related to "Foreign Countries." Besides, Fig. 2 shows that the two descriptors, Information Technology and Instructional Effectiveness, are far from each other, which means that they have the least relationship. Through the five network visualizations, we could see which descriptors are more frequently mentioned in each keyword, how the descriptors are located in each keyword, and how the descriptors are strongly related to each other. Furthermore, future researchers could find opportunities to see the relationships among the descriptors in this study. With such opportunities, they could know what descriptors that they should consider together while they are working on their research regarding HCI education and human-oriented design approaches in the future.

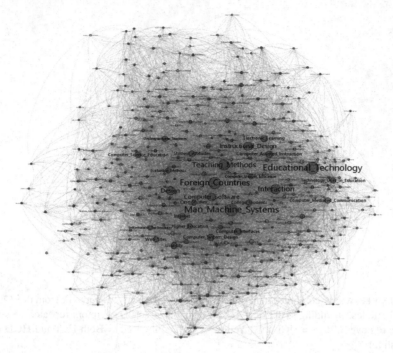

Fig. 9. Two-keywords-combined networks. A comparison descriptor network from the 213 peer-reviewed articles, including "HCI" or "UCD" in the abstract, Descriptors repeated less than 2 times are removed. Blue = HCI only, Light Green = UCD only, Red = Both HCI and UCD (Color figure online)

Figures 7, 8, 9 and 10 help us to understand the relationship between the descriptors of each human-oriented design approach and the descriptors of HCI. When both HCI and an approach have the same descriptor, the node is colored in red. When the descriptor is only in HCI, the node is colored in blue. As shown in the size, number, and color of nodes in the four networks in Figs. 7, 8, 9 and 10, HCI shared the majority descriptors with UX, and then in order of HF, UCD, and HCD. Through this result, we could interpret that UX is the human-related approach that has the closest relationship with HCI education. However, if the total amount of descriptors for two keywords being compared is the same, it might show different results.

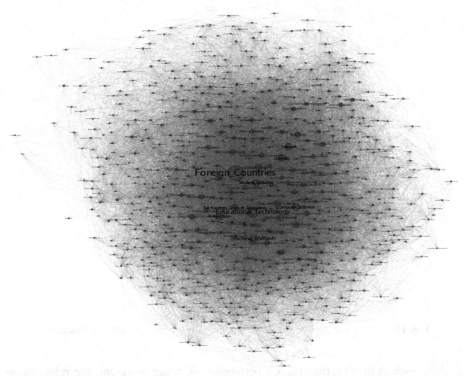

Fig. 10. Two-keywords-combined networks. A comparison descriptor network from the 444 peer-reviewed articles, including "HCI" or "UX" in the abstract, Descriptors repeated less than 2 times are removed. Blue = HCI only, Green = UX only, Red = Both HCI and UX (Color figure online)

Table 3. Author's fields/disciplines related to HCI research in education

Rank	Top 10 author's fields/disciplines related to HCI	Frequency	Percentile
1	Educational Technology	71	8.34
2	Human-computer Interaction	70	8.22
3	Information Science	29	3.40
4	Computer and Society	27	3.17
5	Information Systems (Business Informatics)	26	3.05
6	Teacher Education	25	2.93
7	Artificial Intelligence	24	2.82
7	Teaching Methods	24	2.82
9	Computing in Social science, Arts and Humanities	21	2.46
10	Higher Education	18	2.12

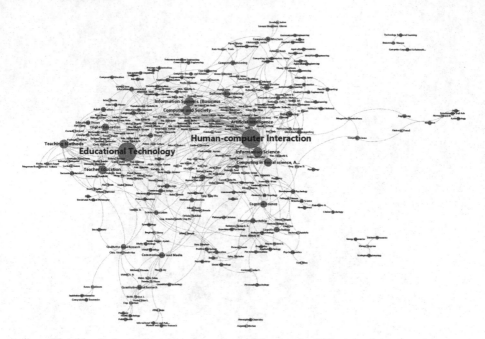

Fig. 11. Author's discipline network visualization for HCI research in education

As shown in Fig. 11, the distance between pink nodes represents the relationship between disciplines, and the distance is determined through the relationship to authors. Typically, an author selected one or more disciplines from the given discipline list on the Research Gate website. When an author, a blue node, is located near a discipline, a pink node, we could say that the author has a relationship with the discipline directly or indirectly. When nodes are connected with an edge, it means a direct relationship, and when nodes are not connected with an edge, it means an indirect relationship. Therefore, the disciplines' network would help HCI researchers in academia who are seeking future research opportunities for interdisciplinary research and new research directions.

References

1. About ResearchGate. https://www.researchgate.net/about. Accessed 19 Oct 2020
2. Bastian, M., Heymann, S., Jacomy, M.: Gephi: an open source software for exploring and manipulating networks. In: Third International AAAI Conference on Weblogs and Social Media (2009)
3. Calma, A., Davies, M.: Studies in higher education 1976–2013: a retrospective using citation network analysis. Stud. High. Educ. **40**(1), 4–21 (2015)
4. Cambrosio, A., Limoges, C., Courtial, J., Laville, F.: Historical scientometrics? Mapping over 70 years of biological safety research with coword analysis. Scientometrics **27**(2), 119–143 (1993)
5. Churchill, E.F., Bowser, A., Preece, J.: The future of HCI education: a flexible, global, living curriculum. Interactions **23**(2), 70–73 (2016)

6. Ding, Y., Chowdhury, G.G., Foo, S.: Bibliometric cartography of information retrieval research by using co-word analysis. Inf. Process. Manag. **37**(6), 817–842 (2001)
7. Education Resources Information Center. ERIC FAQ Home. https://eric.ed.gov/?faq-general. Accessed 10 Sept 2020
8. Garreta-Domingo, M., Sloep, P.B., Hernández-Leo, D.: Human-centred design to empower "teachers as designers." Br. J. Edu. Technol. **49**(6), 1113–1130 (2018)
9. Hewett, T.T., et al.: ACM SIGCHI curricula for human-computer interaction. ACM (1992)
10. Hu, C.-P., Hu, J.-M., Deng, S.-L., Liu, Y.: A co-word analysis of library and information science in China. Scientometrics **97**(2), 369–382 (2013). https://doi.org/10.1007/s11192-013-1076-7
11. ISO 9241-210:2010(en) Ergonomics of human-system interaction—Part 210: Human-centred design for interactive systems. https://www.iso.org/obp/ui/#iso:std:iso:9241:-210:ed-1:v1:en. Accessed 23 Jan 2021
12. Jacomy, M., Venturini, T., Heymann, S., Bastian, M.: ForceAtlas2, a continuous graph layout algorithm for handy network visualization designed for the Gephi software. PLoS ONE **9**(6) (2014)
13. Liu, G.Y., Hu, J.M., Wang, H.L.: A co-word analysis of digital library field in China. Scientometrics **91**(1), 203–217 (2012)
14. Liu, Y., Goncalves, J., Ferreira, D., Xiao, B., Hosio, S., Kostakos, V.: CHI 1994–2013: mapping two decades of intellectual progress through co-word analysis. In: Proceedings of the SIGCHI Conference on Human Factors in Computing Systems, pp. 3553–3562 (2014)
15. Marc, H., Noam, T.: User experience - a research agenda. Behav. Inf. Technol. **25**(2), 91–97 (2006)
16. Norman, D.A., Draper, S.W.: User Centered System Design: New Perspectives on Human-Computer Interaction. Lawrence Erlbaum Associates, Hillsdale (1986)
17. Norman, D.A.: The Design of Everyday Things: Revised and Expanded Edition. Basic Books, New York (2013)
18. Obrist, M., Ranasinghe, N., Spence, C.: Special issue: multisensory human–computer interaction. Int. J. Hum. Comput. Stud. **107**, 1–4 (2017)
19. Still, B., Crane, K.: Fundamentals of User-Centered Design: A Practical Approach. CRC Press, Boca Raton (2016)
20. Wan, X., Rubens, N., Okamoto, T., Feng, Y.: Content filtering based on keyword map. In: 2015 2nd International Conference on Electrical, Computer Engineering and Electronics. Atlantis Press (2015)
21. Wickens, C.D.: An Introduction to Human Factors Engineering, 2nd edn. Pearson/Prentice Hall, Upper Saddle River (2004)
22. Zoltowski, C.B., Oakes, W.C., Cardella, M.E.: Students' ways of experiencing human-centered design. J. Eng. Educ. **101**(1), 28–59 (2012)

Building Common Ground: Applying Mutual Learning in the UI/UX Education

Wan-Ling Chang[1](✉) and Wen-Hsiang Lu[2]

[1] Department of Industrial Design, National Cheng Kung University, Tainan, Taiwan, R.O.C.
wanlingchang@gs.ncku.edu.tw
[2] Department of Computer Science and Information Engineering, National Cheng Kung University, Tainan, Taiwan, R.O.C.
whlu@mail.ncku.edu.tw

Abstract. The spreading of information and communication technology and mobile applications in our everyday contexts retrieve attention to UI/UX design. The education field attempted to train qualified UI/UX professionals to address the job market. However, there is a visible gap between the requirements of education and of professionalization in the job market. The interdisciplinary collaboration and communication with other team members from different fields play a cortical role in UI/UX education. To address the needs, we apply the concept of mutual learning in participatory design practices to design a UI/UX curriculum to enhance students' capacity in interdisciplinary collaboration. We conduct a pilot study to test the mutual learning course design in a joint course of graduate students from industrial design and computer science fields. Students were teamed up for a design project. In the class, they helped their teammates from different fields learn their domain knowledge and the thinking model of problem-solving. At the end of the course, we conducted interviews of twelve students in the course and collected their feedback on the mutual learning course design. The results showed that mutual learning benefited interdisciplinary communication and enabled the students to empathize with their team members of professions.

1 Introduction

Information and communication technology (ICT) and mobile applications spread from the workplace to our everyday lives, such as homes, schools, and other social contexts. The frequent use of digital applications makes the users not satisfied with "workable" or "usable" software or apps. They expect something more. This trend drives the industrial focus on developing an intuitive user interface (UI) and providing a pleasant user experience (UX) of products or services for users [1]. Simultaneously, there is an increasing demand for well-trained UI/UX professionals [2]. Mostly since the COVID-19 drove a major job paradigm shift worldwide, as CNBC and Forbes reported, the industries have a strong demand of UI/UX designers to address the remote work, education, and communication settings [3].

In keeping with the industrial interests in UI/UX professional practices, the academic institutions developed UI/UX programs and courses to prepare qualified students

© Springer Nature Switzerland AG 2021
M. Kurosu (Ed.): HCII 2021, LNCS 12762, pp. 66–76, 2021.
https://doi.org/10.1007/978-3-030-78462-1_5

for the job market. However, there is a visible gap between the requirements of education and the requirements of professionalization [5]. Communicating design is always challenging for interdisciplinary collaboration [6]. Some UI/UX practitioners and product managers reflected that one of the primary challenges of junior UI/UX designers is the communication and collaboration between them and other team members, such as software developers [7]. The insufficient understanding of each professional field uncovered communicational difficulties.

Coaching competent UI/UX practitioners necessitates a new curriculum design to enhance students' capacity for interdisciplinary collaboration and communication with partners who work with programming. We develop a joint course of students from industrial design (ID) and computer science (CS) backgrounds as a pilot study to test the pedagogical design. Students from two fields teamed up and worked together to accomplish a digital application design project. The project-oriented learning style allowed the students to experience the actual work settings of developing digital products or services. The course design intended to apply the "mutual learning" concept in participatory design (PD) [8] to build up the common ground for project members from different domains. PD aimed at having the users and the designers work together to design a product. Mutual learning is one of the central procedures to secure the participants' competence in designing products addressing both users' needs and technical limitations. Participants from different fields learn professional knowledge from other participants. The shared know-how support participants' communication of ideas and leads to a common ground of product design. In this study, we design the curriculum of a mutual learning process of design and CS students. The CS students facilitated their design team members in learning a course of programming exercises to acquire basic Python programming skills. The design students assisted their CS teammates in comprehending the UI/UX design concepts and progressing their design projects with design thinking methodologies.

At the end of this study, we conducted interviews with twelve students attending this course and ask their opinions of the course design. The interview results help us get preliminary feedback on the mutual learning model's effectiveness in UI/UX education. On the basis of this pilot study, we will extend this educational approach in future UI/UX training courses to collect extended data in support of the positive effects of mutual-learning type curriculum design in interdisciplinary collaboration training of UI/UX design.

2 Background

2.1 UI/UX in HCI

UI and UX design are highly related to the academic discipline of Human-Computer Interaction (HCI). HCI is a multidisciplinary field concerning the connections between social and behavioral science and computer and information technology [9]. User interface design is critical for HCI research, practice, and education [10]. As the HCI researchers and practitioners are prone to explore the human's interaction with digital technology beyond the sole considerations of cognitive process and user performance, they navigate the area of user experience [11]. The term of user experience (UX) is firstly proposed by Don Norman [12] and attempt to address human experience from emotional, affective, experiential, hedonic, and aesthetic aspects [11]. The UX research and design practices react to developing the third wave of HCI, which redirected the research and design focus from well-established work setting to private and public spheres and bring the user's element of emotion and experience foreground [13]. Based on this, the designers can understand the dynamics of socio-behavioral contexts of HCI and deal with a complex, networked world of information and computer-mediated interactions [14].

2.2 UI/UX Education in HCI and Design Fields

The strong connection between UI/UX and HCI encouraged many HCI programs offering UI/UX training in their courses [15]. Those courses mean to provide students the UI/UX domain knowledge and preparing them for future UI/UX professionals. Those HCI programs are often operated by the computer science or information department [14, 16], such as the undergraduates and graduate programs in Human-Computer Interaction Human-Computer Interaction Institute at Carnegie Mellon University[1]. While HCI emphasizes on user-centered approach to provide "good" UI and UX, the computer science educators encounter challenges of teaching computer science students to deal with complex and fuzzy human world problems [14, 16, 17]. Students with computational backgrounds get used to thinking problems in a way in which there is a clear, right-or-wrong answer to any question. However, the human-centered HCI design practices did not follow this deterministic approach [17].

HCI educators attempted to appropriate design-oriented programs' teaching practices [18] and developed varied ways of teaching HCI, such as studio-based learning, project-based learning, and problem-based learning [16]. Besides those pedagogical tries of advancing learning models to bridge the gap between traditional course content and design-oriented activities, HCI educators recognized the importance of multidisciplinary perspective inclusion and collaboration in interactive product design [14, 15, 18, 19]. They also identify the challenges and tensions of working with people from different disciplines to design the interface or interaction and the lack of necessary cross-disciplinary HCI training curriculums [15, 19].

Besides HCI, the traditional design domains devoted to UI/UX education in recent years. The user interface is usually part of a product. Many product designers were involved in the UI design practices in early times. As the consumers' preference shifts from a product-based to an experience-based solution, the industrial design field focuses more on designing an experience than designing a product [18, 21]. Some design or industrial design schools or departments include UI/UX courses in design education in response to this trend [21, 22]. Design fields also appropriate the traditional design education to develop UI/UX educational modules [22, 23]. Those course design greatly concentrated on the design practices, such as [22, 23], and paid less attention to the interdisciplinary collaboration works as many HCI programs. This project concentrated on exploring UI/UX pedagogy in the design sphere. We redirect the educational focus to the interdisciplinary design practices and borrow the project-oriented educational practices from the HCI field to build up the backbone of the course design.

---

[1] https://www.hcii.cmu.edu.

2.3 Interdisciplinary Collaboration and Mutual Learning

HCI practitioners and educators draw significant attention to the importance of interdisciplinary collaborations [24]. HCI educators had developed methods to support interdisciplinary collaboration. For example, Altizer Jr et al. adopted a participatory design method -- the design box – to facilitate the collaborative efforts of interdisciplinary teams in designing games [25]. Zeagler et al. used transitional technology artifacts to bring unique expertise in the workshop contexts [26]. Collaboration is about information sharing, decision synchronization, and incentive alignment [27]. Collective learning will contribute to the information sharing and then construct the shared conceptual framework for reaching advanced decisions in synchrony [28]. In this study, we attempt to appropriate the "mutual learning" model in PD [8].

PD is a research field as well as a design methodology [8]. This Scandinavian approach intends to have designers share the power of design decision-making with the users to create a co-design setting for both designers and users. Mutual learning is the cortical process to facilitate democracy and collaboration among different stakeholders. The mutual learning process is collective learning for team participants and helps the information sharing and understanding the incentive of different participants. Mutual learning has been applied in other fields to support interdisciplinary collaboration. For example, Polk and Knutsson presented two cases of transdisciplinary knowledge production of environmental issues. They argued that the mutual learning process contributed to acknowledge the value rationalities of different domains for the extended collaboration [29]. In this educational project, we adopt the mutual learning concept as the core of supporting multidisciplinary learning and effective collaboration with mutually understanding the expertise of other team members.

3 Interdisciplinary Curriculum Design

3.1 Contexts

This pilot study was held in a joint course of an Industrial Design (ID) graduate course (Human-Centered Information Systems & Interaction Experience Design) and a Computer Science (CS) graduate course (Language Processing for Intelligent Service Chatbot) in the spring semester of 2020. The first and second authors were teachers from different departments. They hosted the course and coached student teams together. The goal of this course is to have student teams developing services or applications with language processing technology. Fifteen students from ID graduate school and sixteen students from CS graduate school (including two auditing students) took part in this educational project. Students from two fields were assigned into seven teams and four to five people in a team. Each team had almost equal numbers of ID and CS team members. Students in a team not only worked together with their team project but also helped their teammates learning their domain knowledge in the mutual learning course sections.

3.2 Course Design

The joint course lasted for eighteen weeks. In order to build up the interdisciplinary collaboration in UI/UX practices, this course was primarily constructed by two parts: mutual learning and collaborative design project.

Mutual Learning

The traditional CS education trains students to formulate a problem to admit a computational solution, which was usually called computational thinking [30]. People with computational thinking usually abstract the problems and solutions and analyzed them in the way of the information process. They care more about the effectiveness and efficiency of solutions. Students from design backgrounds are usually well educated with design thinking [31]. Design thinking sustains a human-centered design ethos and enables people to concentrate on people's needs as well as to deal with the complex social context of interaction. Both computational thinking and design thinking are problem-solving methods but had varied considerations in exploring the problem space and solutions.

Besides learning the professional knowledge from different domains, the mutual learning process proposed we designed can support students of different domains understanding problem-solving mindsets by other students. The course design had CS students understand how to design people investigate problems with the design thinking process, methods, and tools. ID students also learned to access and verify a solution with computational thinking. The students from one field were required to help their teammates from the other field learn their field knowledge.

Based on this structure (see Fig. 1), we planned two mutual learning sections for ID students, including a set of python programing courses (three weeks) and an introductory lecture on language process theory and applications (1 week). The python programming course sections mainly focused on teaching ID students basic programming concepts of variable declaration, conditional statements, and function invocation. The CS students will help ID students learn the programing structures and languages use and accomplish their python assignments. ID students were supposed to have some ideas of computational thinking and build up basic programming skills after those course sections.

For the CS students, we introduced the design thinking workshops [32] and UI/UX design lectures to enhance their understanding of the design field. The design thinking workshops were operated as a three-hour challenge workshop and applied in the design project to explore the problem space. The CS students had a basic understanding of the user-centered design process in the three-hour design challenge workshop. Then they advanced their practices of the design procedures when we applied the design process to find out the topic and potential solutions for their design project. The ID students help their CS teammates learned the design methods and tools operated in those workshops. Both ID and CS had four UI/UX design lectures course together (4 weeks). The course sections introduced usability engineering, UI/UX design process, and user patterns for design. Those lectures gave students ideas of how to process a commercial information product design project and design a user-friendly interface and interactive experience in their team design project. Based on this structure (see Fig. 1), we planned two mutual learning sections for ID students, including a set of python programing courses (three weeks) and an introductory lecture on language process theory and applications (1 week). The python programming course sections mainly focused on teaching ID students basic programming concepts of variable declaration, conditional statements, and function invocation. The CS students will help ID students learn the programing structures and languages use and accomplish their python assignments. ID students were supposed to have some ideas of computational thinking and build up basic programming skills after those course sections.

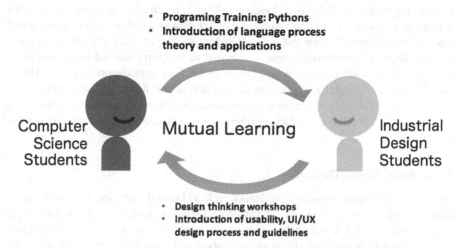

Fig. 1. The mutual learning course contents for CS and ID students.

Collaborative Design Project

The design of this part is based on project-based learning and problem-based learning in HCI education [16]. Students acquired their professional skills during perform their project and accomplish their project work. However, students were not assigned a specific topic for their project. The teacher only provided a general direction – Taiwanese language processing application for older adults -- for students to investigate the solutions of potential users.

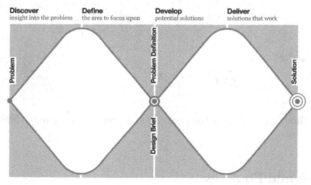

Fig. 2. The "Double Diamond" design process model, developed by the Design Council.[2]

---

[2] http://www.designcouncil.org.uk/designprocess, 2015.

We applied the "Double Diamond" design model (See Fig. 2) in designing activities for students to explore the potential needs and scenarios of senior people who speak Taiwanese. Students were required to conduct interviews and field observation to discover the needs regarding the Taiwanese language. Then, they applied tools (e.g., user journey map, how-might-we) to analyze the collected data and define the problems which needed to be addressed. After the teams decided on the problems they want to solve, they went through brainstorming and storyboard to develop potential solutions. In the final stage of the project, the team selected a technology application scenario. The ID team members designed the physical products, interaction flows, and user interface of their digital solutions. The CS team members were in charge of programming functions that support the effective and efficient interactions between their project product and potential users.

3.3 Students' Design Outcomes

At the end of the course, the seven students developed varied language processing applications for the senior citizens. All of the project outcomes were workable prototypes to demonstrate the functions and interaction in targeted settings. Most of the students developed mobile or desktop solutions to support older adults' everyday livings. For example, one of the student teams found the communicational gap between the older adult and their grandchildren, so they develop an interactive quiz phone app to enhance intergenerational communication. The older people and their children can give quizzes to each other while watching the Taiwanese drama together. Only two students develop a physical interactive product. One of them designed an interactive alarm system, which chatted with the older adults when detecting falling and sent alarm to their family (see Fig. 3).

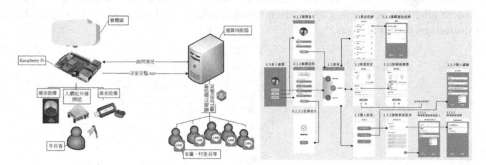

Fig. 3. Students' designs for older adults to alarm the falling in the bathroom

4   Interviews and Findings

4.1   Interviews with Students and Teaching Assistants

Six CS students and six ID students were interviewed about their experiences participating in this course to understand better how the curriculum affects team collaboration.

Two of them are the teaching assistants from CS and ID departments, who support the class's teaching and tutoring activities and help student teams solve problems in their design projects. Since the teaching assistants had close interactions with student teams, they got better insights into students' learning attitudes and ideas about this course. The interviews were conducted individually or in a pair depending on how comfortable the students are. The semi-structured interview questions intend to collect student participants' feedback to verify the effectiveness of mutual learning and project-based learning. The analyzed interview results help us identify whether the curriculum design fosters students' collaborative work in UI/UX design. The interviews were recorded on the voice recorder with permission from the participants. The recorded voice data was coded with qualitative coding analysis [33].

4.2 Findings

The analyzed data demonstrated four major findings in regards to the mutual learning and projected-based learning course design.

ID Students Request Advanced Programming Training

Five out of six ID students thought the programing training in the course was not enough for them in the interviews. Some of them have learned python or other program languages before. They thought the course training content was fundamental, and UI/UX work practices required better programming training in the work practices. One of the ID students went to take other programming courses after this course. In addition to advancing programming skills, more than half of the ID interviewees suggested that it will be much better to teach the programing language or functions that can be applied in UI/UX design directly in the programming learning sections. They thought learning the programing knowledge and applying them in the project immediately not only increased their incentive of learning but also assist them in acquiring the skills in advance.

Programing Training Does Benefit Interdisciplinary Communication

Five ID students mentioned that learning the programing language benefits their communication with software developers. Three ID students said they were more capable of identifying the programming problems and limitations in interface design. One student compared her experience of this course with another cross-disciplinary information design course. Without the programming training, she needed teachers or teaching assistants' assistance to communicate the technical problems with the programmers. After learning to program, she was able to communicate with the software developers in a structured way. Even though she did not know how to program the functions, she could easily understand developers' explanation of the mechanism of how those functions worked. Furthermore, she could propose an alternative programming structure for the function and communicate with the developers for a better UI solution. Another student, who had learned to program before, talked about that learning programming extended her knowledge of technology capacity and enriched her design concepts before consulting the developing team.

Mutual Learning Makes People Empathize with Their Collaborators

All six ID students mentioned that learning the professional makes the CS students respect the UI/UX professionality in collaborative design projects. Some of them found their CS teammates more empathetic in group communication after learning the UI/UX design procedures. They recognized the challenges of design when they were involved in the design activities. Meanwhile, some CS students referred to the capability limitation of performing comprehensive user study in developing a new project. The results reacted to ID students' interview findings. Also, learning programming had the ID students perceive the different thinking models between CS and ID fields. So in their group project, they recognized and appreciated the CS students' programing efforts on solving a minor UI problem.

CS Students Tend to Think Human-Centrically in Their Work
All CS interviewees thought the design thinking training course design benefits their ideas of developing an information product. Most of them mentioned that those training might not directly contribute to their programming skill to enhance their future workplace communication capability. Some CS students who knew human-centered design before thought the course content advanced their knowledge and skill in practices. Three CS interviewees also discovered the change of their colleagues. They all mentioned, after taking the class, one CS student paid more attention to think about users' needs and interaction flow in their lab programming projects.

5 Conclusion

To enhance the interdisciplinary communication training in UI/UX education, we developed a mutual learning and project-based learning curriculum for a joint course with students from ID and CS backgrounds. The course design enabled ID and CS students to help their teammates learning their profession and thinking mode (computational thinking or design thinking). Then, the mutual learning model's effect showed in the collaborative activities in the team design project. This study is a pilot test for the mutual learning teaching modules for UI/UX design education. After this initial investigation of the course design, the interviews of students showed that mutual learning does benefit group communication in the design project. Understanding what other people did their work drove people to respect their collaborators' professionality and appreciate their work effort. Those also led to better communication among team members in the product developing team. In the future, we will extend this study and apply the mutual learning course design in other UI/UX training courses to collect advanced data and verify this pedagogical approach.

References

1. Paun, G.: Council post: the bottom line: why good UX design means better business. https://www.forbes.com/sites/forbesagencycouncil/2017/03/23/the-bottom-line-why-good-ux-design-means-better-business/. Accessed 16 Oct 2020
2. Getto, G., Beecher, F.: Toward a model of UX education: training UX designers within the academy. IEEE Trans. Prof. Commun. **59**, 153–164 (2016)

3. Ioannou, L.: 5 freelance jobs where you can earn $100,000 or more during the pandemic. https://www.cnbc.com/2021/02/02/5-freelance-jobs-where-you-can-earn-100000-or-more-during-pandemic.html. Accessed 11 Feb 2021
4. Younger, J.: Creative and experience economy freelancers see growth ahead for freelancing in (2021). https://www.forbes.com/sites/jonyounger/2020/12/11/creative-and-exp erience-economy-freelancers-forecast-growth-ahead-for-freelancing-in-2021/. Accessed 11 Feb 2021
5. Yu, F., et al.: Innovative UX methods for information access based on interdisciplinary approaches: practical lessons from academia and industry. Data Inf. Manag. 4, 74–80 (2020)
6. Hendry, D.G.: Communication functions and the adaptation of design representations in interdisciplinary teams. In: Proceedings of the 5th Conference on Designing Interactive Systems: Processes, Practices, Methods, and Techniques, pp. 123–132 (2004)
7. YUJ Designs: 8 Must-Have Skills for a UX Designer. https://medium.com/@yujsocial/8-must-have-skills-for-a-ux-designer-6adf224b4b6e. Accessed 26 Feb 2021
8. Simonsen, J., Robertson, T.: Routledge International Handbook of Participatory Design. Routledge, London (2012)
9. Carroll, J.M.: Introduction: toward a multidisciplinary science of human-computer interaction. In: HCI Models, Theories, and Frameworks: Toward a Multidisciplinary Science, pp. 1–9. Elsevier Inc. (2003)
10. Helander, M.G.: Handbook of Human-Computer Interaction. Elsevier, Amsterdam (2014)
11. Law, E., Roto, V., Vermeeren, A.P., Kort, J., Hassenzahl, M.: Towards a shared definition of user experience. In: CHI'08 Extended Abstracts on Human Factors in Computing Systems, pp. 2395–2398 (2008)
12. Nielsen, J.: A 100-year view of user experience (by Jakob Nielsen). https://www.nngroup.com/articles/100-years-ux/. Accessed 11 Feb 2021
13. Bødker, S.: When second wave HCI meets third wave challenges. In: Proceedings of the 4th Nordic Conference on Human-Computer Interaction: Changing Roles, pp. 1–8 (2006)
14. Faiola, A.: The design enterprise: rethinking the HCI education paradigm. Des. Issues 23, 30–45 (2007)
15. Churchill, E.F., Bowser, A., Preece, J.: The future of HCI education: a flexible, global, living curriculum. Interactions 23, 70–73 (2016)
16. Koutsabasis, P., Vosinakis, S.: Rethinking HCI education for design: problem-based learning and virtual worlds at an HCI design studio. Int. J. Hum.-Comput. Interact. 28, 485–499 (2012)
17. Edwards, A., Wright, P., Petrie, H.: HCI education: we are failing–why. In: Proceedings of HCI Educators Workshop 2006 (2006)
18. Greenberg, S.: Embedding a design studio course in a conventional computer science program. In: Kotzé, P., Wong, W., Jorge, J., Dix, A., Silva, P.A. (eds.) Creativity and HCI: From Experience to Design in Education. IIFIP, vol. 289, pp. 23–41. Springer, Boston, MA (2009). https://doi.org/10.1007/978-0-387-89022-7_3
19. Adamczyk, P.D., Twidale, M.B.: Supporting multidisciplinary collaboration: requirements from novel HCI education. In: Proceedings of the SIGCHI Conference on Human Factors in Computing Systems, pp. 1073–1076 (2007)
20. Budd, J., Taylor, R., Wakkary, R., Evernden, D.: Industrial design to experience design: searching for new common ground. In: The Proceedings of the ICSID 2nd Educational Conference, pp. 5–7 (2003)
21. King, S., Chang, K.: Understanding Industrial Design: Principles for UX and Interaction Design. O'Reilly Media Inc., Sebastopol (2016)
22. Budd, J., Wang, W.: Industrial design education: taming technology to enhance user experience. Arch. Des. Res. 30, 17–27 (2017)

23. Qian, Z.C., Visser, S., Chen, Y.V.: Integrating user experience research into industrial design education: the interaction design program at Purdue. In: VentureWell. Proceedings of Open, the Annual Conference, p. 1. National Collegiate Inventors & Innovators Alliance (2011)
24. Blackwell, A.F.: HCI as an inter-discipline. In: Proceedings of the 33rd Annual ACM Conference Extended Abstracts on Human Factors in Computing Systems, pp. 503–516 (2015)
25. Altizer Jr, R., et al.: Design box case study: facilitating interdisciplinary collaboration and participatory design in game developm. In: Extended Abstracts Publication of the Annual Symposium on Computer-Human Interaction in Play, pp. 405–412 (2017)
26. Zeagler, C., Audy, S., Pobiner, S., Profita, H., Gilliland, S., Starner, T.: The electronic textile interface workshop: facilitating interdisciplinary collaboration. In: 2013 IEEE International Symposium on Technology and Society (ISTAS): Social Implications of Wearable Computing and Augmediated Reality in Everyday Life, pp. 76–85. IEEE (2013)
27. Simatupang, T.M., Sridharan, R.: The collaboration index: a measure for supply chain collaboration. Int. J. Phys. Distrib. Logist. Manag. (2005)
28. Pennington, D.D.: Cross-Disciplinary Collaboration and Learning. Ecol. Soc. **13**, 8 (2008)
29. Polk, M., Knutsson, P.: Participation, value rationality and mutual learning in transdisciplinary knowledge production for sustainable development. Environ. Educ. Res. **14**, 643–653 (2008)
30. Wing, J.M.: Computational thinking benefits society. In: 40th Anniversary Blog of Social Issues in Computing, p. 26 (2014)
31. Brown, T.: Design thinking. Harv. Bus. Rev. **86**, 84 (2008)
32. Levy, M., Huli, C.: Design thinking in a nutshell for eliciting requirements of a business process: a case study of a design thinking workshop. In: 2019 IEEE 27th International Requirements Engineering Conference (RE), pp. 351–356. IEEE (2019)
33. Gibbs, G.R.: Thematic coding and categorizing. Analyzing Qual. Data. **703**, 38–56 (2007)

Smart Speakers for Inclusion: How Can Intelligent Virtual Assistants Really Assist Everybody?

Eliseo Sciarretta[✉] and Lia Alimenti

Link Campus University, Rome, Italy
{e.sciarretta,l.alimenti}@unilink.it

Abstract. Smart speakers equipped with intelligent virtual assistants allow people to look for information, complete tasks and control other devices without using their hands and eyes, just their voice. Humans can finally use natural language utterances and be fully understood, without being forced to learn the machine language or to handle more or less complicated interaction techniques. Their potential in terms of inclusive design is therefore very high. However, it is important not to fall into the opposite problem, that is, to limit their use to the voice/auditory channel only, excluding all those who can't or don't want to use it. In this paper, the authors analyze the current situation, highlighting the peculiarities of these systems and the reasons why they are quickly gaining ground. Then, they focus on the potential interaction issues and on the challenges still open. After studying the main use cases relating to people with disabilities, elderly and accessibility, the authors can draw a list of suggestions addressing the inclusive design of virtual assistants and smart speakers.

Keywords: Virtual assistants · Natural language processing · Inclusion · Accessibility · Smart speakers · Conversational agents

1 Introduction

Virtual assistants, that can converse with humans in natural language to provide services, are becoming increasingly popular, pervasive and ubiquitous.

Amazon Alexa, Apple Siri, Google Assistant and Microsoft Cortana (but the full list is much longer) are all variants - produced by different manufacturers - of the same product, which in this paper is usually referred to as Intelligent Virtual Assistant (or IVA), but which is known by many other names: Voice Activated Personal Assistant, Conversational Agent, Virtual Personal Assistant, Voice-Enabled Assistant or Intelligent Personal Assistant (Cowan et al. 2017).

All of these systems share the use of voice as the main interaction channel, through natural language processing (NLP) and speech synthesis processes.

As for the interaction, for the first time in history the visual channel is not essential and is replaced by the hearing one (Cohen Cohen and Balogh 2004). For decades, since the introduction of the first graphical user interfaces (GUI), sight has been the main

© Springer Nature Switzerland AG 2021
M. Kurosu (Ed.): HCII 2021, LNCS 12762, pp. 77–93, 2021.
https://doi.org/10.1007/978-3-030-78462-1_6

sense used to convey information from machines to humans. Hearing, on the other hand, has always been little used in human-computer interaction, where it has generally been limited to the sound being responsible for alerts when something goes wrong, as well as its use for multimedia content, of course.

Now, it seems that "the hottest thing in technology is your voice" (Brunhuber 2018).

When these systems are integrated into devices to be installed at home - in the form of smart speakers - and connected to other smart appliances, people can use them to perform several actions without moving, for example turning on and off lights without reaching the switches or opening the window without moving from the sofa (Masina et al. 2020).

The inclusive potential of IVAs is enormous, as they can be used effortlessly by people who, due to the visual nature of most interactive systems so far, have always been disadvantaged, such as those with limited vision or limited dexterity. Furthermore, voice interaction is considered simpler, and therefore also more acceptable by people with limited literacy on technologies.

Elderly people, for example, can exploit these systems to listen to radio or news and to be assisted in daily services, without having to learn complicated metaphors and gestures to interact with computers or smartphones, and thus maintaining independent living (Kobayashi et al. 2019) without having to be assisted by a caregiver.

But this new perspective can bring problems to other people, such as individuals with speech or hearing disorders.

To achieve full inclusion, it is necessary to ensure that such systems accommodate and can manage everyone's needs. The purpose of this paper is precisely to understand what can be done to maximize the profitable use of IVAs by the largest possible number of individuals, following the inclusive design approach.

The remaining of the paper is structured as follows: Sect. 2 offers an overview on the current state of the market of IVAs and smart speakers, providing definitions, explanations on the functioning of these systems, usage stats and background. Section 3 highlights the main problems identified in the literature regarding the use of assistants, both of a technical nature (recognition problems, irrelevant answers) and of a social nature (excessive personification leading to too much confidence). Section 4, on the other hand, shows the main benefits brought by these systems in terms of interaction, justifying their rapid expansion on the market. Finally, before the conclusion, Sect. 5 illustrates the scenarios related to inclusive design, analyzing the main problems and drawing possible solutions.

2 Background

Since the birth of computers and intelligent machines humans have cultivated the dream of being able to interact with them through natural speech language (Hoy 2018) and to receive answers accordingly.

Science fiction, from the 1960s onwards, is full of examples (Chkrou and Azaria 2019), and while some foreshadowed alarmist scenarios (such as HAL 9000 in "2001: A space odyssey"), others were definitely more optimistic, depicting scenarios of seamless integration between humans and machines (Star Trek can also be cited, but the example that best illustrates the idea is K.I.T.T., the talking artificial intelligence installed on the Pontiac Firebird Trans Am, star of the 1980s TV series Knight Rider).

Today, thanks to Intelligent Virtual Assistants, that dream is becoming reality.

IVAs, which, as mentioned, can have different names, are software applications capable of providing real-time services and assistance to users by "answering questions in natural language, making recommendations, and performing actions" (Baber et al. 1993). But unlike other applications, they can take advantage of a voice interface and a conversational dialogue system (Yang et al. 2019).

Aside from the science fiction imagination, the goal of being able to talk to computers has long been pursued; this type of research is part of the broader sector of natural user interfaces (NUI), i.e. systems that allow the user to use them through intuitive and invisible actions (Berdasco et al. 2019), such as touch and gestures, in order to minimize complexity of the systems. In this sense, voice has always been considered as a promising channel, so much so that the first successful experiments in the field of speech recognition are due to studies carried out in the 1950s (Davis 1952).

Other important moments in this approach march, as reported by Rzepka (2019), are the use of pattern recognition methods (1960s), and subsequently the application of statistical methods.

Only in the 1990s the first systems capable of recognizing speech with a certain reliability and responding thanks to text-to-speech synthesis were developed. However, the technology was still at early stages and these systems were mostly used to "dictate" more or less long texts to computers.

With the new millennium, however, the steps forward in the field of AI, cloud computing and the Internet of Things open up new scenarios, so much so that the IT giants are engaged in a competition to be the first to hit the market with a solution that can be controlled by voice. The competition had a winner in 2011, when Apple launched Siri, the first modern commercial virtual assistant, changing the whole scenario: it is no longer just a system capable of managing simple question/answer cycles, but a real assistant able to extrapolate data and keywords from the user's speech to obtain in-depth knowledge and offer services in exchange (Knote et al. 2019).

Siri is the result of a long research carried out by Apple, which began with the CALO project (Mark and Perrault 2004), but since then the competition has been tight thanks to solutions developed by, among others, Microsoft, Google and Amazon. The latter, thanks to its suite of products connected to Alexa intelligence, has quickly become the industry leader. To get an idea of the proportions, it may be useful to remember that Amazon's market share in US households in 2018 was about 70% (Griswold 2018).

Aside from the competition in the industry, it can be said that all the players involved have contributed to change the way people can receive services, search for information and control their devices. In fact, already in 2018, the data (McCue 2018) showed that over a quarter of people who use online services are already accustomed to voice search, with a marked growth trend.

Juniper Research (2018), indeed, predicts a 1000% increase in the use of IVAs in the home environment from 2018 to 2023.

As for smart speakers, the data are comparable: the study conducted by Markets and Markets (2018) indicates an estimated growth in the value of the global market from 1.5 billion in 2017 to almost 12 billion in 2023.

Indeed, home-environment smart speakers are the most gaining ground form among those that so-called conversational agents can take: being integrated into smartphones (Apple Siri), operating on regular computers or tablets (Microsoft Cortana, Samsung Bixby), through online services (the various chatbots that handle the customer care for many companies), or even be installed on cars (Mercedes Benz User Experience).

Smart speakers are relatively simple devices, equipped with at least one microphone and a loudspeaker to be able to receive user inputs and provide answers. Some may also have a touch screen, and therefore integrate GUI and can also be controlled through other channels. The difference, in this case, is between voice-based devices, which have a single interaction mode, and voice-enhanced devices (Rzepka 2019), with multimodal interfaces.

The speaker intelligence, however, does not reside within it, but relies on a cloud-based architecture. For example, the line of smart speakers launched by Amazon is called Echo, but the beating heart is Alexa, the artificial intelligence that resides on Amazon's servers and is invoked every time. The speaker is therefore configured as an IoT device, which requires an always-on connection to be operational.

Each time the user makes a request to Echo (but the same applies to similar products from other manufacturers), speech is recorded by the microphones, sent over the connection to the servers and there it is converted into text and interpreted, so that Alexa can process an appropriate response, which is ultimately sent back to the smart speaker and delivered to the user through the hearing channel.

The assistant is always listening, but to limit privacy problems it is activated only when a certain wake word (like "Alexa", or "Ok Google", or "Hey Siri") is spoken; from that moment it starts recording.

Thanks to these features, IVAs can handle complex conversations with users, up to the point of giving the illusion of talking to another human being.

Moreover, the potential of these tools can be increased thanks to the openness that producers have granted to third-party developers: smart speakers can thus continuously learn new "skills" (in the case of Amazon), or "actions" (as far as concerns Google), which are nothing more than plug-ins created by independent companies and developers, through the platforms made available by the producers themselves.

In this way, it is possible to extend the functionalities of IVAs and integrate other devices, such as smart home appliances, within a single ecosystem.

Skills and actions play the same role as mobile applications in Android or iOS, but they are not comparable, as they are not software hosted on the device, but only extensions of services available in the cloud and which can be invoked by users.

From a technical point of view, the rise of IVAs can be explained by the maturity of the NLP sector, due to four main factors, according to Hirschberg and Manning (2015):

1. a vast increase in computing power,
2. the availability of very large amounts of linguistic data,
3. the development of highly successful machine learning methods,

4. a much richer understanding of the structure of human language and its deployment in social contexts.

3 Issues and Challenges

Given the increasing interest in the sector of smart speakers, IVAs and voice interaction, these issues have been widely analyzed in recent years research, leading to the emergence of some specific characteristics but also of possible problems to be taken into consideration.

The first question that can be asked when approaching a system like Echo and Alexa is: how should we talk, considering that we are talking to a machine? Can we use the same techniques as in conversation with other humans?

Or, in other words, is the interaction with an assistant really a conversation? This problem was addressed by Arend (2018), with results leading us to think that there are considerable differences in various facets: when we talk to other human beings, we can assume that they remember the previous turns of the conversation, that they have memory of what has already happened, while this is not always true for IVAs, even if for example the developers of Siri are working to let it keep track of the conversation and bind the commands to the previous ones.

Furthermore, during a face-to-face conversation the voice channel is only one of those involved, while we also make a lot of use of the visual one, for example, to interpret the signals that our interlocutor sends us, such as his willingness to listen, or recipiency: to comply, IVAs use visual cues, such as lights, to show that they are active and ready to answer (or that something is wrong).

This, however, leads to further consideration that the hearing channel alone is not enough.

The choice of several manufacturers to integrate in their devices other input and output systems (physical buttons, lighting systems, companion apps) (Spallazzo et al. 2019) shows that to exploit the potential of IVAs it is necessary to expand the spectrum of possible interactions. Fortunately, as far as the purpose of this paper is concerned, this discovery is very useful in terms of inclusive design, because it allows the designers to manage the interaction through multi-modality and thus satisfy a wide range of preferences.

Furthermore, looking at the rules of conversation, it should be noted that due to their design, IVAs fail to replicate the ability of human beings to speak and listen at the same time, and therefore to manage speech overlaps with elegance. An assistant either speaks or listens, it can't do both things at the same time, so it is the human being who has to adapt to this mechanism.

From what has been said, a consideration emerges that designers are learning: it is better not to make the user believe that the assistant is like a real human being. IVAs should not be anthropomorphized.

In fact, the possibility of speaking to these systems and obtaining an answer leads to the attribution of human characteristics to IVAs (Friederike et al. 2012; Lopatovska and Williams 2018). To acknowledge that, it's enough to think that almost all agents have a name (Purington et al. 2017), which is associated with a gender identity (almost always female, which can lead to an amplification of gender stereotypes (Habler et al. 2019)) and a consistent personality, generally using helpful and submissive language.

Dazzled by these characteristics, we tend to socialize with agents, almost to consider them friends. It often happens with technological devices (Schwind et al. 2019), but the phenomenon is observed to happen more with assistants.

This trend is settled above all in younger people, while adults manage to consider them as productivity tools, as emerged in the studies of Sciuto (2018) and Li and Yangisawa (2020).

Still, the personification can lead users to overestimate the capabilities of IVAs, expecting unattainable results from them, ultimately generating frustration with the interaction.

Manufacturing companies themselves are promoters of this behavior, pushing designers, through their guidelines, to use everyday language (Branham and Mukkath Roy 2019), slang and avoid "robotic" conversation, so that it is as natural as possible, and to limit the length (the number of words) and complexity (the number of intents) of the communication.

Recognition of intents is the core of how IVAs work. The systems must be able to fill in the empty slots and obtain all the fundamental variables for understanding the request starting from what is said by the user, thus identifying the keywords (Li and Yangisawa 2020). Each intent can be uttered in a number of different ways and IVAs need to be able to recognize as many of them as possible. To facilitate the purpose, designers can therefore try to reduce the complexity, guiding the user to provide the necessary information from time to time.

However, setting levels of complexity calibrated downwards is not always the best possible choice, especially in terms of inclusion.

For example, it can be hypothesized that blind people, with a more sensitive hearing and already accustomed to the use of assistive technologies with speech output, can sustain a higher level of complexity, and indeed they may prefer it (Abdolrahmani et al. 2018), to optimize the use experience.

Even the choice of speech speed and intonation can vary from case to case: blind people, accustomed to the use of synthetic voices of screen readers, may prefer more robotic voices and a speech output at a rate far faster than a human could.

Therefore, focusing on the average user would be a mistake for designers, because they would risk excluding the vast majority of individuals. Instead, they should prefer to offer the possibility of customizing the experience.

The use of voice as the main output system brings a challenge regarding the discoverability of the services available and the learnability of the system in general, as defined by Grossman (2009) "the ease with which new users can begin effective interaction and achieve maximal performance".

The voice is by its nature ephemeral (Corbett and Weber 2016), it does not allow users to build an adequate mental model of how the system works, because they risk losing important information if they get distracted even for just one moment.

Users are completely unaware of the features that the system offers and can only discover them if they make the right requests. But many get stuck because they don't even know what they can ask for. They cannot explore the system by casually wandering around and then interpreting the responses as in GUIs.

The problem was also studied by White (White 2018), according to whom it remains an open challenge, also because it is further magnified by the presence of skills or actions, which continues to increase day after day with minimal tracking possibilities.

In the case of Alexa, for example, there are thousands of skills available, created by third party developers, but among these very few are known and used: the result is that many features remain hidden (Spallazzo et al. 2019).

Therefore, IVAs implement strategies to help users, such as suggestions on new things to try, but a list of suggestions pronounced one after the other is likely to get the user even more confused.

To make complex responses more effective, IVAs should offer the possibility of using other channels as well, through companion apps or connected devices, and be able to better exploit context information (for example about environment and time), especially in mobility contexts.

In general, it would be useful to improve assistants' proactivity in providing useful advice on their abilities, possibly at the right time, exactly when needed.

Assistants, to improve their efficiency, should be able to understand when users are turning their attention to them and respond accordingly, perhaps through sensors that can detect presence, so as to be activated when users are passing by (Spallazzo et al. 2019).

As specified by Iannizzotto (2018), "Current smart assistants can talk and listen to their users, but cannot 'see' them". Plus, they are often faceless. This makes the communication somehow incomplete and therefore less effective. If until a few years ago facial recognition was inaccurate due to technological limitations, today limitations have gone and recognition is already used in smartphones, so it could be applied also to IVAs.

Of course, the use of similar techniques and sensors inevitably triggers a potentially endless discussion on privacy and data security issues. This is certainly a fundamental theme, already much explored in the literature, but in this paper is deliberately omitted in order not to shift attention from the subject of the research.

Similarly, in this paragraph some challenges have been highlighted that need to be addressed also from the point of view of inclusion, but it has been chosen to leave out further problems present in the sector, of a more technical nature, such as the recognition of multiple voices, background noises, the need to repeat the same command several times (Pyae and Joelsson 2018), the interferences that can arise in case of involuntary pronunciation of the wake word, etc.

4   Interaction

Challenges still need to be faced, but IVAs and smart speakers are showing unique characteristics in the field of human-machine interaction, which can be exploited to optimize the user experience for certain tasks and in certain contexts, and which can bring benefits also in terms of inclusive design. According to many, in fact, voice assistants are changing traditional forms of human-computer interaction (Feng et al. 2017). Further-more, conversational technologies are considered "transformative" and represent a shift towards a more "natural" computing paradigm (The Economist 2017).

First of all, we need to wonder what drives users to use such systems: the studies by Rzepka (2019) indicate efficiency, convenience, ease of use, minimal cognitive effort, and enjoyment as the main objectives to increase the value of IVAs perceived by users.

To this extent, agents offer numerous benefits, as they can be used hands-free, with-out worrying too much about grammatical errors (especially if compared to written communication) and in a way that intrigues users and entertains them (Terzopoulos and Satratzemi 2019).

The main and most evident advantage in terms of interaction proposed by IVAs is the possibility of freeing the hands. As a result, users can do other things in the meantime, supporting multi-tasking, with obvious time advantages (Luger and Sellan 2016).

But not only the hands are free, the eyes are too (Moussawi 2018), giving us the opportunity to focus our attention on something else.

Of course, what for some is at best a competitive advantage, for others becomes a necessity and the only way to obtain services: these systems therefore are very promising in relation to the needs of people with visual and motor disabilities (Branham and Mukkath Roy 2019), as will be explained below.

As mentioned previously, however, hands-free and eyes-free interaction is actually achieved only in some cases, depending on the characteristics of the tasks, objectives and contexts that define the degree of complexity of the situation.

Speech interaction offers its best in situations of low complexity (Zamora 2017) or when multi-tasking can be exploited (Luger and Sellan 2016).

Therefore, IVAs, at home, act as assistants in the daily life of users (McLean and Osei-Frimpong 2019), able to offer simple but useful services such as setting timers and alarms, managing the agenda, searching for information and also the management of connected smart appliances, leaving users free to think about other things. These systems offer greater convenience than any other kind of device, allowing users to complete tasks with little effort and without the need to type, read or hold a device (Hoy 2018).

From what has been said, also in the previous paragraph, the need emerges for a hybrid use of IVAs, which ranges, depending on the occasion, from an exclusively vocal interaction, to one that also integrates other methods, which can be conveyed through touch screens on the devices themselves, tactile buttons, but also through the so-called companion apps. These are mobile apps that have the basic task of guiding the user through the configuration of the device, but which can then be exploited in all cases where complexity requires it. Indeed, all manufacturers are doing this by providing support apps and a range of devices for all needs.

As a result, simple tasks can also be performed through voice alone, in this way the process is lighter and thanks to a single spoken command, a series of gestures such as touch, scrolling and input are avoided (McTear et al. 2016). And this mode also proves perfect when dealing with small screens, where the physical limitations of the device's real estate make it difficult to provide input differently.

But when dealing with complex tasks, the most effective model is rich interaction, where the auditory channel is joined and supported by the visual, and possibly also by the haptic one. Siri, for example, has long been providing multimodal answers, with the transcription on the screen of what it says verbally, together with the relevant information found based on the request made. Not only that: the request made by the user is also shown as written text, as proof of the correct understanding of the command.

The feedback of the system is therefore composed of multiple interactions: lights, verbal expressions, screens and in some cases even movements (Spallazzo et al. 2019) signal the status of the system at all times, and this also helps in terms of inclusive design.

5 Inclusive Design

As already mentioned several times in the previous paragraphs, the purpose of this article is to frame the growing phenomenon of IVAs and connected smart speakers in an inclusive design perspective, which therefore favors the greatest number of people, regardless of their skills and preferences (Sciarretta 2020).

For this it is useful to analyze the accessibility characteristics identified in these systems, in order to highlight what needs to be done to ensure inclusion.

In general, smart speakers, especially when connected to other smart appliances (Abdolrahmani et al. 2018), are showing great potential in terms of assistance, because they allow people to have a single hub to control the home environment without having to learn complicated interfaces.

After all, technologies such as automatic speech recognition (ASR) and text-to-speech (TTS) are well known in the world of accessibility as assistive technologies used for decades (Ballati et al. 2018).

However, they are generally used as a sort of alternative to the main mode of interaction, for example to convert visual elements into auditory feedback, as happens in the case of screen readers, which transform the visual information present on a screen into synthetic speech (Jacko et al. 2008).

In the case of IVAs, instead, the perspective is reversed because the voice becomes the main channel of interaction, if not the only one. However, a consideration arises: as mentioned above, very often IVAs are accompanied by companion apps for smartphones, which are used for setup but which can also be useful for inclusion purposes, since they offer the possibility of providing richer feedback. Obviously, this happens as long as the app is also designed in an accessible way, to ensure that the entire ecosystem is inclusive (Pradhan et al. 2018).

Furthermore, the vocal interaction mode is very successful among people with disabilities, making it the preferred choice by those with limited hand dexterity (Peres 2019), but also by those with intellectual disabilities (Balasuriya et al. 2018), the elderly (Schlögl et al. 2013) and of course by the blind (Corbett and Weber 2016).

However, there are still numerous accessibility challenges (Morris and Thompson 2020), mainly due to the fact that what is accessible to one person is not necessarily accessible to another.

Exactly for this reason, in the remaining part of the paragraph the information provided will be divided by type of user, in order to evaluate the gray areas more carefully, focusing in particular on physical problems, such as vision disorders, hearing problems, speech difficulties and motor limitations, without, however, forgetting the large category of elderly people, who may have one or more of these problems.

Instead, no discussion will be provided about the category of people with cognitive disabilities, due to the impossibility of reducing all possible cases to a single one. But it is clear that to achieve true inclusion, solutions capable of meeting their multiple needs must also be designed.

This division is necessary because every situation is unique and brings different needs: for example, it is intuitive to think that people with motor disabilities can enjoy the greatest benefits from IVAs (Ballati et al. 2018), while deaf people may have greater difficulties.

Hearing and Speech. People with hearing problems, who can also experience language difficulties, are among those who can have the greatest complications in using voice-based virtual assistants. Studies carried out on Google's speech recognition system have shown poor results in the presence of deaf or hard of hearing people (Bigham et al. 2017).

Furthermore, as mentioned, language difficulties must also be considered, which can be blocking: in the studies conducted by Pradhan (2018), for example, it emerged that the greatest problems are the need to speak loudly, otherwise the assistant will not be able to perceive the command, and respecting a precise timing in uttering the request; in fact, systems are generally designed for people who can make intelligible and clear speeches (Masina 2020).

IVAs may misinterpret slightly longer pauses, and think they are sentence delimiters (Kobayashi et al. 2019). In addition, the user can speak at different speeds and the assistant, which instead requires a fairly precise timing, could get confused. When the wake word is pronounced, for example, the device switches to listening mode for a specific amount of time; if the user waits too long, the system times out. For those with speech problems, the time available may be too short.

In this case, therefore, the accessibility challenge is to design assistants so that they can adapt to users' needs, with algorithms that can improve their speech comprehension skills. Furthermore, it is necessary to offer users the ability to manage settings in order to select their preferences.

Vision. There are approximately 285 million people with severe vision impairment worldwide (WHO 2010).

The difficulties related to the visual spectrum have always been among the most limiting ones in the use of computers, the Internet and technologies that rely on graphical user interfaces (Iyer et al. 2020). On the other hand, research on accessibility has often put these problems first, identifying solutions that today allow blind people to effectively use an iPhone or other technologies.

However, from an inclusion perspective, being able to count on devices that are not based on graphic interfaces but on conversational interfaces is a huge step forward, because it makes the visual impairment completely marginal, granting people with visual disabilities the same usability of the tools that everyone else can experience.

Assistive technologies, on the other hand, immediately make it clear that the users need them, risking making them feel disadvantaged (Desmond et al. 2018).

Also, assistive technologies can be very expensive (Beksa and Desmarais 2020). Instead, as already noted by Gill (2017), IVAs are low-cost solutions.

For the blind, the problems that can arise in the use of these tools are linked to their over-ability: being people used to exploiting the hearing channel in interactions with machines, they may not like the excessive verbiage of IVAs, preferring instead a more direct communication.

Therefore, a different approach to the use of these systems emerges, where they are considered as serious tools by the blind (Azenkot and Lee 2013), one of the best possibilities for completing complex tasks, while for sighted users they can become an entertainment pastime (Luger and Sellan 2016; Pradhan et al. 2018).

Furthermore, due to the habit of using the voice channel, blind people prefer much faster speech (Branham and Kane 2015) and consider the default speed to be a waste of time.

For this reason, IVAs designers should provide the ability to set different preferences regarding speed but also word count and general complexity, which would allow better use of the tool.

Although in many smart speakers the voice is used as the main interaction mode, some feedback, as already mentioned, is also provided in other ways, for example through lighting systems. Obviously, to ensure accessibility to the blind, these visual cues must be presented effectively through alternatives (Abdolrahmani et al. 2018), perhaps through short auditory icons, otherwise known as earcons.

Limited Dexterity. For people with limited dexterity some of the same points are valid as for people with vision problems: IVAs are an exceptional opportunity because they allow them to complete tasks without having to use their hands or perform gestures, guaranteeing levels of independence never experienced before.

However, some problems remain, mostly related to the usability of the systems, such as the difficulty in discovering and learning the features, as already seen.

Furthermore, it must also be considered that some motor problems lead, as a secondary effect, to language problems (Duffy 2013), which involve everything that has already been discussed.

Designers must therefore try to properly manage the voice as a primary interaction mode, leaving more complex tasks to other types of interaction. The advantages of this type of design would be perceived not only by those who have limited dexterity due to physical causes, but also by those who are unable to use their hands due to the context.

Elderly. The elderly belong to a category of people very different from those investigated so far, but they share some of the same problems, related to skills that are no longer 100% efficient, with a decline in multiple fields related to the sensory, motor or cognitive sectors (Kobayashi et al. 2019), such as sight or motor abilities (Ho 2018).

Furthermore, elderly people are recognized as those who can receive more benefits from the use of IVAs, because they allow them to bypass the use of more complicated technologies and therefore reduce the generational digital divide.

The extensive use of graphic user interfaces, in fact, makes the interaction implicitly more complex, because GUIs allow people to manage complex tasks. The use of the voice as the main channel, on the other hand, allows to reduce the difficulty, as a result of the limitation of the complexity of the tasks (Sayago et al. 2019).

The popularity of assistants among the elderly is growing, not only for the reasons just mentioned, but also for the possibility of completing tasks without disturbing other processes (Terzopoulos and Satratzemi 2019); voice inputs are the most effective modality according to Smith's studies (2015).

To optimize the user experience of the elderly, it is necessary to overcome the accessibility challenges already described, always providing customization options.

The main problems are in fact due to the management of pauses and the difficulties related to the occasions when there is a need for a repetition of what has been said or, worse, a rephrasing (Kobayashi et al. 2019); on these occasions, it would be necessary to manage the error messages in a more complete and personalized way, which can better explain what went wrong and how to remedy it.

From the considerations made in this paragraph we can draw a list of suggestions that can help in designing for inclusion. Designers of virtual assistants should make sure that their systems:

- use voice as a primary channel of interaction, but also offer richer feedback through integrated screens or connected devices;
- provide auditory alternatives to visual cues such as lights through earcons;
- offer a wide range of customizations in terms of modes, times and speed of speech input and output, like

  - waiting time,
  - output speed,
  - complexity of speech;

- handle errors and misunderstandings more comprehensively, including by providing examples;
- clearly indicate when the request is accepted by the system and when it is completed;
- avoid a one-size-fits-all design approach, trying instead to adapt to be used by as many people as possible;
- clearly show they are artificial intelligence, to avoid marked anthropomorphization phenomena, which can push people to overestimate the skills of assistants;
- (connected to the previous point) are also visually represented, to facilitate interaction and rich feedback; the representation should be abstract, not human-like;
- offer the users a way to teach them new commands or offer shortcuts to issue multiple commands at once;
- exploit additional input channels (such as cameras and sensors) to be proactive and to activate at the right time depending on the context.

6   Conclusion

In this paper we have tried to highlight the inclusive aspects of smart speakers and Intelligent Virtual Assistants. To do so, we analyzed the interaction characteristics of these systems, the possible problems, the challenges still open and their use made by different categories of people.

What emerged is that IVAs have shown a high degree of acceptance by people, and therefore their use as assistive technologies and for inclusion purposes is very promising, as they can allow people to improve their quality of life (Masina et al. 2020), are less expensive and non-stigmatizing, since they can be used by people with or without disabilities.

However, problems remain to be addressed and in the course of the discussion we have identified some of them, also providing suggestions for improvement.

But apart from the specific problems, designers should adopt a more inclusive approach, considering the needs and preferences not only of as many categories of people as possible, but also in relation to a wide variety of situations and contexts.

Voice promises to change the way of interacting with machines, offering an engaging and natural user interface (Luger and Sellan 2016), but to allow this promise to come true some work is needed to identify ways that can help people manage more complex tasks, without falling into the trap of recognition errors or inconclusive answers.

References

Abdolrahmani, A., Kuber, R., Branham, S.M.: Siri talks at you: an empirical investigation of voice-activated personal assistant (VAPA) usage by individuals who are blind. In: Proceedings of the 20th International ACM SIGACCESS Conference on Computers and Accessibility (ASSETS 2018), pp. 249–258 (2018). https://doi.org/10.1145/3234695.3236344

Arend, B.: Hey Siri, what can I tell about Sancho Panza in my presentation? Investigating Siri as a virtual assistant in a learning context? pp. 7854–7863 (2018). https://doi.org/10.21125/inted.2018.1874

Azenkot, S., Lee, N.B.: Exploring the use of speech input by blind people on mobile devices. In: Proceedings of the 15th International ACM SIGACCESS Conference on Computers and Accessibility (ASSETS 2013), pp. 11:1–11:8 (2013). https://doi.org/10.1145/2513383.2513440

Baber C.: Developing interactive speech technology. In: Interactive Speech Technology: Human Factors Issues in the Application of Speech Input/Output to Computers. Taylor & Francis, Inc., Bristol (1993)

Balasuriya, S.S., Sitbon, L., Bayor, A.A., Hoogstrate, M., Brereton, M.: Use of voice activated interfaces by people with intellectual disability. In: Proceedings of the 30th Australian Conference on Computer-Human Interaction (OzCHI 2018), pp. 102–112 (2018). https://doi.org/10.1145/3292147.3292161

Ballati, F., Corno, F., De Russis, L.: Assessing virtual assistant capabilities with Italian dysarthric speech. In: Proceedings of the 20th International ACM SIGACCESS Conference on Computers and Accessibility (ASSETS 2018), pp. 93–101, Association for Computing Machinery, New York (2018). https://doi.org/10.1145/3234695.3236354

Berdasco, A., López, G., Diaz, I., Quesada, L., Guerrero, L.A.: User experience comparison of intelligent personal assistants: Alexa, Google Assistant, Siri and Cortana. In: Proceedings of the 13th International Conference on Ubiquitous Computing and Ambient Intelligence UCAmI, vol. 31, no. 1, p. 51 (2019). https://doi.org/10.3390/proceedings2019031051

Beksa, J., Desmarais, A., Terblanche, M.: Usability study of blind foundation's Alexa library skill & low vision NZ (formerly the Blind Foundation) (2020)

Bigham, J.P., Kushalnagar, R., Huang, T.K., Flores, J.P., Savage, S.: On how deaf people might use speech to control devices. In: Proceedings of the 19th International ACM SIGACCESS Conference on Computers and Accessibility (ASSETS 2017), pp. 383–384 (2017). https://doi.org/10.1145/3132525.3134821

Branham, S.M., Kane, S.K.: The invisible work of accessibility: how blind employees manage accessibility in mixed-ability workplaces. In: Proceedings of the 17th International ACM SIGACCESS Conference on Computers & Accessibility (ASSETS 2015), pp. 163–171 (2015). https://doi.org/10.1145/2700648.2809864

Branham, S.M., Mukkath Roy, A.R.: Reading between the guidelines: how commercial voice assistant guidelines hinder accessibility for blind users. In: The 21st International ACM SIGACCESS Conference on Computers and Accessibility (ASSETS 2019), pp. 446–458. Association for Computing Machinery, New York (2019). https://doi.org/10.1145/3308561.3353797

Brunhuber, K.: The hottest thing in technology is your voice. http://www.cbc.ca/news/technology/brunhuber-ces-voice-activated-1.4483912. Accessed Feb 2021

Chkrou, M., Azaria, A.: LIA: a virtual assistant that can be taught new commands by speech. Int. J. Hum.-Comput. Interact. **35**(17), 1596–1607 (2019). https://doi.org/10.1080/10447318.2018.1557972

Cohen, M.H., Giangola, J., Balogh, J.: Voice User Interface Design. Addison-Wesley Professional, Boston (2004)

Corbett, E., Weber, A.: What can I say? Addressing user experience challenges of a mobile voice user interface for accessibility. In: Proceedings of the 18th International Conference on Human-Computer Interaction with Mobile Devices and Services (MobileHCI 2016), pp. 72–82. Association for Computing Machinery, New York (2016). https://doi.org/10.1145/2935334.2935386

Cowan, B.R., et al.: What can I help you with?: Infrequent users' experiences of intelligent personal assistants. In: Proceedings of the 19th International Conference on Human-Computer Interaction with Mobile Devices and Services (MobileHCI 2017), pp. 43:1–43:12 (2017). https://doi.org/10.1145/3098279.3098539

Davis, K.H., Biddulph, R., Balashek, S.: Automatic recognition of spoken digits. J. Acoust. Soc. Am. **24**, 637–642 (1952)

Desmond, D., et al.: Assistive technology and people: a position paper from the first global research, innovation and education on assistive technology (GREAT) summit. Disabil. Rehabil. Assist. Technol. **13**, 1–8 (2018)

Duffy, J.: Motor Speech Disorders E-Book: Substrates, Differential Diagnosis, and Management. Elsevier Health Sciences, Philadelphia (2013)

Feng, H., Fawaz, K., Shin, K.S.: Continuous authentication for voice assistants. In: Proceedings of the 23rd Annual International Conference on Mobile Computing and Networking, pp. 343–355 (2017)

Friederike, E., Kuchenbrandt, D., Bobinger, S., de Ruiter, L., Hegel, F.: If you sound like me, you must be more human: on the interplay of robot and user features on human-robot acceptance and anthropomorphism. In: Proceedings of the Seventh Annual ACM/IEEE International Conference on Human-Robot Interaction, pp. 125–126. ACM (2012)

Gill, M.: Adaptability and affordances in new media: literate technologies, communicative techniques. J. Pragmatics **116**, 104–108 (2017)

Griswold, A.: Even Amazon is surprised by how much people love Alexa (2018). https://qz.com/1197615/even-amazon-is-surprised-by-how-much-people-love-alexa/. Accessed Feb 2021

Grossman, T., Fitzmaurice, G., Attar, R.: A survey of software learnability: metrics, methodologies and guidelines. In: Proceedings of the 27th International Conference on Human Factors in Computing Systems (CHI 2009), pp. 649–658 (2009). https://doi.org/10.1145/1518701.1518803

Habler, F., Schwind, V., Henze, N.: Effects of smart virtual assistants' gender and language. In: Proceedings of Mensch und Computer 2019 (MuC 2019), pp. 469–473. Association for Computing Machinery, New York (2019). https://doi.org/10.1145/3340764.3344441

Hirschberg, J., Manning, C.D.: Advances in natural language processing. Science **349**(6245), 261–266 (2015). https://doi.org/10.1126/science.aaa8685

Ho, D.K.: Voice-controlled virtual assistants for the older people with visual impairment. Eye (Lond) **32**(1), 53–54 (2018). https://doi.org/10.1038/eye.2017.165

Hoy, M.B.: Alexa, Siri, Cortana, and more: an introduction to voice assistants. Med. Ref. Serv. Q. **37**(1), 81–88 (2018)

Iannizzotto, G., Bello, L.L., Nucita, A., Grasso, G.M.: A vision and speech enabled, customizable, virtual assistant for smart environments. In: 2018 11th International Conference on Human System Interaction (HSI), Gdansk, pp. 50–56 (2018). https://doi.org/10.1109/HSI.2018.843 1232

Iyer, V., Shah, K., Sheth, S., Devadkar, K.: Virtual assistant for the visually impaired. In: 5th International Conference on Communication and Electronics Systems (ICCES), Coimbatore, India, pp. 1057–1062 (2020). https://doi.org/10.1109/ICCES48766.2020.9137874

Jacko, J.A., Leonard, V.K., McClellan, M., Scott, I.U.: Perceptual impairments: new advancements promoting technological access. In: Sears, A., Jacko, J.A. (eds.) The Human-Computer Interaction Handbook: Fundamentals, Evolving Technologies and Emerging Applications, pp. 853–870, Taylor & Francis Group, New York (2008)

Juniper Research: voice assistants used in smart homes to grow 1000%, reaching 275 million by 2023, as Alexa leads the way (2018). https://www.juniperresearch.com/press/press-releases/voice-assistants-used-in-smart-homes. Accessed Feb 2021

Knote, R., Janson, A., Söllner, M., Leimeister, J.M.: Classifying smart personal assistants: an empirical cluster analysis. In: Proceedings of the 52nd Hawaii International Conference on System Sciences, Maui (2019)

Kobayashi, M., et al.: Effects of age-related cognitive decline on elderly user interactions with voice-based dialogue systems. In: Lamas, D., Loizides, F., Nacke, L., Petrie, H., Winckler, M., Zaphiris, P. (eds.) INTERACT 2019. LNCS, vol. 11749, pp. 53–74. Springer, Cham (2019). https://doi.org/10.1007/978-3-030-29390-1_4

Li, C., Yanagisawa, H.: Intrinsic motivation in virtual assistant interaction for fostering spontaneous interactions. ArXiv abs/2010.06416 (2020)

Lopatovska, I., Williams, H.: Personification of the Amazon Alexa: BFF or a mindless companion. In: Proceedings of the 2018 Conference on Human Information Interaction & Retrieval (CHIIR 2018), pp. 265–268. Association for Computing Machinery, New York (2018) https://doi.org/10.1145/3176349.3176868

Luger, E., Sellen, A.: Like having a really bad PA: the gulf between user expectation and experience of conversational agents. In: Proceedings of the 2016 CHI Conference on Human Factors in Computing Systems (CHI 2016), pp. 5286–5297 (2016). https://doi.org/10.1145/2858036.285 8288

Mark, W., Perrault, R.: Calo: a cognitive agent that learns and organizes (2004)

Markets and Markets: Smart speaker market by IVA (Alexa, Google Assistant, Siri, Cortana), Component (Hardware (Speaker Driver, Connectivity IC, Processor, Audio IC, Memory, Power IC, Microphone,) and Software), Application, and Geography - Global Forecast to 2023 (2018). https://www.marketsandmarkets.com/Market-Reports/smart-speaker-market-44984088.html?gclid=EAIaIQobChMIs6Sn3abE5AIVFozICh1-PQLgEAAYASAAEgIZSv D_BwE. Accessed Feb 2021

Masina, F., et al.: Investigating the accessibility of voice assistants with impaired users: mixed methods study. J. Med. Internet Res. **22**(9), e18431 (2020). https://doi.org/10.2196/18431

McCue, T.J.: Okay Google: voice search technology and the rise of voice commerce. Forbes Online (2018). https://www.forbes.com/sites/tjmccue/2018/08/28/okay-google-voice-search-technology-and-the-rise-of-voice-commerce/#57eca9124e29. Accessed Feb 2021

McLean, G., Osei-Frimpong, K.: Hey Alexa … examine the variables influencing the use of artificial intelligent in-home voice assistants. Comput. Hum. Behav. **99**, 28–37 (2019)

McTear, M., Callejas, Z., Griol, D.: The Conversational Interface: Talking to Smart Devices. Springer, Cham (2016). https://doi.org/10.1007/978-3-319-32967-3

Morris, J.T., Thompson, N.A.: User personas: smart speakers, home automation and people with disabilities. J. Technol. Persons Disabil. **8** (2020)

Moussawi, S.: User experiences with personal intelligent agents: a sensory, physical, functional and cognitive affordances view. In: Proceedings of the 2018 ACM SIGMIS Conference on Computers and People Research, pp. 86–92. ACM (2018)

Peres, S.: 39 million Americans now own a smart speaker, report claims. TechCrunch (2019). https://techcrunch.com/2018/01/12/39-million-americans-now-own-a-smart-speaker-report-claims/. Accessed Feb 2021

Pradhan, A., Mehta K., Findlater, L.: Accessibility came by accident: use of voice-controlled intelligent personal assistants by people with disabilities. In: Proceedings of the 2018 CHI Conference on Human Factors in Computing Systems. Paper 459, pp. 1–13. Association for Computing Machinery, New York (2018). https://doi.org/10.1145/3173574.3174033

Purington A., Taft, J.G., Sannon, S., Bazarova, N.N., Hardman Taylor, S.: Alexa is my new BFF: social roles, user satisfaction, and personification of the Amazon Echo. In: Proceedings of the 2017 CHI Conference Extended Abstracts on Human Factors in Computing Systems, pp. 2853–2859. Association for Computing Machinery, New York (2017). https://doi.org/10.1145/3027063.3053246

Pyae, A., Joelsson, T.N.: Investigating the usability and user experiences of voice user interface: a case of Google home smart speaker. In: Proceedings of the 20th International Conference on Human-Computer Interaction with Mobile Devices and Services Adjunct (MobileHCI 2018), pp. 127–131. Association for Computing Machinery, New York (2018). https://doi.org/10.1145/3236112.3236130

Rzepka, C.: Examining the use of voice assistants: a value-focused thinking approach. In: AMCIS (2019)

Sayago, S., Barbosa Neves, B., Cowan, B.R.: Voice assistants and older people: some open issues. In: Proceedings of the 1st International Conference on Conversational User Interfaces (CUI 2019), Article 7, pp. 1–3. Association for Computing Machinery, New York (2019). https://doi.org/10.1145/3342775.3342803

Schlögl, S., Chollet, G., Garschall, M., Tscheligi, M., Legouverneur, G.: Exploring voice user interfaces for seniors. In: Proceedings of the 6th International Conference on Pervasive Technologies Related to Assistive Environments (PETRA 2013), pp. 52:1–52:2 (2013). https://doi.org/10.1145/2504335.2504391

Schwind, V., Deierlein, N., Poguntke, R., Henze, N.: Understanding the social acceptability of mobile devices using the stereotype content model. In: Proceedings of the 2019 CHI Conference on Human Factors in Computing Systems (CHI 2019), Article 361, 12 p. ACM, New York (2019). https://doi.org/10.1145/3290605.3300591

Sciarretta, E.: Libri digitali per tutti - Inclusione sociale tramite gli eBook. Eurilink University Press, Roma (2020) ISBN 979 12 80164 04 9

Sciuto, A., Saini, A., Forlizzi, J., Hong, J.I.: Hey Alexa, what's up? A mixed-methods studies of in-home conversational agent usage. In: Proceedings of the 2018 on Designing Interactive Systems Conference, pp. 857–868. ACM (2018)

Smith, A.L., Chaparro, B.S.: Smartphone text input method performance, usability, and preference with younger and older adults. Hum. Factors **57**(6), 1015–1028 (2015)

Spallazzo, D., Sciannamè, M., Ceconello, M.: The domestic shape of AI: a reflection on virtual assistants. In: DeSForM19 Proceedings (2019). https://doi.org/10.21428/5395bc37.8108aa03

Terzopoulos, G., Satratzemi, M.: Voice assistants and artificial intelligence in education. In: Proceedings of the 9th Balkan Conference on Informatics (BCI 2019), Article 34, pp. 1–6. Association for Computing Machinery, New York (2019). https://doi.org/10.1145/3351556.3351588

The Economist: Now we're talking, 7th Jan 2017. http://www.economist.com/news/leaders/21713836-casting-magic-spell-it-lets-people-control-world-through-words-alone-how-voice. Accessed Feb 2021

White, R.W.: Skill discovery in virtual assistants. Commun. ACM **61**(11), 106–113 (2018). https://doi.org/10.1145/3185336

World Health Organization: Global data on visual impairments (2010). https://www.who.int/blindness/GLOBALDATAFINALforweb.pdf. Accessed Feb 2021

Yang, X., Aurisicchio, M., Baxter, W.: Understanding affective experiences with conversational agents. In: Proceedings of the 2019 CHI Conference on Human Factors in Computing Systems (CHI 2019), Paper 542, pp. 1–12. Association for Computing Machinery, New York (2019). https://doi.org/10.1145/3290605.3300772

Zamora, J.: I'm sorry, Dave, I'm afraid we can't do that: chatbot perception and expectations. In: Proceedings of the 5th International Conference on Human Agent Interaction, pp. 253–260. ACM (2017)

A Panel to Confront the Differences in Intersectional HCI

Pricila Castelini[1](✉) and Marília Abrahão Amaral[2]

[1] Postgraduate Program in Technology and Society, Federal University of Technology, Curitiba, Paraná, Brazil
[2] Academic Department of Informatics and Postgraduate Program in Technology and Society, Federal University of Technology, Curitiba, Paraná, Brazil
mariliaa@utfpr.edu.br

Abstract. Computer science history better known in society is predominantly male, white, and heteronormative. It is also part of our culture, discourse, and society. We base our research on the third-wave of Human-Computer Interaction Studies. We bring a feminist technoscience perspective to investigate the disparities in gender, race, ethnicity, and class. From our systematic mapping, we learn that third-wave HCI studies are organized in three strands: Feminist HCI, Gender HCI, and Intersectional HCI. In the Intersectional HCI perspective, we identified that the proposals generally use just one category (for example: gender), and forget that intersectionality is a crossing categories. From this contradiction, we identified the gaps in 11 publications and produce a panel, that discusses the re-signification of categories. Our main objective is to create the panel to criticize the differences when HCI researches appropriate intersectional theory without considering black women's struggles and resistance. The study results are: a) structural barriers in low women participation; b) gender, race and ethnicity and class disparities is in computer science area but also in society and culture; c) intersection of race, class, and gender in third-wave HCI is controversially appropriate; d) power relations in macro axes reveal intentions of the majority in computer science and also in power spaces in society.

Keyword: Computer science · Third-wave HCI · Intersectional HCI · Feminist technoscience

1 Introduction

One can retell computer science story depending on who is narrating. For a long time, computer science story was (and still is) male. Retelling the story from Donna Haraway [1, 2] is a way of subverting the existing narratives to include and involve people who were part of it but were silenced and removed from the record.

As examples, we can list Katherine Johnson, Dorothy Vaughan, and Mary Jackson stories that in the 1940s contributed to computations, codes and mathematical calculations to the National Aeronautics and Space Administration (NASA) [3, 4]. These three women's contributions are not the most culturally and historically known in computer

© Springer Nature Switzerland AG 2021
M. Kurosu (Ed.): HCII 2021, LNCS 12762, pp. 94–106, 2021.
https://doi.org/10.1007/978-3-030-78462-1_7

science and society. This scenario is due to the fact that they were black women (gender intersection) (race and ethnicity intersection).

Recently (2016), these women were protagonists of Hidden figures book and movie adaptation. Katherine, Dorothy, and Mary went through multiple oppressions that can be observed by intersectional theory by Kimberly Crenshaw [5] that aimed to understand black women oppressions concerning gender, race and ethnicity, and class.

This intersectional theory has been used in several areas. From a systematic mapping, we identify that Human Computer-Interaction (HCI) has a subfield called Intersectional HCI, a recent area with the first publication in 2016. This Intersectional HCI approach is located in the third-wave HCI studies that appropriate cultural, social and gender perspectives to look at designs, uses and appropriations of technologies.

Our study analyzes 11 publications that discuss Intersectional HCI, from the perspective of gender, and which ignores that intersectionality crosses categories. From this contradiction identified we explore the gaps in the proposals and create a panel that appropriates the intersectional theory [5, 6] that discusses the re-signification of categories.

The intersectional movement started with black scholars and feminists in the late 1980s who recognized multiple identities also in women studies but without the intention of creating a global identity theory. Kimberly Crenshaw [5] first used the term in 1989. Intersectionality was a way of observing the multiple oppressions of African American women. She theorizes that women were often obscured from ethnic or racial groups and also within race and gender categories.

NiraYuval-Davis [6] comments that scholars see categories as deceptive constructions that do not readily allow the diversity and heterogeneity of the experience to be represented. The point is not to deny the importance - material and discursive - of categories but to focus on the process by which they are produced, experienced, reproduced and resisted in everyday life.

Our paper is grounded in the feminist technoscience study from Haraway [1, 2]. Technoscience concept is the basis to discuss democracy, empowerment in the resignification of people's realities, as well the process, the situated context, the collective, the individual, and the contradictions. This is our theoretical background that helps to form the critical construction of our final product - a panel that confronts the differences in Intersectional HCI.

This work is divided in: a) theoretical background discussion in third-wave HCI and feminist STS studies; b) methodological research paths to create the panel to confront differences in Intersectional HCI; c) data analysis from a systematic mapping and d) results.

2 Situating the Feminist Technoscience

Technoscience is the term used by Donna Jeane Haraway [1, 2] to consider Science and Technology (S&T) inseparable and interconnected. For her, it is essential to put herself in research/writing in order to situate and embody where people speak to highlight the privileges. She uses technoscience concepts in order to reinforce democracy, people empowerment to re-signification of their realities, the situated knowledge, the collective and also the contradictions.

We use Haraway's approach [1] as the basis of our research to understand computer science in HCI as embodied from a situated perspective [2]. We identify quantitatively that women are less represented in computer science and when it comes to issues of race and ethnicity, social class, disability the discussions and proposals are scarcer considering the Brazilian context.

The women absence in computer science and in the power positions in technoscience involves ideological doctrines according to Haraway [1]. This point of view involves the rhetoric about who is in the power spaces? Who produces, creates S&T and knowledge? For Haraway [1] we need the power of modern critical theories about how meanings and bodies are constructed not to deny but to live in meanings and bodies that have a future possibility. This possibility to criticize the meanings that are in the social, cultural imaginations can be understood from an *embodied objectivity*. This term is related to a doctrine that accommodates critical and paradoxical feminist scientific projects known as *situated knowledge* [1, 2].

The feminist technoscience based on Haraway [1, 2] emphasizes the importance of transcendence, and the division between subject and object. In this way we can become responsible for what we learn to see. *Embodied objectivity* [1, 2] shows different ways of seeing, interacting and mediating people relations in computer science and HCI but also in society.

Situated knowledge [1, 2] involves historicity and culture. It is not limited or determined. From this point of view this perspective criticizes the rhetoric that scientific knowledge is that manufactured and objective. This vision situates where people speak, for what and for whom. For a long time, these were the only recognized and reproduced convictions, however it is from a critique that is possible to identify power and structures as a way to present different approaches. These approaches may be issues of gender, race and ethnicity that can cause a distortion effect on the border of what is recognized as 'natural' [1].

In the next section, we map the third-wave HCI publications to find disparities in gender, race and ethnicity and class. The next section presents third-wave HCI context and feminist HCI, gender HCI and intersectionality HCI, and the publications mapped.

2.1 Third-Wave HCI

Before describing third-wave HCI proposals we consider important to explain why we use waves HCI perspective. According to Bødker [7] the waves are not chronological or linear but the approaches and appropriations are diverse. What are HCI waves? As a metaphor for the sea waves meet, mix, are never the same and bring elements from the surface of the earth. Therefore, thinking about HCI metaphor in waves it involves understanding that there are changes in ways of interacting and values.

The first wave HCI is concerned with cognitive science and human factors, focusing on the human being as a subject to be studied through strict guidelines, formal methods and systematic tests [7]. The second wave HCI concerns "from human factors to human actors" [8]. The focus started to be on groups that worked on applications collection in work-oriented environments. In this wave, the work configurations and practical inter-actions in the communities are important. Concepts and research on situated action, cognition and activity theory contemplate the sources of this wave.

In the third-wave, HCI people's experiences are observed, who develop and use technologies, emancipation, the domestic context, sustainability, gender among others. Bødker [7] said that the studies question the values related to technology because technologies are in people's daily lives.

Besides, the environmental issues and problems that arise from micro-decisions there are other borders elements which involve people's daily lives as a reflection of culture and history [7], such as issues of gender, race and ethnicity, social class, disability. The importance for this study is to bring people closer to decision-making not only at the micro level but also at the macro level to expand the decisions as a whole. How is this shift to action and recognition possible? In third-wave HCI context it can be observed with three approaches that are systematically mapped in this study: feminist HCI, gender HCI and intersectionality HCI.

Systematic Mapping Third-Wave HCI. Based on Petersen et al. [9] and Kitchenham [10] we systematically mapped (SM) the last eleven years of publications in HCI that are related to feminism, gender and intersectionality based on six phases (see Fig. 1).

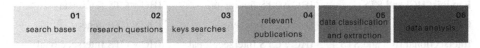

Fig. 1. Systematic mapping phases

(01) Search Bases Choice
The six search bases are the most recurring and recognized in Brazilian academia: ACM, IEEE, Science Direct, Scopus, Springer, Scielo.

(02) Research Questions Elaboration
The research questions were organized based on our theoretical background, as shown in Table 1.

Table 1. Research questions

How many publications approach feminisms, gender and intersectionality in HCI?
How can publications be classified in relation to the approach?
Which publications are in the feminist technoscience perspective?

The first research question - how do many publications approach feminisms, gender and intersectionality in HCI? - it was to identify quantitatively the total of the publication.

From 2009 to 2021 it was found 4.344 publications in English; 4.149 in Portuguese and 3.962 in Spanish.

The second research question - how can publications be classified in relation to the approach? - it can be classified with gender, sexuality, feminisms and intersections of race and ethnicity, social class discussions. In this first selection the data was extracted from abstract, keywords and in some cases, it was necessary to read part of the introduction.

The third research question - which publications are in the feminist technoscience perspective? - this analysis was made from reading the bibliographic references and the theoretical background of each work.

(03) Key Searches in Primary Studies
The search keys were organized in English, Portuguese and Spanish Table 2.

Table 2. Search keys

English	Portuguese	Spanish
Feminist HCI	IHC feminista	IHC feminista
Gender HCI	IHC gênero	IHC género
Intersectional HCI	IHC interseccional	IHC interseccional
Feminist HCI and STS	IHC e CTS feminista	IHC y CTS feminista
Gender HCI and STS	IHC e CTS gênero	IHC y CTS género
Intersectional HCI and STS	IHC e CTS Interseccional	IHC y CTS Interseccional

(04) Selection of Relevant Publications
In some cases just reading titles and abstracts was not enough to decide the relevance for the study so we resorted to reading introduction, conclusion and references. The listed criteria were:

Inclusion criteria:

– complete publications that address feminisms, gender and intersectionality in HCI;
   Exclusion criteria:
– summarized publications;
– publications that was paid or closed for access in the institution proxy;
– publications that do not explicitly gender, feminisms and intersectionality in HCI;
– publications that uses gender linked to literature and/or linguistics such as literary genre, literary category;
– publications that uses the term intersectionality between disciplinary areas, for example, computer science and philosophy.

After the inclusion and exclusion filter 130 publications remained in English and none in Portuguese and Spanish.

(05) Data Classification and Extraction
86 publications from the final list were relevant for this study considering the searches in English, Spanish and Portuguese. It was noticed that there are until now only publications in English language. After, we added some information in the SM in order to identify trends in the publication. For the selection and identification of trends we organized 5 categories: a) publication year; b) authorship; c) publication place; d) keywords; e) title.

(06) Data Analysis
Publications in third-wave HCI especially on feminisms, gender and intersectionality are recent in the area. The first work identified was by Bardzell in 2010 that proposed a feminist agenda for people who develop and use technologies. This work is taken up in many subsequent publications in feminism HCI. We identified that most research is published in the Conference on Human Factors in Computing Systems which started in 1982 in the United States. In its history until 1992 the meetings were held in Canada or in the United States and after that expanded to Europe, in particular Amsterdam and Holland. (Fig. 2) presents the publications graphical representation.

Fig. 2. Third-wave HCI publications geographically situated

The (Fig. 2) highlights and situates the publications and which approach the authors used is important for this study considering our theoretical background discussed in the previous section. There are also other elements that were analyzed in this SM such as: publication year, most cited authors, publication places, keywords but it will not be discussed in this study because it is not aligned with the main objective of focusing on intersectional HCI perspective which is explored in the next section.

Intersectional HCI. The first mention in intersectional movement emerges from black women studies with a collective criticism turned radically against white, heteronormative, middle-class feminism [11]. This movement started with black feminists in the late 1980s who recognize multiple identities in women's studies but without the intention of creating a theory of global identity.

Kimberly Crenshaw [5] first used the intersectional term in 1989. For her intersectionality was a way of observing multiple oppressions of African American women. She theorizes that women were often obscured from ethnic or racial groups and also within the race and gender categories. According to her [5] intersectionality theory can be seen in two ways:

a) structural intersectionality: which has the position of black women at the intersection of race and gender in daily violence experiences;
b) political intersectionality: feminist and anti-racist policies that intensify violence towards black women.

We consider import to bring an intersectionality approach from Crenshaw [5] because she first uses and writes about the intersectional theory. She also considered intersectionality as a crossroads in which the crossing roads collide and the multiple oppressions appear. For this study we also highlight another author called Nira Yuval-Davis [6] who discuss intersectionality under the discursive prism.

The author [6] said that scholars see categories as deceptive constructions that do not readily allow the diversity and heterogeneity experience to be represented. The point is not to deny the importance - material and discursive - of the categories but to focus on the process by which it is produced, experienced, reproduced and resisted in everyday life.

Social divisions are macro axes of social power but also involve concrete people. Social divisions have organization, intersubjectivity, experiential and representational forms and this affects what way is theorized [6]. In other words, it is expressed in institutions and organizations through state laws, agencies, unios and in the family. In addition, it involves specific power and affective relationships between people and their roles as agents of specific social institutions and organizations. It also exists at the representation level being expressed in images, symbols, texts and ideologies including those related to legislation [6].

The theoretical background on intersectionality [5, 6] are important for this study to understand the theory, the contradictions and gaps that exist in talking about intersectionality as a white woman and privileged. It is worth mentioning that the resistance of black women to intersectional theory is understood as a form of struggle that clashes from the multiple oppressions at the social crossroads [6]. Yuval-Davis [6] sees differences as ontological and not homogenize but situates and differentiates within the limits of belonging.

Here, it is understood that intersectionality is not to prioritize a category only because in doing so a structure is prioritized and this is not the objective of bringing theory in fact this is one of the contradictions of those who does it.

3   Research Methodology

This research is qualitative, exploratory, and critical along its four stages: a) bibliographic survey; b) systematic mapping; c) data analysis; d) panel construction.

We began our methodological research by bibliographic research in Science, Technology and Society (STS) from a feminist perspective based on Donna Haraway [1, 2]. In the sequence, we conducted research on Human-Computer Interaction feminist approach that articulated with Haraway's theory [1, 2] and it was found the third-wave HCI approximation.

The second stage was a systematic mapping [9, 10] described in the 2.1.2. Section with six development phases. From the SM results, we analyzed all publications (n = 86) and observed that intersectional HCI approach presented gaps in the theory understanding. Therefore, this aspect was used as a clipping. The mapping resulted in 11 publications from the SM filter from 2009 to 2021.

In the third stage of data analysis, we observed that the intersectional HCI appropriation presents contradictions in some publications. The first step was to understand intersectional theory from [5, 6, 11]. After understanding intersectional theory [5, 6] we read the 11 Intersectional HCI publications that resulted from SM presented in Sect. 2.1.2. For the analysis, we used the intersectional theoretical basis [5, 6, 11] and feminist technoscience perspective from Haraway [1, 2] in conversation with discourse analysis [12]. The discourse analyst [12] says that every discourse in specific contexts. Therefore the analysis of the panel creation categories involves the dialogue between embodied objectivity, situated knowledge, intersectionality and discourse.

The last stage a panel construction is the joining of theories, proposals, and criticisms to situate the intersectional perspective to propose a situated, embodied way of comprehending the differences and recognizing and understanding its importance. The first and second stage was presented in Sect. 2. The next section presents the third and fourth stages.

4   Data Analysis

Research on intersectional HCI is recent with only 11 publications. (See Fig. 3) shows the first publication in 2016 and the last in 2019. A deepening area that is promising because some research has epistemological gaps by understanding the theory and using the term.

4.1   Intersectional HCI

Hankerson et al. [13] analyzed the most recurrent race representation in technology design. The authors bring case studies of how technologies do not recognize race and ethnicity, class and gender in the area.

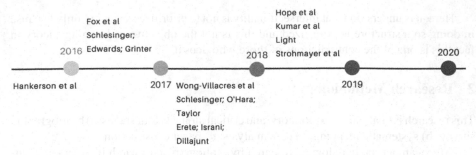

Fig. 3. Intersectional HCI authors (2016–2019)

Thinking of inclusive practices mentioned by [13] Fox et al. [14] proposes a workshop to explore theoretical and methodological approaches considering gender, sexual orientation, power and studies on race and ethnicity. The authors proposal is to analyze existing research and practices to identify concerns and approaches in design and evaluation with an intersectional bias in HCI.

Research by [13] and [14] aims to consider the user representation in third-wave HCI because for them the user represents an expansion, a diverse set of people. In this sense the discussion central question is how the user's identity is represented in gender, race and class dimensions. The authors map publications that are inclined to intersectional discussions and one aspect identified is that a large part of the researchers that use intersectionality general focus mainly on gender category.

Schlesinger; Edwards; Grinter [15] identified that the intersections between race and class are responsible for a small number of publications. They emphasize the importance of encouraging intersectional research to expand identity representations. Intersectionality for them has a wide range of applications in HCI, such as strengthening reports between people relationship with technology and their surrounding context.

Wong-Villacres et al. [16] compares situations to identify possible paths in interaction design. These authors conduct a multisectoral ethnographic study in seven low-resource learning environments in the India states of Maharashtra, Tamil, Nadu, West Bengal to encourage community participation to explore gender and diversity in technologies use and development.

Erete; Israni; Dillahunt [17] describe the approach with communities on the margins of design process. Researchers generally go to communities to conduct research and do not contribute with feedbacks to the communities. This situation is recurrent when it comes to ethnographic research. One way is to have activist posture and reflective thinking that can be organized with Participatory Design (PD) practices which can be used as a means to reach communities as protagonists in the process. Hope et al. [18] also points to PD to involve people in technology design process.

Strohmayer et al. [17] in their workshop proposal for CHI 2017 analyze the #CHIversity campaign highlighting feminist issues related to diversity and inclusion. The examples include: a) promoting connections between participants; b) discuss research polarization in a conservative political climate; c) encourage contributions to the growing body of feminist literature in HCI. For the authors, when diversity is mobilized through the inclusion and intersectionality vehicles it becomes an active and dynamic process.

Schlesinger; O'Hara; Taylor [19] analyze race in chatbots. They do not bring Crenshaw research to discuss identity and difference with chatbots when dealing with race categories but use it to discuss intersections of race and racism. Light [19] analyzes a design experience for social innovation in the local and situated context of northern Finland to understand and expand plural dimensions in design.

From the above-mentioned publications, we highlight the importance of recognizing the theory in its idealization - multiple oppressions in black women experience. Although several authors [16, 18, 19] point to use theory in other contexts, the original perspective aimed strengthening black women's oppression in relation to race, gender and social class as inseparable.

4.2   A Panel to Confront Differences in Intersectional HCI

The idea of a critical panel (see Fig. 4) is to present a broad vision, an overview of a situated and embodied perspective. With this panel a critical proposal is organized based on the interaction between the situated knowledge and embodied objectivity from Haraway [1, 2] and intersectional theory from Crenshaw [5] and Yuval-Davis [6]. Therefore, this panel composes the (dis)connections between theories, contradictions, gaps and boundaries.

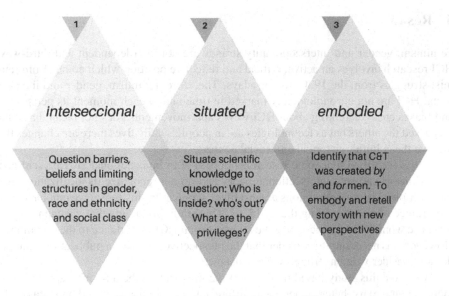

Fig. 4. A critical panel for third-wave HCI

1. The *intersectional* perspective adopted involves understanding that are multiple oppressions in black women experience in relation to gender, race and ethnicity and social class [5]. In addition to this perspective from Crenshaw [5] who first used

the term, another proposal to think about intersectionality based on Yuval-Davis [6] points out the categories and the complexity in a material and discursive level.

2. *Situating* scientific knowledge considering where people speak, why adopt such approach, what are the privileges and boundaries? Haraway [1, 2] based this questions to think of scientific knowledge as partial and situated. The author points out the need to identify it in S&T to question them, pointing out new possibilities for retell stories as an example of the three black women mentioned in the beginning of this study who contributed to computer science however their history were not known socially and culturally. To retell the stories is also to identify the hidden spaces, the contradictions to reframe something that cannot be modified but with the help of other narratives may provide new interpretations.

3. A critique in scientific objectivity in which represented the partial view that came from white, heterosexual men who made and are still the dominant part of computer science area. Understanding that scientific knowledge is not objective, linear and neutral is a way to other representations. The example about the three women is a form of *embodied* objectivity. It is to identify that there are power and privilege relationships in social, discursive and cultural structures but beyond these barriers there are people who contribute and participate, therefore embodied S&T is to confront such are differences and that are differences in the scientific knowledge.

5   Results

Feminism, gender and intersectionality strands are not interdependent and third-wave HCI research involves an active, critical and reflective position which comes from feminist struggles from the 1980s to nowadays. Therefore, feminism, gender and intersectional HCI are not chronologically marked in time and in each moment its perspective and biases change. Talking about HCI waves and movements does not mean that it has surpassed the others but as technologies are in people's daily lives there are changes that involve the cultural, historical and social context.

It was identified that some researchers [16–19] in intersectional HCI present contradictions when using intersectional theory and do not recognize its idealization from the multiple existing oppressions against black women. In this sense, we emphasize the importance of understanding theory [5, 6]. This study highlights that we cannot speak for these women but we recognize the intersectional HCI importance to the community. However, it is necessary to consider that the perspective adopted in publications mapped do not consider women struggles and resistance.

We wrote this study based on different theories and on the author's perspective, so there is complexity, heterogeneity and difference. We emphasize based on Haraway [1, 2] Crenshaw [5] Yuval-Davis [6] theoretical background that failures, contradictions and gaps happen in research because it is based on author experience and epistemology to create meanings. In this sense, we create the panel based on the dialogue between theorists considering the situated, partial and embodied knowledge of each approach.

The panel creation is a proposal that is not static, linear and much less an absolute truth. The panel is a way to understand intersectional theory in dialogue with feminist technoscience and discourse analysis. This dialogue in HCI from a Brazilian situated context is pioneering research discussed in Brazil. Considering that the area is also recent in other research centers, this study will continue in future studies in order to deepen the third-wave HCI perspective that brings more participation and diversity to computer science.

Acknowledgment. This study was financed in part by the Coordenação de Aperfeiçoamento de Pessoal de Nível Superior - Brasil (CAPES) - Finance Code 001.

References

1. Haraway, D.J.: Saberes localizados: a questão da ciência para o feminismo e o privilégio da perspectiva parcial. Cadernos Pagu (5), 07–41 (1995). https://periodicos.sbu.unicamp.br/ojs/index.php/cadpagu/article/view/1773 Accessed 01 Oct 2020
2. Haraway, D.J.: Donna Haraway: story telling for earthly survival. Roteiro e Direção: Fabrizio Terranova (2016). (77 min).
3. Favili, E., Cavallo, F.: Histórias de ninar para garotas rebeldes 2. V&R Editoras, Buenos Aires (2018)
4. Sanz, B.: Quem são as cientistas negras brasileiras? El País Brasil. São Paulo. 28 Feb 2017. https://brasil.elpais.com/brasil/2017/02/24/ciencia/1487948035_323512.html. Accessed 01 Sep 2020
5. Crenshaw, K.: Documento para o encontro de especialistas em aspectos da discriminação racial relativos ao gênero. Revista Estudos Feministas (2002)
6. Yuval-Davis, N.: Intersectionality and feminist politics. Eur. J. Women's Stud. SAGE Publications (UK and US), **13**(3), 193–209 2006. https://hal.archives-ouvertes.fr/hal-00571274. Accessed 14 Oct 2020
7. Bødker, S.: Third-wave HCI, 10 years later - participation and sharing. Mag. Interact. **22**(5), 24–31 (2015). https://dl.acm.org/citation.cfm?id=2804405 Accessed 08 Jan 2021
8. Bannon, L.: From human factors to human actors: the role of psychology and human-computer interaction studies in system design. In: Readings in Human-Computer Interaction. Interactive Technologies, pp. 205–214 (1995)
9. Petersen, K., et al.: Systematic mapping studies in software engineering (2008). http://www.robertfeldt.net/publications/petersen_ease08_sysmap_studies_in_se.pdf. Accessed 10 Jan 2021
10. Kitchenham, B.: Guidelines for performing systematic literature reviews in software engineering. University of Durham, UK (2007). https://www.elsevier.com/__data/promis_misc/525444systematicreviewsguide.pdf. Accessed 11 Jan 2021
11. Hirata, H.: Gênero, classe e raça: Interseccionalidade e consubstancialidade das relações sociais. Gênero, classe e raça, pp. 61–73 (2014)
12. Pêcheux, M.: Análise automática do discurso. In: Mariani, B.S. et al. (eds.)Por uma análise automática do discurso: uma introdução a ohra de Michel Pêcheux. 3a ed. Campinas, SP (1997). http://www.sergiofreire.pro.br/ad/GADET_HAK_PUAAD.pdf. Accessed 12 Sept 2020
13. Hankerson, A., et al.: Hackathons as participatory design: iterative feminist utopias. In: CHI 2019 (2019). https://dl.acm.org/citation.cfm?id=3300291. Accessed 11 Jan 2021
14. Fox, S., et al.: Imagining intersectional futures: feminist approaches in CSCW. In: CSCW 2017 Companion (2017). https://dl.acm.org/citation.cfm?id=3022665. Accessed 11 Jan 2021

15. Schlesinger, A., Edwards, K., Grinter, R.: Intersectional HCI: engaging identity through gender, race and class. In: CHI (2017). https://www.semanticscholar.org/paper/Intersect ional-HCI%3A-Engaging-Identity-through-Race%2C-Schlesinger-Edwards/27b49a706d90 7c5d6858068ba97bbe873fcf687f. Accessed 08 Jan 2021
16. Wong-Villacres, M., et al.: Design for intersections. In: DIS'18 Proceedings of the 2018 Designing Interactive Systems Conference, pp. 45–58. https://dl.acm.org/doi/abs/10.1145/ 3196709.3196794. Accessed11 Jan 2021
17. Erete, S., Israni, A., Dillahunt, T.: An intersectional approach to designing in the margins. Mag. Interact. **25**(3) (2018). https://dl.acm.org/citation.cfm?id=3194349. Accessed 02 Jan 2021
18. Hope, A., et al.: Hackathons as participatory design: iterative feminist utopias. In: CHI 2019 (2019). https://dl.acm.org/citation.cfm?id=3300291. Accessed 10 Jan 2021
19. Schlesinger, A., O'Hara, K., Taylor, A.: Lets talk about race: identity, chatbots, and AI. Paper presented at the CHI 2018, Montreal, Canada, 21–26 April 2018 (2018). https://openaccess. city.ac.uk/id/eprint/19124/. Accessed 11 Jan 2021
20. Light, A.: Design and social innovation at the margins: finding and making cultures of plurality. Design Cult. **11**, 13–35 (2019)

Information Differentiation in the Information Society: From the Perspective of All Stages of Human Information Activities

Ying Zhao[1], Ting Xiong[1], Liang Zhou[1(✉)], Lijia Hu[2], and Guangyao Li[1]

[1] Department of Information Management and Technology, School of Public Administration, Sichuan University, Chengdu, China
[2] Yibin Public Security Bureau, Yibin, Sichuan, China

Abstract. With the rapid development of the information society, the phenomenon of information differentiation caused by the gap of information resources has also emerged. To explore the influencing factors of information differentiation is of great significance for governments to reduce the degree of information differentiation. The existing researches only focus on the part of information activities. To solve this problem, this paper measures the information social status from the perspective of the whole process of information activities. Information differentiation is the embodiment of social differentiation in the information society, and the traditional social differentiation factors will affect information differentiation to some extent. This paper discusses the impact of stratification index of social stratification theory and age stratification theory on individual status in the information society. From this, we can conclude the key factors affecting the degree of information differentiation, which is conducive to the government to take measures to construct the information society and promote social equality and sustainable development.

Keywords: Information differentiation · Information activity · Social stratification

1 Introduction

The development of information and communication technology has brought about the explosive growth of information. At the same time, it has also brought about a significant gap between different social groups in the possession and use of information, resulting in a universal phenomenon of "information differentiation" in the world [1, 2].

As an emerging developing country, China's information society has made great achievements in the past two decades. China's Social Information Society Index (ISI) increased from 0.231 in 2001 to 0.4749 in 2017, ranking 81/126 in the world. However, with the rapid development of the information society, the Chinese people in the information society also have different status based on regions, urban and rural areas and social strata [3]. Today, when information has become an increasingly important factor of production, people's position in the hierarchical information society will directly

© Springer Nature Switzerland AG 2021
M. Kurosu (Ed.): HCII 2021, LNCS 12762, pp. 107–122, 2021.
https://doi.org/10.1007/978-3-030-78462-1_8

reflect their political and economic status [4]. It means that information differentiation will further aggravate the inequality between urban and rural areas, different regions and different social strata in China, and pose a challenge to the sustainable development of the whole country.

Like governments all over the world, the Chinese government is trying to reduce the degree of social information differentiation. The premise and key to solving this problem are to understand the form factors of information differentiation among different social groups, as well as the influencing factors. To sum up, combined with the national conditions of our country, it has become an important issue for the Chinese government to explore the influencing factors of the information differentiation of social groups.

2 Theoretical Basis and Literature Review

2.1 Information Differentiation

The concept of information differentiation was first put forward by Martin. He described information differentiation as isolation, a situation separated from society, a feeling that individuals could not catch up with new technological developments [5]. With the development of information differentiation research, the connotation of information differentiation is more clear and rich. The most common definition is the gap between the information rich and the information poor in terms of access, possession and utilization of information resources [6].

At present, there are two main aspects of the research on information differentiation, including theoretical and empirical aspects.

(1) Theoretical research: many studies have discussed the related concepts and development of information differentiation. With the development of information technology, many related concepts of information differentiation continue to emerge, such as information inequality, information gap, information poverty, information divide and so on [7]. Through the study of the related concepts of information differentiation, scholars can better grasp the complexity of the phenomenon of information differentiation.

(2) Empirical research: the research content mainly includes the performance, causes and coping strategies of information differentiation, in which the reasons or influencing factors of information differentiation are the focus of scholars' attention. The related research on influencing factors mainly focuses on the information differentiation of special groups or specific regions [8], such as the influencing factors of information differentiation of farmers and disabled people, and the influencing factors of rural areas and western China [9–11] and so on. These studies have a strong regional or crowd color and are not suitable for the information society at the national level. In the research process of influencing factors, an important problem is how to measure the degree of information differentiation. The measurement of the degree of information differentiation has only considered the information differentiation in part of information activities, such as information acquisition behavior [11, 12], and has not completely explored the whole picture of information inequality.

In different information activities, measurement methods mainly through the transformation of other related information concepts [13], such as "personal information world". "Personal information world" measure information differences from space, time, intelligence three aspects.

Most of the existing research on information distribution only pays attention to a specific stage of information activities and discusses information differentiation by quantitative analysis of the position of individuals in information socialization. However, information differentiation is an objective phenomenon in the information society. It is not limited to a certain process of information activities. It exists in the whole process of human information activities. In view of this, from the view of the whole process of information activities, this paper describes the information gap comprehensively from five stages: information demand, information acquisition, information evaluation, information organization, information innovation, and information ethics six aspects [14].

2.2 Social Stratification Theory

Information differentiation is the embodiment of social differentiation in the information society, and the traditional factors of social differentiation will also affect the information differentiation to some extent. Therefore, based on the theory of social stratification and age stratification theory this paper extracts the traditional social differentiation index, and explores its influence on the information differentiation.

Social stratification refers to the process and phenomenon that social members and social groups are gradually divided into different levels according to the attributes of certain social significance [15]. Different scholars put forward different theories of social stratification, among which Marx's social stratification theory and Weber's social stratification theory are the most representative social stratification theory. Marx's social stratification theory and Weber's social stratification theory are also the basic model and analytical framework of social stratification theory research. The former emphasizes that the possession of production is the most critical factor directly affecting social stratification, and is also the standard for the division of social strata [16]. The latter advocates hierarchical research from economic, political and social three aspects, such as personal property (economy), control and influence over the actions of others (political), identity and educational level (society), etc. [17].

2.3 Age Stratification Theory

The theory of age stratification is also called age sociology theory. It divides members of society into different simultaneous groups marked by age. The social events and social processes experienced and felt within the same group in the same period are the same. There are various differences in different groups in the same period [18]. On the one hand, these differences are reflected in demography, such as birth rate and mortality rate. On the other hand, differences are also reflected in sociology, such as social characteristics (such as status, income, prestige, etc.) and social behavior (economic behavior, information behavior, etc.). The theory of age stratification emphasizes that age is the main factor affecting the different behavior choices of individuals. In the information age, the members of Chinese society also show obvious age differences in the possession and use of information.

The difference in individual information society status is the direct embodiment of information differentiation in individuals. Therefore, this paper measures the information society status of the individual from the whole process of information activities and explores the influencing factors of information differentiation by studying the influencing factors of the individual status in the information society. With regard to the extraction of influencing factors, this paper abstracts eight representative indexes according to the theory of social stratification and the theory of Age stratification, puts forward the **age** factors based on the theory of age stratification, puts forward six influencing factors of **sex**, **education level**, **income**, **social support**, **information consumption level** and **occupation** based on the theory of social stratification, and puts forward the **Health** factors based on the theory of age stratification and the theory of social stratification.

3 Put Forward a Hypothesis

3.1 The Influence of Age on the Status of Individual Information Society

According to the theory of age stratification, the behavior of people of different ages is "heterogeneous". With the increase of age, the physical function of individuals decreases, and the information demand and information skills will degrade [19], which will further affect their position in the information society. Therefore, this paper puts forward the H1 that age will negatively affect the information society status of the individual.

3.2 The Influence of the Level of Education and the Status of Individual Information Society

According to the theory of social stratification, the level of individual education affects the individual information demand, possession and utilization. It also determines the individual information skills [20] and then produces the status difference of individuals in the information society. Therefore, this paper puts forward the H2 that the level of education will positively affect the information society status of individuals.

3.3 The Influence of Personal Income and Individual Information Society Status

According to the theory of social stratification, in the information society, the acquisition of information will produce different degrees of economic costs. Individuals with high income have more advantages in information demand, access to information and information ideology and morality. So they are in a favorable position in the information society. Therefore, this paper proposes H3 that personal income will positively affect the status of the individual information society.

3.4   The Influence of the Degree of Social Support and the Status of Individual Information Society

According to the theory of social stratification, in the information society, social support shows the degree of individual acquisition and satisfaction of information needs from many aspects, such as emotional support, resource support, technical support and so on. The integration caused by social support and the estrangement caused by social non-support are bound to lead to the division of society [21]. This makes people with insufficient social support at a disadvantage in the information society. Therefore, this paper puts forward H4 that the degree of social support will positively affect the status of personal information society.

3.5   The Influence of Information Consumption and Individual Information Society Status

According to the theory of social stratification, information consumption refers to the expenses incurred in any information service or activity, which can reflect the information possession ability of individuals to a certain extent. The status of people with high information consumption is also relatively high. Therefore, this paper puts forward the H5 that information consumption will positively affect the status of individual information society.

3.6   The Influence of Occupation on the Status of Individual Information Society

According to the theory of social stratification, in the information society, workers of the same occupation will have similar professional knowledge structure and way of thinking. Workers of different occupations will have different information needs, information skills and ideas because of their different status, job requirements and needs in labor relations, resulting in information gap and different position in the information society. Therefore, this paper puts forward the H6 that occupation will affect the status of individual information society.

4   Research Design

4.1   Data Resource

In this paper, 1–2 cities in North China, Central China, East China, South China, Northeast, Northwest and Southwest were selected as the survey sites for online questionnaire survey. According to the data of the sixth census released by the National Bureau of Statistics of China, stratified sampling was conducted for respondents of different ages. A total of 439 valid questionnaires were collected by cleaning and filling out questionnaires for less than 15 min. Among them, 67, 194, 146 and 32 questionnaires were filled out by people aged 0–14, 15–40, 41–64 and over. It is basically in line with the 16:43:31:9 population distribution in China.

4.2 Research Ideas and Methods

This study measures the position of individuals in the information society by evaluating the five stages of information demand, information acquisition, information evaluation, information organization and information innovation, as well as the six dimensions of information ethics. Then, by observing whether there are significant differences in the overall position of different social groups in the information society, the influencing factors of information differentiation in Chinese society are obtained. And then it reflects the overall situation of social information differentiation in China.

Firstly, the factor analysis method is used to find the potential structure of the six observation variables and reduce the dimension, and some core observation variables are obtained. After that, single factor variance analysis was used to determine the significant influencing factors of social information differentiation in China. Finally, the mean value of each individual core observation variable is taken as the explained variable. The explanatory variables are selected according to the results of single factor analysis, and the multiple linear regression model of information differentiation is constructed to quantitatively determine the influence of each influencing factor on the individual's position in the information society.

4.3 Explanatory Variables and Expanded Variables

The research measures the individual's performance in the six dimensions of information ethics, such as information demand, information acquisition, information evaluation, information organization, information innovation, and so on. All the questions in the questionnaire were based on Likert 5-scale. According to their degree of agreement with the statements of each question, the respondents chose five options including "completely disagree", "not quite agree", "neutral", "relatively agree" and "completely agree". Among them, the dimensions of information demand and information ethics each contain four measurement questions, and the other four dimensions contain five measurement questions. The whole questionnaire contains 28 questions in total.

According to the theory of social stratification, the research measures the gender, education level, income, social support level, information consumption level and occupation of the respondents. The study measured the age and health status of the participants based on the age stratification theory, combined with the life cycle theory. Age (1 = 0–14 years (reference), 2 = 15–40 years, 3 = 41–64 years, 4 = 65 years and over), gender (1 = male (reference item), 2 = female), educational level (1 = primary school and below, 2 = junior middle school, 3 = high school, 4 = technical secondary school, 5 = junior high school, 6 = undergraduate, 7 = graduate student and above (reference item)), Health status (1 = very poor, 2 = poor, 3 = general (reference item), 4 = better, 5 = very good), Annual income (1 = less than 10, 000 RMB, 2 = 1,0000–6,0000 RMB, 3 = 6,0000–20,0000 RMB (reference item), 4 = more than 200000 RMB), Degree of social support (1 = very unsupportive, 2 = less supportive, 3 = general support (reference item), 4 = more support, 5 = very supportive), Monthly information consumption (1 = less than 50 RMB (reference item), 2 = 50–100 RMB, 3 = 101–200 RMB, 4 = 201 RMB or more), Occupation (1 = state organs, party organizations, enterprises,

the person in charge of the institution (reference item), 2 = professional and technical personnel, 3 = agriculture, forestry, animal husbandry, fishing, water conservancy
production personnel, 4 = commercial, service industry personnel, 5 = production,
transportation equipment operators and related personnel, 6 = clerks, 7 = students) are
encoded separately.

5   Research Results

5.1   Factor Analysis

Principal component analysis (PCA) was used for exploratory factor analysis. The results
of KMO and Bartlett test showed that KMO = 0.940 > 0.90, which indicated that the
data set had excellent suitability for factor analysis. Through observation, the steep slope
map (see Fig. 1. Factor steep slope map) or gradually becomes flat after 3–4 factors,
and the characteristic value of the four factors is more than 1, so the study considers
extracting four factors.

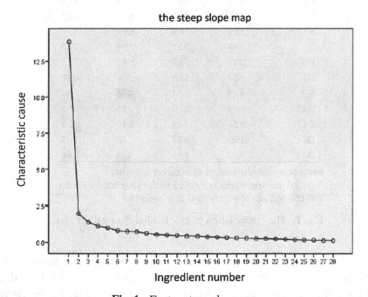

Fig. 1. Factor steep slope map

    After using the maximum variation method to deal with the data matrix, it is found that
the fifth and sixth factors contain only one item of IE3 and one item of ID4 respectively.
The content of the item under these two factors is too little. Therefore, the second factor
analysis was carried out after deleting IE3 and ID4, and the data matrix after rotating
the axis is shown in Fig. 2.

    According to the results of the second factor analysis, four core factors were deter-
mined. The first factor includes eight items of IE3, IE4, IO1, IO2, IO3, II3 and II4,
which are named information evaluation and management; the second factor includes

	component			
	1	2	3	4
IO2	.793	.268	.227	.142
II4	.777	.284	.267	.062
IE4	.769	.331	.201	.132
IO3	.746	.288	.300	.179
IE3	.662	.357	.104	.226
IO4	.658	.361	.323	.109
IO1	.649	.283	.266	.331
II3	.627	.251	.423	.034
ID2	.127	.785	.208	.211
IA1	.223	.759	.198	.203
IA4	.359	.754	.242	.144
ID4	.324	.699	-.008	.129
ID1	.298	.689	.119	.143
IA2	.401	.687	.203	.143
IA5	.271	.665	.357	.121
IA3	.361	.531	.379	.164
II1	.359	.208	.699	.217
IO5	.369	.260	.615	.170
II5	.494	.055	.596	.290
IE1	.087	.549	.587	.111
II2	.547	.188	.554	.068
IE5	.422	.244	.436	.234
IM3	.000	.029	.315	.762
IM2	.324	.345	.049	.713
IM4	.190	.343	.186	.705
IM1	.429	.455	-.074	.466

Extraction method: Analysis of main components
Rotation method: **Varimax** method with **Kaiser** normalization
The rotation axis of **a** converges to 9 iterations

Fig. 2. The composition matrix behind the rotation axis

eight items of ID1, ID2, ID4, IA1, IA2, IA3, IA4 and IA5, which are named information demand and acquisition. The third factor includes six items of IE1, IE5, IO5, II1, II2 and II5, which are named as information understanding and utilization, and the fourth factor includes four items of IM1, IM2, IM3 and IM4, which are named information ethics.

The Cronbach's Alpha value was used to test the reliability of the four dimensions of the scale. The results show that the confidence values of the four dimensions are 0.922, 0.938, 0.864 and 0.783, respectively, all of which are on 0.7. Therefore, the reliability level of the scale can be considered as better as a whole.

5.2 Single Factor Analysis of Variance

Using single factor variance analysis test, this paper analyzes the influence of each explanatory variable on individual scores in the four dimensions of information demand

and acquisition, information evaluation and management, information understanding and utilization, and information ethics, as well as its influence on the overall position in the information society.

Taking age as an example, the results of variance analysis of the total scores of different age groups in each stage of information activities are as Table 1:

Table 1. Variance analysis of information differentiation dimensions in different age groups

		Sum of squares	Degree of freedom	Average sum of squares	F	Significance
Information demand and acquisition score	Between groups	44.187	3	14.729	25.688	0.000
	Within group	249.420	435	.573		
	Sum up	293.607	438			
Information evaluation and management score	Between groups	67.214	3	22.405	39.583	0.000
	Within group	246.218	435	.566		
	Sum up	313.432	438			
Information understanding and utilization score	Between groups	15.066	3	5.022	10.598	0.000
	Within group	206.125	435	.474		
	Sum up	221.191	438			
Information ethics score	Between groups	10.348	3	3.449	5.417	0.001
	Within group	276.997	435	.637		
	Sum up	287.345	438			

The results of variance analysis showed that age has a significant impact on the performance of individuals in the four dimensions of information demand and acquisition, information evaluation and management, information understanding and utilization, and information ethics. So it can be considered to be a significant influencing factor of social information differentiation in China.

The study carried out the same single factor variance analysis of seven explanatory variables: gender, educational level, health status, personal annual income, social support level, information consumption level and occupation. The results show that the level of

education, the degree of social support, the level of information consumption and occupation have significant effects on the performance of individuals in the four dimensions,
and the annual income of individuals has a significant impact on the performance of
individuals in the three dimensions of information demand and acquisition, information
evaluation and management, and information ethics. Personal health status has a significant impact on individual performance in the three dimensions of information demand
and access, information evaluation and management, and information understanding and
utilization. Gender has no significant effect on the performance of individuals in all four
dimensions.

Based on the results of single factor variance analysis of each variable, seven variables, age, education level, health status, individual annual income, social support degree,
information consumption level and health status, were identified as the significant influencing factors of social information differentiation and were included as explanatory
variables in the subsequent regression analysis without considering gender.

5.3 Multiple Linear Regression Analysis

Both normal distribution and equal dispersion of residuals are prerequisites for linear
regression. Therefore, residual analysis and equal dispersion test of the explained variables are carried out in this study. The residuals histogram and P-P graph (see Fig. 3,
Fig. 4, Fig. 5) show that the standardized residuals of the samples basically meet the
normal distribution. The points in the cross-dispersion graph are randomly distributed
horizontally near 0 value, satisfying the dispersity of residual error. In summary, the
study data set meets the prerequisites for linear regression.

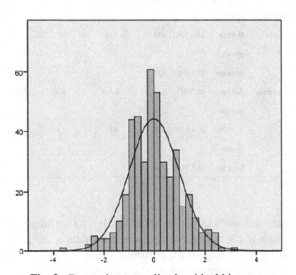

Fig. 3. Regression normalized residual histogram

The average score of an individual in 26 items is calculated to represent the overall
performance of the individual's position in the information society and as an explanatory variable of the regression model. In this study, seven explanatory variables, age,

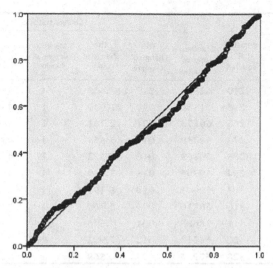

Fig. 4. Normalized residual normal probability distribution diagram

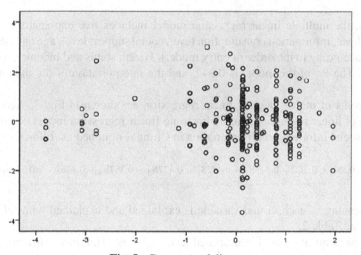

Fig. 5. Cross spread diagram

education level, health status, personal annual income, social support level, health status and information consumption level, were studied by stepwise regression strategy, and the forward selection method was selected to construct the model. The process of establishing the regression model is shown in the following Fig. 6:

model	R	R squared	Adjusted R squared	Standard error of estimation	Change statistics				
					The change of R square	The change of F	Molecular degrees of freedom	Denominator degree of freedom	Significant F change
1	.461^a	.212	.210	.62820	.212	117.689	1	437	.000
2	.499^b	.249	.246	.61386	.037	21.649	1	436	.000
3	.520^c	.271	.266	.60573	.021	12.781	1	435	.000
4	.530^d	.281	.274	.60238	.010	5.854	1	434	.016
5	.539^e	.291	.283	.59869	.010	6.372	1	433	.012
6	.551^f	.304	.294	.59395	.013	7.939	1	432	.005
7	.560^g	.314	.303	.59041	.010	6.195	1	431	.013
8	.568^h	.323	.310	.58710	.009	5.865	1	430	.016
9	.567^i	.322	.311	.58685	-.001	.636	1	430	.426
10	.578^j	.334	.322	.58215	.012	7.992	1	430	.005
11	.585^k	.342	.328	.57955	.007	4.869	1	429	.028

Fig. 6. Test results of regression coefficient

Finally, the multiple linear regression model includes five explanatory variables: education level, information consumption level, social support level, age and occupation (arranged according to the order of entry model). Health status and income do not enter the model. The R^2 of the model is 0.342, and the interpretation of the model is good (Fig. 6).

The results of multi-selection linear regression are shown in Fig. 7. According to the results of linear regression, the multivariate linear regression model of influencing factors of social information differentiation in China is obtained as follows:

$$I = 3.465 - 0.89E + 0.28C - 0.773S_1 - 0.442S_2 - 0.477S_3 - 0.357S_4 + 0.436A_1 + 0.319A_2 - 0.224P \tag{1}$$

The meaning of each virtual variable is explained and explained with reference to the following Table 2:

From the point of view of educational level, there are significant differences in the status of graduate students and above in the information society. The population with graduate students and above is in a dominant position in the information society, which supports H2.

From the level of information consumption, there is a significant difference in the status of people with monthly information consumption of more than 200 yuan and consumption of less than 50 yuan in the information society. The population with monthly consumption of more than 200 yuan occupies a dominant position, supporting H5.

model	Nonstandardized coefficient		Standardization coefficient	t	Significance	Collinearity statistics	
	Estimate of B	Standard error	Beta distribution			Permissible error	VIF
11 (constant)	3.553	.090		39.295	.000		
primary school and below& graduate student and above	-.890	.142	-.303	-6.248	.000	.653	1.531
201 RMB or more& less than 50 RMB	.280	.073	.158	3.843	.000	.907	1.103
General& Constants are very supportive	-.477	.088	-.330	-5.393	.000	.410	2.438
Very unsupportive& Very supportive	-.773	.204	-.186	-3.796	.000	.642	1.558
Supportive& Very supportive	-.357	.088	-.249	-4.037	.000	.405	2.472
15-40years& 0-14years	.436	.081	.307	5.365	.000	.470	2.128
41-64years& 0-14years	.319	.083	.213	3.864	.000	.505	1.982
unsupportive& Very supportive	-.442	.172	-.114	-2.568	.011	.784	1.276
Clerks& state organs, party organizations, enterprises, The person in charge of the instit ution	-.224	.101	-.089	-2.207	.028	.941	1.063

a. Dependent variable : I

Fig. 7. Test results of the regression coefficient of 5 regression equation

Table 2. The meaning and reference explanation of variables in the regression equation

Variable name	Meaning	Reference
E	Education level = Primary school and below	Education level = Postgraduate or above
C	Level of information consumption = 201 RMB or more	Level of information consumption = Less than 50 RMB
S1	Degree of Social Support = very unsupportive	Degree of Social Support = very supportive
S2	Degree of Social Support = less supportive	Degree of Social Support = very supportive
S3	Degree of Social Support = general support	Degree of Social Support = very supportive
S4	Degree of Social Support = more support	Degree of Social Support = very supportive
A1	Years = 15–40	Years = 0–14
A2	Years = 41–64	Years = 0–14
P	Occupation = Clerks	Occupation = state organs, party organizations, enterprises, The person in charge of the institution

From the point of view of the degree of social support, the people with strong social support have the highest position in the information society, and the people with very weak social support have the lowest position in the information society. There is a positive correlation between the status of different groups in the information society and the degree of social support they receive, that is, the higher the degree of social support, the higher the status in the information society, supporting H4. As shown in the following Fig. 8.

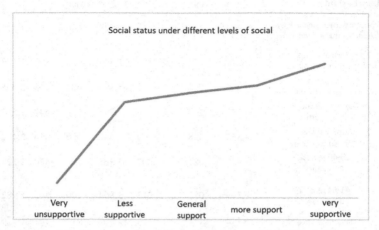

Fig. 8. Changes in the status of the information society with the level of social support

In terms of age, children under 14 years of age are at a disadvantage in the information society compared with young people aged 15–40 and middle-aged people aged 40–64, supporting H1.

From a professional point of view, the population of professional clerks is in a dominant position in the information society compared with the group of people who are responsible for state organs, party and mass organizations, enterprises and institutions, and supports H6.

The failure of the individual's annual income to be included in the regression model indicates that this factor is not a key factor affecting the position of the individual in the information society, so H3 is not supported.

6   Discussion

Based on the theory of age stratification and social stratification, this study puts forward the factors, and then quantitatively measures the position of individuals in the information society from the six stages of information activities. By comparing the status of different groups in the information society, this paper comprehensively discusses the influencing factors of information differentiation in China. Based on the sampling survey of 24 cities in China, this paper constructs a model of influencing factors of information differentiation and makes an empirical analysis.

The results show that: 1) Age, educational level, social support level and information consumption level are all important factors affecting the differentiation of social information in China. This also shows that age stratification theory and social stratification theory have certain applicability in information activities. 2) The level of education is the most important factor affecting the differentiation of social information. The higher the level of education, the more individuals can be in a dominant position in the information society. 3) Income level has no significant effect on information differentiation. This is different from the conclusions of relevant scholars on the digital divide in other countries [22]. This is mainly due to the remarkable progress of information construction in China in recent years, the low cost of Internet use, the high level of user access and use. So low-income people can have a better performance in the process of information activities.

This paper has made great contributions in theory and practice. At the theoretical level, the results show that the age stratification theory and the social stratification theory are not only suitable for the economic society and the political society, but also suitable for the information society. It expands the application scenarios of the social stratification theory and the age stratification theory. This can provide a new way for scholars to carry on the research of information differentiation and information related fields in the future. At the practical level, the influencing factors of information differentiation provide a reference for Chinese government decision-makers to determine the relevant policies. The results show that the level of education and social support have an important impact on the information differentiation among different groups. The government and all sectors of society should take positive measures to promote education, especially to strengthen the education of information knowledge. It can improve the level of national education in our country, and reduce the degree of social information differentiation. At the same time, the government should strengthen social support, actively hold all kinds of information lectures, social training and so on, in order to enhance the level of publicity and education of information activities, and make more people aware of the problem of information differentiation. These measures can effectively narrow the status gap of social groups in the information society, and then reduce the level of information differentiation. It also can help the information vulnerable groups to gradually integrate into the information society, to build a harmonious society has a certain reference significance.

References

1. Zhang, L.B., Yang, J.H.: Sociologically ponder on the question of information differentiation. Inf. Sci. **27**(11), 1611–1614 (2006). https://doi.org/10.1016/0013-7944(94)90124-4
2. Xie, J.G.: Information differentiation in the development of social informationization. J. Hunan City Univ. **27**(3), 1–7 (2006)
3. Zhong, W.D.: The causes of economic poverty and its policy inspiration for anti-poverty from the perspective of information poverty. Library **48**(4), 8–13 (2020)
4. Yu, L.Z., Zhou, W.J., Yu, B.B., Liu, H.F.: Towards a comprehensive measurement of the information rich and poor. J. Doc. **72**(4), 614–635 (2016). https://doi.org/10.1108/jdoc-03-2015-0032
5. Martin, W.J.: The Information Society. Aslib, London (1988)
6. Nolin, J.: Review of: Feather, John the information society: a study of continuity and change. 6th ed. Facet Publishing, London (2013). http://hdl.handle.net/2320/13094. Information Research 18(2)

7. Yu, L.Z.: Understanding information inequality: making sense of the literature of the information and digital divides. J. Librariansh. Inf. Sci. **38**(4), 229–252 (2006). https://doi.org/10.1177/0961000606070600
8. Mou, X.B., Xu, F.: Examining the factors influencing information poverty in Western China. Electron. Libr. **38**(5/6), 1115–1134 (2020). https://doi.org/10.1108/EL-04-2020-0095
9. Nam, S.J., Park, E.Y.: The effects of the smart environment on the information divide experienced by people with disabilities. Disabil. Health J. **10**(2), 257–263 (2016). https://doi.org/10.1016/j.dhjo.2016.11.001
10. Ramírez, A.S., Estrada, E., Ruiz, A.: Mapping the health information landscape in a rural, culturally diverse region: implications for interventions to reduce information inequality. J. Prim. Prev. **38**(4), 345–362 (2017). https://doi.org/10.1007/s10935-017-0466-7
11. Liu, H.F., Wang, J.L.: A study of individual's information world of peasants and factors affecting information divide. Libr. Tribune **37**(10), 54–63 (2017)
12. Yu, L.Z., Xie, H.X.: Peasants' information access in contemporary China: a structural analysis and its limitations. J. Libr. Sci. China **39**(6), 9–26 (2013). https://doi.org/10.13530/j.cnki.jlis.2013.06.004
13. Yu, L.Z.: The information worlds of individuals: the discovery and exposition of a concept for information inequality. J. Libr. Sci. China **39**(1), 4–12 (2013). https://doi.org/10.13530/j.cnki.jlis.2013.01.001
14. Fan, Z.: Study on content framework of information literacy in social media context. J. Intell. **31**(10), 170–174 (2012)
15. Li, Q.: Fairness and justice in the areas of social stratification and social space. J. Renmin Univ. China **26**(1), 2–9 (2012)
16. Waters, M.: Modern Sociological Theory. Sage, Thousand Oaks (1994)
17. Fu, Y.L., Liu, J., Lu, W.J.: Analysis on the causes of american poverty from the perspective of Max Weber's social stratification theory. Chin. Public Adm. **31**(4), 134–139 (2015)
18. Riley, M.W.: Social gerontology and the age stratification of society. Gerontologist **11**(1), 79–87 (1971). https://doi.org/10.1093/geront/11.1_part_1.79
19. Blackburn, C., Read, J., Hughes, N.: Carers and the digital divide: factors affecting Internet use among carers in the UK. Health Soc. Care Commun. **13**(3), 201–210 (2005)
20. Yang, F., Zhang, X.: Focal fields in literature on the information divide: the USA, China, UK and India. J. Doc. **76**(2), 373–388 (2019). https://doi.org/10.1108/JD-02-2019-0032
21. Huang, J.Q.: Segregation of migrant workers: the inevitable choice and the mechanism on realizing the urbanization of migrant workers. Issues Agric. Econ. **32**(11), 28–33 (2011). https://doi.org/10.13246/j.cnki.iae.2011.11.005
22. Michael, H., Anabel, Q.H., Corbett, B.A.: Revisiting the digital divide in Canada: the impact of demographic factors on access to the internet, level of online activity, and social networking site usage. Inf. Commun. Soc. **17**(4), 503–519 (2014). https://doi.org/10.1080/1369118X.2014.891633

Machine-Human Interaction: A Paradigm Shift?

Hervé Saint-Louis(✉)

Université du Québec À Chicoutimi, Chicoutimi, QC G7H 2B1, Canada
`Herve_saint-louis@uqac.ca`

Abstract. The abstract should summarize the contents of the paper in short terms, i.e. 150–250 words. In this article, I perform a preliminary exploration on hypothesised the paradigm shift from human-initiated interaction to machine-initiated interaction. There are consequences and structural issues that need to be highlighted when considering such an important topic beyond the academic setting and ontological issues. While continuing to develop the theoretical work related to evaluating this shift, I use this as an opportunity to ask a classic "so what" question. What matters when machines are the ones trying to initiate interactions with humans? Specifically, what happens to parts of humanity that are often excluded from issues related to the deployment of AI in society? How can such groups, which are often marginalised react and to machines that act autonomously? To do this, I chose Black Twitter as the main case study of this article to explore if and how marginalisation can occur when machines initiate interactions with humans. Recently, Twitter has become the ground of much experimentation with AI deployed by its operators. However, it is also the experiment ground for third-party "bots" that interact with humans, often, without the latter being aware that of the interaction undertaken is with a machine. The article is part of a larger study investigating if there are significant differences between the way machines and members of Black Twitter interact with one another.

Keywords: Human-computer interaction · Artificial intelligence · Paradigm shift · Twitter · Black twitter · Bots · Marginalisation

1 Introduction

When Thomas Kuhn [1] wrote on the structure of scientific revolutions in his seminal history of science, he argued that scientific communities of practices reconfigure knowledge to tackle unforeseen ontological inadequacies in research. These reconfigurations, he argued were paradigm shifts that changed the perceptions of sciences [1]. Discussions and inquiries about paradigm shifts in the field of human-computer interaction (HCI) are not rare. Starting at the discipline's beginning, J.C.R. Licklider [2] theorised that there would be paradigm shifts in HCI related to how humans and machine interact with one another. He argued that HCI would gradually shift from interaction to symbiosis, and then, to advanced artificial intelligence (AI). For Licklider, HCI was a discipline focused on the extension of people's capabilities through technology, while human-machine symbiosis was the intermediary step between autonomous machines endowed

© Springer Nature Switzerland AG 2021
M. Kurosu (Ed.): HCII 2021, LNCS 12762, pp. 123–136, 2021.
https://doi.org/10.1007/978-3-030-78462-1_9

with AI [2]. Similar to Licklider, I argue that there is a paradigm shift in HCI but from human-machine to machine-human interaction. However, I challenge the efficacy and simplicity of the interaction and the symbiosis he predicted. As machines take a leading role in understanding and initiating humans, it often marginalises or fails to take into account parts of humanity for whom technology was not designed for. This question has been an important one raised several times by ethics scholars such as Timmit Gebru and it has been controversial enough to lead to her firing from Google, in December 2020. In this article, I ask if the hypothesised paradigm shift from human-machine to machine-human interaction reinforces the marginalisation of certain groups in society and their access to technology. Further, I argue that the individual level of analysis often used in HCI fails methodologically to analyse how intelligent and autonomous machines, such as AI affect societal structures that affect whole groups such as Black users of Twitter (otherwise known as Black Twitter).

This refection is part of an ongoing research project laying the groundwork of an evaluation of the shift from subject-to-object interaction to object-to-subject interaction that could lead to a reframing of some of the theoretical foundations of HCI. While I argue that there is a paradigm shift from human-machine to machine-human interaction in HCI, my interest in this ongoing project is to develop the proper methodological tools to analyse what are the consequences for some marginalised groups, like Black Twitter. What is at stake in the shift from human-led to machine led interactions is the marginalisation of groups who do not participate in the shaping of evolving technologies.

2 Background

This research continues work that I have elaborated [3] about how to use sociological critical approaches with HCI to answer structural questions that are usually limited social sciences. In previous research, I analysed the commodification of users' attention while they attempted to use third-party authentication on Facebook, Google, and Twitter. That study relied on both an experiment and a policy analysis. HCI, as a discipline is focused on how people use and perceive technology. Much like psychology, knowledge about human behaviour and practices in HCI are inferred through the study of individuals. HCI relies more on experiments and observations rather than collecting existing data from existing documents or recollections of users set after an initial event. My research on Black Twitter integrates experimental work evaluating participants' actions and reactions to machine-initiated interaction with policy analyses on the marginalisation of that group.

3 Related Works

The strength of HCI is that its methodological approaches can directly evaluate phenomena such as the digital literacy of Black Twitter members and their responses to prompt initiated by AI, serving as the springboard for more structural queries. For example, many HCI scholars have embraced research about other marginalised groups such as disabled users [4–8] and aging ones [9–11].

Although the literature about other marginalised groups such as disabled and aging populations is well represented in HCI, research that focuses specifically on race and to some extent intersectionality is surprisingly fairly recent. Beginning in 2010, the Conference on Human Factors in Computing (CHI) held a panel on politics where issues related to privacy, surveillance and diversity were discussed [12]. This was a departure for a community of practice that often saw technology as neutral [13]. Hankerson et al. [14] provide an overview of everyday problems related to technology and race, describing technological errors often related to sensors failing to detect and respond to racialized individuals. They also mention biases in games where the representation favours White men who often attack dehumanised Black people [14]. Schlesinger et al. [15] focus on the representation of diverse scholarship in CHI and found low levels of intersectionality. Rankin and Thomas [16] review and criticise the use of intersectionality in HCI research. Ogbonnaya-Ogburu et al. [17] go further and call for the inclusion of critical race theory in HCI research to deal structural racism in the knowledge creation practices of the discipline. While this research is questioning the ideals of inclusion in HCI, there are few studies that tackle interaction between machines and racialised groups like Gebru's. A noteworthy one is Schlesinger et al.'s study [18] on how chat bots can talk to people about race, suggesting solutions to pervasive problems. Though it is tempting to label discussions about inclusion, intersectionality, and diversity in HCI as paradigm shifts, it is more a process of the discipline catching up to a cultural and sociological context that it had avoided for years, while benefitting from an influx of newer researchers whose voice is finally being heard. If there has been a paradigm shift related to structural questions about race and marginalisation thus far, it has been more epistemological, where a wider breadth of knowledge is researched rather than ontological, where the nature of the discipline itself is challenged.

Queries about paradigm shifts in HCI are not novel. Scholars' perceptions of the discipline have changed and led to calls for labels describing ongoing paradigm shifts since 1960. For example, Grudin [19, 20] focused on the historical development and changes in HCI. Suchman [21] argues that the classic opposition of humans and technology is rather an entanglement of both that challenges classical instrumental perceptions of machines as objects used by subjects, there is another perspective in this intricate relationship worth considering. Dourish [22] has modelled paradigm shifts as the type of interaction between people and machines. Norman [23, 24] has spearheaded an entire branch of HCI focused on the intrinsic values design generates when humans interact with machines, suggesting that user experience matters more than task completion [25]. Harrison et al. [26, 27] have made repeated calls for critical and phenomenological approaches to HCI. Guzman [28] has argued that the communicative practices between humans and machines create meaning, thereby suggesting a human-machine communication between them. More recently, Farooq and Grudin [29, 30] have attempted to refresh Licklider's theory of human-machine symbiosis by arguing that integration between people and technology is replacing interaction. As I wrote above, questions about paradigm shifts in HCI rarely consider issues of marginalisation and structural effects and consequences.

Warnings about the limits and consequences of technology is a common argument that has been made repeatedly in both HCI [31–35] and STS [36–39]. Research about how things (objects) can create inequalities in human groups (subjects) [40–43] is not new either. While authors such as Nakumura wrote about the representation of marginalised communities on the internet [44] and how racialized groups chose to use technology [45], there is now dedicated literature on inequalities generated by machines that interact with marginalised groups. Noble [46] wrote about how search engine algorithms present sexual contents or negative stereotypes when searching for terms such as black girls. Benjamin [47] adds to this that automation can increase White supremacy and reinforce social inequality while appearing neutral. Eubanks [48] argues that algorithmic governance, where AI and big data are used by policymakers indiscriminately to predict outcomes or classify groups, create machine-initiated inequalities that affect people's lives. Broussard [49] continues this perspective when she writes that the beliefs that AI is neutral, always right, and capable of solving all of our problems is an error. An important gap is the study of interactions when members of marginalised groups interact with machines. For example, in her upcoming article with six other authors, Gebru discusses the risk of biases with language learning where siphoning existing writing found on the web, the authors argue that machine-learning operations could create biases that leads AI to discriminate further against marginalised groups [50]. This unpublished article [50], and others authored by Gebru and her colleagues [51–53] remain at the structural level by analysing existing datasets and drawing inferences from them. They do not analyse users' reactions to machines that search, use and share their data. In my evaluations, I want evaluate interactions to uncover the processes that make a member of Black Twitter react to a bot suggesting topics of interests as they navigate Twitter's interface.

Research on Black Twitter has not focused on how people and machine interact. Instead, the scholarship has remained in the realm of entertainment [54–59], media [60, 61], and politics [62–64]. I shall focus on media and politics which are more relevant for this article. Brock [65] offers one of the earliest scholarly articles on Black Twitter, explaining its origin, its particularities and how it inscribes itself in the continuity of American Black culture. In the media realm, Clark [66] relying on mixed methods wrote a dissertation on Black Twitter looking at the networking and identity building processes that generated and sustain Black Twitter. In an earlier study, she researches how community building occurs around hashtags as topics are used maintain Black Twitter's group cohesion [67]. Murthy et al. [68] generated demographic data on urban Twitter users to understand African Americans' social interaction on the platform. Lee [69] observes how Twitter is used by African Americans to correct what they perceive as media biases. Freelon et al. [70] wrote a comprehensive quantitative report on Black, feminist, and Asian Twitter to map out the relationships between the groups and traditional media and implications for journalists. In the political realm, Edrington and Lee explore how the #BlackLivesMatter movement used Twitter for community building and remedial action against systemic oppression. Prasad [71] analysed two hashtags (#IfTheyGunnedMeDown and #AliveWhileBlack) used by Black Twitter in resistance of police oppression. Chaudhry [72] investigates discussions about race and racism following the shooting of youth Mike Brown in Ferguson, Missouri. Maragh [73] studies the identity performance and reappropriation on Twitter centred around "acting white" or "acting black" on the platform. Graham and Smith [74] use Habermas's public sphere theory to empirically determine if Black Twitter is a counterpublic. Hill [75] follows this by using first-hand ethnographic research, defends the position that Black Twitter serves as a counterpublic, a form counterculture resistant to hegemonic discourses that can affect African Americans. Tillery [76] examines social movements' use of #BlackLivesMatter as a messaging tool arguing for individual rights. My contribution to Black Twitter scholarship fills gaps in areas related to individuals' actions and reactions with machines which differs from the conventional entertainment, media, and political investigations.

4 Methods

The issue of bridging the divide between agency-based research such as HCI with structural approaches has been a major epistemological concern. Traditional usability and even user experience studies with Black Twitter users observing their interaction with Twitter would probably lead to validity concerns by not testing potential marginalisation or related factors. In such a study, there is a need to observe some form of valid user interaction with Twitter-based AI. Then, there is a need to understand these users' perceptions with these intelligent machines. Finally, there is a need for a more systematic understanding of who is part of this group.

I selected three approaches to obtain relevant data on Black Twitter users' potential marginalisation because of the shift to machine-initiated interaction. The first is a social network analysis of Black Twitter members to map out who these users are, who they are linked to, who they follow, who they retweet, and who they like. This evaluation constitutes the main structural part of the project. The second evaluation method used is an experiment consisting of three benign Twitter bots that initiate interactions with a database of Black Twitter members collected from the social network analysis. The bots perform three operations. The first bot creates lists of Black Twitter users. The second bot collects threads from multi-tweet discussions based on relevant hashtags by Black Twitter members that can be downloaded by the public. The third bot is a video clip download bot that collects videos posted on Twitter from relevant hashtags and threads that the public can download. Twitter users can call upon this bot to generate downloadable videos that they can download. These Twitter-based third—party bots allow us to evaluate how Black Twitter members react to the AI-initiated interactions. This part of the evaluation is the micro-level HCI-based analysis of users' machine-human interaction. Finally, the third evaluation approach used in this study bridges the two other evaluations by as we will conduct surveys with Black Twitter members that we have identified. We will invite Black Twitter users to participate in this study.

4.1 Measurement

Social network analysis is a theoretical approach derived from the social sciences, in particular, sociology and anthropology [77]. It explains the interactions and links between actors who are part of a social network [78]. A social network is the confluence of links between nodes (in other words, actors) in a network [79]. Nodes are individuals or other observational variables such as companies, countries, cities, colours, objects, or abstract concepts. The relationships between these observation variables pique the researcher's curiosity because they are dynamic [80], therefore changing and evolving over time and space. We rely on ORA Pro and NodeXL for social networking analysis and the data collection. The construction of the Twitter bots is relatively simple and only requires a proper registration with Twitter before being deployed on the platform. Because the bots are designed to initiate interaction with people, they must be benign. The data collected is already public and can be deleted at any time by a simple request to the tweet and to an email address located on the website where respondents can download compiled threads and videos. Respondents only have access to the URLs provided by the bots and cannot search nor browse the entirety of stored conversations and videos. After 48 h, the links to threads and videos are disabled. We use benign deception by not informing respondents that the bots are operated as part of a university research project. We want to limit learning biases. However, supplemental information on the operators of the bots will always be indicated on the website where the collected data will be stored. To understand their perceptions, the survey asks participants questions about their interaction with Twitter-operated AI. Typical questions ask the following; what has account has Twitter recently suggested that you follow; Did you follow any of the suggested account; Do you browse Twitter using the suggested top tweets or as they happen; What interests has Twitter suggested that you follow? These questions and more will allow us to understand how Twitter performs machine learning with Black Twitter members without needing access to participants' accounts. The surveys are conducted online though a university-hosted questionnaire.

5 Discussion

Licklider's predictions did not account for societal and structural consequences of the symbiosis between human and machine, and even less about the advent of AI for society. Licklider's insight is a common one in HCI where the level of analysis is centred on individuals (user agency) as opposed to structural actors such as groups, organisations, and institutions. The debate between methodological individualism and methodological structuralism in social sciences is one that began early on in sociology. Scholars such as Weber [81] and Boudon [82] maintains that individual actors influence structures and societal structures while Durkheim [83], Parsons [84], and Bourdieu [85], contend that society and its structures influence individual norms and practices. HCI's level of analysis being the individual, it rarely accounts for how societal structures can affect individual interaction with machines. Instead, the user is the dominant actor upon which HCI researchers draw their conclusions on human behaviour and practice with machines. This individual conception of the discipline leaves it ill-prepared to tackle societal issues related to race, gender, and even class, when related to machine-initiated interaction with humans.

Gebru's controversial firing by Google in 2020 called to attention a major concern of paradigm shifts to machine-human interaction in the area of AI. Gebru's exit from Google was caused in part by criticisms of the limitations of AI and the risks of exclusion of people based on their race, gender [52], and language [86]. The issues raised by Gebru are structural as they relate to race and gender. Yet, to test issues such as AI failing to identify Blacks in pictures [51], micro-level evaluations prevalent in HCI were required.

Such work tends to describe implications of technologies but stop short of evaluating deeper structural consequences such as what happens to some of the people that are left behind and further marginalised when methodological approaches frequently used in HCI fail to address the consequences of machines' interactions with entire groups, such as users of Black Twitter. Twitter, like many other leading social media platforms, has been leaning towards automation and machine learning to better understand its users such. Users' use of the platform is monitored and studied by AI trying to understand and predict future behaviour. However, Twitter is used by African Americans as their main social media platform to the extent that they have appropriated it for themselves, the way women appear to favour Pinterest, the way LGBT groups congregated around Tumblr at one time or how millennials seem to abandon Facebook for Instagram.

5.1 On Human-Computer Interaction

Human-computer interaction has been an important discipline and area of research since scientist Vannevar Bush [87] suggested how technology could aid society manage knowledge. Studying HCI helps us understand how we use machines at work, school, and in our everyday lives. One concern of HCI has been to help people understand and improve their interaction with technology. Major research areas in HCI that embody this concern are usability and user experience. Usability seeks to measure and minimize friction in human-machine interaction [88]. User experience seeks to improve the level of satisfaction and qualitative experiences of those interactions [89]. An underlying theme in both usability and user experience research is that machines are tools used by humans who must learn to decode them. Refreshing Licklider's proposed symbiotic phase of HCI Suchman [21] suggested that observing interactions between humans and machines as one where one dominates the other ignored the reconfiguration that occur through their interplay. Although steeped in phenomenological and critical approaches, Suchman's contention seeks to break the subject-object hierarchy seen in usability and user experiences HCI research.

My arguments for a paradigm shift in HCI are based on observations of the leading role machines take when interacting with people. Virtual assistants aiding users with mobile devices seek to understand the humans who interact with them. In social media, bots are amassing and learning about human behaviour and practices to predict and understand them better. AI in vehicles attempts to predict and learn human behaviour well enough to operate on roads without harming people and animals. In the previous examples, human-created machines attempt to improve their interaction with people. In some instances, humans are not aware that interaction with a machine is occurring, especially when the AI is trying to mimic people [90].

5.2 Black Twitter?

As of February 2019, African Americans use Twitter disproportionately in comparison to other US groups at 21% [91]. Black Twitter is an unorganised group of mainly African American Twitter users who exchange, and comment on common topics of interests such as entertainment, politics, and economics. Black Twitter often initiates novel expressions and cultural signs that other groups later adopt [92–94]. When Black Twitter mobilises its resources, it can create movements such as #MeToo or #BlackLivesMatter. Thus, Black Twitter can generate norms through a social media platform that influences African Americans and society at large. Recently, Twitter has become the ground of much experimentation with AI deployed by its operators. However, it is also the experiment ground for third-party "bots" that interact with humans, often, without the latter being aware that of the interaction undertaken is with a machine.

Black Twitter is an interesting case study to explore the potential if and how marginalisation can occur when machines initiate interactions with humans. Twitter's operators use machine learning to understand users. They use AI to analyse users' tweets, their images, their connections to other users, whom they retweet, to understand whose tweets they like, to make data-driven suggestions about whom they should follow, and to moderate hate speech. The practices that I just listed do not even include those that are performed by third parties that rely on data generated by Twitter users. For example, there are bots that correct people's grammar, some that add people to lists, retweet, or follow users automatically when they mention certain terms or follow some Twitter accounts. Sometimes, Twitter users with high levels of digital literacy invite bots in to interact with them, such as when they request threads to be compiled into a single article, or to extract videos from tweets, so they can be downloaded. The level of interaction with AI can be deep in the Twitter environment and often it is unbeknownst to people.

Typical approaches to tackle questions about the consequences of technologies such as bots, AI, and their effects on human groups are often answered through sociological studies such as those found in the field of science and technology studies (STS). Research in these areas ask macro-level questions that are well suited to answer questions related to algorithmic governance [95, 96]. However, such studies do not completely address crucial questions related to end users and their direct interactions with machines, which is usually the purview of disciplines such as HCI. There is a methodological bridge required to evaluate individual members of groups such as Black Twitter and their interaction with technology. The methodological bridge that I seek to develop through this research project draws on micro-levels of analyses such as those used in HCI and macro-levels of analyses, much like those used in STS, communications, and sociology. Such research informs scholars, developers, public policy wonks, and the public about the consequences of machine-initiated interaction with humans. While the first contribution of this ongoing project seeks to evaluate the consequences for some marginalised groups, such as Black Twitter users, the second contribution seeks to form a methodological framework that can analyse situations (such as group marginalisation) where intelligent machines through direct interaction with people affect society and its structures.

The challenge of researching a phenomenon like Black Twitter is that usual approaches that deal with marginalised groups often rely on critical approaches stemming from cultural studies and other disciplines concerned with structural investigations. When studies look at direct cases of marginalisation and technology misunderstanding humans, such as I n the cases of the soap dispensers and cameras that cannot recognize darker skin tones, little is spent of the perceptions of marginalised users and their reactions. Instead, discussions tend to focus on the flaws of the instruments which inevitably leads to the blaming of the developers and operators of the faulty technology. Yet, one rich aspect of HCI research is understanding users as they interact with machines. For example, as well as observing the difficulties Black Twitter users may have with Twitter-based AI, one question that is rich in understanding is to ask how do such marginalised users cope work around possibly unresponsive technologies.

5.3 Measuring Marginalisation in HCI

Our project, as mentioned above is built around three evaluation methods which bridge the micro (agency) and macro (structural) limits of studies that focus exclusively on only one approach. Authors such as Giddens [97] have argued that mixed micro-macro approaches when studying human phenomena yield more comprehensive and precise understanding. Network analysis is seldom used with HCI-based approaches. While the two approaches are both quantitative and qualitative, they appear as direct opposites. Yet, social network analysis is based on the individual actor as a part of a structure that influences its behaviour and practices. As Carley [80] reminds us, relationships between members of a social network are dynamic. They change constantly. Thus, who is a member of Black Twitter does not have to constitute a contested classification. We can determine who is a member of Black Twitter based on who they follow and who follows them on Twitter. This approach is more inclusive of minute differences between users and those on the fringes of belonging formally to Black Twitter or not. It follows the famous *Don Quixote* proverb about telling a person who they are based on whom they follow [98]. Thus, once we can determine a cluster of users that we can quantitatively and qualitatively assign to Black Twitter, we can best study their interaction with machines. Understanding who the group is, we can then observe how it influences individuals and how in turn, individuals affect social network cliques, such as Black Twitter. This is work on Black Twitter has not been done in social sciences nor in HCI.

Nevertheless, it is necessary to help in the recruitment of Black Twitter users for the survey and the deployment of Twitter-based bots that will initiate interaction with this group. Previous work on Twitter-based bots has focused on evaluating the population of bots [99, 100], determining if humans could detect and differentiate them from other humans [101, 102] Gilani large scale in order to assess their social influence on users [103, 104]. Here the bots will take the lead in adding Black Twitter to lists, in creating collected threads from their discussions, and to generate downloadable videos from relevant discussions. I hypothesise that Black Twitter users do not use Twitter the way other groups such as academics, or political junkies would, and thus they would not initiate requests from Twitter-based third-party bots. As African Americans use Twitter as an oral communication platform [105, 106], I am interested in determining if there are missed interaction opportunities when AI interact with Black Twitter users in non-oral modalities. The technology "is neutral mantra" transforms Twitter into a platform adopted by one community into one whose development alienates the very core group of users that have propelled it and sustained it.

6 Conclusion

As human-computer interaction seemingly changes and progresses into a domain where the machine is no longer a mere object controlled and operated by humans into a field where AI initiates interaction with people. I maintain for a paradigm shift where machines are the principal actors attempting to understand and fine-tune their interactions with humans. However, the objective of this inquiry into the paradigm shift from human-machine to machine-human interaction is to ask valuable questions about the populations and groups that are at risk of marginalisation because of the growing changes in HCI.

While this question has been tackled in fields such as STS and communications, it is usually studied through structural and macro-level sociological lenses. I presented here a preliminary discussion on ongoing research where I investigate the consequences of machines leading the interaction process with humans that attempts to bridge the gap between sociological approaches and the kind of analyses usually performed in HCI.

References

1. Kuhn, T.S.: La structure des révolutions scientifiques. Flammarion, Paris (2008)
2. Licklider, J.C.R.: Man-computer symbiosis. In: IRE Transactions on Human Factors in Electronics, vol. HFE-1, pp. 4–11 (1960)
3. Saint-Louis, H.: User Perceptions of Security Risks in Multiple Authentications. University of Toronto Libraries, Toronto (2018)
4. Lewis, C.: HCI for people with cognitive disabilities. Accessibility Comput. **83**, 12–24 (2005)
5. Wandke, H.: Assistance in human–machine interaction: a conceptual framework and a proposal for a taxonomy. Theor. Issues Ergon. Sci. **6**(2), 129–155 (2005)
6. Mankoff, J., Hayes, G.R., Kasnitz, D.: Disability studies as a source of critical inquiry for the field of assistive technology. In: Proceedings of the 12th International ACM SIGACCESS Conference on Computers and Accessibility, New York (2010)
7. Armagno, G.: The role of HCI in the construction of disability. In: The 26th BCS Conference on Human Computer Interaction, vol. 26, Swinton (2012)
8. Frauenberger, C.: Disability and technology: a critical realist perspective. In: Proceedings of the 17th International ACM SIGACCESS Conference on Computers & Accessibility, Lisbon (2015)
9. Czaja, S.J.: The impact of aging on access to technology. Accessibility Comput. **83**, 7–11 (2005)
10. Baecker, R.M., Moffatt, K., Massimi, M.: Technologies for aging gracefully. Interactions **19**(3), 32–36 (2012)
11. Sin, J., Munteanu, C.: An empirically grounded sociotechnical perspective on designing virtual agents for older adults. Hum.-Comput. Interact. **5–6**(35), 481–510 (2020)
12. DiSalvo, C., Light, A., Hirsch, T., Le Dantec, C.A., Goodman, E., Hill, K.: HCI, communities and politics. In: CHI EA 2010: CHI 2010 Extended Abstracts on Human Factors in Computing Systems, New York (2010)
13. Rode, J.A.: A theoretical agenda for feminist HCI. Interact. Comput. **23**(5), 393–400 (2011)
14. Hankerson, D., Marshall, A.R., Booker, J., El Mimouni, H., Walker, I., Rode, J.A.: Does technology have race? In: CHI EA 2016: Proceedings of the 2016 CHI Conference Extended Abstracts on Human Factors in Computing Systems, 2016 (2016)
15. Schlesinger, A., Edwards, W.K., Grinter, R.E.: Intersectional HCI: engaging identity through gender, race, and class. In: CHI 2017: Proceedings of the 2017 CHI Conference on Human Factors in Computing Systems, New York (2017)
16. Rankin, Y., Thomas, J.: Straighten up and fly right: rethinking intersectionality in HCI research. Interactions **26**(6), 64–68 (2019)
17. Ogbonnaya-Ogburu, I.F., Smith, A.D., To, A., Toyama, K.: Critical race theory for HCI. In: HI 2020: Proceedings of the 2020 CHI Conference on Human Factors in Computing Systems, New York (2020)
18. Schlesinger, A., O'Hara, K.P., Taylor, A.S.: Let's talk about race: identity, chatbots, and AI. In: Proceedings of the 2018 chi Conference on Human Factors in Computing Systems, New York (2019)

19. Grudin, J.: A moving target: the evolution of human-computer interaction. In: Jacko, J.A. (ed.) The Human-Computer Interaction Handbook: Fundamentals, Evolving Technologies, and Emerging Applications, 3 edn., pp. xxvii–lxi. CRC Press, Boca Raton (2012)
20. Grudin, J.: From Tool to Partner: The Evolution of Human-Computer Interaction. Morgan and Claypool, Williston, Vermont (2017)
21. Suchman, L.: Human-Machine Reconfigurations: Plans and Situated Actions, 2nd edn. Cambridge University Press, Cambridge (2007)
22. Dourish, P.: Where the Action Is: The Foundations of Embodied Interaction. MIT Press, Cambridge (2001)
23. Norman, D.A.: Design rules based on analyses of human error. Commun. ACM **26**(4), 254–258 (1983)
24. Norman, D.A.: The Design of Everyday Things: Revised and Expanded. Basic Books, New York (2013)
25. Hassenzahl, M., Tractinsky, N.: User experience – a research agenda. Behav. Inf. Technol. **25**(2), 91–97 (2006)
26. Harrison, S., Tatar, D., Sengers, P.: The three paradigms of HCI. In: CHI, San Jose (2007)
27. Harrison, S., Sengers, P., Tatar, D.: Making epistemological trouble: third-paradigm HCI as successor science. Interact. Comput. **23**, 385–392 (2011)
28. Guzman, A.L.: Introductions: "what is human-machine communication, anyway?" In: Guzman, A.L. (ed.) Human-Machine Communication: Rethinking Communication, Technology, and Ourselves, pp. 1–28. Peter Lang, New York (2018)
29. Farooq, U., Grudin, J.: Human-computer integration. ACM Interact. **23**(6), 26–32 (2016)
30. Farooq, U., Grudin, J.T.: Paradigm shift from human computer interaction to integration. In: CHI 2017, Denver (2017)
31. Shneiderman, B.: Fighting for the user. Bull. Am. Soc. Inf. Sci. **9**, 27–29 (1982)
32. Shneiderman, B.: Leonardo's Laptop: Human Needs and the New Computing Technologies. MIT Press, Cambridge (2003)
33. Vincente, K.: The Human Factor. Alfred A. Knopf Canada, Toronto (2003)
34. Cranor, L.F., Garfinkel, S. (eds.): Security and Usability: Designing Secure Systems that People Can Use. O'Reilly, Sebastapol (2005)
35. Garfinkel, S., Ritcher Lipford, H.: Usable Security: History, Themes, and Challenges. Morgan & Claypool Publishers, Williston, Vermount (2014)
36. Winner, L.: Do artifacts have politics? In: MacKenzie, D., Wajcman, J. (eds.) The Social Shaping of Technology: HOW the Refrigerator Got its Hum, pp. 26–38. Open University Press, Philadelphia (1985)
37. Bijker, W.E., Law, J.: Postrcript: technology, stability, and social theory. In: Bijker, W.E., Law, J. (eds.) Shaping Technology/Building Society: Studies in Sociotechnical Change, pp. 290–308. MIT Press, Cambridge (1992)
38. Sclove, R.: Democracy and Technology. The Guilford Press, New York (1995)
39. Williams, R., Edge, D.: The social shaping of technology. Res. Policy **25**, 865–899 (1996)
40. Foucault, M.: Surveiller et punir: naissance de la prison. Gallimard, Paris (1975)
41. Latour, B.: Where are the missing masses? The sociology of a few mundane artifacts. In: Bijker, W.E., Law, J. (eds.) Shaping Technology/Building Society: Studies in Sociotechnical Change, pp. 225–258. MIT Press, Cambridge (1992)
42. Dyer-Witheford, N.: Cyber-Marx: Cycles and Circuits of Struggle in High Technology Capitalism. University of Illinois Press, Urbana (1999)
43. Bowker, G.C., Star, S.L.: Sorting Things Out: Classification and Its Consequences. MIT Press, Cambridge (2000)
44. Nakamura, L.: A Review of Cybertypes: Race, Ethnicity, and Identity on the Internet. Routledge, London (2002)

45. Nakamura, L.: Digitizing Race: Visual Cultures of the Internet. University of Minnesota Press, Minneapolis (2007)
46. Noble, S.U.: Algorithms of Oppression : How Search Engines Reinforce Racism. New York University Press, New York (2018)
47. Benjamin, R.: Race After Technology: Abolitionist Tools for the New Jim Code. Wiley, Cambridge (2019)
48. Eubanks, V.: Automating Inequality: How High-Tech Tools Profile, Police, and Punish the Poor. St. Martin's Press, New York (2019)
49. Broussard, M.: Artificial Intelligence: How Computers Misunderstand the World. The MIT Press, Cambridge (2019)
50. Hao, K.: We read the paper that forced Timnit Gebru out of Google. Here's what it says, December 2020. https://www.technologyreview.com/2020/12/04/1013294/google-ai-ethics-research-paper-forced-out-timnit-gebru/
51. Buolamwini, J., Gebru, T.: Gender shades: intersectional accuracy disparities in commercial gender classification. In: Conference on Fairness, Accountability and Transparency (2018)
52. Gebru, T.: Race and gender. In: Dubber, M.D., Pasquale, F., Das, S. (eds.) The Oxford Handbook of Ethics of AI, pp. 251–269. Oxford Press, Oxford (2020)
53. Jo, E.S., Gebru, T.: Lessons from archives: strategies for collecting sociocultural data in machine learning. In: Proceedings of the 2020 Conference on Fairness, Accountability, and Transparency, New York (2020)
54. Maragh, R.S.: "Our struggles are unequal": black women's affective labor between television and twitter. J. Commun. Inq. 40(4), 351–369 (2016)
55. Chatman, D.: Black Twitter and the politics of viewing Scandal. In: Gray, J., Sandvoss, C., Harrington, C.L. (eds.) Fandom: Identities and Communities in a Mediated World, Second Edition edn., pp. 299–314. New York University Press, New York (2017)
56. Harlow, S., Benbrook, A.: How #Blacklivesmatter: exploring the role of hip-hop celebrities in constructing racial identity on Black Twitter. Inf. Commun. Soc. 22(3), 352–368 (2017)
57. Williams, A., Gonlin, V.: I got all my sisters with me (on Black Twitter): second screening of how to get away with murder as a discourse on black womanhood. Inf. Commun. Soc. 20(7), 984–1004 (2017)
58. Gutiérrez, A.: Situating representation as a form of erasure: #OscarsSoWhite, black twitter, and latinx twitter. Telev. New Med. (2020)
59. Smit, A., Bosch, T.: Television and black twitter in South Africa: our perfect wedding. Media Cult. Soc. 42(7–8), 1512–1527 (2020)
60. Ince, J., Rojas, F., Davis, C.A.: The social media response to black lives matter: how twitter users interact with black lives matter through hashtag use. Ethn. Racial Stud. 40(11), 1814–1830 (2017)
61. Edrington, C.L., Lee, N.: Tweeting a social movement: black lives matter and its use of twitter to share information, build community, and promote action. J. Publ. Interest Commun. 2(2), 289–306 (2018)
62. Schiappa, J.: #IfTheyGunnedMeDown: the necessity of "Black Twitter" and hashtags in the age of ferguson. ProudFlesh: New Afrikan J. Cul. Polit. Conscious. (10) (2014)
63. Lavan, M.: The Negro tweets his presence: black twitter as social and political watchdog. Mod. Lang. Stud. 45(1), 56–65 (2015)
64. Stevens, L., Maurantonio, N.: Black twitter asks Rachel: racial identity theft in "Post-Racial" America. Howard J. Commun. 29(2), 179–195 (2018)
65. Brock, A.: From the blackhand side: twitter as a cultural conversation. J. Broadcast. Electron. Med. 56(4), 529–549 (2012)
66. Clark, M.: To Tweet Our Own Cause: A Mixed-Methods Study of the Online Phenomenon "Black Twitter." University of North Carolina at Chapel Hill Graduate School, Chapel Hill (2019)

67. Clark, M.: Black twitter: building connection through cultural conversation. In: Rambukkana, N. (ed.) Hashtag Publics: The Power and Politics of Discursive Networks, pp. 205–215. Peter Lang, New York (2015)
68. Murthy, D., Gross, A., Pensavalle, A.: Urban social media demographics: an exploration of twitter use in major american cities. J. Comput.-Mediat. Commun. **21**(1), 33–49 (2015)
69. Lee, L.A.: Black twitter: a response to bias in mainstream media. Soc. Sci. **6**(2), 1–17 (2017)
70. Freelon, D., Lopez, L., Clarck, M.D., Jackson, S.J.: How Black Twitter and Other Social Media Communities Interact With Mainstream News. John S. and James L. Knight Foundation, Miami (2018)
71. Prasad, P.: Beyond rights as recognition: black twitter and posthuman coalitional possibilities. Prose Stud.: History Theory Criticism **38**(1), 50–73 (2016)
72. Chaudhry, I.: "Not So Black and White": discussions of race on twitter in the aftermath of #Ferguson and the shooting death of mike brown. Cult. Stud. ↔ Critic. Methodol. **16**(3), 296–304 (2016)
73. Maragh, R.S.: Authenticity on "Black Twitter": reading racial performance and social networking. TEMA J. Land Use Mobil. Environ. **19**(7), 591–609 (2017)
74. Graham, R., Smith, S.: The content of our #Characters: black twitter as counterpublic. Sociol. Race Ethn. **2**(4), 433–449 (2016)
75. Hill, M.L.: "Thank You, Black Twitter": state violence, digital counterpublics, and pedagogies of resistance. Urban Educ. **53**(2), 286–302 (2018)
76. Tillery Jr., A.B.: What kind of movement is black lives matter? The view from twitter. J. Race Ethn. Polit. **4**(2), 297–323 (2019)
77. Mercklé, P.: Sociologie des réseaux sociaux, Troisième édition ed., Paris: La découverte (2016)
78. Wasserman, S.: Social Network Analysis: Methods and Applications. Cambridge University Press, Cambridge (1994)
79. Mercklé, P.: Les réseaux: un nouveau concept, une vieille histoire. Ressources en Sci. économiques et sociales **06**, 03 (2012)
80. Carley, K.: A theory of group stability. Am. Sociol. Rev. **56**(3), 331–354 (1991)
81. Weber, M.: Max Weber: Selections in Translation. Cambridge University Press, Cambridge (1978)
82. Boudon, R.: Raison, Bonnes Raisons. Presses Universitaires de France, Paris (2003)
83. Durkheim, E.: De la division du travail social. Presses universitaires de France, Paris (1973)
84. Parsons, T.: The Structure of Social Action; A Study in Social Theory with Special Reference to a Group of Recent European Writers. Free Press, New York (1949)
85. Bourdieu, P.: Choses dites : Le sens commun. Éditions de Minuit, Paris (1987)
86. Simonite, T.: Behind the Paper That Led to a Google Researcher's Firing. Accessed 8 Dec 2020. https://www.wired.com/story/behind-paper-led-google-researchers-firing/
87. Bush, V.: As we may think. Atlantic **1**(176), 101–108 (1945)
88. Albert, W., Tullis, T.: Measuring the User Experience: Collecting, Analyzing, and Presenting Usability Metrics, 2nd edn. Morgan Kaufmann, Amsterdam (2013)
89. Hassenzahl, M.: User experience (UX): towards an experiential perspective on product quality. In: Proceedings of the 20th International Conference of the Association Francophone d'Interaction Homme-Machine, Metz (2008)
90. Turing, A.: Computing machinery and intelligence (1950). In: Copeland, B.J. (ed.) The Essential Turing: Seminal Writings in Computing, Logic, Philosophy, Artificial Intelligence, and Artificial Life plus The Secrets of Enigma, pp. 441–464. Oxford University Press, London (2004)
91. Pew Research Center: Social Media Fact Sheet, 19 June 2019. https://www.pewresearch.org/internet/fact-sheet/social-media/. Accessed 01 Feb 2021

92. Florini, S.: Tweets, tweeps, and signifyin': communication and cultural performance on "Black Twitter." TEMA J. Land Use Mob. Environ. **15**(3), 223–237 (2013)
93. Jones, T.: Toward a description of african american vernacular english dialect regions using "Black Twitter. Am. Speech **90**(4), 403–440 (2015)
94. Sharma, S.: Black Twitter? Racial hashtags, networks and contagion. New Formations **19**(78), 46–64 (2013)
95. Katzenbach, C., Ulbricht, L.: Algorithmic governance. J. Internet Regul. **8**(4), 1–18 (2019)
96. König, P.D.: Dissecting the algorithmic leviathan: on the socio-political anatomy of algorithmic governance. Philos. Technol. **33**(3), 467–485 (2019). https://doi.org/10.1007/s13347-019-00363-w
97. Giddens, A.: The Constitution of Society. Polity Press, Cambridge (1984)
98. Cervantes Saavedra, M.D.: L'ingénieux Hidalgo Don Quichotte de la Manche, Éditions du Seuil, Paris (1997)
99. Beskow, D.M., Carley, K.M.: Bot conversations are different: leveraging network metrics for bot detection in twitter. In: IEEE/ACM International Conference on Advances in Social Networks Analysis and Mining (2018)
100. Gilani, Z., Farahbakhsh, R., Tyson, G., Wang, L., Crowcroft, J.: Of bots and humans (on Twitter). In: ASONAM 2017: Proceedings of the 2017 IEEE/ACM International Conference on Advances in Social Networks Analysis and Mining 2017, New York (2017)
101. Gilani, Z., Farahbakhsh, R., Tyson, G., Crowcroft, J.: A large scale behavioural analysis of bots and humans on twitter. ACM Trans. Web **13**(1), 2–24 (2019)
102. Varol, O., Ferrara, E., Davis, C.A., Menczer, F., Flammini, A.: Online human-bot interactions: detection, estimation, and characterization. In: Proceedings of the Eleventh International AAAI Conference on Web and Social Media (2017)
103. Duh, A., Rupnik, M.S., Korošak, D.: Collective behavior of social bots is encoded in their temporal twitter activity. Big Data **6**(2), 113–123 (2018)
104. Wald, R., Khoshgoftaar, T.M., Napolitano, A., Sumner, C.: Predicting susceptibility to social bots on twitter. In: 2013 IEEE 14th International Conference on Information Reuse & Integration, San Francisco (2013)
105. Knight Steele, C.: The Digital Barbershop: Blogs and Online Oral Culture Within the African American Community, vol. 2, no. 4. Social Media + Society, October 2016
106. Long, T.: As Seen on Twitter: African-American Rhetorical Traditions Gone Viral. Eastern Michigan University Library, Ypsilanti (2012)

Understanding Agency in Human-Computer Interaction Design

Romualdo Gondomar[1] and Enric Mor[2(✉)]

[1] Elisava, Barcelona School of Design and Engineering, Barcelona, Spain
rgondomar@elisava.net
[2] Universitat Oberta de Catalunya, Barcelona, Spain
emor@uoc.edu

Abstract. This paper presents the research around the concept and idea of agency in the context of human-computer interaction (HCI) design. The notion of agency is made up of several elements and therefore should not be considered as a rigid concept. This work proposes a framework for understanding agency in HCI that considers the main elements that must be taken into account in the design and evaluation of interactive artifacts. The framework is composed of four main elements: mental models, affordances, reciprocity and responsiveness. Two elements related to the cognitive processes that allow people to perceive and make decisions and two elements related to the response processes generated by technological devices to people's actions. Each of these four main elements is specified by three attributes organized in levels. The proposed framework has been evaluated through focus groups, involving design practitioners. The results show that the concept of agency not well known in interaction design practice and that a framework can facilitate its implementation in design processes and projects.

Keywords: Human-computer interaction · Interaction design · Agency · Design theory · Design practice

1 Introduction

Interactivity, as the quality or condition of the interaction process, is shown to be effective when its technological configuration or representation stimulates the agent's or person's impulse for action [1]. Dewey [2] used the term "impulse" to designate the organism's active response from interaction with the context. This response derives from a need that arises from the interaction process. From this point of view, the agent establishes a close connection between the environment (as a physical-representative element) and the type of actions carried out [3]. The concept of interactivity is based on the agency that artifacts offer people and is inseparable from the formal configurations that technology supports. We can consider agency as an essential attribute of the interactive process if we adopt the conception of interactive experience as the set of actions carried out by people with technological devices.

© Springer Nature Switzerland AG 2021
M. Kurosu (Ed.): HCII 2021, LNCS 12762, pp. 137–149, 2021.
https://doi.org/10.1007/978-3-030-78462-1_10

The notion of agency of technological devices is manifested when an agent interacts with the environment. People can infer the potentiality of agency of technological artifacts from observing the qualitative configuration of designed resources and interfaces. This potentiality of agency is verified when people perform actions that they perceive and discover in this attribute of the interactive process [4].

The idea of agency is central to human-computer interaction (HCI) design and evaluation [5, 6]. When interacting with computing devices people want to experience control. Shneiderman states that "users strongly desire the sense that they are in charge of the interface and that the interface responds to their actions [7]. Keeping users in control is one of the Shneiderman's eight golden rules for designing interactive systems and relates with the sense of agency. The sense of agency refers to the feeling of being in control over actions and their consequences [8]. This feeling is central on people's daily life and especially on their interactions with everyday technology.

The sense of agency in HCI mostly "puts" the agency on the agent or human side. Conversely, Janlert and Stolterman state that "the notion of agency in relation to interactivity has to do with the idea that the actions of both parties (human and artifact/system) are guided by some internal design to achieve certain goals" [1]. The idea of agency is not only applicable to humans but also on systems is especially important in interaction design and HCI.

Although the concept of agency is significant in the field of HCI and it is relevant in the professional practice of interaction design [6], it is a little-known concept and, designers who are aware of it, don't have clear guidelines in terms of applying and developing it in design projects. Literature related to user experience (UX) and interaction design usually has limited evidence around the concept of agency. However the studies that discuss agency emphasize on theoretical aspects or have a focus on psychological measures [8]. The same limited scope can be observed in HCI education [9] and human-centered design education [10]. We believe that there is a need to structure and organize the notion of agency into elements that can be understandable and actionable to designers, that are manageable and applicable in design projects. This constitutes the motivation of this work where we propose a framework to approach the notion of agency in a way that structures its key elements and articulates its fundamental attributes in an accessible way for design practitioners. A theoretical approach to the main elements and attributes of the concept of agency will be needed in order to support interaction design practice.

This paper is organized as follows: Sect. 2 presents the main definitions of agency and the areas where it has been used and developed. Section 3 introduces the framework of agency for interaction design. Section 4 presents the main attributes of agency framework and the field research conducted with design practitioners and, finally, Sect. 5 presents the discussion and conclusions.

2 The Concept of Agency

The concept of agency has been extensively studied and analyzed throughout the history of philosophy. From a broad point of view, the concept refers to causal relationships between different entities as they interact with each other. While in a more restricted sense it focuses on the relationship between intentional actions that take place in an interactive process. Here lies the importance of the concept of agency for interaction design, in its definition as the capacity and condition to promote human action [11, 12]. The most relevant philosophical contributions to the concept of agency are developed through activity and structure theories. Activity theory analyzes in particular the formation and evolution of the activities, while structure theory provides the reflexive capacity on the actions executed, that is, it allows to reflect on the needs, motives and objectives of the activities of the people [13, 14]. Both structure an agency concept that can contribute significantly to understanding the extent of user interactions with technological-digital systems and contribute to HCI research. Given that the interactive relationships led by agency occur between people and technological systems, and that intentional actions are decisive to generate activity, we consider important to obtain an idea of agency from the human perspective (cognitive psychology); of technological- digital systems (software design) and of the communication process that links the two areas, that is, the human-computer interaction.

Agency From the Perspective of Human Behavior (Cognitive Psychology)
The human being develops self-awareness, thought, sensitivity, emotions and his own personal identity as he interacts with the real world. Archer [15] states that the human being depends on interaction with the environment and that practice takes on a fundamental role. The whole set of facts that make up the practical activities, also the language and the gestures, order our communication and our interactive behavior.

The human being, based on deductive reasoning, connects his thought and action with reality. In this way, active experience facilitates the construction of sequential perceptions that facilitate the construction of meaning [16]. This view led Piaget [17] to connect practical interaction, which involves the use and development of sensory-motor skills, with the emergence of the concept of object which, in his opinion, depends on the interpretations formed in the context of practical action. For Archer [15], the incorporated knowledge, called "knowing how to," is based on sensory-motor interactions, its content is derived from the physical world and is exercised directly in a context. While practical knowledge connects the knowledge that emerges from the physical world with social order.

Understanding how human cognition works is crucial to understanding the dynamic relationship of human beings with the interactive context, composed of physical, social and cultural components. The reasoning processes allow human beings to think critically about their social context and can redefine it, designing or devising new forms of interaction that take advantage of the contextual resources that have acquired meaning throughout their experiences.

Agency From the Perspective of Software Design
The ideas and concepts associated with agency are also taken into account in software design, specifically in agent-oriented software modeling. The design of agents and multiagent systems have gained significant importance in technological contexts such as artificial intelligence, distributed computing and complex interactions between software-software or software-human. Agent-based software modeling is a relatively young field in software development and computing and had a significant growth in artificial intelligence. An agent can be defined as "an entity that performs a specific

activity in an environment of which is aware and that can respond to changes" [18]. Under this definition, people can also be considered agents and, this perspective, opens up the possibility of designing software that interacts with people in a more natural way, as equals, taking into account the agency of both software and people.

A set of agents can be grouped together and form a system, that is, a multi-agent system. When this happens, we have a set of entities connected to each other that constitute a complex entity that can perform a complex function.

There is a set of properties and attributes of agent modeling and multiagent systems that are of particular interest in this work. The software attributes of multi-agent systems: adaptivity, intelligence (awareness), efficiency, purposefulness and understability. The qualities of agents as defined entities: 1) being purposeful: agents have goals and can adopt roles; 2) controlled autonomy: agents pursue their own goals and 3) situated: agents are aware of their environment, capable of perceiving changes and respond accordingly [18]. And the anthropomorphic qualities used for modelling software agents such as beliefs, desires, intentions, goals, capabilities responsibilities and expectations that mostly came from the extensive influence of the Belief-Desire-Intention (BDI) agent architecture and execution model [19].

All these qualities and attributes are of great importance in the design and evaluation of multi-agent systems from the point of view of interactive systems. They are characteristics intrinsically related to the concept of agency that are expressed in order to achieve a better software design that interacts with the environment, with other software or with people.

Agency From the Perspective of the HCI
Some significant HCI research focuses on the analytical frameworks that take into account the needs, motives and objectives of people and how these human conditions are manifested through the activities they carry out. Consequently, this HCI research tries to integrate people and technology as agents that determine the contextual activity of an interactive process mediated by technological devices into the same conceptual model of analysis [5, 7].

Among the different perspectives that have explored the analysis of agency and/or agents in the HCI process itself we can find models that consider users as agents that prioritize the user experience over the characteristics of interaction interfaces; models that focus on the specific needs of actors and use technology to increase interaction capabilities by improving the autonomy of digital devices; interactive models that are based on how people perceive the agency of technological devices and their social implications and, finally, models that investigate the collective involvement of the agency based on the social and cultural factors of the community. We can delve into the particular characteristics of the models listed in the compilation by Zacarias & Oliveira: Human-Computer Interaction: The Agency Perspective [6].

To reveal the ability of agency we cannot rely on certain physical qualities and specific forms. Therefore, we can state that its configuration does not depend on a direct application of the general principles that configure human-computer interaction design. For this reason, agency cannot be defined as a principle or a design premise, but rather as a compound of several manifestations and representations exposed by interactive devices. In the analysis of the ontological dimension of digital artworks, Lopes [20] claims that the interactive potentiality derives from the capacity of the system to exhibit agency to induce action. A configuration or design formalization that must be guided by the basic principles that inform action.

Additionally, the agency of an interactive system/artifact must be based on the basic principles that articulate the human communication process. In this way, the value of agency will be useful and effective [21]. The principles of human communication that are relevant in this context are: a common conceptual space, a communicative intentionality and a cooperative motivation. In the human-computer interaction field these principles can be translated into: sharing a common conception of reality, transmitting information using codes or shared systems and promoting or encouraging the purposes of the agent, that is, adopting a cooperative attitude in the interactive process (shared agency) [22]. From the perspective of the basic models of communication, agency is effective if it explores or extends its common and shared attributes.

One of the most comprehensive studies on the social dimension of the agency is the model developed by Enfield & Kockelman [23], called distributed agency. The authors analyze how agency is experienced in human societies and conclude that one of the components that integrates the concept of agency derives directly from the social life of people and is proportional to the degree of complexity of culture and society. The concepts they use to define the agency that relates people to their actions and the effects produced are flexibility and accountability. The first, flexibility, related to human behavior, while the second, responsibility, relates human behavior to the sociocultural environment in which the agency occurs.

3 Towards a Framework for Agency in Interaction Design

In order to understand and extend the agency of technological artifacts in human-computer interaction design, we created a first proposal of the guiding principles of design that we consider to be part of the agency of interactive products. We selected two principles related to the cognitive processes that allow people to perceive and make decisions and two principles related to the response processes generated by technological devices to people's actions. These principles are decisive to promote fluid communication between the agents that participate in the interactive process.

On the one hand, mental models and affordances are directly related to cognitive processes of people (agents), and allow us to understand the interactive situation in relation to what they perceive from the outside world. On the other hand, reciprocity and responsiveness regulate communication processes and the information that technological devices offer to people's actions.

We believe that this basic scheme of how interaction works responds adequately to the concept of agency presented above. Mental models structure and support how people act. Affordances are presented as stimuli that people interpret in the characteristics of the objects to trigger the sequence of action that can be inferred from the qualities of the objects. Reciprocity articulates the dialogic process between the person and the device, generating and providing continuity to the communicative sequence. Finally, responsiveness constitutes the ability and sensitivity to generate the appropriate information of technological-digital scenarios so that the agency or interactivity is maintained over time.

The goal of this work is not to theorize about agency and related concepts but to propose a framework to promote the use and application of the notion of agency in interaction design. However, in order to define and provide justification of the framework it is necessary a theoretical approach to the main elements of the framework. This work follows the idea that interaction design research is needed in order to support interaction design practice [24].

Mental Models. One of the theoretical proposals that highlights the importance of understanding multidimensional experiences from mental models is that formulated by Lakoff and Johnson [25]. The authors propose the idea of domains of experience. This conception considers the experience composed of various dimensions that are present in a situation where people participate. The concepts that arise from the correlations that are established between the different components involved in the activity determine a significant *gestaltic* whole. For Lakoff and Johnson [25] these conceptual relationships and their interdependence on multidimensional experience allow us to structure a basic system of mental models that we use to interact with our physical and sociocultural environment. These mental models, which we assume as our own, allow us to understand and relate the similarities between the diverse concepts that we know and are able to handle. These basic schemes make it easier for us to understand our environment.

Metaphors, as conceptual instruments that facilitate comparisons between different elements, establish the resources that structure the mental models that we use to understand everyday situations. In their theoretical proposal they identify different types of metaphors that configure mental models to approach the understanding of reality: structural, orientational and ontological. Structural metaphors link different concepts. Orientational metaphors facilitate the dimensional comparison between spatial experiences, whether physical or sociocultural. Finally, ontological metaphors establish a set of mental models that are born from one's own experience with physical objects. It is these, the ontological ones, that define a set of relationships between experiential concepts and those that we use to understand the events, actions and activities that we carry out. At the same time, and as a result of reasoning processes, this experience with physical objects, structured from ontological mental models, provides us with the possibility of establishing reflective conclusions that enable us to understand reality.

The natural dimensions of experience that Lakoff and Johnson consider essential to structure the conceptual system that shapes our mental models are spatial, emotional and sociocultural. Spatial mental models allow our own experimentation in relation to the rest of the elements that shape our environment. Emotional models, linked to the sensoriality of our experiences, allow us to establish direct correlations with each situation. Finally, sociocultural mental models structure our experiences from a set of values and habits that act as a conventional and limiting basis for our activities.

Affordances. The concept of affordance gained special importance thanks to the speed of technological change and the advancement of digital technologies and interactive devices. Affordances were introduced by perception psychologist J.Gibson [26] and refer to the possible actions of an agent in a specific environment. The affordance defined by Gibson did not require to be perceived or recognized. Donald A. Norman, a few years later, connected the concept of affordance with design [27]. For Norman, affordances must be perceptible and he referred to them as perceived affordances. Norman's work had a great impact first in the design field and later in the HCI field. Affordance, according to Norman, should not be confused with signifier, an indicator or signal in the physical or social world that can be interpreted. Affordances are of particular importance since people need them to operate (function) in the world (environment) socially or individually. In addition, people also need to organize the perception of the environment, the meaning of things, and how they work through the development of internal models. This connects affordances with mental models, which on the one hand help people understand the environment and objects and how to use them, but also leads to the creation of stereotypes with the consequent risk of perpetuating systems of discrimination and power.

One way to articulate the idea of affordance in technological and design contexts is the Mechanisms and Conditions Framework proposed by Jenny L. Davis [28]. The framework is based on a definition of affordance that takes into account that is not a binary construct, not uniform, is relational and conditional and refers to how objects enable and constrain. Davis addresses affordances with an analytic approach asking what technologies afford and how they afford. The proposed framework pursues the operationalization of affordances through a structure and vocabulary to approach affordance analysis. Using a vocabulary, a list of keywords, provides an actionable approach to bring the framework closer to design practice.

Reciprocity. People's relationships with technology are dominated by the communicative relationships that are established between them. It is mainly based on the information that is constantly exchanged between participants in order to generate a flow of meaning that provides sense to the process of interaction that individuals perform through technological devices. In each of the interactive situations mediated by technology, a constant flow of information must be generated. This bidirectional flow supports the actions that are carried out and reciprocity is the driving force behind this process.

From a phenomenological perspective, reciprocity provides continuity to the meaning of the interactive process between people and technology. Ihde [29] considers that between the human being, technology and the world, different types of relationships are generated, among which the use of technology as a means of the perceptive experience of the individual stands out. It is, in this way, how technology integrates, subjectively, in the sense of the process itself. A technological embodiment of the individual in which devices go from being external objects to being integrated into the process of technological interaction.

This process of technological interaction will make sense and acquire meaning if it integrates the communicative reciprocity between agents, technology and the context of each situation. This interaction requires a dialogue between the user and the system that generates a flow of information that enables the continuity of the process and, at the same time, complements senses and shows possible meanings [30]. For that to happen, the reciprocity of technological devices, such as communication vehicles, must indicate the necessary and appropriate information, intentionally direct the proposed action and use codes or messages that are common and widely known.

Responsiveness. In the context of HCI responsiveness has different meanings. On the one hand, responsiveness refers to the ability of an interface to adapt to different screen sizes. On the other hand, responsiveness refers to the response time of a system. Although this approach is not central to this work, it is interesting to highlight its key elements. One of the first works from HCI's point of view was [31] that considered interaction with a computer as a dialogue: the user provides commands, and the computer produces answers. In this context responsiveness is defined in relation to response time from a user making a request to an interactive computational system providing a response. This measure of time is called system response time and is considered a key factor that directly impacts the user experience [32]. In this context, the concept of feedback holds significance as part of this dialog: it provides the user a sense of control reducing uncertainty as it reinforces the idea that the system is working based on the user's commands.

From a communicative point of view, the responsive aspects of the interaction relate to the resources that the system uses to react, generating and directing the timely response [30, 33]. Response time must be synchronized with the type of activity the user performs and, finally, the media used must be appropriate and relevant (McLuhan's emphasized the importance of the medium as the message [34] to promote the meaning and flow of the interactive activity (Fig. 1).

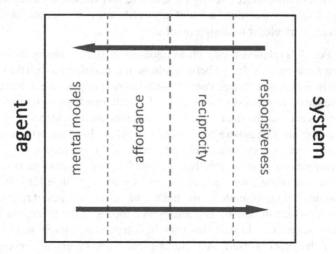

Fig. 1. The main elements of the agency framework for interaction design

The agency framework for interaction design that we propose in this work is based on the concepts highlighted above and on the idea that derives from the general conception of the process of interactive communication between agent and system. A process of interaction based on the dialogue that occurs between two agents who pursue a fluid process of communication. For this reason, we understand agency as a face-to-face relationship. On the agent's side, led by the mental models that structure the general understanding of the system and by the ability to perceive and understand the affordances shown by technological resources. On the system's side, interactivity is sustained by the resources and reactions generated by systems to provide relevant information and by the means they use to promote a fluid and interactive dialogue.

4 Mapping Agency to Interaction Design

In order to facilitate the understanding of the proposed agency framework a set of attributes for each of its main elements was identified. The selection criteria used to assign these attributes is based on three levels that derive from people's interaction process with systems.

The first level designates the characteristics that can be decisive in the execution of actions: orientational mental models (orientational), perception of affordances (perceptual), indicators that promote communication (indicative) and direct immediacy of the response of the devices (reactive).

The second level specifies characteristics of the dynamics of action: structural mental models that are used as a basis of action (structural), functional affordances (functional), communicative objectives (intentional) and the production of concurrent responses by the system (synchronous).

Finally, the third level describes the reflexive processes induced by the understanding of the actions carried out: ontological mental models (ontological), the meaning of affordances (meaningful), the use of common socially well-established concepts (common) and the relevance of the response generated to induce the communicative flow (relevant) (Fig. 2).

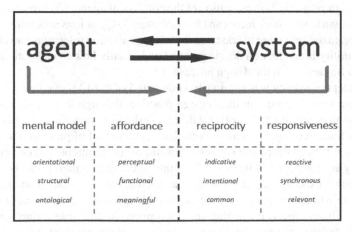

Fig. 2. The main elements of the agency framework with attributes

We believe that the selection of the aforementioned attributes helps to clarify the importance of each of the four main elements of the framework, that is, the elements involved in the generation of agency. Additionally, the organization of these attributes according to the three levels that structure action (performing, meaning and reflection) constitute a reliable approach for understanding how agency contributes to interaction (Table 1).

With the aim of reviewing the suitability and usefulness of the framework, it was presented and discussed with design practitioners and academics through a set of focus groups. Focus groups are especially suitable for a wide range of opinions, feelings,

Table 1. Description of the attributes of the agency framework.

Participant	Element	Attribute	Description
Agent	Mental Model	Orientational	*Facilitates the dimensional comparison of experiences, both physical and sociocultural*
		Structural	*Connects concepts referentially*
		Ontological	*The basis of relationships between known experiential concepts*
	Affordance	Perceptual	*Perceiving possibilities to act*
		Functional	*Facilitates activity operability*
		Meaningful	*Connects the action to the result obtained*
System	Reciprocity	Indicative	*Displays a particular meaning*
		Intentional	*The message has a certain purpose*
		Common	*The dialogue is established from a few common and well-known bases*
	Responsivity	Reactive	*Generates direct and immediate information*
		Synchronous	*Promotes continuity of the communication process*
		Relevant	*The response that promotes the flow of communication*

attitudes and experiences [35]. In this research 4 focus groups have been held where 13 designers have participated. 4 participants were product designers and 9 were interaction designers. To recruit the participants, a call was made to a total of 21 designers.

All focus groups sessions were conducted following a shared outline: 1) A small set of opening questions about whether they know the concept of agency and whether they use it in their design projects; 2) Presentation of the concept of agency; 3) Presentation of the agency framework with its elements and its attributes; 4) Questions about the framework that were organized into three blocks: framework organization (elements and attributes), framework utility in interaction design practice and, finally how to integrate the agency concept and framework in the design process.

The concept of agency was previously known to 4 of the 13 participants, who stated that they take it into account in their design practice although they don't have a clear process or strategies to do it. The other 9 designers did not know the concept of agency. When the definition of agency was presented, more than half of participants stated that they understood the concept and considered it important in interaction design practice and that they are interested in ways to take it into account into their projects.

In relation to the agency framework, the participants consider it interesting and appropriate to articulate a complex concept through specific and manageable elements. Overall, participants found interesting and appropriate to articulate a complex concept through specific and manageable elements. Three participants from two different sessions stated that the four elements of the framework clarified the complicated concept of agency and provided them with clues to incorporate it into their design projects. On the other hand, four participants commented that the concept of agency was too new for them and they did not have an opinion on the proposed elements and attributes of the framework. Three participants commented that while the elements of the framework provided clarity and invited them to take action, the proposed attributes for each element seemed confusing. They suggested adding a checklist to convert elements and attributes into actionable guidance for design practice.

In relation to the three blocks of questions on the framework, the results are structured as follows:

Organization. The majority of participants, nine, positively valued the organization of the framework with its elements and attributes while four of them claimed not to have an opinion on it. All participants stated that the visual presentation of the elements of the framework was important for understanding the idea of agency and for understanding how the elements relate to each other. The importance of structuring the attributes of each element based on some sort of classification was also discussed to help visualize the relationship between them.

Usefulness. Participants who previously knew the concept of agency as well as those who learned it in the session, considered useful to deploy a framework to take into account the idea of agency in design projects. The rest of participants, four, said they did not have an opinion on the matter.

Design Process. All participants agreed on the importance of taking into account the concept of agency in design projects. When participants were asked about which phase of the design process agency should be taken into account, they stated that in all phases of the design process but especially in the phase of generating design ideas and in the evaluation phase.

5 Discussion and Conclusions

This research proposes a framework that aims to bring the notion of agency to interaction design practice. The framework is composed of four elements: mental models, affordances, reciprocity and responsiveness and three attributes for each element.

The choice to broadly approach the notion of agency makes it possible to interrelate the capacity and condition of promoting the interaction of all the entities that participate in the process, in our case, mainly people and technological systems. The communicative perspective of HCI facilitates the understanding of the basic models that are involved in the mutual (reciprocal) participation to generate information and in the ways of transmitting it. For this reason, we believe that proposing the framework of agency in terms of elements that facilitate dialogue between people and technological-digital systems can enhance the exhibition of agency and, therefore, promote interaction.

The proposed framework is based on the "face-to-face" communication process between users and systems. The selection of agency elements for the framework has been focused on aspects that, based on the design theory and practice, we considered central, relevant and necessary in order to present a simple scheme that favors the understanding of the notion of agency in interaction design.

We have been able to validate that the concept of agency is not widespread in the field of interaction design and, therefore, there is a lack of knowledge about its definition and scope. The proposed framework can help to spread the concept and, its organization in main elements and attribute levels, can facilitate its implementation and use in design processes and projects. In fact, the results obtained in the focus groups with designers show that the framework can be useful in both ways. Once the extension of the agency concept had been assimilated and understood, the participants considered that a framework such as the one proposed could be useful in different phases of the design process. In our research, once the participants understood the scope of the agency concept, they considered that a framework such as the one proposed could be useful in different phases of the design process.

However, taking into account that we are still in the early steps of research on agency in interaction design, we think we should explore the appropriateness of the proposal more widely. In the following steps, it will be necessary to review whether the proposed elements are the most appropriate to clearly present and define the notion of agency. It will also be necessary to analyze the three levels of specific attributes of each element, develop an actionable checklist for the interaction design practice, and consider whether the attributes can be valid to establish measures to assess the potential agency that technological-digital systems can offer.

References

1. Janlert, L.-E., Stolterman, E.: The meaning of interactivity-some proposals for definitions and measures. Hum.-Comput. Interact. **32**(3), 103–138 (2017)
2. Dewey, J.: Art as Experience. Perigee Book, New York (2005)
3. Mele, A.R.: Aspects of Agency: Decisions, Abilities, Explanations, and Free Will. Oxford University Press, New York (2017)
4. Soler-Adillon, J.: The intangible material of interactive art: agency, behavior and emergence. Artnodes, [online] Num. **16** 43–52 (2015)
5. Limerick, H., Coyle, D., Moore, J.W.: The experience of agency in human-computer interactions: a review. Front. Hum. Neurosci. **8**, 643 (2014)
6. Zacarias, M., de Oliveira, J.V.: Human-Computer Interaction: The Agency Perspective. Springer, Heidelberg (2012). https://doi.org/10.1007/978-3-642-25691-2
7. Shneiderman, B., Plaisant, C., Cohen, M.S., Jacobs, S., Elmqvist, N., Diakopoulos, N.: Designing the User Interface: Strategies for Effective Human-Computer Interaction. Pearson (2016)
8. Moore, J.W.: What is the sense of agency and why does it matter? Front. Psychol. **7**, 1272 (2016)
9. Khademi, K., Hui, B.: Towards understanding the HCI education landscape. In: Koli Calling 2020: Proceedings of the 20th Koli Calling International Conference on Computing Education Research, pp. 1–2, November 2020
10. Gondomar, R., Mor, E.: From UCD to HCD and beyond. Conciliating the human aims between philosophy and design education. In: International Conference on Human-Computer Interaction, pp. 108–122. Springer, Cham, July 2020. https://doi.org/10.1007/978-3-030-601 14-0_7
11. Barker, T.S.: Time and the Digital: Connecting Technology, Aesthetics, and a Process Philosophy of Time. Dartmouth College Press, Hanover (2012)
12. Shepherd, J.: The Shape of Agency: Control, Action, Skill, Knowledge. Oxford University Press, Oxford, New York (2021)
13. Neumann, M., Cowley, S.J.: Human agency and the resources of reason. In: Cowley, S.J., Vallée-Tourangeau, F. (eds.) Cognition Beyond the Brain, pp. 175–192. Springer, Cham (2017). https://doi.org/10.1007/978-3-319-49115-8_9

14. Kögler, H.-H., Stueber, K.R.: Empathy and Agency: The Problem of Understanding in the Human Sciences. Westview Press, Boulder, Colo (2000)
15. Archer, M.S.: Being Human: The Problem of Agency. Cambridge University Press, Cambridge (2000)
16. Gondomar, R.: Pragmatic experience of digital media and environments. Hipertext.net: Revista Académica sobre Documentación Digital y Comunicación Interactiva, 17: The Digital Future of Facts. Universitat Pompeu Fabra, Barcelona (2018). https://doi.org/10.31009/hipertext.net.2018.i17.03
17. Piaget, J.: The Construction of Reality in the Child. Routledge & Kegan Paul, London (1955)
18. Sterling, L., Taveter, K.: The Art of Agent-Oriented Modeling. MIT Press, Cambridge (2009)
19. Rao, A.S., Georgeff, M.P.: BDI agents: from theory to practice. In: Proceedings of the First International Conference on Multiagent Systems (ICMAS 1995), June 1995
20. Lopes, D.M.M.: The ontology of interactive art. J. Aesthetic Educ. **35**(4), 65–81 (2001)
21. Tomasello, M.: Origins of Human Communication. MIT Press, Cambridge, Mass (2008)
22. Bratman, M.: Shared Agency: A Planning Theory of Acting Together. Oxford University Press, Oxford (2014)
23. Enfield, N.J., Kockelman, P.: Distributed Agency. Oxford University Press, New York (2017)
24. Stolterman, E.: The nature of design practice and implications for interaction design research. Int. J. Des. **2**(1), 55–65 (2008)
25. Lakoff, G., Johnson, M.: Metaphors We Live By. University of Chicago Press, Chicago [etc.] (1980)
26. Gibson, J.J.: The Senses Considered as Perceptual Systems. George Allen & Unwin, London (1968)
27. Norman, D.A.: The Psychology of Everyday Things. Basic Books, New York (1988)
28. Davis, J.L.: How Artifacts Afford: The Power and Politics of Everyday Things. MIT Press (2020)
29. Ihde, D.: Heidegger's Technologies: Postphenomenological Perspectives. Fordham University Press, New York (2010)
30. Johnson, G., Bruner, G., Kumar, A.: Interactivity and its facets revisited: theory and empirical test. J. Advert. **35**, 35–52 (2006)
31. Miller, R.B.: Response time in man-computer conversational transactions. In: International Business Machines (IBM) Corporation, Fall Joint Computer Conference, Poughkeepsie, New York (1968)
32. Doherty, R.A., Sorenson, P.: Keeping users in the flow: mapping system responsiveness with user experience. Proc. Manuf. **3**, 4384–4391 (2015)
33. Ishizaki, S.: Improvisational Design: Continuous, Responsive Digital Communication. MIT Press, Cambridge (Mass.) (2003)
34. McLuhan, M.: Understanding Media: The Extensions of Man. MIT Press, Cambridge (Mass.) (1994)
35. Lazar, J., Feng, J.H., Hochheiser, H.: Research Methods in Human-Computer Interaction . Morgan Kaufmann, Cambridge (2017)

Grounding of Concept, Indexical, and Name

Roland Hausser[✉]

Universität Erlangen-Nürnberg (em.), Erlangen, Germany

Abstract. The semantics of agent-based DBS is 'grounded' in that the Content kinds *concept, indexical,* and *name* have their foundation in the agent's recognition and action, whereby each Content kind has its own computational Mechanism. For a concept it is pattern *matching* between the type provided by memory and raw data provided by the agent's interface component. For an indexical it is *pointing* at a STAR value of the agent's on-board orientation system (OBOS). For a name it is the address of the 'named referent' which is inserted as the core value into a lexical name proplet in an act of *baptism*.

Orthogonal to the Content kinds and their computational Mechanisms are the Semantic kinds *referent, property,* and *relation* with their associated Syntactic kind *noun, adj* and *intransitive verb,* and *transitive verb.* It is shown that the Semantic kind of *referent* is restricted to the Syntactic kind of noun, but utilizes the computational Mechanisms of matching, pointing, and baptism. Furthermore, figurative use is restricted to the computational Mechanism of matching, but uses the Semantic kinds referent, property, and relation.

Keywords: Syntactic kinds of noun, adj, verb · Semantic kinds of referent, property, relation · Content kinds of concept, indexical, name · Computational mechanisms of matching, pointing, baptism · Recognition vs. action · Type vs. token · Speak mode vs. hear mode · Language vs. nonlanguage content

1 Apparent Terminological Redundany

The notions noun, verb, and adjective from linguistics (philology) have counterparts in analytic philosophy, namely referent, relation, and property, and in symbolic logic, namely argument, functor, and modifier:

1.1 Three Times Three Related Notions

	(a) *linguistics*	(b) *philosophy*	(c) *symbolic logic*
1.	noun	referent (object)	argument
2.	verb	relation	functor
3.	adj	property	modifier

© Springer Nature Switzerland AG 2021
M. Kurosu (Ed.): HCII 2021, LNCS 12762, pp. 150–160, 2021.
https://doi.org/10.1007/978-3-030-78462-1_11

We take it that these variants are not merely different terms for the same things, but different terms for different aspects of the same things. In particular, the linguistic terminology may be viewed as representing the syntactic aspect, the philosophical terminology as representing the associated semantic aspect, and the logical terminology as a preparatory step towards a computational implementation.

In DBS, the distinctions are related as follows:

1.2   1st Correlation: Semantic and Syntactic Kind

Semantic kind	*Syntactic kind*
1. referent	noun
2. property	adn, adv, adnv, intransitive verb
3. relation	transitive verb

The Semantic kinds *referent, property*, and *relation* correspond to argument, 1-place functor, and 2- or 3-place functor, respectively, in Symbolic Logic. Syntactically, *property* splits up into adn, adv, prepnoun, and 1-place verb. *Relation* splits up into 2- and 3-place verbs.

The distinction between (i) Semantic and (iii) Syntactic kinds is complemented by a second, orthogonal pair of triple distinctions, namely (ii) Content kinds and associated (iv) computational Mechanisms:

1.3   2nd Correlation: Content Kind and Comput. Mechanism

Content kind	*computational Mechanism*
a. concept	matching
b. indexical	pointing
c. name	baptism

The terms of the three Content kinds and the correlated Mechanisms have had informal use in the literature,[1] but without an agent-based ontology. The essential points of the Mechanisms in DBS are their obvious computational realizations (Sects. 4–6), which have not been utilized until now.

The dichotomies Sects. 1.2 and 1.3 provide 12 ($2 \times 2 \times 3$) basic notions. Empirically, they combine into six classes of proplets which constitute the semantic building blocks of DBS cognition in general and natural language communication in particular. The six classes form what we call the *cognitive square*[2]:

---

[1] Examples of precomputational uses are (i) matching for concepts but without the type-token relation and its computational implementation based on content and pattern proplets, (ii) pointing for indexicals but without an on-board orientation system (OBOS), and (iii) baptism but without the named referent as the core value for use in the speak and the hear mode.

[2] 'Triangle' would be appropriate as well, but the term "cognitive triangle" is already used by the cognitive behavioral therapists (CBT). Earlier it was used by Ogden and Richards (1923) for their "Semiotic Triangle." The term 'square' is well suited to express the orthogonal relation between the Syntactic_kinds-Semantic_kinds and the Content_kinds-computational_Mechanisms.

1.4   Cognitive Square of DBS

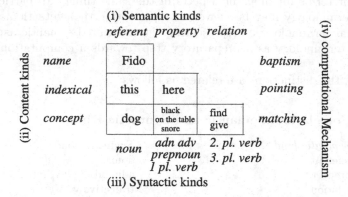

The twelve basic notions of this NLC 2.6.9 extension are distributed over six basic proplets kinds such that no two are characterized the same:

1.5   Closer View of the Cognitive Square

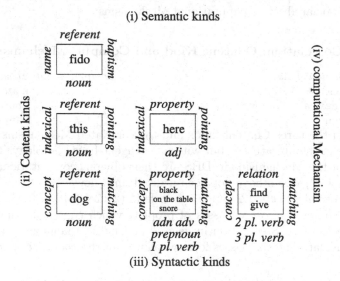

The surfaces inside the rectangles have the following proplet definitions:

1.6   Proplets Instantiating the Cognitive Square of DBS

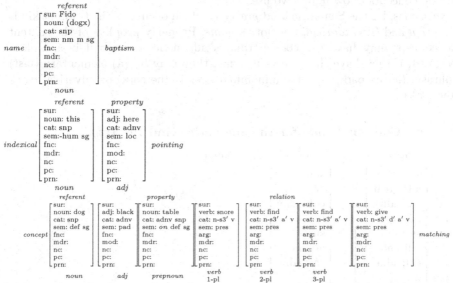

In a proplet, the Semantic kind *referent* is limited to the core attribute noun, *property* is limited to the core values adn, adv, adnv and to verbs characterized by their cat value as intransitive, and *relation* is limited to verbs characterized by their cat value as transitive.

The Content kind *name, indexical*, and *concept* is specified by the core value of a proplet. The corresponding computational Mechanisms *baptism, pointing*, and *matching* are implemented by inserting a 'named referent' as core value into *names*, by indexicals pointing at a STAR value of the onboard orientation system, (OBOS) and by computational type-token matching in the case of *concepts*.

The cognitive square of DBS is empirically important because (i) figurative use is restricted to concepts, i.e. the bottom row in Sects. 1.4–1.6, and (ii) reference is restricted to nouns, i.e. the left-most column. Thus only concept nouns may be used both figuratively and as referents, while indexical properties like here and now may not be used as either, and names only as referents.

2   Restriction of Figurative Use to Concepts

To show the restriction of figurative use to the Content kind concept let us go systematically through the three Semantic kinds:

2.1   Three Content Kinds for the Semantic Kind *Referent*

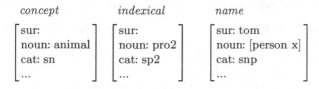

The three Content kinds of the Semantic kind *referent* all have literal use, but only the concepts allow figurative use.

Next consider the Semantic kind *property*, which occurs as the Content kinds (i) *concept* and (ii) *indexical*, but not as *name*. Property proplets of the content kind concept may have the core attributes adj, noun, or verb if it is 1-place (Sect. 1.6). If they have the core value adnv, they may be (a) elementary (fast) or phrasal (in the park), and (b) adnominal (tree in the park) or adverbial (walk in the park).[3]

2.2   Two Content Kinds for the Semantic Kind *Property*

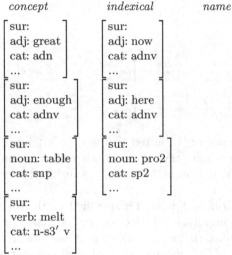

concept   indexical   name

$$
\begin{bmatrix} \text{sur:} \\ \text{adj: great} \\ \text{cat: adn} \\ \text{...} \end{bmatrix}
\quad
\begin{bmatrix} \text{sur:} \\ \text{adj: now} \\ \text{cat: adnv} \\ \text{...} \end{bmatrix}
$$

$$
\begin{bmatrix} \text{sur:} \\ \text{adj: enough} \\ \text{cat: adnv} \\ \text{...} \end{bmatrix}
\quad
\begin{bmatrix} \text{sur:} \\ \text{adj: here} \\ \text{cat: adnv} \\ \text{...} \end{bmatrix}
$$

$$
\begin{bmatrix} \text{sur:} \\ \text{noun: table} \\ \text{cat: snp} \\ \text{...} \end{bmatrix}
\quad
\begin{bmatrix} \text{sur:} \\ \text{noun: pro2} \\ \text{cat: sp2} \\ \text{...} \end{bmatrix}
$$

$$
\begin{bmatrix} \text{sur:} \\ \text{verb: melt} \\ \text{cat: n-s3' v} \\ \text{...} \end{bmatrix}
$$

Of the Semantic kind *property*, only the concepts may be used nonliterally.[4]

The Grammatical kind transitive verb with its single Semantic kind *relation* exists as the Content kind *concept*, but not as *indexical* or *name*:

2.3   One Content Kind for the Semantic Kind *Relation*

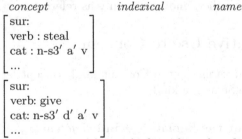

concept   indexical   name

$$
\begin{bmatrix} \text{sur:} \\ \text{verb : steal} \\ \text{cat : n-s3' a' v} \\ \text{...} \end{bmatrix}
$$

$$
\begin{bmatrix} \text{sur:} \\ \text{verb: give} \\ \text{cat: n-s3' d' a' v} \\ \text{...} \end{bmatrix}
$$

Being concepts, transitive verbs have literal and nonliteral use.

---

[3] Phrasal modifiers, called prepnouns in DBS, are derived from a referent by means of a preposition or an affix, depending on the language. Therefore, a prepnoun like in the park refers by means of park, in contradistinction to the other modifiers, e.g. elementary fast or intransitive snore, which do not refer.

[4] For a nonliteral use of *on the table* see CC 9.2.4 and of *melt* CC 9.5.1.

3 Additional Constraint on Figurative Use

The restriction of figurative use to concepts is constrained further by the condition that the literal term and its figurative counterpart must be grammatically equivalent:

3.1 Invariance Constraint

A figurative use and its literal counterpart must be of the same Syntactic and Semantic kind.

Thus, one cannot use a 1-place verb like bark to refer figuratively to a dog unless bark is nominalized, as in the little barker (i.e. by turning the property of intransitive bark into the referent barker, sleep into sleeper, stink into stinker, etc.). Similarly for the adj fat, which for figurative use must be nominalized, as in the old fatso. Functionally, the constraint helps the hearer to find the literal counterpart of a figurative use by reducing the search space.

The systematic examples in CC Chap. 9 all satisfy the invariance constraint:

3.2 Syntactic-Semantic Invariance of Figurative Use

Semantic kind	Syntactic kind	Nonliteral use	Literal counterpart	in CC
noun	referent	animal	dog	9.1.2
property	prepnoun	on the table	on the orange crate	9.2.1
property	adn	great	greater than average	9.6.3
property	adv	enough	more than enough	9.6.6
property	intransitive verb	melt	disappear	9.5.1
relation	transitive verb	steal	take over	9.4.2

The Semantic kind *property* has several Syntactic kinds, while each Syntactic kind, e.g. prepnoun, has only one Semantic kind, i.e. *property*, regardless of whether it is used literally or figuratively. The other two Semantic kinds, i.e. *referent* and *relation*, each have only a single syntactic counterpart.

As an example of using all three Semantic kinds figuratively consider the following description of a dog contorting itself catching a frisbee in mid air:

3.3 Example Using All Three Semantic Kinds Figuratively

The animal flew acrobatically towards the disc.

The content obeys the invariance constraint: literal dog and figurative animal are both singular nouns, literal jumped and figurative flew are both finite verbs in the indicative past, literal in a spectacular gymnastic feat and figurative acrobatically are both adverbials (one phrasal, the other elementary), and literal frisbee and figurative disc are both singular nouns. For successful communication, the hearer-reader must relate figurative animal to literal dog and figurative disc to literal frisbee. The relation flew and the property acrobatically, in contrast, do not refer directly, but only indirectly via their function as relation or modifier.

4 Declarative Specification of Concepts for Recognition

Concepts are the only Semantic kind which interacts directly with the agent's cognition-external environment. The interaction consists of matching between (i) raw data provided by sensors and activators of the agent's interface component and (ii) concept types provided by the agent's memory.[5]

Consider the rule for the recognition of a color:

4.1 Declarative Specification for Recognizing the Color Blue

$$
\begin{array}{ll}
\textit{concept type} & \textit{concept token} \\
\begin{bmatrix}
\text{place holder: blue} \\
\text{sensory modality: vision} \\
\text{semantic field: color} \\
\text{content kind: concept} \\
\text{wavelength: 450--495nm} \\
\text{frequency: 670--610THz} \\
\text{samples: a, b, c, ...}
\end{bmatrix}
\Rightarrow
\begin{bmatrix}
\text{place holder: blue} \\
\text{sensory modality: vision} \\
\text{semantic field: color} \\
\text{content kind: concept} \\
\text{wavelength: 470nm} \\
\text{frequency: 637THz} \\
\text{samples: ...}
\end{bmatrix}
\end{array}
$$

⇑ *analyzed output*

sensory modality vision

raw input   sensor values: 470nm
637 THz

The raw input data 470nm and 637 THz are provided by the agent's interface component and recognized as the color blue because they fall into the type's wavelength interval of 450–495nm and the frequency interval of 670–610 THz. The analyzed output token results from replacing the wavelength and frequency intervals of the type with the raw data measurements of the input.

The place holder value of the recognized token, i.e. the letter sequence b l u e, is used for lookup of the lexical proplet which contains the place holder as its core value (CC 1.6.3):

---

[5] From a theory of science point of view, computational pattern matching based on the type-token relation constitutes a fruitful interaction between the humanities and the sciences.

4.2   Place Holder Value of Concept Used for Lexical Lookup

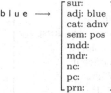

Like the concept type, the proplet is retrieved from the artificial agent's memory (on-board database). Computationally, the lookup is based on string search (Knuth et al. 1977) in combination with a trie structure (de la Briandais 1959).

The language counterpart to the recognition of nonlanguage concepts is the interpretation of language-dependent surfaces. As an example, consider the DBS robot's recognition of the letter sequence blue by matching raw visual input data with letter patterns as shape types, resulting in a surface token:

4.3   Sensor Interacting with Lang. Concept Type (Surface)

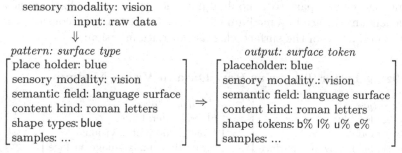

Raw data input is matched by the shape types of the letters b l u e. The output replaces the matching shape types with the shape tokens b% l% u% e%[6] to record such accidental properties as the font, size, color, etc. in the sensory medium of print, and pronunciation, pitch, speed, loudness, etc. in the sensory medium of speech. The shape types are used (i) for matching the raw data and (ii) for lookup of the lexical definition. For developing the linguistic side of automatic word form recognition, the type-token matching of raw data in different media may be cut short temporarily by typing letters directly into a standard computer.

5   Declarative Specification of Concepts for Action

The action counterpart to the recognition of nonlanguage concepts is their cognition-external realization as raw data. It consists in adapting a type to the agent's purpose as a token which is passed to the appropriate actuator. As an example, consider a cuttlefish (Metasepia pfefferi) turning on the color blue:

---

[6] For ease of illustration, the letter shapes are represented by the letters themselves, e.g. e (type) and e% (token).

5.1   Rule for Producing the Color Blue

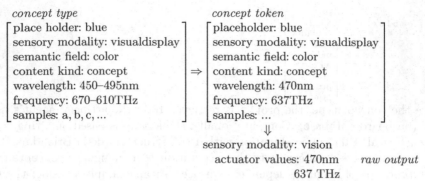

Semantic Field

The type is adapted into a token by replacing the wavelength interval of 450–495 nm and frequency interval of 670–610 THz with the agent-selected values of 470 nm and 637 THz. In the cuttlefish, these values are realized by natural actuators for color control (chromatophores) as raw data.

The language counterpart to a nonlanguage action is the realization of a language-dependent surface in a medium of choice. As an example, consider the DBS robot's production of the surface blue as raw data in vision:

5.2   Realizing Letter Tokens as Raw Data in Vision Medium

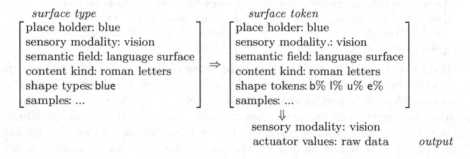

The input to the actuator consists of a sequence the shape tokens representing roman letters. The output replaces the shape tokens, here b% l% u% e%, with matching raw data, for example on a computer screen.

6   Indirect Grounding of Indexicals and Names

In DBS, the second computational Mechanism of *indexicals* is pointing at STAR values of the agent's on-board orientation system (OBOS) and is as such cognition-internal. However, because the STAR values originate as concept recognitions, past or present (CC Chaps. 7, 8), indexicals rely indirectly on the Mechanism of computational pattern matching. More specifically, the indexical pro1 points at the A value of the STAR, pro2 at the R value, pro3 at the 3rd value, here at the S value, and now at the T value (with S and T values nominalized).

The third computational Mechanism of *names* relies on an act of baptism, which inserts the 'named referent' as the core value into the lexical name proplet (CTGR (Hausser 2017)). Because the named referent originates as concept recognition, names – like indexicals – rely indirectly on the first computational Mechanism of *concepts*, i.e. computational pattern matching.

After working out the basic functioning of the computational Mechanism for the recognition and action of certain concepts in a codesigned but real environment, more concepts of the same kind (semantic field) may be added routinely, as shown by the following example:

6.1   Similarity and Difference Between Color Concept Types

$$
\begin{bmatrix}
\text{place holder: red} \\
\text{sensory modality: vision} \\
\text{semantic field: color} \\
\text{content kind: concept} \\
\text{wavelength: 700-635 nm} \\
\text{frequency: 430-480 THz} \\
\text{samples: a, b, c, ...}
\end{bmatrix}
\begin{bmatrix}
\text{place holder: green} \\
\text{sensory modality: vision} \\
\text{semantic field: color} \\
\text{content kind: concept} \\
\text{wavelength: 495-570nm} \\
\text{frequency: 526-606THz} \\
\text{samples: } a', b', c', ...
\end{bmatrix}
\begin{bmatrix}
\text{place holder: blue} \\
\text{sensory modality: vision} \\
\text{semantic field: color} \\
\text{content kind: concept} \\
\text{wavelength: 490-450nm} \\
\text{frequency: 610-670THz} \\
\text{samples: } a'', b'', c'', ...
\end{bmatrix}
$$

Once the recognition and action side of these concepts is working as intended, more colors may be easily added as an efficient, transparent upscaling.[7]

Similarly for geometric forms: once the concepts of square (CC 1.3.2) and rectangle work as intended, more two-dimensional forms, such as triangle, heptagon, hexagon, and rhombus, may be added routinely. After implementing the concept pick including the associated hand-eye coordination and the semantic relation of object\predicate (CC 2.5.1, 2), the robot should be able to execute language-based requests like Pick the blue square or Pick the green rectangle correctly from a set of items in its task environment.

7   Conclusion

In data-driven agent-based DBS, recognition and action must be *grounded* in the form of a computational interaction between raw data and a robot's digital cognition. For practical reasons, grounding may be temporarily suspended by the shortcut of typing place holder values into a standard computer's key board and displaying output on the screen. This allows systematic upscaling of an artificial cognition even today, yet prepares for integrating operational core values for referents, properties, and relations when they become available in robotics.

---

[7] Set-theoretically, the colors red, green, and blue are (i) disjunct and (ii) subsets of color. This structure is inherent in the color concepts, but regardless of being true, it is neither the only nor the predominant aspect of their meaning: knowing that red and green are disjunct, for example, is not sufficient for naming these colors correctly.

Computational upscaling has two basic aspects: the *declarative specification* and the *procedural implementation*. A declarative specification must be both, (i) easily readable by humans and (ii) easily translatable into a general purpose programming language like Lisp, C, Java, or Perl. From a humanities point of view, a declarative specification must represent the necessary properties of a software solution by omitting the accidental properties which distinguish the individual programming languages and make them difficult to read. Methodologically, a procedural implementation complements a declarative specification with automatic verification, which supports systematic incremental upscaling.

References

de la Briandais, R.: File searching using variable length keys. In: Proceedings of the Western Joint Computer Conference, vol. 15, pp. 295–298 (1959)

Hausser, R.: Computational Cognition; Integrated DBS Software Design for Data-Driven Cognitive Processing (2019). https://lagrammar.net/

Hausser, R.: A computational treatment of generalized reference. Complex Adapt. Syst. Model. **5**(1), 1–26 (2017)

Knuth, D.E., Morris, J.H., Pratt, V.R.: Fast pattern matching in strings. SIAM J. Comput. **6**(2), 323–350 (1977)

Hausser, R.: A Computational Model of Natural Language Communication; Interpretation, Inferencing, and Production in Database Semantics, 2nd edn, pp. 360, 363. Springer, Heidelberg (2006). https://lagrammar.net

Ogden, C.K., Richards, I.A.: The Meaning of Meaning. Routledge and Kegan Paul, London (1923)

Quillian, M.: Semantic memory. In: Minsky, M. (ed.) Semantic Information Processing, pp. 227–270. MIT Press, Cambridge (1968)

Quine, W.V.O.: Word and Object. MIT Press, Cambridge (1960)

Hausser, R.: Twentyfour Exercises in Linguistic Analysis; DBS Software Design for the Hear and the Speak Mode of a Talking Robot, p. 318 (2020). https://doi.org/10.13140/RG.2.2.13035.39200. https://lagrammar.net

Ethics in Human-Centered Design

Jun Iio[1]([⊠]) [iD], Atsushi Hasegawa[2] [iD], Shigeyoshi Iizuka[3], Seiji Hayakawa[4],
and Hiroshi Tsujioka[5]

[1] Chuo University, Shinjuku-ku, Tokyo 162-8478, Japan
iiojun@tamacc.cho-u.ac.jp
[2] Concent, Inc., Shibuya-ku, Tokyo 150-0022, Japan
hase@concentinc.jp
[3] Kanagawa University, Yokohama-shi, Kanagawa 220-0012, Japan
iizuka@kanagawa-u.ac.jp
[4] HCD YOROZU Consulting, Toshima-ku, Tokyo, Japan
seiji.hayakawa@cilas.net
[5] Human-Centered Design Organization, Shinjuku-ku, Tokyo 162-0056, Japan
pxs02147@nifty.ne.jp

Abstract. In recent years, ethical considerations have become a primary concern across all fields of research. Human-Centered Design (HCD) is no exception.
When the subjects of an experiment are human beings, rigid ethical consideration
is required. User researchers must be careful about HCD-specific research ethics
regardless of whether their work is carried out in laboratories or in industry. In
view of this, the Human-Centered Design Organization (HCD-net) organized a
particular working group (WG) to discuss the matter in early 2020. The group
discusses three ethical concerns: (1) What ethical guidelines are necessary for
specialists studying any HCD-related issues? (2) What ethical guidelines are necessary for HCD researchers conducting user research or user tests? (3) Should
the HCD professionals have an ethical policy on their services or products? As a
starting point for their discussion, the WG conducted a questionnaire asking about
several ethical problems. This paper contains a summary of the comprehensive
debate conducted in the WG and the results of the questionnaire, suggesting focal
points for the WG to address in determining ethical guidelines for HCD activities.

Keyword: Human-centered design · Ethical considerations · Research ethics

1 Introduction

With the evolution of advanced information processing technology, computers have
come to be used in various fields. High-performance computers enable unprecedented
information processing, such as big data analysis, large-scale computer simulation, and
bioinformatics. In many ways, technological innovation has contributed to the prosperity
of society. At the same time, ethical considerations have come to be questioned in all
situations. For example, bioinformatics and biomedical research [1] face the ethical
judgment of creating artificial life based on genetic engineering [2, 3], and big data

© Springer Nature Switzerland AG 2021
M. Kurosu (Ed.): HCII 2021, LNCS 12762, pp. 161–170, 2021.
https://doi.org/10.1007/978-3-030-78462-1_12

analysis must handle sensitive and personal information [4–6]. Artificial intelligence also requires ethical considerations [7, 8]; in applied artificial intelligence research, philosophical judgments, such as the so-called trolley problem, are important [9, 10]. Research ethics, too, require the careful consideration of researchers in all fields.

The field of Human-Centered Design (HCD) is no exception [11]. In one sense, design and ethics are tightly connected [12]. In the research of HCD, User-Centered Design (UCD), and User Experience (UX), the subjects of experiments are usually human beings; hence, rigid ethical considerations are of utmost importance.

This is not only true of laboratory research. User researchers must be mindful of HCD-specific research ethics in industry research, as well, as their research targets are still humans. As described previously, researchers have become accustomed to consideration of ethical issues due to the requirement from the recent research norms. However, many HCD practitioners and businesspersons are not familiar with these issues, even as they face pressure to keep their business compliant with laws and regulations. It would therefore be useful to determine certain ethical guidelines for all scientists and practitioners working on HCD-related activities.

The rest of this paper is structured as follows. In Sect. 2, our research questions are described. In Sect. 3, an overview of the investigation and the questionnaire results are presented. In Sect. 4, the discussion ensuing from those results is reported. Finally, conclusions and future work close the article in Sect. 5.

2   Research Questions

Under the background previously laid out, the Human-Centered Design Organization (HCD-net) organized a particular working group (WG) to discuss this problem in early 2020. The WG's goal is to determine ethical guidelines for experts working on all kinds of HCD activities.

As the described previous section, the ethical consideration in the HCD field is slightly more complicated than that in other areas because it varies from the laboratory level to the industry level. Therefore, the WG decided to discuss the following three ethical concerns:

1. What ethical guidelines are necessary for specialists studying any HCD-related issues?
2. What ethical guidelines are necessary for HCD researchers conducting user research or user tests?
3. Should the HCD professionals have an ethical policy or responsibility for their services or products?

The first question is a fundamental one; it is the question of baseline ethical guidelines to be referred to by every HCD expert.

The second question comes from the character of HCD, which includes not only laboratory studies but activities in the industry. The WG's challenge is to figure out the ethical difference between user research carried out by the researchers in a laboratory context and user tests carried out by practitioners in the industry.

The third question is practical and crucial for the practitioners because they provide their services or products to a market. Due to the heavy compliance requirements in their business recently implemented, businesspersons have more to worry about regarding their services and products every day. Although ethical considerations are essential, their burden grows more and more if ethical consideration is added to their responsibilities.

3   The Questionnaire Survey

As a starting point for the WG's discussion, we conducted a questionnaire asking about several ethical problems. The questionnaire was prepared in Google Forms (see Fig. 1), and it had eleven questions (plus several sub-questions).

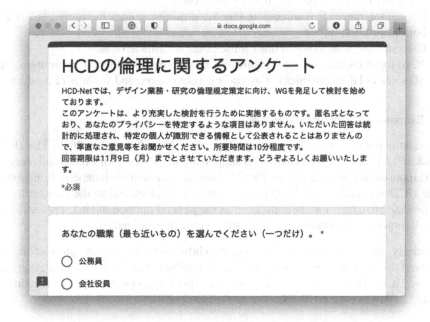

Fig. 1. A screenshot of the questionnaire, which was titled "Ethical Considerations Regarding HCD." It explains that the HCD-net has created a working group to determine ethical guidelines for design and research; that the answers will be anonymized to protect respondents' privacy; that approximately ten minutes are required to fill in the responses; and that the due date is November 9th, 2020.

3.1   The Questions

The questions included in the questionnaire are as follows:

1. Directivity to HCD: Are your company's services or products produced using user- or HCD?

2. Taking action: What action do you take if your company uses an inappropriate strategy?
3. Representativity: Have you had an experience in which your choice or activity was representing your organization?
4. Choice of options: Do you choose appropriate options to act as an HCD specialist when behaving as consumer?
5. Ethicality of deliverables: Are the services or products of your company ethical?
6. Ethical experiences: Do you have any examples in which you feel that "ethics" are of concern in your daily businesses?
7. Bad experiences: Can you think of an experience in which you felt something was lost due to a malformed user interface?
8. Ethical responsibility: What is the ethical responsibility of HCD specialists and designers for the outputs of your organization?
9. Ethical tolerance: Is it admissible that the gimmick guides the users to click any buttons or URL-links?
10. Case studies: which do you think those cases are ethical or not?
11. Need for an ethical guideline: Please give us your opinion about determining a code of ethics in HCD activities for specialists, researchers, and services or products.

3.2 Responses to the Questionnaire

The questionnaire was conducted from October 2020 to November 2020. The HCD-net asked 1,019 members (including 66 supporting members) to fill it out and received 105 responses (a response rate of 10.3%). Note that almost all independent members of the HCD-net are certified HCD professionals or HCD specialist; the answers to this questionnaire can therefore be considered as the general opinion of HCD professionals. Table 1 shows the responses to each question in the questionnaire.

Directivity to HCD and Taking Appropriate Actions. Nearly all respondents answered that they recognized their services or products were designed using user centered or HCD. Then, they responded that they hired appropriate actions indirectly or actively as they are the HCD specialist to the next question.

Representativity. To the third question, approximately half of respondents said that they represent a part of their organizations. Adding 21% of respondents who considered that they represented the whole company, nearly three-quarters of responses indicated representativity.

Choice of Options to Act as the HCD Expert. To the fourth question, 82% of responses answered that they behave as specialists. It implies the nature of the HCD specialist who thought anything from users' or consumers' view.

Ethicality of the Services / Products, Ethical Experiences, and Bad Experiences. Regarding the ethics of the services and products of the companies, 80% of answers chose the option showing yes or almost yes. Furthermore, approximately 80% of respondents answered that they were conscious of ethical issues in their businesses. To the seventh question, more than 90% of the answers selected the options showing "yes, I have

Table 1. The questions and answers to the questionnaire.

Questions	Answers (in percentages)
Directivity to HCD	Applicable (27%), Somewhat applicable (47%), Not applicable (25%), Not applicable at all (5%), I do not care (2%)
Taking actions	Take actions aggressively (42%), Take actions indirectly (44%), Take no actions (11%), I have no idea (3%)
Representativity	I am a representative of the whole organization (21%), of part of the organization (55%), I am not a representative (15%), I have no idea (7%), I do not care (2%)
Choice of options	I act as the HCD experts properly (82%), I do not consider it as consumers (13%), I have no idea (5%)
Ethicality of deliverables	Applicable (30%), Somewhat applicable (50%), Not applicable (10%), Not applicable at all (3%), I have no idea (6%), I do not care (1%)
Ethical experiences	Yes (42%), Sometimes (37%), No 16%), Not at all (2%), I have no idea (2%), I do not care (1%)
Bad experiences	Yes (57%), No but I have similar problems (34%), No (9%)
Ethical responsibility	Agree (47%), Totally agree (41%), disagree (7%), totally disagree (4%), I have no idea (1%)
Ethical tolerance	Acceptable (5%), Somewhat acceptable (13%), Acceptable if the users do not get disadvantages (62%), Not acceptable (19%), I have no idea (1%)
Case studies	No problems at all (2%), No problems (4%), Problematic (67%), I have no idea (27%)
Need for an ethical guideline	It is necessary, and it should be determined (36%), Should be defined, but guidelines for deliverables are not needed (57%), No need to do that (5%), I do not care (2%)

experiences of getting lost something" or "no, but sometimes I was confused by the bad user interface." The sixth and seventh questions were open-ended, and many descriptions were reported from the respondents.

Typical responses were chosen by the authors as follows:

- The case of making things without consideration for nature and the environment.
- The time when I considered the quality to be sacrificed.
- Does the convenience in which the product aims to make the users happy?
- When I consider how to deliver the information to users, which is valuable to the users but has some disadvantage to the company.
- Considering not only how the human acts but whether it is appropriate or not.
- When I raise the UCD as an indulgence.
- When I notice that we were designing a specification which placed the user at a disadvantage.

– When I imagine whether I can recommend a product whose design I was involved in to my family.
– When decisions were made using political rather than logical consideration.

We also conducted text analysis on the open-ended answers. Figure 2 shows the results of Primary Component Analysis (PCA) to the open-ended question results asking about situations when the respondent has been conscious of ethics. The horizontal axis represents the abstractness or concreteness of an idea, and the vertical one denotes whether the field was business or research. (Note that these labels were assigned manually according to the scattered keywords.)

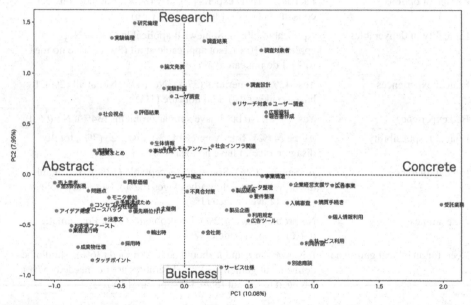

Fig. 2. This graph shows the results of PCA for the sixth question. The natural language processing software extracted the noun phrases. Then, the word vectors were calculated for each phrase. The word vectors have 100-dimensional elements, they but were compressed to two-dimensional values to plot the plane shown in this figure.

We also conducted a similar analysis to the open-ended answers to the following sub-question of the sixth question (see Fig. 3).

Ethical Responsibility and Ethical Tolerance. For the next question, approximately nine out of ten respondents replied that they have ethical responsibilities. However, regarding the following question about a nudge, 62% of respondents responded that it was permissible if the user did not suffer a disadvantage.

Figure 4 shows the cross-tabulation graph with one row for ethical tolerance and one column for the experiences suffering from disadvantage. There is a loose relationship between the two tendencies.

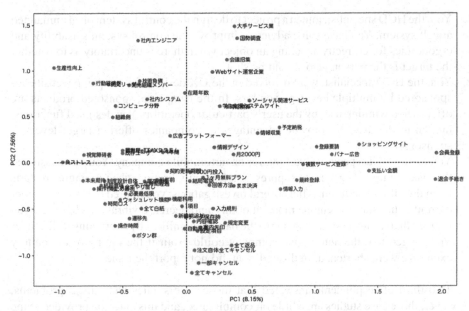

Fig. 3. This graph shows the results of PCA for the seventh question. Some clusters showing common keywords such as "cancellation," "subscription or un-subscription procedure," etc., appear in this graph.

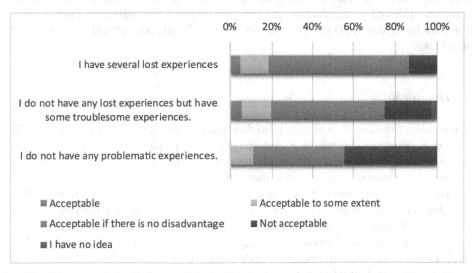

Fig. 4. This graph shows the cross-tabulation with one row for ethical tolerance and one column for the bad experiences. The respondents who had some bad experiences tended to be amenable to the gimmick which induces the users explicitly or implicitly.

Case Studies. The tenth question asked about case studies. The question presented three cases and asked whether those cases contained ethical problems.

1. You, the HCD specialist, joined a project to design the control system of an unmanned attack system. You gave some advice to improve the control system's usability and ergonomics for correctly attacking an object when there is uncertainty as to whether the target is the person who should be shot.
2. You, the HCD specialist, were involved in the UX design of a campaign website co-sponsored by multiple beverage vendors. In the campaign, sponsored products are offered to a winning user by the user's particular operation. You designed functions, hidden to the users, to provide advantages to companies offering larger levels of sponsorship.
3. You are an HCD specialist working for an automobile company. You were assigned the task of improving a car to suppress unpleasant vibration when its engine restarts from the idling condition. After several investigations, you figured out that a stronger current could start the engine more smoothly and decrease vibration. However, you noticed that it caused some damage to the battery, significantly shortening its lifetime. You judged that the automobile company could profit if the timing of the battery exchange were shortened. In the end, you did not report the issue.

Two-third of respondents answered that those case studies had ethical problems. However, those case studies are a little bit complicated, and this question provided some difficulty. Therefore, it is better to consider these answers as a reference.

Need for an Ethical Guideline. The last question is the most critical and explicit. More than half of the respondents selected the option of "The code of ethics is meaningful. However, it should not regulate the services or products." The answers to the last question may imply that HCD professionals are also confused about ethical issues in HCD activities.

4   Discussions

The results of the questionnaire revealed that many respondents proudly work as HCD specialists. However, it should be considered that the respondents are HCD-net members who were already interested in this issue. It is obvious that they actively cooperated with this survey because of their interest in these ethical considerations.

The respondents seem to believe that almost all services and products they provide are ethically sound under the pressure of keeping compliance in their daily businesses, so it does not seem to determine the ethical guideline. On the other hand, there is room to improve ethical conscientiousness; many respondents answered that they have had troublesome experiences from a consumer's perspective.

It remains unclear whether the difference in ethical consciousness was between laboratory and industry research. To answer this question, we need to conduct further investigations on the researchers and practitioners responding to the questionnaire and more intensive qualitative surveying, such as semi-structured interviews and other methodologies.

The most important finding is the implication derived from answers to the last question. On the one hand, the answers to the previous questions revealed that almost all respondents understood that ethical issues should be adequately treated. On the other hand, though, they seem to hesitate to create additional burden in their daily business activities. That resulted in the answer that they did not consider that the ethical guideline should regulate their services or products. It can easily be imagined that researchers and practitioners will have to prepare more and more things to adapt to ethical requirements if HCD-net provides ethical guidelines.

The WG believes that HCD-specific ethical guidelines must be prepared in three stages. The first is a fundamental guideline, which provides a behavioral criterion that all HCD professionals should have. The second is the ethical guidelines for conducting user surveys and user tests; existing ethical guidelines in other fields can be used as references. The third is the ethical standards for services or products created by HCD professionals. It is considered essential to formulate these guidelines. However, the questionnaire's results revealed this as a matter to be carefully discussed, as many people in charge tended to reject the necessity of this regulation.

5 Conclusions and Future Work

In the today's highly information-based society, considering ethical issues has become necessary in any social activity. HCD activities, such as user surveys and user tests, are no exception. Therefore, it is necessary to define certain ethical guidelines for HCD activities. By an implicit request from the industries, a WG discussing the ethical guidelines in HCD fields was established by HCD-net.

At the beginning of their discussion, they conducted a questionnaire to gauge the consciousness of HCD specialists regarding ethical issues. The results of the questionnaire revealed that nearly all the respondents were highly interested in ethical problems. However, they tended to hesitate regarding the determination of guidelines for their products or services. The results of the survey encourage us to draw a blueprint of HCD-specific ethical guidelines, which remains as a future work.

References

1. Council for International Organizations of Medical Sciences: International ethical guidelines for biomedical research involving human subjects. Bull. Med. Ethics (182), 17–23 (2002)
2. Rollin, B.E.: Bad ethics, good ethics and the genetic engineering of animals in agriculture. J. Anim. Sci. **74**(3), 535–541 (1996)
3. Polkinghorne, J.C.: The person, the soul, and genetic engineering. J. Med. Ethics **30**(6), 593–597 (2014)
4. Xu, L., Jiang, C., Wang, J., Yuan, J., Ren, Y.: Information security in big data: privacy and data mining. IEEE Access **2**, 1149–1176 (2014)
5. Wu, X., Zhu, X., Wu, G.Q., Ding, W.: Data mining with big data. IEEE Trans. Knowl. Data Eng. **26**(1), 97–107 (2013)
6. Tene, O., Polonetsky, J.: Big data for all: privacy and user control in the age of analytics. Nw. J. Tech. Intell. Prop. **11**, xxvii (2012)
7. Bostrom, N., Yudkowsky, E.: The ethics of artificial intelligence. In: The Cambridge Handbook of Artificial Intelligence, vol. 1, pp. 316–334 (2014)

8. Etzioni, A., Etzioni, O.: Incorporating ethics into artificial intelligence. J. Ethics **21**(4), 403–418 (2017)
9. Renda, A.: Ethics, algorithms and self-driving cars–a CSI of the 'trolley problem'. CEPS Policy Insight (2018/02). (2018)
10. Moolayil, A.K.: The modern trolley problem: ethical and economically-sound liability schemes for autonomous vehicles. Case W. Res. JL Tech. Internet **9**, 1 (2018)
11. Ramírez, R.H.: The meaning of 'Good Design' in the age of smart automation. J. Sci. Technol. Arts **12**(3), 100–114 (2020)
12. Mulvenna, M., Boger, J., Bond, R.: Ethical by design: a manifesto. In: Proceedings of the European Conference on Cognitive Ergonomics 2017, pp. 51–54. (2017)

AI Creativity and the Human-AI Co-creation Model

Zhuohao Wu[1]([✉]), Danwen Ji[2], Kaiwen Yu[3], Xianxu Zeng[4], Dingming Wu[5],
and Mohammad Shidujaman[6]

[1] School of Animation and Digital Arts, Communication University of China, Beijing, China
[2] College of Design and Innovation, Tongji University, Shanghai, China
[3] San Jose State University, San Jose, CA 95112, USA
[4] Department of Mathematics, University of British Columbia, Vancouver, Canada
[5] College of Computer Science and Software Engineering,
Shenzhen University, Shenzhen, China
[6] Department of Information Art and Design, Academy of Arts and Design, Tsinghua
University, Beijing, China

Abstract. Artificial intelligence (AI) is bringing new possibilities to numerous fields. There have been a lot of discussions about the development of AI technologies and the challenges caused by AI such as job replacement and ethical issues. However, it's far from enough to systematically discuss how to use AI creatively and how AI can enhance human creativity. After studying over 1,600 application cases across more than 45 areas, and analyzing related academic publications, we believe that focusing on the collaboration with AI will benefit us far more than dwelling on the competing against AI. "AI Creativity" is the concept we want to introduce here: the ability for human and AI to co-live and co-create by playing to each other's strengths to achieve more. AI is a complement to human intelligence, and it consolidates wisdom from all achievements of mankind, making collaboration across time and space possible. AI empowers us throughout the entire creative process, and makes creativity more accessible and more inclusive than ever. The corresponding Human-AI Co-Creation Model we proposed explains the creative process in the era of AI, with new possibilities brought by AI in each phase. In addition, this model allows any "meaning-making" action to be enhanced by AI and delivered in a more efficient way. The emphasis on collaboration is not only an echo to the importance of teamwork, but is also a push for co-creation between human and AI. The study of application cases shows that AI Creativity has been making significant impact in various fields, bringing new possibilities to human society and individuals, as well as new opportunities and challenges in technology, society and education.

Keywords: Creativity · Artificial intelligence · Design methods and techniques · Design process management · HCI theories and methods · Education

1 Introduction

In recent years, Artificial intelligence (AI) is bringing new possibilities to numerous fields from everyday life, industry application to scientific research. There have been a

© Springer Nature Switzerland AG 2021
M. Kurosu (Ed.): HCII 2021, LNCS 12762, pp. 171–190, 2021.
https://doi.org/10.1007/978-3-030-78462-1_13

lot of discussions about the development of AI technologies and the challenges caused by AI such as job replacement and ethical issues. However, it's far from enough to systematically discuss how to use AI creatively and how AI can enhance human creativity. After studying over 1,600 application cases across more than 45 areas, and analyzing related academic publications, we believe that focusing on the collaboration with AI will benefit us far more than dwelling on the competing against AI [1, 2]. Among the human dominant abilities, creativity is one of the most im-portant yet the least understood of all intellectual abilities until today. It is a popular topic yet remains underdiscussing. It is being refocused in the era of AI as the debate arose whether AI has creativity.

The purpose of this paper is to introduce the preliminary definition of "AI Creativity" and the corresponding Human-AI Co-Creation Model. AI Creativity refers to the ability for human and AI to co-live and co-create by playing to each other's strengths to achieve more. AI is a complement to human intelligence, and it consolidates wisdom from all achievements of mankind, making collaboration across time and space possible. AI empowers us throughout the entire creative process, and makes creativity more accessible and more inclusive than ever. The corresponding Human-AI Co-Creation Model we proposed explains the creative process in the era of AI, with new possibilities brought by AI in each phase. In addition, this model allows any "meaning-making" action to be enhanced by AI and delivered in a more efficient way. The emphasis on collaboration is not only an echo to the importance of teamwork, but is also a push for co-creation between human and AI.

By illustrating the application cases in various areas, this paper explains that AI Creativity is a new philosophy to collaborate with all achievements of mankind across time and space, a new strategy to boost productivity and to inspire innovation, and a new force to empower human to access creativity inclusively more than ever.

2 Related Work

2.1 The Rise of AI and Potential Impacts

The application of AI has already made significant impacts in businesses around the world. Between 34% and 44% of global companies surveyed are using AI in their IT departments mainly in information technology, marketing, finance and accounting, and customer service, monitoring huge volumes of machine-to-machine activities [3].

AI Industries is becoming the new engine of economic development. According to recent reports, the potential contribution of AI to the global economy will reach $15.7 trillion, bringing a GDP boost of up to 26% to local economies [4]. 29–62% of annual growth rate of GVA (gross value added) comes from AI by 2035 across 16 industries in 12 economies, which could lead to an economic boost of US$14 trillion [5].

In these circumstances, people are concerned that AI is on the verge of reaching and challenging "human-level intelligence," with recent evidences suggesting that workforce transitions from human to AI has been triggered. A report by McKinsey [6] says, "50% of the time spent on work activities in the global economy could theoretically be automated by adapting currently demonstrated technologies". The most quoted study of occupations likely to be automated in the next decade by Oxford University [7] also predicted up to 47% replacement of the workforce in US. A following study by Asian Development Bank

[8] concluded that routine, cognitive and manual work would be the most vulnerable, and the time spent on different activities which can be replaced ranges from 9% to 78%.

2.2 Collaboration Between Humans and AI

AI is relatively strong when it comes to repetitive and predictable workflow, and super good at dealing with complexity and multi-tasking; while humans are flexible and creative, and adept at knowledge understanding and strategic thinking, as is summarized in the figure below. Collaboration between humans and AI varies across domains [9, 10]. Human leads where tasks are more about creative or strategy and compassion is needed, while AI leads where tasks are more about routine or optimization and compassion is not needed (Fig. 1).

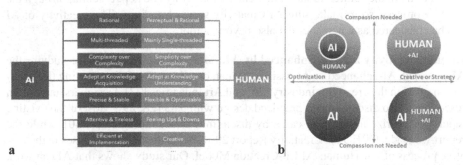

Fig. 1. (a) Human-AI complement each other, (b) Blueprint of Human-AI collaboration [10]

2.3 AI and Creativity

Creativity Research is Mainly About People, Methods and Tools Before the Era of AI. Creativity is often considered as an "intuition" and can't be easily interpreted in a rational way. The creative industries often refer to graphic design, film, music, video game, fashion, advertising, media, or entertainment industries [11], related to the extraordinary thinking by supreme creative individuals [12]. However, creativity actually lies in all creating activities, from art to science, from everyday life to industry production. And the thinking behind creativity and all those great creations can be acquired by ordinary people with deliberate practice [12]. Some recent studies summarized creativity as a "multifaceted phenomenon to form value and produce innovation entailing the generation of new intangible or physical item" [13, 14]. In discussing how to define, measure, and enhance the impact of creativity, scholars have proposed three dichotomies: firstly, whether creativity orginates within individual or comes from social; secondly, whether creative artifacts should be of novelty or value; and thirdly, whether creative activity is a thought or an action [15].

In recent decades, great progress has been made by an increasing number of scholars and researcher with different backgrounds, including cognitive science, psychology, philosophy, computer science, logic, mathematics, sociology, architecture, design and etc. The emerging concepts such as digital creativity [16] and computational creativity[1] [17] also shed some light on the concept of AI Creativity. With the new possibilities AI bringing in, the research on AI Creativity will help us use AI creatively and enhance human creativity efficiently and effectively.

The Creativity of AI is Inseparable from Human's. From AlphaGo to AlphaFold [18, 19], AI created something which have never existed before, although researchers still hold different viewpoints on whether AI has creativity [20–23]. Theories and algorithms were invented to imitate and go beyond human's ways of thinking, using the past achievements of mankind, such as internet data, as training data for AI. Furthermore, as lack of understanding causality of the real world, AI has to be designed for interactive use by humans and enhance human creativity [20, 24]. No matter how far AI can go on creativity in the future, human judgment should always be kept essential through the creative process, so to make sure AI Creativity serves humanity. The creativity of AI can be considered as a new tool but also beyond a tool.

Human Creativity is to be Enhanced by AI. More and more scholars are studying the AI-powered, AI-enhanced or AI-assisted human creativity [24, 25], reporting the application of AI in the creativity industry [26] and Art industries [27]. Designers and design researchers also discussed and practiced design with data [28, 29]. Most of the existing reports categorize application cases by disciplines or technologies [1, 30], while the report we made, CREO AI Creativity Report 2021, presents the typical cases in the creative process of our Human-AI Co-Creation Model. Our study shows that AI can work far more than a black box, but can assists humans throughout the entire creative process. Human input serves as the framework of this process.

2.4   The Study of Creativity

The Theories of Creativity. One major opinion in early creativity research argued whether creativity is "unconscious thinking" or "unconscious processing" [31, 32], a sudden appearance of an idea [33] or leaps of insight [34, 35]. These theories undoubtedly demonstrated the mysterious nature of creativity or the extraordinary thinking of some creative individuals, which makes ordinary people think that creativity is far away from them.

Measurement psychology suggested that every individual has creativity, with "divergent thinking" and "convergent thinking" involved [36]. Their study identified the main components in creative thinking, but lacked the analyzing of the functional mechanisms of creative process. Guilford [37] further construed creativity as a form of problem-solving and argues that the creator's sensitivity to the problem is the key to initiating creation. In the era of AI, various sensors and big data gives humans expanded views in both perceptual and rational perspectives.

---

[1] Computational creativity also known as artificial creativity, mechanical creativity, creative computing or creative computation.

Evolutionary theories of creativity [38] suggested that the creative process is similar to Darwinian evolution: Innovative ideas are generated based on early ones and tested with the latest conditions [35]. The Human-AI Co-Creation Model is consistent with this theory: Upon input, AI can generate a myriad of explorations and present the preliminary selections for humans to choose for further "evolving".

Cognitive theories of creativity believed that the processes of creative thinking and thinking involved in solving ordinary problems are basically the same [39], and creative products come through the process of ordinary thinking [12]. This view brings creativity and ordinary people closer together. With AI empowering in all phases of the creative process, people can access creativity inclusively more than ever.

In recent years, new theoretical frameworks proposed from the perspective of brain science have systematically elaborated the interaction between knowledge and creative thinking [40]. The studies of creative cognition through medical imaging have opened up new possibilities for the measurement of creativity [41]. It also provides valuable references for the development of AI.

The Methods of Creativity. These methods encourage creative actions and have demonstrated their usefulness in both arts and sciences [42], usually covering information acquisition, idea generation, problem reframing, prototyping, testing, iterating and etc. [43].

Some of them are for guiding the creative process, such as TRIZ [44] (and its modifications and derivatives such as SIT and USIT), CPS (Creative Problem Solving) [45], Design Thinking [46], Double Diamond Model [47], First Principles [48]. Others provide different thinking principles and toolkits, such as Six Thinking Hats [49], Herrmann Brain Dominance Instrument [50], Lateral Thinking, Brainstorming, Brainwriting, Think Outside the Box, SWOT Analysis, Thought Experience, and Five Ws. As internet technology advanced, new methods came in such as Data-Driven Design [28], HEART & GSM [51], Agile Development [52], Design Sprint [53].

Most of the methods listed above are in the context of problem solving. However, meaning making including painting and music composing, is not necessarily only about problem solving.

The Abilities of Creativity. Creativity tests summarized the abilities of creativity. Structure of Intellect theory (SOI) [54] by Guilford organizes intellectual abilities in three categories: operations, content and products. Operations dimension included six general intellectual processes. Built on SOI, Torrance Tests of Creative Thinking (TTCT) [55] involves simple tests of divergent thinking and other problem-solving skills. Several controversial creativity tests, such as Getzels and Jackson's exploration [56] and Wallach and Kogan's study [57] had significant impact in the research area (Table 1).

Future-oriented creativity requires people to learn and create in a constantly evolving technological landscape. ISTE (International Society for Technology in Education) provided a well-recognized standard for student to become a transformative learner [58]. AIK12 [59] provided a list of criteria of competencies for young people to have in the era of AI.

From the current study of creativity, some characteristics were found: The classical creativity theories have less discussion on the discovery strategies before the problem emerges. The existing creativity methods are mainly for problem solving or product innovation, but not for other meaning-making activities; Besides, these methods lay no emphasis on collaboration. The Human-AI Co-Creation Model we proposed introduces new possibilities brought by AI throughout the creative process, allows any "meaning-making" action to be enhanced by AI and delivered in a more efficient way, and emphasizes on collaboration no mater it's interpersonally or between hu-man and AI. This model also well supports the creativity abilities reflected in the ex-isting creativity assessment standards such as ISTE and aik12.

Table 1. Main process/components in current study of creativity

Theories/methods/abilities	Main process/components
Psychometrics	Divergent thinking, Convergent thinking
Evolutionary Theories	Randomness, Conditions, Selection
Cognitive Perspective	Remembering, Imagining, Planning, Deciding
Brain Research	Knowledge Domain: Emotional, Cognitive Processing Model: Deliberate, Spontaneous
TRIZ (ARIZ)	Abstraction, Solution, Concretization
CPS (Creative Problem Solving)	Clarify, Ideate, Develop, Implement
Design Thinking	Empathize, Define, Ideate, Prototype, Test
Double Diamond	Challenge, Discover, Define, Develop, Deliver, Outcome
First Principles Thinking	Identify problems and define assumptions, Breakdown the problem into its fundamental principles, Create new solutions based on the deductions of those principles
Six Thinking Hats	White Hat – Facts and Information. Red Hat – Feeling and Intuition. Black Hat – Caution and Problems. Yellow Hat – Benefits and Advantages. Blue Hat – Managing Thinking. Green Hat – Creativity and Solution.
The Whole Brain Thinking Model	Analytical Thinking, Structural Thinking, Relational Thinking, Experimental Thinking
Data-Driven Design	Goal, Problem/Opportunity Area, Hypothesis, Test, Result
HEART & GSM	Happiness, Engagement, Adoption, Retention, Task Success; Goals, Signals and Metrics
Agile Development	Requirements, Design, Development, Testing, Deployment, Review
Design Sprint	Map, Sketch, Decide, Prototype, Test
SOI's (Structure of Intelligence) Operations Dimension	Cognition, Memory recording, Memory retention, Divergent production, Convergent production, Evaluation
TTCT (Torrance Tests of Creative Thinking)	Fluency, Flexibility, Originality, Elaboration
5C Core Competences	Cultural Competence, Creativity, Collaboration, Critical Thinking, Communication
ISTE	Empowered learner, Digital citizen, Knowledge constructor, Innovative Designer, Computational Thinker, Creative communicator, Global Collaborator
Human-AI Co-Creation Model	Perceive, Think, Express, Collaborate, Build, Test

3   The "AI Creativity"

3.1   Preliminary Definition of AI Creativity

Combining the above points of view, we make our own preliminary definition: AI creativity is the ability for human and AI to live and create together by playing to each other's strengths. It is a new philosophy, a new strategy, and a new force.

AI Creativity can be perceived as a new philosophy. Through AI, people can collaborate with all achievements of mankind across time and space. It's well demonstrated in the making of Portrait of Edmond Belamy: the original algorithm by Americans, the implementation by Frenchmen, and the AI trained with 15,000 human paintings from between the 14th and 20th centuries.

AI Creativity can be conceived as a new strategy. Human and AI can play to each other's strengths and embrace more possibilities efficiently. Thus human and AI can complement each other throughout the entire creative process, boosting productivity and inspiring innovation.

AI Creativity can be regared as a new force. Empowered by AI, human can access creativity inclusively more than ever. AI creativity can lower the bar to enter an area and enable human to focus on the most creative part, leaving the complex or time-consuming tasks to AI.

3.2 AI Creativity Reshapes Creative Process

The "Human-AI Co-Creation Model" is a circular process model including 6 major phases: perceiving, thinking, expressing, collaborating, building and testing (Fig. 2).

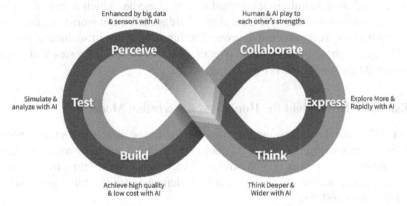

Fig. 2. The Human-AI co-creation model

The first phase is to persive, where human perception can be enhanced by big data and sensors with AI. Beyond the Senses that humans normally perceive the world with, AI can turn big data into meaningful information and knowledge using all kinds of sensors and networks, giving human expanded views in both perceptual and rational perspectives. The second phase is to think, where humans can think deeper and wider with AI. Inspiration and exploration that AI brings can go far more than human considerations. This will break the limits of resource and help human think deeper, wider, in a more thorough but also efficient way, potentially leading to unexpected accomplishments. The third phase is to express, where humans can explore more and rapidly with AI. Various ideas and diverse people need their optimal ways to present, such as painting, designing, composing, writing, performing, coding, prototyping… Empowered by AI tools, people won't be stopped for lack of talent or training. Creativity matters more than skills. The fourth phase is to collaborate, where human and AI play to each other's strengths. Whether working alone or with others, people can always team up with AI. Just fully understand the strengths and limitations of both human and AI, and give each side the best assignment. The fifth phase and the sixth are to build and test, where production can achieve higher quality and lower cost by simulating and analyzing with AI. Rehearsing gives people a chance to predict how things will go and to prepare ourselves for real-world events. With detailed simulation and calculation offered by AI, the process and result of building and testing can be handled effectively and efficiently. During this creative process, human and AI can complement each other and unleash the great potential of both sides.

4   The Application of "AI Creativity"

4.1   AI Creativity Prospering Across Industries

We analyzed over 1,600 AI Creativity cases across more than 45 areas from 2017 to 2020. An AI application is only qualified as an AI Creativity case when AI is used creatively or AI enhances human creativity. Culture and entertainment contributes the most cases until now, mainly in the format of digital media, which is easier to go with AI; Cases in industry and lifestyle are trying to bridge the virtual world and the physical world, which has a great potential to grow; The big percentage in science suggests that it's still the early phase of exploration overall; A lot more subcategories will rise from the misc. as AI moves forward (Fig. 3).

4.2   Examples Throughout the Human-AI Co-creation Model

Perceive. The sound of cellphone-recorded coughs can be used to detect asymptomatic Covid-19 infections (Fig. 4a). Only AI could achieve high accuracy and efficiency for this purpose because neither doctor can be effectively trained on this, nor can enough doctors be trained around the globe for this. It demonstrates the huge potential of AI assisted diagnosis [60, 61].

Sensors such as cameras, LiDAR and millimeter-wave radar on autonomous driving cars (Fig. 4b), do not only help humans get an all-direction and all-weather view, but also give humans smart advice based on object detection and analysis [62].

IoT connects machines, objects, animals and people in increasingly numerous ways (Fig. 4c). As each pig is recognized and traced, customized plans can be applied. Such a detailed overview enables humans to have a better understanding and greater control over their work and life [63].

Ambient Intelligence makes physical spaces sensitive and responsive to the presence of humans (Fig. 4d). It enables more efficient clinical workflows and improved patient safety in hospital spaces. It could also help the elderly with chronic diseases in daily living spaces [64].

Think. Predicting the protein structure, AlphaFold unlocked a greater understanding of what it does and how it works (Fig. 5a). From AlphaGo, AlphaStar to AlphaFold, AI demonstrated new methods and great potential to learn and solve complex problems effectively and efficiently through massive exploration [19].

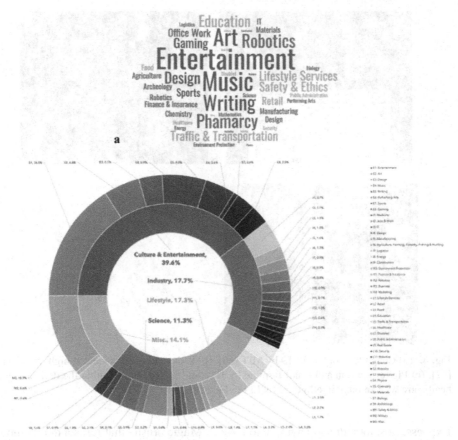

Fig. 3. AI creativity cases across industries: (**a**) By name of subcategories, (**b**) By number

Multi-Channel human-machine interaction allows humans to communicate with AI in a natural way [68], such as searching by color and shape (Fig. 5b). Making AI adapt to the human way, it brings not only comfort, but also efficiency [65].

Inspired by the knowledge graph based on the search queries on internet, people can get a better overview of the object studied and can trigger more relevant ideas around it (Fig. 5c). With the help of AI, the world's knowledge can be organized and accessed more than ever, and then further developed into new concepts [66].

Simulating a simple game of hide-and-seek, agents built a series of distinct strategies and counterstrategies, some of which were unexpected (Fig. 5d). This further suggests extremely complex and intelligent behaviors could be synthesized [67].

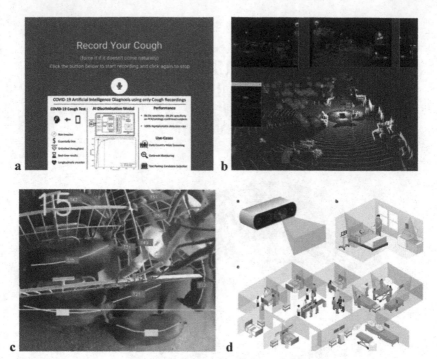

Fig. 4. (**a**) Cough test for Covid-19 by MIT [60]. (**b**) Lidar and camera view at night by Waymo [62]. (**c**) Pig recognition and smart farming by JD.com [63]. (**d**) Illuminating the dark spaces of healthcare with ambient intelligence by Li Fei-Fei et al. [64]

Express. It's not a dream anymore to have a "Magic brush" that turns a doodle into a photo. As if done by an experienced artist or designer, AI turns people's rough ideas into reality (Fig. 6a). AI helps humans focus more on generating and testing ideas without worrying about the presenting skills [69]. And DALL·E released in Jan 2021 is pushing this to the next level.

AI can work as a friend sharing ideas with humans, responding and inspiring each other to make a story gradually (Fig. 6b). From such a game today, we can foresee that the future of collaborative writing between human and AI is coming [70].

With the help of AI, humans can play any role in any context by controlling characters through body and face movements (Fig. 6c). The making of animations and demonstrations becomes easier [71].

Coding has a history of becoming easier to use, and AI will speed up this process (Fig. 6d). Although the making of high-quality software still requires experienced engineers, it will be world-changing to enable everyone to create their own software by talking, writing, drawing, playing with building blocks, not only by coding [72].

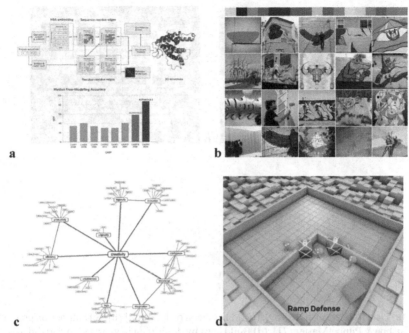

Fig. 5. (**a**) AlphaFold on protein folding problem by DeepMind [19]. (**b**) Street art by color by Google Arts & Culture [65]. (**c**) Knowledge graph of google searches by Anvaka [66]. (**d**) Simulation of multi-agent hide and seek by OpenAI [67]

Build and Test. In the context of product manufacturing, AI allows designers and engineers to input their design goals, along with parameters such as materials, manufacturing methods, and cost constraints (Fig. 7a). Then AI explores all the possible solutions by testing and iterating [73].

Qualitative changes can happen when quantitative changes are big enough. Personalization comes after. Alibaba Luban's design engine has demonstrated how powerful the true personalization is, as so does TikTok's recommendation engine (Fig. 7b). AI is the key to enable massive design and implementation efficiently at low cost [74].

A process that takes generations of evolution in the physical world can be simulated in the virtual world at much higher speeds. Through the design and making of Xenobots, biology and computer scientists worked together and significantly speeded up the process of trial and error (Fig. 7c) [75].

Digital Twin brings parallel universe to reality. Building and testing happens in the virtual world and the best solution can be chosen to implement in the physical world (Fig. 7d). Meanwhile, anything manifesting in the physical world can be reflected in the virtual world for further analysis and exploration [76].

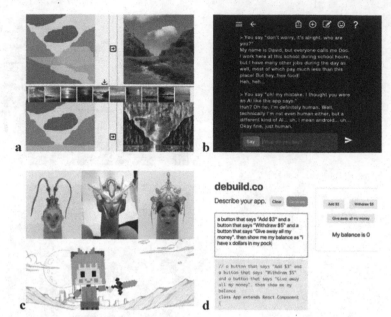

Fig. 6. (**a**) GauGAN by NVIDIA [69]. (**b**) AI Dungeon by Latitude [70]. (**c**) Animation production with Kuaishou & PuppetMaster [71]. (**d**) Build apps by describing in words with debuild, powered by GPT-3 [72]

Collaborate. We placed collaborating at the end instead of as its sequence in the model, because it's a great example demonstrating the creative process enhanced by AI. Art styles are among the great achievements of civilizations. It's almost impossible for a human to master every style of art, but it's not hard for AI (Fig. 8a). Trained with examples of various artistic styles, AI can imitate any one of them. Based on the variations developed upon the input, the best parts can be picked for further development[2].

Expressing in an ancient language is much harder than understanding it. However, given enough training materials, it's no different for AI to learn a modern language or an ancient one (Fig. 8b). Such a poetry AI can give human many inspirations, although it's not perfect, nor does it have a soul[3].

---

[2] The painting by Mr. HOW with Deep Dream Generator: https://deepdreamgenerator.com/.

[3] The poem Mr. HOW with Tsinghua JiuGe: http://118.190.162.99:8080/, Microsoft JueJu: http://couplet.msra.cn/jueju/ and SouYun: https://sou-yun.cn/MAnalyzePoem.aspx.

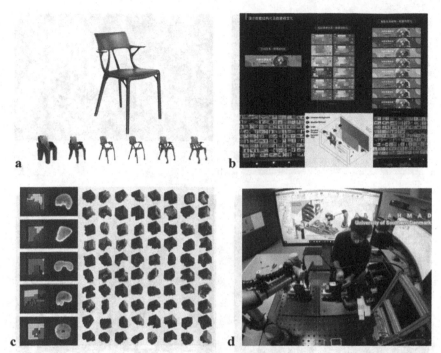

Fig. 7. (a) "The first chair created with AI" by Philippe Starck, Autodesk & Kartell [73]. **(b)** Alibaba Luban's AI banner design [74]. **(c)** Xenobots: first living robots by University of Vermont [75]. **(d)** Collaborative robots in assembly by University of Southern Denmark [76]

Breaking language barriers, AI helps regular people to enjoy different cultures and create things more easily (Fig. 8c) [77]. In this case, the poem in ancient Chinese was firstly translated into modern Chinese by human, then into English by AI, and then fine-tuned by human in the end[4].

Not everyone can make music although it's a universal language (Fig. 8d). Music AI allows people to bring out the rhythm and rhyme from their heart and mind. Based on the initial input, variations will be generated for picking for further developing[5].

As the ending of a traditional Chinese painting, a stamp was used, which is actually a QR code linked to the video of the making of this artwork[6].

---

[4] The poem translated by Mr. HOW with Google, Apple and Microsoft Translation.

[5] The music by Mr. HOW with LingDongYin: https://demo.lazycomposer.com/compose/v2/.

[6] The making of the artwork, The Mind of AI Creativity: http://qr09.cn/Ew06EW.

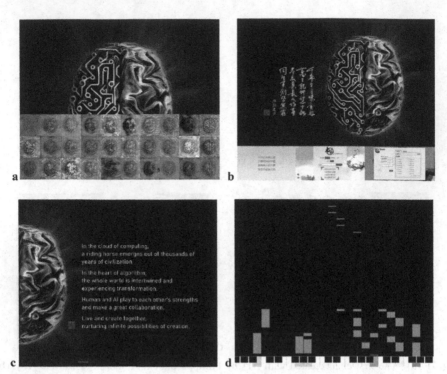

Fig. 8. The mind of AI creativity (**a**) Painting, (**b**) Poem in Chinese, (**c**) Poem in English, (**d**) Music composing

5　The Future of AI Creativity

5.1　Developing AI Creativity

The adoption of AI is expected to run high across industries, company sizes and geography [78]. Skills of using AI as a demand in all online job vacancies have been rapidly increasing especially since 2015 [79]. AI talents include technology developers, technology-product transformers [80], and product utilizers. All of them need AI Creativity, mastering AI thinking and skills. Regardless of interests or specialties, people can always find effective ways to develop their AI Creativity.

Collaborative creation between human and AI will be seen everywhere. Processes are enhanced or even evolved in every step where AI enters. STEM-DAL [81] is a new way to inspire and leverage AI Creativity in cross-disciplinary learning and creation. Science and Art stand at the two ends. Technology brings Science into application, while Design brings Art into application. Meanwhile, Engineering merges Technology and Design, while Mathematics and Literature serve as foundations (Fig. 9).

In recent years, some educational initiatives have proposed some new concepts and practices for AI education in addition to coding, such as AI4ALL [82], aik12-MIT [59] and Mr. HOW AI Creativity Academy [81]. These initiatives are trying to make AI education inclusively accessible for all people with different interests and specialties, beyond technology perspectives only. Great potential remains yet to be unleashed.

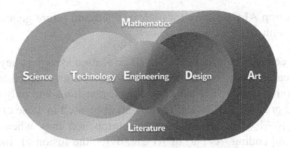

Fig. 9. The STEM-DAL model

5.2 Challenges and Opportunities

Technology Perspective. Pre-Mature AI technologies are still the norm, although there has been a huge leap since the modern era of deep learning began at the 2012 ImageNet competition. Scientists are working hard on the next generation of AI to break today's constrains. New initiatives such as GPT-3 aren't perfect, but it did unleash new potentials.

Incomplete solutions built on separate technologies according to proprietary standards are very common. Doing anything with AI often relies heavily on experts and well-funded organizations. This stands in the way of more people adopting AI technologies and unleash the great potential of AI Creativity.

Limited Resources invested in the industry today are mainly driven by capital for to maximize financial returns. As more scientists, engineers and other resources are added to transform AI technologies into more products, more areas will be covered and driven by AI Creativity.

Attacks on AI raises the alert of AI security. A simple attack can cause AI to see something different than what an image really looks like, so a T-shirt with a special pattern can render someone "invisible" to cameras, or an autonomous car misread an altered traffic sign. Addressing the security issue also needs AI Creativity.

Society Perspective. Privacy could become very vulnerable in the era of AI. Individuals could become transparent to all kinds of ubiquitous sensors and AI applications with recognition and analysis abilities. It's not always easy to balance privacy with convenience. AI Creativity may help to make smart decisions.

Abuse of AI has been documented, such as unwanted facial recognition, spam calls, deepfake videos, etc. Anyone of those could set you in trouble. As more people access more AI applications, potential for abuse will increase. AI Creativity can contribute in preventing this.

Discrimination follows from human behaviors, as AI is trained with materials that humans generated. As a technical issue, things like accuracy of facial recognition across different human races can be easily improved. However, things like the bias in resume screening may need a lot of AI Creativity to address.

Job Replacement is a hot topic, especially for parents. However, many parents wouldn't necessarily want their children to do the jobs AI is going to replace. Rather than worrying about potential job replacement, it's more important to think about how to inspire and develop AI Creativity for both yourself and future generations, and how to live and create with AI.

Education Perspective. Exploration in the AI education system is key for developing talents. What to learn, how to train, whether AI should be an independent discipline or intertwined with other ones… The answers to these questions will only emerge through deep thinking and practice. AI Creativity itself shall be used in these explorations.

Liberal Arts + AI education is almost an untouched area, when compared with STEM, robotics and coding. As part of AI Creativity, the fusion of liberal arts and AI will be critical. It's not only to give all kids a balanced education in addition to STEM learning, but also to provide a method of development for kids who do not have an aptitude for STEM.

Thinking vs Skills are both important things to learn for AI Creativity. AI thinking is for choosing the right strategy, while skills are for choosing the right tactics. They support each other and can't live without each other.

Democratizing AI and Creativity will be a key outcome of AI Creativity education. People will be empowered to go beyond their current level, to live and create with AI by playing to each other's strengths.

6 Conclusion

AI Creativity has been making significant impact in various fields, bringing new possibilities and challenges to human society and individuals. The topic of cultivating AI Creativity has a great value and potential to be explored. For professionals, the evolved thinkings and methods need to be built up, such as the Human-AI Co-Creation Model we proposed; For educators, the inclusive AI education system needs to be built up, such as the STEM-DAL system we proposed, which will be discussed in another paper; For scholars, the framework of measuring AI Creativity needs to be built up. For everyone, how to unleash the great potential of AI Creativity and how to prevent the unexpected consequences need to be discussed. We initiated CREO (Creativity Renaissance in Education and Organizations) with experts around the world, and will keep pushing the boundary of AI Creativity.

Acknowledgements. The authors like to thank Qinwen Chen, Guojie Qi, Peiqi Su, Qing Sheng, Jieqiong Li, Qianqiu Qiu, Linda Li and all the volunteers for their contribution in this paper.

References

1. Mueller, S.T., Hoffman, R.R., Clancey, W., Emrey, A., Klein, G.: Explanation in Human-AI Systems: a Literature Meta-Review, Synopsis of Key Ideas and Publications, and Bibliography for Explainable AI (2019)
2. Peeters, M.M.M., van Diggelen, J., van den Bosch, K., et al.: Hybrid collective intelligence in a human-AI society. AI Soc. **36**, 217–238 (2021). https://link.springer.com/article/10.1007/s00146-020-01005-y

3. Tata Consultancy Services: How Companies are Improving Performance using Artificial Intelligence (2017)
4. PwC: Sizing the prize. What's the real value of AI for your business and What's the real value of AI for your business and how can you capitalise? (2017)
5. Accenture: How AI Boosts Industry Profits and Innovation (2017)
6. McKinsey Global Institute: Jobs Lost, Jobs Gained. Workforce Transitions in A Time of Automation (2017)
7. Frey, C.B., Osborne, M.A.: The Future of Employment. How Susceptible Are Jobs to Computerisation (2013)
8. Asian Development Bank: Asian Development Outlook. Asian Development Bank, Manila, Philippines (2018)
9. Amershi, S., et al.: Guidelines for human-AI interaction. In: CHI 2019 Proceedings of the 2019 CHI Conference on Human Factors in Computing Systems, Glasgow, Scotland UK, 4–9 May, 2019. ACM, New York (2019)
10. Lee, K.F.: How AI can save our humanity. https://www.ted.com/talks/kai_fu_lee_how_ai_can_save_our_humanity
11. Howkins, J.: The Creative Economy: How People Make Money from Ideas. Penguin, UK (2002)
12. Weisberg, R.W.: Creativity: Understanding Innovation in Problem Solving, Science, Invention, and the Arts. John Wiley (2006)
13. Palmiero, M., Piccardi, L., Nori, R., Palermo, L., Salvi, C., Guariglia, C.: Editorial: creativity: education and rehabilitation. Front. Psychol. **10**, 1500 (2019)
14. Wikipedia: Creativity. https://en.wikipedia.org/w/index.php?title=Creativity&oldid=999304631
15. Kaufman, J.C., Sternberg, R.J. (eds.): The Cambridge Handbook of Creativity. Cambridge University Press, Cambridge (2019)
16. Owen Kelly: Digital creativity (1996)
17. Colton, S., Wiggins, G.A.: Others: computational creativity: the final frontier? ECAI **12**, 21–26 (2012)
18. OpenAI: AlphaFold : a solution to a 50-year-old grand challenge in biology. https://deepmind.com/blog (2020)
19. Deepmind: AlphaFold: a solution to a 50-year-old grand challenge in biology. https://deepmind.com/blog/article/alphafold-a-solution-to-a-50-year-old-grand-challenge-in-biology
20. Boden, M.A.: Creativity and artificial intelligence. Artif. Intell. **103**, 347–356 (1998)
21. Erden, Y.J.: Could a created being ever be creative? Some philosophical remarks on creativity and AI development. Minds Mach. **20**, 349–362 (2010)
22. Fetzer, J.H., Dartnall, T.: Artificial Intelligence and Creativity. An Interdisciplinary Approach. Springer Netherlands, Dordrecht (2010).
23. Dartnall, T. (ed.): Artificial Intelligence and Creativity. An Interdisciplinary Approach. Springer Netherlands, Dordrecht (1994)
24. Miller, A.I.: The Artist in the Machine. The World of AI-Powered Creativity. The MIT Press, Cambridge, Massachusetts (2019)
25. Fischer, G., Nakakoji, K.: Amplifying designers' creativity with domain-oriented design environments. In: Dartnall, T. (ed.) Artificial Intelligence and Creativity. An Interdisciplinary Approach, pp. 343–364. Springer Netherlands, Dordrecht (1994)
26. Anantrasirichai, N., Bull, D.: Artificial Intelligence in the Creative Industries: A Review (2020)
27. Chen, W., Shidujaman, M., Tang, X.: AiArt: Towards Artificial Intelligence Art (2020)
28. King, R., Churchill, E.F., Tan, C.: Designing with Data: Improving the User Experience with A/B Testing. O'Reilly Media, Incorporated (2017)

29. Graham Michael Dove: CoDesign with data (2015)
30. JSAI AI Map task force: AI Map Beta (English), 6 June 2019
31. Poincaré, H.: The Foundations of Science (GH Halstead, Trans.). Science , New York (1913)
32. Miller, A.I.: Insights of Genius: Imagery and Creativity in Science and Art. Springer Science & Business Media (2012)
33. Wertheimer, M.: Max Wertheimer Productive Thinking. Springer (2020). https://doi.org/10.1007/978-3-030-36063-4
34. Csikszentmihalyi, M.: Flow and the Psychology of Discovery and Invention, vol. 39. HarperPerennial, New York (1997)
35. Simonton, D.K.: Origins of Genius: Darwinian Perspectives on Creativity. Oxford University Press (1999)
36. Mumford, M.D.: Something old, something new: revisiting Guilford's conception of creative problem solving. Creat. Res. J. **13**, 267–276 (2001)
37. Guilford, J.P.: Varieties of creative giftedness, their measurement and development. Gifted Child Q. **19**, 107–121 (1975)
38. Campbell, D.T.: Blind variation and selective retentions in creative thought as in other knowledge processes. Psychol. Rev. **67**, 380 (1960)
39. Newell, A., Shaw, J.C., Simon, H.A.: The processes of creative thinking. In: Contemporary Approaches to Creative Thinking, 1958, University of Colorado, CO, US; This paper was presented at the aforementioned symposium (1962)
40. Dietrich, A.: The cognitive neuroscience of creativity. Psychon. Bull. Rev. **11**, 1011–1026 (2004)
41. Arden, R., Chavez, R.S., Grazioplene, R., Jung, R.E.: Neuroimaging creativity: a psychometric view. Behav. Brain Res. **214**, 143–156 (2010)
42. Chen, W., Shidujaman, M., Jin, J., Ahmed, S.U.: A methodological approach to create interactive art in artificial intelligence. In: Stephanidis, C., et al. (eds.) HCII 2020. LNCS, vol. 12425, pp. 13–31. Springer, Cham (2020). https://doi.org/10.1007/978-3-030-60128-7_2
43. Wikipedia: Creativity techniques. https://en.wikipedia.org/w/index.php?title=Creativity_techniques&oldid=996672803
44. Al'tshuller, G.S.: The Innovation Algorithm: TRIZ, Systematic Innovation and Technical Creativity. Technical innovation center, Inc. (1999)
45. Creative Education Foundation: The CPS Process. https://www.creativeeducationfoundation.org/creative-problem-solving/the-cps-process/
46. Brown, T.: Others: design thinking. Harv. Bus. Rev. **86**, 84 (2008)
47. Design Council: What is the framework for innovation? Design Council's evolved Double Diamond. https://www.designcouncil.org.uk/news-opinion/what-framework-innovation-design-councils-evolved-double-diamond
48. Merrill, M.D.: First principles of instruction. Educ. Tech. Res. Dev. **50**, 43–59 (2002)
49. de Bono, E.: Six Thinking Hats. Penguin,s UK (2017)
50. Herrmann: HBDI (Herrmann Brain Dominance Instrument)® Assessment I Herrmann. https://www.thinkherrmann.com/hbdi
51. Rodden, K., Hutchinson, H., Fu, X.: Measuring the user experience on a large scale: user-centered metrics for web applications. In: Proceedings of the SIGCHI Conference on Human Factors in Computing Systems, pp. 2395–2398 (2010)
52. Abrahamsson, P., Salo, O., Ronkainen, J., Warsta, J.: Agile Software Development Methods: Review and Analysis (2017)
53. Banfield, R., Lombardo, C.T., Wax, T.: Design Sprint. A Practical Guidebook for Building Great Digital Products. O'Reilly Media, Ind, Sebastopol (2016)
54. Guilford, J.P.: The structure of intellect. Psychol. Bull. **53**, 267 (1956)
55. Torrance, E.R.: The torrance tests of creative thinking. Norms-technical mannual (1990)

56. Getzels, J.W., Jackson, P.W.: Creativity and intelligence: explorations with gifted students. AAUP Bull. **48**, 186 (1962)
57. Wallach, M.A., Kogan, N.: Modes of Thinking in Young Children: A Study of the Creativity-Intelligence Distinction. Holt Rinehart and Winston (1965)
58. ISTE: ISTE Standards for Students. https://www.iste.org/standards/for-students
59. k12 AI Education MIT: aik12-MIT. https://aieducation.mit.edu/
60. MIT: MIT Covid-19 Initiative. https://opensigma.mit.edu/
61. Laguarta, J., Hueto, F., Subirana, B.: COVID-19 artificial intelligence diagnosis using only cough recordings. IEEE Open J. Eng. Med. Biol. **1**, 275–281 (2020). https://doi.org/10.1109/OJEMB.2020.3026928
62. Waymo: Waymo Open Dataset: Sharing our self-driving data for research. https://blog.waymo.com/2019/08/waymo-open-dataset-sharing-our-self.html
63. JD.com: Pig Facial Recognition – YouTube. https://www.youtube.com/watch?v=BECDKKYi-48
64. Johnson, J., Alahi, A., Fei-Fei, L.: Perceptual losses for real-time style transfer and super-resolution. In: Leibe, B., Matas, J., Sebe, N., Welling, M. (eds.) ECCV 2016. LNCS, vol. 9906, pp. 694–711. Springer, Cham (2016). https://doi.org/10.1007/978-3-319-46475-6_43
65. Google Arts & Culture: Color Explorer: Street Art - Google Arts & Culture. https://artsandculture.google.com/color?project=street-art&col=RGB_1BE5E1
66. Kashcha, A.: Autocomplete VS graph. https://anvaka.github.io/vs/?query=creativity
67. Baker, B.: Emergent Tool Use from Multi-Agent Interaction. OpenAI (2019)
68. Shidujaman, M., Zhang, S., Elder, R., Mi, H.: "RoboQuin": a mannequin robot with natural humanoid movements. In: 2018 27th IEEE International Symposium on Robot and Human Interactive Communication (RO-MAN), pp. 1051–1056 (2018)
69. Park, T., Liu, M.-Y., Wang, T.-C., Zhu, J.-Y.: Semantic image synthesis with spatially-adaptive normalization. In: Proceedings of the IEEE/CVF Conference on Computer Vision and Pattern Recognition, pp. 2337–2346 (2019)
70. Latitude: AI Dungeon. https://play.aidungeon.io/
71. Mr. HOW: Animation with Facial Recognition & Motion Capture on Mobile Phone. https://v.kuaishou.com/7reyAJ
72. Debuild: Build web apps lightning fast. https://debuild.co/
73. STARCK Site web officiel: A.I. - Introducing The First Chair Created With Artificial Intelligence. https://www.starck.com/a-i-introducing-the-first-chair-created-with-artificial-intelligence-p3801
74. Alibaba Cloud Community: The Evolution of Luban in Designing One Billion Images. https://www.alibabacloud.com/blog/the-evolution-of-luban-in-designing-one-billion-images_596118
75. University of Vermont: Team Builds the First Living Robots. https://www.uvm.edu/uvmnews/news/team-builds-first-living-robots
76. University of Southern Denmark: Collaborative Robots in Assembly: A Digital-Twin Approach. https://www.youtube.com/watch?v=lWHT3_B2spg
77. Shidujaman, M., Mi, H.: "which country are you from?" A cross-cultural study on greeting interaction design for social robots. In: International Conference on Cross-Cultural Design, pp. 362–374 (2018)
78. Ransbotham, S., Kiron, D., Gerbert, P., Reeves, M.: Reshaping Business with Artificial Intelligence. Closing the Gap Between Ambition and Action (2017)
79. Alekseeva, L., Azar, J., Gine, M., Samila, S., Taska, B.: The demand for AI skills in the labour market. https://voxeu.org/article/demand-ai-skills-labour-market

80. Wang, K.-J., Shidujaman, M., Zheng, C.Y., Thakur, P.: HRIpreneur thinking: strategies towards faster innovation and commercialization of academic HRI research. In: 2019 IEEE International Conference on Advanced Robotics and its Social Impacts (ARSO), pp. 219–226 (2019)
81. Mr. HOW AI Creativity Academy: Inspire Kids to Live and Create with AI by Playing to Each Other's Strength. http://qr09.cn/CVUI2H
82. AI4ALL: AI4ALL Annual Report 2019 (2019)

Two-Way Human-Agent Trust Relationships in Adaptive Cognitive Agent, Adaptive Tasking Scenarios: Literature Metadata Analysis

Daniel Kennedy[✉] and Maartje Hidalgo[✉]

Institute for Simulation and Training, University of Central Florida, Orlando, FL, USA
{dkennedy,mhidalgo}@ist.ucf.edu

Abstract. Rapid development of autonomous systems, that act independently and are deeply integrated with humans, necessitates trust-based cooperation and collaboration between these agents and the humans they interact with. A greater understanding of two-way trust between humans and artificial agents is a topic of interest for situations when the human makes mistakes or an anomalous situation such as an enemy combatant taking control of friendly AI. The purpose of this paper is to review the state-of-the-art regarding two-way trust research in Human-Adaptive Agent teams. A systematic review of academic and technical literature from the last ten years (2010–2020) was performed to collect metadata for analysis and discussion. Details of the literature review to include search databases, search terms, and inclusion-exclusion filtering is provided. A metadata analysis is discussed comparing measurements of human trust and agent trust; adaptive-scenario and adaptive-agent mechanisms; type of collaborative human-agent tasking; and level of automation and embodiment of the agent.

Keywords: Adaptive agent · Adaptive tasking · Mutual trust

1 Introduction

The use of artificial intelligence (AI) is growing rapidly, becoming more integrated with our daily lives. AI started as simple automation and has become more and more autonomous, able to make decisions and given the agency to act on those decisions [1, 2]. As AI has evolved, it has also become more pervasive with humans increasingly relying on it. AI has become a critical asset for the military with unmanned vehicles (UVs), and human-robot teaming is poised to be an important element in the future of warfare [3]. Outside of the military, AI is becoming ever more present as intelligent personal assistants [4], learning thermostats [5], and automotive driver assistants [6]. The rise of human and AI collaboration [2] has led to levels of performance greater than human and AI alone [7], but what are the risks?

A warning and call to action was provided by Hancock [8] that humans need to stay in the loop and retain control of autonomous systems. There are times when automation must react without human consent in an emergency [9], but what if it makes the wrong

© Springer Nature Switzerland AG 2021
M. Kurosu (Ed.): HCII 2021, LNCS 12762, pp. 191–205, 2021.
https://doi.org/10.1007/978-3-030-78462-1_14

decision? As humans and AI are working together, it is important for the human to appropriately trust and distrust the AI's recommendations or decision logic to make an effective team. Research has shown that once the AI's performance drops below approximately 70%, using the AI results in worse performance than not having it at all [10]. A poor performing AI team member can lead to the human distrusting the agent in such a way that he or she could abandon it all together. However, what about situations when the human makes mistakes, or the wrong human takes control of the AI, such as an enemy combatant? It is also important for the AI to know when to trust the human, illuminating the importance of two-way trust.

As agents increasingly integrate into human lives [11], two-way trust calibration becomes a topic of interest. In this paper, we use the terms artificial intelligence and agent interchangeably. As will be discussed, a plethora of research exists of human trust in the agent. However, little research has been done into AI trust of the human. With vast technological improvements and in accordance with Hancock's [8] warning, scientists need to stay ahead of these developments and aim for a greater understanding of two-way trust between humans and artificial agents. In this paper, we review the literature for insights to how dynamics have been explored for mutual trust within human-adaptive agent teams in changing environments.

1.1 Agent Capabilities

Two entities are involved in two-way trust: the artificial agent and the human that work together. Human-agent teams "are formed by one or more humans and intelligent agents that collaborate in a joint activity with a shared goal in mind" [12] (p. 3). Here, collaboration is intelligent in nature [13]. In this context, AI agents are intelligent, autonomous, and adaptive [12].

Intelligent agents are rational, use built-in knowledge, sense their environment, and perform actions that maximize their performance measure [14]. This definition shows that agents are no longer mere automated systems. Agents are becoming increasingly autonomous. From Hancock [8], automation can be defined as a system "designed to accomplish a specific set of largely deterministic steps, most often in a repeating pattern, in order to achieve one of an envisaged and limited set of pre-defined outcomes" (p. 284); autonomy or autonomous systems "are generative and learn, evolve and permanently change their functional capacities as a result of the input of operational and contextual information. Their actions necessarily become more indeterminate across time" (p. 284).

Automation and autonomous systems can either be embodied, such as a UAV, or disembodied, such as a grammar recommendation engine [15, 16]. If an AI agent is intelligent and autonomous, it follows that the AI agent can also either be embodied or disembodied. Autonomous systems may have varying levels of autonomy, authority, adaptiveness, and adaptability. Levels of autonomy are based on how much assistance the autonomous system needs from a human or how much self-governance it is afforded by the human [17–19].

An agent is adaptive if it can dynamically change in level of automation in response to changing situational demands [20]. This definition can be further clarified into adaptable vs. adaptive automation. Adaptable automation changes level of automation based on the human operator's control, whereas adaptive automation can change level of automation by itself as well as by operator control [21]. The adaptation could be in the form of changing control laws, control interfaces, goals, or internal simulations [18]. These internal changes may manifest in improving data classification ability, reinforcement learning using goal driven behavior, improved recommendations, or improved context awareness.

In the natural environment, the actors adapt autonomously to changing internal or external conditions. Thus, the AI is assumed to be placed in a context or scenario that is changing, mirroring the natural environment. For this paper, a scenario is defined as the combined environment and tasking associated with human-agent collaboration. An adaptive scenario is therefore an environment or tasking that can change in a dynamic way during the collaboration event. Examples of adaptive scenarios could be spontaneous "pop-up" threats in a military exercise, an unexpected change in road conditions during autonomous navigation, or a change in mission objectives. For the adaptive scenario, the scenario may change due to either intentional or unintentional human or agent control.

1.2 Importance of Trust

As mentioned, two-way trust is here situated in a human-agent collaboration or team effort. Like human-human teams, human-agent teams are only as good as its constituents [12] and their ability to appropriately rely on each other. Working in teams can improve performance in many situations where many actors or many disparate skills are needed. Moreover, human-agent collaboration is by design viewed from the human perspective, as the agent is developed to augment the human or team's performance [22, 23]. Whether the human collaborates with a human or an agent, teaming principles are assumed to function similarly for the human, since the agent is developed with the human in mind [24–26]. As such, theoretical constructs from human-human teaming could be applied (and tested) in human-agent teaming.

Salas et al. [27] identified core components and coordinating mechanisms in effective human-human teamwork. The five core components are: team leadership, mutual performance monitoring, backup behavior, adaptability, and team orientation. The core components are maintained by three coordinating mechanisms: shared mental models, closed-loop communication, mutual trust. Closed-loop communication involves one entity communicating, another receiving and acknowledging the communication, and then the first verifying that the original communication was understood [27]. Closed-loop communication has been shown to be beneficial in human-agent teaming [24, 28]. Mutual trust opens the door for team members to be more willing to share information, facilitating mutual performance monitoring and backup behaviors. Moreover, mutual trust affects how willing team members are to participate and contribute [27].

Many definitions of trust exist. Mayer et al. [29] summarizes trust as "a willingness to be vulnerable to another party (i.e., to trust), but there is no risk involved with holding such an attitude" (p. 724). Feitosa et al.[30] defines team trust as "an emergent and dynamic shared state at the team level whereby team members believe in one another's competence and are willing to be vulnerable beyond task related issues" (p. 480). This definition is similar to the construct of trust in human-agent teaming [31]. Hancock et al. [32] found three factors that are important of human trust in an agent: human related factors (ability-based and characteristics), robot related factors (performance-based and attribute-based), and environment related factors (team collaboration and task-based). Within these three factors, the meta-analysis showed that the most important factor for human trust is robot performance and attributes.

However, human trust is not a mere all-or-nothing construct. Trust is a process [33]. Human relationships lead to a network of varying degrees of trust and distrust [34]. In human-agent teaming, a lot of work has been done to understand the process of trust repair [35], which can be defined as a return to a positive trust state and willingness to be vulnerable after a trust transgression [36, 37]. Furthermore, it is not merely on a relationship level important that the human appropriately trusts the agent. On a functional level, the human also needs to maintain supervisory control [8] and not inappropriately neglect [32] or over-rely on an agent that may be unreliable [31]. This notion refers to trust calibration, the matching "between the perceived and the actual system performance and capabilities" [38]. Research has shown that the degree of humanness of an agent affects human trust and the human-agent team performance [39].

For an adaptive agent that is responsive to human feedback, how responsive should it be? Mutual transparency is important for human-agent communication [22]. Human team member's consistent transparency in actions, motivations, and feedback, could lead to emergent agent-based trust in the human. Historical transparency might be leveraged by an adaptive agent to provide greater weight to adaptation functions resulting in more efficient adaptation or learning. Conversely, behaviors and feedback signals from some human team members could be interpreted as more ambiguous or noisy if this trust has not been established, necessitating a more cautious adaptation approach. For an embodied agent that must have safe close-quarters collaboration with human team members, this agent-based trust might allow fewer resources to be spent monitoring for human safety so that more resources can be devoted to task performance, anticipation of team member needs, or analyzing unexpected events and ambiguous situations.

There may one day be a case where an adaptive intelligent agent is best suited to be a team leader, not just team member. This might be driven by the need for large scale data analysis and integration for coordinating and prioritizing tasking, detecting inefficiencies and adjusting workload, or managing dependencies that are too complex for humans to fully reason about or too complicated for humans to manage efficiently. Salas et al. [27] identified team leadership as one of the "Big Five" components of teamwork and argued that trust is important for acceptance of team leadership to support effective team performance. It follows that not only would the human team members need to trust the intelligent agent team leader, but this leader must also trust the human team members to make an effective team.

With human-agent teaming flourishing in this Fourth Industrial Revolution [11], important questions remain to be answered. The question to be answered in this paper is: what is the state-of-the-art regarding two-way trust research in Human-Agent teams? Specifically, to promote future research, we are interested in identifying measurements of human trust and agent trust; adaptive-scenario and adaptive-agent mechanisms; type of collaborative human-agent tasking; and level of automation and embodiment of the agent.

2 Method

Academic and technical literature was systematically reviewed to collect metadata for analysis. Information sources included literature from academic journals and conferences as well as technical reports published within the last ten years (2010–2020). Literature was collected from search databases to include: Springer Link, Sage Publishing, Engineering Village, Web of Science, EBSCOhost, IEEE Xplore, ACM Digital Library, and Science Direct. Search terms were selected based on review of a scoping set of articles covering Human-Agent Trust, Cognitive Agents, Adaptive Agents, and Team Performance. An initial search was performed using the terms of Table 1 in the form of a Boolean equation.

Table 1. Initial search terms.

Search term group	Search terms
Trust terms	"Trust", "Reliability"
Task terms	"Adaptive Task", "Adaptive Scenario", "Adaptive Goal", "Changing Task", "Changing Scenario", "Changing Goal"
Adaptation terms	"Learning", "Adaptive", "Cognitive", "Intelligent", "Autonomous"
Agent terms	"Agent", "Robot", "Automation"

After collecting references from the initial search, a second search was performed to expand the search pool with autonomy related terms from Table 2.

Table 2. Additional search terms.

Search term group	Search terms
Trust terms	"Trust", "Reliability"
Task terms	"Adaptive Task", "Adaptive Scenario", "Adaptive Goal", "Changing Task", "Changing Scenario", "Changing Goal"
Autonomy terms	"Autonomy", "Autonomous System", "Adaptive Autonomy", "Adjustable Autonomy"
Agent terms	"Agent", "Robot"

The search engines had different limitations on Boolean operators allowed in the search phrase. The most limiting search engine was used as a basis for breaking the search into ten unique search strings that provided complete coverage of the terms while maintaining the correct AND-OR Boolean relationships (eight strings in initial search, two strings in second search). Table 3 lists the search strings that were used on all search engines with the exception of Web of Science, where the trust terms were removed due to lack of results.

Table 3. Search strings.

("Learning automation" OR "Adaptive automation" OR "Cognitive automation" OR "Intelligent automation") AND ("adaptive task" OR "adaptive scenario" OR "adaptive goal") AND (trust OR reliability)
("Learning agent" OR "Adaptive agent" OR "Cognitive agent" OR "Intelligent agent") AND ("adaptive task" OR "adaptive scenario" OR "adaptive goal") AND (trust OR reliability)
("Learning robot" OR "Adaptive robot" OR "Cognitive robot" OR "Intelligent robot") AND ("adaptive task" OR "adaptive scenario" OR "adaptive goal") AND (trust OR reliability)
("Autonomous automation" OR "Autonomous agent" OR "Autonomous robot") AND ("adaptive task" OR "adaptive scenario" OR "adaptive goal") AND (trust OR reliability)
("Learning automation" OR "Adaptive automation" OR "Cognitive automation" OR "Intelligent automation") AND ("changing task" OR "changing scenario" OR "changing goal") AND (trust OR reliability)
("Learning agent" OR "Adaptive agent" OR "Cognitive agent" OR "Intelligent agent") AND ("changing task" OR "changing scenario" OR "changing goal") AND (trust OR reliability)
("Learning robot" OR "Adaptive robot" OR "Cognitive robot" OR "Intelligent robot") AND ("changing task" OR "changing scenario" OR "changing goal") AND (trust OR reliability)
("Autonomous automation" OR "Autonomous agent" OR "Autonomous robot") AND ("changing task" OR "changing scenario" OR "changing goal") AND (trust OR reliability)
("autonomy" OR "autonomous system" OR "adaptive autonomy" OR "adjustable autonomy") AND ("agent" OR "robot") AND ("changing task" OR "changing scenario" OR "changing goal") AND (trust OR reliability)
("autonomy" OR "autonomous system" OR "adaptive autonomy" OR "adjustable autonomy") AND ("agent" OR "robot") AND ("adaptive task" OR "adaptive scenario" OR "adaptive goal") AND (trust OR reliability)
("Learning automation" OR "Adaptive automation" OR "Cognitive automation" OR "Intelligent automation") AND ("adaptive task" OR "adaptive scenario" OR "adaptive goal") AND (trust OR reliability)

To qualify for inclusion in the reference set, references must discuss experimental results measuring human trust of an autonomous agent collaborator and/or autonomous agent trust in human collaborator. Additionally, the scenario tasking must change and the autonomous agent must adapt on its own (adaptive automation) in response to changes in the task, human or agent workload, interaction with the environment, or interaction with the human collaborator. Adaptation or change of scenario tasking could occur continuously within a scenario or between scenarios. Learning and adaptation of the autonomous agent could occur continuously within a scenario or between scenarios in response to results from the previous scenario.

Two-hundred-seventy-four (274) unique references were collected for the starting reference pool. References were excluded if they were: a book chapter; a survey or review of other papers; or if they were a model, architecture, or framework without experimental results that involved a human or simulated human. This resulted in fifty-seven (57) papers remaining. Next, references were excluded if the word "trust" was not present or was only used as background or introduction material. The remaining references were checked to verify all inclusion criteria were met, resulting in a final reference set of six (6) articles.

Table 4 lists the total results returned from the ten search strings for each search engine as well as the number of references selected for the starting reference pool and the final reference set (N = 6).

Table 4. Search result breakdown.

Search Engine	Total Results	Initial Set Qty.	Final Set Qty.	Final Reference Set
ACM digital library	25	19	1	[40]
EBSCO host	82	15	2	[41, 42]
Engineering village	22	8	0	–
IEEE xplore	71	35	1	[43]
Sage publications	26	10	1	[44]
Science direct	317	91	0	–
Springer Link	496	91	1	[45]
Web of science	9	5	0	–

3 Results

Each paper from the final reference set was reviewed to understand and compare the following metadata questions:

1. How was human trust measured or operationalized?
2. How was agent trust measured or operationalized?
3. How did the scenario adapt or change?
4. How did the agent adapt or change?
5. What form of human-agent collaborative tasking was used?
6. What level of automation was the agent?
7. Was the agent embodied or disembodied?
8. How did agent adaptiveness affect trust?

The answers to these questions were then used for metadata analysis. Table 5 provides a high-level summary of these metadata topics and corresponding metadata points. Analysis and comparison of these points are discussed in Sect. 4.

Table 5. High-level summary of metadata points.

Metadata Topic	Metadata Point	Reference
Measurement of human trust	Trust questionnaire (adapted from [46])	[41]
	Trust questionnaire (adapted from [47])	[44]
	Trust questionnaire (interval scale); real-time dynamic measurement	[40]
	Trust questionnaire (questionnaire details not described)	[45]
	Measure of level of agreement with agent	[42]
	Trust simulation model	[43]
Measurement of agent trust	None	[41, 42, 44, 45]
	None; Time-delayed model to estimate human's trust in agent	[43]
	None; Near real-time model to estimate human's trust in agent	[40]
Adaptive scenario mechanism	Workload; Surprise loss of automation	[41]
	Task load; Agent reliability	[44]
	Human-Agent task allocation	[43]
	Type of scenario hazards	[45]
	Task demand; Level of automation; Reliability of agent	[42]
	Changing terrain; Dynamic paths	[40]
Adaptive agent mechanism	Activated based on task load	[41, 42, 44]
	Human-Agent task allocation based on task load and human trust	[43]
	Haptic feedback, automatic steering control, and sound alerts based on hazard sensing	[45]
	Adaptive steering behavior based on reinforcement learning	[40]
Type of collaborative tasking	Contact tracking; Situational awareness	[41]
	Detection tasks	[44]
	Human-Agent task sharing	[43]
	Automotive driving simulator	[45]
	Identification tasks	[42]
	Autonomous navigation with human intervention allowed	[40]
Level of automation of agent	Information and analysis only	[41]
	Autonomous navigation; Identification	[44]
	Recommendation and direct action; Human override allowed	[43]
	Variable haptic feedback; Direct action; Partial human override allowed	[45]
	Recommendation; Human can disable completely	[42]
	Direct action; Human override allowed	[40]
Embodiment of agent	Disembodied	[41, 43]
	Embodied	[45]
	Simulated embodied	[42, 44]
	Embodied; Simulated embodied	[40]
Trust in adaptive agent	No significant difference between trust in static, adaptable, and adaptive agents	[41]
	Higher trust in adaptive agent	[44]
	Higher performance with adaptive trust agent	[43]
	Higher trust and acceptance for adaptive agent	[45]
	Neuroticism significantly correlated with agreement, but not related to agent adaptiveness	[42]
	Dynamic trust model predicted higher performance than reference works	[40]

4 Discussion

The following sections describe a metadata analysis comparing and contrasting the metadata points collected from the reference set.

4.1 Measurement of Human Trust

Most articles in the reference set performed experiments with human participants. Each of these articles discussed the use of a trust questionnaire, reflecting a subjective measure of trust. Chen et al. [41] used a questionnaire adapted from Merritt [46] and de Visser & Parasuraman [44] used a questionnaire adapted from Lee & Moray [47]. Muslim & Itoh [45] discussed using a questionnaire of trust and acceptance of automated assistance, but did not provide details of the questionnaire contents or methodology. Xu & Dudek [40] described using an interval scale for users to report absolute trust value. Additionally, users were able to use a gamepad controller during tasks to provide indication of trust lost, gained, or if trust level had not changed. Szalma & Taylor [42] operationalized trust by measuring level of agreement with the agent in relation to stress, workload, coping, and results from a personality questionnaire using the Five Factor Model (neuroticism, extraversion, conscientiousness, openness, and agreeableness).

The work by Dubois & Le Ny [43] did not use a human participant, but instead used a simulation of a mixed-initiative human-agent team that performed task sharing. The authors created a simulation of human trust in the adaptive agent using a mathematical model of trust level and belief in the automation's capability. This human trust model, along with a workload model, was used by the agent to recommend tasking allocation dynamically while allowing a simulated human the opportunity to accept the recommendation or manually choose how many tasks to perform. The human trust level was modeled as a function of the agent's previous ability to correctly complete its tasks as well as the quality of the agent's recommended task distributions. This trust level affects the amount of work the human chooses to do in contrast to the amount of work recommended by the agent. This mismatch in actual workload is then used to inform the next round of recommendations, resulting in adaptation through an attempt at objectively measuring trust.

4.2 Measurement of Agent Trust

In all of the experiments reviewed in the reference set that allowed direct agent action, the agent was always obedient to the human unless given the authority to override the human in an emergency. While none of the papers included measurement of agent trust in the human teammate, two of the papers directly involved the agent's estimation of human trust in the agent. Dubois & Le Ny [43] described their system as "human-aware" in which the automation uses previous task allocation and performance to estimate human trust in the agent and inform the next task allocation. Xu & Dudek [40] collected real-time data on the participant's trust in the agent, participant's manual interventions, and the agent's task performance. This data was used to create a Dynamic Bayesian Network near-real-time model of the human's trust in the agent.

4.3 Adaptive Scenario Mechanism

In the article by de Visser and Parasuraman [44], the authors performed two experiments in a high-fidelity 3D virtual simulation where participants collaborated with unmanned airborne (UAV), ground (UGV), and experimental (XUV) vehicles to perform reconnaissance missions and identify targets. Scenario adaptiveness was provided by varying levels of task load, static imperfect agent reliability (30%, 70%, 100%), and agent adaptive aiding (no automation, static automation, adaptive automation based on mission task load).

Szalma & Taylor [42] also adjusted agent reliability as a means of adjusting the scenarios. The participants were tasked with collaborating with a simulated autonomous uninhabited ground vehicle (UGV) to identify terrorists, friendly forces, civilians, and improvised explosive devices (IEDs) with or without the aid of the autonomous agent. The task load was varied high or low and the agent reliability was at a level of 75% or 95%.

All but one of the articles created scenarios that had a dynamic environment as part of the experiment [40–42, 44, 45]. Many of the articles adapted the scenario using task or workload [41–44]. Lastly, an important factor of an experiment in Chen et al. [41] was a surprise loss of automation resulting in a return to manual control condition. This situation was presented in a mission operation context that prevented interpretation as a loss of reliability.

4.4 Adaptive Agent Mechanism

Many of the articles in the reference set used a form of adaptive automation that was triggered by tasking or workload [41–44]. The driver assistance agent in Muslim & Itoh [45] used a haptic steering wheel which provided force against steering, a fly-by-wire steering wheel that removed lateral control from the driver, and an adaptive system that used both and was triggered based on hazard sensing features of the vehicle. The agent in Xu & Dudek [40] was the only agent that employed a learning adaptation, in this case a reinforcement learning algorithm.

4.5 Type of Collaborative Tasking

Three of the articles involved collaboration with some form of UAV, UGV, or XUV. [40, 42, 44]. In the article by Chen et al. [41] the authors performed three experiments of a submarine track management scenario in which participants on a simulated submarine performed track and classification tasks of other ships with the aid of automation under varying task loading. The simulations in Dubois & Le Ny [43] provided simple tasking that involved binary yes-no decision-making modeling as hypothesis testing. Muslin & Itoh [45] discussed experiments using multiple types of driver assistance automation systems during hazardous lane changing scenarios.

4.6 Level of Automation of Agent

The level of automation of the agents in the reference set spanned between information and analysis to direct-action. A low level of automation in the form of information, identification, or analysis was used in four articles [41–44]. Three of the articles involved direct action by the agent [40, 43, 45]. In Dubois & Le Ny [43], the human and agent could equally perform each task. Muslin & Itoh [45] was the only article that presented a direct-action agent that could override human control in an emergency. Two of the experiments included agents with autonomous navigation, however this navigation was not central to the human tasking [42, 44]. Additionally, two of the experiments offered the human the ability to disable the automation completely [41, 42].

4.7 Embodiment of Agent

The embodiment of the agents in the reference set spanned from disembodied to simulated embodied to embodied. Most of the experiments in the reference set either involved embodied or simulated-embodied agents [40, 42, 44, 45]. Two of the articles used purely disembodied agents [41, 43].

4.8 Trust in Adaptive Agent

For most of the articles in the reference set, collaborating with an adaptive agent resulted in higher trust and/or performance. The work by de Visser & Parasuraman [44] found that trust was higher in the context-sensitive adaptive automation vs. the static automation. Muslin & Itoh [45] found that trust and acceptance were higher for the adaptive driver assistance vs. non adaptive assistance. In Xu & Dudek [40], the dynamic trust model predicted higher performance than other reference works that the authors used for comparison. Dubois & Le Ny [43] found that the Markov Decision Process task allocation using dynamic trust and workload modeling improved performance vs. static workload-based task allocation. Contrary to these findings, Chen et al. [41] found no significant difference between trust in static, adaptable, and adaptive agents for their experiments. Lastly, in Szalma & Taylor [42], neuroticism was significantly correlated with agreement with the agent, but this was not related to agent adaptiveness.

4.9 Limitations

A potential limitation to the SLR performed was the emphasis on an adaptive tasking/scenario. While all of the references in the final reference set contained experiments where the participants experienced differing scenarios, the SLR may have resulted in a greater quantity of qualified results if the requirement for the adaptive tasking/scenario terms was not included.

5 Conclusion

In this paper, we seek to gain a greater understanding of two-way trust between humans and artificial agents. A systematic review of academic and technical literature from the last ten years (2010–2020) was performed and a metadata analysis was presented comparing measurements of human trust and agent trust; adaptive-scenario and adaptive-agent mechanisms; type of collaborative human-agent tasking; and level of automation and embodiment of the agent.

Eight academic search engines were used to collect two-hundred-seventy-four (274) unique references for the starting reference pool. Of these, inclusion and exclusion criteria were applied resulting in a final reference set of six (6) articles. To qualify for inclusion, references were required to discuss experimental results measuring human trust of an autonomous agent collaborator and/or autonomous agent trust in human collaborator. Additionally, the experimental scenario must change and the autonomous agent must adapt on its own (adaptive automation).

The metadata analysis showed that most of the reference set articles employed a form of trust questionnaire for measuring human trust in the agent and one article used agreeability related personality traits as a proxy for trust, a potential attempt to objectively measure trust. Agent trust in the human was not measured in any of the experiments, however two articles employed a trust simulation model to estimate human trust in the agent.

The experimental scenarios provided adaptiveness related to level of workload and task load, level and reliability of the agent, and environmental factors such as hazards, paths, and terrain. Experiments provided agent adaptiveness to include task load, level of human trust, level of automation, and reinforcement learning. The collaborative tasking across the reference set included contact tracking and detection tasks, mixed initiative task sharing, automotive driving assistance, and semi-autonomous navigation. The level of automation ranged between information and analysis only to direct action with full to partial human override allowed. Most of the experiments in the reference set either involved embodied or simulated-embodied agents, while two of the articles used purely disembodied agents. Moreover, most of the articles in the reference set indicated higher trust and/or performance when collaborating with an adaptive agent. One of the articles, in contrast, found no significant difference between trust in static, adaptable, and adaptive agents for their experiments.

The results of this review spanned a variety of mechanisms for agent and scenario adaptiveness as well as level of automation and embodiment. While human trust in the agent was frequently subjectively measured and two of the articles estimated human trust in the agent, estimation or measurement of agent trust in the human was not present at all. However, there may be an opportunity to objectively measure trust in automation through measuring agreement with automation in relation to personality traits, stress, workload, and coping to inform development of algorithms of agent trust in the human collaborator. This could potentially lead to two-way trust calibration in human-agent teams. From the small quantity of results of the systematic literature search and the lack of results with experiments that include agent-based trust, it appears that two-way mutual trust between humans and adaptive agents is a field with opportunities for further focus and development.

References

1. Barnes, M.J., Chen, J.Y.C., Hill, S.: Humans and Autonomy: Implications of Shared Decision-Making for Military Operations. p. 42 (2017)
2. Bradshaw, J.M., et al.: From tools to teammates: joint activity in human-agent-robot teams. In: Kurosu, M. (ed.) HCD 2009. LNCS, vol. 5619, pp. 935–944. Springer, Heidelberg (2009). https://doi.org/10.1007/978-3-642-02806-9_107

3. Singer, P.W.: Wired for War: The Future of Military Robots, Brookings (2009). https://www. brookings.edu/opinions/wired-for-war-the-future-of-military-robots/. Accessed 10 February 2021
4. Han, S., Yang, H.: Understanding adoption of intelligent personal assistants: a parasocial relationship perspective. Ind. Manag. Data Syst. **118**(3), 618–636 (2018). https://doi.org/10. 1108/IMDS-05-2017-0214
5. Yang, R., Newman, M.W.: Living with an intelligent thermostat: advanced control for heating and cooling systems. In: Proceedings of the 2012 ACM Conference on Ubiquitous Computing, New York, NY, USA, pp. 1102–1107, September 2012. https://doi.org/10.1145/2370216.237 0449.
6. Rupp, J.D., King, A.G.: Autonomous Driving - A Practical Roadmap, October 2010. https:// doi.org/10.4271/2010-01-2335
7. Kasparov, G.: The Chess Master and the Computer. The New York Review of Books, February 2010
8. Hancock, P.A.: Imposing limits on autonomous systems. Ergonomics **60**(2), 284–291 (2017). https://doi.org/10.1080/00140139.2016.1190035
9. Parasuraman, R., Bahri, T., Deaton, J., Morrison, J., Barnes, M.: Theory and design of adaptive automation in aviation systems, July 1992
10. Wickens, C.D., Dixon, S.R.: The benefits of imperfect diagnostic automation: a synthesis of the literature. Theor. Issues Ergon. Sci. **8**(3), 201–212 (2007). https://doi.org/10.1080/146392 20500370105
11. Schwab, K.: The Fourth Industrial Revolution: What it means and how to respond, Science & Technology. https://www.foreignaffairs.com/articles/2015-12-12/fourth-industrial-revolu tion. Dec 2015
12. Hidalgo, M.: An Approach to Modeling Simulated Military Human-agent Teaming, Electronic Theses and Dissertations, January 2020. https://stars.library.ucf.edu/etd2020/439
13. Grosz, B.J.: Collaborative Systems, AI Magazine, pp. 67–85 (1996)
14. Russell, S.J., Norvig, P., Davis, E.: Artificial Intelligence: a Modern Approach, 3rd edn. Prentice Hall, Upper Saddle River (2010)
15. Sukthankar, D.G., Sycara, K., Giampapa, J.A., Burnett, C.: A model of human teamwork for agent-assisted search operations. Carnegie Mellon University, p. 22 (2008)
16. Sukthankar, G., Shumaker, R., Lewis, M.: Intelligent agents as teammates. In: Salas, E., Fiore, S.M., Letsky, M.P. (eds.) Theories of team cognition: Cross-disciplinary perspectives, pp. 313–343. Routledge, Taylor & Francis Group (2012)
17. Bradshaw, J.M., Hoffman, R.R., Woods, D.D., Johnson, M.: The Seven Deadly Myths of 'Autonomous Systems.' IEEE Intell. Syst. **28**(3), 54–61 (2013). https://doi.org/10.1109/MIS. 2013.70
18. Sheridan, T.B.: Adaptive automation, level of automation, allocation authority, supervisory control, and adaptive control: distinctions and modes of adaptation. IEEE Trans. Syst., Man, Cybern. - Part A: Syst. Hum. **41**(4), 662–667 (2011). https://doi.org/10.1109/TSMCA.2010. 2093888
19. Sheridan, T.B., Verplank, W.L.: Human and computer control of undersea Teleoperators, massachusetts inst of tech Cambridge man-machine systems lab, Jul. 1978. https://apps.dtic. mil/sti/citations/ADA057655. Accessed 18 Nov 2020
20. Parasuraman, R., Sheridan, T.B., Wickens, C.D.: A model for types and levels of human interaction with automation. IEEE Trans. Syst., Man, Cybern. - A **30**(3), 286–297 (2000). https://doi.org/10.1109/3468.844354
21. Scerbo, M.W.: Adaptive Automation, International Encyclopedia of Human Factors. pp. 1077–1079 (2011)
22. Barnes, M., Elliott, L.R., Wright, J., Scharine, A., Chen, J.: Human–Robot Interaction Design Research: From Teleoperations to, p. 54

23. Chen, J.Y.C.: Human-autonomy teaming in military settings. Theor. Issues Ergon. Sci. **19**(3), 255–258 (2018). https://doi.org/10.1080/1463922X.2017.1397229
24. Demir, M., McNeese, N.J., Cooke, N.J., Ball, J.T., Myers, C., Frieman, M.: Synthetic team-mate communication and coordination with humans. In: Proceedings of the Human Factors and Ergonomics Society Annual Meeting, vol. 59(1), pp. 951–955, September 2015. https://doi.org/10.1177/1541931215591275
25. Demir, M., McNeese, N.J., Cooke, N.J.: The Evolution of Human-Autonomy Teams in Remotely Piloted Aircraft Systems Operations. Front. Commun. **4**, 50 (2019). https://doi.org/10.3389/fcomm.2019.00050
26. McNeese, N.J., Demir, M., Cooke, N.J., Myers, C.: Teaming with a synthetic teammate: insights into human-autonomy teaming. Hum Factors **60**(2), 262–273 (2018). https://doi.org/10.1177/0018720817743223
27. Salas, E., Sims, D.E., Burke, C.S.: Is there a 'big five' in teamwork? Small Group Res. **36**(5), 555–599 (2005). https://doi.org/10.1177/1046496405277134
28. Teo, G., Reinerman-Jones, L., Matthews, G., Szalma, J., Jentsch, F., Hancock, P.: Enhancing the effectiveness of human-robot teaming with a closed-loop system. Appl. Ergon. **67**, 91–103 (2018). https://doi.org/10.1016/j.apergo.2017.07.007
29. Mayer, R.C., Davis, J.H., Schoorman, F.D.: An integrative model of organizational trust. Acad. Manag. Rev. **20**(3), 709–734 (1995). https://doi.org/10.2307/258792
30. Feitosa, J., Grossman, R., Kramer, W.S., Salas, E.: Measuring team trust: a critical and meta-analytical review. J. Organ. Behav. **41**(5), 479–501 (2020). https://doi.org/10.1002/job.2436
31. Lee, J.D., See, K.A.: Trust in automation: designing for appropriate reliance. Hum Factors **46**(1), 50–80 (2004). https://doi.org/10.1518/hfes.46.1.50_30392
32. Hancock, P.A., Billings, D.R., Schaefer, K.E., Chen, J.Y.C., de Visser, E.J., Parasuraman, R.: A meta-analysis of factors affecting trust in human-robot interaction. Hum Factors **53**(5), 517–527 (2011). https://doi.org/10.1177/0018720811417254
33. Khodyakov, D.: Trust as a process: a three-dimensional approach. Soc.-J. Brit. Soc. Assoc. – Soc. **41**, 115–132 (2007). https://doi.org/10.1177/0038038507072285
34. Victor, P., Verbiest, N., Cornelis, C., Cock, M.D.: Enhancing the trust-based recommendation process with explicit distrust. ACM Trans. Web, vol. 7(2), p. 19
35. de Visser, E.J., Pak, R., Shaw, T.H.: From 'automation' to 'autonomy': the importance of trust repair in human–machine interaction. Ergonomics **61**(10), 1409–1427 (2018). https://doi.org/10.1080/00140139.2018.1457725
36. Dirks, K.T., Lewicki, R.J., Zaheer, A.: Repairing relationships within and between organizations: building a conceptual foundation. Acad. Manage. Rev. **34**, 68–84 (2009)
37. Kramer, R.M., Lewicki, R.J.: Repairing and enhancing trust: approaches to reducing organizational trust deficits. Annals **4**(1), 245–277 (2010). https://doi.org/10.5465/19416520.2010.487403
38. McGuirl, J.M., Sarter, N.B.: Supporting trust calibration and the effective use of decision aids by presenting dynamic system confidence information. Hum Factors **48**(4), 656–665 (2006). https://doi.org/10.1518/001872006779166334
39. de Visser, E.J., et al.: The world is not enough: trust in cognitive agents. In: Proceedings of the Human Factors and Ergonomics Society Annual Meeting, vol. 56(1), pp. 263–267, September 2012. https://doi.org/10.1177/1071181312561062
40. Xu, A., Dudek, G.: Towards efficient collaborations with trust-seeking adaptive robots. In: Proceedings of the Tenth Annual ACM/IEEE International Conference on Human-Robot Interaction Extended Abstracts, Portland Oregon USA, pp. 221–222 March 2015. https://doi.org/10.1145/2701973.2702711
41. Chen, S.I., Visser, T.A.W., Huf, S., Loft, S.: Optimizing the balance between task automation and human manual control in simulated submarine track management. J. Exp. Psychol. Appl. **23**(3), 240–262 (2017). https://doi.org/10.1037/xap0000126

42. Szalma, J.L., Taylor, G.S.: Individual differences in response to automation: the five factor model of personality. J. Exp. Psychol. Appl. **17**(2), 71–96 (2011). https://doi.org/10.1037/a00 24170
43. Dubois, C., Le Ny, J.: Adaptive task allocation in human-machine teams with trust and workload cognitive models. In: 2020 IEEE International Conference on Systems, Man, and Cybernetics (SMC), Toronto, ON, pp. 3241–3246, October 2020. https://doi.org/10.1109/SMC42975.2020.9283461
44. de Visser, E., Parasuraman, R.: Adaptive Aiding of Human-Robot Teaming: Effects of Imperfect Automation on Performance, Trust, and Workload. J. Cogn. Eng. Decis. Making **5**(2), 209–231 (2011). https://doi.org/10.1177/1555343411410160
45. Muslim, H., Itoh, M.: Trust and acceptance of adaptive and conventional collision avoidance systems. IFAC-PapersOnLine **52**(19), 55–60 (2019). https://doi.org/10.1016/j.ifacol.2019.12.086
46. Merritt, S.M.: Affective processes in human-automation interactions. Hum Factors **53**(4), 356–370 (2011). https://doi.org/10.1177/0018720811411912
47. Lee, J.D., Moray, N.: Trust, self-confidence, and operators' adaptation to automation. Int. J. Hum Comput Stud. **40**(1), 153–184 (1994). https://doi.org/10.1006/ijhc.1994.1007

A Review of Multimodal Interaction in Intelligent Systems

May Jorella Lazaro[1](✉), Sungho Kim[1], Jaeyong Lee[2], Jaemin Chun[2],
Gyungbhin Kim[1], EunJeong Yang[1], Aigerim Bilyalova[1], and Myung Hwan Yun[1]

[1] Seoul National University, Seoul, South Korea
ellalazaro@snu.ac.kr
[2] UX Innovation Lab, Samsung Research, Samsung Electronics Co., Ltd, Seoul, South Korea

Abstract. Interest in the development of multimodal interaction modalities (e.g. visual, auditory, haptics etc.) has become more prominent. Despite this strong interest in multimodality, research on this domain remains to be quite a few. The present study aims to review the current literature regarding multimodal interaction in intelligent systems, specifically in extended realities (XR) and robots. 961 research articles gathered through engineering and science databases were subjected to rigorous screening. The articles were evaluated by multiple researchers based on its quality and relevance. 30 highly-relevant empirical research papers about multimodal interaction in the context of XR and robot systems were chosen and were subjected for review. Reviewed papers were summarized through descriptive statistics and qualitative analysis. It was revealed that although multimodal interaction is being utilized in various intelligent systems, there are still gaps in the literature that needs to be filled in order to completely understand the concept. The lack of user-centered and human factor-based investigation indicates that the current intelligent systems that require human interaction still need to be improved further. The results of this study can be utilized by system developers and designers in order to create systems that would better accommodate the needs and capabilities of its users.

Keywords: Multimodal interaction · Augmented reality · Virtual reality · Extended reality · Robot · Intelligent systems

1 Introduction

The growth of technology has spiked in recent years. According to the Data Bridge Market Research report, the global virtual market size was approximately 10.32 billion USD in 2019 and it is expected to reach 2,094.08 billion USD by 2027 [1]. Intelligent devices and virtual technologies have been applied in various domains such as medicine, education, online shopping and e-commerce sector. This enhanced growth may lead to a leap in investment by economically leading companies for the retail industry in the forecast period of 2020–2027 [1]. The increasing attention towards such technologies has led to the development of different intelligent systems equipped with sophisticated pattern recognition and classification technologies. Intelligent systems are technologically

© Springer Nature Switzerland AG 2021
M. Kurosu (Ed.): HCII 2021, LNCS 12762, pp. 206–219, 2021.
https://doi.org/10.1007/978-3-030-78462-1_15

advanced machines, which are able to process information and respond to the physical world around them [2]. Nowadays human beings constantly interact with intelligent systems on a daily basis. Those intelligent systems can take many forms, from personal computers, automobiles, and smart appliances to advanced systems that emerged into technologies that are able to learn from experience and adapt to a given data [3, 4]. In this study, we have categorized intelligent systems into two groups – the first-person perspective system and the third-person perspective system. The first-person perspective system refers to XR systems which include augmented reality (AR) and virtual reality (VR). The third-person perspective system refers to systems that require a separate intelligent agent such as robots and artificial intelligence (AI) speakers. Within this context, this research is going to focus on finding the interaction techniques used to perform multimodal interactions in such an environment.

The human-machine system interaction is essentially comprised of an exchange of information between a computer and a human through different input and output modalities [5]. Input to systems consists of the information sent by the user, and output from systems typically refers to feedback that supports and guides a user to accomplish one's task, thus forming an input and output bridge between systems' inner world and real physical world [6]. If the system has multiple modalities implemented, that is considering multiple sensory channels, it is referred to as a multimodal system. Humans naturally interact with the world multimodally, utilizing multiple sensory channels to perceive and respond to another human or the external environment. In order to achieve this natural interaction experience that exists between humans, technology is being developed to enable such multimodal interaction between humans and intelligent systems. However, most of the studies regarding human-computer interaction are mostly based on unimodal interaction [7].

The goal of intelligent systems is to help users to complete tasks and requirements with comfort, ease and high efficiency. Therefore, the preferred combination of modalities can differ for each intelligent systems and tasks. For example, according to a study, AR utilizes visual signal as the main output modality to visualize information [8]. Moreover, in the study by Zhu et al. (2014) user can ask questions to AR using auditory modality and the system responds based on the user's voice as well as tracking user's gaze to output tasks on the visual display [9].

It was proved by several studies that implementing a multimodal interaction system is important for natural and realistic interaction due to increased flexibility in delivering or exchanging information between intelligent systems and users [10]. For example, combining any type of feedback modality with visual feedback modality improves task completion time and effectiveness of telerobotic assistance [11]. However, this field of study lacks in number yet to enhance the user experience. Currently, most research regarding multimodal interaction systems are focused on technological advancement without taking into account the human factors perspective, such as how the system should be designed to provide users with a natural interaction to perform various task and achieve their goals. Multimodal interaction systems that do not consider major human factor principle and guidelines can cause problems such as human error and poor acceptance of the technology. According to a review on multimodal interaction frameworks, the majority of existing frameworks generally discussed the overall system framework but overlooked specific details about interaction modalities [12]. Thus, this suggests that a further investigation in designing multimodal interaction between humans and intelligent systems in consideration with the human factors perspective is essential.

The present study aims to review the current literature regarding multimodal interaction in intelligent systems, specifically in extended realities (XR) and robots. More particularly, it aims (1) to determine different interaction modalities used in different intelligent system domains, (2) to identify factors that might affect human-system multimodal interaction and (3) to derive insights as to how such interactions should be designed based on human factors perspective.

2 Method

This study was conducted in adherence to the Preferred Reporting Items for Systematic Reviews and Meta-Analyses (PRISMA) guidelines [13]. The data was searched and gathered through multiple academic research databases in August 2020. The details of the review processes are indicated below and is shown in Fig. 1.

2.1 Information Source

The primary search was conducted in four major research databases namely SCOPUS, Web of Science, Science Direct and ProQuest. These databases were chosen as it covers a wide range of studies in the field of engineering and social sciences. Secondary search was also conducted through backward referencing in Google Scholar.

2.2 Inclusion and Prescreening Criteria

Journal articles in English published from 2015 to 2020 (5-year span) were collected from the aforementioned databases. The keyword formula used for all databases are as follows: ("multimodal" OR "cross-modal" OR "modality") AND ("interaction" OR "interface" OR "techniques" OR "feedback") AND ("augmented reality" OR "AR" OR"virtual reality OR "VR" OR"robot" OR "intelligent machines"). The records were screened based on the title and abstract. Only empirical studies were included during the screening, leaving out review articles, short reports, critiques, proceeding papers, books and dissertations.

2.3 Eligibility Criteria

Screened records were subjected to full-text evaluation based on the eligibility criteria set by the researchers. Articles that focuses on interaction modalities were given high regards for relevance. Articles are considered eligible for synthesis if it discusses more than one interaction modality and it empirically investigated multimodal interaction in the context of intelligent systems on actual users. Records that are focused on the development of algorithms and multimodal hardware systems were excluded in this review.

2.4 Data Synthesis

A total of 961 records were identified during the initial phase of the review. After removing the duplicate records and screening the title and abstract, 183 records were rigorously assessed for eligibility. As a result, a total of 30 articles were included for the final synthesis. Each article was organized and classified based on factors related to the users, tasks, system and the environment.

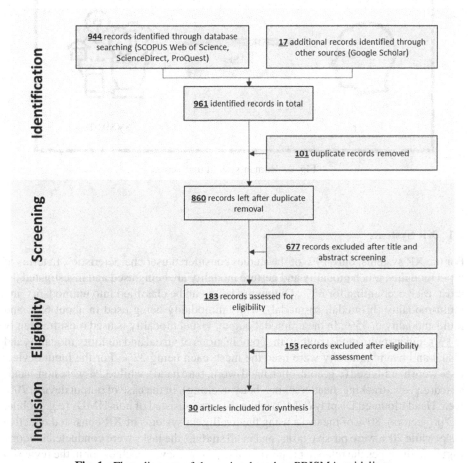

Fig. 1. Flow diagram of the review based on PRISMA guidelines

3 Results

A total of 30 empirical research papers were reviewed (Table 1). Findings of the review showed that different combinations of input and output modalities were used depending on user characteristics, task, system, and environment (Fig. 2). User characteristics are classified into age, gender/sex, prior experience, and personality. The type of task is classified into whether it is passive or active from the user's perspective, and for system, different types of input and output device are found. And lastly, environment refers to where the task took place, whether it was indoors or outdoors.

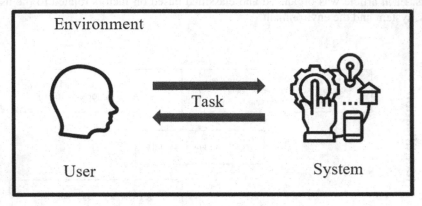

Fig. 2. Human-system interaction

3.1 XR Systems

For the XR systems, only 19% of the studies considered user characteristics. In terms of input modality, touch modality and gesture modality are being used and investigated the most, each accounting for 33%. Output modality can be classified into unimodality and multi-modality (bi-modal, tri-modal), with unimodality being used in about 65% and multi-modality in 35%. In the unimodal output, visual modality is used most frequently (51%), and in multi-modal output, the combinations of visual and auditory modality, and visual and haptic modality were used the most, each being 32%. For the input device, 68% were hand-based (e.g. controller, hand-worn, bare hand), while 32% were non-hand-based(e.g. eye-tracking, head tracking, body tracking). In the case of output device, 70% were Head Mounted Display (HMD) while the rest consisted of non-HMDs (e.g. mobile, PC/projectors). 80% of the tasks using the intelligent systems of XR consisted of active tasks while 20% were passive tasks, and in all studies, the tasks were conducted indoors. Figure 3 illustrates the relative proportion of the frequency of each factor in the reviewed studies.

3.2 Robot Systems

In robot systems, the proportion of studies that considered user characteristics and the proportion of studies that do not were equal. In interactions, touch modality (34%) was used the most, with speech modality (33%) following. For output modality, in contrast to XR systems, unimodal output modality was mostly used. Overall, visual-based modalities were used most commonly, with visual modality (unimodal) accounting

Table 1. List of reviewed articles

No.	Author(s)	Year	Title	Source
1	Shwarz & Fatenmeier	2017	Augmented Reality Warnings in Vehicles: Effects of Modality and Specificity on Effectiveness	Accident Analysis and Prevention
2	Ren et al.	2017	Towards the design of effective haptic and audio display for AR and MR applications	Advances in Multimedia
3	Nuamah et al.	2019	Neural efficiency of human-robotic feedback modalities under stress differs with gender	Frontiers in Human Neuroscience
4	Montuwy et al.	2019	Helping older pedestrians navigate in the city: comparisons of visual, auditory, and haptic guidance instructions in a virtual environment	Behaviour & Information Technology
5	Triantakfyllidis et al.	2020	Study of multimodal interfaces and the improvements of teleoperation	IEEE Access
6	Nuovo et al.	2018	The multimodal interface of robot-era multi-robot services tailored for the elderly	Intel Serv Robotics
7	Luzio et al.	2020	Visual vs vibrotactile feedback for posture assessment during upper limb robot-aided rehabilitation	Applied Ergonomics
8	Cho et al.	2019	The effects of modality, device, and task differences on perceived human likeness of voice activated virtual assistants	CYBERPSYCHOLOGY, BEHAVIOR, AND SOCIAL NETWORKING

(*continued*)

Table 1. (*continued*)

No.	Author(s)	Year	Title	Source
9	Merkouris et al.	2019	Understanding the notion of friction through gestural interaction with a remotely controlled robot	Journal of Science Education and Technology
10	De Carolis et al.	2017	Recognizing users feedback from non-verbal communicative acts in conversational recommender systems	Pattern Recognition Letters
11	Hepperle et al.	2019	2D, 3D or speech? A case study on which user interface is preferable for what kind of object interaction in immersive virtual reality	Computers & Graphics
12	Doukakis et al.	2019	Audio-visual-olfactory resource allocation for tri-modal virtual environments	IEEE TRANSACTIONS ON VISUALIZATION AND COMPUTER GRAPHICS
13	Wang et al.	2016	Multi-modal augmented-reality assembly guidance based on bare-hand interface	Advanced Engineering Informatics
14	Brito & Stoyanova	2018	Marker versus markerless augmented reality. Which has more impact on users?	INTERNATIONAL JOURNAL OF HUMAN–COMPUTER INTERACTION
15	Wang et al.	2016	Haptic communication in collaborative virtual environments	Human Factors
16	Kim et al.	2018	Augmented reality-based remote coaching for fast-paced physical task	Virtual Reality
17	Zsiga et al.	2018	Evaluation of a companion robot based on field tests with single older adults in their homes	Assistive Technology

(*continued*)

Table 1. (*continued*)

No.	Author(s)	Year	Title	Source
18	Clerk et al.	2019	User centered design of interaction techniques for VR-based automotive design reviews	Frontiers Robotics AI
19	Kim et al.	2019	Blowing in the wind: increasing social presence with a virtual human via environmental airflow interaction in mixed reality	Computers and Graphics (Pergamon)
20	Patrick et al.	2020	Distractive effect of multimodal information in multisensory learning	Computers and Education
21	Schüssel et al.	2013	Influencing Factors on Multimodal Interaction During Selection Task	Journal on Multimodal User Interfaces
22	Esteves et al.	2020	Comparing selection mechanisms for gaze input techniques in head-mounted displays	International Journal of Human-Computer Studies
23	Heller et al.	2019	Touching the Untouchable: Exploring Multi-Sensory Augmented Reality in the Context of Online Retailing	Journal of Retailing
24	Bajpai et al.	2020	Enhancing Physical Human Evasion of Moving Threats Using Tactile Cues	IEEE Transactions on Haptics
25	Bell & Macuga	2019	Goal-directed aiming under restricted viewing conditions with confirmatory sensory feedback	Human Movement Science
26	Richer et al.	2020	Exploring Smart Agents for the Interaction with Multimodal Mediated Environments	Multimodal Technologies and Interaction

(*continued*)

Table 1. (*continued*)

No.	Author(s)	Year	Title	Source
27	Rau & Zheng	2019	Modality capacity and appropriateness in multimodal display of complex non-semantic information stream	International Journal of Human-Computer studies
28	Gibson	2018	Evaluation of a visual-tactile multimodal display for surface obstacle avoidance during walking	IEEE TRANSACTIONS ON HUMAN-MACHINE SYSTEMS
29	Jevtic	2019	Personalized robot assistant for support in dressing	IEEE TRANSACTION ON COGNITIVE AND DEVELOPMENTAL SYSTEMS
30	Xiao	2018	MRTouch: Adding touch input to Head-Mounted Mixed Reality	IEEE ON VISUALIZATION AND COMPUTER GRAPHICS

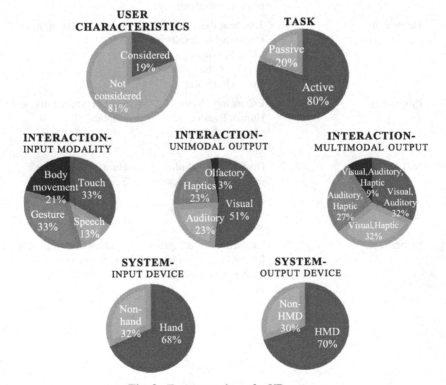

Fig. 3. Frequency charts for XR systems

for 54% and a combination of visual and auditory modality accounting for 8%, thus resulting in a total of 62%. Of input devices, the proportion of non-hand devices (e.g. microphone, body tracking), which is 64%, turned out to be larger than the proportion (36%) of hand-based devices (e.g. bare hand, controller). Physical robots are commonly used for output devices, as found in 56% of the reviewed studies. All tasks while using the intelligent systems of this domain are active tasks, and all interactions take place indoors. Figure 4 illustrates the relative proportion of the frequency of each factor in the reviewed studies.

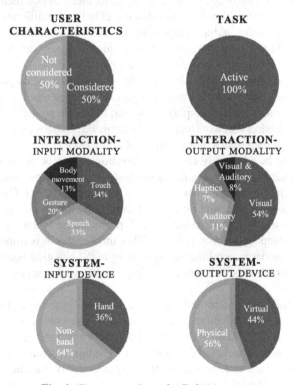

Fig. 4. Frequency charts for Robot systems

4 Discussion

The aim of this study was to review the literature related to multimodal interaction in intelligent systems. The papers reviewed in this study were systematically investigated through procedures such as keyword selection, application of inclusion and exclusion criteria, and evaluation of research relevance level. As a result, the main modalities for each domain were quantitatively analyzed. Also, design considerations for multimodal interaction were derived from a human factors perspective. This review paper gives an overview of the system design characteristics of modalities that can contribute to the development of intelligent systems or interface design.

The characteristics of input and output modality in the intelligent systems were analyzed based on human factors elements including user, system, task, and environment. In addition, design considerations for multimodal interaction were identified accordingly. Some of the design guidelines proposed in this study are discussed as follows.

• Modality should be determined in consideration of user characteristics such as age, gender, experience, knowledge, and personality. For example, Montuwy et al. (2019) showed that adults aged over 70 years demonstrated a lower task performance than the participants ranging in age from 53 to 70 years under haptic feedback conditions in a virtual environment. This indicates that the elderly have difficulties in accurately perceiving tactile feedback due to loss of skin sensitivity with the aging process [17].
• Modality should follow the principles of affordance design so that humans can easily understand and operate the system. For example, Cho et al. (2019) showed that a laptop display can increase human likeness than a mobile phone display when humans interact with the voice assistant system. This can be interpreted as a relatively high modality affordance of laptop display compared to mobile phone display because the laptop display requires less workload for handling and provides more sensory richness through a large screen than a mobile phone display [21].
• Modality should be adaptively changed according to task or environmental characteristics. For example, in the manipulation task or the position task, the increase of interaction modalities leads to better task performance [18, 37]. On the contrary, in the navigation task or selection task, it was confirmed that the integration of a wider range of modalities had small effect on task performance when compared to utilizing unimodal components only [17, 40]. This implies that it is important to provide an appropriate modality combination according to the situation because the effect of multimodal interaction is different depending on the context scenarios.

Meanwhile, this study identified that the modalities in the specific domain of the intelligent systems, XR and robot domain, are different from each other. The input modalities most commonly used in the XR domain were touch and gesture, and the output modality was visual feedback. On the other hand, the input modalities used most in the robot domain were touch and speech, and the output modality was auditory feedback. In addition, research on the intelligent systems generally focused on single modality, and it was found that the combinations of two or more modalities were insufficient especially in the robot systems. Therefore, it is necessary to perform additional research on the applicability of modality with low frequency of use in each domain and to identify the optimal combination of multimodality in consideration of the context of use.

Based on the review, further work is needed to improve existing evaluation methods for users in the intelligent system. As a result of literature review, it was found that there was a lack of research on the validation of testing protocol for users to confirm the effect of multimodal interaction. Thus, if empirical studies based on systematic evaluation methods are performed to implement user-centered modality in the future, it can help to promote understanding of the characteristics of human factors such as behavior or cognition when designing multimodal interaction in the intelligent system.

5 Conclusion

In conclusion, the present study was able to summarize the current trends in multimodal interaction research in intelligent systems, specifically in XR and robot systems. It was revealed that although multimodal interaction is being utilized in various intelligent systems, there are still gaps in the literature that needs to be filled in order to completely understand the concept. The lack of user-centered and human factor-based investigation indicates that the current intelligent systems that require human interaction still needs to be improved further.

The results of this study can be utilized by system developers and designers in order to create systems that would better accommodate the needs and capabilities of its users. For example, adding interaction modality alternatives to the system may cater a wider range of users with different characteristics such as physical (e.g. height, visual acuity) or cognitive (e.g. attention, memory) abilities.

Acknowledgement. This work is supported by Samsung Research, Samsung Electronics Co., Ltd.

References

1. Data Bridge Market Research. https://www.databridgemarketresearch.com/reports/global-augmented-reality-and-virtual-reality-market. Accepted 22 January 2021
2. Lynn, T., Rosati, P., Endo, P.T.: Toward the intelligent internet of everything: observations on multidisciplinary challenges in intelligent systems research. In: Picazo-Vela, S., Hernández L. R. (eds.) Technology, Science, and Culture: A Global Vision, vol. 116,000 120M, pp. 52–64. (2018). https://doi.org/10.5772/intechopen.83691
3. Agah, A.: Human interactions with intelligent systems: research taxonomy. Comput. Electr. Eng. 27(1), 71–107 (2000)
4. Adhikari, S., Thapa, S., Shah, B.K.: Oversampling based classifiers for categorization of radar returns from the ionosphere. In: 2020 International Conference on Electronics and Sustainable Communication Systems (ICESC), pp. 975–978. Coimbatore, India (2020)
5. Karray, F., Alemzadeh, M., Abou Saleh, J., Arab, M.N.: Human-Computer interaction: overview on state of the art. Int. J. Smart Sens. Intell. Syst. 1(1), 137–153 (2008)
6. Hinckley, K., Jacob, R.J., Ware, C., Wobbrock, J.O., Wigdor, D.: Input/Output Devices and Interaction Techniques. Computing Handbook. 3rd edn. Chapman and Hall (2014)
7. Turk, M.: Multimodal interaction: a review. Pattern Recogn. Lett. 36(15), 189–195 (2014). https://doi.org/10.1016/j.patrec.2013.07.003
8. Kim, J.C.: Multimodal Interaction with Internet of Things and Augmented Reality: Foundations. Systems and Challenges. Lulea University of Technology, Lulea (2020)
9. Zhu, Z., et al.: AR-mentor: augmented reality based mentoring system. In: 2014 IEEE International Symposium on Mixed and Augmented Reality (ISMAR), pp. 17–22. IEEE (2014).
10. Xiao, B., Lunsford, R., Coulston, R., Wesson, M., Oviatt, S.: Modeling multimodal integration patterns and performance in seniors: toward adaptive processing of individual differences. In: Proceedings of the 5th International Conference on Multimodal Interfaces, pp. 265–272, Association for Computing Machinery, USA (2003). https://doi.org/10.1145/958432.958480

11. Bolarinwa, J., Eimontaite, I., Dogramadzi, S., Mitchell, T., Caleb-Solly, P.: The use of different feedback modalities and verbal collaboration in tele-robotic assistance. In: 2019 IEEE International Symposium on Robotic and Sensors Environments (ROSE), pp. 1–8, IEEE (2019)

12. Nizam, S.S.M., Abidin, R.Z., Hashim, N.C., Lam, M.C., Arshad, H., Majid, N.A.A.: A review of multimodal interaction technique in augmented reality environment. Int. J. Adv. Sci. Eng. Inf. Technol. **8**(4–2), 1460–1468 (2018)

13. Moher, D., Liberati, A., Tetzlaff, J., Altman, D.G.: Prisma group: preferred reporting items for systematic reviews and meta-analyses: the PRISMA statement. PLoS med **6**(7), e1000097 (2009). https://doi.org/10.1371/journal.pmed.1000097

14. Schwarz, F., Fastenmeier, W.: Augmented reality warnings in vehicles: effects of modality and specificity on effectiveness. Accid. Anal. Prev. **101**, 55–66 (2017). https://doi.org/10.1016/j.aap.2017.01.019

15. Ren, G., Wei, S., O'Neill, E., Chen, F.: Towards the design of effective haptic and audio displays for augmented reality and mixed reality applications. Advances in Multimedia (2018). https://doi.org/10.1155/2018/4517150

16. Nuamah, J.K., Mantooth, W., Karthikeyan, R., Mehta, R.K., Ryu, S.C.: Neural efficiency of human-robotic feedback modalities under stress differs with gender. Front. Hum. Neurosci. **13**, 287 (2019). https://doi.org/10.3389/fnhum.2019.00287

17. Montuwy, A., Dommes, A., Cahour, B.: Helping older pedestrians navigate in the city: comparisons of visual, auditory and haptic guidance in a virtual environment. Behav. Inf. Technol. **38**(20), 150–171 (2019). https://doi.org/10.1080/0144929X.2018.1519035

18. Triantafyllidis, E., Mcgreavy, C., Gu, J., Li, Z.: Study of multimodal interfaces and the improvements on teleoperation. IEEE Access. **8**, 78213–78227 (2020). https://doi.org/10.1109/ACCESS.2020.2990080

19. Di Nuovo, A., et al.: The multi-modal interface of Robot-Era multi-robot services tailored for the elderly. Intel. Serv. Robot. **11**(1), 109–126 (2017). https://doi.org/10.1007/s11370-017-0237-6

20. di Luzio, F.S., Lauretti, C., Cordella, F., Draicchio, F., Zollo, L.: Visual vs vibrotactile feedback for posture assessment during upper-limb robot-aided rehabilitation. Appl. Ergon. **82**, 102950 (2020). https://doi.org/10.1016/j.apergo.2019.102950

21. Cho, E., Molina, M.D., Wang, J.: The effects of modality, device, and task differences on perceived human likeness of voice-activated virtual assistants. Cyberpsychol. Behav. Soc. Netw. **22**(8), 515–520 (2019). https://doi.org/10.1089/cyber.2018.0571

22. Merkouris, A., Chorianopoulou, B., Chorianopoulos, K., Chrissikopoulos, V.: Understanding the notion of friction through gestural interaction with a remotely controlled robot. J. Sci. Educ. Technol. **28**(3), 209–221 (2018). https://doi.org/10.1007/s10956-018-9760-2

23. De Carolis, B., de Gemmis, M., Lops, P., Palestra, G.: Recognizing users feedback from nonverbal communicative acts in conversational recommender systems. Pattern Recogn. Lett. **99**, 87–95 (2017). https://doi.org/10.1016/j.patrec.2017.06.011

24. Hepperle, D., Weiß, Y., Siess, A., Wölfel, M.: 2D, 3D or speech? a case study on which user interface is preferable for what kind of object interaction in immersive virtual reality. Comput. Graph. **82**, 321–331 (2019). https://doi.org/10.1016/j.cag.2019.06.003

25. Doukakis, E., et al.: Audio-visual-olfactory resource allocation for tri-modal virtual environments. IEEE Trans. Visual Comput. Graph. **25**(5), 1865–1875 (2019). https://doi.org/10.1109/TVCG.2019.2898823

26. Wang, X., Ong, S.K., Nee, A.Y.C.: Multi-modal augmented-reality assembly guidance based on bare-hand interface. Adv. Eng. Inform. **30**(3), 406–421 (2016). https://doi.org/10.1016/j.aei.2016.05.004

27. Brito, P.Q., Stoyanova, J.: Marker versus markerless augmented reality. Which has more impact on users? Int. J. Hum.–Comput. Interac. **34**(9), 819–833 (2018). https://doi.org/10.1080/10447318.2017.1393974

28. Wang, J., Chellali, A., Cao, C.G.: Haptic communication in collaborative virtual environments. Hum. Factors **58**(3), 496–508 (2016). https://doi.org/10.1177/0018720815618808

29. Kim, Y., Hong, S., Kim, G.J.: Augmented reality-based remote coaching for fast-paced physical task. Virtual Reality **22**(1), 25–36 (2017). https://doi.org/10.1007/s10055-017-0315-2

30. Zsiga, K., Tóth, A., Pilissy, T., Péter, O., Dénes, Z., Fazekas, G.: Evaluation of a companion robot based on field tests with single older adults in their homes. Assist. Technol. **30**(5), 259–266 (2018). https://doi.org/10.1080/10400435.2017.1322158

31. De Clerk, M., Dangelmaier, M., Schmierer, G., Spath, D.: User Centered Design of Interaction Techniques for VR-Based Automotive Design Reviews. Frontiers in Robotics and AI 6, 13 (2019). https://doi.org/10.3389/frobt.2019.00013

32. Kim, K., Schubert, R., Hochreiter, J., Bruder, G., Welch, G.: Blowing in the wind: Increasing social presence with a virtual human via environmental airflow interaction in mixed reality. Comput. Graph. **83**, 23–32 (2019). https://doi.org/10.1016/j.cag.2019.06.006

33. Rau, P.L.P., Zheng, J., Wei, Y.: Distractive effect of multimodal information in multisensory learning. Comput. Educ. **144**, 103699 (2020). https://doi.org/10.1016/j.compedu.2019.103699

34. Schüssel, F., Honold, F., Weber, M.: Influencing factors on multimodal interaction during selection tasks. J. Multimodal User Interfaces **7**(4), 299–310 (2012). https://doi.org/10.1007/s12193-012-0117-5

35. Esteves, A., Shin, Y., Oakley, I.: Comparing selection mechanisms for gaze input techniques in head-mounted displays. Int. J. Hum. Comput. Stud. **139**, 102414 (2020). https://doi.org/10.1016/j.ijhcs.2020.102414

36. Heller, J., Chylinski, M., de Ruyter, K., Mahr, D., Keeling, D.I.: Touching the untouchable: exploring multi-sensory augmented reality in the context of online retailing. J. Retail. **95**(4), 219–234 (2019). https://doi.org/10.1016/j.jretai.2019.10.008

37. Bajpai, A., Powel, J.C., Young, A.J., Mazumdar, A.: Enhancing physical human evasion of moving threats using tactile cues. IEEE Trans. Haptics **13**(1), 32–37 (2020). https://ieeexplore.ieee.org/document/8943999

38. Bell, J.D., Macuga, K.L.: Goal-directed aiming under restricted viewing conditions with confirmatory sensory feedback. Hum. Mov. Sci. **67**, 102515 (2019). https://doi.org/10.1016/j.humov.2019.102515

39. Richer, R., Zhao, N., Eskofier, B.M., Paradiso, J.A.: Exploring smart agents for the interaction with multimodal mediated environments. Multimodal Technol. Interact. **4**(2), 27 (2020). https://doi.org/10.3390/mti4020027

40. Rau, P.L.P., Zheng, J.: Modality capacity and appropriateness in multimodal display of complex non-semantic information stream. Int. J. Hum Comput. Stud. **130**, 166–178 (2019). https://doi.org/10.1016/j.ijhcs.2019.06.008

41. Gibson, A., Webb, A., Stirling, L.: Evaluation of a visual-tactile multimodal display for surface obstacle avoidance during walking. IEEE Trans. Hum.-Mach. Syst. **48**(6), 604–613 (2018). https://doi.org/10.1109/THMS.2018.2849018

42. Jevtić, A., et al.: Personalized robot assistant for support in dressing. IEEE Trans. Cogn. Dev. Syst. **11**(3), 363–374 (2018). https://doi.org/10.1109/TCDS.2018.2817283

43. Xiao, R., Schwarz, J., Throm, N., Wilson, A.D., Benko, H.: MRTouch: adding touch input to head-mounted mixed reality. IEEE Trans. Visual Comput. Graphics **24**(4), 1653–1660 (2018). https://doi.org/10.1109/TVCG.2018.2794222

An Unheimlich Media: Bringing the Uncanny into the World

Kenneth Feinstein(✉) ⓘ

Sunway University, No. 5, Jalan Universiti, 47500 Bandar Sunway, Selangor Darul Ehsan, Malaysia
kenf@sunway.edu.my

Abstract. This paper looks at how the uncanny has become a fundamental element in the creation of media art. How the juxtaposition of desperate elements has become central to how we understand the creation of meaning in contemporary culture. It traces how the idea of the uncanny has developed in Western culture and how it has our changing idea of Otherness has influenced and been influenced by the uncanny in the form of montage. Lastly it looks at examples of how contemporary media works as 'pataphysical objects embody the uncanny.

Keywords: The uncanny · Media art · Montage · Martin Buber · Emmanuel Lévinas · Freud · Pataphysics

1 Introduction

Since the invention of photography, we have entered the age of media art and mass media. How we encounter and relate to images and sound has transformed how we experience the world. It has allowed us to see beyond our direct environment and has allowed us to experience the world beyond our physical presence. As such it has concretised Otherness, that which is not the self, as an active agent in our lives. As new mediums have developed this relationship with Otherness has changed. We have moved away from Cartesian thinking, the self is paramount and Otherness is at best an reflection back on the self if not an obstacle to the self [1]. Our devices, the photograph, film, video the smart phone has made us face Otherness as the reality that defines us. In order to understand how we live within otherness we have to understand how it functions and how those forces have moved us away from fearing the other to facing otherness as part of reality. Starting from the classic Freudian understanding of the unheimlich, the uncanny, as a source of terror moving through to an understanding of the montage as a way of using the uncanny as a way for us to face the other. We will see how the uncanny relates to this and how our relationship to the uncanny has changed as we have embraced the Otherness in our cultures.

© Springer Nature Switzerland AG 2021
M. Kurosu (Ed.): HCII 2021, LNCS 12762, pp. 220–229, 2021.
https://doi.org/10.1007/978-3-030-78462-1_16

2 The Uncanny and Montage

2.1 The Unheimlich

Sigmund Freud wrote about what the nature of the uncanny in its various forms in his essay of the same name. [2] the word he used for uncanny was *unheimlich* in German and started the essay with a detailed look at its various meanings. It translates as the unfamiliar or literally the unhomely. Implying the importance of familiarity and comfort to a sense of personal identity. Conversely saying that the unfamiliar is a threat to one's sense of self. Further saying that we naturally shy away from the unfamiliar because we find it threatening. For Freud the confronting of the other in the form of the uncanny is a challenge to the ego. It takes the form of confusing the internal (the ego) with the external (the other). As such the emphasis on the idea of terror and a threat to one's sense of personal identity may seem out of proportion in relation to our standards. It is still grounded on Cartesian idea of self. Where Being is grounded in an idea of a self that is singular and its relation to the other is secondary. In this view otherness is either a threat to the sovereignty of the self or it is a necessary inconvenience that we must come to terms with to survive while persevering our identity. For Freud, although we live in a world of otherness, the other possess a threat to the self and the issue is if we allow it to overwhelm us or not.

It is important to note that Freud's essay was written as narrative cinema was being developed and reflects a pre-media view of how we experience the world. It was written before media was a part of how we form our own identity and how it has changed our understanding of the relationship of the individual to others and Otherness.

What is interesting for us in Freud's work is how he defines what works possess the uncanny and why. He states that "an uncanny effect is often and easily produced by effacing the distinction between imagination and reality, such as when something that we have hitherto regarded as imaginary appears before us in reality." [2]. He goes on to say that different works that may possess the same unreal or magical effects or imagery may not be uncanny. He refers specifically to "fairy-tales" as an example of works that do not possess the uncanny. They are complete worlds unto themselves and as such what would seem to be uncanny in our world is just part of the logic of that world. Upsetting the sense of identity for characters in such a world is impossible because what would seem unworldly to us is normal in that world. In A. E. Hoffman's *The Sand-Man* the events that happen to Nathaniel create an uncanny effect because the world created is the same as our normal world. While the events that happen to Harry Potter are not uncanny because they exist in a world where they are just as logical as ours. The uncanny is found when the logical world we live in (the familiar) is put into juxtaposition to something that disrupts it.

The uncanny, unheimlich, exists through the confronting or juxtaposition of the real with something that interrupts or contrasts it. The discomfort found therein is caused by this interruption making us view our own position to the real in a different way. It takes the real from being a given that we live into something which becomes a vehicle for meaning and makes us conscious of our relation to otherness. Such a situation is found in our modern media environment. As we moved from the early mass media of daily newspapers, cheap prints & books to the variety of media that directly challenge our sense of time, place and the sovereignty of the self, montage has been a key tactic that has framed how we encounter the world. It has allowed us to experience fragmentation as being meaningful and made what Freud describes as a threat into a way to find a place for ourselves within society.

2.2   The Montage

About a century and a half ago with the coming of rotogravure cheap mass market periodicals came into being. In the early 20th century photogravure allowed images to be easily incorporated into the newspapers and magazine. Along with this was the development of cinematic language. A consequence of this was forms of artistic practice developed, the collage and montage. It was developed by Dadaists, Russian Constructivist and film artist. As a form it was interested in in finding new ways of communicating a new vision of the world to a general public. While at times collage and montage have been used interchangeably, a distinction needs to be made in order to understand the intentions of the two different image making processes.

There were 19th century examples of collage in photography. Most notably in the Pictorialism of Henry Peach Robinson's *Fading Away and* Oscar Rejlander's *The Two Ways of Life.* Here desperate images were collages together to create a realistic image. The collaging of the image was meant to be hidden. The image was to be read in the same manner as the tableaux vivant as exemplified in works such as Jacques Louis David's *The Death of Socrates* or Gustave Courbet's *The Painter's Studio.* Such images were very easy to read because of how it related back to our reality. We can see a direct relationship between Robinson and David's images. They both depict the climactic moment of their stories, the moment before death, and they follow Diderot's ideas of narrative and tableaux vivant. In the case if Courbet and Rejlander, although they are tableaux vivant images, they are in the tradition allegorical paintings such as Raphael's *School of Athens* or *The Disputation of the Holy Sacrament* in composition and form. They tell a moral tales where the people depicted are there not as a part of a narrative, but for symbolic reasons. This type of photography, Pictorialism, saw itself as extending painting into photography and thus giving it the status of fine art. The use of collage here is to take various images and recreate them into a new image that maintains the language of realism. It is this aspect of what a collage is that I want to distinguish from montage. While montage is a subset of collage, montages allow the viewer to be aware of juxtaposition of the disparate elements that create it. It disrupts the visual plane so that meaning is found through the interrelationship of the various elements as they come together into a new whole.

The Dadaists and Surrealist used montage to find a new visual language that moved beyond the rational and objective world. Trying to find a way of making sense of a world where pure reason had been torn asunder by the irrational chaos of the First World War. In the Dadaists and Surrealists cases they were invoking the irrational. While the Constructivists wanted to find a new vision for a new society. For them the new images had to upset the traditional pictural language, just as their political revolution had the Czarist system. We can see this in the work of the Constructivists like the Stenberg brothers, Alexander Rodchenko and Lyubov Popova, to name a few. In the Western left-wing press artists like John Heartfield were using collage as political commentary.

These types of photomontage worked through the creation of juxtapositions that were contradictory, associative or had a visual continuity that created a new visual world. Meaning was created through how the disparate images came together; the new image's meaning is formed by the relationship of the elements to each other creating a message not found in the original images. In this way photomontage works similarly to Gilles Deleuze explanation of the function of cinematic montage [3]. The significant difference being that cinematic montage can be used to create a seamless feeling of reality and photomontage emphasises the disparity of images.

The nature of these juxtapositions of disparate images is to create an effect that is uncanny. It is the disruptive nature of the final image that makes one stop and question what was happening in the image and what its greater meaning is. Photomontage assumed that the viewer approached the image much like a text. They created works that were meant to be read like a text. Much like Western advertising would do later, they tended to incorporate text into the montages to regulate the meaning of the montage. As a political tool it has had great effect as commentary on the world. We can see this in the works of not only Heartfield in the 1930s, but more recently in the work of contemporary artists such as Peter Kennard, Hans Haacke and Krzysztof Wodiczko. The Surrealist drew directly from Freud and his theories of the unconscious and the uncanny. In their hands, the montage was more derived from the artist's discovering an unconscious that runs under the surface of their psyche. Their images were more confounding in meaning, tended to incorporate text as at title for a work and be less interested in an easily derived meaning from the work; being more ambiguous images.

In both cases, photomontage was used to bring out meaning lying below the surface. It presented us with a strange world residing within our ordinary one. Reflecting on and critiquing the real as we experience it. As such they were linked to the idea of the uncanny. Its uncanniness is what activates it as a form.

Where the Freudian *unhelimlich* has been interpreted as one's relation to dread or terror, in this paper the aim is to look at the uncanny as the facing of otherness as being beyond interpretation and control, dislocation and the unease this causes.

3 Montage and Otherness

3.1 The Self and the Other

Common to Kant's sublime and Freud's uncanny is a confrontation between the self and an otherness bigger than the self. For both of them this confrontation invokes dread and fear. It questions the idea of the self as singular and Being as supreme. It exposes the possibility of Otherness being prior to and fundamental to the establishment of Being. This idea of the self as unique and supreme to world grounded in the Cartesian *cogito* and the establishment of the subjective as identity. The statement, 'I think therefore I am' first defines the speaker as subject and then acknowledges the speaker through self-reflection. I am the subject of the statement and my subjectivity is enunciated. I exist because I can state that I exist. It is propositions that are linked up naturally, because if it is true that a statement is produced by a subject, then for that very reason this subject will be divided into the subject of enunciation and the subject of the statement." [1]. The cogito establishes the importance and supremacy of the self in the world. What we encounter, how we encounter it is based on this split between the subject and an enunciation that goes back to the subject. In Cartesian terms all thought and experience comes from the interaction of the subject with the world. Our desire or *jouissance* comes from how we encounter the word on the one hand, but also how we incorporate it back to ourselves as subject. It acknowledges the world while trying to subsume it to the self. This is why for both Kant and Freud the first reaction to facing the reality of Otherness is terror. Because it cannot be subsumed into the self, it challenges how they have constructed identity and terror is a reaction that goes beyond reason. Otherness is seen as a challenge to the sovereignty of the self which Kant resolves in the divine. For Freud this challenge is subsumed back into the ego. Thus, defusing its threat. In both cases encountering the others or the Other does not challenge supremacy of the cogito. We make our way in the world despite the fact that there are others. The relationship of Otherness.

3.2 The Uncanny as Facing Otherness

In the 20th century a different understanding of the Other was developed. Finding the cogito to be a fallacy it posited that we are defined through our relationship to the Other not despite it. This view of being as in relation to the Other is posited by Martin Buber in *I and Thou*. Cartesian thought sees the self as subjective and the world as objective. Being in the world is interacting with a series of objects as an I-It relationship. Others may be animate, but they remain as It to us. Buber replaces that with I, You and It. For him the I-You relationship is one of dialog and mutual interdependence. We are defined through our interaction with others one which creates a space in between. "There is no I as such but only the I of the basic word I-You and the I of the basic word I-It." [4]. The I-It is the world as we experience in relation to goals. The I-You is experience as relation. "The world as experience belongs to the basic word I-It. The basic word I-You establishes the world of relation." [4]. I-You is defined by relation and not turning that which is before you into a means to an end. For media art practice, this means that even though an image or work is a thing for Buber we can still enter into an I-You relationship.

Emmanuel Lévinas further elaborated on the I-You concept into a fuller understanding of our being-in-the-world as not just a relation with the other, but that we as individuals bare a responsibility for the Other. Taking from Martin Heidegger, the importance of existence of self as being-in-the-world. He moves further to our being-for-the-world. For him we are not merely in relation with the other, but we exist because of and for the Other. Our living in the world can only happen as part of the interrelationship with reality that we call the world. That we come from the other and form the self in relation to the other means that as much as it is responsible for us, we in turn are responsible to it [5]. The means that we must enter into relationship with it without reducing its otherness to symbols or themes. We have to face otherness in its reality. We first experience what the montage as a whole, we look at it in its face only then can we come to terms with it and start to ask what it wants to tell us.

This is in very direct contrast to Freud whose process is to reduce our encounters with the other to understandable symbols and themes. It is in this in this irreconcilable tension between having to face the other in its reality, beyond meaning, and the desire to reduce those encounters to symbols that have meaning to the self that is the source of the terror and threat Freud writes about. The terror of the uncanny is found in the inability to face being in the world with the Other. With the invention of montage, we find that the confrontation of desperate elements with each other creates a new way of presenting meaning. We can see the relationship between montage and to Buber's idea of dialog. On one level conversation is the centre of montage, both between the elements in the image and between the montage and the viewer. On top of this, Lévinas' contention is that we have to face the other head on as something that we cannot reduce to a sign or read just as signification. If we look at montage as a vehicle for communication, we see that the uncanny is the excess that brings us face to face with the work as an experience.

It is a method grounded in a view where we exist because of our being-in-the-world not despite it.

4 The Uncanny as an Artistic Form

The uncanny as a manifestation in art and design is asking us to face that other and accept it as more than a projection of self or a threat. Instead, it presents questions of how we see the world and asks us to be present within it. The montage aesthetic is one that allows disparate elements to interact. They become other than their elements. It makes sense only in how each part makes the different elements face each other without thematizing one to the other. It is the coming together of the elements while maintaining an identity through a medium that gives these works resonance.

If as Lévinas says that the our relationship with the Other grounds us in the ethical, [6] then the uncanny's excess allows such works to function as art. The montage, especially as contemporary media art, moves away from simple meaning in the fashion of semiotics and becomes experiential. As works become more experiential in form they can only become complete works through some type of interaction. They exist through the effects that they present to the viewer. In this way they become conversational. As Freud reminds us the uncanny is an effect, it only exists when it is experienced. It is actualised in its becoming. For works of art we can say that is emphasises interaction as creating a relationship between the work and the viewer, that the situation is one created through being-with. As such the viewer is forced to face the work as another, the experience is an event, a moment out of time where we face the other in their fullness. Such an experience presents an effect that moves beyond programmed meaning into a relationship between the work and the viewer. Making meaning an act of being-with-the-other. And by doing so placing us in the world.

4.1 The Montage Becomes Presence

The nature of our relationship to the uncanny has been transformed by technology. As Freud stated that the "fairy-tales" cannot be uncanny, because they create a whole or unified world. In contrast the montage does use the uncanny because it questions the very idea of a unified or whole world. Starting with photography, we have been able to create images which are direct records of the real world. We have put these images into relation to each other and the viewer to create new ways of seeing and interpreting reality and our relationship to otherness (both people and images). As the technology has developed artists have continued to develop new practises utilising the idea of the montage. From the late Fifties and early Sixties montage started to move in two parallel tracks, the fine art world and independent cinema. In the art world the main focus revolved around Fluxus. Much like Dada before it, Fluxus questioned art practice and reinvented it through a montage aesthetic. They brought in different elements of the world into works by breaking down the relationship of audience to work through what Allan Kaprow called happenings. Where traditional works are objects to be observed, happenings are occurrences that happen in time and space. The work is the unfolding of a planned moment in time and space. They are moments when participants move outside of their daily world and the laws of cause and effect, to become present in a moment of direct relation to the other. The combination of disparate elements now incorporates the viewer, the image, time and space. It becomes pure presence where differing parts exist in relation to each other, what Heidegger has called *being-there* [7].

We can find this creation of the event as being-there in John Cage's *4':33"* (1952) and Nam June Paik's *Zen for Film* (1964). *4':33"* is a performance in which the performer doesn't play music, turning the ambient sound of the environment into music. While *Zen for Film* projects blank filmstock on to the cinema wall making is aware of being in relation to the machinery of cinema, the projector and film. In both cases there is an absence of what is expected in the performance experience which makes us question the nature of the form as well as an uncomfortableness in being present within the event creating an uncanny feeling. Common to both works also is a relationship to the technology of performance. Where we easily understand that Cage's work is never the same twice, Paik's work also has this quality. When a piece of film goes through the gate of the projector a mark is left. A piece of dirt or scratch will occur which demotes the physicality of film as well as marking the movement of time. This trope was later used by Derek Jarman in his film *Blue*. All three works exist as becomings and not as objects or performances in the traditional sense. They unfold via the relationship of the work and the audience.

The other direction where montage was developing as artistic practise was in the experimental and expanded film movements. The earliest experimental films to the 1920's made by artists such as Ferdinand Léger, Hans Richter, Marcel Duchamp and Man Ray. They combined ideas of cinematic montage from Eisenstein and combined it with cubist and photomontage. Creating a new form of cinema. What they gave us was both the beginnings of independent film and a new less narrative film form. This was picked up by post war artists such as Stan Brakhage, Harry Smith, Bruce Conner who use visual montage as well as film makers like Isadore Isou and Guy Debord separated image from sound as a form of montage. For these artists, cinema was becoming a form of expression as unique as painting was for the generations before. Incorporating the ideas of the uncanny and associative thinking within their work, they set out to reinvent film to address the same concepts as the Surrealists and Cubists before them. These artists created films for the cinema. They expected their work to be seen in a black-ened theatre with a seated audience. They pushed what could be seen on the screen but remained within the basic form of film. As they started film collectives and alternative spaces, they tried to turn the cinema (theatre) into a parallel to the art gallery. Giving us a relationship of the white cube (the gallery) to the black box (cinema) [8].

Continuing with fine art practice the gallery was used as a space in which to stage performative events and to be the site of a new sense of montage as objects in physical space. Works like Hans Haacke's are made as dialogs. They continue the use of montage as a way of creating new understanding through the juxtaposition of disparate elements. A work like *Helmsboro Country* (1990) uses not only the 2D montaging of the Marlboro cigarette box with images of Jesse Helms a senator with financial ties to the cigarette industry and the cultural wars of the time, but by making it a three-dimensional object that is human sized the viewer is put in direct relationship to the work presenting the uncanny through scale and proximity. This continues through with artists such as Tiffany Chung, Kara Walker, and Tintin Wulia who use the physicality of the exhibition space to transform it into an environment.

Starting in the 60's with the development of small projectors for film and video art, gallery practice has combined with the expanded cinema movement. Expanded film saw the relationship between the image and the audience as being-with relationship. They called this intermedia. Today we now use names such as Mixed Reality or Installation for similar works. Artists like Stan Vander Beek were interested "intermedia environments [that] turn the participant inward upon himself, providing a matrix for psychic exploration, perceptual, censorial, and intellectual awareness; on the other hand technology has advanced to the point at which the whole earth itself becomes the 'content' of aesthetic activity." [9]. We can see that although the language used may seem dated to us, it is referring to the idea of a facing of Otherness as a method of expanding the consciousness of the self.

As imaging technology developed with video and later digital imaging, the white cube could become a place to present time-based images. The cinema as art space became absorbed into the gallery opening up the ability to create unique environments to present uncanny environments. Where the cinema or even the Movie Drome was fixed in form now each work could create its own form. Allowing a unique way to present the zone for the work and the audience to experience each other. Artists such as Gary Hill, Bill Viola and Isaac Julian have placed fragmented images into galleries as constructed space. They have used multiple screens as a form of fragmentation where it becomes impossible for a viewer to experience as a whole. This turns what in a cinema would be a passive experience into one where the viewer discovers their own relationship with the images before them. The experience of viewing becomes both uncanny and a montage at the same time. Julian even calls his method multiscreen montage. It is this being-with which defines the work. Taking this in a different direction, people like Nam June Paik, Tony Ousler and Daniel Rozin have create time-based media works that are more sculptural based. Works like Paik's *TV Buddha* (1974) and Rozin's mechanical mirrors use the media as a way of the viewer to find a level of self-reflection a way to understand the relationship of self to the Other. Viewers are turned into images of self that they experience as both being and other at the same time. These contemporary works be they multiple images, installations or image/objects all resonate because they have moved away from established form into unique objects. They have used a montage aesthetic to create uncanny objects to communicate to and with us. The individuality of the workplaces us into direct relation to us demanding that we relate it as other to us. As other we first face it in its reality, as something irreducible to the semiotic order and only from there can we start to create meaning. It is the individuality of the viewer and the work, this facing of one to the other which creates an uncanny feeling, forcing us to face Otherness in it s reality. Each object exists as a unique and particular being who we enter into relationship with. This relationship is uncanny and ethical, while the object in its individuality is also a 'pataphysical object.

5   The Montage as the Pataphysical Object

In *The Exploits and Opinions of Doctor Faustroll, Pataphysician*, Alfred Jarry creates and defines as "pataphysics will be, above all, the science of the particular… Pataphysics will examine the laws governing exceptions and will explain the universe supplementary to this one[.]" [10]. We can say that the 'pataphysical is the uncanny brought to life. It is the creation of a unique moment outside of our normal life, which bares meaning on all those involved. It is not exception for the sake of difference, but rather the valorisation of the event. Doctor Faustroll's opinions parody scientific knowledge in a way that puts it in relation to its exception or opposite. His opinion is montage as thought. As a model 'pataphysics becomes a way of understanding and facing the uncanny not as terror, but rather as parody or even joy. It calls the supremacy of logic and reason into question. When we call 'pataphysics parody we do not mean that it is a joke as much as a way of using existing elements in juxtaposition to ideas of fancy or moving accepted reason to a logical conclusion which becomes absurd. As such it incorporates the same type of methods and tools as montage. The 'pataphysical as parody demonstrates that rational knowledge is always a reduction of the experience into a simplified form. Its function is to make us understand our assumptions of reality as being as constructed as any fantasy. It does not deny the Real, rather it reminds us that we find it hard to face and that we create explanations and frameworks so that we don't have to face it in its own reality. 'Pataphysically experiences are more real than explanations.

This is why Jarry and the 'pataphysical were adopted by the Surrealists along with Freudian psychology. From performative art to the Movie Drome and now site-specific art we can see how 'pataphysical has become a model for how art defines its relationship to the Other. That by creating something unique it can create a place and a moment, an event, where the experience of facing the work as other comes first and before any chance to turn the work into a semiotic object. The 'pataphysical aspect of this is the recognition that once we do turn a work into a sign, we have reduced it to a parody of itself. By using the montage aesthetic, contemporary art has tried to make come face to face with Otherness and by doing so they have created 'pataphysical objects.

References

1. Deleuze, G.: Dualism, monism and multiplicities (Desire-Pleasure-Jouissance), Contretemps: Online J. Philos. **2**, 17 (2001)
2. Freud, S., McLintock, D., Haughton, H.: The Uncanny. Penguin Books (2003)
3. Deleuze, G.A.: Cinema I: the movement-image

 4. Buber, M., Kaufmann, W.A.: I and Thou. Scribner (1970)
 5. Lévinas, E.: Entre Nous: on Thinking-of-the-Other. Columbia University Press (1998)
 6. Lévinas, E.: Time and the Other and Additional Essays. Duquesne University Press (1987)
 7. Lévinas, E.: God, Death, and Time. Stanford University Press (2000)
 8. Uroskie, A.V.: Between the Black Box and the White Cube: Expanded Cinema and Postwar Art. University of Chicago Press (2014)
 9. Youngblood, G.: Expanded Cinema, 1st edn. Dutton (1970)
10. Jarry, A., Jarry, A.A.l., Jarry, A.D., Nights Jarry, A.E.: And opinions of doctor Faustroll. In: Three Early Novels. Atlas (2006)

Implementation Goals for Multimodal Interfaces in Human-Computer Interaction

Sónia Rafael[1]([✉]) and Victor M. Almeida[2]

[1] Universidade de Lisboa, Faculdade de Belas-Artes, ITI – Interactive Technologies Institute/LARSyS, Largo da Academia Nacional de Belas-Artes, 1249-058 Lisboa, Portugal
s.rafael@belasartes.ulisboa.pt
[2] Universidade de Lisboa, Faculdade de Belas-Artes, Centro de Investigação e de Estudos em Belas-Artes (CIEBA), Largo da Academia Nacional de Belas-Artes, 1249-058 Lisboa, Portugal
v.almeida@belasartes.ulisboa.pt

Abstract. A multimodal interface will only be adequate if it is validated by usability criteria, namely, if it promotes: a faster interaction; a selective adaptation to different environments, users or usage behaviours; a shorter learning curve or being more intuitive; the recognition of information in a noisy environment (*e.g.* at the sound, visual or tactile level); the connection of presented information to a more global contextual knowledge (enabling an easier interpretation); and the translation of information between modalities. Hence, the option for a multimodal interface, over a unimodal, depends on the type of action to be carried out by the user, its potential for increased usability and experience it can provide. The multimodal interface research area constitutes a very active and constantly expanding interdisciplinary territory, and this fact contributes to the numerous implementation goals attributed to these interfaces. This article seeks to identify and enumerate them, supporting itself on a thorough bibliographic analysis.

Keywords: HCI · Multimodal interfaces · Implementation goals · Usability · Interaction design

1 Introduction

The scope of Human-Computer Interaction today encompasses physical devices of interaction that would otherwise have been inconceivable, such as the use of electrodes introduced at various points in the nervous system that monitor brain activity and use these signals to issue orders or commands; the use of muscle contraction for the production of local electrical signals in the control of myo-electric prostheses in amputated limbs; the control of AI's through variations in the electromagnetic fields generated by the human body; among others. For this reason, the possibility of physical interaction devices that use forms of interaction that are currently functionally impractical or even unimaginable in the contemporary context should not be excluded.

The area of study of interaction has progressively evolved and developed preoccupations increasingly focused on the user's usability and accessibility, as well as on the ubiquity, naturalness and multimodality of interactive processes.

© Springer Nature Switzerland AG 2021
M. Kurosu (Ed.): HCII 2021, LNCS 12762, pp. 230–239, 2021.
https://doi.org/10.1007/978-3-030-78462-1_17

Multimodality is still one of the most important challenges in the scope of HCI, that require your understanding to look into the universe of all usable modalities [1] and that can be implemented in interactive devices. To this end, it is necessary to properly analyse the situations and dimensions in which each of the modalities of a multimodal interface is effectively superior to the typical graphical user interfaces (GUI) [2]. A user should be free to use a combination of modalities or choose to use only the one he considers most appropriate to the characteristics of the task or the interaction environment in which he finds himself [3].

Sharma et al. [61] understand that man perceives the environment in which he lives through the five classic senses – sight, hearing, touch, smell and taste – acting on it through actuators– for example, the body, hands, face and mouth. In this way, human-human interaction will be based on the perception of the actions of the actuators, in a given environment. At HCI, the computer assumes the role of perceiving the actions of the human user. The authors also mention that computers incorporate modalities that man does not have, for example, the ability that they have to estimate the position of the hand through magnetic sensors or subtle changes in the electrical activity of the brain. Thus, there is a vast repertoire of human action modalities that can be perceived by a computer, even though in their investigation they have concluded that the current physical technologies that support common HCI are circumscribed to the human senses to which they apply. Predominantly only three senses are used: sight, hearing and touch, despite finding proposals for integrating other senses in the interaction with the computer.

Multimodality has the potential to increase the usability, flexibility and efficiency of access to information services. Despite recent technological developments in the field of human-computer interaction based on the re-knowledge and interpretation of the message and the understanding of communication processes, the lack of understanding of how interaction modes can be combined in the user interface often originates solutions with poor usability [4]. The option for a multimodal interface, instead of a unimodal interface, depends on the type of task, the added usability and a better experience of use that this interface can provide.

2   Potentialities and Constraints of Multimodal Interfaces

Multimodal interfaces are a class of multimedia systems that integrate artificial intelligence and have gradually acquired the ability to understand, interpret and generate specific data in response to the analysis content, differing from classic multimedia systems and applications that do not understand the semantics of the data (sound, image, video) that they manipulate [4, 5].

Although both types of systems can use similar physical input and output means (acquiring, storing and generating visual and sound information), each serves a different purpose: in the case of multimedia systems, the information is subject to the task being manipulated by the user; in the case of multimodal systems, information is a resource for executing the control processes of the task itself. More than the simple juxtaposition of various modes of interaction, a multimodal system must consider its possible synergistic combinations in order to overcome individual weaknesses and obtain (ideally) the sum of its expressive strengths. This fact will have as main objective to originate a superior usability and a more expressive use experience.

In this regard, Soares and Rebelo refer that "Successful interaction with products, tools, and technologies depends on usable designs, accommodating the needs of potential users and does not require costly training." [6].

Martin *et al.* [7] argue that, in the scope of a computer system, the option for multimodal solutions will only be convenient, if it has been ratified by usability criteria. For example, they mention the following: if it allows a faster interaction; if it allows a selective adaptation to different environments, users or usage behaviours; if it enables a shorter learning curve or is more intuitive; if it improves the recognition of information in a noisy environment (*e.g.* at the sound, visual or tactile level); if it allows the connection of presented information to a more global contextual knowledge (enabling an easier interpretation); and if it allows the translation of information between modalities.

This is also the understanding of [8], when they state that the option for a multimodal interface, instead of a unimodal solution, depends on the type of action to be carried out by the user and its potential for increased usability.

In this line of thought, Martin [9] indicated that an empirical analysis of the results of the use of multimodal interaction is necessary to contextually validate its superiority in relation to unimodality.

Their studies have shown that there are interaction contexts in which the use of more than just one modality can lead to the production of a greater number of errors as well as a lower speed of interaction.

In fact, the various input and output channels usable in HCI (keyboard, mouse, touch screen, microphone, motion sensor, monitor, loudspeaker, haptic receivers, etc.) have their own benefits and limitations, so the multimodal interaction is often used to compensate for the limitations of one modality, making another available [10]. Each input modality must be adapted to a set of interaction contexts, not being ideal or even being inappropriate [3] in others; for this reason, the selection of the interaction modality is a matter of extreme relevance in a multimodal system.

At the heart of multimodal systems, there are also other relevant issues such as information fusion techniques. More than the simple juxtaposition of various modalities in the user interface, their possible synergistic combinations must be considered, in order to overcome individual weaknesses and obtain (ideally) the sum of their expressive strengths. This can lead to greater usability. This superior usability is a possibility that, according to Bretan and Karlgren [34], results from the fact that certain modalities support different communicative intentions through different degrees of adequacy.

However, the implementation of data fusion systems from different sensors is not simple and can even lead to the production of worse results than would be obtained through the selection and use of the most appropriate sensor. Such results could, for example, originate from the combination of an exact set of data, coming from a modal source, with an imprecise set of data, coming from another. For this reason, the structuring of a data fusion system for a given application [14], should address the following fundamental issues:

- which algorithms or techniques are appropriate for an application.
- what data fusion architecture should be used (*i.e.,* at what stage of the process should the data be merged).

- how the data from each sensor should be processed to extract as much information as possible.
- what accuracy can realistically be achieved by the data fusion process.
- how the fusion process can be dynamically optimized.
- how the environmental context of data collection disrupts its processing.
- and under what conditions the fusion of multisensory data improves the system.

In turn, Esteban *et al.* [60] argue that the specific combination of sensors to be used depends on the system requirements, and the following issues should be considered (in the process of defining the type of fusion algorithm used and the phase in which the data must be fused): the way the sensors are distributed; the format, type and accuracy of the data collected; the nature of the sensors used; the resolution of the sensors used; and the computing capacity available for each of the sensors.

On the other hand, the fusion of multisensory data presents, among others, the following difficulties: the diversity of sensors used (their nature, their timing, their location, the format of data collected, etc.); the diversity of data represented (*e.g.* image, space, statistics and text); the checking of the consistency of the data collected, with subsequent elimination of fallacious data sets; the calibration of sensors when errors occur in the operation of the system; the operating limitations of the sensors; and the deficiencies of the statistical models of the sensors and limitations in the development of the algorithm.

Based on the aforementioned understanding, the architecture of the implementation of a specific multisensory data fusion solution is critical to its success, and its selection must be supported by a deep understanding of the countless possibilities for interaction [60].

3 Development Requirements

System designers increasingly resort to a greater number of different input/output modalities (which often present themselves as alternatives), in the exchange of information between systems and their users.

Maybury [62] states that the design of multimodal interfaces needs to be based on a specific set of principles: selection of the content to be transferred; assigning appropriate modalities to the content; and functional implementation of the modality, ensuring the transfer of content.

Bernsen [63] presents an analogous logic of procedures that interface designers must consider identifying the information to be exchanged between users and the system; implement a good correspondence between the information and the available input/output modalities, in terms of functionality, usability, naturalness, efficiency, etc.; and proceed with the design, implementation and testing of the interface.

The usability of multimodal interfaces can, in general, be facilitated if users are familiar with this mode of interaction. To this end, it is important to develop standards across all interfaces [23].

Some interfaces place an excessive cognitive burden on its users, although this is a problem that can be overcome by its "disappearance" so that users focus exclusively on the activity and its implications.

In turn, Reeves et al. [19] mention that it is necessary to define guidelines that facilitate the design of mainstream multimodal systems. They present six initial strategies that, if followed, will constitute a significant step towards their success and general acceptance:

1. Clear specification of requirements for the interface, with particular attention to the concern that it should cover a maximum number of users, contexts of use and possible applications, in order to ensure flexibility for users with skills and limitations and in situations that impose different restrictions or possibilities of use.
2. Concern with the necessary flexibility in the decision, by users, of how their privacy and security will be managed.
3. Option for input and output multimodality, in order to maximize the cognitive and physical capacities, as well as the usage preferences of the various users.
4. Use of consistent terminology, presentation and operation of the interface.
5. Constant feedback to the user from the interface, so that the user is aware of the point of usage at which he finds himself and is constantly aware of the possibilities and channels of interaction available.
6. Prevention and proper management of system and user errors, providing ways for them to be consciously corrected.

4 Objectives for Multimodal Interfaces Implementation

In a context of Human-Computer Interaction, the emitter translates concepts (symbolic information) into physical events that are transmitted to the appropriate receiver and the latter interprets the received signal in terms of abstract symbols. These processes involve the user's senses and motor capabilities and, symmetrically, the input and output mechanisms of the system.

The objective of a multimodal system is to provide the extension of sensorimotor capabilities so that it replicates the processes of natural communication between human beings [11]. As this mode of communication involves the simultaneous use of several modalities, a computer system must be able to support them when interacting with the user. For this to happen, a multimodal computer system must be equipped with hardware that: allows it to acquire and/or transmit multimodal expressions (in a time compatible with the user's expectations); is able to choose the output mode that is appropriate to the content to be transmitted; and can understand multimodal input expressions [12].

The research area in multimodal interfaces is a very active and constantly expanding interdisciplinary territory. This reality contributes to its being assigned numerous implementation objectives, namely those of:

- promoting more natural, intuitive, efficient and, at the same time, less obstructive HCIs, associated with a fast-learning curve [4, 13–26, 49, 51, 52].
- increasing the amount of information transmitted in a timely manner during an HCI, with a consequent decrease in the time required for its execution [2, 4, 15–18, 20, 26–33, 49, 50, 54].
- increasing the robustness of the system, seeking to obtain superior intelligibility in the recognition of information through the crossing of signals received in different

modalities, with a view to resolving ambiguities, preventing errors in communication and/or solving them [4, 13–16, 18, 19, 23, 26, 28, 29, 32–36, 49, 53].

- stimulating the user's commitment to the activity to be developed, promoting the user's satisfaction [20, 26, 37, 38, 51, 52].
- promoting computers' understanding and anticipation of the user/human intentions [15, 17, 21, 31, 55, 58].
- allowing greater flexibility in accessibility to computers in contexts, which, being independent of the user, reveal usability constraints for a given modality (s), through the possibility of selection of the modal channel (s) that are most suitable to the user's preferences, degree of proficiency and/or the nature of the task to be performed [4, 19, 20, 26, 28, 29, 35, 39, 41–43, 49, 51, 52].
- allowing greater accessibility to computers by people with specific disabilities (whether sensory or motor), providing alternative modalities and multimodality styles [29, 35, 44, 45, 48, 51].
- promoting new forms of computing, not previously available [26, 29, 48, 59].
- providing alternation of input channels (modalities), in order to prevent cognitive and/or physical saturation, and consequent degradation, during prolonged use of the interface [19, 29, 35].
- reducing the cognitive load associated with a task and, consequently, the level of attention necessary for its execution [20, 24, 35, 50].
- enabling the adaptation of the computer system to the user's predominant interaction patterns, optimizing the HCI processes [15, 46, 47, 49, 51, 55, 56].

In this context, it is highlighted that there is an urge to resolve a possible confusion between implementation objectives and the results that are effectively produced through the development of the interaction.

5 Conclusion

This article, based on a literature review by the reference authors in the area of multimodality at HCI, identified and listed eleven objectives for the implementation of multimodal interfaces. It reinforces that the use of multimodal solutions must always be contextualized for each interaction and its adoption must be properly considered and evaluated.

The understanding that multimodality at HCI promotes greater naturalness, accessibility, flexibility, usability, as well as the amount of data transmitted and the reliability in its recognition, are common propositions of both academy and industry. These propositions are anchored in the recognition of the multimodal character of the processes of sensory perception and in the conviction that, through interfaces that replicate the modes of action in a human-human or human-environment context, the use of computer systems will be optimized.

However, research does not always support the defence that multimodal solutions alone ensure the development of more natural and effective interactions, as the opposite is sometimes the case. Thus, its adoption must be considered and validated in each context.

References

1. Blache, P., Rauzy, S., Ferré, G.: An XML coding scheme for multimodal corpus annotation. In: Proceedings of Corpus Linguistics (2007)
2. Cohen, P., Johnston, M., McGee, D., Oviatt, S., Clow, J., Smith, I.: The efficiency of multimodal interaction: a case study. In: Proceedings of the 5th International Conference on Spoken Language Processing, pp. 249–252. Sydney, Australia (1998)
3. Oviatt, S., et al.: Designing the user interface for multimodal speech and pen-based gesture applications: state of the art systems and future research directions. Hum. Comput. Interact. **15**(4), 263–322 (2000)
4. Bourguet, M.-L.: An overview of multimodal interaction techniques and applications. In: Zaphiris, P., Ang, C.S. (eds.) Human Computer Interaction: Concepts, Methodologies, Tools, and Applications, pp. 95–101. Information Science Reference, New York, USA (2009)
5. Nigay, L., Coutaz, J.: A design space for multimodal systems: concurrent processing and data fusion. In: Proceedings of INTERCHI 1993 – Conference on Human Factors in Computing Systems, joint conference of ACM SIG-CHI and INTERACT, pp. 172–178. Amsterdam, The Netherlands (1993)
6. Soares M., Rebelo F.: Preface. In: Soares, M., Rebelo, F. (Eds.), Advances in Usability Evaluation. Part 1 of Advances in Human Factors and Ergonomics Series, Xv. CRC Press, New York, USA (2012)
7. Martin, J.C., Veldman, R., Béroule, D.: Developing multimodal interfaces: a theoretical framework and guided propagation networks. In: Bunt, H., Beun, R.-J., Borghuis, T. (eds.) CMC 1995. LNCS, vol. 1374, pp. 158–187. Springer, Heidelberg (1998). https://doi.org/10.1007/BFb0052318
8. Ferri, F., Paolozzi, S.: Analyzing multimodal interaction. In: Grifoni, P. (ed.) Multimodal Human Computer Interaction and Pervasive Services, pp. 19–33. IGI Global, Hershey (2009)
9. Martin, J.-C.: Towards "intelligent" cooperation between modalities. The example of a system enabling multimodal interaction with a map. In: Proceedings of the IJCAI 1997. Workshop on Intelligent Multimodal Systems. Nagoya, Japan (1997)
10. James, F., Gurram, R.: Multimodal and federated interaction. In: Zaphiris, P., Ang, C.S. (Eds.) Human Computer Interaction: Concepts, Methodologies, Tools, and Applications, pp. 102–122. New York, USA (2009)
11. Dutoit, T., Nigay, L., Schnaider, M.: Editorial of the special issue on multimodal human-computer interfaces. Signal Process. **86**(12), 3515–3517 (2006)
12. Coutaz, J., Caelen, J.: A taxonomy for multimedia and multimodal user interfaces. In: Proceedings of the 1st ERCIM Workshop on Multimedia HCI, November 1991, Lisbon, Portugal (1991)
13. Cohen, P., et al.: Synergistic use of direct manipulation and natural language. In: Proceedings of CHI 1989: Conference on Human Factors in Computer Systems, pp. 227–233. New York, USA (1989)
14. Hall, D., Llinas, J.: An introduction to multi-sensor data fusion. In: Proceedings of the 1998 IEEE International Symposium on Circuits and Systems, vol. 6, pp. 6–23. IEEE, Monterey, CA, USA (1998)
15. Oviatt, S., Angeli, A., Kuhn, K.: Integration and synchronization of input modes during multimodal human-computer interaction. In: Proceedings of CHI 1997, pp. 415–422 (1997)
16. Vernier, F., Nigay, L.: A framework for the combination and characterization of output modalities. In: Palanque, P., Paternò, F. (Eds.) Lecture Notes in Computer Science, vol. 1946, pp. 35–50. Leipzig, Germany: Springer – Verlag, Berlin, Heidelberg (2001)
17. Abascal, J., Moriyón, R.: Tendencias en interacción persona computador. Revis. Iberoam. de Intel. Artif. **16**, 9–24 (2002)

18. Ko, T.: Untethered Human Motion Recognition for a Multimodal Interface. Massachusetts Institute of Technology. Cambridge, Massachusetts, USA (2003)
19. Reeves, L., et al.: Guidelines for multimodal user interface. Commun. ACM **47**(1), 57–59 (2004)
20. Anthony, L., Yang, J., Koedinger, K.: Evaluation of multimodal input for entering mathematical equations on the computer. In: ACM Conference on Human Factors in Computing Systems (CHI 2005), pp.1184 - 1187. Portland, OR, USA (2005)
21. Lee, J.: Spatial User Interfaces: Augmenting Human Sensibilities in a Domestic Kitchen. Massachusetts Institute of Technology. Cambridge, Massachusetts, USA (2005)
22. Karam, M., Schraefel, M.: A Taxonomy of Gestures in Human Computer Interaction. University of Southampton, Electronics and Computer Science (2005)
23. Sturm, J.: On the Usability of Multimodal Interaction for Mobile Access to Information Services. PhD Thesis. Radboud University Nijmegen, Nijmegen, The Netherlands (2005)
24. Anthony, L., Yang, J., Koedinger, K.: Entering Mathematical Equations Multimodally: Results on Usability and Interaction Patterns. Technical Report CMU-HCII-06-101 (2006)
25. Inanoglu, Z., et al.: Multimodal speaker identity conversion – continued. In: Preccedings eNTERFACE07 Summer Workshop on Multimodal Interfaces, pp. 51–60. Istambul, Turquia (2007)
26. Dumas, B., Lalanne, D., Oviatt, S.: Multimodal interfaces: a survey of principles, models and frameworks. In: Lalanne, D., Kohlas, J. (eds.) Human Machine Interaction. LNCS, vol. 5440, pp. 3–26. Springer, Heidelberg (2009). https://doi.org/10.1007/978-3-642-00437-7_1
27. Wahlster, W.: Pointing, language and the visual world: towards multimodal input and output for natural language dialog systems (Panel). In: Proceedings of the 10th International Joint Conference on Artificial Intelligence, 1163. Morgan Kaufmann. Milan, Italy (1987)
28. Cohen, P., et al.: QuickSet: multimodal interaction for simulation set-up and control. In: Proceedings of the Fifth Applied Natural Language Processing meeting, pp. 20–24 (1997)
29. Oviatt, S.: Designing robust multimodal systems for diverse users and environments. In: Workshop on Universal Accessibility of Ubiquitous Computing: Providing for the Elderly (2001)
30. Zenka, R., Slavík, P.: Multimodal interface for data retrieval during conversation. In: Proceedings for the 19th International CODATA Conference – The Information Society: New Horizons for Science [CD-ROM]. Paris: CODATA – International Council for Science (2004)
31. Pelachaud, C.: Multimodal expressive embodied conversational agents. In: Proceedings of the 13th annual ACM International Conference on Multimedia, pp. 683–689. Singapore (2005)
32. Bourguet, M.-L.: Towards a taxonomy of error-handling strategies in recognition-based multimodal human-computer interfaces. Signal Process. J. **86**(12), 3625–3643 (2007)
33. Kieffer, S., Carbonell, N.: How really effective are multimodal hints in enhancing visual target spotting? Some evidence from a usability study. J. Multimodal User Interfaces **1**(1), 1–5 (2007)
34. Bretan, I., Karlgren, J.: Synergy effects in natural language based multimodal interaction. In: Proceedings of the ERCIM 1993. Workshop on Multimodal Human-Computer Interaction. Nancy, France (1993)
35. Oviatt, S., Coulston, R., Lunsford, R.: When do we interact multimodally? Cognitive load and multimodal communication patterns. In: Proceedings of the 6th IEEE International Conference on Multimodal Interfaces, pp. 129–136. State College, PA, USA. ACM Press. New York (2004)
36. James, F., Gurram, R.: Multimodal and federated interaction. In: Zaphiris, P., Ang, C.S. (eds.) Human Computer Interaction: Concepts, methodologies, Tools, and Applications, pp. 102–122. Information Science Reference, New York, USA (2009)

37. Anastopoulou, S.: Investigating Multimodal Interactions for the Design of Learning Environments: A Case Study in Science Learning. PhD Thesis. University of Birmingham. Birmingham, United Kingdom (2004)
38. Lisowska, A.: Multimodal Interface Design for Multimedia Meeting Content Retrieval. PhD Thesis. Université de Genève, Geneva, Switzerland (2007)
39. Roth, S., Chuah, M., Kerpedjiev, S., Kolojejchick, J., Lucas, P.: Towards an information visualization workspace: combining multiple means of expression. Hum. Comput. Interact. **12**(1 & 2), 131–185 (1997)
40. Catinis, L.: Etude de L'usage de la Parole dans les Interfaces Multimodales. PhD Thesis. Institut National Polytechnique de Grenoble, Grenoble, France (1998)
41. López-Cózar, R.: Uso de Canales de Comunicación Adicionales en Sistemas Conversacionales. Proces. del Leng. Nat. **30**, 89–97 (2003)
42. D'Ulizia, A., Ferri, F.: Formalization of multimodal languages in pervasive computing paradigm. In: Advanced Internet Based Systems and Applications: 2nd International Conference on Signal-Image Technology and Internet-Based Systems, SITIS 2006. Hammamet, Tunisia (2006)
43. Zhang, Z.: Leveraging pervasive and ubiquitous service computing. In: Zaphiris, P., Ang, C. (Eds.) Human computer interaction: Concepts, Methodologies, Tools, and Applications, pp. 262–278. New York, USA (2009)
44. Mynatt, E.: Transforming graphical interfaces into auditory interfaces for blind users. Hum. Comput. Interact. **12**(1), 7–45 (1997)
45. Vetter, A., Chanier, T.: Supporting oral production for professional purposes in synchronous communication with heterogeneous learners. ReCALL J. EuroCALL **18**(1), 5–23 (2006)
46. Xiao, B., Girand, C., Oviatt, S.: Multimodal integration patterns in children. In: Proceedings of ICSLP 2002, pp. 629–632 (2002)
47. Oviatt, S., et al.: Toward a theory of organized multimodal integration patterns during human-computer interaction. In: Proceedings of the International Conference on Multimodal Interfaces (ICMI 2003), pp. 44–51. ACM Press, New York, USA (2003)
48. Rocha, L., Naves, E., Morére, Y., et al.: Multimodal interface for alternative communication of people with motor disabilities. Res. Biomed. Eng. **36**, 21–29 (2020)
49. Bubalo, N., Honold, F., Schüssel, F., Weber, M., Huckauf, A.: User expertise in multimodal HCI. In: Proceedings of the European Conference on Cognitive Ergonomics, Nottingham, UK (2016)
50. Oviatt, S.: Multimodal interfaces. In: Jacko, J. (Ed.) Human Computer Interaction Handbook: Fundamentals, Evolving Technologies, and Emerging Applications, Third Edition (Human Factors and Ergonomics). CRC Press. NY, USA (2012)
51. GhasemAghaei, R.: Multimodal software for affective education: user interaction design and evaluation. In: Unpublished Doctoral Dissertation. Carleton University, Ottawa (2017)
52. Srinivasan, A., Stasko, J.: Orko: facilitating multimodal interaction for visual exploration and analysis of networks. IEEE Trans. Visual Comput. Gr. **24**(1), 511–521 (2018)
53. Schaffer, S., Minge, M.: Error-prone voice and graphical user interfaces in a mobile application. In: Sprachkommunikation: Beitrage zur 10. ITG-Fachtagung vom 26. bis 28. September 2012 in Braunschweig, pp. 1–4. VDE-Verlag (2012)
54. Schaffer, S.: Modeling Modality Selection in Multimodal Human-Computer Interaction: Extending Automated Usability Evaluation Tools for Multimodal Input. Unpublished Doctoral Dissertation. Technical University of Berlin. Berlin (2016)
55. Keller, I., Ahmad, M., Lohan, K.: Multi-modal measurements of mental load. In: Paper presented at CHI 2019 Workshop 12: "The Challenges of Working on Social Robots that Collaborate with People", Glasgow, United Kingdom (2019)
56. Dermouche, S., Pelachaud, C.: Sequence-based multimodal behavior modeling for social agents. In: Proceedings of the International Conference on Multimodal Interaction (2016)

57. Hung, S.: Enhancing feedback provision through multimodal video technology. Comput. Educ. **98**, 90–101 (2015)
58. Min, W., et al.: Multimodal goal recognition in open-world digital games. In: The Thirteenth AAAI Conference on Artificial Intelligence and Interactive Digital Entertainment (AIIDE-17) (2017)
59. Liarokapis, F., Petridis, P., Andrews, D., Freitas, S.: Multimodal serious games technologies for cultural heritage. In: Ioannides, M., Magnenat-Thalmann, N., Papagiannakis, G. (eds) Mixed Reality and Gamification for Cultural Heritage. Springer, Cham (2017). https://doi.org/10.1007/978-3-319-49607-8_15
60. Esteban, J., Starr, A., Willetts, R., Hannah, P., Bryanston-Cross, P.: A review of data fusion models and architectures: towards engineering guidelines. Neural Comput. Appl. **14**, 273–281 (2005)
61. Sharma, R., Pavlovic, V.I., Huang, T.S.: Toward multimodal human-computer interface. In: Proceedings of the IEEE, Special Issue on Multimedia Signal Processing, 86(5), pp. 853–869 (1998)
62. Maybury, M.: Introduction. In: Maybury, M. (Ed.). Intelligent multimedia interfaces. Cambridge, MA: AAAI Press (1991)
63. Bernsen, N.O.: Modality theory in support of multimodal interface design. In: Proceedings of the AAAI Spring Symposium on Intelligent Multi-Modal Systems, pp. 37–44 (1994)

UX Evaluation Methods, Techniques and Tools

Guidelines for Collecting Automatic Facial Expression Detection Data Synchronized with a Dynamic Stimulus in Remote Moderated User Tests

Félix Giroux[1]([✉]), Pierre-Majorique Léger[1,2], David Brieugne[1],
François Courtemanche[1], Frédérique Bouvier[1], Shang-Lin Chen[1], Salima Tazi[1],
Emma Rucco[1], Marc Fredette[1,4], Constantinos Coursaris[1,2], and Sylvain Sénécal[1,3]

[1] Tech3Lab, HEC Montréal, Montréal, Québec, Canada
`felix.giroux@hec.ca`
[2] Department of Information Technologies, HEC Montréal, Montréal, Québec, Canada
[3] Department of Marketing, HEC Montréal, Montréal, Québec, Canada
[4] Department of Decision Sciences, HEC Montréal, Montréal, Québec, Canada

Abstract. Because of the COVID-19 pandemic, telework policies have required many user experience (UX) labs to restrict their research activities to remote user testing. Automatic Facial Expression Analysis (AFEA) is an accessible psychophysiological measurement that can be easily implemented in remote user tests. However, to date, the literature on Human Computer Interaction (HCI) has provided no guidelines for remote moderated user tests that collect facial expression data and synchronize them with the state of a dynamic stimulus such as a webpage. To address this research gap, this article offers guidelines for effective AFEA data collection that are based on a methodology developed in a concrete research context and on the lessons learned from applying it in four remote moderated user testing projects. Since researchers have less control over test environment settings, we maintain that they should pay greater attention to factors that can affect face detection and\or emotion classification prior, during, and after remote moderated user tests. Our study contributes to the development of methods for including psychophysiological and neurophysiological measurements in remote user tests that offer promising opportunities for information systems (IS) research, UX design, and even digital health research.

Keywords: NeuroIS · User experience · Remote user test · Automatic facial expression analysis · Psychophysiological data · Human-computer interaction

1 Introduction

In Human Computer Interaction (HCI) research, conducting a user experience (UX) study remotely can improve access to participants and provide an ecologically valid environment for tests in remote environments such as a person's living room [1]. Nonetheless, remote user tests are limited in terms of the equipment and measurement tools

© Springer Nature Switzerland AG 2021
M. Kurosu (Ed.): HCII 2021, LNCS 12762, pp. 243–254, 2021.
https://doi.org/10.1007/978-3-030-78462-1_18

that can be used and installed during this distributed setup, preventing scholars from typically collecting psychophysiological data. Therefore, lab-based user tests are still preferable as they allow researchers to enrich their understanding of the user's experience by triangulating traditional self-reported measures via survey scales and interviews with psychophysiological measurements such as automatic facial expression analysis (AFEA) [2, 3]. However, due to the COVID-19 pandemic and the telework policies that have been introduced as part of the public health response, user experience research labs have been forced to suspend in-lab activities and to proceed with their user experience projects remotely. Since most personal computers and mobile devices have an integrated camera, it is possible to record videos of the participants' faces and assess their emotions while they are interacting with a digital interface.

Yet extant HCI literature fails to provide guidelines on how to collect facial expression data associated with the state of a dynamic experimental stimulus such as a webpage in remote moderated user tests. Developing and prescribing such guidelines is critical during the present pandemic, and it may also encourage further methodological development for remote user research. This study addresses the following research question: During remote moderated usability testing sessions, how can the facial expressions that a participant forms in reaction to an external stimulus such as a webpage be detected automatically and synchronously with the state of that stimulus?

This article offers guidelines on how to effectively collect real-time AFEA data in remote moderated user tests by presenting our in-house developed methodology and reflecting on lessons learned from four different UX research projects, which involved a total of 66 participants and many pre-tests, with desktop or mobile websites of companies operating in telecommunications, catering, and banking. The rest of the article is presented as follows. The next section presents background information on remote moderated user testing and how this research method is rapidly developing during the present. We then explain our methodology for designing a remote moderated user test with facial expression measures, describing the selection of an appropriate commercially available remote user testing platform, here, the Noldus FaceReader AFEA software, and the test procedures developed to ensure optimal data quality. Finally, we present and discuss the lessons learned from the application of our test procedures in four different remote moderated user experience projects.

2   Background Literature: Remote Moderated User Testing

According to Black and Abrams [4], user testing involves measuring the ease with which a person uses a system interface to perform a task. User testing can have different purposes and can be done at different stages of the existence of a system interface including the creation, deployment, maintenance, or revision stages [4]. For instance, formative tests, which usually evaluate a mock-up or prototype, can indicate ways of enhancing the general usability of a system interface at the time of its creation. Summative tests are another type of user testing typically performed on a fully functional version of the system interface just prior to its delivery or deployment.

Remote user tests are a kind of user testing that offer many benefits, including the possibility to test context-dependent interfaces anywhere with reduced costs and quicker setup [5]. Remote user testing implies that the researcher or moderator is either physically separated from the participant or both physically and temporally separated from them [4]. In remote moderated user testing, the researcher and participant are not physically in the same room, but they are still in direct communication with each other in real time during the test. In unmoderated remote user testing, there is no real-time communication between the researcher and the participant, who essentially performs the test alone with predetermined and automated instructions. Therefore, since unmoderated tests do not allow the researcher to use semi-guided interviews or to assist the participant in need of help, this type of remote user testing has a tendency to produce data with low granularity whose quality can even deteriorate due to technical issues experienced by the participant [4]. In this article, we focus on remote moderated rather than unmoderated user testing.

During the past few years, researchers have had more access to commercially available online tools such as Lookback.io, UserTesting, Userlytics, or even Skype and Zoom, and this has given them the opportunity to perform remote moderated user tests. With the current pandemic, remote moderated user testing is the only way for many academic and industrial research labs to pursue their activities. This has been particularly problematic for usability labs, because they mainly rely on psychophysiological measurements such as those made possible by AFEA to obtain information on the user's experience. Indeed, to our knowledge, there are few if any commercially available remote moderated user testing tools that can integrate and synchronize psychophysiological data with behavioral and/or subjective data. Since most modern personal computers and mobile devices have a built-in camera that makes it possible to record facial expressions, research should devote more attention to the development of guidelines on how to collect AFEA data in remote moderated user tests effectively and reliably.

3   Method

3.1   Remote User Testing Platform Selection

We began by performing a systematic evaluation of the different commercially available remote user testing platforms. There were several selection criteria. In line with the suggestion by the Nielsen Norman Group [6], the platform should allow for the display of both the moderator's and the participant's faces on the screen, when needed, to improve communication during the test and especially during interviews. The platform should also be able to record both the participant's face and the webpage simultaneously so that the Automatic Facial Expression Analysis (AFEA) data could be related with specific webpages and/or user actions e.g. performed via input devices such as mice. The platform should operate both on a desktop and on a mobile device to allow for the testing of both the screen- and mobile versions of an interface (e.g. screen web vs. mobile web vs. mobile app). We also considered the pricing and the ease of use of each reviewed platform.

From among a dozen products[1] commercially available at the time of this article's writing, we selected Lookback.io (Montréal, Québec), specifically the Remote LiveShare Moderated Testing feature, which satisfied all of our criteria. The desktop version of

---

[1] Evalyzer, HatchTank, iTracks, Lookback.io, Qualaroo, Recollective, Trymyui, Userlook, Userlytics, Usertesting, UXCam, Validately.

Lookback.io operates on Google Chrome, and the mobile version, Participate, can be installed on iOS and Android devices. In both the desktop and the mobile user tests, the recommended bandwidth for the download and upload internet speed is 5 Mbps and the one for the loaded latency is below 300 ms.

3.2 Automatic Facial Expression Analysis (AFEA)

AFEA is an unobtrusive method used to assess human emotions with low equipment costs. It uses a camera with a minimal video resolution of 640 × 480 pixels, and it requires a commercially available and scientifically validated software program like Noldus FaceReader to detect and classify facial expressions of emotion. The video recordings are post-processed by the software program that first detects the participant's face. Each video frame of a detected face is classified as corresponding to the basic emotions of happiness, anger, disgust, sadness, fear, and surprise, using artificial neural networks from a sample of 2000 static images of humans mimicking these emotions [7]. These basic emotions are indicated by configurations of specific facial muscle movements that are recognized as specific facial Action Units (AU) in the Facial Action Coding System (FACS) [8]. For example, the basic emotion of sadness can be predicted from a combination of an Inner brow raiser (AU1), a Brow lowerer (AU4), and a Chin raiser (AU17).

This study used the Noldus FaceReader 8.0 version (Noldus Information Technology Inc, Netherlands). Among the limitations mentioned in the FaceReader Reference Manual [9], we highlight the ones that are relevant to the quality of AFEA data in this study. First, anything partially hiding the face of participants, including their hands, hairs falling on their forehead, the mic of their headphones, or even their prescription glasses, especially ones with a thick, dark frame, may significantly decrease face detection and emotion classification performance. Head movements must be limited, with the horizontal rotation of the head remaining within an angle of less than 40° compared to when the participant is looking straight into the camera. FaceReader is also very sensitive to light conditions. Indeed, strong shadows or reflections in the face caused by ceiling lights or windows located to the sides of participants can also impede or impair facial expression detection and emotion classification.

3.3 User Test Prerequisites and Instructions

Using the above-mentioned Lookback.io and FaceReader software, our team performed over 50 pretests on desktops and mobile devices to build a set of prerequisites and instructions for both the participant and the moderator (see Fig. 1). The prerequisites are mainly related to the requirements for maximizing data quality suggested for the application and the software presented in the previous sections. All six of the prerequisites listed below must be satisfied by the participant, and the moderator must make sure to satisfy the prerequisites regarding the microphone, camera, and internet speed.

1. Before the tests, participants are required to install the Google Chrome browser on their personal computer in order to be able to use the Lookback.io online platform,

and for mobile user tests, it is necessary to have the app Participate and an intact touch screen.

2. The personal computer or mobile device used for the test must have a functioning audio output (e.g. speaker) and input (e.g. microphone) device, which may at times be combined (e.g. headset with an integrated microphone).

3. The personal computer or mobile device used for the test must have a functioning webcam or frontal camera.

4. Participants are required to have an internet speed exceeding 5Mbps and a loaded latency of 300 ms and below. Also, if possible, participants must connect to a 5 Ghz wifi network.

5. While performing the test, the participant must be seated at a work desk that is stable and flat so that they look straight toward the camera at all times. Moreover, the work desk must be in an isolated environment to minimize ambient noise, which can distract the participant from the task and even influence the accuracy of the AFEA. Indeed, there is an association between corrugator supercilii face muscle activity and auditory attention to a stimulus [10]. Since the corrugator supercilii is typically involved in the expression of negative emotions, the previous finding suggests that researchers should avoid using AFEA data that were recorded while the moderator is giving instructions, which can sometimes happen during the test when the moderator needs to guide the participant. In addition, the participant must be placed in front of a light source such as a window so that their face receives equal amounts of light to avoid shadow contrasts.

6. Participants must be able to use their personal computer or mobile device without wearing glasses because the frame for a pair of glasses can hinder face detection.

In addition to the previous prerequisites for participating in the study, we developed specific instructions to ensure the quality of AFEA data during the user tests. Although the instructions presented below are not exclusively used for remote user tests because they should be used for lab experiments as well, we argue that they must be emphasized in the former type of user tests since researchers have less control over various environmental factors. To maximize the quality of AFEA data, the moderator gave four main instructions to the participant:

1. Participants are asked to avoid obstructing the view of their face with anything including hands or hairs falling on their forehead. During the tests, this instruction may need to be communicated more than once because participants often put their hands in their face unconsciously. Other causes are specific to the uncontrolled environment in remote user tests. For example, there may be sunlight variations that create undesirable light contrasts in the participant's face.

2. Participants are asked to stay as steady as possible throughout the user test so that their face remains in the webcam frame. During a user test, the Lookback.io platform does not allow participants to verify that their position is adequate by monitoring the real-time video recording of their face. Although this is also the case for lab experiments, in the latter it is possible to use ergonomic chairs that limit participants' movements. However, in remote user tests, participants may have different types of chairs that

248   F. Giroux et al.

Fig. 1. Displays an example of a resource created and used to communicate the above six prerequisites to the participant in advance of their scheduled session; the prerequisites are adapted for either web- or mobile-based user testing.

allow them to rotate or roll, and this may cause them to move out of their webcam frame more than in lab experiment settings.

3. The system interface being tested should remain steady throughout the user test. This instruction aims at ensuring that the angle or positioning of the camera or interface with respect to the participant's face does not vary during the user test. In lab studies, this is controlled by using a fixed monitor or a support that stabilizes mobile devices in a set angle and position. In remote user tests, participants may tilt their laptop screen to adjust its contrast, thereby modifying the angle and the framing of the

webcam. Similarly, participants may lower the position of a mobile device in front of them, which would naturally lower their visual target. Ergonomic studies have shown that the action of looking down on a monitor at an angle of 30° increases activity in the corrugator supercilii face muscle [11]. The corrugator supercillii face muscle, more commonly known as the eyebrow frown muscle, is also responsible for expressing the basic negative emotions of anger, sadness, and fear [8]. Therefore, this instruction can not only help avoid problems with the detection of participants' faces, it can also help maximize emotion classification performance.

4. Participants are asked not to talk (or whisper) during the user test unless they need to ask the moderator for help. Participants may whisper as they read textual information during a task. As they do so, they naturally engage their mouth and lip muscles, which are also used to predict basic emotions. For instance, a Lip Corner Puller (AU12) contributes to the basic emotion of happiness, a Lip Corner Depressor (AU15), to the basic emotion of sadness or disgust, a Lip Stretcher (AU20), to that of fear, and a Lip Tightener (AU23), to that of anger [8]. Therefore, facial muscle movements that occur in talking, whispering, or even chewing gum could affect emotion classification, and they should be avoided. Throughout the user test, it is important for the moderator to monitor the video showing the participant's face so as to be able to provide instructions to solve issues related to the quality of the AFEA data as quickly as possible.

3.4 Data Analysis and Synchronization

With commercially available AFEA software programs like Noldus FaceReader, it is not possible to synchronize and interpret AFEA data from a temporally occurring dynamic experimental stimulus such as a webpage. Instead, this can be done using other lab management and stimulus presentation tools that triangulate psychophysiological data in a timely manner [12, 13]. Other visualization tools combine AFEA and eye-tracking data to better interpret, via heatmaps, users' emotional reactions according to the spatial location of their fixation gaze in a webpage [14, 15]. However, our remote moderated user tests were limited by our inability to use stimulus presentation software programs (e.g. E-Prime) and eye tracking solutions (e.g. Tobii) remotely. Therefore, we have developed in-house procedures to synchronize the Lookback.io.mp4 file – i.e. the video recording of the screen showing the webpage as it's being used – with the video of the participant's face that is post-processed in FaceReader. Consequently, and although the present study does not use eye tracking measures, it is possible to link AFEA data to a specific webpage or action performed by the participant.

Regarding our measures of interest, to simplify the interpretation of emotion results, we used the Noldus FaceReader emotional valence metric that is calculated as the intensity of happy emotion minus the intensity of the negative emotion with the highest intensity. This metric allows us to compare the average emotional valence, expressed within a range of −1 to 1, exhibited by a participant throughout a webpage or website visit. Among other research objectives, user tests often aim at uncovering bugs or usability issues that may cause a person to experience pain points during a task on a system interface. Pain points are typically peaks of negative emotions with increased arousal, and can be measured with psychophysiological data [16, 17]. Our research team has developed an algorithm to detect psychophysiological pain points based on peaks of negative emotions. The pain points were manually investigated by looking at both the participant's face and the webpage video recording to identify and classify them according to categories of usability issues. Our method for analyzing and interpreting pain points based on AFEA data is out of the scope of this study.

4 Results

The methodology previously described was tested in four different user experience research projects, in which remote moderated user tests were performed on formative or summative, and mobile or desktop website versions of companies operating in telecommunication, catering, and banking. In total, 66 participants (30 males and 36 females) ranging from 20 to 73 years old, with a mean age of 39 years old, took part in the research projects that informed this article. The next section presents the lessons learned from these projects by illustrating potential issues when using AFEA measurement in remote moderated user testing.

4.1 Lessons Learned

In one project, we performed a summative user test on a prototype and compared it with other benchmarks. Although the prototype was clearly preferred and perceived as easier to use, the AFEA data indicated that participants generally experienced higher intensity of negative emotions and a greater amount of psychophysiological pain points when using it as compared to other websites. After performing the verification of pain points, we realized that a few of these experienced moments were caused by natural factors. For instance, one participant was clearly squinting her eyes during a task and repeatedly mentioned having difficulty to read the textual information with pale font on her screen due to monitor brightness issues. Since the action of squinting our eyes, also referred as a lid tightener or AU7 according to the FACS [8], contributes to the detection of basic emotions of fear and anger, it is possible that this facial movement caused by poor visibility can artificially be classified as negative emotions.

In another project, a participant complained about the small font of the text. It is indeed possible that the participant's personal browser settings made the font size smaller than it should. In this case, one should remember that participant's personal computers and browsers have different settings and may affect the size and disposition of text and images. It should also be noted that the Lookback.io platform for desktop displays a window that takes approximately one third of the browser to show instructions for the task. With less space, a webpage can appear smaller or can have its layout modified according to participants' browser settings. Therefore, it is important to help participants adjust their settings to make sure that they all view a similar system interface. It is also possible that the participant had bad eyesight and had to squint his eyes to read text with a smaller font or with poorer readability. In fact, using electromyography (EMG), past studies have found that reading a text with poor typography [18], or focusing our eyes due to poor eyesight [19] increased activity in the corrugator supercilii facial muscle also recognized as AU4 according to the FACS [8]. Since this facial movement also predicts the negative emotions of sadness, anger, and fear, it is quite possible that eye squinting to improve our ability to read text can be erroneously detected as negative emotions.

In the project with mobile devices, although participants were asked to keep their device horizontal to their face, they tended to lower it in a more natural position, thereby creating a low-angle shot of their face. This can be problematic as AFEA systems are sensitive to rotation of the head and may lose track of the participant's face [9]. Moreover, since lowering our gaze engages natural facial muscle activity [11], lowering the position of the interface could impact emotion classification. For future remote research, it would be interesting to think of ways to support and stabilize the device or the arm of participants with personal objects like books or pillows.

5 Discussion and Conclusion

The goal of the present study has been to show that during remote moderated usability testing sessions, the facial expressions formed by participants in reaction to a dynamic stimulus such as a webpage can be measured automatically and synchronously with the state of that stimulus. Our methodology and the lessons learned from the four UX research projects, which involved a total of 66 participants and many pre-test sessions, suggest that researchers using AFEA measurements in remote moderated user tests should devote greater attention to factors that can impede or impair either face detection or emotion classification. The guidelines presented in this article will help future remote UX research projects using AFEA to maximize the quality of data and consequently the validity of HCI research findings. Nevertheless, we do not claim that AFEA alone is a sufficient psychophysiological method for examining user experience in remote moderated user tests. In fact, user experience labs often triangulate AFEA measures with other objective data, including autonomous nervous system measures like electrodermal activity [20–22] or eye-tracking measures [23–25].

AFEA measures are not the only ones that have been used in recent remote user experience research. Electrodermal activity [26], vocal emotion [27], and brain activity assessed via electroencephalography [28, 29] have also been used. The COVID-19 pandemic may have a silver lining to the extent that it has resulted in the rapid development of methods to include these other psychophysiological and neurophysiological measurements in remote moderated user tests [30, 31]. This topic was discussed during a Practice Development Workshop on NeuroIS [32] at the virtual 2020 International Conference on Information Systems. One of the conclusions from the Workshop was that the development of remote data collection methods offers new opportunities to examine phenomena that used to be challenging to investigate through lab-based user testing. For example, it is now possible to do longitudinal studies on habituation using longer experiment sessions in ecologically valid environments. During the Workshop, it was also suggested that improving our ability to collect psychophysiological and neurophysiological data remotely may have benefits that extend beyond information systems (IS) research and user experience design, benefits such as important advances in digital health research. During the Workshop, it was also suggested that improving our ability to collect psychophysiological and neurophysiological data remotely may have benefits that extend beyond information systems (IS) research and user experience design, including advances in digital health research.

Indeed, psychophysiological measures could also be used for self-monitoring purposes to directly inform a user about indicators related to personal health issues. For example, teleworkers could self-monitor their level of stress throughout a working day. In a word, although the increasing need for remote user testing is due to the exceptional circumstances of the COVID-19 pandemic, this has led to the rapid development of multi-method approaches that will enable HCI scholars to undertake a great number of highly interesting remote user studies.

References

1. vom Brocke, J., Hevner, A., Léger, P.M., Walla, P., Riedl, R.: Advancing a NeuroIS research agenda with four areas of societal contributions. Eur. J. Inf. Syst. **29**(1), 9–24 (2020)
2. Alvarez, J., Brieugne, D., Léger, P.M., Sénécal, S., Frédette, M.: Towards agility and speed in enriched UX evaluation projects. In: Human 4.0-From Biology to Cybernetic, IntechOpen (2019)
3. Alvarez, J., Léger, P.M., Fredette, M., Chen, S.L., Maunier, B., Senecal, S.: An enriched customer journey map: how to construct and visualize a global portrait of both lived and perceived users' experiences? Designs **4**(3), 29 (2020)
4. Black, J., Abrams, M.: Remote usability testing. In: The Wiley Handbook of Human Computer Interaction, pp. 277–297 (2018)
5. Bolt, N., Tulathimutte, T.: Remote Research: Real Users, Real Time, Real Research, 1st edn. Rosenfeld Media, LLC, Brooklyn (2010)
6. Remote Moderated Usability Tests: How to Do Them. https://www.nngroup.com/articles/moderated-remote-usability-test/. Accessed 06 Feb 2020
7. Skiendziel, T., Ro, A.G.: Assessing the convergent validity between the automated emotion recognition software Noldus FaceReader 7 and facial action coding system scoring. PLoS One 1–18 (2019)
8. Ekman, P., Friesen, W.V.: Facial Action Coding System: A Technique for the Measurement of Facial Movement. Consulting Psychologists Press, Palo Alto (1978)
9. Noldus FaceReader methodology. https://info.noldus.com/free-white-paper-on-facereader-methodology. Accessed 15 Jan 2020
10. Cohen, B.H., Davidson, R.J., Senulis, J.A., Saron, C.D., Weisman, D.R.: Muscle tension patterns during auditory attention. Biol. Psychol. **33**, 133–156 (1992)
11. Peper, E, Gibney, K.H.: muscle biofeedback at the computer: a manual to prevent repetitive strain injury (RSI) by taking the guesswork out of assessment, monitoring, and training. Association for Applied Psychophysiology & Biofeedback (2006)
12. Léger, P.-M., Courtemanche, F., Fredette, M., Sénécal, S.: A cloud-based lab management and analytics software for triangulated human-centered research. In: Davis, F.D., Riedl, R., vom Brocke, J., Léger, P.-M., Randolph, A.B. (eds.) Information Systems and Neuroscience. LNISO, vol. 29, pp. 93–99. Springer, Cham (2019). https://doi.org/10.1007/978-3-030-01087-4_11
13. Courtemanche, F., et al.: Ambient facial emotion recognition: a pilot study. In: Davis, F.D., Riedl, R., vom Brocke, J., Léger, P.-M., Randolph, A.B., Fischer, T. (eds.) NeuroIS 2020. LNISO, vol. 43, pp. 284–290. Springer, Cham (2020). https://doi.org/10.1007/978-3-030-60073-0_33
14. Courtemanche, F., Léger, P.-M., Dufresne, A., Fredette, M., Labonté-LeMoyne, É., Sénécal, S.: Physiological heatmaps: a tool for visualizing users' emotional reactions. Multimed. Tools Appl. **77**(9), 11547–11574 (2017). https://doi.org/10.1007/s11042-017-5091-1

15. Courtemanche, F., et al.: U.S. Patent No. 10,368,741. U.S. Patent and Trademark Office, Washington, DC (2019)
16. Giroux-Huppé, C., Sénécal, S., Fredette, M., Chen, S.L., Demolin, B., Léger, P.-M.: Identifying psychophysiological pain points in the online user journey: the case of online grocery. In: Marcus, A., Wang, W. (eds.) HCII 2019. LNCS, vol. 11586, pp. 459–473. Springer, Cham (2019). https://doi.org/10.1007/978-3-030-23535-2_34
17. Lamontagne, C., et al.: User test: how many users are needed to find the psychophysiological pain points in a journey map? In: Ahram, T., Taiar, R., Colson, S., Choplin, A. (eds.) Human Interaction and Emerging Technologies. IHIET 2019, vol. 1018, pp. 136–142. Springer, Cham (2019). https://doi.org/10.1007/978-3-030-25629-6_22
18. Larson, K., Hazlett, R.L., Chaparro, B.S., Picard, R.W.: Measuring the aesthetics of reading. In: Bryan-Kinns, N., Blanford, A., Curzon, P., Nigay, L. (eds.) People and Computers XX—Engage, pp 41–56. Springer, London (2007). https://doi.org/10.1007/978-1-84628-664-3_4
19. Kappas, A.: What facial activity can and cannot tell us about emotions. In: Katsikitis, M. (ed.) The human face: Measurement and Meaning, pp. 215–234. Springer, Boston (2003). https://doi.org/10.1007/978-1-4615-1063-5_11
20. Roy, A., Sénécal, S., Léger, P.-M., Demolin, B., Bigras, É., Gagne, J.: Measuring users' psychophysiological experience in non-linear omnichannel environment. In: Stephanidis, C., Marcus, A., Rosenzweig, E., Rau, P.-L., Moallem, A., Rauterberg, M. (eds.) HCII 2020. LNCS, vol. 12423, pp. 762–779. Springer, Cham (2020). https://doi.org/10.1007/978-3-030-60114-0_50
21. Veilleux, M., et al.: Visualizing a user's cognitive and emotional journeys: a fintech case. In: Marcus, A., Rosenzweig, E. (eds.) HCII 2020. LNCS, vol. 12200, pp. 549–566. Springer, Cham (2020). https://doi.org/10.1007/978-3-030-49713-2_38
22. Giroux, F., et al.: Haptic stimulation with high fidelity vibro-kinetic technology psychophysiologically enhances seated active music listening experience. In: 2019 IEEE World Haptics Conference, pp. 151–156 (2019)
23. Giroux, F., Boasen, J., Sénécal, S., Léger, P.-M.: Hedonic multitasking: the effects of instrumental subtitles during video watching. In: Davis, F.D., Riedl, R., vom Brocke, J., Léger, P.-M., Randolph, A.B., Fischer, T. (eds.) NeuroIS 2020. LNISO, vol. 43, pp. 330–336. Springer, Cham (2020). https://doi.org/10.1007/978-3-030-60073-0_38
24. Falconnet, A., et al.: Beyond system design: the impact of message design on recommendation acceptance. In: Davis, F.D., Riedl, R., vom Brocke, J., Léger, P.-M., Randolph, A.B., Fischer, T. (eds.) NeuroIS 2020. LNISO, vol. 43, pp. 185–190. Springer, Cham (2020). https://doi.org/10.1007/978-3-030-60073-0_21
25. Beauchesne, A., et al.: User-centered gestures for mobile phones: exploring a method to evaluate user gestures for UX designers. In: Marcus, A., Wang, W. (eds.) HCII 2019. LNCS, vol. 11584, pp. 121–133. Springer, Cham (2019). https://doi.org/10.1007/978-3-030-23541-3_10
26. Brissette-Gendron, R., Léger, P.M., Courtemanche, F., Chen, S.L., Ouhnana, M., Sénécal, S.: The response to impactful interactivity on spectators' engagement in a digital game. Multimodal Technol. Interact. 4(4), 89 (2020)
27. Le Pailleur, F., Huang, B., Léger, P.-M., Sénécal, S.: A new approach to measure user experience with voice-controlled intelligent assistants: a pilot study. In: Kurosu, M. (ed.) HCII 2020. LNCS, vol. 12182, pp. 197–208. Springer, Cham (2020). https://doi.org/10.1007/978-3-030-49062-1_13
28. Passalacqua, M., et al.: Playing in the backstore: interface gamification increases warehousing workforce engagement. Ind. Manage. Data Syst. (2020)

29. Ruer, P., et al.: Improving driving behavior with an insurance telematics mobile application. In: Davis, F.D., Riedl, R., vom Brocke, J., Léger, P.-M., Randolph, A.B., Fischer, T. (eds.) NeuroIS 2020. LNISO, vol. 43, pp. 198–203. Springer, Cham (2020). https://doi.org/10.1007/978-3-030-60073-0_23
30. Vasseur, A., et al.: Distributed remote psychophysiological data collection for UX evaluation: a pilot project. In: International Conference on Human-Computer Interaction (forthcoming)
31. Demazure, T., et al.: Distributed remote EEG data collection for NeuroIS research: a methodological framework. In: International Conference on Human-Computer Interaction (forthcoming)
32. Riedl, R., Davis, F.D., Leger, P.M., Muller-Putz, G.: NeuroIS: status, rewarding research questions, and future directions. practice development workshop. In: Forty-First International Conference on Information Systems, India (2020)

Distributed Remote Psychophysiological Data Collection for UX Evaluation: A Pilot Project

Aurélie Vasseur[✉], Pierre-Majorique Léger, François Courtemanche,
Elise Labonte-Lemoyne, Vanessa Georges, Audrey Valiquette, David Brieugne,
Emma Rucco, Constantinos Coursaris, Marc Fredette, and Sylvain Sénécal

HEC Montréal, Montréal, QC, Canada
`aurelie.vasseur@hec.ca`

Abstract. User experience (UX) research has been critically impacted by the recent COVID-19 pandemic and the sanitary restrictions put in place. Observational or perceptual studies can be adapted remotely with participants using their own computer and internet access. However, studies based on the unconscious and automatic physiological states of participants use neurophysiological measurements that requires highly specific hardware. Electrodermal activity (EDA) or electrocardiogram (ECG) based studies are complex to transpose to a remote environment since researchers have no physical contact with the participants. To address this concern, our research team previously developed a remote instrument that can collect the EDA and the ECG activity at the participants' location through a moderated self-installation of sensors. We developed a protocol for remote physiological data collection that we pilot tested with 2 UX studies. After each study, we administered an open-ended questionnaire regarding the full experience of remote data-collection from both the moderator's and the participant's side. We collected 92 responses total which provided us with a rich dataset that we analyzed through a thematic analysis lens in order to uncover the success factors of remote psychophysiological data collection. Operational support, moderator-participant collaboration, individual characteristics, and technological capabilities clearly emerged as drivers for success. This project aimed to develop a rigorous and contextually relevant protocol for remote physiological data collection in UX evaluations, train our research team on the developed protocol, and provide guidance regarding remote physiological data collection activities.

Keywords: User experience · NeuroIS · Electrodermal activity · Physiological data · Remote research methods

1 Introduction

User research in human-centered design is critical because each step of the design process revolves around the feedback received by potential users (Alvarez et al. 2019). There are multiple ways to collect data related to the users' experience during their interaction with a technology, ranging from quantitative methods (e.g., clickstream data) to qualitative methods (e.g., interviews) (de Guinea et al. 2014). Certain methods, like think-aloud

© Springer Nature Switzerland AG 2021
M. Kurosu (Ed.): HCII 2021, LNCS 12762, pp. 255–267, 2021.
https://doi.org/10.1007/978-3-030-78462-1_19

usability testing, have been adapted to facilitate remote data-collection (Hammontree et al. 1994). Despite some struggles that may arise with remote data collection, a participant's experience can still be captured with a limited impact on measurement reliability and validity and even offer some efficiency benefits (Vasalou et al. 2005).

These perceptual and observational methods provide perceptual or observational measures that participants are conscious about and that they are willing to share. However, research in Information Systems (IS) and in User Experience (UX) can also take advantage of physiological measurement approaches to record the user's cognitive and/or affective states even before they rise to the participant's consciousness, as well as do so for the entire duration of an experiment, providing the researcher(s) with an extra-rich layer of information that bypasses some common method biases such as memory and social desirability biases (Alvarez et al. 2020; Giroux-Huppé et al. 2019; Roy et al. 2020). The research field using neurophysiological measures to inform IS research is known as NeuroIS (Riedl et al. 2020; Riedl and Léger 2016). NeuroIS has been deeply impacted by the recent COVID-19 pandemic and the consequent sanitary restrictions put in place, given the criticality for NeuroIS to access participants physically in order to record their physiological states. Indeed, once we move away from the use of perceptual and/or observational measures, the difficulty of creating reliable remote experimental protocols involving the collection of psychophysiological data becomes increasingly complicated. In many countries, researchers have suffered negative consequences at different levels depending on their department or research topics (Myers et al. 2020). Laboratories that were able to continue conducting human-computer interaction (HCI) research with participants had to demonstrate a high level of creative thinking to develop remote testing protocols involving the use of behavioral and physiological measures such as brain activity (EEG) (Demazure et al., forthcoming), heart activity (ECG), electrodermal activation (EDA), eye-tracking or facial expression analysis (Giroux et al., forthcoming).

Related to the increased complexity mentioned earlier, not only would technical problems have to be solved remotely, but also participants and moderators would have to collaborate throughout the duration of the study to ensure the correct setup and use of the sensors and other equipment being used in physiological measurement. Hence, there is a need to understand the challenges associated with participant home-based testing in regard to potentially biasing the participants' experience; for example, how would their perceptions of the technology being used and evaluated be biased because the experiment is being carried out in their familiar home and daily environment, rather than in an unknown and neutral space. On the one hand, collecting data from participants' homes allows researchers to collect data that may even be more ecologically valid than when collected in a laboratory. On the other hand, participants are now required to set-up all equipment, both hardware and software, while being remotely guided by a research assistant; this approach makes participants more active than ever in the research protocol. Given this, there is a great need to understand how this shift in the participants' roles may be impacting their experience and what would be the associated implications.

To fill this void, a UX pilot project was undertaken comprised of two remote UX experiments using a measuring instrument developed by our research team that allowed for the remote collection and synchronization of participant physiological data. The aim of this paper is to report results from this pilot UX project, which reveal four key success factors in the successful completion of remote physiological data completion in UX evaluations. A thematic analysis of the qualitative data (Braun and Clarke 2006) resulted in operational support, moderator-participant collaboration, individual characteristics, and technological capabilities clearly emerging as these drivers for success This paper begins with an overview of relevant prior work leading up to this pilot UX project. Then, the research design of each of the two studies is presented, followed by an analysis of collected data. Finally, we discuss the most important methodological contributions for UX along with implications for UX researchers and practitioners. Opportunities for future research are also outlined.

2   Previous Work

Our team designed and manufactured a device enabling the remote data collection of physiological activity for UX research. It is composed of a main 3D printed box (Fig. 1) which is the principal hardware component, and two sets of electrodes: one that records EDA, and another that records ECG. Regarding the technical features, the box has an ON/OFF switch, a slot for a microSD card, a switch to upload the data in the cloud, a charging port, and a set of 4 visual indicators.

Fig. 1. Main component of the instrument for remote data collection of physiological measures

Each of these indicators is related to a specific function of the box and can help in the event of remote troubleshooting. The indicators can inform participants and moderators on (1) whether a microSD card is functional, (2) the state of the Wi-Fi connection, (3) the state of the Bluetooth connection, and (4) the state of the physiological recording (see Fig. 2). This hardware is complemented by our cloud-based software for triangulation of data that allows multimodal data acquisition (Courtemanche et al. 2019; Léger et al. 2019). Experiments can therefore be conducted at the participants' home, workplace, or any venue without the need for a research team to be present on location.

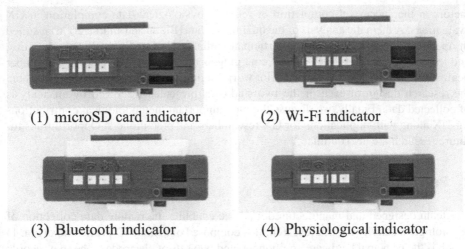

(1) microSD card indicator   (2) Wi-Fi indicator

(3) Bluetooth indicator   (4) Physiological indicator

Fig. 2. Visual indicators of the instrument

To participate in either of our two remote studies, a participant received the main box (device) and two sets of electrodes, but also a set of accessories such as a glove and a wristband to keep the electrodermal sensors in place, and disposable items such as alcohol wipes and sticky sensors. They also received instructions on how to self-install the sensors, while being remotely supported by research assistants (called moderators in the remainder of the paper) via a proprietary test interface used to conduct the experiment (Fig. 3). The test interface allows the recording of the webcam of the participant – so as to observe their reactions - and the recording of their screen, so as to follow their actions on the interface being evaluated during the study.

Fig. 3. Moderated remote self-installation of the sensors

The research team also developed extensive training tools for the moderator to assist the participants in self-installing the sensors remotely. Moderators received training on the instrument, the test interface, and the protocol. They received visual instructions to help the participants install the sensors through their webcam.

3 Pilot Study

3.1 Data Collection

We conducted a pilot study utilizing this new measuring instrument and tailored training protocol with UX professionals in training (i.e., students enrolled in our institution's UX graduate program). In this pilot study, two consecutive experiments were conducted after the installation of the sensors to have participants and moderators experience the full process of remote data collection.

The first experiment was a typical usability study: participants were asked to perform search tasks on a hotel booking website and were subsequently asked about their experience with the website; the second experiment was evaluating the participants' experience with video stimuli by measuring their physiological reaction along with survey-based self-reported measures after each video. Also, after each experiment, participants and moderators answered a number of open-ended questions regarding their experience in the set-up and carrying-out of the user test. Both of these experiments were conducted by our research team with three aims in mind: (i) develop a rigorous and contextually relevant protocol for remote physiological data collection in UX evaluations, (ii) train our research team on the developed protocol, and (iii) provide guidance through methodological contributions to fellow UX researchers along with opportunities for future research. Therefore, task-related results from the two studies are not discussed in this paper, which focuses on the development of the research protocol and the insight generated from both participants and moderators in a remote study involving physiological data collection.

Each UX professional took turns acting as the moderator and participant. A total of 46 test sessions were conducted where all subjects – participants and moderators – answered questionnaires (total n = 92). The protocol applicable to both studies is illustrated in Table 1. The synchronization and sensors' installation steps are specific to data collection with physiological measures, while the other steps are typically found in traditional remote research protocols.

3.2 Measurement

During the post-experiment step, qualitative feedback from both participants and moderators covering each aspect of the experience (i.e., from the installation of the sensors to the interaction between the participant and the moderator) was collected through an open-ended online survey. Additionally, to have a measure of the effort deployed by subjects during their experiment, we measured their Customer Effort Score regarding the critical tasks of the protocol. The list of qualitative and quantitative questions is included in Table 2.

Table 1. Activities performed during each step of protocol

Step	Activities
30 min before	Participant receives email with the preparation information sheet, the test interface link, and the consent form
	Moderator logs in to the test interface and set up their video feed and microphone
Setup	Moderator presents the tools and asks participant for consent
	Moderator checks the technical setting of the participant and ensures the video and microphone quality
Synchronization	Moderator and participant test the synchronization of the tool with the participant's network
Sensor installation	Moderator guides the participant with the sensor positioning
	Moderator does a verification check on the sensors with the help of the participant and the embedded visual checks of the hardware
Experiment tasks	This section refers to the actual study (in our case study 1: website usability study; study 2: video stimuli study)
Post-experiment	Participant uploads the physiological data collected during the experiment assisted by the moderator
	Moderator and participant each complete a questionnaire

3.3 Data Analysis

A thematic analysis was conducted with NVivo (March 2020 release) to uncover patterns from our large qualitative dataset (5 mandatory open-ended questions +4 conditional ones when participants encountered problems, from each of the 96 completed open-ended surveys). Thematic analysis is the method of choice in this paper because of its potential to provide a rich description of the data from a large body of data and its flexibility (Braun and Clarke 2006).

Since remote data collection of physiological measures is an emergingmethodology, the goal of the analysis was to uncover as many themes and/or patterns from the data as possible to reveal key success factors in the remote collection of physiological data. Therefore, the emergence of themes is not bounded by a minimal number of instances: information collected from just one participant can provide relevant feedback that would facilitate future remote research. Themes and subthemes were identified at their semantic (explicit) level under an essentialist approach to theorise the individuals' experience of remote data collection.

Table 2. List of questions of the post-experiment survey

Type of questions	Questions

Open-ended	Describe your personal experience: what did you experience during the **synchronization**? Describe your feelings and your emotions during this step.
	    Did you encounter any technical problems during this step?
	    (if yes to question above) Please describe the problems encountered in connection with the synchronization of the box.
	Describe your personal experience: what did you experience during your **interactions** with the participant / moderator? Describe your feelings and emotions during these interactions.
	Describe your personal experience: what did you experience during the **installation of the sensors**? Describe your feelings and your emotions during this step.
	    Did you encounter any technical problems during this step?
	    (if yes to question above) Please describe the problems encountered in connection with the installation of the sensors.
	(For moderator only) Describe your personal experience: what did you experience while using **the test interface**? Describe your feelings and your emotions during this step.
	    Did you encounter any technical problems during this step?
	    (if yes to question above) Please describe the problems encountered in relation to the test interface.
	Did you experience **stress** at any time before, during or after this remote data collection?
	    (if yes) What was the most stressful during your experience?
	    What do you think we could do to reduce the stress of participating in this type of remote test?

Quantitative (on a scale from 1 to 5)	What do you think is the level of effort that you had to deploy during the synchronization step? How much effort do you think it took to interact with the moderator or participant through the test interface? What do you think is the level of effort you had to deploy during the installation of the sensors? How much effort do you think you had to put into using the test interface?

After each study, the data was inspected by the first author in order to get to know the dataset in depth and facilitate future rounds of analysis. Then, the questionnaires from both studies were aggregated and coded concurrently in a first round. The goal of this round of coding was to extract relevant extract from the data set. The codes were precise and not yet grouped by themes, except for very similar extracts. For example *"my wifi does not work"* and *"I don't have functional wifi"* would be coded similarly, yet, extracts related to other network issues would have their own specific codes. In round 2, codes were grouped based on their similarity and large themes emerged. In round 3, further grouping of codes was conducted and most similar extracts were aggregated into subcategories within their respective themes, while less relevant themes were discarded or reorganised into more prevalent or detailed sub-themes. After round 3, a thematic map of the data was developed to summarize the findings. Figure 4 illustrates our analysis process along with the outcome of each round.

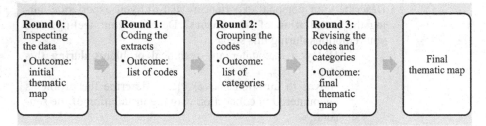

Fig. 4. Qualitative analysis process

4 Analysis and Discussion

4.1 Initial Thematic Map

The initial inspection of the data led to the development of an initial thematic map represented in Fig. 5.

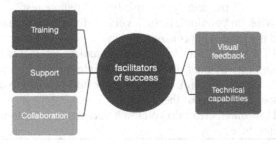

Fig. 5. Initial thematic map

The success factors identified in this step can be divided into two main categories: human and technical factors. Respondents were highly appreciative of the training they received, and of the remote support they had from the operational team during the data collection. Both moderators and participants considered collaboration between them as a key point in their experience. These human factors were often mentioned by respondents as contributing to a good experience, while technical factors were mentioned as limiting or disrupting aspects of their experience. Network issues or technical problems from the test interface were either a stress source or the reason to stop the experiment. Since the information is shared by voice or through visual feedback obtained from the camera of the participant, the technical capabilities of participants and moderators seem to be an important factor to consider.

This initial mapping shown in Fig. 5 was built only from the initial review of the dataset and not from rigorous extraction and coding. The next section presents the final success factors identified with their sub-categories.

4.2 Success Factors of Remote Data-Collection

After coding and grouping the extracts, the final thematic map revealed that four factors are crucial for the success of remote data collection involving physiological measures: operational support, individual characteristics, moderator-participant collaboration and technological capabilities. These categories are similar to those identified during the initial phase of the data analysis. However, they became slightly different and more detailed with each round of the analysis. Each success factor is detailed below.

Support
Support is a success factor that was first identified in the initial inspection of the data. It represents the level of presence of the operational or research team that is in charge of the data-collection tool and protocol. It can be provided by a team in your laboratory and/or by external resources if the equipment (both software and hardware) used for the data collection has been developed by a third-party. Our data analysis revealed three sub-categories within the support theme and found that a successful remote data collection will involve (1) a high level of training of the moderators, (2) the involvement of the research lab's operational team during and around data collection, and (3) a well-written and complete documentation.

Individual Characteristics
Individual characteristics have also been reported as key facilitators of the remote physiological data collection. The level of technical knowledge possessed by the participants and their experience in the use of conferencing remote tools is often referred by respondents as a facilitator of the remote testing experience: it makes the experience more fluid for both participants and moderators. We identified a third category under the individual characteristics theme: the level of individual preparation for the experiment. No matter the amount of training and documentation available and developed by the research team, it is the responsibility of the individuals actively engaged in the remote study (i.e., participants and moderators) to be ready for the experiment. Subsequently, (1) generic technical know-how, (2) experience in conferencing remote tools, and (3) the level of

individual preparation (of both moderators and participants) are the three sub-categories of individual characteristics that emerged from the pilot study data analysis.

Collaboration

The physical distance between moderators and participants put an emphasis on the need for clear and suitable communication. Proper data collection of physiological measures requires that sensors are installed by the participants while being remotely assisted by the moderators. This put the participants' actions at the core of the data-collection process, more so than in a normal laboratory setting. Indeed, not only are their insights needed for the experiment itself, but their role in sensors' installation makes them partially responsible for the accuracy of the data received. The shift in the participant roles from a passive subject to an active collaborator requires a high amount of interaction between the moderator and the participant. The moderator-participant collaboration has to be nurtured through an establishment of trust from the beginning of the test session, during the experiment, and throughout. Respondents who had time before the experiments or between steps to get to know each other reported it being helpful to remain calm and at ease with the remote study. Since we are measuring physiological measures related to stress, such as electrodermal activity, it is important to keep the participant at their normal level of stress (not accounting for study stimulus-evoked stress). It is important that the moderator is present and lets the participant know ahead of time what will happen, but it is also important that the moderator's presence becomes secondary to the experiment. Hence, the moderator has to (1) build trust, (2) be knowledgeable, but also (3) be present without being at the center of the user's experience during the study.

Technological Capabilities

In a controlled laboratory environment, moderators have access to a number of powerful computers that each monitors a specific part of the physiological measurement while participants are performing the user test in a simulated office or home space. However, during a moderated remote experiment, moderators and participants each have their own access to technology, which can be different and limited compared to what a UX lab would typically provide. On the moderators' side, they have to control that the data collection device is functional, that the participant is following instructions and performing the assigned tasks, that the test interface is properly setup and that there are no technical issues, all while reading the protocol. This not only places a high mental load on them, but from a technical side, it is also important to ensure that moderators have the capability to view all the information they need to be checking on during the experiment.

However, the technical capabilities of the moderators and the participants are not the only ones to consider. It is critical that the data collection device itself has some embedded features that renders it user-friendly. Given the remote setup, moderators don't have physical access to the device, which restricts their capabilities in troubleshooting. To conclude, a successful remote data-collection needs to consider the technological capabilities of (1) the moderator, (2) the participant, and (3) the remote data collection device.

4.3 Summary

We conducted a pilot project collecting data from 92 respondents (a 50/50 split between participants and moderators) during two UX experiments. From our thematic analysis of qualitative data, four key success factors emerged in relation to a successful remote physiological data collection: operational support, technological capabilities, moderator-participant collaboration, and individual characteristics. Each of these four factors was decomposed into sub-dimensions. The expanded thematic map of the success factors in remote data collection is shown in Fig. 6.

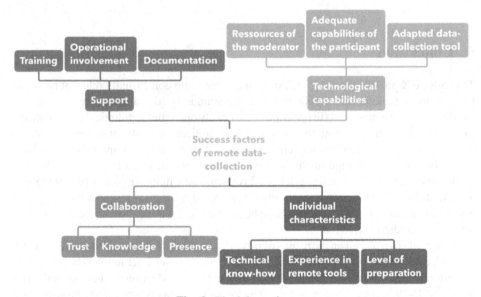

Fig. 6. Final thematic map

Each of these factors was sub-divided into smaller themes (see Table 3) based on the analysis of the data extracts. This qualitative analysis does not speak to the relative importance of each factor in the successful remote physiological data collection; instead, it is an exploration of which factors are important in this context.

Table 3. List of themes and sub-categories with their meanings

Theme	Sub-category	Related to
Support	Training	The amount of training available for moderators and participants with the device, the protocol, and the test interface
	Documentation	The clarity and completeness of the available documentation
	Operational Involvement	The level of involvement before, during, and after the data collection of the research team (research or operational team members)
Individual characteristics	Technical know-how	The level of general technical knowledge possessed by moderators and participants
	Experience in remote tools	The amount of experience in videoconferencing
	Level of preparation	How well-prepared the moderators and the participants are at the beginning of the experiment
Collaboration	Trust	How much is the moderator and participant are able to trust each other in order for them to be confident and calm
	Knowledge	How much does the moderator knows the protocol and how well can they communicate with the participant
	Presence	The availability of the moderator to assist the participant only when needed
Technological capabilities	... of the moderator	The technical setup of the moderator (hardware and network) considerations
	... of the participant	The technical setup of the participant (hardware and network) considerations
	... of the data-collection device	How well the data collection device embeds hardware and software solutions that help with the remote aspect of the data collection (e.g., visual feedback, accessories)

5   Conclusion

This pilot UX project aimed to (i) develop a rigorous and contextually relevant protocol for remote physiological data collection in UX evaluations, (ii) train our research team on the developed protocol, and (iii) provide guidance through methodological contributions to fellow UX researchers with their remote physiological data collection activities along with providing opportunities for future research. Our sample was incredibly involved and willing to provide high quality feedback, which resulted in a large dataset for our qualitative analysis. This rich dataset of 92 response sets helped us identify many problems that could be anticipated for in future remote physiological research by putting an emphasis on the four categories that have been found to be linked to a successful remote physiological data collection.

Our goal is to expand on the results of this pilot study by building a comprehensive list of guidelines that would inspire and guide human-computer interaction (HCI) and UX researchers in setting up their remote physiological data-collection studies. Even though the COVID-19 context accelerated the development of this remote study protocol, we believe that remote data collection has a use potential that goes well beyond the context of this pandemic. Indeed, remote data collection is not just a short-term solution to maintain research activities during mandated physical distancing, rather it opens up incredible opportunities to engage in the study of phenomena longitudinally in an ecologically valid setting, directly from the participants' living room or office, which until now was simulated in a UX research laboratory.

References

Alvarez, J., Brieugne, D., Léger, P.-M., Sénécal, S., Frédette, M.: Towards agility and speed in enriched UX evaluation projects. Hum.-Comput. Interact. (2019). https://doi.org/10.5772/int echopen.89762

Alvarez, J., Léger, P.-M., Fredette, M., Chen, S.-L., Maunier, B., Senecal, S.: An enriched customer journey map : how to construct and visualize a global portrait of both lived and perceived users' experiences? Designs 4(3), 29 (2020). https://doi.org/10.3390/designs4030029

Braun, V., Clarke, V.: Using thematic analysis in psychology. Qual. Res. Psychol. 3(2), 77–101 (2006). https://doi.org/10.1191/1478088706qp063oa

Courtemanche, F., et al.: Method of and system for processing signals sensed from a user (United States Patent N$^{\circ}$ US10368741B2) (2019). https://patents.google.com/patent/US10368741B2/en?oq=10%2c368%2c741%2c+6+ao%C3%BBt+2019.

de Guinea, A.O., Titah, R., Léger, P.-M.: Explicit and implicit antecedents of users' behavioral beliefs in information systems : a neuropsychological investigation. J. Manag. Inf. Syst. 30(4), 179–210 (2014). https://doi.org/10.2753/MIS0742-1222300407

Demazure, T., et al.: Distributed remote EEG data collection for NeuroIS research: a methodological framework. In International Conference on Human-Computer Interaction (forthcoming)

Giroux, F., et al. Guidelines for collecting automatic facial expression detection data synchronized with a dynamic stimulus in remote moderated user tests. In: International Conference on Human-Computer Interaction 2021 (forthcoming)

Giroux-Huppé, C., Sénécal, S., Fredette, M., Chen, S.L., Demolin, B., Léger, P.-M.: Identifying psychophysiological pain points in the online user journey: the case of online grocery. In: Marcus, A., Wang, W. (eds.) HCII 2019. LNCS, vol. 11586, pp. 459–473. Springer, Cham (2019). https://doi.org/10.1007/978-3-030-23535-2_34

Hammontree, M., Weiler, P., Nayak, N.: Remote usability testing. Interactions 1(3), 21–25 (1994). https://doi.org/10.1145/182966.182969

Léger, P.-M., Courtemanche, F., Fredette, M., Sénécal, S.: A cloud-based lab management and analytics software for triangulated human-centered research. In: Davis, F.D., Riedl, R., vom Brocke, J., Léger, P.-M., Randolph, A.B. (eds.) Information Systems and Neuroscience. LNISO, vol. 29, pp. 93–99. Springer, Cham (2019). https://doi.org/10.1007/978-3-030-01087-4_11

Myers, K.R., et al.: Unequal effects of the COVID-19 pandemic on scientists. Nat. Hum. Behav. 4(9), 880–883 (2020). https://doi.org/10.1038/s41562-020-0921-y

Riedl, R., Fischer, T., Léger, P.-M., Davis, F.D.: A decade of NeuroIS research : progress, challenges, and future directions. Data Base Adv. Inf. Syst. 51(3), 13–54 (2020)

Riedl, R., Léger, P.-M.: Fundamentals of NeuroIS: Information Systems and the Brain. Springer, Heidelberg (2016). https://doi.org/10.1007/978-3-662-45091-8

Roy, A., Sénécal, S., Léger, P.-M., Demolin, B., Bigras, É., Gagne, J.: Measuring users' psychophysiological experience in non-linear omnichannel environment. In: Stephanidis, C., Marcus, A., Rosenzweig, E., Rau, P.-L.P., Moallem, A., Rauterberg, M. (eds.) HCII 2020. LNCS, vol. 12423, pp. 762–779. Springer, Cham (2020). https://doi.org/10.1007/978-3-030-60114-0_50

Vasalou, A., Oshlyansky, L., Cairns, P., Savakis, K.: Human-moderated remote user testing : An empirical evaluation. In: HCI (2005)

A Chatbot Solution for eGLU-Box Pro: The Usability Evaluation Platform for Italian Public Administrations

Stefano Federici[1](✉)(iD), Maria Laura Mele[1](✉)(iD), Marco Bracalenti[1](✉),
Maria Laura De Filippis[1](✉)(iD), Rosa Lanzilotti[2](✉)(iD), Giuseppe Desolda[2](✉)(iD),
Simone Borsci[3](✉)(iD), Giancarlo Gaudino[4](✉), Antonello Cocco[4](✉),
Massimo Amendola[4](✉), and Emilio Simonetti[5](✉)

[1] Department of Philosophy, Social and Human Sciences and Education University of Perugia,
Perugia, Italy
{stefano.federici,marialaura.mele,marco.bracalenti,
marialaura.defilippis}@unipg.it
[2] Department of Computer Science, University of Bari Aldo Moro, Bari, Italy
{rosa.lanzilotti,giuseppe.desolda}@uniba.it
[3] Department of Learning, Data analysis, and Technology – Cognition,
Data and Education – CODE group, Faculty of BMS, University of Twente,
Enschede, The Netherlands
[4] DGTCSI-ISCTI – Directorate General for Management and Information and Communications
Technology, Superior Institute of Communication and Information Technologies, Ministry of
Economic Development, Rome, Italy
{giancarlo.gaudino,antonello.cocco,massimo.amendola}@mise.gov.it
[5] Department of Public Service, Prime Minister's Office, Rome, Italy
e.simonetti@funzionepubblica.it

Abstract. This paper shows a chatbot solution for eGLU-box Pro, a usability testing platform for Italian Public Administration (PA). eGLU-box Pro is a web-based tool designed to help PA practitioners in creating remote usability tests and analyzing participants' answers and interaction data after they complete the usability tasks. The impact of the chatbot solution on users' experience was assessed by bio-behavioral evaluation methods such as eye tracking, electroencephalography, and facial expression recognition. This work describes the platform and its integrated chatbot solution and shows the results of a preliminary laboratory study involving 20 end-users. The study is part of an ongoing design and development project based on a user-centered approach.

Keywords: Chatbots · Usability testing tools · User experience evaluation · Psychophysics

1 Introduction

Chatbots are intelligent conversational agents that interact with users by textual dialogues written in a natural language [1]. The use of chatbots aims at supporting interpersonal services, decision-making processes, and training in different contexts [2–5].

© Springer Nature Switzerland AG 2021
M. Kurosu (Ed.): HCII 2021, LNCS 12762, pp. 268–279, 2021.
https://doi.org/10.1007/978-3-030-78462-1_20

A recent review by Abd-Alrazaq and colleagues [6] highlighted that chatbots are usually assessed only in randomized controlled trials. The literature also shows that chatbot interaction efficiency is rarely assessed and, when assessments are performed, they are usually done on qualitative or non-standardized aspects of the interaction, thus providing data that cannot be statistically compared [1, 7, 8]. Because chatbots are interaction systems, their design should include users from the earliest stages by following a user-centered approach rather than a system-centered approach [1].

This study describes the user-centered design of a chatbot component of eGLU-box Pro, which is a digital web platform designed to support Italian Public Administration (PA) in conducting usability evaluation studies. The platform is based on the eGLU 2.1 protocol, which has been recently developed by the Working Group for the usability of the PA (https://www.agid.gov.it). The latest released version of the platform is eGLU-box PA v. 2018.1, which is now an integral part of the design guidelines for PA web services promoted by the Agency for Digital Italy (AGID) and by the Digital Team. The previous versions of eGLU-box have been validated in several studies [9–11] based on heuristic assessments and both user experience (UX) and psychophysical usability evaluations with PA practitioners in workplace conditions, web end-users in experimental laboratory conditions, and web end-users in remote online conditions.

This paper describes a new version of eGLU-box, called eGLU-box Pro, which allows for the improvement of the functionality of the platform, achieved through the development of an interface for the virtual management of remote tests (chatbot). In this study, the UX evaluation of the eGLU-box Pro chatbot was conducted by comparing the bio-behavioral components of the user experience of interaction derived from a usability test on a website. This study uses psychophysiological measures because they reflect top-down factors of human–computer interaction such as interest, attention, active participation, and mood. Eye-tracking technologies, facial expression recognition algorithms, and electroencephalography (EEG) can accurately measure the psychophysiological components of users' experience while interacting with a chatbot.

The paper is organized as follows. Section 2 describes the user-centered technology. Section 3 describes in detail the experimental methodology used for the assessment of the chatbot solution for eGLU-box Pro. Sections 4 and 5 present and discuss the results of the experimental assessment. Section 6 summarizes the findings.

2   eGLU-Box Pro

eGLU-box Pro is a web platform designed and developed during two previous research projects, funded and coordinated by the Superior Institute of Communication and Information Technologies (ISCTI) and the scientific and technical body of the Italian Ministry of Economic Development (MISE). The main goal is to improve the usability of Italian PA websites by involving the users of these websites in the evaluation, with a low-cost methodology (eGLU-LG 2.1 protocol) and an ad hoc technology (eGLU-box Pro). Another important goal is to increase the awareness of those who work in PA, from employees to managers, on the importance of usability, a fundamental element to be able to encourage citizens in using PA digital services.

2.1 The Platform

eGLU-BOX Pro supports the execution of remote asynchronous usability tests [12] according to the eGLU-LG 2.1 protocol. Two types of users are involved in remote usability tests with eGLU-box Pro, namely the evaluators and the participants. Different activities are supported by eGLU-box Pro according to such user types.

- *Evaluators* can create usability tests and visualize the analysis of the data automatically performed by the platform. When creating a test, evaluators have to define: the welcome script, the list of tasks to be performed by participants (specifying the URL where the task starts and the URL where the task is considered completed), possible questionnaires to administer to participants after the tasks have been executed (choosing between SUS [System Usability Scale], UMUX-Lite [Usability Metric for User Experience]; NPS [Net Promoter Score], and custom; [13, 14]), the data to be automatically collected during the user interaction with the website under evaluation (i.e., desktop recording and video and/or audio recording), and the participants to be invited.
  eGLU-box Pro automatically stores and analyzes all the collected data, showing in an aggregated form all the results of the performed test. Specifically, it shows the time and the success of each task and of each user as well as the task success of all tasks and all participants, the average score of each administered questionnaire, and a summary report exportable as a PDF. In addition, eGLU-box Pro allows the evaluator to analyze and annotate the video and audio of each user and each task.
- *Participants*, on the other hand, are guided in carrying out the usability test they are invited to complete. The platform, through a wizard process, first tests the peripherals that may be necessary to record the data selected by the evaluator (e.g., webcam and microphone), and then administers one after the other the tasks the participant has to carry out and, finally, the questionnaires.

This platform has been developed as a web app; thus, it does not require the installation of plug-ins or specific software because it has been realized through the use of solid web programming tools such as the PHP Laravel 5.6 framework, together with the use of HTML 5, Bootstrap 4, CSS 3, and jQuery. eGLU-box Pro has been certified according to ISO/IEC 25010:2005 "Software Engineering – Software product Quality Requirements and Evaluation (SQuaRE)".

2.2 The Chatbot

eGLU-box Pro has been used during more than 1,000 usability tests, allowing us to gather important feedback on different aspects. One of the most interesting results regards the absence of a real conductor that typically guides participants during an in-lab user test. We observed that participants, acting alone during a remote test, sometimes experience difficulties. For example, they need clarifications on aspects such as the use of audio/video registrations or need to solve some technical problems (e.g., peripherals not working). It emerged that, in a large number of cases, this negatively affects the user test results [paper under review]. For this reason, to compensate for the absence of a real conductor during the remote user test with eGLU-box Pro, we designed a chatbot that emulates all possible help and support that a conductor typically provides during an in-lab synchronous user test as a response to participants' requests.

The chatbot was implemented using Google Dialogflow. The chatbot is always visible and active from the moment the participant logs into the platform homepage until the end of the user test. The chatbot assumes three different faces, one for each state it may be in: inactive (Fig. 1, left), meaning that the user has closed the chatbot; active (Fig. 1, center), meaning that the user is interacting with the chatbot; and alert (Fig. 1, right), when the chat window is closed but the chatbot wants to communicate something to the participant.

Fig. 1. Expressions of the chatbot.

Users can also interact with the chatbot by means of specific buttons: increase/decrease font size; reset the chat history; enable or disable voice reading because the audio may be annoying; send the message, avoiding pressing "Enter" on the keyboard every time; and minimize the chatbot.

The design of the chatbot conversation follows the design patterns proposed by the Natural Conversation Framework, inspired by the natural way people speak [15]. These design patterns are specific to the creation of conversational agents such as chatbots and help to structure the dialogue in naturalistic conversational sequences between a chatbot and a real user through four components:

1. an interaction model based on expandable sequences;
2. a format based on the interaction model;
3. reusable templates for common speaking activities; and
4. a method of navigation by conversation.

The resulting chatbot interacts with the test participant in the following way (see Fig. 2). After logging into the platform, the chatbot welcomes the participant with a short message. The chatbot also explains that to start a test the participant must click the "Start" button next to the name of the study. The welcome message ends by explaining that by saying or typing the word "Help," the test participant will be supported with additional information. Help can be requested during any time in the user test and allows the participant to choose from a menu displayed by the chatbot to have more support on:

• How to run the task
• How to start a test
• What is a user test

- How to move to the next task
- What is the purpose of eGLU-box Pro
- What the recordings will be used for
- How to abandon a test
- How to fill out the questionnaires

Fig. 2. Chatbot integrated in eGLU-box Pro.

Once the participant has selected a specific user test, before starting the task execution he/she has to test the peripherals that the evaluator has selected for data capture, namely webcam, microphone, and desktop recording. For each peripheral, if the check is successful, the chatbot informs the participant that the test has been correctly executed, and vice versa it provides the participant with useful information to solve technical problems.

After the peripheral check, the test starts. In particular, all the tasks are administered in sequence. At the beginning of each task, the chatbot, simulating the behavior of an in-person conductor, tells the participant that he or she has to execute a task. In addition, the chatbot announces that the test is about to end with the evaluation by administering questionnaires that the user must complete. For each questionnaire administered by eGLU-box Pro, the chatbot briefly describes what the user is about to fill out, in terms of the name of the questionnaire (e.g., SUS), number of questions (10), and the type of answers they will be able to give (choice of 1 to 5). When the last questionnaire is completed, the chatbot thanks and dismisses the participant.

3   Method

This work is part of an ongoing study to assess eGLU-box Pro. The user-centered design of the chatbot integrated in eGLU-box Pro is here described as the first part of a multi-step process. This study evaluates the performance of the first version of the chatbot. A laboratory study has been conducted as described in Sect. 3.2. to investigate with psychophysics whether providing the automatic usability assessment tool with a chatbot affects the user experience.

Eye tracking methodology usually combines near-infrared technology with high-resolution optical sensors to measure where an observer is looking based on the pupil center corneal reflection (PCCR). The two main dynamics of eye movements, namely saccades and fixations, reveal the underlying cognitive processes of interaction, such as reasoning, problem solving, or attention [16].

Facial expression recognition uses patterns of involuntary facial muscular movements with algorithms to measure affective valence and seven universal basic emotions (joy, sadness, anger, contempt, disgust, fear, and surprise) as proposed by Paul Ekman and coded by the Facial Action Coding System (FACS) [17].

Frontal EEG alpha asymmetry is related to processes of approach/withdraw from affective or unexpected stimuli [18]. EEG measures the electrical field produced by the neural activity. EEG rhythms can reveal several components of cognition. In human–computer interaction research, one of the most studied rhythms is related to alpha activity. A decrease or desynchronization in alpha waves happens when cortical activity increases [19]. In particular, alpha frontal asymmetry may reveal approach or withdrawal cognitive processes [20]. An alpha lateralization to the left frontal lobe is related to approach, and a right lateralization appears as a withdrawal response from unexpected stimuli [21].

3.1 Apparatus and Measures

The version of eGLU-box Pro evaluated in this study runs on a PC with an Intel® Core™ i7-4710MQ CPU @ 2.50 GHz/2.49 GHz, RAM 8 GB, and 2880 × 1620 screen resolution. The experimental assessment was carried out using iMotions (www.imotions. com), a research platform that synchronizes biometric sensors in a single platform for psychophysical experiments. In this study, an eye tracker, a facial expression recognition software, and EGG technology were used.

The eye tracker model was a Tobii X2-30 Eye Tracker Compact Edition, with a 30 Hz gaze sample rate and 0.4° accuracy. In this study, the fixation number and duration (in milliseconds) were calculated.

The Affectiva Affdex technology was used to measure facial expressions to determine emotional valence (-100 = negative valence, 100 = positive valence) and seven emotions (0 = absent, 100 = present) with a 20% confidence threshold.

An EEG Emotiv Epoc+ was used. This wireless EEG headset records 16 channels based on the international 10–20 system at 2048 Hz internal, filtered, and downsampled to 128 or 256 per second per channel. The EEG device was used to calculate the frontal alpha asymmetry index by the difference between the alpha EEG power in the frontal right electrode and the alpha EEG power in the frontal left electrode [22].

3.2 Procedure

A usability test of an Italian PA website (http://www.sviluppoeconomico.gov.it) was performed. The test was administered through either the eGLU-box Pro tool with the integrated chatbot (experimental condition) or the eGLU-box tool without the integrated chatbot (control condition).

The experimental sessions were carried out in line with the COVID-19 prevention procedures recommended by the World Health Organization (https://www.who.int/eme

rgencies/diseases/novel-coronavirus-2019). Before entering the laboratory, each participant was asked to read and sign an informed consent document that asked epidemiologi-
cal and clinical questions aimed at self-certifying that each participant had no symptoms
and no risk of having come into contact with people that were COVID-19 positive within
the last 14 days.

The test comprised four tasks showing four user scenarios asking participants to
search for specific information, which is shown in a certain landing page that participants
do not know before completing the task. Participants are free to follow the path they want
to search for the required information. Each task lasts a maximum of 5 min, an average
time beyond which users generally lose interest in the interaction. After 5 min from the
beginning of each task, the eGLU-BOX platform automatically stops the current task
and shows a new task or the ending pages of the test.

Both experimental and control conditions were monitored using the iMotions platform. The test was conducted under an artificial constant dim light. Participants were
seated at about 600 mm from the screen. A 9-point eye-tracking calibration and
EEG benchmark data acquisition after the EEG electrode impedance assessment were
conducted.

3.3 Participants

An experimental test with 20 participants was conducted (10 control condition participants, 10 experimental condition participants). Participants (50% female, mean age
23.55 years old) declared they had normal or corrected-to-normal vision, no color blind-
ness, and no professional experience in usability studies. Two outliers per condition were
removed by the eye tracking dataset. One outlier was removed from the experimental
condition of the EEG dataset.

4 Results

The results show the data on eye tracking, facial expression, and EEG measured in both
conditions during the test.

4.1 Facial Expressions

The participants' emotions were computed by analyzing the webcam videos with the
Affectiva software. For each frame, the analyzed emotions were joy, anger, disgust, surprise, fear, sadness, and contempt (from 0 to 100, where 100 indicates the maximum
level of emotion), as well as valence (from -100 to $+100$, where -100 indicate negative emotion and $+100$ positive emotion). Affectiva produced 1,549,481 data points
associated with emotions.

The mean value of basic emotions and valence measured during the four tasks was
calculated for both control and experimental conditions (Table 1). All the emotion statistics have been calculated by removing frames whose values were <5, because emotions
under this threshold were considered noise.

Table 1. The mean (M) and standard deviation (SD) and *t*-test comparisons for basic emotions and valence in the control (condition 0) and experimental (condition 1) groups.

	Condition	M	SD	Welch's *t*-test
Engagement	0	47.687	47.602	$t = 0.233, p > .05$
	1	47.602	34.191	
Anger	0	16.078	13.934	$t = 1.858, p = .001$
	1	18.007	24.641	
Sadness	0	25.939	26.977	$t = 2,725.321, p = .000$
	1	12.373	8.331	
Disgust	0	20.473	25.898	$t = 201.995, p = .000$
	1	11.212	13.007	
Joy	0	82.670	28.934	$t = 59.709, p = .000$
	1	79.260	31.152	
Surprise	0	21.849	17.921	$t = 0.965, p > .05$
	1	22.232	17.498	
Fear	0	8.857	6.088	$t = 276.526, p = .000$
	1	23.724	20.232	
Contempt	0	68.692	34.877	$t = 53.094, p = .000$
	1	23.724	20.232	
Valence	0	−1.445	13.453	$t = 3,425.220, p = .000$
	1	−.314	8.745	

Welch's *t*-test was performed to determine if there was a statistically significant difference on basic emotions between the control and the experimental group (Table 1). No significant difference between the two groups was found for engagement and surprise ($p > .05$). As Table 1 shows, the control group (condition 0) showed significantly higher scores of sadness, disgust, joy, contempt, and overall negative valence, whereas the experimental group had significantly higher mean values for anger and fear.

A one-way analysis of variance (ANOVA) was performed on affective valence and the mean time percent of each basic emotion, showing no significant difference among the four experimental tasks, $p > 0.05$, meaning that the content of each task did not emotionally affect the participants. Further investigation using Welch *t*-test did not reveal any additional significance.

4.2 EEG Alpha Asymmetry

The effect of test condition on participants' approach/avoidance states was studied. After a previous automatic decontamination process for artefact removal, the FAA mean values were calculated (Table 2).

Table 2. The mean (M) and standard deviation (SD) for frontal alpha asymmetry in the control (condition 0) and experimental (condition 1) groups.

	Condition	M	SD
Frontal alpha asymmetry	0	0.7165	5.926
	1	−0.1641	0.864

A one way analysis of variance (ANOVA) was performed on FAA mean values, showing no significant difference among the four experimental tasks, $F(3, 75)$ = 0.639, $p > 0.05$, meaning that the content of each task did not affect the participants' approach/avoidance EEG correlates.

A one way ANOVA on FAA mean values also showed no significant difference between the two groups (control and experimental), $F(3, 75) = 0.639$, $p > .05$.

4.3 Eye Tracking

The mean values of both the duration and number of eye fixations measured during the four tasks were calculated for both control and experimental conditions (Table 3).

Table 3. The mean (M) and standard deviation (SD) for the duration and number of eye fixations in the control (condition 0) and experimental (condition 1) groups.

	Condition	M	SD
Duration of fixations (ms)	0	175.095	25.810
	1	161.998	26.820
Number of fixations	0	101.773	118.080
	1	117.136	84.500

No significant difference among the four experimental tasks was found by a one way analysis of variance (ANOVA) performed on mean values of duration, $F(3, 56) = 1.033$, $p > .05$, and number of eye fixations, $F(3, 56) = 1.444$, $p > .05$. Hence, the content of each task did not significantly affect the eye movements of participants.

A one way ANOVA between the two groups (control and experimental) showed no significant differences in the duration, $F(1, 63) = 3.061$, $p = .51$, or the number of fixations, $F(1, 63) = 0.358$, $p > .05$.

5 Discussion

The aim of this work was to introduce the user-centered design of a chatbot solution integrated in eGLU-box Pro, a usability assessment platform for Italian PA.

An experimental investigation was performed to analyze the impact on psychophysiological measures of experience when using a chatbot solution during a typical usability test of a website with eGLU-box PA Pro. Two groups were compared: One group performed the test with the chatbot version of the platform (experimental condition), while the other group used the platform without the chatbot solution enabled (control condition).

Statistical comparisons of the results of the experimental condition with the control condition were performed. Overall, there were no significant differences between the two groups for the number and duration of eye fixations and the approach/withdrawal motivation measured with EEG methods. The only significant differences were for facial expression recognition, with mean negative valence values higher for the control group performing the usability test without the aid of the chatbot compared with the experimental group using the chatbot solution. In particular, on the one hand, higher mean values of sadness, disgust, and contempt were found for the control group, but also higher values of joy. On the other hand, participants in the experimental condition showed higher mean values of anger and fear than the control condition. Finally, based on within-subject analyses, there was no difference for any of the three psychophysiological measures among the four tasks of the usability test meaning that the test difficulty was balanced across tasks.

The literature shows that eye fixations reflect cognitive processes in terms of mental load. Specifically, the more a visual stimulus demands analytic processes, the more fixation time and number of fixations is higher [23]. The average eye fixation in the experimental condition (about 161 ms per task) and number of fixations (about $N = 117$ per task) did not significantly differ from the control condition (with a mean fixation time of about 175 ms per task and a mean number of fixations of about $N = 101$ per task). This result means that the introduction of a conversational agent during a typical usability assessment test with eGLU-box did not increase cognitive workload in participants.

The findings on EEG measures also showed no differences in FAA mean values between the two groups, meaning that users' approach/withdrawal motivation processes did not significantly change in either condition. Introducing a conversational agent in an automatic usability assessment procedure did not significantly affect the quality of interaction in terms of user experience.

The main difference between the groups was in basic emotions. Overall, the control group had a significantly higher negative-valence experience, showing emotions such as sadness, disgust, and contempt that we did not find in the group using the chatbot as a source of help while performing the tasks. Those results might be due to the absence of a supervisor monitoring the user on the control group. Hence, the participant is free to complete the tasks without any tips or feedback, thus leading to more negative emotions during the test. The chatbot group experienced significantly higher emotional states related to anger and fear and lower emotional states related to joy. Those results might be due to usability issues related to the introduction of the chatbot, which might have prompted a decrease in enjoyment and an increase in negative emotions because of a reduction of perceived freedom if compared to the group that has not received any help or feedback during the test. Further studies will focus on the emotional aspects of the user experience with the proposed chatbot solution and investigate which usability aspects of it negatively affect user's emotions.

6 Conclusions

In this paper, we presented the user-centered design of a chatbot solution integrated in a usability assessment platform called eGLU-box Pro. The platform aims at helping the Italian PA in the assessment of their digital web-based services. The user experience of the integrated chatbot was compared with a control condition without the chatbot through three bio-behavioral measures: eye tracking, EEG, and facial expression recognition. There was no noteworthy difference among the four tasks comprising the test between the conditions, meaning that the difficulty of the tasks was well balanced across the test. Participants in both conditions did not show differences in psychophysiological measures of subjective experience such as eye movements and approach/withdrawal processes measured by EEG. Only basic emotions and emotional valence highlighted differences between the two groups. On the one hand, the chatbot users experienced higher anger and fear and lower joy than the control users, probably due to usability issues strictly related to the chatbot presence during the tasks. On the other hand, the tests conducted with no chatbot providing them feedback and help in following some correct procedures increased general negative-valence emotions, in particular sadness, disgust, and contempt. This result might be related to the absence of any help during the test. Overall, the study shows that introducing the eGLU-box PA conversational agent in an automatic usability assessment procedure did not significantly affect the quality of interaction in terms of user experience except for emotions. Future phases of the ongoing project presented here will focus on the usability aspects of the chatbot solution related to emotions, satisfaction and pleasantness of use.

Funding. This study was supported by the Directorate General for Management and Information and Communications Technology, Superior Institute of Communication and Information Technologies (DGTCSI-ISCTI), Ministry of Economic Development, Rome, Italy, under the grant project "eGLU-box Pro".

References

1. Radziwill, N.M., Benton, M.C.: Evaluating quality of chatbots and intelligent conversational agents. arXiv preprint arXiv:1704.04579 (2017)
2. Ammari, T., Kaye, J., Tsai, J.Y., Bentley, F.: Music, search, and iot: how people (really) use voice assistants. ACM Trans. Comput.-Hum. Interact. **26** (2019). https://doi.org/10.1145/331 1956
3. Beaudry, J., Consigli, A., Clark, C., Robinson, K.J.: Getting ready for adult healthcare: designing a chatbot to coach adolescents with special health needs through the transitions of care. J. Pediatr. Nurs. **49**, 85–91 (2019). https://doi.org/10.1016/j.pedn.2019.09.004
4. Costa, S., Brunete, A., Bae, B.C., Mavridis, N.: Emotional storytelling using virtual and robotic agents. Int. J. Hum. Robot. **15** (2018). https://doi.org/10.1142/S0219843618500068
5. Dmello, S., Graesser, A.: Autotutor and affective autotutor: learning by talking with cognitively and emotionally intelligent computers that talk back. ACM Trans. Interact. Intell. Syst. **2** (2012). https://doi.org/10.1145/2395123.2395128

6. Abd-Alrazaq, A.A., Alajlani, M., Alalwan, A.A., Bewick, B.M., Gardner, P., Househ, M.: An overview of the features of chatbots in mental health: a scoping review. Int. J. Med. Inf. **132**, 103978 (2019). https://doi.org/10.1016/j.ijmedinf.2019.103978

7. Balaji, D., Borsci, S.: Assessing user satisfaction with information chatbots: a preliminary investigation. University of Twente, University of Twente repository (2019). http://essay.utw ente.nl/79785/

8. Tariverdiyeva, G., Borsci, S.: Chatbots' perceived usability in information retrieval tasks: an exploratory analysis. University of Twente, University of Twente repository (2019). http://essay.utwente.nl/77182/

9. Federici, S., et al.: Heuristic evaluation of eGLU-Box: a semi-automatic usability evaluation tool for public administrations. In: Kurosu, M. (ed.) HCII 2019. LNCS, vol. 11566, pp. 75–86. Springer, Cham (2019). https://doi.org/10.1007/978-3-030-22646-6_6

10. Catarci, T., et al.: Digital interaction: where are we going? In: Proceedings of the 2018 International Conference on Advanced Visual Interfaces: AVI 2018, pp. 1–5 (2018). https://doi.org/10.1145/3206505.3206606

11. Federici, S., Mele, M.L., Bracalenti, M., Buttafuoco, A., Lanzilotti, R., Desolda, G.: Bio-behavioral and self-report user experience evaluation of a usability assessment platform (UTAssistant). In: VISIGRAPP 2019: Proceedings of the 14th International Joint Conference on Computer Vision, Imaging and Computer Graphics Theory and Applications. Volume 2: HUCAPP, pp. 19–27 (2019)

12. Hammontree, M., Weiler, P., Nayak, N.: Remote usability testing. Interactions **1**, 21–25 (1994). https://doi.org/10.1145/182966.182969

13. Borsci, S., Federici, S., Bacci, S., Gnaldi, M., Bartolucci, F.: Assessing user satisfaction in the era of user experience: comparison of the Sus, Umux and Umux-lite as a function of product experience. Int. J. Hum.-Comput. Interact. **31**, 484–495 (2015). https://doi.org/10.1080/104 47318.2015.1064648

14. Reichheld, F.F.: The one number you need to grow. Harv. Bus. Rev. **82**, 133 (2004)

15. Moore, R.J.: A natural conversation framework for conversational UX design. In: Moore, R.J., Szymanski, M.H., Arar, R., Ren, G.-J. (eds.) Studies in Conversational UX Design. HIS, pp. 181–204. Springer, Cham (2018). https://doi.org/10.1007/978-3-319-95579-7_9

16. Duchowski, A.T.: Eye Tracking Methodology: Theory and Practice. Springer, London (2007). https://doi.org/10.1007/978-1-84628-609-4

17. Ekman, P., Friesen, W.V.: The Facial Action Coding System (Facs): A Technique for the Measurement of Facial Action. Consulting Psychologists Press, Palo Alto (1978)

18. Schur, M., Ritvo, L.B.: A principle of evolutionary biology for psychoanalysis: schneirla's evolutionary and developmental theory of biphasic processes underlying approach and withdrawal and freud's unpleastire and pleaswe principles. J. Am. Psychoanal. Assoc. **18**, 422–439 (1970). https://doi.org/10.1177/000306517001800210

19. Pizzagalli, D.A.: Electroencephalography and high-density electrophysiological source localization. In: Caccioppo, J.T., Tassinary, L.G., Berntson, G. (eds.) Handbook of Psychophysiology, pp. 56–84. Cambridge University Press, Cambridge (2007)

20. Schneirla, T.C.: An evolutionary and developmental theory of biphasic processes underlying approach and withdrawal. In: Jones, M.R. (ed.) Nebraska Symposium on Motivation, vol. 7, pp. 1–42. University of Nebraska Press, Lincoln (1959)

21. Coan, J.A., Allen, J.J.B.: Frontal EEG asymmetry as a moderator and mediator of emotion. Biol. Psychol. **67**, 7–49 (2004). https://doi.org/10.1016/j.biopsycho.2004.03.002

22. Allen, J.J.B., Coan, J.A., Nazarian, M.: Issues and assumptions on the road from raw signals to metrics of frontal EEG asymmetry in emotion. Biol. Psychol. **67**, 183–218 (2004). https://doi.org/10.1016/j.biopsycho.2004.03.007

23. Jacob, R.J.K.: The use of eye movements in human-computer interaction techniques: what you look at is what you get. TOIS **9**, 152–169 (1991). https://doi.org/10.1145/123078.128728

ERM-AT Applied to Social Aspects of Everyday Life

Masaaki Kurosu[1](✉) and Ayako Hashizume[2](✉)

[1] The Open University of Japan, Chiba-shi 261-8586, Japan
nigrumamet-s23@mbr.nifty.com
[2] Hosei University, Machida-shi 194-0298, Japan
hashiaya@hosei.ac.jp

Abstract. Based on the notion of quality characteristics in design and quality characteristics in use in terms of the UX for products and services, authors tried to apply the ERM that was originally developed for measuring (and evaluating) the UX to the new field "social aspects of everyday life" based on the idea that the UX is just a part of the total experience and that we have to make efforts to improve the total experience of human life.

The ERM was originally developed to let users write down episodes in terms of some specific product or service with the rating value from 10 to -10 on the rough time scale. We could examine how the positive and negative episodes were experiences. It should serve as a basis for the improvement of the UX. But unfortunately, the original ERM lacked the linkage to the improvement from finding problems. ERM-AT was thus proposed to provide the analytical clues where quality characteristics in design caused the (negative) quality characteristics in use.

The challenge in this paper is to expand the scope of the ERM-AT to be applied from just the products and services to the social aspects of everyday life. For that purpose we changed the quality characteristics in design and in use to the independent variables and dependent variables that will include different set of keywords depending on the type of social aspect of everyday life.

A trial application to the university life suggested the successful expansion of the method. Finally, a vast map of applicable domain was shown.

Keywords: ERM-AT · Everyday life · User experience (UX)

1 Measurement of User Experience

1.1 Structure of User Experience

When the UX (User eXperience) was a buzzword in 2000s, it was necessary to clarify its structure before discussing the measurement method. But some people identified it as the same concept with the usability and insisted that the usability testing can be used to evaluate the UX, others claimed that the UX can be predicted before users start using products or services, and others even regarded the UX as the positive aspects

© Springer Nature Switzerland AG 2021
M. Kurosu (Ed.): HCII 2021, LNCS 12762, pp. 280–290, 2021.
https://doi.org/10.1007/978-3-030-78462-1_21

of the use of products and services and UX design can make users happy. All these misunderstandings can be traced back to the ambiguous definition, the lack of logical description of the concept and no mention to the evaluation method of the UX by Norman [1] who coined the term. As he complained later [2], there was a wide-spread turmoil in terms of the use of this concept.

In order to clarify the vagueness of UX concept, 30 researchers came together to Dagstuhl, Germany in 2010 and in the next year the UX White Paper [3] that compiled the discussion was issued. It proposed the temporal structural model of UX but did not provided the formal definition of the concept.

For promoting the logical understanding on this concept, authors proposed a conceptual model of UX in 2015 [4] and revised it in 2018 [5] as shown in Fig. 1. In this figure, the quality in design and the quality in use and the objective quality and the subjective quality are distinguished respectively. Thus, four groups of quality characteristics can be generated: the objective quality in design, the objective quality in use, the subjective quality in design and the subjective quality in use. The usability, in this diagram, is one of the objective quality characteristics in design (upper left in Fig. 1) and the UX is related to the quality in use (right side half in Fig. 1).

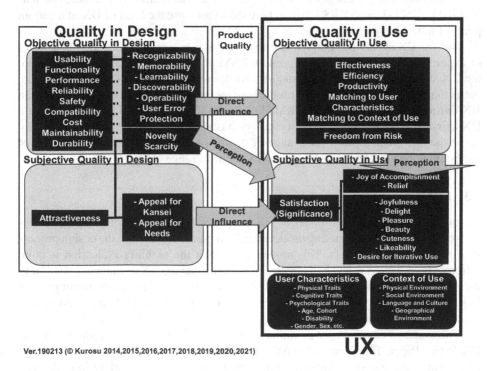

Fig. 1. Diagram of four quality characteristics that shows the difference between usability and UX

It should be noted that the quality in design and the quality in use are in a kind of causal relationship. We can hear the users' voice mainly after they used the product or service and that voice represent the evaluation of UX and we can measure the degree and content of UX from their utterance or written records. In other words, the quality in use is related to the evaluation of UX and it can be analyzed by going back to the quality in design as to which quality in design was not made properly or adequately. It must be a useful feedback to the development process including the design process.

1.2 UX Measurement Methods

Many methods to measure the UX have been proposed reflecting the confusing situation on the concept of UX. Examples can be found at the website of ALL ABOUT UX [6]. This big list is, though, not complete because it includes, for example, the usability evaluation methods reflecting the confusion of UX and usability.

Because the UX is the experience of user at the time of using some product or service, it is thought to be the best to measure it while the user is using such product or service. A typical example of such method is the ESM (Experience Sampling Method) [7]. But the ESM is invasive as the user may not know in advance when the triggering bell starts to ring during the user's daily life. The questionnaire method SUS [8] can be applied for the measurement of UX albeit the name of the method. Other questionnaires such as SUPR-Q, NPS [9], and QUIS [10] can be used to measure the level of UX at a certain point of time.

But the UX should be regarded not an experience at one point of time but a series of experiences from the past to the present. ESM and questionnaires can only measure the UX at a specific point of time. And authors thought that memory-based methods are better than the ESM and questionnaires because memory-based methods can measure the UX during certain range of time. DRM [11], TFD [12], CORPUS [13], iScale [14] and UX Curve [15] are examples of such memory-based methods. These methods basically adopt the line graph to show the change of degree of UX and the visual impression of the graph is easy for grasping the whole UX within a range of time.

1.3 ERM

By examining the temporal model of UX proposed by the UX White Paper, authors revised it as Fig. 2 by juxtaposing the development process (including the design process in it) and the usage process. This model shows that the usability evaluation is quite different from the UX evaluation (measurement) and that the UX evaluation is similar to the survey activity, the second activity in the design process. The development process is also called a Decagon model because of 10 activities included in it and round shaped model is shown in another reference [16].

The usage process in Fig. 2 is similar to the temporal model of UX proposed by the UX White Paper. The important point is that the UX is not only reflecting the usage alone, but is influenced by the whole stages in the usage process starting from the past experience.

Regarding stages consisting of the past experience, expectation, purchase, usage with sometimes the waste where the user stops using the product or service, there are various kinds of episode some positive and some negative as can be revealed by such evaluation method as the UX graph [17] that is a revision of the UX curve [15].

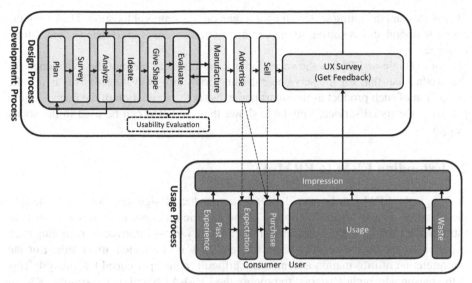

Fig. 2. Relationship between the development process and the usage process. The development process includes the design process in it. This also shows that the usability evaluation and the UX survey are completely different.

Considering the inaccurateness of the abscissa of the graph and curve, authors proposed the ERM (Experience Recollection Method) that put more emphasis on the content

Table 1. Sample ERM sheet in terms of the university experience.

Recording Sheet for ERM: Experience Recollection Method   Target Item _University_   ⟨Male⟩/Female Age _18_

1. Write what you experienced at each phase and fill in the evaluation by +10 to -10 rating.

Phase		What you experienced	Evaluation
Expectation before the purchase		_Expecting that I can learn what I could not learn at high school._	3
Evaluation at the time of start of usage	Year 2016	_May be able to learn various subjects._	4
Evaluation at early days from the start of usage		_It's located very far from home_	-7
		Interesting to study, but teachers don't let me know how to study.	-3
Evaluation during the use		_Science and technology are interesting_	2
		Could get many good friends.	4
		Very interesting to go to the university.	6
		Too much home tasks and have little time to do them.	-8
Recent evaluation		_There are many interesting lectures._	1
		There is a limit of the number of lectures that I can take.	-2
Present evaluation	Year 2017	_There are many restrictions._	2
Estimation in the near future		_Would like to study more seriously._	4

of episodes and the rating scale value for it than on the temporal location. Thus, only the rough temporal stages similar to the one mentioned before is used than the exact time position.

An example of ERM is shown in Table 1. In this example, not the experience for the product but that for the service or the university life is evaluated. This is not the evaluation of such product as the smart phone but is the evaluation of the service, more precisely the social service. This table shows that the ERM can be used in the social design too.

2 Extending ERM to ERM-AT

Although the ERM can be used both for the product design and the service design, the obtained data is just a description of the experiential episode with the evaluative rating scale value. It is a good material that contains various information regarding each experiential episode, especially when the interview is conducted afterwards. But the interpretation of information is sometimes difficult to unexperienced UX analyst. This is the reason why authors started to propose the ERM-AT based on the simple ERM.

The idea to facilitate the analysis of ERM data is to make a cross-table based on the quality characteristics mentioned in Subsect. 1.1. The quality characteristics in design as the cause of the experience and the quality characteristics in use as the result of the experience will be listed on the column of the table. Each row of the ERM representing

Table 2. An example of ERM-AT for the cellphone.

Phase	Episode	Rating	Usability	Functionality	Performance	Reliability	Safety	Compatibility	Cost	Maintainability	Durability	Novelty	Scarcity	Attractiveness	Effectiveness	Efficiency	Productivity	Matching to user characteristics	Matching to context of use	Freedom from Risk	Satisfaction
			Quality in Design											Quality in use							
Expectation before the use	I expected to get the latest model of iPhone on the day of sale	8																			8
Evaluation at the start (2014)	I was astonished by the large screen compared to my previous model (iPhone 5)	5		5											5	5					5
Evaluation during early use	I got used to the large screen soon. And I felt the advantage of large screen for enjoying the game	10		10										10				10	10		10
Evaluation during the use	The body was bent, but was straighten back by pushing it harder	-5				-5									-5	-5					-5
Evaluation during recent use	The power loss of battery is unexpectedly fast	-5			-5	-5					-5				-5	-5					-5
Present evaluation (2016)	It's now a must to carry the backup battery	-5			-5	-5									-5	-5					-5
Expectation for the future	I will use this until the next model will appear	-2																			-2

Smartphone (iPhone 6)   Age 27

different experiential episodes will be analyzed one by one by checking if that episode is related to the quality characteristics in each column. If the match was found, the rating value from 10 to −10 will be copied to that cell. This is how the ERM-AT (ERM Analytic Table) is used.

An example is shown in Table 2 (for the cellphone) and in Table 3 (for the automatic driving car) [18]. By comparing these two tables, we can find different cells filled with the different rating values, thus facilitating the analysis of each episode. For example, in Table 2, "the evaluation at the start (2014)" was "I was astonished by the large screen compared to my previous model (iPhone5)" with the rating 5. The experience value of satisfaction was 5 and that rating was also related to the effectiveness and efficiency.

Table 3. An example of ERM-AT for the automatic driving car.

Phase	Episode	Rating	Usability	Functionality	Performance	Reliability	Safety	Compatibility	Cost	Maintainability	Durability	Novelty	Scarcity	Attractiveness	Effectiveness	Efficiency	Productivity	Matching to user characteristics	Matching to context of use	Freedom from Risk	Satisfaction
Expectation before the use	I was interested in it by watching the TV commercial. But still not assured for the precision and performance. Automated car is still expensive and it will be 3 years from now for me to buy it when there will be many cars and the price and performance may be stable.	3			3				3												3
Evaluation at the start (2014)	At the automobile inspection, the dealer let me have an automatic car as a substitute for 10 days. Because it was uneasy to drive it in mountains, I tried it on the flat road. Driving was easy by skillfully follow the car ahead of me.	8	8	8			8								8	8					8
Evaluation during early use	On the highway, I used it in fixed speed mode. It was easy by driving in a steady speed and keeping the adequate distance to the car ahead.	8	8	8	8															-5	-5
Evaluation during the use	In the auto-driving mode, the handle was locked. It seemed to be of no use of holding the handle. But when I left the hand from handle, the alarm buzzed and I had to put my hand on the handle with nothing to do.	-5	-5																	-5	-5
	I had an impression that it is convenient for the long driving or on the highway after several times of using it.	6		6	6										6	6					6
Evaluation during recent use	I understood that the level of auto-driving cannot set higher thus the driver has to put the hand on handle. But it is nice that the level can be set higher from the technological point. That's nice.	5		5	5																5
	After returned the substitute car, I do not feel any difficulties without the automatic driving function	0													0						0
Present evaluation (2021)	Now I'm not anxious about the precision and performance, but the problem now is if it is installed in the car or not that I will purchase. I will buy the automatic car if it is at a reasonable price.	6									6										6
Expectation for the future	I will use it if the car that I want to drive will equip that function.	7																			7

These quality in use cells might have been caused by the performance in the quality in design.

In short, when all the rating values are copied to the relevant cells, the analysis on the quality characteristics in terms of the quality in use and quality in design will be started. The point of analysis is (1) which quality characteristics have many cells with values without regard to the value, and (2) whether the values are generally positive or negative. Thus, the kind of quality in design that caused the positive or negative quality in use will be shown. Based on negative cell values in the quality in design, the direction of next design process will be clarified.

3   ERM-AT Applied to Social Aspects of Everyday Life

Based on the success of applying the ERM-AT to various products and services, authors thought of applying it to social aspects of everyday life. But we had to reconsider about the quality characteristics in the social design. All those quality characteristics in Fig. 1 were for the design and use of products. But services and social aspects of everyday life will have different set of quality characteristics. Regarding the service, we had some questions if the durability and reliability is relevant or not. Usually, the service will be short in time and the durability and reliability is not relevant in most cases. In addition to this, the social aspects of everyday life should have quite a different set of quality characteristics from both the product or the service. What we had in mind as the social aspects of everyday life is the school life, marriage life, regional activity, local government activity, etc. What we concluded is that the set of quality characteristics will have to be redesigned each time the targeted activity will change.

The first example we adopted was the university life as shown in Table 4. Students were given the ERM sheet to write down their experience before the entrance, when they entered the university, at the beginning of their school life, during the school life, recent experience, what they are experiencing now and in the near future (after the graduation) as an expectation. If the informants were the graduates, the graduation of the university and the retrospective view should be written. In such a way, the ERM sheet can be used similarly for the products and the services to the social aspects of everyday life. The difference exists in the set of quality characteristics.

Regarding the service, there are phases both in design and usage in a kind of the causal relationship. Thus, the similar terminologies in Fig. 1 can be applied. Similarly, the social aspects of everyday life will indeed have the design phase and the use phase. For example, the university life is designed by the university personnel in its selection of the geographic location, its campus layout, its building design, school expenses, quality of lectures, facility design, etc. Other factors such as the academic level of the university, the employment rate and so on will affect the attractiveness of the university. These design qualities are quite different from products and services. Furthermore, the quality characteristics in use are mainly the emotional ones, i.e., positive and negative feelings, such as attractive, joyful, anxiety and so on in the form of adjectives.

But in the everyday life situation, the term "quality characteristics" does not completely match to the situation because the life is not the product nor the service. Authors decided to change the terms "quality characteristics in design" and "quality characteristics in use" to "independent variables" and "dependent variables" by clearly showing the nature of both concepts in the causal relationship.

Both variables will include different terms depending on the type of everyday life situation. For example, the independent variables for the marriage life will include the age of marriage, personality, fidelity, feelings among kinship members, income level, housing, etc. while the independent variables for the social service will include the subject of activity, level of cohesion, financial background, etc. The set of variables may have some default concepts, such as the location, campus, facility, school expenses, etc. but some more concepts should be added by analyzing the data. Anyways, all the list of variables should be exactly the same so that the comparison among informants can be possible.

An example ERM-AT in Tables 4 and 5 are about the university life based on the description by two students. The general view of informant A is the one who is intending to enjoy the university as much as possible while informant B is the one who is eager to study but motivated to only those subjects of which he is interested in. This difference between two students is reflected on the right side of tables (AT parts) of Table 4 and Table 5.

Note that new columns curriculum in independent variables and interesting in dependent variables were added. Hence, Table 4 should also have to be added these two columns afterwards so that both tables in terms of the university life have the same structure and allows an easy comparison.

Table 4. An example of ERM-AT for the university life by the informant A.

Phase	Episode	Rating	location	campus	facility	school expense	quality of lecture	level of university	employment rate	level	difficulty of learning	part time job	enjoyment	happiness	expectation	anxiety	regret	achievement
			Independent Variables										Dependent Variables					
Expectation before the use	Before the entrance, I had an image that the university life is full of freedom. I was expecting the happy campus life.	10											10	10				
Evaluation at the start (2015)	I had a bit of anxiety for selecting the lecture for myself. But I was motivated that I can learn professional caliculum that the high school does not provide.	8									8					8		
Evaluation during early use	There were difficult lectures, but they must be useful in the future.	8					8				8					8		
	I failed a class that was so difficult to learn.	-10									-10						-10	-10
Evaluation during the use	I adapted the university life and enjoyed it with no classes to fail.	10									10		10					10
	Some classes were difficult, but I studied hard to avoid failing it.	7									7		7					7
Evaluation during recent use	Because I got enough credits, I focused on the parttime job.	8										8	8					
Present evaluation (2017)	Choosing the adequate class is difficult.	5									5		5					
Expectation for the future	I'll be busy for job searching	-5							-5	-5						-5		

Table 5. An example of ERM-AT for the university life by the informant B.

			Independent Variables											Dependent Variables						
Phase	Episode	Rating	location	campus	facility	school expense	quality of lecture	level of university	employment rate	level	difficulty of learning	curriculum	part time job	enjoyment	happiness	expectation	anxiety	interesting	regret	achievement
Expectation before the use	There are many faculties and the university campus is modern.	7		7	7									7						
Evaluation at the start (2015)	Many buildings are large and I thought learning here will be interesting.	6		7	7											7				
Evaluation during early use	The street up to the university has a steep slope. It's very hard.	-7	-7												-7					
	Studying many subjects is interesting and useful.	8										8						8		
Evaluation during the use	Many professors simply rate the grade D and there are no remedies.	-10									-10				-10					-10
	It is not clear how students can express their opinions to the university authorities. It is not good for improving the university system.	-10			-10															
	Got acquaintance to the professor who is friendly, and the lecture has come to be interesting.	9					9											9		
	Lectures have wide range of genres. It is a pleasure to take them.	7										9		9						
Evaluation during recent use	It is uneasy that we can not get enough units for grduation if we take only interesting ones.	-8									-8				-8					
	University as a whole is a small community to find good friends.	-9			-9														-9	
Present evaluation (2017)	Some lectures are interesting, but necessary units are far large. Furthermore, the commuting is not easy. I'm not completely enjoying the university life.	-4	-4									-4		-4						
Expectation for the future	I wonder if I may withdraw from the university or stay another year.	-6					-6					-6							-6	

4 Conclusion

Combining the list of quality characteristics of Fig. 1 and the temporal process framework in Fig. 2, authors proposed ERM as a measurement method of the UX. Because the original ERM lacked the tool for analysis, we proposed the ERM-AT that cross-checks each of the episodes and the quality characteristics. Applying the ERM-AT to products and services were successful. By tracing back the episode that the informant experienced to the quality characteristics, we could clarify what should be improved, especially, in the quality characteristics in design.

But for applying the method to the social aspects of everyday life, we had to make a small change to the original method. Because the basic nature of columns are not the quality characteristics but just the variables in the causal relationship, we now call them as the independent variables and dependent variables. Further, the nature of the experience will differ from one social aspect to another, we allowed to collect a list of most adequate variables (especially, the independent variables) depending on the type of the experience.

Finally, for further application of ERM-AT, a list of social aspects of everyday life is shown in Fig. 3.

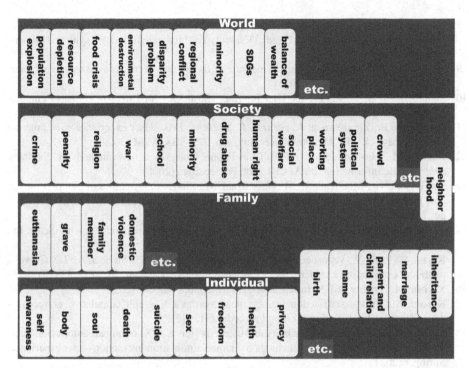

Fig. 3. A list of further topics that ERM-AT should be applied. There are four layers included: world level, society level, family level and individual level (this might be disregarded). At least three levels, there are very many subject areas that should be analyzed by ERM-AT for their own improvements.

References

1. Norman, D.A.: The Invisible Computer – Why Good Products Can Fail, the Personal Computer is So Complex, and Information Appliances Are the Solution. The MIT Press (1998)
2. Merholz, P.: Peter in conversation with Don Norman about UX & innovation (2007). https://adaptivepath.org/ideas/e000862/
3. Roto, V., Law, E., Vermeeren, A., Hoonhout, J.: User experience white paper – bringing clarity to the concept of user experience. Result from Dagstuhl Seminar on Demarcating User Experience, 15–18 September 2010 (2011). https://www.allaboutux.org/uxwhitepaper
4. Kurosu, M.: Usability, quality in use and the model of quality characteristics. In: Kurosu, M. (ed.) HCI 2015. LNCS, vol. 9169, pp. 227–237. Springer, Cham (2015). https://doi.org/10.1007/978-3-319-20901-2_21
5. Kurosu, M., Hashizume, A., Ueno, Y.: User experience evaluation by ERM: experience recollection method. In: Kurosu, M. (ed.) HCI 2018. LNCS, vol. 10901, pp. 138–147. Springer, Cham (2018). https://doi.org/10.1007/978-3-319-91238-7_12
6. All About UX. http://www.allaboutux.org/all-methods
7. Larson, R., Csikszentmihalyi, M.: The experience sampling method. New Direct. Methodol. Soc. Behav. Sci. **15**, 41–56 (1983)

8. Brooke, J.: SUS: A 'quick and dirty' usability scale. In: Jordan, P.W., Thomas, B., Weerdmeester, B.A., McClelland, I.L. (eds.) Usability Evaluation in Industry. Taylor and Francis, London (1996)

9. Sauro, J.: SUPR-Q: a comprehensive measure of the quality of the website user experience. J. Usabil. Stud. **10**(2), 68–86 (2015)

10. Shneiderman, B.: Designing the User Interface: Strategies for Effective Human-Computer Interaction. 3rd edn. Addison-Wesley (1998)

11. Karapanos, E., Zimmerman, J., Forlizzi, J., Martens, J.-B.: User experience over time: an initial framework. In: CHI 2009 Proceedings, pp. 729–738. ACM (2009)

12. Kurosu, M., Hashizume, A.: TFD (Time Frame Diary) – a new method for obtaining ethnographic information. In: APCHI 2008 Proceedings (2008)

13. von Wilamowits-Moellendorff, M., Hassenzahl, M., Platz, A.: Dynamics of user experience: how the perceived quality of mobile phones changes over time. In: UX WS NordiCHI 2006, pp. 74–78 (2006)

14. Karapanos, E., Martens, J.-B., Hassenzahl, M.: Reconstructing experiences with iScale. Int. J. Hum.-Comput. Stud. 1–17 (2012)

15. Kujala, S., Roto, V., Vaananen-Vainio-Mattila, K., Karapanos, E., Sinnela, A.: UX Curve: a method for evaluating long-term user experience. Interact. Comput. **23**, 473–483 (2011)

16. Kurosu, M.: Theory of UX (in Japanese), Kindaikagaku-sha Co. (2020)

17. Kurosu, M.: Is the satisfaction measurement by the UX graph cumulative or recency-dependent? In: JSKE Spring Meeting Proceedings (2015)

18. Kurosu, M., Hashizume, A.: Usability and user experience (UX) of human-automation interaction – concept and measurement method - human automation interaction – user experience. Springer (2021)

Civil Aircraft Cockpit Human Machine Interactive Dynamic Assessment Quality Improvement Based on System Engineering

Qun Kuang[✉], Jingjin Zhang, and Fei Li

Shanghai Aircraft Design and Research Institute, Shanghai 201210, China

Abstract. The quality improvement of cockpit human machine interactive dynamic assessment based on the system engineering of a certain civil aircraft cockpit assessment task was presented in this paper. Firstly, by applying the theoretical method of system engineering and combining the practical experience of cockpit integration design, evaluation, development and verification of civil aircraft, the double-V process of civil aircraft cockpit integration design process and the components in the double-V process are sorted out and determined which can be used for the guidance of the cockpit design and assessment. Secondly, the design of cockpit human machine interactive assessment platform is performed from four aspects of requirement capture, requirement verification, project design and requirement validation, the scheme design and components of the evaluation platform are described in detail. Finally, the correctness and integrity of requirements fulfillment were verified through performing cockpit human machine interactive assessment on the platform. The practice was a successful application of system engineering in civil aircraft cockpit design and assessment domain.

Keywords: System engineering · Cockpit assessment · Human machine interactive · Civil aircraft

1 Foreword

Cockpit is the only place in which pilots interact with the aircraft, which is also the very important place for the control inputs and information display outputs of all the systems. The cockpit is the concentrated embodiment of safety and advancement. Civil aircraft cockpit design is integrated with the requirements and design characteristics of multiple systems' display, control, alarm and human machine interactive, design inputs, design criterion and design needs of multiple branches of learning. Civil aircraft cockpit design is an integrated design process of multiple branches of learning.

2 Cockpit Assessment

During the development of civil aircraft design process, cockpit design is a multilevel iterative optimization design process. After the cockpit integrated design finished, requirement validation and evaluation of cockpit design shall be performed. Flight experts and

© Springer Nature Switzerland AG 2021
M. Kurosu (Ed.): HCII 2021, LNCS 12762, pp. 291–298, 2021.
https://doi.org/10.1007/978-3-030-78462-1_22

experts majored in human factors are usually invited to perform the static evaluation of cockpit physical ergonomics (cockpit environment, layout, visuality and reachability) based on document, drawing and cockpit samples.

Integrated with different flight scenes, aircraft configuration (weight, center of gravity, flap/slat configuration and so on), flight conditions, dynamic evaluation of cognitive ergonomics (display elements, control devices and flight crew alarm), operational procedure (normal operating procedure, abnormal operational procedure, emergency procedure) are performed.

After the evaluation, combined with evaluation results, the decision of whether cockpit optimal design needs to be performed is made. Performing the requirement validation, cockpit design results check and evaluation as early as possible and fully before the real aircraft is ready, the prime costs and periods of iterative developments of cockpit software and hardware can be reduced effectively, the risk of cockpit major changes at the later stage of development can be reduced. At present, the platform supporting the cockpit human machine interactive dynamic evaluation is lacked. Therefore, the quality improvement of performing cockpit human machine interactive dynamic evaluation is raised.

3   Implementation Steps of Quality Improvement

Cockpit is an integrated multidisciplinary design, and the development of the dynamic evaluation platform for cockpit human machine interaction is a complex system engineering. In order to grasp the overall contents of cockpit design evaluation, the theoretical method of systems engineering is used to sort out the cockpit design evaluation work from four aspects, namely requirement capture, requirement validation, scheme

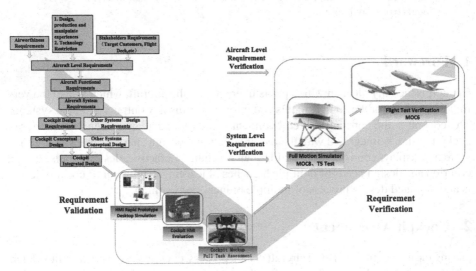

Fig. 1. Civil aircraft cockpit integration design process (requirements validation and requirements verification)

design and requirement verification, and establish the cockpit integration design process (requirement validation and requirement verification). Refer to Fig. 1 for the detailed information.

The system engineering concept is adopted to guide the cockpit integration design. In accordance with the forward design and double V process, the requirements of stakeholders of the cockpit integration design are fully captured. Functional analysis, demand analysis, conceptual design and integration design of the cockpit and various systems are carried out. After the completion of the cockpit integration design, requirements validation was carried out in the form of human machine interactive desktop simulation and cockpit human machine interactive evaluation, requirements verification was implemented in the form of simulator test and flight test, and requirements verification was completed at aircraft level and system level.

3.1 Requirements Capture

After requirements analysis, the requirements for dynamic evaluation of cockpit human machine interaction are mainly divided into "airworthiness" and "cockpit design requirements confirmation and evaluation". The sources of requirements mainly involve airworthiness regulations, cockpit design requirements confirmation and cockpit evaluation.

a) Airworthiness Requirements Capture
   The objective of capturing airworthiness requirements is to meet the requirements of airworthiness regulations and terms and to ensure the safety and airworthiness of the aircraft, which is also the most basic requirements to be met in cockpit design evaluation. The airworthiness requirements to be met for cockpit evaluation are shown in Table 1.

Table 1. Airworthiness requirements of cockpit evaluation

Number	Airworthiness regulations	Airworthiness terms/Requirements
1	CCAR 25R4	25.671(a), 25.672(a)(b), 25.677(a)(b), 25.685(b), 25.697(a)(b), 25.699(a)(b)(c), 25.703(b), 25.729(e)(2)(3)(4), 25.771(c)(e), 25.773(a)(b)(1)(i)(ii)(2)(d), 25.775(e), 25.777(a)(b)(c)(d)(e)(f)(g), 25.779, 25.781, 25.785(k)(l), 25.807(j), 25.841(b)(5)(6), 25.863(c), 25.1141(a)(d)(f)(2), 25.1143(c)(e), 25.1145(c), 25.1155, 25.1189(f), 25.1303(a)(1)(2)(3)(b)(c), 25.1307(d)(e), 25.1321(a)(b)(c), 25.1322, 25.1325(f), 25.1326(a), 25.1329(a)(f)(i)(j)(k)(l)(m), 25.1351(b)(5)(6), 25.1357(d), 25.1381(a)(b), 25.1383, 25.1403, 25.1541, 25.1543(b), 25.1545, 25.1551, 25.1553, 25.1555, 25.1563, 25.1142
2	CS 25	25.1302

b) Cockpit Design Requirements Validation and Evaluation Requirements Capture
   In the preliminary design and detailed design stages of the cockpit, the design schemes of display, control, alarm and human machine interaction of each airborne

system (e.g., power system, etc.) in the cockpit shall be confirmed, so as to ensure that the design results are complete and correctly meet the design requirements.

In addition, the evaluation of cockpit human machine interaction and operation procedures should be carried out in combination with different operational scenarios and tasks, cockpit human factor evaluation methods and guidelines.

3.2 Scheme Design

According to the captured dynamic evaluation requirements of cockpit human machine interaction, the design of dynamic evaluation platform for cockpit human machine interaction is carried out. Planning the cockpit human machine interactive dynamic evaluation platform by the visual simulation station, audio simulation, integrated control workstation, display control workstation, engineer development workstation, hardware interface system, real-time simulation workstation(including flight simulation, aircraft system function simulation, cockpit environment and equipment(maneuvering devices and control panels) simulation, human machine interface (HMI) simulation), cockpit control device, control panel, light guide plate, etc. Refer to Fig. 2 for the structural block diagram of cockpit human machine interactive dynamic evaluation platform.

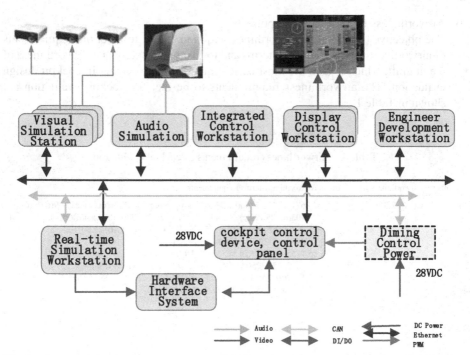

Fig. 2. The structural block diagram of the cockpit human machine interactive dynamic evaluation platform

During the evaluation, the evaluator controls the aircraft through cockpit maneuvering devices and control panels. The hardware interface system collects the operating inputs of the evaluator and sends them to a real-time simulator. In the real-time simulator, aircraft dynamics simulation model, aircraft system function model, environment simulation model, control interface logic model, display and alarm logic model and other simulation models are solved. The flight status data of the aircraft and the status data of the aircraft system are calculated and transmitted to the display control workstation and the visual simulation station to generate the instrument display screen and display it on the cockpit instrument panel.

The flight control system receives the flight status data and changes the status of the joystick, pedal and throttle according to the flight status data. The control board receives the status data of the aircraft system, and feeds back the status information of the aircraft system to the pilot through the character light display of the control board. The visual simulation station receives the current flight status data and generates the high-fidelity and aviation-perspective images of the scene outside the cockpit. The sound server receives flight status data and generates current aerodynamic noise, engine noise, airborne equipment alarm, etc. providing an intuitive, visual, fully immersive cockpit evaluation environment for evaluators.

a) Visual Simulation Station

Using high-performance graphics computer as the carrier, the visual simulation station is configured with multichannel graphics card, and the graphics computer application invokes software to generate the scene that needs to be displayed in real-time. It drives the graphics card to output three channels and displays the visual picture on three large-screen monitors, dynamically presenting the external scene and changes of the aircraft. The visual picture mainly includes aircraft attitude change, airport (including surrounding buildings, trees, mountains, water and other surrounding environment), runway, horizon and other scenes.

b) Audio Simulation

The audio simulation integrates the audio alarm logic into the executable file, integrates audio files with physical audio equipment in hardware, and realizes the voice alarm function by calling and executing audio files.

The audio simulation combines the environmental sound with the actual situation of the aircraft (e.g., the sound of engine starting when the engine starts), and emits the environmental sound in combination with the flight scenes, tasks and operations, so as to create a relatively realistic cockpit auditory environment. Environmental impacts mainly include but are not limited to:

1. Power unit acoustics: such as engine start, fan sound, exhaust sound, intake sound, rotor sound, etc.;
2. Aerodynamic acoustics: noise caused by airflow noise and buffeting of spoiler, landing gear and flap stall, etc.;
3. Landing gear acoustics: landing gear locking, landing ground sound, etc.;
4. Other sounds: such as flaps/flaps, sound of crashed aircraft, etc.

c) Integrated Control Workstation

As a platform for evaluating platform operation and monitoring, integrated control workstation can monitor and control the whole platform system effectively. The integrated console takes high-performance computer hardware as the carrier, combines with touch screen display and integrated control software, and carries out data interaction with display control workstation, visual workstation and simulation workstation through Ethernet, so as to realize the flexible setting of evaluation scenarios and tasks.

The integrated control workstation performs the following main tasks:

1) Initialization Settings: Initialize the simulation platform (display control workstation, visual simulation workstation, audio simulation and so on);
2) Setting functions

   i)   Aircraft state setting: aircraft mass, center of gravity, fuel loading and distribution, external power control, etc.;
   ii) Airport setting: airport selection, runway selection and light setting;
   iii) Setting of external environment, including setting of operating period (such as early morning, noon, dusk, night, etc.), setting of weather conditions (such as sunny day, cloudy, fog, rain, snow, lightning, etc.), setting of visibility, setting of temperature, setting of wind direction and speed, setting of sea pressure and field pressure;

3) Display of relevant parameters of each subsystem, including: aircraft flight speed, altitude, flight path, attitude display, etc.;
4) Fault setting: Provide fault setting, default fault, and support fault insertion and deletion;
5) Functions of freezing model, aircraft re-positioning and model balancing.

d) Display Control Workstation
The display control workstation is used to realize the graphic drive of cockpit display consistent with the aircraft, and drive the sound alarm according to the alarm information drive logic or fault equation calculation results. The visual simulation station takes high-performance graphics computer as the carrier to generate the scene that needs to be displayed in real-time and dynamically present the external scene and changes of the aircraft. The integrated control workstation is used to set aircraft status, external environment, system failure and reset.

e) Real-time Simulation Workstation
The real-time simulation workstation takes civil aircraft as the simulation object, and simulates aerodynamic characteristics, various aircraft systems function, cockpit environment and equipment (maneuvering devices and control panels), human machine interface and typical failure models of aircraft.
According to the captured dynamic evaluation requirements of cockpit human machine interaction, the dynamic evaluation platform of cockpit human machine interaction can simulate typical failure scenarios of civil aircraft and major failures of various systems (such as power supply and flight control system). Therefore, the aircraft system function model includes the fault simulation function of each system.

Taking the power supply system as an example, it can simulate the failure of main battery/standby battery, single or all generators, auxiliary power unit generators, ac transmission bus bars and standby bus bars, etc.

f) Engineers Development Workstation

Engineers development workstation is used for off-line desktop simulation, development, online debugging and downloading, such as flight simulation, aircraft system function simulation, aircraft system display control logic, etc.

g) Hardware Interface System

The hardware interface system is mainly used to collect the state of various cockpit switches, buttons, knobs, joysticks, steering discs and other control equipment, and convert it into the input quantity of control commands required by the aircraft system and avionics system. At the same time, the flight state output of the real-time flight simulation system is converted to drive the cockpit instruments and indicators. The hardware interface system includes signal conditioning box, signal testing box and wiring box. The signal conditioning cabinet is responsible for converting the output signals of the cockpit control devices and control panels into signals that can be collected by the interface board of the real-time simulation system, or converting the output signals of the interface board of the real-time simulation system into the driving signals of the cockpit control panel. The signal test box provides a signal separation surface between the cockpit control device and the control panel and the real-time simulation system for signal extraction and testing. The distribution box provides switching between cockpit controls and control panel signals and signal test boxes.

3.3 Requirements Verification

The dynamic evaluation platform for cockpit human machine interaction is a complex integrated system, and the requirement validation runs through the design and implementation process. Before the platform is implemented, the completeness and correctness of requirements capture are confirmed through changeability and engineering review. After the requirements are captured, the cockpit integration design requirements, aircraft system requirements and aircraft functional requirements are traced upward, and the correctness of requirements implementation is confirmed. Experts with rich experience in cockpit design, flight technology and aircraft systems are invited to form a review group to review the platform to ensure the completeness and correctness of requirements capture.

After the product is realized, requirements are confirmed again by means of test method and engineering review method. Professional technical personnel such as aircraft hydraulic and power systems are invited to confirm the requirements for the realization of the platform by comparing the design features of the cockpit human machine interaction and the evaluation of the cockpit tasks of each system. The pilot is invited to test and evaluate the platform based on a specific flight scenario.

3.4 Requirements Verification

The requirement verification of dynamic evaluation platform for cockpit human machine interaction is carried out by the experimental method. By carrying out cockpit subtask and full mission evaluation tests such as aircraft hydraulic and power systems, the human machine interaction logic of each system on the platform, normal, abnormal and emergency use scenarios of the aircraft were evaluated and requirements were verified. Invite the pilot to validate the implementation of the operating program on the platform.

The result of requirement verification shows that the dynamic evaluation platform of cockpit human machine interaction established by the quality improvement can undertake the requirement validation and evaluation of civil aircraft cockpit integration design.

4   Conclusion

The system engineering based dynamic evaluation of civil aircraft cockpit human machine interaction improves the quality, which solves the problem of lack of dynamic evaluation platform for cockpit integration design requirements validation and evaluation. Cockpit human machine interactive dynamic evaluation platform for the design and evaluation of the pilot in the cockpit work provides a work platform, support the cockpit rounds of iterative design and assessment of the integrated design, reduce the cost of the cockpit design change, significantly reduce the risk of a civil aircraft cockpit integration design and schedule risk. It is a successful application of system engineering theory in the field of civil aircraft cockpit design and assessment.

Is Usability Evaluation of DSL Still a Trending Topic?

Ildevana Poltronieri[1]([⊠])(iD), Allan Christopher Pedroso[2](iD),
Avelino Francisco Zorzo[1]([⊠])(iD), Maicon Bernardino[2](iD),
and Marcia de Borba Campos[3](iD)

[1] PUCRS - Pontifical Catholic University of Rio Grande do Sul, Porto Alegre, Brazil
ildevana.rodrigues@acad.pucrs.br, avelino.zorzo@pucrs.br
[2] UNIPAMPA - Federal University of Pampa, Alegrete, Brazil
bernardino@acm.org
[3] CESUCA, Cachoeirinha, Brazil
marciabcampos@hotmail.com

Abstract. In the past, several works have considered usability, user experience, and design principles when developing Domain-Specific Languages (DSL). To understand those principles, when developing and evaluating a DSL, is a challenge since not all design goals have the same relevance in different types of systems or DSL domains. Researchers from the Software Engineering and Human-Computer Interaction fields, for example, have mentioned in the recent past that usability or user experience evaluations usually do not use well-defined techniques to assess the quality of software products, or do not describe them accurately. Therefore, this paper will investigate whether the usability methods or techniques are still a trending topic to the DSL developers. To do that, we present an update to a Systematic Literature Review on usability evaluation that was performed in 2017. As a result, we identified that usability evaluation of DSLs is not only a trending topic but the discussions have increased in the past years. Furthermore, in this paper, we present an extension of a taxonomy on usability evaluation of DSLs.

Keywords: Evaluation methods and techniques · Human-computer interaction · Domain-specific languages · Systematic literature review · Usability evaluation

1 Introduction

A Domain-Specific Language (DSL) is a language with a high level of abstraction optimized for a specific class of problems. It is generally less complex than a General-Purpose Language (GPL) [23], *e.g.* Python or C#. Commonly, DSLs are developed in coordination with experts in the field for which the DSL is being designed for. In many cases, DSLs should be used not by software teams, but by non-programmers who are fluent in the domain of the DSL [9]. The implementation of DSLs can bring several benefits, such as efficiency, clearer thinking,

© Springer Nature Switzerland AG 2021
M. Kurosu (Ed.): HCII 2021, LNCS 12762, pp. 299–317, 2021.
https://doi.org/10.1007/978-3-030-78462-1_23

stakeholder integration, and quality [15]. Nonetheless, despite the increase in the number of DSLs, several of them are not successful since their usability is not properly evaluated.

Usability evaluation can improve DSLs since its main goal is to identify problems that might occur during DSLs use. Furthermore, usability solutions can address cognitive, perceptive, or motor capacity from users during system interaction. Nonetheless, usually, usability evaluation is dealt with in a generic process. However, some authors [3,21] have shown that usability should be related to the evaluated domain, varying the evaluation method, performance metrics, or even the order of efficiency, efficacy, and satisfaction metrics, for example, depending on the application area. We believe the same can be applied to DSLs evaluation since there is no ready solution once DSL varies according to its purpose [30]. Usability is an important requirement in DSL evaluation. Although several different authors consider that concern [3,5–7,30–32,34], we believe there are several trending topics on the usability evaluation of DSLs that should be investigated.

Previously, a Systematic Literature Review (SLR) carried out by Rodrigues *et al.* [32] identified that DSL designers consider aspects of usability in the creation of DSL. In that SLR twelve studies were selected for analysis, those studies were used to answer three research questions and understand how usability was dealt with in a DSL project. Furthermore, it also presented the techniques or approaches used to evaluate the usability of DSLs, as well as identified what kind of problems were found during the evaluation process.

The results helped to build a taxonomy that helped researchers to design new DSLs or mainly to evaluate the usability of DSLs. Besides, the results of that SLR relied on identifying problems and resources for the Usa-DSL Framework [30,31] to evaluate the usability of a DSL, in addition to assisting in the design of the Usa-DSL Process [29]. Although the SLR has shown that most researchers evaluate their DSL on an *ad hoc* basis, or do not describe the used methods, it was important to obtain the state of the art up to that moment.

Therefore, this paper presents an update on the study from Rodrigues *et at.* [32]. It improves on the previous study, updating the Usa-DSL Framework and also extending the usability evaluation taxonomy regarding usability heuristics and specific guidelines for DSLs evaluation.

For this study, the Systematic Literature Review (SLR) protocol [16] and Thoth[1] [20], a web-based tool to support systematic reviews, were used. The main digital libraries used were from ACM, IEEE, ScienceDirect, and Scopus. The SLR searched papers from June 2016 to September 2020. The study allowed us to identify primary studies in both Human-Computer Interaction (HCI) and Software Engineering (SE).

In order to understand how usability evaluation of DSLs has been investigated in the past few years, we set the following three research questions: i) Was the importance of usability considered during DSL development? ii) What were the

---

[1] Thoth: http://lesse.com.br/tools/thoth/.

evaluation techniques that were applied in the context of DSLs? iii) What were the problems or limitations identified during the DSL usage?

During the analysis of our SLR, we found several papers that consider DSL usability evaluation an important topic [3, 5–7, 25, 30, 31, 34]. Other papers, even though in a general way, present DSL usability evaluation and discuss the importance of preparation, data collection, analysis, and results' consolidation for the evaluation [13, 14, 27]. Some papers propose the use of a framework for DSL usability evaluation, *e.g.* USE-ME [5], whose main goal is to help DSL developers and it is used in the development life cycle that follows the Agile Manifesto; and, Usa-DSL [30, 31], whose main goal is to guide the DSL usability evaluation process, in a high-level abstraction regarding the metrics that will be used.

In this paper, we will also show that metrics regarding efficiency, efficacy, usage simplicity and easiness, usefulness, time spent to fulfill tasks are discussed in several papers [2, 18, 19, 28]. Those metrics are aligned to the metrics used in the Usa-DSL framework, *i.e.*, easy to learn, remember, effort/time, perceived complexity, satisfaction, conclusion rate, task error rate, efficiency, or effectiveness. Furthermore, some papers use questionnaires [26, 33, 35], some are based on cognitive dimensions [7, 14], and others propose manual evaluation techniques [3].

Few works discuss limitations and usability problems in the analyzed DSLs [2, 13, 17, 26]. They usually discuss problems related to lack of expressiveness, either from their grammar or the domain they intend to represent. Another problem that we could identify is related to the subjects that participate in the evaluation. Usually, researchers invite DSL developers and not specialists in the DSL domain or even DSL final users.

Finally, we will present the SLR protocol and discuss the results of the SLR, which point out that usability evaluation of DSLs is still a trending topic and further research is needed. We will also present an extended taxonomy used in the Usa-DSL framework and in the Usa-DSL process to guide the development of DSL usability evaluation artifacts.

This paper is organized as follows. Section 2 presents the SLR protocol and discusses the main findings of this work as well as discussions on the usability evaluation of DSL trending topics. Section 5 presents a Taxonomy for DSL Evaluation. Section 6 presents the final remarks of this work.

2   Systematic Literature Review

This section presents a Systematic Literature Review (SLR) protocol, in which the main focus was to identify and analyze the trending topics of the evaluation process of DSLs. To assist the SLR protocol we use the Thoth tool. The period in which the SLR was executed was from June 2016 to September 2020. This study allowed us to identify primary studies in both Human-Computer Interaction (HCI) and Software Engineering (SE) fields.

2.1 SLR Planning

In the planning stage, we performed the following activities in order to establish an SLR protocol: the establishment of the research goals and research question, definition of the search strategy, selection of primary studies, quality assessment, definition of the data extraction strategy, and selection of synthesis methods.

The goals of the study were to examine whether HCI aspects were considered or not during the development of a DSL, to know the techniques and approaches used to evaluate DSLs, and whether there were problems and limitations regarding DSL evaluation when HCI techniques were used. To do achieve those goals we set the following three research questions:

– *RQ1.* Was the importance of usability considered during DSL development?
– *RQ2.* What were the evaluation techniques that were applied in the context of DSLs?
– *RQ3.* What were the problems or limitations identified during the DSL usage?

Search Strategy: the following digital libraries were used: ACM[2]; IEEE[3]; ScienceDirect[4]; and Scopus[5].

Selection Criteria: the following inclusion (IC) and exclusion (EC) criteria were used:

– *IC1*: The study must contain at least one of the terms related to HCI evaluation in DSLs in the title or abstract;
– *IC2*: The study must present some type of DSL evaluation;
– *EC1*: The study is about evaluation but not DSLs;
– *EC2*: The study is not written in English;
– *EC3*: The study is about DSL but does not present an evaluation;
– *EC4*: The study is about HCI but not DSL evaluation.

2.2 SLR Execution

During this phase, the search string construction, studies selection, quality assessment, data extraction and synthesis were performed. The information produced during the execution of the RSL can be accessed at Zenodo[6].

Search String Construction: The search string was built based on terms from DSL and HCI, from usage evaluation and usability, and their synonyms. Figure 1 shows the generic string used in the digital libraries.

Quality Assessment: This step was performed by two evaluators who analyzed each one of the studies and answered the quality assessment questions as follows:

---

[2] ACM: http://portal.acm.org/.
[3] IEEE: http://ieeexplore.ieee.org/.
[4] ScienceDirect: http://www.sciencedirect.com/.
[5] Scopus: https://www.scopus.com/.
[6] DOI 10.5281/zenodo.4563198.

> ((''domain specific language'' OR dsl OR dsm OR ''domain
> specific modeling'' OR, ''domain specific modeling language''
> OR dsml) AND (evaluation OR evaluating OR experiment) AND
> (usability OR ''user centered design'' OR ''user experience'' OR
> hci OR ''human computer interaction''))

Fig. 1. Search string

yes, partially, and no. Each answer was graded as: 1 for yes, 0.5 for partially, and 0 for no. After answering the 5 quality assessment questions, only studies that were scored 2.5 to 5 were considered for further analysis. Table 1 shows only the articles that were considered to be read. The final quality score is the average from the assessment of the two evaluator. The quality assessment questions were:

- *QA1.* Did the article make any contribution to HCI?
- *QA2.* Did the article present any usability evaluation technique?
- *QA3.* Did the article present the analysis of the results?
- *QA4.* Did the article describe the evaluated DSL?
- *QA5.* Did the article describe the encountered usability problems?

Table 1. Quality assessment

Studies reference	Evaluator 1						Evaluator 2					Quality score
	Year	QA1	QA2	QA3	QA4	QA5	QA1	QA2	QA3	QA4	QA5	
[2]	2018	Y	Y	Y	Y	Y	N	P	Y	N	P	3.5
[3]	2017	P	N	Y	Y	N	N	Y	Y	N	Y	2.8
[5]	2018	Y	Y	Y	Y	P	P	Y	Y	Y	Y	4.5
[6]	2018	P	N	Y	Y	P	N	Y	Y	Y	Y	3.5
[7]	2019	P	N	Y	Y	P	N	N	Y	Y	N	2.5
[11]	2018	P	N	Y	Y	N	N	P	Y	P	P	2.5
[12]	2018	Y	Y	Y	Y	Y	Y	Y	Y	Y	Y	5.0
[13]	2019	Y	Y	Y	Y	Y	Y	P	Y	Y	P	4.5
[14]	2019	Y	Y	Y	P	P	P	P	N	Y	N	2.8
[17]	2018	N	Y	Y	Y	P	N	Y	Y	P	Y	3.5
[18]	2019	N	N	Y	Y	N	N	Y	Y	Y	Y	3.0
[19]	2018	P	N	Y	P	Y	P	N	Y	P	Y	3.0
[25]	2020	Y	Y	P	P	Y	Y	Y	Y	Y	Y	4.5
[26]	2019	P	N	Y	Y	N	N	P	Y	Y	P	2.8
[27]	2019	N	N	Y	Y	Y	P	Y	Y	Y	Y	3.8
[28]	2017	P	N	Y	Y	P	P	N	Y	Y	P	3.0
[31]	2018	Y	Y	Y	N	Y	Y	Y	N	N	N	3.0
[30]	2018	Y	Y	Y	N	N	Y	Y	Y	N	Y	3.5
[33]	2019	Y	Y	Y	Y	Y	N	Y	Y	Y	N	4.0
[34]	2019	Y	N	Y	Y	Y	N	N	Y	N	Y	3.0
[35]	2018	P	N	Y	Y	P	N	Y	N	Y	P	2.5

Score: (P) Partially = 0.5, (Y) Yes = 1; (N) No = 0

Primary Studies Selection: The performed search, based on the search string for each database, returned the number of studies presented in Fig. 2.

Fig. 2. Studies selection process

In the first phase of the SLR, 44 papers returned from ACM, 39 from IEEE, 146 from Scopus, and 14 from ScienceDirect, resulting in 243 papers. When eliminating duplicate papers and applying the inclusion, exclusion, and quality criteria, 21 papers remained, which were thoroughly read. Figure 2 shows the number of papers that were selected after each phase.

3   SLR Analysis and Answers to Research Questions

This section presents the answers to the research questions from Sect. 1. The answers are based on the 21 studies selected in Sect. 2.2.

RQ1. Was the importance of usability considered during DSL development?

The importance of usability in the development or evaluation of DSL was discussed in most of the selected studies. However, some studies quote usability evaluation instruments but do not describe the process itself. In a nutshell: i) some of these studies evaluate the environment in which the DSL is developed, without evaluating the language itself; ii) some define usability criteria to evaluate the language, but without relating them to the quality of use criterion; iii) some studies compared GPL with the DSL also without discussing the usability process, which could be involved in the development and evaluation of these languages. In the next paragraphs we summarize each of the studies analyzed in this paper.

First we mention papers that are related to usability of DSL somehow, but do not consider usability during the DSL development [2,12,13,18,19,27,28,33].

Alhaag *et al.* [2] presented a user evaluation to identify language usefulness. The effectiveness and efficiency characteristics were measured based on the results of a task given to the participants and the time spent to complete the task. Furthermore, five other characteristics were evaluated: satisfaction, usefulness, ease of use, clarity, and attractiveness, through a subjective questionnaire created in accordance with the Common Industry Format (CIF) for usability test reports.

Nandra and Gorgan [27] adopted an evaluation processes to compare the use of GPL to a DSL, but there was no discussion on usability criteria. They made a comparison between Python and the WorDel DSL, using as criteria the average time in which the participants perform a certain task, code correctness, syntax errors, number of interactions in the editing area code (such as mouse clicks and key presses), and task execution precision.

Nosál et al. [28] addressed the user experience, without relating that to the usability criteria. This study presented an experiment with participants who had no programming knowledge, which they were organized into two groups to verify whether a customized IDE would facilitate the syntax comprehension of a programming language when compared to a standard IDE.

Finally, Henriques et al. [12] presented a DSL usability evaluation through SUS (System Usability Scale), which is a numerical usability evaluation scale with a focus on effectiveness, efficiency, and user satisfaction; Liu et al. [18] evaluated the web platform that runs a DSL, but not the language itself; and, Rodriguez-Gil [33] used an adaptation of UMUX (Usability Metric for User Experience), which is an adaptation of SUS.

Regarding usability analysis during the DSL development process, the following studies considered that in their research [3, 5–7, 11, 14, 17, 25, 26, 30, 31, 34, 35].

Shin-Shing [34] indicated that more studies evaluate usability in terms of effectiveness and efficiency than about other usability criteria. In that study, a measure of the feasibility of Model Driven Architecture (MDA) techniques was also made in terms of effectiveness and efficiency. However, there was no description of the process for usability evaluation.

Cachero et al. [7] presented a performance evaluation between two DSL notations, one textual and one graphical. For their evaluation, a Cognitive Dimensions Framework (CDF) was used. This framework defines a set of constructions to extract values for different notations, so that at least, partially, the differences in language usability are observed. For example, the extent to which a product can be used by participants to achieve particular goals such as effectiveness, efficiency and satisfaction in a specific use context.

Hoffmann et al. [14] stated that, despite being a very important task, usability evaluation is often overlooked in the development of DSLs. For DSLs that are translated into other languages, a first impression of the efficiency of a DSL can be obtained by comparing the number of lines of code (LoC) to the generated output. In their paper, they presented a heuristic evaluation in which some cognitive dimensions of the CDF are observed. However, an evaluation is not performed.

Msosa [26] observed through a survey of studies that the Computer-Interpretable Guideline (CIG) has no emphasis on the usability of the modeling language, since aspects of usability or human factors are rarely evaluated. This can result in the implementation of inappropriate languages. Furthermore, incompatible domain abstractions between language users and language engineers remain a recurring problem with regard to language usability. To evaluate the presented language, a survey was conducted, using the System Usability Scale (SUS) questionnaire, in order to obtain the participants' perception of the DSL.

Le Moulec *et al.* [17] focused on the importance of DSL documentation, which, they claimed, imply in a better understanding of the language. In their study, a tool was proposed to automate the production of documentation based on artifacts generated during the DSL implementation phase, and an experiment was carried out using the tool in two DSLs. Furthermore, they observed the efficiency in automating language documentation and, consequently, improving usability.

Barisic *et al.* [6] defined DSL usability as the degree to which a language can be used by specific users, to meet the needs of reaching specific goals with effectiveness, efficiency and satisfaction, within a specific context of use. The authors also mentioned that, although there is a lack of general guidelines and a properly defined process for conducting language usability evaluation, they are slowly being recognized as an important step. In another study, Barisic *et al.* [5] argued that there is still little consideration to user needs when developing a DSL. They also mentioned that, even though, the creation of DSLs may seem intuitive, it is necessary to have means to evaluate its impact. This can be performed using a real context of use, with users from the target domain.

Bacíková *et al.* [3] indicated that DSLs are directly related to the usability of the their domain. They also argued that it is important to consider domain-specific concepts, properties and relationships, especially when designing a DSL. The study also considered discussions related to the User Interface.

Poltronieri *et al.* [31] mentioned that domain engineers aim, through different languages, to mitigate difficulties encountered in the development of applications using traditional GPLs. One way to mitigate these difficulties would be through DSLs. Therefore, DSLs should have their usability adequately evaluated, in order to extract their full potential. In their study, a framework for evaluating the usability of DSLs was proposed.

Mosqueira-Rey and Alonso-Ríos [25] also indicated an increase in research related to the evaluation of usability of DSLs through subjective and empirical methods. Although there are studies based on heuristics for interface evaluation, there is a shortage with regard to heuristic methods.

In order to reflect the user needs, Gilson [11] found that usability related to Software Language Engineering (SLE) has been poorly addressed, despite DSLs directly involving end users. For the author, evaluating the theoretical and technical strength of a DSL structure is very common. Nonetheless, usability issues are often overlooked in these evaluations.

Table 2 presents a summary of the topics that were discussed in each analyzed paper regarding the importance of usability considered during the DSL development.

Table 2. Importance of usability

Paper	RQ1	Main topic regarding DSL usability analysis
Alhaag et al. [2]		Observes metrics of effectiveness and efficiency
Bací-ková et al. [3]	✓	Presents a survey in which the authors claim that DSLs are directly related to domain usability
Barisic et al. [5]	✓	Authors argue that it is necessary to have means to evaluate the impact of usability on DSL
Barisic et al. [6]	✓	Usability is the degree to which a language can be used by specific users, to meet the needs of reaching specific goals with effectiveness, efficiency and satisfaction, within a context of specific use
Cachero et al. [7]	✓	The authors apply the Cognitive Dimensions Framework(CDF) in their evaluation
Gilson [11]	✓	The author mentions that evaluation of the theoretical and technical strength of the structure of a DSL is very common, however usability issues are often neglected in those evaluations
Henriques et al. [12]		Does not consider or mention usability in the development of DSL
Hesenius and Gruhn [13]		Does not consider or mention usability in the development of DSL
Hoffmann et al. [14]	✓	Cite other studies that argue that the evaluation of usability is a very important task but often neglected in the development of DSL
Le Moulec et al. [17]	✓	They emphasize the documentation of DSL, a factor that is considered essential in the understanding and use of languages, directly implying their usability
Liu et al. [18]		Presents a usability evaluation of the web platform that runs a DSL
Logre and Déry Pinna [19]		Does not consider or mention usability in the development of DSL
Mosqueira-Rey [25]	✓	Authors present a set of heuristics to evaluate usability of DSLs
Msosa [26]	✓	The authors used the System Usability Scale (SUS) Questionnaire in their study to evaluate their DSL
Nandra and Gorgan [27]		Does not consider or mention usability in the development of DSL
Nosál et al. [28]		Analyzes the user experience when using a DSL
Poltronieri et al. [31]	✓	Presents a framework to evaluate usability of DSLs
Poltronieri et al. [30]	✓	Presents a framework to evaluate usability of DSLs
Rodriguez-Gil [33]		They mention the concern to develop their DSL as close as possible to the domain user reality
Shin-Shing [34]	✓	Presents a survey that somewhat evaluates this aspect
Silva et al. [35]	✓	Presents a comparative evaluation between two languages in order to evaluate the usability of their DSL

Legend: **RQ1** Was the importance of usability considered during the DSL development?

RQ2. What were the evaluation techniques that were applied in the context of DSLs?

Researchers use quantitative (14/21) or qualitative (13/21) data to analyze the DSL usability. Several use both (8/21) and only in two situations we could not identify the data type that was used by the researchers.

Regarding technique, Usability Evaluation (8/21) was the most used one. Other techniques were also used, *i.e.*, Usability Testing and Heuristic Evaluation. Several papers (8/21) did not describe which technique was used.

Different instruments were applied in the usability evaluation. Questionnaire was the most used instrument (13/21), but other instruments to support data gathering, such as logs, scripts, interviews, audio and video recordings and other tools that observe the tasks performed by the users during the evaluation were also used. Only two papers did not describe the instruments that were used in the usability evaluation.

Table 3 shows a summary of the evaluation techniques, instruments and data types that each study uses.

RQ3. What were the problems or limitations identified during the DSL usage?

The analyzed papers present some limitations or problems regarding, either the evaluated DSL or the evaluation process that they performed. From the 21 selected articles, not all of they present the problems found in their DSL (see Table 4). Only Hesenius and Gruhn [13], Henriques *et al.* [12], Liu *et al.* [18] and Nosal *et al.* [28] somehow present the encountered problems. The other articles have limitations found in general, that is, in the designed DSL or in the evaluations. Bacíková *et al.* [3], Rodriguez *et al.* [33] and Silva *et al.* [35] did not present any problem or limitation in their studies.

Regarding the study by Hesenius and Gruhn [13], the GestureCards notation has some limitations in special circumstances, and two potential problems were described: being voluminous and in the description of spatial gestures. These problems occur because GestureCards uses spatial positioning to denote temporal relations of partial gestures. Thus, the volume problem occurs when the gestures are composed of multiple partial gestures that are defined separately. It was suggested that to avoid those problems, the parallel gestures can be combined in a graphic representation when shared with the other features. The authors argue that this will be sufficient for most of the use cases.

Liu *et al.* [18] discussed the organizational problems for business people, as employees use their own mobile devices to process workflow tasks. Due to that, a middleware-based approach, called MUIT (Mobility, User Interactions and Tasks), was introduced to develop and deploy mobility, user interactions and tasks in Web Services Business Process Execution Language (WS-BPEL) mechanisms. This DSL allows to significantly reduce the manual efforts for developers with regard to user interactions, avoiding to use more than one type of code and thus offering satisfactory support for user experiences. On the one hand, the

Table 3. Evaluation data

Paper	Data type		Evaluation techniques	Instruments
	Quantitative	Qualitative		
Alhaag *et al.* [2]	✓		Not described	Questionnaire
Bacikova *et al.* [3]		✓	Usability Evaluation	Task Recording
Barisic *et al.* [5]	✓	✓	Usability Evaluation	Questionnaire
Barisic *et al.* [6]	✓	✓	Usability Evaluation	Questionnaire; Video recordings
Cachero *et al.* [7]	✓		Not described	Manual Evaluation of Tasks
Gilson [11]	✓		Not described	Questionnaire
Henriques *et al.* [12]	✓		Usability Evaluation	Questionnaire
Hesenius and Gruhn [13]	✓	✓	Evaluates some HCI metrics (*e.g.* efficiency and effectiveness)	Recording of Sessions
Hoffman *et al.* [14]	Undefined	Undefined	Heuristic Evaluation	Undefined
Moulec *et al.* [17]	✓	✓	Not described	Questionnaire
Liu *et al.* [18]		✓	Usability Evaluation	Data Logs; Interviews
Logre and Déry Pinna [19]	✓	✓	Not described	Manual Method
Mosqueira-Rey and Alonso-Ríos [25]	Undefined	Undefined	Heuristic evaluation	Undefined
Msosa [26]	✓	✓	Usability Evaluation	Questionnaire
Nandra and Gorgan [27]	✓		Not described	Questionnaire; Recorded Actions
Nosal *et al.* [28]		✓	Not described	Task Recording
Poltronieri *et al.* [31]		✓	Usability Evaluation	Questionnaire
Poltronieri *et al.* [30]		✓	Usability Testing and Heuristic Evaluation	Questionnaire
Rodríguez-Gil *et al.* [33]	✓		Not well defined, observes efficiency and effectiveness metrics	Questionnaire (UMUX)
Shin [34]	✓	✓	Not described	Questionnaire
Silva *et al.* [35]	✓	✓	Usability Evaluation	Questionnaire (SUS)

authors pointed out that some users from the healthcare area still complain that MUIT touch controls are not good when they process electronic patient records. On the other hand, no limitations were pointed out.

Henriques *et al.* [12] presented the OutSystems platform, a development environment composed of several DSLs, used to specify, build and validate data from Web applications on mobile devices. The DSL for Business Process Technology

Table 4. DSL constraints and evaluation constraints

Reference	Description
DSL Constraints	
Henriques *et al.* [12]	Not all stakeholders participate in the evaluation
Hesenius and Gruhn [13]	Notation introduced in this paper present problems in description of space gestures and bulky gestures
Moulec *et al.* [17]	The use learning curve of the DSL is a challenge to participants
Nosál *et al.* [28]	The syntactic noise still remains the main problem of pure EDSL when used by non-programmers
Evaluation Constraints	
Alhaag *et al.* [2]	The evaluation was made by expert users and do not show the full potential of solution
Barisic *et al.* [5]	The reliability of participants answers in the questionnaires, since they were young
Cachero *et al.* [7]	According to the values observed in the cognitive dimensions (CDF), it can be inferred that these dimensions do not affect the same way that the maintenance of the domain model and the tasks of creating the domain model
Mosqueira-Rey and Alonso-Ríos [25]	Some identifiers are not so clear and not so easy to remember
Nandra and Gorgan [27]	GPL demonstrates better performance than DSL in syntax and time required for task description
Poltronieri *et al.* [31]	Provide a Usability Framework. Does not provide a process that guides the user in decision-make
Poltronieri *et al.* [30]	Does not provide a process that guides the user in decision-make
Shin *et al.* [34]	Use of participants without professional experience in the sampling of the experiment

(BPT) process modeling, had a low adoption rate due to usability problems, increasing maintenance costs. Furthermore, they found a limitation related to population selection, because, due to resource limitations, all participants in the usability experiments were members of OutSystems. The authors believe that business managers should also be invited and that more experiments should therefore be conducted with interested parties.

Mosqueira-Rey and Alonso-Ríos [25] also identified usability problems in their case study, which uses heuristics that help to identify real usability problems. As problems they pointed out that DSL identifiers do not have a clear meaning, some acronyms have no obvious meaning and certain identifiers are difficult to remember.

Nosal *et al.* [28] results indicate that even IDE customizations can significantly alleviate the problems caused by syntactic problems in the language. As limitations, the authors mentioned the low representativeness of Embedded DSLs (EDSL) when compared to real-world DSLs. An EDSL can be much more complex from a syntactic point of view, as it can include variables, functions, structures, etc. The benefits of the proposed technique (for example, file templates) may become insignificant due to the complexity of the language syntax. Therefore, generalization of the results for all EDSLs is not possible and a replication of the experiment with a more complex EDSL is necessary. In terms of domain abstractions, the study by Msosa [26] mentioned that the incompatibility of some domain abstractions is a limitation that can present some barriers and negatively impact the usability of a DSL.

Shin-Shing [34] analyzed techniques for reverse engineering and model transformations in Model Driven Architecture (MDA). Their evaluation was performed using usability metrics, *i.e.* productivity and efficiency. In their paper, they concluded that such techniques are still immature and superficial, requiring further studies in order to improve them. They emphasized that, before performing further usability evaluations, they first needed to pay more attention to the techniques and methods used during the MDA development phases.

Nandra and Gorgan [27] presented and evaluated the DSL WorDeL interface, which was designed to facilitate the connection of existing processing operations in high level algorithms. The authors compared the WordeL DSL with the Python language. In their comparison, Python showed better results in terms of time to describe each task. Besides, the WorDeL DSL produces better results in terms of accuracy, with higher percentages of tasks completed correctly. WorDeL was also better in terms of accuracy when evaluated for its expressiveness.

Hoffmann *et al.* [14] did not present limitations on the evaluation, but mentioned that the number of lines of code can be considered a problem with regard to DSL usability. The authors mentioned that "For DSLs that are translated into other languages, the efficiency of a DSL can be obtained by comparing the number of lines of code between the source program and the generated output". They also used the McCabe's cyclomatic complexity [22] to analyze the language. Both lines of code and cyclomatic complexity are quantitative measures that can be applied to roughly estimate the effort to understand, to test and to maintain a program. Furthermore, the DSL was not used by end users.

Le Moulec *et al.* [17] found limitations regarding the contextualization of the documentation. Specifically, the model is customized to correspond to the

DSL documentation concept. However, the provided examples had no context that were easily related to the original model. Another limitation was related to code compliance, the generated documentation did not help new users to make the models faster. Furthermore, some participants read all the available documentation before starting the exercises, while others did that when they started to use the editor. Therefore, the subjects spent around 30 min to perform the basic exercise, showing that the initial learning curve is a challenge to be faced in future works. Similarly, Le Moulec et al., and Logre and Déry-Pinna [19], mentioned that the relevance of the participants' choice was not analyzed, making this a limitation.

Barisicic et al. [6] mentioned that the selection of participants might be a limitation in their study. They tried to mitigate the problem through tutors that would help the participants when they needed to answer the questions. This helped to guarantee the validity and integrity of the results. Likewise, the study by Alhaag et al. [2] also presented the background of the participants as a limitation for their study. As a solution to mitigate this threat, Alhaag et al. indicated that the platform should be evaluated by domain experts with little technical knowledge in order to better explore new metadata in their domain. Like the previous two studies, Gilson et al. [11] also described the lack of evaluation with end users as a limitation for their study.

Poltronieri et al. [30,31] presented a framework focused on evaluating the usability of DSLs, called Usa-DSL framework. The authors pointed out the lack of a flow or process that would help the participants in the creation of the evaluation, guiding their steps, what should be done and at what time to perform a certain activity. Unlike the framework of Poltronieri et al., Barisic et al. [5] focused only on evaluating usability with end users and through experimental studies.

4   Evolution of Usability Evaluation for DSL

This section summarizes the evolution on research of usability evaluation of DSL from Rodrigues et al. [32]. In the past 5 years there was a significant increase in published studies on usability evaluation of DSL. The previous Systematic Literature Review (SLR) was performed without limiting the initial year and looked for papers that were published until 2016. In that SLR, 12 papers were selected. The current SLR selected 21 papers that were published from 2016 to 2020. This showed an increase of 75% in the number of selected papers that somehow are related to usability evaluation of DSLs. Hence, **usability evaluation of DSL is still a trending topic**. Actually, it seems that **there is an increase on the research in this area**. Some of the analyzed papers are more straightforward to mention that [1,5,12,14,18,31,36] than others.

One interesting point from the previous SLR to this one, is that, in the previous SLR authors seemed to be interested to evaluate their DSL, without any concern on the protocol, technique and instruments that were used [1,8, 10]. In the current SLR it was clear the increased concern on the development or organization of the techniques and instruments that are used to evaluate the DSL usability [4,12,13,35]. Furthermore, new protocols, frameworks and even processes to evaluate the DSL usability have been proposed. For example, Barisic *et al.* [5] and Poltronieri *et al.* [31] developed frameworks to evaluate DSL usability focusing on the ease of use. On the one hand, Bacikova *et al.* [3] presented ways to automatize the evaluation, while Mosqueira-Rey *et al.* [24] have created some heuristics to evaluate DSL usability.

Although authors have increased their preoccupation to use well-defined techniques, instruments and processes to evaluate usability of DSLs, they are still neglecting to better describe the problems or limitations that they find when evaluating DSL usability. Usually, authors describe problems or limitations when the DSL is used, but neglect to describe the DSL usability problems. It seems that the focus has been on whether users can use the language rather than to identify usability problems that the language contains. For example, few studies present user perception, use satisfaction, system intuitiveness, real-world representation, among others. Some authors [13,14] even use some terms (*i.e.* number of lines of code, usage time, efficiency and efficacy) that are not directly related to usability. This might be one of the reasons that several DSLs are not successful.

5   Evolution taxonomy for DSL evaluation

Based on the selected studies and the research questions, this section presents a taxonomy extension of terms used during the evaluation of DSLs. This taxonomy was structured as a conceptual mapping (see Fig. 3). This taxonomy was based on the terms that were mentioned in the studies selected in our previous SLR [32] and in the SLR presented in this paper.

Figure 3 shows the main groups of categories represented as the external rectangles: framework/approaches, data type, usability evaluation methods, instruments, profile user, software engineering evaluation method and evaluation metrics. In each of these groups, there is a set of categories, for example, a user profile can have the following categories: HCI expert, DSL expert, potential user, final user. This figure also presents new categories and one new group (*i.e.* process) that were not present in the previous taxonomy. These new categories are represented by gray rectangles in the figure. Basically the new categories are: i) frameworks: Usa-DSL framework and USE-ME; ii) process: Usa-DSL process; iii) instruments: data log, challenge solution, video recording, task recording; iv) Software Engineering Evaluation Method: *quasi*-experiment; and, v) metrics: conciseness, readability and comprehensibility. Furthermore, the figure also shows some categories represented by dashed round rectangles. These categories are not directly mentioned in the studies presented neither in the previous or in this SLR, but are important in the development of a framework and process to evaluate DSLs.

Similarly from what we found when answering the research questions presented in this paper, this taxonomy reflects the lack of standards when planning and applying DSL usability evaluation. We can highlight that many of the

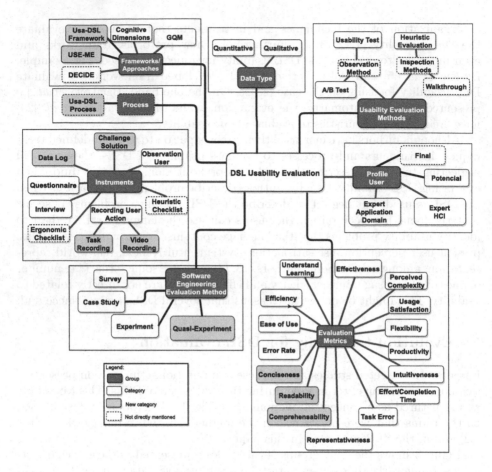

Fig. 3. DSL usability evaluation taxonomy

authors mention that they do not use standard techniques, methods or instruments when they evaluate their DSL. However, some authors have been developing new frameworks and processes to systematize and help language engineers to use standard methods, instruments and metrics for usability evaluation of DSLs.

6 Final Remarks

The literature has shown that issues related to usability, user experience and design principles have been increasingly considered in the DSL project. Recognizing and understanding the relationship among these principles in the development and evaluation of DSL has been a challenge, as not all interaction design goals have the same relevance in all types of systems and, in the case of DSL, in the DSL domain.

Therefore, DSL usability evaluation still remains an important research topic [3, 5, 6, 25, 30, 31], since there are still several issues that need to be improved. For example, several authors that evaluate DSL usability do not use HCI methods and in several papers they do not describe the evaluation execution in a proper way [2,7,11,17,19,27,28,34]. Some of the authors evaluate the usability using well-defined instruments, but do not use specific methods, while others use *ad-hoc* methods to do that [13,33]. Sometimes this lack of proper evaluation leads to the DSL being unsuccessful, because when the users are unable to use the language in its full, or need to follow many steps and remember different paths, they end up giving up.

Another relevant point is that language developers still do not use available usability frameworks or processes. Nonetheless, some researchers have proposed new ways to evaluate DSL usability. In this paper we presented an extension to the previous published taxonomy for usability evaluation of DSLs. It interesting to notice that after five years of the first published taxonomy, new categories were used by the researchers when evaluating their DSL.

Although the focus of this SLR was not to analyze tools to support the usability evaluation of DSLs, this is a subject that should be better investigated. This would allow researchers to understand how usability evaluation of DSLs is planned, executed, analyzed and reported by those tools.

Acknowledgements. This study was financed in part by the Coordenação de Aperfeiçoamento de Pessoal de Nível Superior - Brasil (CAPES) - Finance Code 001. Avelino F. Zorzo is supported by CNPq (315192/2018-6).

References

1. Albuquerque, D., Cafeo, B., Garcia, A., Barbosa, S., Abrahão, S., Ribeiro, A.: Quantifying usability of domain-specific languages: an empirical study on software maintenance. J. Syst. Softw. **101**, 245–259 (2015)
2. Alhaag, A.A., Savic, G., Milosavljevic, G., Segedinac, M.T., Filipovic, M.: Executable platform for managing customizable metadata of educational resources. Electron. Libr. **36**(6), 962–978 (2018)
3. Bacikova, M., Galko, L., Hvizdova, E.: Manual techniques for evaluating domain usability. In: 14th International Scientific Conference on Informatics, pp. 24–30 (2017)
4. Bacikova, M., Maricak, M., Vancik, M.: Usability of a domain-specific language for a gesture-driven IDE. In: Federated Conference on Computer Science and Information Systems (FedCSIS), pp. 909–914, September 2015
5. Barisic, A., Amaral, V., Goulão, M.: Usability driven DSL development with USE-ME. Comput. Lang. Syst. Struct. **51**, 118–157 (2018)
6. Barisic, A., Cambeiro, J., Amaral, V., Goulão, M., Mota, T.: Leveraging teenagers feedback in the development of a domain-specific language: the case of programming low-cost robots. In: 33rd Symposium on Applied Computing (SAC), pp. 1221–1229. SAC, ACM (2018)
7. Cachero, C., Melia, S., Hermida, J.M.: Impact of model notations on the productivity of domain modelling: an empirical study. Inf. Softw. Technol. **108**, 78–87 (2019)

8. Cuenca, F., Bergh, J., Luyten, K., Coninx, K.: A user study for comparing the programming efficiency of modifying executable multimodal interaction descriptions: a domain-specific language versus equivalent event-callback code. In: 6th Workshop on Evaluation and Usability of Programming Languages and Tools, pp. 31–38. ACM, New York (2015)
9. Fowler, M.: Domain Specific Languages. 1 edn. Addison-Wesley (2010)
10. Gibbs, I., Dascalu, S., Harris, F.C., Jr.: A separation-based UI architecture with a DSL for role specialization. J. Syst. Softw. **101**, 69–85 (2015)
11. Gilson, F.: Teaching software language engineering and usability through students peer reviews. In: 21st International Conference on Model Driven Engineering Languages and Systems: Companion Proceedings, pp. 98–105 (2018)
12. Henriques, H., Lourenço, H., Amaral, V., Goulão, M.: Improving the developer experience with a low-code process modelling language. In: 21th International Conference on Model Driven Engineering Languages and Systems, pp. 200–210 (2018)
13. Hesenius, M., Gruhn, V.: GestureCards-a hybrid gesture notation. Human-Computer Interaction **3**(EICS), 1–35 (2019)
14. Hoffmann, B., Chalmers, K., Urquhart, N., Guckert, M.: Athos - a model driven approach to describe and solve optimisation problems: an application to the vehicle routing problem with time windows. In: 4th International Workshop on Real World Domain Specific Languages (RWDS). ACM (2019)
15. Kelly, S., Tolvanen, J.: Domain-Specific Modeling: Enabling Full Code Generation. IEEE Computer Society, Wiley-Interscience, Hoboken (2008)
16. Kitchenham, B.: Guidelines for performing systematic literature reviews in software engineering. Technical report, Keele University, Durham, UK (2007)
17. Le Moulec, G., Blouin, A., Gouranton, V., Arnaldi, B.: Automatic production of end user documentation for DSLs. Comput. Lang. Syst. Struct. **54**, 337–357 (2018)
18. Liu, X., Xu, M., Teng, T., Huang, G., Mei, H.: MUIT: a domain-specific language and its middleware for adaptive mobile web-based user interfaces in WS-BPEL. IEEE Trans. Serv. Comput. **12**(6), 955–969 (2019)
19. Logre, I., Déry-Pinna, A.M.: MDE in support of visualization systems design: a multi-staged approach tailored for multiple roles. Hum.-Comput. Interact. **2**, 1–17 (2018)
20. Marchezan, L., Bolfe, G., Rodrigues, E., Bernardino, M., Basso, F.P.: Thoth: a web-based tool to support systematic reviews. In: 2019 International Symposium on Empirical Software Engineering and Measurement, pp. 1–6 (2019)
21. Mator, J., Lehman, W., Mcmanus, W., Powers, S., Tiller, L., Unverricht, J., Still, J.: Usability: adoption, measurement, value. Hum. Factors J. Hum. Factors Ergon. Soc. (2020)
22. McCabe, T.J.: A complexity measure. IEEE Trans. Softw. Eng. **SE–2**(4), 308–320 (1976)
23. Mernik, M., Heering, J., Sloane, A.: When and how to develop domain-specific languages. ACM Comput. Surv. **37**, 316–344 (2005)
24. Mosqueira-Rey, E., Alonso-Ríos, D.: Usability heuristics for domain-specific languages (DSLs). In: 35th Symposium on Applied Computing, pp. 1340–1343. ACM (2020)
25. Mosqueira-Rey, E., Alonso-Ríos, D.: Usability heuristics for domain-specific languages. In: 35th Symposium on Applied Computing (SAC), pp. 1340–1343 (2020)
26. Msosa, Y.J.: FCIG grammar evaluation: a usability assessment of clinical guideline modelling constructs. In: Symposium on Computers and Communications, pp. 1141–1146 (2019)

27. Nandra, C., Gorgan, D.: Usability evaluation of a domain specific language for defining aggregated processing tasks. In: 15th International Conference on Intelligent Computer Communication and Processing, pp. 87–94 (2019)
28. Nosal, M., Poruban, J., Sulir, M.: Customizing host IDE for non-programming users of pure embedded DSLs: a case study. Comput. Lang. Syst. Struct. **49**, 101–118 (2017)
29. Poltronieri, I., Zorzo., A.F., Bernardino., M., Medeiros., B., de Borba Campos., M.: Heuristic evaluation checklist for domain-specific languages. In: 16th International Joint Conference on Computer Vision. Imaging and Computer Graphics Theory and Applications - Volume 2 HUCAPP: HUCAPP, pp. 37–48. SciTePress, INSTICC (2021)
30. Poltronieri, I., Zorzo, A.F., Bernardino, M., de Borba Campos, M.: USA-DSL: Usability evaluation framework for domain-specific languages. In: 33rd Symposium on Applied Computing (SAC), pp. 2013–2021. ACM (2018)
31. Poltronieri, I., Zorzo, A.F., Bernardino, M., de Borba Campos, M.: Usability evaluation framework for domain-specific language: a focus group study. ACM SIGAPP Appl. Comput. Rev. **18**, 5–18 (2018)
32. Rodrigues, I., de Borba Campos, M., Zorzo, A.: Usability evaluation of domain-specific languages: a systematic literature review. In: 19th International Conference on Human-Computer Interaction, pp. 522–534 (05 2017)
33. Rodríguez-Gil, L., García-Zubia, J., Orduña, P., Villar-Martinez, A., López-De-Ipiña, D.: New approach for conversational agent definition by non-programmers: a visual domain-specific language. IEEE Access **7**, 5262–5276 (2019)
34. Shin, S.S.: Empirical study on the effectiveness and efficiency of model-driven architecture techniques. Softw. Syst. Model. **18**(5), 3083–3096 (2019)
35. Silva, J., et al.: Comparing the usability of two multi-agents systems DSLs: SEA_ML++ and DSML4MAS study design. In: 3rd International Workshop on Human Factors in Modeling, vol. 2245, pp. 770–777 (2018)
36. Sinha, A., Smidts, C.: An experimental evaluation of a higher-ordered-typed-functional specification-based test-generation technique. Empir. Softw. Eng. **11**, 173–202 (2006)

A Sentiment Analysis Web Platform for Multiple Social Media Types and Language-Specific Customizations

Stavros Giannakis[1,2](✉), Christina Valavani[1,2], and Christina Alexandris[1,2]

[1] National and Kapodistrian University of Athens, Athens, Greece
calexandris@gs.uoa.gr
[2] European Communication Institute (ECI), Danube University Krems and National Technical University of Athens, Athens, Greece

Abstract. The designed and implemented web platform for extracting sentiment from texts consists of a machine learning model retrieving sentiment from a text by categorizing the input into three different classes: positive, negative or neutral. Additionally, this model can be used via a web application processing two different types of text input, namely tweets and (movie) reviews. The web interface allows users to analyze their sentences and evaluate batches of opinions and comments based on specific keywords, retrieved from not one but from various types of online sources, namely Twitter, Reddit, and Youtube. Customizations for additional languages are an additional target.

Keywords: Sentiment analysis · Multiple social media · Multiple text types

1 Introduction

The present application concerns the creation of a web platform for extracting sentiment from texts. Specifically, the designed and implemented platform consists of a machine learning model that manages to retrieve sentiment from a text by categorizing the input into three different classes: positive, negative or neutral. Additionally, this model can be used via a web application processing two different types of text input, namely tweets and (movie) reviews. The platform also provides the possibility to retrieve comments and opinions from different social media platforms such as Reddit, Twitter and Youtube by searching any keyword and classifying the results. The results are presented with a distinctive visualization to the users, giving a better perspective of what people think about specific topics.

Specifically, the web interface allows users (1) to analyze their sentences and (2) to evaluate batches of opinions and comments based on specific keywords, retrieved from not one but from various types of online sources. The online sources concerned include: (a) Twitter, a microblogging website, (b) Reddit, a social news aggregation, web content rating, and discussion website and, finally, (c) Youtube, an online video-sharing platform. The sentiment analysis of the input data will be based on custom machine learning models, trained by different datasets and based on probabilistic algorithms.

© Springer Nature Switzerland AG 2021
M. Kurosu (Ed.): HCII 2021, LNCS 12762, pp. 318–328, 2021.
https://doi.org/10.1007/978-3-030-78462-1_24

The advantages of the proposed application are the following: (1) the user-friendly interface, providing an easy way for users to perform sentimental analysis on their input, (2) the customized machine learning models, trained for two different types of text and document categories (tweets and (movie) reviews) and targeting to provide accurate results, (3) the communication with multiple social media platforms for data retrieval based on specific topics.

The application is designed to be adapted for processing and predicting the polarity and emotion of other languages, except from English, especially for less resourced languages such as Greek.

2 The "How Do You Feel" Platform and Application

The application, named 'How do you feel?', is intended as a user-friendly web interface platform and middleware for the broad user-group of Sentiment Analysis applications. The 'How do you feel? platform offers an easy to use, user-friendly user interface where users are provided with the following functionalities:

Analyze their own text (1): The interface provides a textbox that a user can type or paste a text of their choice, or even use an implemented speech-to-text feature to dictate a phrase and then perform on it sentiment analysis. The interface analyzes the text in real time and returns the result to the user.

Extract other peoples' opinions from a list of social media networks (2): While extracting the polarity of an inputted text could provide benefits to a user, Sentiment Analysis is especially remarkable when it can be applied on a wide variety of data while simultaneously, providing statistics about a specific topic. This facilitates the study of the way people think and the way they express themselves. Thus, the second feature of the platform is the possibility to communicate with a variety of websites that people use to express their opinions. Specifically, these websites are: Twitter, the popular micro-blogging social network, Reddit, a collection of forums with an overwhelming number of topics and subjects and, finally, Youtube, the most popular video streaming platform.

These functionalities have to be powered by a sentiment analysis mechanism that actually processes the text and outputs the polarity of the documents. A machine learning approach was used [1].

While any input can be analyzed, the application is of particular efficiency and performs better when the texts belong to the following categories:

Social media quotes (1): Any opinion expressed on social media networks like Twitter or Facebook is ideal for sentiment analysis. People often resort to their social media accounts to voice their beliefs on various subjects or products and services. Mining the sentiment from these kinds of texts is one of the main functions of the application [2, 3].

Reviews (2): People criticize products or services, with well-structured text bodies that express their positive and negative impressions. These reviews can be inputted into the application and extract accurate results, especially when it comes to movie reviews [4].

The above categories are aligned with the datasets used to train the proposed machine learning model (Fig. 1).

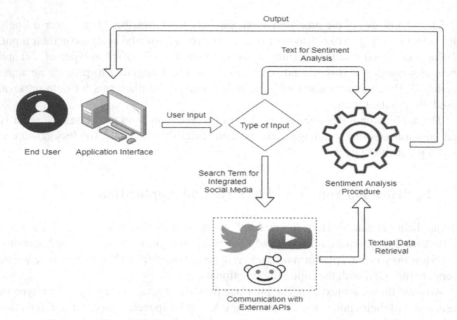

Fig. 1. Outline of sentiment analysis with the "How Do You Feel" platform.

3 Datasets

The datasets used are the Sentiment140 [5], containing textual data extracted from Twitter, and the IMDB dataset [6], concerning movie reviews extracted by the IMDB website.

For our model, we used the dataset from Sentiment140 which is a popular Sentiment Analysis project. The dataset contains 1.6 million tweets targeted to be completely balanced between sentiments and opinions, with 800 thousand being positive and 800 thousand being negative. No "neutral" label is used. The dataset contains a large amount of information such as dates, users and is tagged with a label "0" if the sentiment of the tweet is negative and "4" if it is positive. To visualize the words of the dataset, we created three wordclouds. These wordclouds present the most used words of the whole dataset, the most used words of the positive tagged tweets and, finally, the most used words of the negative tagged tweets (Fig. 2).

The first dataset contained short texts, and the second selection of training data is completely different and opposite from the above-described first one. The IMDB dataset contains movie reviews extracted from the well-known online movie repository, IMDB. The dataset, similar to its sentiment140 counterpart, was assembled in scope of another project and was released on the web for use in other sentiment analysis applications. It contains 50 thousand movie reviews, with half of the dataset being positive and the other half being negative. The selection of this dataset was based on the fact that, since the platform offers a "Free-text" section, where the user can input any text of choice, some users may select to input long, well-structured texts to quickly sentimentally analyze them. While the first dataset would still be accurate to an extent, the model trained with

Fig. 2. Sentiment140 dataset wordcloud

similar data would provide better results. For this reason, to offer a better user experience, both datasets were included.

4   Prediction Models and Application Programming Interface

4.1   Prediction Models

Three (3) prediction models of 'How do you feel?' were created. All of the data was preprocessed [7] with the same function what removed noise from the input texts and the TF-IDF [8] method was selected for feature extraction. It was previously described that we wanted to classify our data as neutral, though there is no neutral class in the used datasets. To achieve this goal, the selected classification algorithms that were used for experimentation were probabilistic [9]. In the end, the classification algorithms selected for the models were: Multinomial Naïve Bayes [10] for the IMDB dataset and Logistic Regression [11] for the remaining two models (Sentiment140 and the combination of the two). The final models were then evaluated using random English phrases, yielding satisfying results with accuracy percentages of around 85%.

4.2   Data Access Layer and External API Communication

As most Sentiment Analysis applications, the 'How do you feel?' application is observed to perform well when used on a lot of data, to extract verdicts and conclusions about how people feel, retrieve their opinions and use this information to one's advantage. A way to achieve this functionality is to retrieve data from popular social networks, where people express themselves. For the retrieval of the data, while crawling and scraping techniques would have worked, it would have been difficult to clean the results and costly in terms of time. To confront this issue, communication with external APIs was chosen to be implemented. Since some of the most widely used social networks such as Facebook and Instagram do not offer their data accessing APIs to the public, the choices narrowed down to Twitter, Reddit and Youtube. All three of these options can contain opinions on products, services or even politics, which is beneficial when using a Sentiment Analysis application.

To access all of the Application Programming Interfaces (APIS) of the web pages mentioned above, developer accounts had to be created to get API keys. All of these API Keys (which are mandatory for the authentication phase during the communication with the endpoints) are stored into three separate configuration files, one for each Application Programming Interface provider. The configuration files serve as an extra layer of security in order to avoid hard coding credentials and authorization tokens into the code that requests the resources from the endpoints and in order to be manageable in case there is a need to change them.

4.3 Twitter

Twitter, being one of the most researched and studied social network when it comes to Sentiment Analysis, was one of the basic pillars on which the application 'How do you feel?' was built on. To retrieve tweets and the information of the authors, for convenience, Tweepy [12] was used. Tweepy is a Python module that communicates with ease with the Twitter API, fetching data in an easy and feasible way. It converts the response JSON in a Python object form, making it easy to manage and obtain the valuable parts.

Twitter API's responses hold plenty of information. One request for a tweet returns a JSON response that contains information about the tweet (such as the time of the post, language and geographic information), statistics (such as number of retweets) and favorites, but it also contains details about the user that posted the tweet. These details feature if the user is validated or not, user name and location that the user states in his profile, number of followers and accounts following and many more. The fact that this amount of information is returned in a single request is convenient, needing less requests even when requesting a huge number of tweets to be returned.

Tweepy assists with the type of tweets that the application fetches. It filters out retweets, since we do not want to include duplicates, and also helps with the language of the texts, since our application works with English data.paragraphs.

4.4 Reddit

Similarly to Tweepy, for the retrieval of data from Reddit, the Python Reddit API Wrapper library (PRAW) [13] is utilized. PRAW offers multiple functionalities such as search per user, subbredit or even with submission and random search terms in the whole reddit website. After authenticating with API keys, provided by the configuration files mentioned earlier, data is conveniently acquired in the same manner as Tweepy; Python objects that can be iterated are created.

One major issue with the Reddit Application Programming Interface is that the responses, on the contrary to Twitter's implementation, contain much less information. For example, the request for a specific comment contains the comment's details like time and the actual text, as well as a unique ID for the user that posted it. To retrieve the user's information, a separate request has to be made. Also, we are considering only the top comments in our data retrieval function. This is because the replies are additional requests and, furthermore, when replying to a top-level comment, sometimes the content of the reply does not hold sentimental value. Taking all the above into consideration, for a large amount of data, multiple requests have to be made, which leads to delays due to a bottleneck; Reddit allows maximum 60 requests per 1 min, resulting in our application responding slower than usual when using the Reddit functionalities.

4.5 YouTube

As a member of the Google API ecosystem, retrieving data from YouTube's API is effortless. Google offers a well-structured solution, making the communication very easy, with the Google API Python Client [14] library connecting and serving the data the users request quickly and easily. This Application Programming Interface offers a modular approach; the request can be modified to ask about more information in one request. The parameter that allows this functionality is named "part" and it can be modified to include statistics about videos, comments, user and channel information, as well as playlists and many more features.

While Google does restrict the API requests to around 8000 per day, these are more than enough to satisfy the needs of our application. Since the threshold is daily and not by the minute, it does not affect the speeds of our application.

5 User Interface

The landing page of the application, accessible through the root URL ("/"), displays buttons which correspond to the four core functionalities of the platform. These buttons perform the same routing action to the respective URI as the navigation sidebar, which is on the left side of the interface. The buttons in the center do not include the "About" page, which is only visible on the sidebar, for aesthetic and symmetry reasons. The icons feature animations achieved via custom CSS, included in the styling sheet file of the homepage component. The sidebar can also be expanded, offering a better view and description of each icon, as seen in Fig. 3.

Sentiment Analysis is performed in selected social media types (Twitter, Youtube, Reddit) (Fig. 4) and as Free-text sentiment analysis (Fig. 5). The Free-text sentiment analysis part of the platform uses the same square-card layout as the rest of the website. On the left component there is a text area that the user can input the text of his choice for Sentiment Analysis. A dropdown menu is offered for the user to select the prediction model of choice.

The results are presented to the user in the respective charts and diagrams generated after sentiment analysis, according to the selected social media type. Figure 6 displays the results for Youtube.

Fig. 3. Homepage layout in user interface with extended sidebar

Fig. 4. Twitter sentiment analysis user interface.

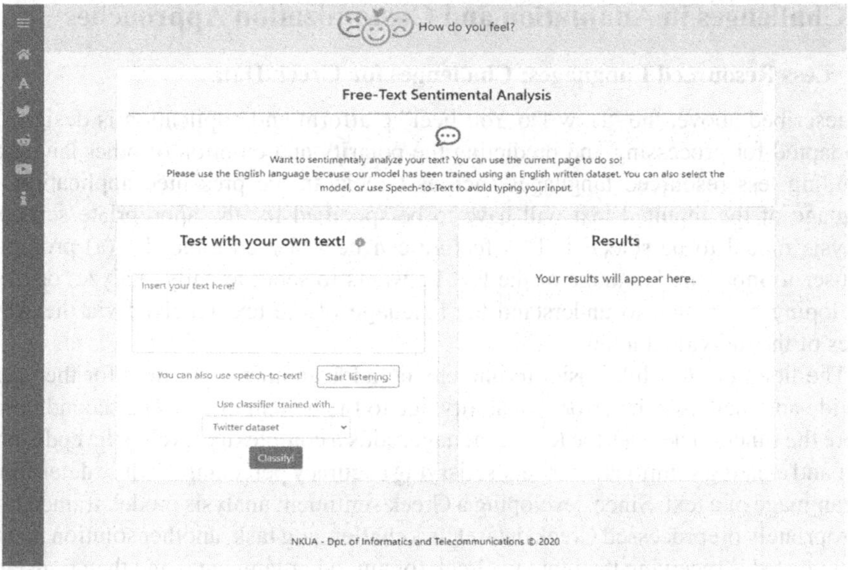

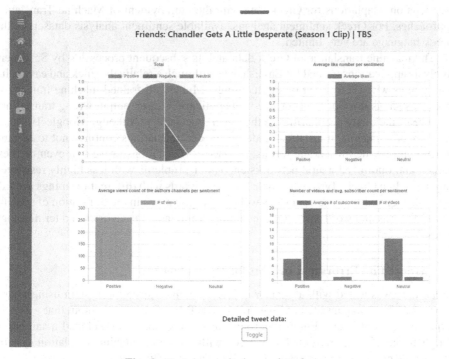

Fig. 5. Free-text sentiment analysis user interface.

Fig. 6. Youtube results in user interface.

6 Challenges in Adaptation and Customization Approaches

6.1 Less Resourced Languages: Challenges for Greek Data

As described above, the "How Do You Feel" platform and application is designed to be adapted for processing and predicting the polarity and emotion of other languages, including less resourced languages such as Greek. In the presented application, the language of the inputted text will have to be specified for the appropriate sentiment analysis model to be selected. This feature can be achieved either by (a) prompting the user to input the language of the text he wants to sentimentally analyze, or (b) by developing a function to understand the language of the text received via the ASCII codes of the individual letters.

The first option, while easier to implement, adds another input field for the user to provide and increases the error probability due to the human factor. The second option, where the function decides the text's language, adds a complexity level to the code, but is safer and existing solutions offer very satisfying accuracy percentages while determining the language of a text. Since developing a Greek sentiment analysis model, trained by an appropriately preprocessed Greek dataset, is a challenging task, another solution that can be suggested is receiving the input in Greek (or any other language) and then translating it in English, to perform sentiment analysis on the translated text. This way, an already implemented model that has been trained by an English dataset can be used. Here, we focus on adaptations for Greek data with the employment of Machine Translation approaches, For Greek sentiment analysis, available sentiment analysis datasets in the Greek language are very limited.

The machine translation of Greek data and its subsequent processing by Sentiment Analysis applications trained for English data, although a relatively quick and easy solution, comes with its own set of shortcomings. Many well-trained machine translation models, such as the Google Translate web application, often output wrong translations because of the many peculiarities of the Greek vocabulary. Although Google Translate uses a neural machine translation model, incorrect translations continue not to be rare. which can provide misleading results. Erroneous translations prove that even the best trained and optimized neural networks encounter problems with less highly resourced languages like Greek. Typical examples concern words with different meanings according to the context they are used in, as well as complications in the translation of specific types of words and word categories, including grammatical categories and terminology types.

6.2 Translation Errors and Insights for Upgrading

Greek data was tested with a popular online machine translation system using neural networks. The data consisted of Twitter and YouTube social media input that was subsequently translated into English and vice versa. The data also included a sample of (English) Reddit data translated into Greek with the same machine translation system. The results produced the following five (5) main error categories:

Errors in syntax (Divergencies), especially in regard to translating elliptical phrases and sentences or producing incorrect and/or ungrammatical elliptical phrases and sentences (a).

No recognition or incorrect translation of exclamations, including exclamation types typical of Social Media (for example "wow" and "lol") (b).

No recognition or incorrect translation of abbreviations, mostly non-standardized abbreviations used by Social Media users (not registered in dictionaries and lexicons) (c).

Errors in generated translated phrases and sentences containing expressions from another natural language (for example, Spanish) (d).

Errors in generated translated phrases and sentences containing emoticons (e).

The above-presented error categories are directly related to linguistic features typical of texts in Social Media. In this case, a machine translation system must process input containing linguistic features of written language and of spoken language, in addition to expressions and other elements characteristic of Social Media text types. Furthermore, code-switching and the use of expressions from other natural languages is common in Social Media texts, posing an additional challenge to machine translation systems. Finally, it should be noted that texts in Social Media come with their own sets of idiosyncrasies when it comes to variations across languages, even to variations in English used by the international public.

Considering all of the above, it proposed to adopt a "hybrid" approach, making full use of the advantages of neural network-based online machine translation systems but also in combination with a preprocessing module for eliminating problematic input and errors in generated translated data. The preprocessing module may isolate emoticons and exclamations for their separate processing. In addition, similarly to a text editor, it may make predictions involving abbreviated words and elliptical sentences and phrases. These predictions may also include foreign words in sentences where they may be assigned default meaning and part-of-speech types to facilitate processing. The preprocessing module approach is a subject of further testing and investigation.

7   Conclusions and Further Research

We presented a designed and implemented platform performing sentiment analysis from texts with input classification: positive, negative or neutral. The "How Do You Feel" platform and web application processes comments and opinions from different social media platforms, namely Reddit, Twitter and YouTube. The "How Do You Feel" platform includes a user-friendly interface, customized machine learning models, trained for two different types of text and document categories (tweets and (movie) reviews) and allows communication with multiple social media platforms for data retrieval based on specific topics.

The proposed adaptations in further research may also contribute to the customization and development of the Sentiment Analysis web platform in different languages. Further research will target to customized language-specific adaptations designed to contribute to the considerable reduction and elimination of problematic machine-translation output. The "How Do You Feel" platform and web application, combining different social media platforms, is intended to be upgraded and adapted in languages other than English, facilitating its use by a broader, international public.

References

1. Garg, S., Verma, N.: Study of sentiment classification techniques. https://www.researchgate.net/publication/332343554_Study_of_Sentiment_Classification_Techniques. Accessed 20 Dec 2020
2. Agarwal, A., Xie, B., Vovsha, I., Rambow, O., Passonneau, R.: Sentiment analysis of Twitter data. https://www.aclweb.org/anthology/W11-0705.pdf. Accessed 20 Dec 2020
3. Go, A., Huang, L., Bhayani, R.: Twitter sentiment analysis. https://nlp.stanford.edu/courses/cs224n/2009/fp/3.pdf. Accessed 20 Dec 2020
4. Yasen, M., Tedmori, S.: Movies reviews sentiment analysis and classification. https://www.researchgate.net/publication/332321070_Movies_Reviews_Sentiment_Analysis_and_Classification. Accessed 20 Dec 2020.
5. Go, A., Bhayani, R., Huang, L.: Sentiment140. http://help.sentiment140.com/. Accessed 20 Dec 2020
6. Maas, A., Daly, D., Pham, P., Huang, D., Ng, A., Potts. C.: Large movie review dataset. http://ai.stanford.edu/~amaas/data/sentiment/. Accessed 20 Dec 2020
7. Krouska, A., Troussas, C., Virvou, M.: The effect of preprocessing techniques on Twitter sentiment analysis. https://www.researchgate.net/publication/311755864_The_effect_of_preprocessing_techniques_on_Twitter_sentiment_analysis. Accessed 20 Dec 2020
8. Qaiser, S.: Text mining: use of TF-IDF to examine the relevance of words to documents. https://www.researchgate.net/publication/326425709_Text_Mining_Use_of_TF-IDF_to_Examine_the_Relevance_of_Words_to_Documents. Accessed 20 Dec 2020
9. Colace, F., Santo, M., Greco L.: A probabilistic approach to tweets' sentiment classification. https://www.researchgate.net/publication/256472988_A_Probabilistic_Approach_to_Tweets'_Sentiment_Classification. Accessed 20 Dec 2020
10. Kibriya, A., Frank, E., Pfahringer, B., Holmes, G.: Multinomial naive bayes for text categorization revisited. https://perun.pmf.uns.ac.rs/radovanovic/dmsem/cd/install/Weka/doc/pubs/2004/KibriyaAI04-MultinomialNBRevisited.pdf. Accessed 20 Dec 2020
11. Hamdan, H., Bellot, P., Bechet, F.: Lsislif: CRF and logistic regression for opinion target extraction and sentiment polarity analysis. https://www.aclweb.org/anthology/S15-2128/. Accessed 20 Dec 2020
12. Tweepy Homepage. https://www.tweepy.org/. Accessed 20 Dec 2020
13. PRAW Official Documentation. https://praw.readthedocs.io/. Accessed 20 Dec 2020
14. Google API Client Documentation. https://github.com/googleapis/google-api-python-client. Accessed 20 Dec 2020

FLM-2A: Towards Automated HCI Modeling of Android Applications Based on a Modified Version of the Keystroke Level Model

Savvas Theofilou, Nikolas Vardas, and Christos Katsanos[✉]

Department of Informatics, Aristotle University of Thessaloniki, Thessaloniki, Greece
savvasth@protonmail.com, ckatsanos@csd.auth.gr

Abstract. Keystroke-Level Model (KLM) is an established HCI model for predicting users' time on task. KLM was originally developed for desktop systems, but it has been extended for different interaction contexts. Fingerstroke-Level Model (FLM) is such an extension for touch-sensitive interactions with direct finger movements. This paper presents a novel tool, named FLM for Android Apps (FLM-2A), that supports automated FLM modeling of tasks performed in Android apps. The tool aims to support design and evaluation of Android apps in an effective and efficient manner. A study investigated the accuracy of FLM-2A predictions by comparing them to participants' interaction times for three custom-built Android apps. Results showed that the error rate for the FLM-2A predictions with Fitts' Law enabled were 0.3% and 2.8% for the first and second apps respectively. However, the error rate for the third custom-built Android app was 40.0%, indicating that additional steps are required to finetune the FLM-2A predictions.

Keywords: Keystroke-Level Mode (KLM) · Fingerstroke-Level Model (FLM) · Mobile interaction · Android apps usability · Automated tool

1 Introduction

Nowadays, people use mobile apps for a wide range of daily activities. Thus, ensuring good user experience (UX) while interacting with mobile apps is important. In this mobile context, interaction efficiency is a parameter that plays a central role in the usability and consequently in the overall UX of an application on a mobile device.

However, modern mobile application development often requires a fast pace with limited resources for UX design and evaluation. Predictive HCI models, such as GOMS (Goals, Operators, Methods, Selection Rules) [1], can be particularly useful in the design and evaluation of mobile apps. An essential benefit of such models is that they can substantially reduce the number of time-consuming and resource-demanding experiments in the early phases of design [2–4].

The Keystroke Level Model (KLM) [5] is the simplest and most widely used variant of the GOMS family. KLM predicts the time it takes for an experienced user to perform a specific task without making any errors while using a specific user interface. To achieve

© Springer Nature Switzerland AG 2021
M. Kurosu (Ed.): HCII 2021, LNCS 12762, pp. 329–342, 2021.
https://doi.org/10.1007/978-3-030-78462-1_25

this, the KLM model defines a set of seven operators [3, 5]: a) K: pressing a key, and not a character, on the keyboard, b) P: pointing to a target on the display with a mouse, c) B: pressing or releasing the mouse button, d) H: homing hands to keyboard or mouse, e) D: drawing manually straight-line segments, f) M: mentally preparing for executing physical actions, and g) R: waiting for the system to respond. KLM is an accurate model with a standard error range of 21% [6].

The original KLM [5] includes operators and associated times for desktop-based interaction using a mouse and a keyboard. However, various KLM extensions have been proposed. Regarding modeling user interaction with mobile devices, one of the earliest KLM variants is the Mobile KLM [7]. The latter considered key-based smartphones and introduced new operators for this context. It was later refined [8] to consider short-range device communication (NFC). Li et al. [9] proposed a KLM model for stylus-based interaction with a mobile phone. They introduced 14 new operators and the concept of an operator block.

The Touch-Level Model (TLM) [10] and Fingerstroke Level Model (FLM) [11] address interactions with modern touch-based mobile devices. Both models use operators from the original KLM, but they also introduce new ones, such as tapping and swiping. However, only the FLM provides baseline time values for the new operators and has been validated in experimental studies [4, 11]. It has been also extended to the Blind FLM [12], which models interaction between visually impaired users and touch devices.

Watch KLM [13] extends KLM to model smartwatch interaction. The new model contains 14 operators, some of which were inherited from KLM and other extensions, and some other operators were created specifically for smartwatch interaction. The Watch KLM has an error rate of 12.07% [13].

This paper presents a novel tool, named FLM for Android Apps (FLM-2A), that supports the automated FLM modeling of Android apps. The tool aims to support design and evaluation of Android apps in an effective and efficient manner. FLM-2A is a desktop application implemented in Python.

2   GOMS-Based Software Tools for HCI Modeling

Various software tools have been proposed in the literature to facilitate GOMS-based predictive modeling in HCI.

CogTool [14] is a general-purpose open source tool for UI prototyping[1] that produces model-based predictions from tasks demonstrated on storyboard mockups of a user interface. CogTool uses the KLM model implemented in the ACT-R cognitive architecture [15]. The storyboard mockups are created using CogTool's Frame objects for each different screen and predefined widget overlays to define which part of the Frame is interactive. CogTool has been used in various studies, such as evaluating programming environments [16] and supporting better real-time software development [17]. Cogtool-Explorer [18] extends Cogtool to predict novice exploration behavior.

The Stochastic Activity Network Laboratory for Cognitive Modeling (SANLab-CM) [19] is an open source software tool[2] that produces CPM-GOMS models [20] for routine

---

[1] https://github.com/cogtool.
[2] https://github.com/CogWorks/SANLab-CM.

interactive behavior. Unlike other tools, it can add variability to the operator execution times and offers functionality to visualize and compare critical paths. A study [21] compared SANLab-CM and CogTool for entering the landing speed into the Boeing 777 Flight Management Computer using the Control and Display Unit. It was found that SANLab-CM can model the individual differences within a method but not across different methods for completing a task.

Cogulator is an open source human performance modeling tool[3] for estimating task time and mental workload. Unlike other modeling tools, Cogulator provides a text-based interface for the user to build models, it supports multitasking of the modeled user and building of multiple GOMS-based models, such as KLM and CPM-GOMS. Cogulator has been used to model a pilot's task times, heads down times and working memory load during the approaching phase of flight [22].

The presented general-purpose modeling tools require non-trivial manual work (e.g., design UI prototypes) to perform predictive modeling. In addition, the plethora of available functions and generic modeling nature of existing tools can overwhelm and discourage practitioners who, in most cases, need a simple tool focused on the problem at hand. These observations motivated us to develop software tools that support effortless HCI modeling for specific design and evaluation contexts, such as FLM-2A presented in this paper and the Keystroke Level Model Form Analyzer (KLM-FA) presented in our previous work [23, 24].

KLM-FA is a freely-available Windows-based software tool[4] that uses KLM and Fitts' Law [25] to automate modeling of web form filling tasks for various interaction strategies and modeled users' characteristics. To this end, KLM-FA runs an algorithm that first parses an HTML form to identify each element. The evaluator can then simply select the sequence of form elements that are required for the task. Text elements can be also associated to predefined types (e.g., email, password) that come with a research-based estimated number of characters to be filled. Next, KLM-FA produces the sequence of KLM operators and time required for the form filling task. A study [24] found that KLM-FA had a mean error rate of 10.9% against empirical data. KLM-FA has been also used to support instruction of KLM. Three studies [26–28] showed that the KLM-FA learning activity had a significant positive effect on students' learning gain in various education delivery methods (campus-based, blended, and distance learning) and levels (undergraduate, postgraduate). The Web-based KLM-FA (WKLM-FA) [29] is a recent web-based implementation of KLM-FA, which, amongst other improvements, can be also used by non-Windows users.

3 The FLM-2A Tool

The purpose of FLM-2A is to support design and evaluation of Android apps in an effective and efficient manner. The tool employs an algorithm that first parses the UI elements in the display screen of a running Android app using the Appium[5] and the

---

[3] https://cogulator.io.

[4] http://klmformanalyzer.weebly.com.

[5] http://appium.io.

Android SDK Platform Tools[6]. FLM-2A then executes FLM modeling to calculate the time required to perform the modeled user task.

FLM-2A is a desktop application implemented in Python which uses the tkinter library for its Graphical User Interface (GUI). FLM-2A is a flexible application as it allows the user to change various parameters to meet his/her modeling needs. Figure 1 presents the main interface and functionality of FLM-2A, and Table 1 provides brief information about the available buttons in the menu bar of FLM-2A. Figure 2 presents the high-level architecture of FLM-2A.

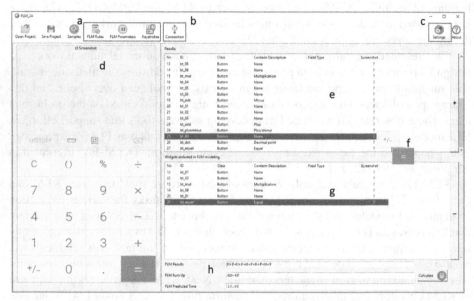

Fig. 1. Overview of the FLM-2A interface and functionality while using the tool to model a user task (i.e., 73 * 91) performed with a Calculator mobile app: (a) Modeling preferences, (b) Button to connect the Android device running the evaluated mobile app with the computer running FLM-2A, (c) Settings that can show or hide specific Android classes of UI elements, (d) UI screenshot of the app under evaluation, (e) Numbered list of the automatically identified UI elements, (f) Screenshot of the automatically identified UI element, (g) Modeled interaction task based on the sequence of the selected UI elements, (h) Sequence of the FLM operators and predicted task completion time.

3.1 Typical Usage Scenario of FLM-2A

First, the evaluator connects an Android device to the computer running FLM-2A and then opens the app under evaluation in the mobile device. Next, through the "Connection" button in the tool interface (Fig. 1-b), the evaluator connects FLM-2A with the mobile device and the tool employs an algorithm to automatically identify the UI elements of the Android app screen. As a result, FLM-2A presents a screenshot of the evaluated UI

---

[6] https://developer.android.com/studio/releases/platform-tools.

Table 1. Overview of the available buttons provided in the menu bar of FLM-2A.

Button	Functionality description
Open Project	Open a saved project. All projects come with a screenshot of the UI so that they can be easily identified
Save Project	Save a project for future use. The tool does not save modeled tasks
Samples	A few sample applications including the three applications used for the evaluation study reported in this paper
FLM Rules	Choose the value for the P Operator (FLM value, Fitts' Law) and the starting position of the finger
FLM Parameters	Change the values of the currently-supported FLM operators and the values of the Fitts' Law constants
Keystrokes	Change the keystrokes of ready-to-use FLM-2A field types that can be assigned to editable textboxes (e.g., email, username etc.)
Connection	Connect a mobile app running on an Android device with FLM-2A so that the tool can automatically parse its UI elements
Settings	Change which classes of widgets appear in the results frame
About	Show the current version of the application, information about FLM-2A creators and references for the graphics used

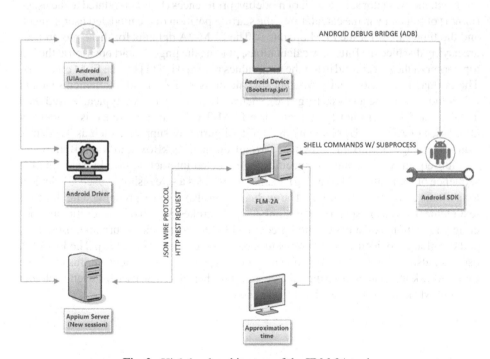

Fig. 2. High-level architecture of the FLM-2A tool.

(Fig. 1-d) and a numbered list of the identified UI elements (Fig. 1-e). This list includes the following columns for each element:

1. No: a unique ascending number assigned by FLM-2A.
2. ID: the value of the android:id attribute of the widget. This is a unique resource name for an Android widget that typically provides information about how the widget is used. For instance, the id "btn_add" is used for the button that performs addition in the Calculator app of Fig. 1.
3. Class: the Android class that the widget belongs to (e.g., Button, EditText).
4. Content-Description: the value of the android:contentDescription attribute of a widget. This attribute is used to make apps more accessible by linking a text description to a widget that has no text content. Thus, it provides additional information about how the widget is used. For instance, the mobile Calculator app (Fig. 1) has a widget with id "btn_dot" which the content description clarifies as "Decimal point".
5. Field Type: the FLM-2A type of the field assigned by the evaluator. This can be only assigned to editable textboxes (i.e., EditText widgets) and defines the number of keystrokes to be used for this field in the FLM modeling.
6. Screenshot: a screenshot of the widget. This facilitates the evaluator to find the placement of a specific widget in the overall user interface of the evaluated app (e.g., Fig. 1-f).

Next, the evaluator selects a set of modeling preferences (Fig. 1-a) related to the usage (or not) of Fitts' law in the calculations, the starting position of the modeled user's finger, and the time values for the FLM operators. The FLM-2A defaults for these preferences are having disabled the Fitts' law calculations, placing the finger's start position at the left top corner of the screen, and using the time values reported in [11] for the FLM operators. The evaluator can also specify whether specific classes of Android UI elements should be excluded from the analysis (Fig. 1-c), such as TextViews that are typically used only as labels and thus are not tap targets. The FLM-2A default preference is to identify all classes of Android UI elements that the tool currently supports, such as TextView, EditText, ImageView, Button, Switch, ToggleButton, CheckBox, and RadioButton.

Subsequently, the evaluator specifies the modeled interaction task by selecting the sequence of elements used (Fig. 1-g). FLM-2A provides a screenshot of each UI element to facilitate this process (Fig. 1-f). The evaluator can also assign a predefined field type to text elements to easily specify their number of keystrokes, which offers additional modeling automation. A list of common predefined field types, such as surname, username, and email are provided with default values based on empirical data [23]. The FLM-2A user can also assign the "Insert Manually" field type to a text element. In this case, the tool will ask the evaluator to type the desired number of keystrokes for each such text element when the "Calculate" button is pressed.

The output of the tool is the sequence of FLM operators and predicted task completion time (Fig. 1-h). Depending on the evaluation scenario, UI elements can be included or excluded from the analysis by simply using the plus and minus buttons in the FLM-2A user interface. In addition, modeling preferences can be modified (e.g., enable Fitts' law calculations). In all such cases, the tool updates the results in real time when the "Calculate" button is pressed. If desired, the evaluator can save a project so that the next time it would not be necessary to have the Android device connected to his/her computer and the mobile app running in the Android device.

3.2 Architecture and Reasoning of FLM-2A

Parsing Module. This FLM-2A module combines Appium and the Android SDK Platform Tools to automatically identify the UI elements in the display screen of the evaluated Android app. Appium is an open source software used for automated testing of iOS, Android and Windows applications. It supports testing for web, native and hybrid mobile apps. Appium uses the client-server architecture for communication. The Android SDK Platform Tools is a component of the Android SDK. It includes tools that interface with the Android platform, such as adb, fastboot and systrace.

First, FLM-2A uses the Android Debug Bridge (adb) tool[7], a versatile command-line tool that enables communication with a device, to find the Desired Capabilities[8]. The latter are keys and values encoded in a JSON object, which are required by the Appium when a new automation session is requested. These Desired Capabilities are the name of the device in which the Android application runs, the package of the application and the activity of the application.

Next, FLM-2A employs functionality provided by Appium to parse the display screen of the mobile app under evaluation and find its UI elements. In specific, the Appium server is used to first connect with the Android device (treated as an Appium client) and then the Appium library to find all the widgets of the application. These widgets are returned in the form of WebElement[9] objects which have various properties and methods. The latter provide to FLM-2A the information used by the FLM modeling algorithm, such as the class of widgets, their position and size in the UI etc.

The following pseudocode sketches the FLM-2A parsing module algorithm.

---

[7] https://developer.android.com/studio/command-line/adb.

[8] http://appium.io/docs/en/writing-running-appium/caps.

[9] https://www.selenium.dev/documentation/en/webdriver/web_element.

```
getDesiredCapabilities(){
  //Use adb to Find Device name, Package and Activity
  device, package, activity = getDevicePackageActivity()
  desired_capabilities.add(device, package, activity)
  return desired_capabilities
}
connectToServer(Port){
  desired_capabilities = getDesiredCapabilities()
  //Send a request to Appium server
  Driver = Webdriver.remote(port, desired_capabilities)
  return Driver
}
FindUIElements(){
  //Connect to the Appium server
  Webdriver = ConnectToServer(Port)
  //Find all the UI Elements using the Webdriver object
  TextViews[] = Webdriver.findElementsByClass("TextView")
  Buttons[] = Webdriver.findElementsByClass("Button")
  //[..] continue for all Android classes of UI elements
}
```

Analysis Module. This FLM-2A module performs the FLM modeling. The main function involved is the "FLMcost", which takes as arguments the list of elements of the modeled task (Fig. 1-g), the modeling assumptions and the FLM operator values.

Initially, the time values for the FLM operators are set to either the defaults [11] or the ones defined by the user through the "FLM parameters" button of FLM-2A (Fig. 1-a). For each element in the modeled task, the algorithm first checks whether Fitts' Law is enabled. If it is enabled then the Fitts' Law formula by MacKenzie [30] is used to calculate the value of the P operator in this iteration. Next, the algorithm checks if the element belongs to the EditText class and sets the T operator value according to the number of assigned finger keystrokes. Then, the "analyzeElement" function returns the sequence of FLM operators and total time to interact with this element. The latter are added to the sequence of FLM operators and total time for the whole modeled task. This iterative process stops when all the elements in the list are examined.

The following pseudocode sketches the FLM-2A analysis module algorithm.

```
FLMcost(elements, assumptions, flm){
  M, P, T, R = flm.getFLMoperatorsValues()
  foreach element in elements{
    If (assumptions.getFittsLaw() == True){
      P = Fitts_Law(element, elements)
    }
    If (element.getType() == EditText){
      T = T * element.getKeystrokes()
    }
    result = analyzeElement(element, M, P, T, R)
    operator_seq += operator_seq + result.operator_seq
    time += time + result.time
  }
  return operator_seq, time
}
```

4 Evaluation Study

An evaluation study was conducted to compare the FLM-2A predictions with users' observed interaction times for three custom-built Android apps (Fig. 3).

4.1 Methodology

Participants. Twenty users, 9 female and 11 male, with a mean age of 24.3 years old (SD = 2.9) participated in the study. All the participants had a smartphone. Fifteen of them (75%) owned an Android device and the rest five (25%) owned an iPhone device. The participants rated their previous experience in using mobile apps as high to very high (M = 4.5, SD = 0.6 on a scale from 1 = very low to 5 = very high).

Evaluated Android Apps and User Tasks. Three custom-built apps were developed for the needs of the study. Figure 3 presents the UI of these mobile apps.

The apps were designed to include a variety of UI elements typically used in Android apps. More importantly, they included source code that logged participants' interaction actions and time per UI element. The Android Studio 3 was used to develop the three evaluated apps.

Participants used an OnePlus 5T smartphone with a 6 inches display and the Microsoft SwiftKey Keyboard to interact with the three evaluated Android apps. Users were given specific data that they had to fill out for each field in each application. An attempt was made to make the information easy to remember (e.g., using the first name and last name of a popular singer for AppA).

Procedures. The participants performed a task on each of the three custom-built apps and their interaction actions and time were logged. The order in which the participants interacted with the three apps was counterbalanced to minimize serial order effects.

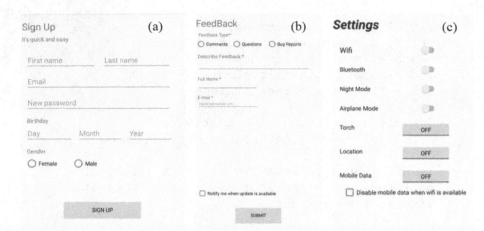

Fig. 3. The applications used for the FLM-2A evaluation study: (a) AppA: Signup app, (b) AppB: Feedback app, (c) AppC: Device settings app.

The participants were asked to complete each task as fast and correct as possible. They were instructed to: a) fill in the fields of each app from top to bottom and from left to right, b) not use copy-paste functionality, c) insert text in Greek and only using capital letters, and d) perform each task at least 10 times.

Ten task repetitions have been also used in similar previous research efforts [24, 31] so that the participants can reach skilled performance. If the tenth trial was not error-free then the participant was asked to perform additional trials. Task execution times were derived from participants' last error-free trial and they were informed about this before starting the study. They were also informed that their interaction actions and times would be recorded as soon as they opened an evaluated app.

4.2 Results

The results of the user study were compared with the calculated times of FLM-2A.

The following assumptions were used for the FLM-2A modeling: a) system response time was negligible (i.e., set to zero), b) the finger's initial position was at the left top corner of the screen, c) tool defaults for all analysis parameters were used, except for the keystrokes for EditTexts that were appropriately adjusted for each task and the Fitts' law constants that were determined empirically by regression analysis. In addition, we run two modeling approaches, one using the mean value of 0.43 for the P operator [11] and one using Fitts' Law to accurately measure each P operator. In the following, these approaches are referred as FLM-2A (P = 0.43) and FLM-2A (P = Fitts) respectively.

Table 2 presents participants' task execution times and the FLM-2A predicted times for each modeling approach, along with the FLM-2A error rate. The error rate was calculated as the difference between the FLM-2A predictions and participants' mean task time, and this difference divided by the participants' mean task time.

The results showed that the error rate of FLM-2A (P = 0.43) predictions for AppA and AppB fell well within the standard error range of 21% for KLM models [6]; 6.3%

Table 2. Study results showing the mean observed user time (standard deviation in parentheses), the predicted FLM-2A time and the error rate for the two modeling approaches used.

App	Users' task time (sec)	FLM-2A (P = 0.43) predicted time (sec)	Error rate (P = 0.43)	FLM-2A (P = Fitts) predicted time (sec)	Error rate (P = Fitts)
AppA	42.32 (3.34)	45.00	6.3%	41.14	2.8%
AppB	36.11 (5.00)	36.43	0.9%	35.99	0.3%
AppC	4.82 (0.27)	8.90	84.6%	6.75	40.0%

and 0.9% for AppA and AppB respectively. This was also true for the FLM-2A (P = Fitts) predictions, which further improved the error rate as expected; 2.8% and 0.3% for AppA and AppB respectively. However, the error rate for AppC was very high for both modeling approaches; 84.6% for FLM-2A (P = 0.43) and 40.0% for FLM-2A (P = Fitts) respectively.

AppC had a rather large deviation from participants' observed times. Users' mean task time in this mobile app was rather low (M = 4.82 s, SD = 0.27), thus even slight deviations in FLM-2A predictions result in a substantially higher error rate compared to the rest two apps; M = 42.32 s (SD = 3.34) and M = 36.11 s (SD = 5.00) respectively. AppC uses only elements of the Button Android class (i.e., Switch, ToggleButton, CheckBox), which means that the predicted time is largely dependent on the time value of the P operator. Indeed, the initial error rate of 84.6% for the fixed P value of 0.43 s [11] dropped to 40.0% after using Fitts' Law for estimating the pointing time.

However, an error rate of 40.0% is still high for KLM modeling. The FFitts model [32] is an expansion of Fitts' Law, which has been found to be more accurate in modeling finger input on touchscreens. Implementing the FFitts model in FLM-2A could further improve its predictions, particularly for UIs that depend only on pointing, such as AppC in this evaluation study. Similarly, time estimates based on regression models have been also proposed [4] for FLM, which may also improve the FLM-2A predictions.

5 Conclusion

The modeling of human interaction with modern touch-sensitive portable devices is quite recent. The classic KLM model is not suitable for its study. Our goal in this paper was to develop a software that can provide automation in this modeling context.

The FLM-2A tool was presented, a tool that automates modeling of interaction on Android touch-based mobile devices. FLM-2A uses the FLM model, a KLM variant for touch-sensitive interaction, to provide predictions of task time while interacting with Android apps. This paper also presented an evaluation study involving 20 users. The users were asked to interact with three experimental applications and their task completion times were compared to the FLM-2A predictions for the same tasks. A rather low error rate was found for the first two apps (0.3% and 2.8%). By contrast, the FLM-2A error rate was 40.0% for the third app.

The latter highlights the need for further study of the FLM-2A predictions in various evaluation contexts. Particular emphasis should be placed in providing accurate predictions for the P (pointing) operator. Thus, we plan to implement the FFitts model [32] in FLM-2A. One additional future goal is to support the S (sliding) and F (flicking) operators of FLM in the FLM-2A modeling. Finally, we plan to support automated identification of more Android app components.

References

1. Card, S.K., Moran, T.P., Newell, A.: The Psychology of Human-Computer Interaction. Lawrence Erlbaum Associates (1983)
2. Jimenez, Y., Morreale, P.: Design and evaluation of a predictive model for smartphone selection. In: Marcus, A. (ed.) DUXU 2013. LNCS, vol. 8015, pp. 376–384. Springer, Heidelberg (2013). https://doi.org/10.1007/978-3-642-39253-5_41
3. Kieras, D.: Using the keystroke-level model to estimate execution times (2001)
4. Lee, A., Song, K., Ryu, H.B., Kim, J., Kwon, G.: Fingerstroke time estimates for touchscreen-based mobile gaming interaction. Hum. Mov. Sci. **44**, 211–224 (2015). https://doi.org/10.1016/j.humov.2015.09.003
5. Card, S.K., Moran, T.P., Newell, A.: The keystroke-level model for user performance time with interactive systems. Commun. ACM **23**, 396–410 (1980). https://doi.org/10.1145/358886.358895
6. John, B.E., Suzuki, S.: Toward cognitive modeling for predicting usability. In: Jacko, J.A. (ed.) HCI 2009. LNCS, vol. 5610, pp. 267–276. Springer, Heidelberg (2009). https://doi.org/10.1007/978-3-642-02574-7_30
7. Holleis, P., Otto, F., Hussmann, H., Schmidt, A.: Keystroke-level model for advanced mobile phone interaction. In: Proceedings of the SIGCHI Conference on Human Factors in Computing Systems, pp. 1505–1514. ACM, New York (2007). https://doi.org/10.1145/1240624.1240851
8. Holleis, P., Scherr, M., Broll, G.: A revised mobile KLM for interaction with multiple NFC-tags. In: Proceedings of the 13th IFIP TC 13 International Conference on Human-Computer Interaction - Volume Part IV, pp. 204–221. Springer, Heidelberg (2011)
9. Li, H., Liu, Y., Liu, J., Wang, X., Li, Y., Rau, P.-L.P.: Extended KLM for mobile phone interaction: a user study result. In: CHI 2010 Extended Abstracts on Human Factors in Computing Systems, pp. 3517–3522. Association for Computing Machinery, New York (2010). https://doi.org/10.1145/1753846.1754011
10. Rice, A.D., Lartigue, J.W.: Touch-level model (TLM): evolving KLM-GOMS for touchscreen and mobile devices. In: Proceedings of the 2014 ACM Southeast Regional Conference, pp. 1–6. Association for Computing Machinery, New York (2014). https://doi.org/10.1145/2638404.2638532
11. Song, K., et al.: The fingerstroke-level model strikes back: a modified keystroke-level model in developing a gaming UI for 4G networks. In: CHI 2013 Extended Abstracts on Human Factors in Computing Systems, pp. 2359–2362. ACM, New York (2013). https://doi.org/10.1145/2468356.2468769
12. Al-Megren, S., Altamimi, W., Al-Khalifa, H.S.: Blind FLM: an enhanced keystroke-level model for visually impaired smartphone interaction. In: Bernhaupt, R., Dalvi, G., Joshi, A., Balkrishan, D.K., O'Neill, J., Winckler, M. (eds.) INTERACT 2017. LNCS, vol. 10513, pp. 155–172. Springer, Cham (2017). https://doi.org/10.1007/978-3-319-67744-6_10
13. Al-Megren, S.: A predictive fingerstroke-level model for smartwatch interaction. Multimodal Technol. Interact. **2**, 38 (2018). https://doi.org/10.3390/mti2030038

14. John, B.E., Prevas, K., Salvucci, D.D., Koedinger, K.: Predictive human performance modeling made easy. In: Proceedings of the SIGCHI Conference on Human Factors in Computing Systems, pp. 455–462. ACM, Vienna (2004). https://doi.org/10.1145/985692.985750
15. Anderson, J.R., Lebiere, C.J.: The Atomic Components of Thought. Psychology Press, Mahwah (1998)
16. Bellamy, R., John, B., Richards, J., Thomas, J.: Using CogTool to model programming tasks. In: Evaluation and Usability of Programming Languages and Tools, pp. 1–6. Association for Computing Machinery, New York (2010). https://doi.org/10.1145/1937117.1937118
17. Bellamy, R., John, B., Kogan, S.: Deploying CogTool: integrating quantitative usability assessment into real-world software development. In: 2011 33rd International Conference on Software Engineering (ICSE), pp. 691–700 (2011). https://doi.org/10.1145/1985793.198 5890
18. Teo, L., John, B.E.: Cogtool-explorer: towards a tool for predicting user interaction. In: CHI 2008 extended abstracts on Human Factors in Computing Systems, pp. 2793–2798. ACM, Florence (2008). https://doi.org/10.1145/1358628.1358763
19. Patton, E.W., Gray, W.D.: SANLab-CM: a tool for incorporating stochastic operations into activity network modeling. Behav. Res. Methods 42, 877–883 (2010). https://doi.org/10.3758/ BRM.42.3.877
20. Gray, W.D., John, B.E., Atwood, M.E.: The precis of Project Ernestine or an overview of a validation of GOMS. In: Proceedings of the SIGCHI Conference on Human Factors in Computing Systems, pp. 307–312. Association for Computing Machinery, New York (1992). https://doi.org/10.1145/142750.142821
21. John, B.E., Patton, E.W., Gray, W.D., Morrison, D.F.: Tools for predicting the duration and variability of skilled performance without skilled performers. Proc. Hum. Factors Ergon. Soc. Ann. Meeting. 56, 985–989 (2012). https://doi.org/10.1177/1071181312561206
22. Wilkins, S.A.: Examination of pilot benefits from cognitive assistance for single-pilot general aviation operations. In: 2017 IEEE/AIAA 36th Digital Avionics Systems Conference (DASC), pp. 1–9 (2017). https://doi.org/10.1109/DASC.2017.8101987
23. Karousos, N., Katsanos, C., Tselios, N., Xenos, M.: Effortless tool-based evaluation of web form filling tasks using Keystroke Level Model and Fitts Law. In: CHI 2013 Extended Abstracts on Human Factors in Computing Systems, pp. 1851–1856. ACM, New York (2013). https://doi.org/10.1145/2468356.2468688
24. Katsanos, C., Karousos, N., Tselios, N., Xenos, M., Avouris, N.: KLM form analyzer: automated evaluation of web form filling tasks using human performance models. In: Kotzé, P., Marsden, G., Lindgaard, G., Wesson, J., Winckler, M. (eds.) INTERACT 2013. LNCS, vol. 8118, pp. 530–537. Springer, Heidelberg (2013). https://doi.org/10.1007/978-3-642-40480-1_36
25. Fitts, P.M.: The information capacity of the human motor system in controlling the amplitude of movement. J. Exp. Psychol. 47, 381 (1954)
26. Katsanos, C., Xenos, M., Tselios, N., Karousos, N.: Tool-mediated HCI modelling instruction: evidence from three studies. Behav. Inf. Technol. (2020). https://doi.org/10.1080/0144929X. 2020.1790661
27. Katsanos, C., Xenos, M., Tselios, N.: Tool-mediated HCI modeling instruction in a campus-based software quality course. In: Kurosu, M. (ed.) HCI 2018. LNCS, vol. 10901, pp. 114–125. Springer, Cham (2018). https://doi.org/10.1007/978-3-319-91238-7_10
28. Katsanos, C., Tselios, N., Karousos, N., Xenos, M.: Learning web form design by using the KLM Form Analyzer: a case study. In: Proceedings of the 19th Panhellenic Conference on Informatics, pp. 44–49. ACM, New York (2015). https://doi.org/10.1145/2801948.2801990

29. Karousos, N., Tatsis, F., Karousos, D., Katsanos, C., Tselios, N., Xenos, M.: WKLM-FA: a web application for automated human-computer interaction modeling of web form filling tasks. In: Proceedings of the 24th Panhellenic Conference on Informatics, pp. 183–187. ACM, New York (2020). https://doi.org/10.1145/3437120.3437303
30. MacKenzie, I.S.: A note on the information-theoretic basis for Fitts' Law. J. Mot. Behav. **21**, 323–330 (1989). https://doi.org/10.1080/00222895.1989.10735486
31. Luo, L., John, B.E.: Predicting task execution time on handheld devices using the keystroke-level model. In: CHI 2005 Extended Abstracts on Human Factors in Computing Systems, pp. 1605–1608. ACM, New York (2005). https://doi.org/10.1145/1056808.1056977
32. Bi, X., Li, Y., Zhai, S.: FFitts law: modeling finger touch with fitts' law. In: Proceedings of the SIGCHI Conference on Human Factors in Computing Systems, pp. 1363–1372. Association for Computing Machinery, New York (2013). https://doi.org/10.1145/2470654.2466180

Quality in Use -Case Study for Evaluation-

Shin'ichi Fukuzumi[1](✉) and Noriko Wada[2]

[1] Center for AIP, RIKEN, Tokyo, Japan
Shin-ichi.fukuzumi@riken.jp
[2] Meditrina, Yamanashi, Japan

Abstract. As system and software products are widely used in our life, use of them is influence on not only their direct uses but also organizations and society.

However, it is responsibility for society of the manufacturer to be controllable these influences as much as possible. From this, quality is regarded influence on stakeholders by using. The purpose of quality in use is that manufacturers and managers are able to enforce to "use" for improvement of quality by measuring and evaluating.

"Quality in use" is defined as "degree to the system satisfied the stakeholder needs related to use when operator uses the system and software" and stakeholders are classified into four groups, they are "operator", "customer", "responsible organization" and "society".

Analyzing the relationship among them, quality characteristics as quality in use model are extracted. They are "beneficialness", "freedom from risk" and "acceptability". And subcharacteristics for each quality characteristics are also extracted. In the future, we continue to collect any examples and improve the accuracy of the model.

Keywords: Software · Quality · Usability · Risk · Acceptability

1 Introduction

From the end of the last century, importance of usability has been considered in not only ergonomics area but also software engineering area. Quality model in SQuaRE (System and software Quality Requirement and Evaluation) series which are dealt with in ISO/IEC JTC1SC7 defined effectiveness, efficiency, satisfaction freedom from risk and context coverage as elements of "Quality in Use" [1]. Figure 1 shows the Quality in Use model defined in ISO/IEC 25010. In this document, Quality in Use is defined that "Quality in use is the degree to which a product or system can be used by specific users to meet their needs to achieve specific goals with effectiveness, efficiency, freedom from risk and satisfaction in specific contexts of use.

In this figure, three quality characteristics (effectiveness, efficiency, satisfaction) are same as usability elements defined in ergonomics standard ISO 9241–11: 2018 [2]. About freedom from risk and context coverage, though influence on economy and health is described in the definition, there is no concrete contents. Context of use is mainly focused on interaction directly.

© Springer Nature Switzerland AG 2021
M. Kurosu (Ed.): HCII 2021, LNCS 12762, pp. 343–350, 2021.
https://doi.org/10.1007/978-3-030-78462-1_26

As system and software products are widely used in our life, use of them is influence on not only their direct uses but also organizations and society.

However, it is responsibility for society of the manufacturer to be controllable these influences as much as possible.

From this, quality is regarded influence on stakeholders by using. The purpose of quality in use is that manufacturers and managers are able to enforce to "use" for improvement of quality by measuring and evaluating.

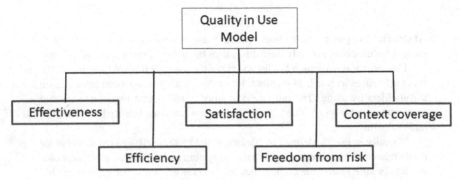

Fig. 1. Quality in Use model defined in ISO/IEC 25010 [1]

2   Issues of Previous Quality in Use Model

As shown in Fig. 1, there are five quality characteristics. However, this model has some issues. They are:

- Effectiveness, efficiency and satisfaction: they are elements for usability (ISO9241–11:2018).
- Freedom from risk: Though this means influence on circumstance, description is not concrete (current definition: degree to which a product or system mitigates the potential risk to economic status, human life, health, or the Environment).
- About "context coverage", because the definition is "degree to which a product or system can be used with effectiveness, efficiency, freedom from risk and satisfaction in both specified contexts of use and in contexts beyond those initially explicitly identified". this is not a subcharacteristics but a prerequisite.

The target stakeholders which are influenced by use of system and software are not only their direct users but also various kinds of stakeholders. Contents of influence (quality characteristics) are different by the difference of objects. From this, the paper classifies these objects into four groups shown below. The rationale is as follows: Firstly, operators and customers are different. Secondly, organization and/or people who has responsible by use of system or product are influenced by use. And there are the other stakeholders around these three kinds of stakeholders. They can be called "society". Four stakeholders and their definitions are shown below [3].

– Operator of system and/or software. Definition is "(1) entity that performs the operation of a system (2) individual or organization that performs the operations of a system (ISO/IEC/IEEE 12207:2017 Systems and software engineering--Software life cycle processes, 3.1.29)" [4].

– Organization which has responsibility for system and/or software management. Definition is "group of people and facilities with an arrangement of responsibilities, authorities and relationships (ISO/IEC/IEEE 12207:2017 Systems and software engineering--Software life cycle processes, 3.1.30)" [4].

– Customer using system and/or software. Definition is "organization or person that receives a product or service (ISO/IEC/IEEE 12207:2017 Systems and software engineering--Software life cycle processes, 3.1.16)" [4].

– Society which exists system and/or software (definition is general).

When "quality in Use" is considered, it is necessary to clarify which group is focused. Even though target system or product are same, influence is different by different of target when considering quality of same product or system by use.

3   Approach to New Quality in Use Model Proposal

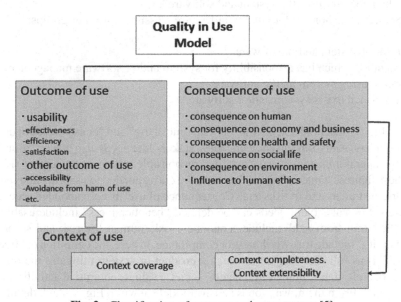

Fig. 2. Classification of outcome and consequence [5].

To modify the previous model and propose new model, we tried two approach. They were "classification of outcome and consequence" and "classification of stakeholders' view". Figure 2 shows former approach and Fig. 3 shows latter approach.

In ISO/IEC25011:2011, Quality models is defined as follows: "The quality of a system is the degree to which the system satisfies the stated and implied needs of its

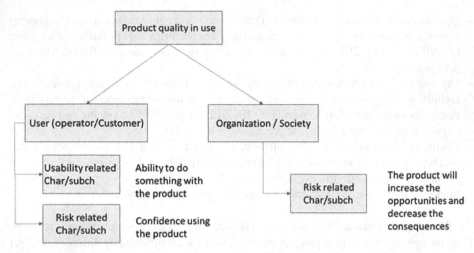

Fig. 3. Classification of stakeholders' view.

various stakeholders, and thus provides value". According to this definition, the definition of "Quality in Use" shall be "Degree to the system satisfied the stakeholder needs related to use when operator uses the system and software".

In Sect. 2, stakeholders for Quality in Use are classified into four groups:

- Operator of system and/or software.
- Organization which has responsibility for system and/or software management.
- Customer using system and/or software.
- Society which exists system and/or software.

From Fig. 2, stakeholder needs maybe "outcome of use" and "consequence of use" for all stakeholders. And from stakeholders' view, stakeholder needs also maybe "usability", "risk" for operator/customer and "risk" for responsible organization/society (Fig. 3). From these figures, "Outcome of use" seems to be corresponded to usability and risks for operators, customers and to risks and "Consequence of use" is corresponded acceptance for society. So, stakeholder needs can be defined "beneficialness" include usability or utility, "freedom from risk" include economical risk, human life risk and so on, and "acceptability" include trustworthiness or compliance. In here, the definition of "freedom form risk" is as follows: "degree to which a product or system mitigates the potential risk to economic status, human life, health, society, values, enterprise activities, or the environment". From them, we propose a new model shown in Fig. 4. And, detail items relationship between quality subcharaceristics in quality in use model and stakeholders are shown in Fig. 5.

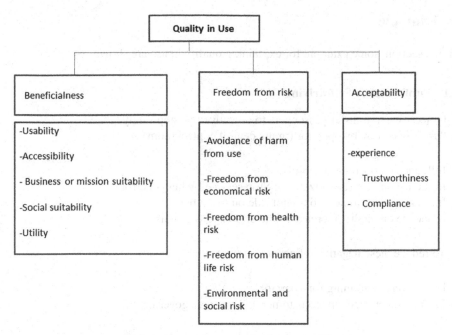

Fig. 4. Proposal new quality in use model

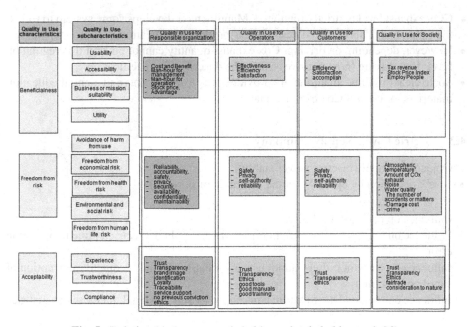

Fig. 5. Relationship between stakeholder and stakeholder needs [6]

4 Examples

In this section, some example for explaining quality in use are shown [6].

4.1 Public Bus by Self-driving

- Objectives: to transfer passengers to objective bus stop safely.
- "use": operation by operator (in the central control room).

- Influence on operator: usability.
- Influence on user (organization): Stop service by human error.
- Influence on customer: could not ride on /off a bus.
- Influence on public: Increase of the effluent gas or noise.

- To reduce these negative influences,

- Education and training for operators.
- Prompt announcement to customer and /or local government.

4.2 COx Exhaust Level by Driving Car

- COx exhaust level is strictly regulated. Manufacturer develops some system to follow the regulation. This could be described as product specification.
- However, depending on driving, Cox exhaust quantity cannot be kept this regulation level. But, driving (how to drive) cannot be described in specification.
- So, to clear this issue, manufacture provide a way to drive, tools and manual/education materials for control Cox exhaust quantity.

4.3 Electric Power Supply Company

- Objectives: supply electric power stably.
- "use": operation by operator (in the central control room).

- Influence on operator: usability.
- Influence on user (organization): interrupted the supply of electricity due to operation error.
- Influence on customer: they cannot use any electric appliances due to interruption of supply of electricity.
- Influence on society: Due to traffic jam caused by stop of signal, increase exhaust gas.

4.4 Online Shopping and Delivery Service

- Objectives: to be able to buy a variety of goods, to be able to sell a variety of goods, to operate physical distribution smoothly.
- "use": (1) operation by buyer.

- Influence on operator: usability, certainly.
- Influence on organization: Stop physical distribution, cannot reach a goods to a buyer, lose operation company credit.
- Influence on customer: could not receive a goods.
- Influence on society: increase of the traffic.

- "use": (2) operation by people who put up for sale.

- Influence on operator: usability, certainly, safety, trustworthy.
- Influence on user (organization): Stop physical distribution, cannot reach a goods to a buyer, lose seller's credit.
- Influence on customer: could not deliver a goods to a buyer.
- Influence on society: increase of the traffic, confusion of a distribution system.

- "use": (3) operation by system operator.

- Influence on operator: usability, certainly, safety, trustworthy.
- Influence on organization: Stop physical distribution, cannot reach a goods to a buyer, lose operation company credit.
- Influence on customer: could not deliver a goods to a buyer, could not put up a goods for sale.
- Influence on society: increase of the traffic, confusion of a distribution system.

5 Conclusion

In this research, we classified stakeholders of quality in use into four groups and proposal a new quality in use model. The usage of this model is shown in below.

- The model and characteristics give manufacturers indices to measure and evaluate quality in use.
- However, these measurement value and/or evaluation value are depended on "use" by users.
- Unlike product quality, it is difficult to describe quality in use as specification.

So, to improve quality in use, important points are as follows:

1. Supporting tools for using system and product.
2. Clear procedure for using system and product.
3. Education and training for using system and product.

In the future, we continue to collect any examples and improve the accuracy of the model.

Acknowledgement. We appreciate Mr. Raúl Martínez to give us Fig. 4 for discussing quality in use.

References

1. ISO/IEC 25010: Systems and software engineering -Systems and software Quality Requirements and Evaluation (SQuaRE)—System and software quality (2011)
2. ISO 9241–11:2018, Ergonomics of human system interaction—Part 11: Usability: concept and definition
3. Fukuzumi, S., Hirasawa, N.: Usability in software development process -Proposal of Society/Stakeholder Centered Design (SCD). In: 1st International Workshop on Experience with SQuaRE series and their Future Direction (IWESQ2019), pp. 18–19 (2019). http://www.sic.shibaura-it.ac.jp/~tsnaka/iwesq_program.html
4. ISO/IEC 12207:2008, Systems and software engineering—Software life cycle processes
5. Fukuzumi, S., Hirasawa, N.: Proposal of Quality in Use in software quality, IPSJ SIG Technical report, Information Processing Society of Japan (2019). (In Japanese)
6. Fukuzumi, S., Wada, N., Hirasawa, N.: Quality in Use -Issues and proposal-, IWESQ2020 (2020). http://ceur-ws.org/Vol-2800/paper-07.pdf

How to Evaluate a Good Conversation?
An Evaluation Framework for Chat Experience
in Smart Home

Xiantao Chen[1](✉), Liang Ma[2], Menghua Jia[1], Yajuan Han[1], Jiaqi Mi[1], and Meng Xu[1]

[1] Baidu AI User Experience Department, Beijing, China
chenxiantao@baidu.com
[2] College of Engineering, Heilongjian Bayi Agricultural University, Daqing, China

Abstract. With the development of artificial intelligence technology, more and more smart devices equipped with smart conversational agents, which can engage in chat or free conversation with human. However, the human-machine chat is still in the early stage of development, and there is a lack of effective methods to evaluate chat experience. In this study we proposed a framework to evaluate chat experience with smart conversational agents in smart home. Firstly, we collected evaluation metrics, and then applied them in the first user test and optimized the metrics and constructed an evaluation system. Finally, we carried out the second user test to validate the evaluation system with SEM. The results indicated that the evaluation system had good reliability, validity and internal consistency, which can be used to evaluate the user experience of smart conversational agents' chat-oriented dialogue.

Keywords: Smart conversational agents · Chat-oriented dialogue · Evaluation metrics · Smart speaker · Smart home

1 Introduction

With the development of artificial intelligence technology, natural language dialogue has been widely used in recent years as a new way of human-computer interaction. People can talk with more and more intelligent devices through natural language. Compared with traditional interaction, natural language dialogue makes full use of human's perception, cognition and understanding, and greatly improves the naturalness and efficiency of human-computer interaction. At present, natural language dialogue has been particularly prevalent among smart home, intelligent vehicle, smart wearable, robot, smart customer service and other fields.

According to the purpose and content of people's conversation with smart devices, natural language dialogue can be divided into two types: task-oriented dialogue and chat-oriented dialogue [1]. The goal of task-based dialogue is to help people finish specific tasks in specific situations, such as booking air tickets and service appointments [2–5]. In the past, many researchers have paid attention to the design of task-based dialogue. Different from task-oriented dialogue, chat-oriented dialogue usually does not specifically

© Springer Nature Switzerland AG 2021
M. Kurosu (Ed.): HCII 2021, LNCS 12762, pp. 351–362, 2021.
https://doi.org/10.1007/978-3-030-78462-1_27

help people complete specific tasks but appease people's emotions or meet the needs of chat and communication [6, 7]. With the development of technologies such as natural language processing (NLP) and knowledge graph (KG), more and more intelligent devices provide chat functions. Many research have shown that chat function can help to increase people's trust and emotional connection to the product, and also can obtain more user preference information for personalized recommendation [8–10]. Take smart home products as an example, such as Google Home, Amazon Echo, Xiaomi Xiaoai, Xiaodu smart speaker all provide chat functions. According to a IDC (International Data Corporation) report, the sales volume for smart speakers in China reached 36.76 million units in 2020.

Evaluating and optimizing natural language dialogue experience between people and smart devices is currently a research focus in the field of HCI. For the task-oriented dialogue experience evaluation, it usually focuses on the user's task completion and the common evaluation indicators include task success rate, efficiency and usefulness [11–13]. As the purpose of chat-oriented dialogue is to conduct open chat and communication, which is different from the task-oriented dialogue, many indictors of task-oriented dialogue are not suitable for the evaluation of chat-oriented dialogue. Many research had been carried out to evaluate chat-oriented dialogue, Zhou [14] proposed the conversation-turns per session (CPS) as a key indicator to evaluate Microsoft Xiaoice. Although CPS can evaluate user engagement of the conversation, CPS is not suitable to evaluate the entire experience of the user's dialogue with smart devices. Bayan [15] proposed a Loebner Prize Competition method to evaluate chat system, the performance of different chat systems was compared through ranking method. For example, many experts were invited to have 10–15 min chat with different chat systems and then ranked their naturalness respectively. In essence, Loebner Prize Competition is a kind of Turing test and its accuracy and reliability have been questioned, moreover it is not suitable for the evaluation of single chat system. Zhou [6] proposed an approach for investigating non-goal oriented dialogue system, each turn dialogue was evaluated using the Likert 5-point scale from "very uninterested" to "very interested". Many other approach evaluated whether chat systems were appropriate, coherent or logical [16–19], for example Gandhe [18] designed various chat scenarios and invited users to evaluate whether the responses of different inputs were appropriate (5-point scale from "very inappropriate" to "very appropriate"). Above evaluation approach have many deficiencies in systematically and scientifically evaluating chat system experience. On the one hand, most approach focus on the single turn chat evaluation and do not consider the overall interaction process. On the other hand, many evaluation methods themselves lack quantitative verification and standardization. As a result, the evaluation system can not be popularized and compared between different chat systems.

Aimed at evaluating chat experience and building an evaluation system, we focused on the smart home scenario and explored the evaluation method for chat experience of smart speakers. In this study, we combined the qualitative and quantitative methods. First, we collected the evaluation metrics by qualitative methods, and then optimized and verified the evaluation system by quantitative methods. The evaluation system can be used to compare different chat-oriented systems and discover usability issues.

2   Method, Process and Result

Our research was divided into three phases, as shown in Fig. 1. Firstly, we collected qualitatively the evaluation metrics of chat conversations and ensured them be comprehensive and easy to understand. Secondly, we carried out the first user test to apply the metrics in the test and constructed the evaluation system through quantitative analysis. Finally, we validated the framework of the evaluation system and ensured the evaluation system was reliable and scientific. The specific process of each phase will be described in detail in the following sessions.

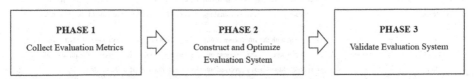

Fig. 1. Research process of chat-oriented dialogue evaluation system.

2.1   Collection of Evaluation Metrics

In order to ensure the metrics were comprehensive and easy to understand, the collection process undergone three steps.

Step 1: By reviewing the existing evaluation dimensions of task-oriented dialogue and chat-oriented dialogue, we obtained some metrics such as Grace's "cooperative principle" [20] and Leech's "politeness principle" [21]. Then a brainstorming was carried out, ten users (five males and five females, age between 20–40 years old) with experience in chatting with smart speakers were involved to speak out factors that influence chat experience during the past usage. A total of 45 metrics was collected at this stage.

Step 2: A total of thirteen practitioners in smart conversational agent's industry were invited to evaluate the metrics in terms of their importance and comprehensibility respectively, including UX researchers, product managers (PM) and designers. Through this step, we deleted the unimportant indicators that were not suitable to evaluate the chat experience, finally 24 indicators were remained.

Step 3: We invited ten smart speaker users (five males and five females, age between 20–40 years old) to evaluate the comprehensibility of the metrics and their descriptions, and then we modified or deleted metrics indicators that were either unclear, difficult to understand or ambiguous. Finally, a chat experience evaluation metrics consisting of 20 indicators was formed, as shown in Table 1.

Table 1. 20 Evaluation metrics collected in phase 1.

Metric	Description
Understand what I say	Smart Conversational Agents can understand what I say
Have a natural voice	The tone of voice and punctuation of smart conversational agents are natural, not like mechanical voice
Speak at a moderate speed	Smart Conversational Agents speak at moderate speed
Have a pleasant voice	The voice of smart conversational agents is pleasant
Inform its state timely and effectively	Be able to let me know in time the current state of the smart conversational agent (e.g. whether it is listening to me)
Be not inconsistent	When chatting with the smart conversational agents, there is no inconsistency
Be colloquial expression	Smart conversational agents speak naturally, which conforms to daily language and habits
Be diverse expression	The response of smart conversational agents is diverse, and the expression of the same meaning is changeable
Be easy to understand	When chatting with the smart conversational agents, it is easy to understand the dialogue contents
Have accurate and believable content	When it comes to facts, the response of the smart conversational agents is accurate and believable
Be Relevant	The response of the smart conversational agents is related to the current topic
Have rich and diverse content	The smart conversational agents can give me rich and diverse information about this topic
Have valuable content	The response of the smart conversational agents is valuable
Understand context	The smart conversational agents can connect with the context for continuous conversation
Be Interactive	The response of the smart conversational agents is interactive, to maintain multi-turn conversation
Initiate a new topic appropriately	The smart conversational agents can actively initiate new topics at appropriate time to attract me to continue chatting
Be friendly	Smart conversational agents speak in a kindly and friendly manner
Be Humorous	The smart conversational agent is humorous and interesting
Have adorable persona	I like the personality traits of the smart conversational agents
Situation awareness	Smart conversational agents can pay attention to the current time, occasion, my preferences, etc

2.2 Construction and Optimization of Evaluation System

In order to optimize the structure of the evaluation metrics collected, we conducted the first chat experience test to collect user's evaluation data. In total, five smart conversational agents in Chinese market were evaluated in the tests, they were Baidu NLP (A), Trio (B), Deep Brain (C), Microsoft Xiaoice (D) and Xiaomi Xiaoai (E). All above agents support chat-oriented dialogue, each of them was different in both content of speech and voice.

Subjects. A total of thirty-eight subjects (eighteen males and twenty females, age between 20–40 years old) participated the test. All participants had experience in using smart speaker's chat system. Fifteen subjects usually chatted more than 3 times a week and twenty-three subjects chatted 1 to 3 times a week.

Procedure. Subjects were asked to chat with smart conversational agents A, B, C, D and E in random order. Four types of chat topics in smart home were joking, seeking suggestions, talking about specific topics and communicating emotions, as shown in Table 2. Every topic included 5–7 different queries, and subjects could choose three queries among them to talk with the smart speakers separately.

When the participants finished the four topics with each smart conversational agent, they evaluated the chat experience of the smart conversational agents in terms of the

Table 2. Chat topics and query in user test.

Chat topics	Context description	Query
Joking	You just bought the smart conversational agent and learned that it can chat. You want to know it better and crack a joke	What's your age?
		What's your gender?
		What's your IQ?
		What star sign are you
		What are your hobbies?
		Can you lie?
		Can you speak English?
		How stupid you are?
Seeking good ideas	Choosing gifts or losing sleep at night makes you upset. You want to ask the smart conversational agent for some good ideas	What gifts do you recommend for my lover's birthday/on Valentine's Day?
		What if I can't sleep?
Talking about a topic	You are bored at home alone and want to talk with the smart conversational agent	Do you like Mi Yang?
		Do you like the TV play such as XXX?
		Do you like Ronaldo?
		Let's talk about life
		What do you think of our human beings?
Venting emotions	Scenario 1: Recently, you feel pressure from work or life and talk to the smart conversational agent for relaxation	I'm tired
		I don't want to go to work
		I don't want to get married
	Scenario 2: Recently, you have a quarrel with your lover and you are in the cold war. You want to talk to the smart conversational agent for good ideas	I have a quarrel with my lover

20 metrics, using a 10-point Likert scale, from "strongly disagree" to "strongly agree". Then they filled the Kano questionnaire to evaluate the importance of the metrics.

Evaluation Metrics Optimization

The score of each user participants of each smart conversational agent was regarded as a sample data. The total sample size was 168. Then we used the Kano model, correlation analysis and qualitative interview data to optimize the metrics. The analysis process included the following steps:

1. Deleted the indifferent attributes in Kano model, including "Be easy to understand", "Speak at a moderate speed", "Inform its state timely and effectively".
2. Deleted or merge the highly relevant metrics, the correlation coefficient between "Be interactive" and "Initiate a new topic appropriately", "Be interactive" and "Understand context", "Initiate a new topic appropriately" and "Be interactive" are 0.90, 0.83 and 0.82 respectively. From user feedback in qualitative interviews, subjects regarded "Understand context" as an independent metric, so it was retained in the evaluation metrics. And subjects thought that "Be interactive" is analogous to "Initiate a new topic appropriately", so we merge the two metrics as "Initiate a new topic appropriately"
3. Optimized severe multiple collinearity metrics. Multiple collinearity diagnosis results displayed that the tolerance of "Be relevant" is 0.178 (<0.2), which indicated the metric could be largely replaced by other metrics. Combine findings from

user interviews, we found that subjects' perception of "Understand what I say" was mainly related with whether the response was relevant. Therefore, we merged "Understand what I say" and "Be relevant" into "Understand what I say and give relevant response".

4. Modified the description of several indicators from the user feedbacks. As current technology is difficult to accurately identify the situational dialogues such as "emotional recognition", "mood recognition" and "intimacy recognition". The subjects' perception of situational awareness was mainly related with "whether the chat dialogue can comfort or inspire them when they felt bad emotional state or frustrated". Therefore, the metric of "Situational awareness" was modified to "Be conciliatory and encouraging".

The final optimized evaluation metrics are shown in Table 3, which included 15 indicators.

Table 3. Optimized evaluation metrics.

Metric	Description
Understand what I say and give relevant response	When chatting, the smart conversational agents understands what I say and do not give an irrelevant respond
Have a natural voice	The tone of voice and punctuation of smart conversational agents are natural, not like mechanical voice
Have a pleasant voice	The voice of smart conversational agents is pleasant
Be not inconsistent	When chatting with the smart conversational agents, there is no inconsistency
Be colloquial expression	The smart conversational agents speak naturally, which conforms to daily language and habits
Be diverse expression	The response of smart conversational agents is diverse, and the expression of the same meaning is changeable
Have accurate and believable content	When it comes to facts, the response of the smart conversational agents is accurate and believable
Have rich and diverse content	The smart conversational agents can give me rich and diverse information about this topic
Have valuable content	The response of the smart conversational agents is valuable
Understand context	The smart conversational agents can connect with the context for continuous conversation
Initiate a new topic appropriately	The smart conversational agents can actively initiate new topics at appropriate time to attract me to continue chatting
Be friendly	The smart conversational agents speak in a kindly and friendly manner
Be humorous	The smart conversational agents are humorous and interesting
Have adorable persona	I like the personality traits of the smart conversational agents
Be conciliatory and encouraging	The smart conversational agents can comfort or inspire me in an appropriate manner

Evaluation Metrics Optimization

The Cronbach's alpha coefficient was 0.954 (>0.8), which indicated that the reliability of the data was good. Moreover, the KMO value was 0.928 (>0.9) and the Bartlett spherical test result was significant, indicating that the data had good structural validity and was suitable for exploratory factor analysis.

We used the maximum variance method to rotate the factors and extract the factors whose eigenvalue was greater than 1. Finally, two factors were extracted, and the cumulative variance contribution rate was 68.0%, as shown in Table 4.

Table 4. Total variance explained.

Factors	Initial eigenvalues	% of variance	Cumulative %
1	8.837	58.916	58.916
2	1.369	9.126	68.043

As the result shown in Table 5, there were five metrics: "Be diverse expression", "Have adorable persona", "Be Humorous", "Be colloquial expression" and "Have accurate and believable content", that had high weight on both two factors. For the remaining metrics, Factor 1 was mainly related to the quality of chat content and multi-turn conversations, and Factor 2 was mainly about voice and expressions other than chat content. Among the 5 metrics with high weight on both factors, "Have accurate and believable content" laid more emphasis on the quality of chat content, so it was classified into Factor 1, while the metrics of "Be diverse expression", "Have adorable persona", "Be Humorous", "Be colloquial expression" were less related to Factor 1, instead they belonged to the form of expression other than chat content, so they were classified into Factor 2. In addition, as "Situation awareness" was modified to "Be conciliatory and encouraging", it was also classified into Factor 2.

As each factor involved a large number of metrics, and some of them were differences in the evaluation dimension. On the basis of exploratory factors analysis, we further split factor 1 into "Continuous conversation" and "Content quality", and split factor 2 into "Expression" and "Voice". Finally, we obtained four factors (as shown in Fig. 2), and then we further verified the structure of evaluation metrics system.

2.3 Validation of the Evaluation System

In order to further validate above evaluation metrics system, we conducted the second user test and applied the optimized metrics in Xiaodu smart speaker test. Based on user test data, we used structural equation model (SEM) to validate the evaluation metrics system.

Subjects. A total of 162 subjects (82 males and 80 females, aged between 20 and 40 years old) participated the test. All participants were experienced users of smart conversational agents' chat function.

Procedure. In this test, we choose Xiaodu smart speaker as the evaluation object, which was embedded with Baidu NLP (A). Except for the optimized evaluation metrics (Table 3), the procedure and user tasks were consistent with the first user test.

Table 5. Exploratory factor analysis results.

Metric	Factor 1	Factor 2
Initiate a new topic appropriately	0.84	
Understand context	0.83	
Have valuable content	0.82	
Have rich and diverse content	0.78	
Be not inconsistent	0.78	
Understand what I say and give relevant response	0.72	
Be diverse expression	0.64	0.44
Situation awareness	0.64	
Have adorable persona	0.55	0.52
Have pleasant voice		0.86
Have natural voice		0.82
Be Humorous	0.50	0.74
Be friendly		0.74
Be colloquial expression	0.56	0.67
Have accurate and believable content	0.47	0.58

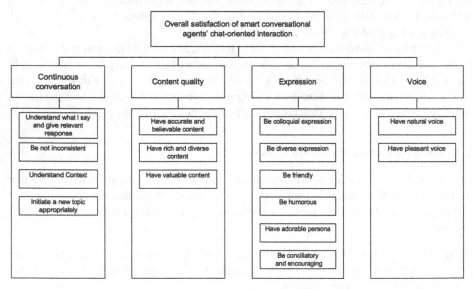

Fig. 2. The structure of evaluation metrics system.

Analysis and Result. We removed 5 invalid samples and remained 157 valid samples. Based on the test data, we used the structural equation model by AMOS23 to verify the fit indices of the evaluation system.

Free Parameters Estimation and Fit Indices Test of SEM

The covariance coefficients of the secondary metrics were all more than 0.5, so there was a moderate-high correlation between the metrics. Therefore, we could establish a second-order CFA model. The final evaluation system of smart conversational agents' chat-oriented dialogue is shown in Fig. 3.

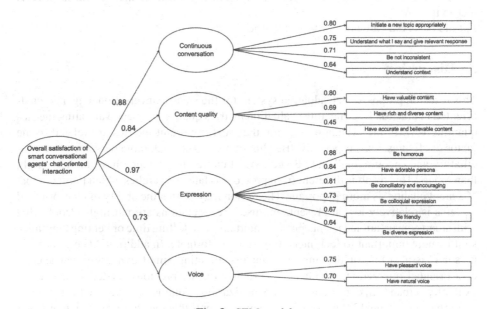

Fig. 3. SEM model.

Then we tested the fit indices of SEM, as shown in Table 6. The SEM model had a good fit. Therefore, we could accept the hypothetical evaluation system obtained in the previous stage.

Table 6. Fit Indices of SEM.

X^2/df	RMSEA	GFI	AGFI	CFI	NFI	TLI	PGFI	PNFI
0.99	0.00	0.938	0.906	1.00	0.94	1.00	0.62	0.71

Criterion Validity of SEM

We used correlation analysis to verify the consistency between manual scoring and machine scoring. The correlation coefficient was 0.85 ($p < 0.05$), which reached a very high correlation level (correlation coefficient > 0.8), indicating that the model had good criterion validity.

The formula for calculating the machine scoring S_X was as follows:

$$S_X = \frac{\sum_{i=1}^{M} \sum_{j=1}^{N} \left(a_i^2 * b_{ij}^2 * F_{ij} \right)}{W_{sum}}, \quad W_{sum} = \sum_{i=1}^{M} \sum_{j=1}^{N} \left(a_i^2 * b_{ij}^2 \right) \ (M = 4, \ N \in \{2, 3, 4, 6\})$$

a_i: the standardized regression weights between first-level metric and second-level metric in SEM.

b_{ij}: the standardized regression weights between second-level metric and third-level metric in SEM.

F_{ij}: the observed value of third-level metric.

3 Discussion

This research proposed an evaluation system for the smart conversational agents' chat-oriented interaction by collecting evaluation metrics qualitatively and validating metrics quantitatively. In the evaluation system, the most important metrics are related to the factor of "Expression", especially "Be Humorous", "Have adorable persona", "Be conciliatory and encouraging" and "Be colloquial expression", which have higher weight than others. This result is different from previous related researches which point out that "Content quality" is more important. The reason may be that the ability of chat-oriented systems is relatively low at present, and users' expectations are not high. People chat with smart conversational agents just for entertainment, killing time or venting emotions, so it is more important to feel interesting and comfortable. In addition, "Have adorable persona" is also one of the important factors affecting smart conversational agents' chat-oriented interaction, which is consistent with the previous related research, for example, Serban [22] considered the personalization of dialogue system to be an important topic, and Zhang [23] proved through experiments that the chat-oriented interaction with personalized traits will make the users experience better.

Although this research built an evaluation system with high reliability and validity, which can be applied to measure the user experience of smart conversational agents' chat-oriented interaction, there are still some limitations. Firstly, the evaluation system focuses on the chat function built in smart conversational agents, which may not apply to other chat-oriented systems, such as chat applications in mobile phone, which involve text input and output, while voice is not necessary. Secondly, the participants in this study are all 20–40 years old. Their expectations and behaviour may be different with other years old people. So, the evaluation system may not be extended to other groups. Thirdly, different brands may have different weight coefficients in SEM, because of their different basic capabilities. So, it is necessary to test the criterion validity of SEM when applying it to measure other brands' user experience. If the criterion validity is not good, the weight coefficients of the evaluation system should be recalculated.

As the chat function of smart conversational agents is still in the early stage, products and user expectation will change faster. Therefore, the weight coefficients of the evaluation system may also change. In the future, we will continue to revise the evaluation system. In addition, groups aged under 20 and over 40 are also our potential users, so we will test the validity extension for these groups in the future.

4 Conclusion

This study proposed an evaluation method for smart conversational agents' chat experience. Firstly, we collected evaluation metrics through desk study, brainstorming and expert evaluation to ensure that the metrics are comprehensive, meaningful and easy to understand. Secondly, we applied the evaluation metrics into user testing and optimized the metrics by Kano model, correlation analysis, multiple collinearity diagnosis. And then we constructed the evaluation system by exploratory factor analysis. Finally, we applied the optimized evaluation metrics into user testing again and used structural equation model to verify the evaluation system. The final evaluation system consists of 4 factors and 15 metrics. The 4 factors are as "Continuous conversation", "Content quality", "Expression" and "Voice". The system has good reliability, validity and internal consistency, which indicates that the evaluation system can be used to evaluate the user experience of smart conversational agents' chat-oriented interaction.

References

1. Banchs, E., Li, H.: IRIS: a chat-oriented dialogue system based on the vector space model. In: Proceedings of the ACL 2012 System Demonstrations, pp. 37–42 (2012)
2. Busemann, S., Declerck, T., Diagne, A., Dini, L., Klein, J., Schmeier, S.: Natural language dialogue service for appointment scheduling agents. In: Proceedings of the 5th Conference on Applied NLP, pp. 25–32 (1997)
3. Seneff, S., Polifroni, J.: Dialogue management in the Mercury flight reservation system. In: Proceedings of the ANLP-NAACL 2000 Workshop on Conversational Systems, pp. 11–16 (2000)
4. Stallard, D.: Talk'n'travel: a conversational system for air travel planning. In: Proceedings of the 6th Conference on Applied NLP, pp. 68–75 (2000)
5. Bordes, A., Boureau, Y.-L.,Weston, J.: Learning end-to-end goal-oriented dialog. In: Proceedings of ICLR (2017)
6. Yu, Z., Papangelis, A., Rudnicky, A.: Ticktock: a non-goal-oriented multimodal dialog system with engagement awareness. In: 2015 AAAI Spring Symposium Series, pp. 108–111 (2015)
7. Yu, Z., Xu, Z., Black, A.W., Rudnicky, A.I.: Strategy and policy learning for non-task-oriented conversational systems. In: Proceedings of the SIGDIAL 2016 Conference, pp. 404–412 (2016)
8. Bickmore, T., Cassell, J.: Relational agents: a model and implementation of building user trust. In:Proceedings of the SIGCHI Conference on Human Factors in Computing Systems, pp. 396–403 (2001)
9. Wilcock, G., Jokinen, K.: WikiTalk human-robot interactions. In: Proceedings of the 15th ACM on International Conference on Multimodal Interaction, pp. 73–74 (2013)
10. Bang, J., Noh, H., Kim, Y., Lee, G.G.: Example-based chat-oriented dialogue system with personalized long-term memory. In: 2015 International Conference on Big Data and Smart Computing (BIGCOMP), pp. 238–243 (2015)
11. Deriu, J., et al.: Survey on evaluation methods for dialogue systems. Artif. Intell. Rev. **54**(1), 755–810 (2020). https://doi.org/10.1007/s10462-020-09866-x

12. Hassenzahl, M., et al.: The Thing and I: understanding the relationship between user and product. In: Blythe, M.A., Overbeeke, K., Monk, A.F., Wright, P.C. (eds.) Funology. HCIS, pp. 31–42. Springer, Cham (2004). https://doi.org/10.1007/1-4020-2967-5_4

13. Radziwill, N.M., Benton, M.C.: Evaluating Quality of Chatbots and Intelligent Conversational Agents. Computing Research Repository (CoRR), pp. 1–21 (2017)

14. Zhou, L., Gao, J., Li, D., Shum, H.-Y.: The design and implementation of xiaoice, an empathetic social chatbot. Comput. Linguist. **46**(1), 53–93 (2020)

15. Shawar, B.A., Atwell, E.: Different measurements metrics to evaluate a chatbot system. In: Bridging the Gap: Academic and Industrial Research in Dialog Technologies Workshop Proceedings, pp. 89–96 (2007)

16. Papineni, K., Roukos, S., Ward, T., Henderson, J., Reeder, F.: Corpus-based comprehensive and diagnostic MT evaluation: initial Arabic, Chinese, French, and Spanish results. In: Proceedings of the Second International Conference on Human Language Technology Research, pp. 132–137 (2002)

17. Liu, C.W., Lowe, R., Serban, I.V., Noseworthy, M., Charlin, L., Pineau, J.: How not to evaluate your dialogue system: an empirical study of unsupervised evaluation metrics for dialogue response generation. In: EMNLP, Association for Computational Linguistics, pp. 2122–2132 (2016)

18. Gandhe, S., Traum, D.R.: Creating spoken dialogue characters from corpora without annotations. In: INTERSPEECH, pp. 2201–2204 (2007)

19. Dubuisson Duplessis, G., Letard, V., Ligozat, A.L., Rosset, S.: Purely corpus-based automatic conversation authoring. In: Proceedings of the Tenth International Conference on Language Resources and Evaluation (LREC 2016), pp. 2728–2735 (2016)

20. Grice, P.: Logic and conversation. In: Cole, P., Morgan, J. (eds.) Syntax and Semantics 3: Speech Acts, pp. 41–58. Academic Press, New York (1975)

21. Leech, G.N.: Principles of Pragmatics. Longman, London (1983)

22. Serban, I.V., Lowe, R., Henderson, P., Charlin, L., Pineau, J.: A survey of available corpora for building data-driven dialogue systems. Comput. Sci. **33**(16), 6078–6093 (2015)

23. Zhang, S., Dinan, E., Urbanek, J., Szlam, A., Kiela, D., Weston, J.: Personalizing dialogue agents: I have a dog, do you have pets too? In: Proceedings of the 56th Annual Meeting of the Association for Computational Linguistics, pp. 2204–2213 (2018)

Collaborative Heuristic Inspection: Evaluator Experiences and Organization of Work

Yavuz Inal[1]([⊠]) [iD], Jo D. Wake[2] [iD], and Frode Guribye[1] [iD]

[1] Department of Information Science and Media Studies, Faculty of Social Sciences, University of Bergen, Bergen, Norway
yavuz.inal@uib.no
[2] NORCE Norwegian Research Centre, Bergen, Norway

Abstract. Usability inspection is a key part of professional practice in user experience, and continued research into inspection practices is essential to move the field forward. While usability inspections are traditionally portrayed as individual work, a number of studies have established that group-based inspections can yield better results. As many collaborative inspection studies have focused on outcomes, there is a need to learn more about how collaborative usability inspections are experienced by evaluators, and how these collaborative efforts can be organized. To study this process, we had 23 evaluators self-organize in unmoderated groups to conduct a usability inspection of a new mHealth web service. The evaluators valued the group work because it presented them with opportunities to learn from others. Additionally, a workflow that starts with individual evaluations and moves into group discussions to validate identified problems and generate more issues is a fruitful way of organizing a collaborative heuristic inspection process.

Keywords: Usability · Usability evaluation · Collaborative heuristic inspection · Evaluator experience

1 Introduction

Usability inspections are conducted to improve the usability of software and services, and constitute a key part of professional practice in user experience. The motivation for performing inspections is to identify usability problems, which usually result in additional requirements and interface design updates. Inspection is traditionally portrayed as a solitary process and as individual work. Evaluators work alone when testing usability of a system and follow a guideline to identify usability problems. However, previous studies show that evaluators report different outcomes when evaluating the same application while following the same guidelines [1, 9, 12].

The average agreement between two evaluators who have appraised the same system using the same method varies between 5% and 65% [8]. This results from the subjective nature of the usability evaluation process, where each evaluator analyzes a system to find the flaws and interprets the outcomes using their judgments [8]. Furthermore, the lack of a clear evaluation process, lack of domain knowledge of evaluators, and lack

© Springer Nature Switzerland AG 2021
M. Kurosu (Ed.): HCII 2021, LNCS 12762, pp. 363–372, 2021.
https://doi.org/10.1007/978-3-030-78462-1_28

of powerful evidence to decide whether a usability issue exists cause an increase in variations between evaluators [9]. In heuristic usability testing, there is also a high risk of overlooking critical usability issues, whilst simultaneously identifying large numbers of false positives [2].

Variation between evaluators affects the reliability and validity of the evaluation outcomes [10]. Usability problems identified by the involvement of different evaluation parties in the process needs to be aggregated from multiple evaluators [13] and consolidated [14] in order to enhance reliability and validity in the group, and thereby the quality of the evaluation. Here, a collaborative process facilitates the usability testing in which users, experts or moderators work together to discuss identified problems.

Collaborative evaluation, an alternative method that has been receiving increased attention recently [4, 18], can address the challenges of individual work and improve the quality of evaluation outcomes. Group discussions help improve the productivity of evaluators [5, 7, 18], minimize differences in the identified issues generated by different evaluators [6], normalize highly rated severity of problems, and prioritize them accordingly [9]. Lowry and colleagues [15, 16] compared two modes of heuristic usability evaluation. Standard, individual heuristic usability evaluation was compared with computer-supported collaborative heuristic evaluation, and they found two major differences between the modes: First, the process became more efficient, as evaluators could see the results of others, and did not have to duplicate their work. Second, the evaluators developed an "implicit agreement on how to categorize [the usability issues]" [15, p. 2210].

Many of these studies have focused on evaluation outcomes [e.g., 10, 11]; however, there is a need to learn more about how collaborative usability inspection is experienced by evaluators and how they can organize the work in practice. The focus of our study was, therefore, on the evaluator experience and their organization of evaluation work. Given the advantages of collaborative inspection, it is a pertinent research challenge to build knowledge about how to support, facilitate and scaffold collaborative processes.

For this study, we orchestrated a group-based, collaborative, unmoderated heuristic inspection process. The research goal was to observe how the evaluators organized their work and understand their experiences in the collaborative process. We labelled our method "collaborative heuristic inspection", in which evaluators worked together in groups to identify usability problems and reported the outcomes. Aspects of the collaborative process deemed consequential to the evaluation outcomes include division of labor, the perceived value of group work, challenges, resolutions of discrepancies, and the lessons learned. The following research questions guided the study;

- How did the evaluators organize the work in groups?
- What did the evaluators value working in a group when performing the usability evaluation?
- What challenges did the evaluators encounter in the group work?
- How did the evaluators resolve disagreements between the group members?
- What did the evaluators learn about usability evaluation from the group work?

2 Methods

The evaluation was performed by 23 Master's students in information science, with the goal of the identification and analysis of usability problems in an online cognitive remediation program for patients in remission from depression, called RestDep. The student evaluators were enrolled in a master-level human-computer interaction course. They had previous experience in inspection methods and were provided with a training exercise in heuristic evaluation before taking part in the evaluation. The heuristic scale created by Nielsen [17] was used for usability testing. As recommended by Nielsen, the evaluators categorized the usability problems according to their severity as cosmetic, minor, major, and catastrophic.

The evaluators formed six groups, and evaluation work lasted two weeks. The evaluators were free to choose how to organize their work, and each group evaluated the program independently. All the groups tested both desktop and mobile versions of the program and were instructed to use the same web browser (Google Chrome) to ensure a similar experience of the RestDep interface. RestDep was developed using responsive design; thus, the mobile version was very similar to the desktop version. Following the evaluation, the evaluators composed a reflection document including open-ended questions about their experience and reflections on the collaborative evaluation process. These reflection documents and evaluation reports were subsequently analyzed for patterns and themes by the researchers. Thematic analysis [3] was employed to interpret the qualitative data.

3 Results

3.1 Self-organizing Process of the Groups

The self-organizing process in the groups was undertaken in the five sequential steps of (1) division of labor, (2) identification, (3) aggregation, (4) consolidation, and (5) finalization. Figure 1 illustrates the self-organizing process for all the groups.

Division of labor describes how the usability evaluation tasks were distributed between group members. Four groups (G1, 3, 4 and 5) split into two sub-groups, in which each sub-group was responsible for either the mobile or desktop version of the program (platform-based division of labor). The sub-groups then presented their findings to the other half to obtain feedback and ensure there was an agreement in the discussions in which they engaged through the process. The group-based division of labor was applied by only one group (G2), in which the group members took part in the evaluation process, attended a series of meetings, and performed the evaluation together. The final group (G6) evaluated the program individually (person-based division of labor). After each group member finished the evaluation of each version, they jointly reviewed the results. Although the evaluators in this group tested the program alone, they did organize several meetings to discuss the identified problems throughout the process.

Identification means finding the usability problems in the evaluated program. The majority of those who evaluated the mobile version of the program adjusted the screen display to resemble a mobile format. When they found a problem, they created and recorded the problem description. Some groups included problem fixes and notes for later discussions. The groups in which the evaluators worked individually (G6, n = 37) or split into sub-groups (G1,3,4,5, mean = 21.5) reported more usability problems than those where all group members worked together to identify the problems during the evaluation process (G2, n = 18).

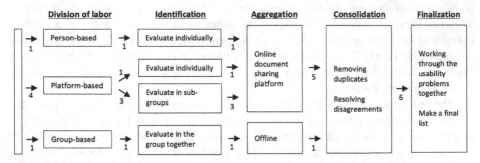

Fig. 1. Self-organizing process of the groups.

Aggregation pertains to gathering feedback during the process and achieving a raw list of usability problems. The only group that performed the evaluation together used an offline word document and recorded all identified problems in a single file. Other groups used an online document sharing platform to record their findings, access the inputs of others and collaborate simultaneously. It was also possible to view the duplicates there.

Consolidation refers to discussing the aggregated data in the group, removing duplicates, and resolving disagreements. There were generally few disagreements in the groups; yet, they reported the consolidation process to be essential when they disagreed about the problem definition. Consolidation was performed by categorizing problems encountered by the group members and noted after each reported issue was agreed upon. Each group discussed the usability problems together to decide where to put them on the heuristic scale and how to phrase it. Thus, all group members came to an agreement on the problems before they were recorded in the heuristic evaluation table.

In *finalization*, the groups completed the evaluation process. Each group discussed the usability problems together, made a final list of the identified problems, and completed the evaluation report.

3.2   Value of Group Work in Collaborative Heuristic Inspection

Affording Opportunities to Learn from Peers. The value of group work in the collaborative inspection process was appreciated by many. *"It is nice to have someone to bounce your ideas off. You also get more input, so you might see something that you wouldn't have seen doing the task alone."* (G2P2) The discussions encouraged the group members to put more effort into the process and learn about the problems. *"The constructive feedback from the group helped us to improve by feeling valued and motivated to keep up the good work". (G6P1)* This was an advantage since each group member might have a different perspective on the system, and aggregating the ideas helped in perceiving the system from new angles.

Group discussions were also considered as valuable to increase the evaluation accuracy, as well as learning from other group members during the process. *"I learned the most from the group meetings through the discussions we had while going through all the comments in the form."* *(G6P2)* Group work allowed the evaluators to share ideas and knowledge, and to learn from each other. *"Some group members are more creative when it comes to testing systems, some members are more precise and that benefits us all in the group."* *(G3P2)* Even though some performed the evaluation independently, they gathered to discuss the discrepancies, consolidate aggregated problems, and reach an agreement before completing the evaluation process.

Performing a More Thorough Evaluation in a Short Time. Collaborative inspection was seen as time-saving, allowing immediate discussions of discovered problems and help in identifying usability problems with higher precision compared to an independent evaluation. *"It can help find problems one person might overlook when doing it alone; it also provides several layers of evaluation due to several people assessing the same subject".* *(G6P3)* Each member of the group found different problems, which created a more substantial list in a short time.

Achieving More Precise, Accurate and Valid Outcomes. Working in a group helped confirm the validity and accuracy of decisions made by individual members independently. They were able to validate their decisions when categorizing the problems each group member had found. It was also deemed helpful to obtain a second opinion on unsure categorization and ratings. *"Having other people seeing the same issues as me and confirming its validity give more credibility to the usability evaluation".* *(G4P1).*

Reporting Quality Evaluation Reports. The evaluators were able to minimize the risk of describing something that only one group member, who identified the problem, could understand. *"Working together helps when writing a description of the problems. It can sometimes be challenging to describe the problems accurately and in a way that readers can understand it."* *(G5P3).*

3.3   Challenges of Working in a Group in Collaborative Heuristic Inspection

Identifying Usability Problems. The group members sometimes had different understandings of what was to be considered a problem. Some group members felt that something was obvious while others did not think it was that obvious and therefore stated problems that the others did not.

Categorizing Usability Problems. The evaluators found it challenging to categorize the problems as many of them could fit in more than one category. *"Some of the categories were somewhat overlapping, at least in the sense of how the group members understood the heuristics, which made it hard to determine the category that would be most suitable."* *(G3P3)* There were disagreements between group members in terms of relating the same usability problems to one of the heuristic items. *"It was difficult at times to know which heuristic item an identified usability problem should fall under as some overlapped several different heuristic items. We spent more time discussing these items".* *(G2P1).*

Rating Severity of Problems. There were discussions on the severity of the identified usability problems. *"Deciding whether the usability problems were minor or major was also hard due to the group members' different perceptions of the system." (G3P3)* They spent a considerable amount of time discussing how to rate the severity of each usability problem. *"But the more we worked together on the evaluation, the easier the rating became." (G3P1).*

Aggregating Sub-groups' Findings. The evaluators who split their groups into sub-groups reported that it was challenging to aggregate the sub-groups' findings during the consolidation process. Even though most of the findings were overlapping, they disagreed on how to describe, categorize and rate severity.

3.4 Resolution of Discrepancies Between Group Members

The evaluators were eager to reach an agreement whenever a discussion occurred to complete the evaluation in a timely fashion. *"The disagreements were discussed in an orderly manner, where we went back and forth explaining our point of view." (G6P4)* In order to resolve discrepancies, each group listened to the opinions of others, discussed, and found a compromise, and arrived at a shared conclusion or a majority decision. *"If we disagreed on the importance of a problem, we simply included it and let the person who came up with the problem put it in the list." (G1P2)* Discrepancies were resolved through the final discussions, where the group members were open to hearing other members' thoughts on each identified problem. *"There were no quarrels, only small disagreements that were valued for bringing insight from differences in opinions." (G6P3).*

3.5 Lessons Learned from the Collaborative Process

Usability Evaluation of a System in a Group. The evaluators reported gaining more understanding of the usability inspection process using a heuristics scale. Having knowledge about how to discern good and bad usability features was useful when an evaluator reviewed the system from different angles. *"When working in a group, you get input from other people about the process which was useful" (G2P2)* and *"[…] made the evaluation less biased." (G1P4)* The evaluators also reported gaining the ability to locate, define, categorize and rate the usability problems together, which was a good way to conduct a heuristic inspection, giving a much better basis for locating problems in a system due to having several perspectives on the same matter.

The Value of Collaboration. Many evaluators highlighted the importance of working collectively when performing an evaluation, allowing them to see problems they possibly would not have noticed otherwise. *"It helped give a better overview of different problems. I believe it made us aware of more problems than we otherwise would have noticed if we were to complete the evaluation individually." (G1P2)* A thorough walkthrough by multiple evaluators was important to detect problems. Since the evaluators had different expectations of how a system should work, this provided important insights into how an evaluator might interpret issues differently. *"It can be really useful to listen* *to people with different perspectives in order to uncover problems you might not see by yourself." (G1P3)* Furthermore, it helped improve the overall quality of the end results and increased individual knowledge throughout constructive discussions. *"The discussions that arose were also helpful in identifying what we thought of as the right category for a problem, and whether or not a specific problem would be categorized as a minor or major problem." (G3P3).*

4 Discussion

We derived five sequential steps, namely division of labor, identification, aggregation, consolidation, and finalization, which cover the inter-group variation in the activity and are deemed to be of critical importance to the outcome of a collaborative inspection process. In line with previous research [4, 6], the evaluators valued collaborative heuristic inspection because they could split the workload, speed up the evaluation process and perform the evaluation without spending too much time. They found the collaborative process to be a useful and promising approach for the evaluation of digital systems in order to learn from others in the group, obtain more precise, accurate and valid outcomes, and better report the identified problems.

The main challenges of working in a group were lack of powerful evidence to decide whether a usability issue exists, discrepancies in categorizing usability problems, and rating the severity of problems. This indicates that problems arising from the subjective nature of heuristic inspections still exist in the collaborative inspection process. Furthermore, the evaluators reported that two main lessons were learned: how to evaluate the usability of a system in the group and the value of collaboration.

Some evaluators were familiar with most of their group members and were comfortable with each other. They reported less challenges and valued the collaborative heuristic inspection more. However, the evaluation process was not so comfortable and efficient when the evaluators had concern about the performance of group work. The group members reporting such concerns either split into sub-groups or performed the evaluation independently. Following an independent evaluation, they discussed their findings with others in the group, and then consolidated the outcomes together. These groups reported more usability problems than the groups where all group members worked together to identify usability problems. This indicates the possibility that the evaluators contributed more when they worked alone, and group discussions helped generate more usability issues, in addition to individual work.

Constructive discussions among group members may generate a substantial set of high-quality usability issues, making an impact on the interplay between usability inspection and evaluated systems. These results corroborate the findings of Følstad [7], who found that a considerable number of usability problems was reported during group discussions which were not generated by evaluators working independently. Furthermore, the evaluators who identified the usability problems together in a group added suggestions on how to fix a problem they identified in the evaluation report which was of high quality and included usability problems with screenshots from the program, detailed explanations, and suggestions on how to solve them.

Overall, we found that collaborative evaluation increases the quality of evaluation outcomes both in terms of identification and validation of usability issues, and reporting of them. However, collaborative evaluations require more and different forms of work to achieve the end result, namely that the evaluation needs to be practically coordinated with others. Additionally, disagreements require negotiation and resolution. Group work also afforded opportunities for individuals to learn from their peers both in terms of understanding the added perspectives of others and the requirement of being articulate and making problems explicit.

4.1 Implications for Collaborative Heuristic Inspection

When doing collaborative usability inspections, a fruitful way of organizing the work is to begin with individual and independent evaluation and then move to group to discussions to validate identified problems and generate user experience issues. Further, while it might be more time consuming, a collaborative process can present opportunities for participants to learn, so especially in situations where there are inexperienced evaluators or when there is a need to train someone it might be particularly valuable.

When doing collaborative evaluations, it is key to plan for discussions and resolving problems arising from the subjective nature of the evaluation process. Group meetings can serve a key role in improving the quality of evaluation reports and to ensure that it conveys necessary information clearly to the design and development team.

5 Conclusion

The main goal of the current study was to determine how the evaluators organized their work and their experiences in the collaborative process. To this end, we orchestrated a group-based, collaborative, unmoderated heuristic inspection process. The evaluators valued the group work because it presented them with opportunities to learn from others. Most disagreements were related to the subjective nature of heuristic inspections, such as how to describe, categorize and rate the severity of the identified problems. A workflow that starts with independent evaluations and then moves into group discussions to validate identified problems and generate more issues is a fruitful way of organizing a collaborative heuristic inspection process. It is also useful to form a group of evaluators who are familiar with each other, aware of each person's strengths and weaknesses, and able to work constructively.

Based on the findings from orchestrating collaborative usability inspections presented here, we plan to go forward with investigating how teams involved in collaborative evaluations can organize their work where the evaluators are physically separated, working with online collaboration tools. We plan to analyze how physical separation affects the collaborative aspect of the process, and what the ideal infrastructure for supporting teams in this condition are.

Acknowledgements. This publication is part of the INTROducing Mental health through Adaptive Technology project, funded by the Norwegian Research Council (259293/o70).

References

1. Andre, T.S., Hartson, H.R., Belz, S.M., McCreary, F.A.: The user action framework: a reliable foundation for usability engineering support tools. Int. J. Hum. Comput. Stud. **54**(1), 107–136 (2001). https://doi.org/10.1006/ijhc.2000.0441
2. Bailey, R.W.: Heuristic evaluation vs. user testing. UI design update newsletter (2001). http://www.humanfactors.com/downloads/jan01.asp. Accessed 14 Jan 2021
3. Braun, V., Clarke, V.: Using thematic analysis in psychology. Qual. Res. Psychol. **3**(2), 77–101 (2006). https://doi.org/10.1191/1478088706qp063oa
4. Chen, C.J., Lau, S.Y., Chuah, K.M., Teh., C.S.: Group usability testing of virtual reality-based learning environments: a modified approach. Procedia-Soc. Behav. Sci. **97**, 691–699 (2013). https://doi.org/10.1016/j.sbspro.2013.10.289
5. de Vreede, G.J., Fruhling, A., Chakrapani, A.: A repeatable collaboration process for usability testing. In: Proceedings of the 38th Annual Hawaii International Conference on System Sciences, p. 46 (2005). https://doi.org/10.1109/HICSS.2005.46
6. Downey, L.L.: Group usability testing: evolution in usability techniques. J. Usability Stud. **2**(3), 133–144 (2007)
7. Følstad, A.: The effect of group discussions in usability inspection: a pilot study. In: Proceedings of the 5th Nordic Conference on Human-Computer Interaction: Building Bridges, pp. 467–470 (2008). https://doi.org/10.1145/1463160.1463221
8. Hertzum, M., Jacobsen, N.E.: The evaluator effect: a chilling fact about usability evaluation methods. Int. J. Hum.-Comput. Interact. **15**(1), 183–204 (2003). https://doi.org/10.1207/S15 327590IJHC1501_14
9. Hertzum, M., Molich, R., Jacobsen, N.E.: What you get is what you see: revisiting the evaluator effect in usability tests. Behav. Inf. Technol. **33**(2), 144–162 (2014). https://doi.org/10.1080/0144929X.2013.783114
10. Hoffmann, R., Jónsdóttir, A.H., Hvannberg, E.T.: Consolidation of usability problems with novice evaluators re-examined in individual vs. collaborative settings. Interacting Comput. **31**(6), 525–538 (2019). https://doi.org/10.1093/iwc/iwz034
11. Hollingsed, T., Novick, D.G.: Usability inspection methods after 15 years of research and practice. In: Proceedings of the 25th Annual ACM International Conference on Design of Communication, pp. 249–255 (2007). https://doi.org/10.1145/1297144.1297200
12. Hornbæk, K., Frøkjær, E.: A study of the evaluator effect in usability testing. Hum.-Comput. Interact. **23**(3), 251–277 (2008). https://doi.org/10.1080/07370020802278205
13. Kessner, M., Wood, J., Dillon, R.F., West, R.L.: On the reliability of usability testing. In: CHI 2001 Extended Abstracts on Human Factors in Computing Systems, pp. 97–98 (2001). https://doi.org/10.1145/634067.634127
14. Law, E.L.C., Hvannberg, E.T.: Consolidating usability problems with novice evaluators. In: Proceedings of the 5th Nordic Conference on Human-Computer Interaction: Building Bridges, pp. 495–498 (2008). https://doi.org/10.1145/1463160.1463228
15. Lowry, P.B., Roberts, T.: Improving the usability evaluation technique, heuristic evaluation through the use of collaborative software. In: Proceedings of 9th Annual Americas Conference on Information Systems (AMCIS). 9th Annual Americas Conference on Information Systems, pp. 2203–2211 (2003)

16. Lowry, P.B., Roberts, T.L., Dean, D., Marakas, G.M.: Toward building self-sustaining groups in PCR-based tasks through implicit coordination: the case of heuristic evaluation. J. Assoc. Inf. Syst. (JAIS) **10**(3), 170–195 (2009)
17. Nielsen, J.: 10 usability heuristics for user interface design (1995). http://www.nngroup.com/articles/ten-usability-heuristics/. Accessed 14 Jan 2021
18. Solano, A., Collazos, C.A., Rusu, C., Fardoun, H.M.: Combinations of methods for collaborative evaluation of the usability of interactive software systems. Adv. Hum.-Comput. Interact. Article ID 4089520 (2016). https://doi.org/10.1155/2016/4089520

Emotional and Persuasive Design

Blossoms: Preliminary Experiment on Sharing Empathy Online

Chizumi Shimamura, Peeraya Sripian[✉], and Midori Sugaya

Shibaura Institute of Technology, 3-7-5 Toyosu, koto-ku, Tokyo 135-8504, Japan
peeraya@shibaura-it.ac.jp

Abstract. Due to the recent spread of COVID-19 infection, online communication tools are rapidly becoming widespread. However, it is difficult to convey nonverbal information online, therefore, it is difficult to obtain "empathy," which is important in communication. Although there are methods to convey empathy in existing SNS platform such as using buttons, people may feel reluctant to consciously convey their feeling. In our study, we propose a system that will extract empathy feeling from biological signals, heart rate variability and brain waves. With our proposed method, it is possible to generate and share empathy reaction automatically and unconsciously. As a preliminary study toward creating such a system, we assess the method for analyzing empathy in this study by calculating correlation of biological signals of two persons communicating in online environment under two conditions: video on and off. The results showed significant effects of correlation coefficient, suggesting that empathy could be measured.

Keywords: Brain wave · Heart rate variability · Emotion · Empathy · Online communication · Feedback · COVID-19

1 Introduction

Online communication tools are becoming popular due to the recent spread of COVID-19 pandemic. Face to face communication becoming dangerous because of the infection possibility, online communication is employed instead in many situations such as online classes, online meetings, and online interviews. This enable teleworking to be actively in many workplaces. Also, teleworking is expected to be recommended even after the pandemic situation has settled because it has the advantages of achieving work-life balance and reducing office costs and transportation costs [1]. One of the challenges of online communication is that it is difficult to understand the reaction of the person we are communicating with. This is because online communication lacks the presentation of emotion using nonverbal communication, which is usually transmitted unconsciously, like gestures and atmosphere.

To compensate for the lack of nonverbal information in these online communications, existing online communication tools are equipped with reaction features, such as reaction buttons, that users consciously press. However, while non-verbal information

M. Kurosu (Ed.): HCII 2021, LNCS 12762, pp. 375–383, 2021.
https://doi.org/10.1007/978-3-030-78462-1_29

is transmitted unconsciously, these conscious representations require a conscious push, which makes it difficult for reluctant people to use them.

Meanwhile, one of the goals of general communication is empathy. Empathy was an effective element in promoting mutual reliability and construction of a good relationship [2]. It is defined as the ability of people to recognize and respond to the emotions of others. By sharing empathy, a sense of communication can be created, which reduces anxiety in building a relationship. In online communication, the lack of non-verbal information made it difficult to obtain empathy.

Therefore, it is possible to promote more comfortable online communication if there is a mechanism for sharing empathy, even in unconscious and reluctant situation.

To determine unconscious emotions, Ikeda et al. introduced an emotion estimation method using biological data such as heart rate variability (HRV) and brain wave (EEG). They found that the estimated emotion and subjective emotion are close with small errors [3]. Based on Ikeda et al.'s emotion estimation method, many application have been proposed such as robot personal space estimation [4], social network evaluation [5], and so on. Feng et al. compared the effectiveness of online transmission of subjective emotional information and estimated emotion based on Ikeda's method [6]. They found that transmitting only subjective emotional information performed better. However, their study aimed to compare the communication methods, "empathy," which created from emotion of both sender and receiver were not considered.

In this study, we use biological information to estimate the "empathy" emotions that occur unconsciously on both sides. We analyze emotional synchronization using a cross-correlation function [7] to assess empathy and discuss whether it is effective in determining empathy. A preliminary experiment was performed by measuring biological information of two participants communicating online. Biological information was analyzed during two experiment condition: video on and off. The results showed significant effects of correlation coefficient, suggesting that empathy could be measured.

2 Proposed Method

One of the challenges in online communication is that it is difficult to understand the reaction of the person we are communicating with because it is difficult to convey non-verbal information. The purpose of this study is to clarify how to share unconscious "empathy" feelings and apply them to online communication to facilitate communication. In order to achieve this goal, we examine (1) the detection of empathy and (2) effective feedback methods for empathy.

2.1 Empathy Extraction Method

This study defines empathy as "emotion synchronization" and proposes a method for estimate empathy by the estimation of emotion from unconscious expression [8].

Emotion Estimation from Biological Signals. To estimate emotion from unconscious expression, we used brain waves and heart rate variability, which are biological indicators used in Ikeda et al.'s study, to evaluate emotion using biological information [3].

For the brainwave, we measure the activity of the central nervous system using EEG. NeuroSky'S MindWave Mobile 2 is used in our study to measure the EEG where Attention, a measure of arousal, was subtracted from Meditation, a measure of sleepiness. Since the range of values ranges from 0–100, larger values indicate a predominantly awake state, and smaller values indicate a drowsy state.

Nervous system indices that indicate the sympathetic and parasympathetic states of the body can be used as values for states such as relaxation and tension. The heart rate variability index has been used in various emotional analyses because it can determine the relationship between respiration and blood pressure as fluctuations in the heart rate interval. In this study, we used the pNN50, a time-domain measure of heart rate variability, which is a measure of heart rate variability. pNN50 is a time-domain measure of heart rate variability. pNN50 is a measure of heart rate variability, with higher values indicating parasympathetic dominance, or a relaxed state, and lower values indicating sympathetic dominance, or a nervous state.

Correlation Analysis with Biological Values. Watanabe et al. conducted experiments comparing face-to-face and non-face-to-face communication and analyzed the respiratory and heart rate interval data obtained from the experiments using the cross-correlation function equations. The results showed that the breath drawdown of both sides could significantly smooth the communication [7].

In this study, we first examine the values of respiration and heart rate interval used by Watanabe et al. [7]. Generally, RR_i, the interval between R waves in the ECG that indicates the peak, is used for examining the heart rate interval. Because the RR_i is affected by respiration, the RR_i alone would be practically sufficient as an indicator. Instead, pNN50, which reveals the effects of respiration and blood pressure in the time-domain analysis, can be included to get more effective result than using the RRI alone. In order to measure unconscious emotion, the brain wave, which cannot be controlled consciously, that could be used to identify state of arousal can be used. By substituting the values obtained by these two indices into the equation of the cross-correlation function, "empathy" can be evaluated by obtaining the correlation value of the feelings of the two experimental collaborators.

The biological measurements of two experimental collaborators A and B, taken at 1-s intervals, were evaluated by the following cross-correlation function $C(\tau)$

$$\frac{\sum_{i=1}^{n-\tau}(x_i - \overline{x})(y_{i+\tau} - \overline{y})}{\sqrt{\sum_{i=1}^{n}(x_i - \overline{x})^2}\sqrt{\sum_{i=1}^{n}(y_i - \overline{y})^2}} \tag{1}$$

x_i: EEG or heart rate variability of participant A*
y_i: EEG or heart rate variability of participant B*
$\overline{x}, \overline{y}$: Average values of x, y
n: Number of sample
τ: Time delayed

The time interval used for analysis was set at 10 s. The time delay τ was set to 1 s. We calculated Eq. 1a and 1b, with the values of x and y interchanged between participant A and B, respectively. Empathy is considered when a correlation value of 0.7

~ 1.0 is observed. This range is considered quite strong and widely accepted as positive correlation.

3   Preliminary Experiment

In order to clarify the evaluation index for measuring empathy, we measure the biological signals of two participants having conversation online, using Zoom web conferencing application. There are two conditions in the experiment: video off and video on. In order to determine the evaluation method for the empathy feedback system, we check whether the degree of synchronization of biological information changes according to the two conditions.

3.1   Experimental Procedure

The participant is asked to wear the EEG sensor and a pulse sensor during the whole experiment.

1. The participants stay still for one minute for baseline measurement.
2. The participants can talk to each other freely for 10 min.

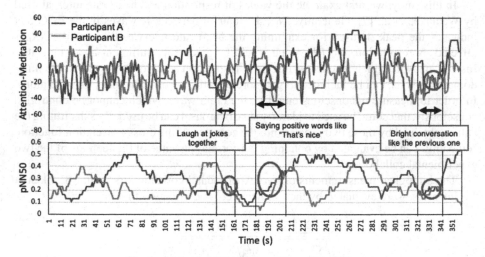

Fig. 1. Biological data during video off condition

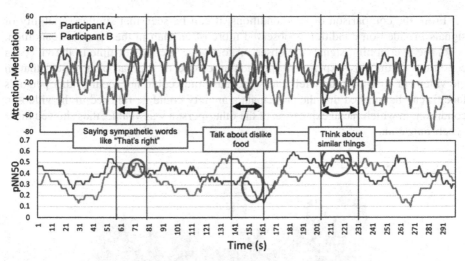

Fig. 2. Biological data during video on condition

The above steps 1–2 were performed for the video-off condition. In the video-on condition, the video was turned on before step 2. There was also a 10-min break between the video-off and video-on conditions.

3.2   Experiment Result

First, we performed a time-series analysis of the biological information obtained in the experiment, represented as line graphs for the two conditions. Next, the model of correlation analysis was validated in order to reveal the optimal correlation analysis method. Finally, correlation analysis is performed for the evaluation of the relationship between the biological signals of two participants.

Time Series Analysis. Figure 1 and 2 shows the time series data and the recorded conversation for the two participants in the video-off and video-on condition, respectively. The detail of the conversation is shown as comments in the graph only when the data of two participants cross and there are some noticeable topic in the conversation. It can be implied that the biological data of participants A and B were synchronized in both video-off and video-on conditions. Especially when both participants saying sympathetic words such as "That's nice" or "That's right", and when they were laughing at each other.

Table 1. Comparison of correlation analysis models

Biological index	Equation 1a x = A, y = B	Equation 1b x = B, y = A	Equation 2 General equation
Brain waves (A-M)	65	95	93
Heart rate variability (pNN50)	93	83	69

From the comparison of two conditions, it can be seen that similar variability of signals in video-on condition is observed more often than in the video-off condition. Also, the overlapping signals are observed for longer periods of time in the video-on condition. In the post-experiment questionnaire, one of the participants said that in the video-off condition, they felt uneasy because they could not see the other person's face. It can be implied that the participant's anxiety could be relieved in the video-on condition, in which facial expression of the other person was visible, thus showed more synchronization.

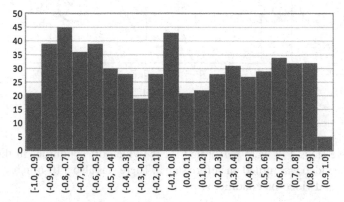

Fig. 3. The number of correlation coefficients (Using general equation: pNN50)

Comparison of Correlation Analysis Models. The biological information of two subjects was evaluated by the cross-correlation function equation. Unlike Watanabe et al.'s experiment, we did not explicitly separate the speaker and the listener in the experiment, therefore both A and B subjects were evaluated for the time delay. Also, Watanabe et al.'s work did not take in to account the EEG signals. In this work, we compare general correlation function equation (Eq. 2) to determine whether this evaluation model is appropriate for the present study.

$$r = \frac{\sum_{i=1}^{n}(x_i - \bar{x})(y_i - \bar{y})}{\sqrt{\sum_{i=1}^{n}(x_i - \bar{x})^2}\sqrt{\sum_{i=1}^{n}(y_i - \bar{y})^2}} \tag{2}$$

Figure 3 shows the summarization of number of correlation data at 0.1 increment.Table 1 shows the total number of data with positive correlation coefficients greater than or equal to 0.7, i.e., the sum of the three right-hand sides of the graph shown in Fig. 3. For the τ, time delay, shown in Eq. 1, we denote the case where B is delayed as $x = A, y = B$ and the case where A is delayed as $x = B, y = A$.

From the comparison of the results obtained by Eq. 1a, 1b (Table 1 shows the comparison of the results obtained by Eq. 1a, 1b (equation proposed by previous research [7]) and Eq. 2 (general correlation coefficient equation), it can be seen that the values obtained from Eq. 1 did not necessarily yield higher positive correlation ($> = 0.7$) coefficients with higher data values of correlation coefficients than those obtained from

Eq. 2. Also, since we did not separate the role of speaker and listener explicitly, it is difficult to determine which of the participants' data should be set for time-delayed.

Table 2. EEG's correlation coefficients and p-value

	(1)	(2)	(3)	(4)	(5)
Correlation coefficients	.371	.772**	−.829	.846**	.233
p-value	.291	.009	.003	.002	.518

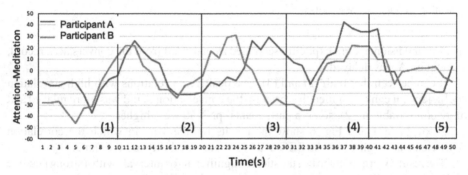

Fig. 4. Time interval when the correlation coefficient of brain wave is above 0.7, indicating strong positive correlation.

Table 3. Heart rate variability's correlation coefficients and p-value

	(1)	(2)	(3)	(4)	(5)
Correlation coefficients	−.120	.861**	−.722*	−.404**	.405
p-value	.741	.001	.018	.247	.246

Therefore, in this work, we focus on the correlation coefficients calculated by Eq. 2, the general equation, and proceed with the correlation analysis in the next section.

Correlation Analysis. The correlation coefficients and p-values were calculated in 10-s cycles, similar to the emotion estimation method by Kajihara et al. [8].

The results of 50 s interval signals of similar variability for EEG and heart rate variability are shown in Fig. 4 and Fig. 5, respectively. Table 2 and 3 shows the p-values of correlation coefficients for EEG and heart rate variability. There was a significant difference between EEG and heart rate for intervals with a strong positive correlation of 0.7 or greater. The time intervals are shown as (1)–(5) from the left.

Strongly positively correlation observed in intervals (2) and (4) indicated that the participants communicated with similar levels of arousal. In contrast, the negative value of (3) indicates a strong negative correlation. We consider that during this period, the

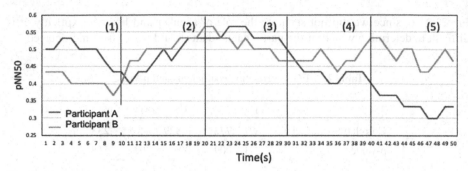

Fig. 5. Time interval where the correlation coefficient of heart rate variability is above 0.7, indicating strong positive correlation.

speaker and listener were explicitly separated as observed from the conversation record, participant A was delayed.

It can be seen that both (2) and (3) have positive correlations with high correlation coefficients. It can be implied that because the conversation detail was more relaxed and more comfortable in (2), so both participants' pNN50 were higher.

Next, Table 4 and Fig. 6 show the results for the 10 s in which the correlation coefficients are high when the EEG and heart rate variability are the same.

The results were found to be statistically significant for intervals with a strong positive correlation of 0.7 or greater.

These results suggest that positive correlation coefficients above 0.7 can be used as an indicator of empathy.

4 Summary and Future Works

In this work, we analyzed the biological information of two participants talking online and captured the characteristics of their biological information while they were feeling empathy. Since the value of the correlation coefficient was found to be significant at 10-s intervals, it could be implied that a positive correlation coefficient of more than 0.7 could be used as an index of empathy.

In the future, we plan to conduct the experiment again with more number of participants to increase the validity of the result. Also, we plan to examine effective feedback methods by developing an actual system based on the results of this experiment. We will also conduct experiments with the system and evaluate the impressions of the feedback.

Table 4. Correlation coefficients and p-value for EEG and HRV

	EEG	HRV
Correlation coefficients	.768**	.765**
p-value	.009	.010

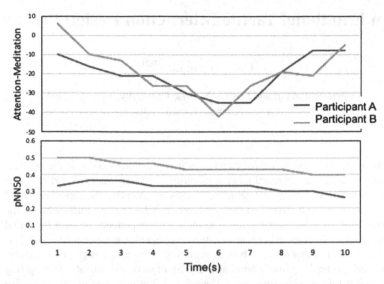

Fig. 6. Time interval when the correlation coefficients of both EEG and heart rate are above 0.7

References

1. Proactive use of telework as a countermeasure against new coronavirus infections (in Japanese). https://www.soumu.go.jp/main_sosiki/joho_tsusin/telework/02ryutsu02_0400 0341.html. Accessed 15 Dec 2020
2. Satoshi, U., et al.: Cognitive Science in Comminication 2: Empathy (Iwanami lecture) [in Japanese]. In: Iwanami Shoten (2014)
3. Ikeda, Y., Horie, R., Sugaya, M.: Estimate emotion with biological information for robot interaction. Paper presented at the 21st International Conference on Knowledge-Based and Intelligent Information & Engineering Systems (KES-2017), Marseille, France
4. Someya, E., Tobe, Y., Kagawa, R., Matsuhira, N., Sugaya, M.: Emotional evaluation and location estimation of personal space during robot approach using bio-emotional estimation method (in Japanese). Proc. 80th Natl. Convention Lect. **2018**(1), 281–282 (2018)
5. Feng, C., Liu, Y., Sugaya, M.: Presentation system of estimated emotion based on biological information while sending SNS (in Japanese). 人間工学 **54**(Supplement), 1E4–2–1E4–2 (2018). https://doi.org/10.5100/jje.54.1E4-2
6. Feng, C., Ikeda, Y., Sugaya, M.: Comparison of emotional communication method in remote place (in Japanese). In: The proceedings of DICOMO2017 Multimedia, Distributed, Cooperative, and Mobile Symposium **2017**, 149–153 (2017)
7. Watanabe, T., Okubo, M.: Physiological analysis of entrainment in communication (special issue on next generation human interface and interaction). J. Inf. Process. Soc. Japan **39**(5), 1225–1231 (1998)
8. Kajihara, Y., Sripian, P., Feng, C., Sugaya, M.: Emotion synchronization method for robot facial expression. In: Kurosu, M. (ed.) HCII 2020. LNCS, vol. 12182, pp. 644–653. Springer, Cham (2020). https://doi.org/10.1007/978-3-030-49062-1_44

An Emotional Tactile Interaction Design Process

Chor-Kheng Lim[✉]

Department of Art and Design, YuanZe University, Taoyuan, Taiwan
kheng@saturn.yzu.edu.tw

Abstract. This research explores whether it is possible to maintain the existing, most natural, and emotional touch relationship between "human" and "human" or "human" and "object" in interactive designs by observing the user's behavioral experience without relying on the operation of technology products while at the same time allowing users to enjoy the innovative experience brought by digital technology. "Interactive behavior is natural, but emotional experience is novel" is the core idea of this research behind exploring interactive design. This research conceals technology inside familiar everyday objects and activates them giving them sensitive sensing capabilities. Detection and provision of timely interactive feedback are used in the emotional interactive touch mode that exists between "human" and "object", allowing users to experience an emotional interactive experience. The research analyzes and summarizes the design process and steps through four interactive design projects executed by the author (inter-generational interactive design for older adults and interactive space design) [8–11], and finally integrates familiar artifacts (everyday object) as a device and provides a process and framework for emotional, physical touch, interactive experience designs.

Keywords: Interaction design · Intuitive behavior · Familiar artifact

1 Background and Objective

In addition to verbal, human communicates using non- verbal communication means, such as facial expressions, gesture, and touch. Among all means, "touch" is a significant way of conveying affection, thus playing an essential role in improving mental and physical health [1–3]. In daily life, physical contact and touch behavior happen frequently both between "human" and "human," and "human" and "object." According to research, affective touch can regulate physiological reactions, build up relationships, and alleviate disruptive behavior [4, 5]. Researches Hector, et al. also suggest in their Human-Computer Interaction study that affective touch can function as a regulator with positive effect, not only between "human" and "human," but also "human" and "robot," which operates in digital computation [6]. Due to the recent progress in technology, the design of Human-Computer Interaction Interface is shifting from Graphical User Interface (GUI) toward a more natural and human-centric Natural User Interface (NUI). NUI focuses more on natural human behaviors, such as touch, body gesture recognition, and language recognition.

© Springer Nature Switzerland AG 2021
M. Kurosu (Ed.): HCII 2021, LNCS 12762, pp. 384–395, 2021.
https://doi.org/10.1007/978-3-030-78462-1_30

The research literature reveals that the focus of interaction design is shifting toward more intuitive NUI design; however, how to turn the behavior patterns obtained from observing user behavior to a more adaptive interaction interface is the major focus of this study. Some studies have explored how to understand user behavior through "observation," with User-Centered Design in mind, and have successfully applied it during the design process. They use "observation" as the primary design method in the course of design and propose its value [7]. The study under Kang and Suto also suggests the theoretical model of ADT Design, indicating the close relationship among designer, user, and artifact. Such a relationship shows that the observation of the designer on user behavior must be based on his/her behavior pattern and the physical laws applicable to the artifact he/she contacts. It is therefore understood that user experience emphasizes his/her behavior of "human" and "object" or physical properties, and on the inseparable, interactive behavior relationship between the two.

As a result, technologies such as Ubiquitous Computing, Mobile Computing, Sensors and Actuators, and even Internet of Things, Ambient Intelligence (Aml), and Affective Computing have been adopted to meet the needs of interactive design that are more natural and human-centric. This is so because there exist many interactive behaviors and patterns in human events. However, despite these proven technologies, the interaction interface or devices for the current interaction designs are still presented in a way that depends mostly on existing input interfaces offered by the digital interactive products, including touch screens, keyboard and mouse, joysticks, buttons control devices, etc. The interactive behaviors are still based on the operation behavior patterns provided by such digital devices and it will raise the learning threshold of operation. Therefore, this research explores whether it is possible to maintain the existing, most natural, and emotional touch relationship between "human" and "human" or "human" and "object" in interactive designs by observing the user's behavioral experience without relying on the operation of technology products while at the same time allowing users to enjoy the innovative experience brought by digital technology. "Interactive behavior is natural, but emotional experience is novel" is the core idea of this research behind exploring interactive design. This research conceals technology inside familiar everyday objects and activates them giving them sensitive sensing capabilities. Detection and provision of timely interactive feedback are used in the emotional interactive touch mode that exists between "human" and "object", allowing users to experience an emotional interactive experience. The research analyzes and summarizes the design process and steps through four interactive design projects executed by the author (inter-generational interactive design for older adults and interactive space design), and finally integrates familiar artifacts (everyday object) as a device and provides a process and framework for emotional, physical touch, interactive experience designs.

2 Research Method and Analysis

Based on the goal of this research to understand the user's behavioral experience through observation for creative application in design solutions, this research uses a commonly-used method in user experience research, the AEIOU observation method, to test and analyze the design process for 4 interactive design projects done by the author from 2010 to 2020 (Fig. 1). The pain points of each design, design solutions, and technologies used are shown in Tables 1 and 2.

Project 1: Pillow Fight

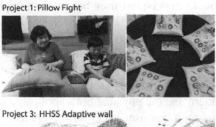

Project 2: Wonder Corner

Project 3: HHSS Adaptive wall

Project 4: Shape, Cloud

Fig. 1. Four interactive design projects done by the author

Table 1. Interaction design for inter-generational care.

Paint Point (P) - Solution(S)	Technology
Project 1: Pillow Fight (2019) **(P).** Through observation, author's mother in the terminal phase of cancer was found to be less and less capable of playing with grandchildren. The experiences that remain most intimate to mother was only holding a pillow sitting on the wheelchair or sitting on the bed side, watching her grandchildren playing tablet games by themselves. How to create more interaction between these two generation in intuitive way? **(S).** By combining the familiar objects dear to them, the pillow and computer games played by the grandchildren, and grandparents can enjoy intimate family relationships anytime through intuitive interaction pattern (touching)	• Capacitive touch sensors design (conductive thread, fabric) • PCB design • Bluetooth BLE • App games • Digital fabrication (lasercut, 3D print) • Mass production
Project 2: Wonder Corner (2019) **(P).** Living room is the space where family members spend time together most often. Is it possible for the family members to physically interact more intimately with the objects in such a space, instead of playing with a cell phone, with head down? **(S).** By connecting the sofa, cushions, TV, stereo, lights, and floor in the living room through IoT technology, we built an interaction pattern that allows family members to enjoy entertainment together. Sitting on a sofa, holding a cushion, and sitting on the floor could be the inputs to the game. Lights, TV, and stereo then can be the audio and video outputs of the game. In the design, the most natural way of contact between body and object can be used to replace an electronic game's joystick or controller. The information of activities happening in the space is collected through the transmission of messages by the objects endowed with the ability to sense	• Capacitive touch sensors design (conductive thread) • PCB design • Bluetooth BLE • MQTT (IoT) • App games • Parametric design • Digital fabrication (lasercut, 3D print)

Table 2. Interaction space design.

Paint Point (P) - Solution(S)	Technology
Project 3: HHSS Adaptive Wall (2015) (A soft illuminating wall that detects hear beat) **(P).** How to allow the physical space to reflect the heart rates of those in action in the space? How to enable the space to visualize the physiological information of those who are experiencing such space through dynamic feedback from the structure? How to allow the space to feel the heartbeats of the people? **(S).** We designed a two-meter long tunnel in which the spatial structure pulses mechanically in a rhythmic following the heart rates of the people who act in it. By illuminating a piece of soft cloth, the skin layer of such a spatial structure reacts with feedback to such a rhythmic pulse. Those who experience must put on headphones first when entering the entry and listen to their favorite music. They then enter the tunnel to experience the visualization of their heart rates. The soft illuminating cloth also changes its color and presentation following the change of the rhythmic pulse. The design receives the heart rates of the visitors most naturally with a receiver hidden in the headphone. The heart rate is then transmitted via Bluetooth connection to the control end of the spatial structure, allowing the motor on the structure to operate	• EL fabric • Arduino (heart sensors, motors, speakers) • Bluetooth • Parametric design • Digital fabrication (lasercut)
Project 4: Shape, Cloud (2015) **(P).** How to let the visitors interact with and feel through an interactive device, with fun, the natural elements, namely, cloud, wind, thunder, and rain **(S).** We designed a cloud and a fan for visitors to blow air. "Invisible wind" serves as an input while "visible cloud," as an output. When visitors blow air together, thunder will come from a big cloud; a muffled thunder will be heard if blowing continues; a big thunder will be heard with further blowing; and finally, it begins to rain when the maximum value is reached. Let the children work with the parents and have fun from experiencing interactively with the changes in the natural phenomena	• Arduino (sound sensors, LEDs, speakers) • Bluetooth • Parametric design • Digital fabrication

2.1 "Problem Finding" Method and Process in Early Phase of the Design

The AEIOU method emphasizes five levels of observation: Activity, Environment, Interaction, Object, and User are used as analysis factors for users in each design project. Table 3 and Table 4 show the AEIOU factor analysis summarized from the pain points observed in the designs. Through the empirical analysis of these designs, this research summarizes the pain points or "problem finding" methods and processes in the initial design stage: At the beginning, the author observed the pain points of everyday familiar objects through the author's own emotional orientation, then familiar patterns of interaction were found from the people and objects observed, and finally the familiar life objects that have a relationship with people were compiled from these interactions. The main process is shown in Fig. 2. The familiar artifacts compiled are used as the main design carrier used in the design solution.

Table 3. AEIOU factor analysis of inter-generational care design projects.

AEIOU	Project 1: Pillow fight	Project 2: Wonder corner
User	• Grandmother • Grandchild	• Family members
Activity (paint point)	Grandmother was unable to accompany her grandchild due to illness, so she could only watch her grandchild play by himself	The whole family gathered together but looking at their respective phones/tablets
Environment	Living room	Living room
Object	• Pillow • Wheelchair • Bed • Tablet	• Mobile phone • Tablet • Pillow • Sofa • Floor • TV • Lamp
Interaction	• (touch) Grandmother holding the pillow • (touch, sight) Grandmother sitting on the wheelchair and watching her grandchildren playing tablet games by themselves • (touch) Grandmother sitting on the bed side • (touch) Grandchild playing tablet on the floor	• (touch, sight) Adults sitting on the sofa and playing their mobile phones • (touch, sight) Adults sitting on the sofa, holding the cushions and all become phubbers • (touch, sight, hear) Children sitting on the floor and playing tablet games • (sight, hear) The TV is on and sometimes someone looks up and watching

Table 4. AEIOU factor analysis of interactive space design project.

AEIOU	Project 3: HHSS adaptive Wall	Project 4: Shape, Cloud
User	• Visitors (All age groups)	• Visitors (All age groups)
Activity (paint point)	How to make the tunnel response the physiological state of people who walking into the space, can the space feel like people are alive?	How to represent natural phenomena in a fun and interactive way? Natural phenomena related to a cloud: wind, thunder, rain
Environment	Exhibition Hall	Exhibition Hall
Object	• Tunnel wall • Earmuff headphones	• Windmill • Cloud
Interaction	• (touch, hear) Wear headphones to listen to music • (touch, sight) Walk through the tunnel, the wall will give feedback in time	• (touch) Blow • (hear) Thunder in the distance before the wind was blowing • (hear) The closer the thunder, the louder • (sight, listening) raining

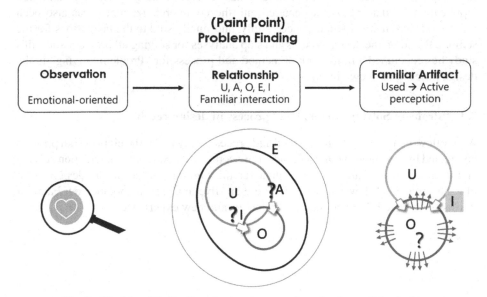

Fig. 2. "Problem Finding" method and process in early phase of the design

2.2 "Problem Solving" Method and Process in the Design Process

The findings and phenomenon based on the observations from AEIOU in the previous phase will be applied effectively in the design process as operating elements for the creative concept. The relationship between Users and Objects, i.e., Interaction, concluded from the "Problem Finding" stage in the early phase of design will continue serving as a familiar interaction pattern for the design concept. The concluded object, especially the familiar artifact in life then serves as the author's major design carrier or interaction interface in each design project. And these familiar artifacts will be redefined for their roles in the design process. Their roles will change from the original status of passive usage to the activated objects with active perceiving ability by using ubiquitous computing or the method on how the sensing technology is hidden.

Figure 3a & 3b shows how to make a familiar object the interaction carrier in each interaction design project; and how to keep the object maintaining at its familiar interactive behavior and pattern designated by the design concept. Since this phase is the implementation and modification process from the abstract concept to the material object, it is, therefore, one with the major steps and processes in which the manufacturing technology and application are validated in the transformation from concept to tactile object. Most of the design projects in this study are mainly those for prototype design and development in the design process. However, "Pillow Fight" has undergone many cycles of V-validation (application validation) and has entered into the commercialization; it has also been mass-produced in small volume successfully, and finally sold to the institutions for the seniors. Based on the design process and step analyses for solving all project issues, this study has concluded a framework of method and process for "Problem Solving" in the design process, as shown in Fig. 4.

2.3 "Problem Solving" method and process in design result

As a follow-up from the design method and process analysis for the eight design projects conducted by the author within a decade, this section will explore the interaction solving and its interaction characteristics sought for the familiar artifact in the design result of each project, as shown in Table 5. There are five analysis factors include: Familiar Artifact, Activated, Method, Intuitive behavior and new experience.

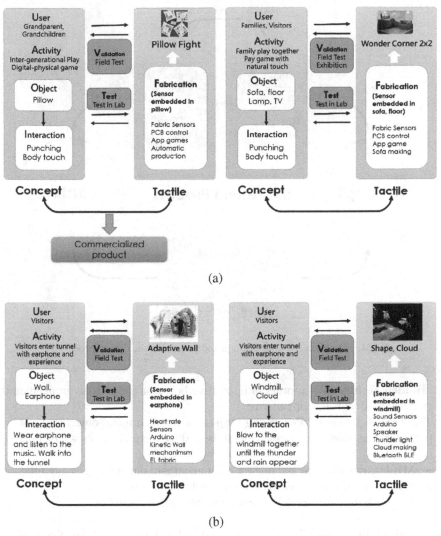

Fig. 3. (a) The process of how to make a familiar object as the interaction carrier (Project 1 & 2). (b) The process of how to make a familiar object as the interaction carrier (Project 3 & 4)

3 Research Results

Based on the analysis shown as Table 6, this study concludes a design process that start from observation AEIOU method, and focus on the intuitive interaction behavior design by activated daily life familiar object to become the input sensor devices. Through the analysis of the four design projects by author, it can be concluded some characteristics and methods as below (Fig. 5):

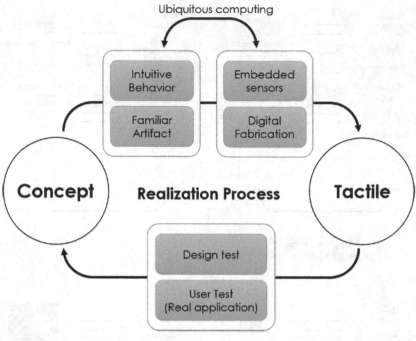

Fig. 4. "Problem Solving" method and process in the design process.

1. **"Hidden Technology"** appears in interactive behavior and persists in maintaining original intuitive behavior patterns.
2. Three methods of how **"Perceiving Object"** activates original object into one with perceiving function. The comparison of these three methods as shown in Table 6.

   - M1: Use raw material and make a component into one with a sensing function.
   - M2: Combine original object with interactive controls.
   - M3: Redesign show rack by combining interactive controls.

3. **"Feedback mechanism"** is based on visual and auditory senses. Feedback mechanism and actuation object for the inter-generation caring design process: APP provided to the younger generation, dynamic (original object changing from passive dynamic to active variation). The feedback mechanism of interaction space design project is based on visual and auditory senses.

Table 5. The interaction solving and its characteristics sought for the familiar artefact.

Project Name	Familiar Artifact	Activated Perception	Method	Intuitive behavior	New experience
2019 Pillow Fight	Pillow	Sense by users' punching and touching	Make the original material of the object into sensor cotton + conductive thread (Developed and manufactured sensing element. The sensing layer hide in the cotton, then sewn into a pillow core	Punch pillow Touch pillow	**Intergenerational care, parent-child entertainment.** Play games with App
2019 Wonder Corner	Sofa Floor Lamp	Sense by users' punching and touching	Make the original material of the object into sensor Original sofa fabric + conductive fiber (Developed and manufactured sensing element. The sensing layer hide in the cotton, then sewn into a sofa cover)	Touch sofa Touch floor	**parent-child entertainment.** Play games with App
2015 HHSS Adaptive Wall (A soft illuminating wall that detects hear beat)	Headphone Wall	Can sense the heartbeat of visitors who listen to music with headphones in the space	**Redesign** space structure and combined with interactive control In order to combine sensing and control, the tunnel of a free-form wooden structure similar to blood vessels was redesigned. (sensor and dynamic mechanisms was made to be hidden in space)	Listening to music with headphone while walking through the tunnel	**Physiological Information Visualization** Combined with dynamic soft wall dynamic changes

(continued)

Table 5. (*continued*)

Project Name	Familiar Artifact	Activated Perception	Method	Intuitive behavior	New experience
2015 Shape, Cloud	Windmill Cloud	Can sense the volume of the air that visitors blow out	**Reproduce** cloud shape structure and combined with interactive control In order to combine the sensing and control, natural phenomenon, thunder, lightning was reproduced by the feedback of LED and sound control	Parents and children work together to blow at the windmill	**Parent-child entertainment.** Natural phenomenon reproduction, combined with natural action entertainment experience

Table 6. The comparison of three methods of activated original object to become the sensors.

Method	Fabrication time	Ease of production	Familiarity to users
M1	Long	High	High
M2	Middle	Middle	Middle
M3	Short	Middle	Low

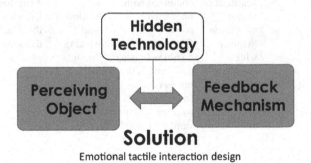

Fig. 5. Solution" Emotional tactile interaction design process

References

1. Field, T.: Touch for socioemotional and physical well-being: a review. Dev. Rev. **30**, 367–383 (2010). https://doi.org/10.1016/j.dr.2011.01.001

2. Morrison, I., Löken, L., Olausson, H.: The skin as a social organ. Exp. Brain Res. **204**, 305–314 (2010). https://doi.org/10.1007/s00221-009-2007-y
3. App, B., McIntosh, D.N., Reed, C.L., Hertenstein, M.J.: Nonverbal channel use in communication of emotion: how may depend on why. Emotion **11**, 603–617 (2011). https://doi.org/10.1037/a0023164
4. van Erp, J.B.F., Toet, A.: Social touch in human-computer interaction. Front. Digit. Hum. **2**, 1–14 (2015). https://doi.org/10.3389/fdigh.2015.00002
5. Burleson, M.H., Trevathan, W.R., Todd, M.: In the mood for love, or vice versa? Understanding the relations among physical affection, sexual activity, mood, and stress in the daily lives of mid-aged women. Arch. Sex. Behav. **36**, 357–368 (2007)
6. Guthier, B., Dörner, R., Martinez, H.P.: Affective computing in games. In: Dörner, R., Göbel, S., Kickmeier-Rust, M., Masuch, M., Zweig, K. (eds.) Entertainment Computing and Serious Games. LNCS, vol. 9970, pp. 402–441. Springer, Cham (2016). https://doi.org/10.1007/978-3-319-46152-6_16
7. Kang, N., Suto, H.: How to observe, share and apply in design process? In: Marcus, A. (ed.) DUXU 2013. LNCS, vol. 8012, pp. 498–505. Springer, Heidelberg (2013). https://doi.org/10.1007/978-3-642-39229-0_53
8. Chang, Y.L., Lim, C.K., Chou, C.M., Huang, H., Sun, T.L., Liu, I.C.: Using facial emotion recognition to observe the emotional changes of the elderly playing the pillow type device. In: The 20th Asia Pacific Industrial Engineering and Management Systems (APIEMS 2019). Kanazawa City, Japan (December 2019)
9. Huang, H., Lim, C.K., Sun, T.L., Chou, C.M., Liu, I.C.: Evaluation of elderly gaming devices using openpose. In: The 4th International Conference on Ambient Intelligence & Ergonomics in Asia (AmI&E 2019). Taoyuan, Taiwan (October 2019)
10. Lim, C.K.: Pillow Fight: application of conductive fabric technology in activities for dementia. In: Physical Ergonomics and Human Factor, the 10th International Conference on Applied Human Factors and Ergonomics (AHFE 2019) Washington D.C. USA (July 2019)
11. Lim, C.K.: "Pillow Fight" board game design. In: 21 st International Conference on Human-Computer Interaction. Orlando, Florida, USA (July 2019)

Continuous Monitoring of Interactive Exhibits in Museums as Part of a Persuasive Design Approach

Walter Ritter[1]([✉]), Andreas Künz[1], Katrin Paldán[1], Guido Kempter[1], and Mathias Gort[2]

[1] UCT Research, Vorarlberg University of Applied Sciences, Dornbirn, Austria
`walter.ritter@fhv.at`
[2] inatura – Erlebnis Naturschau GmbH, Dornbirn, Austria

Abstract. Museums are no longer places where guests aren't allowed to touch anything. They have increasingly become adventure parks, where visitors are invited to directly interact with exhibits to discover new knowledge. This raises questions regarding how to design such interactive exhibits, so they invite and persuade people to interact with them and therefore help visitors to learn new things. How to optimize exhibitions so exhibits are exposed to visitors in effective ways has been the subject of many studies. Most of them rely on resource intensive observations and interviewing of visitors. In this paper, a privacy-savvy and automated method for observing, how exhibits are actually used by visitors, is presented, and the benefits of such long-term monitoring for improving the exhibit design process are discussed. Long-term usage is an often-neglected factor in existing studies. Differences in exhibit usage are mostly attributed to changed versions or changed arrangements of exhibits within an exhibition rather than time of day or season. Results of the case study presented in this paper show that listening durations for an audio player exhibit varied slightly during daytimes, and seasons, but not between weekdays and weekends. Also, an effect on listening durations between different dynamic social settings could be observed. These results give an indication that besides the variation of the exhibits, the consideration of the time of day, season, and variation of social setting is important when different versions of persuasive objects are to be compared in terms of their use in a live setting in a museum. In a next step, the automated interaction monitoring setup will be used to investigate combined effects of time and variations of persuasive exhibits on visitor interactions.

Keywords: Exhibit design · Interaction · Museum · Logging · Optimization · Persuasive design

1 Introduction

The role of museums has long been that of education and social action (Hein 2005). According to Graf et al., museums have been seen as places for education and research

© Springer Nature Switzerland AG 2021
M. Kurosu (Ed.): HCII 2021, LNCS 12762, pp. 396–411, 2021.
https://doi.org/10.1007/978-3-030-78462-1_31

and thus are here for transferring knowledge (Graf et al. 2016). Similarly, the Network of European Museum Organisations (NEMO) attributes social, collection, educational and economic value to museums and stresses their role in knowledge creation and lifelong learning (NEMO 2015). Whether museums show pieces of art, historical documents, skeletons of dinosaurs, historic technical masterpieces - they all should ignite inspiration and a thirst for knowledge. But due to the immense value of the pieces exhibited, many of them are only shown behind glass or are protected in other ways (Friedman 2010). However, museums like the Exploratorium in San Francisco[1] or the Ontario Science Center[2] started a new trend in the late 60s. Museums are increasingly becoming more like activity and adventure parks, not only meant for transferring knowledge, but also doing that in a fun and experience-rich way (Friedman 2010) and thus have also become an important touristic factor (Aalst and Boogaart 2002). Even the effects of marketing museums as theme parks have been investigated (Zbuchea 2015), which further underscores the expanding role of museums in the tourism sector. However, Zbuchea also stresses the importance of not losing sight of a museum's core values in the process of it.

Interactive exhibits play a major role in this shift towards a more fun- and adventure-park-related view of museums. The use of new technology should also assist museums in staying relevant and generating the needed income (Wilson-Barnao 2018). Even though new technologies offer a broad range of new possibilities regarding interactive exhibit design, it's still important that these technologies are used in a way that supports the original goal of museums and not act as self-promotion of the technologies (Economou 2008). Allen (2004) points out that while interactive exhibits can increase engagement, they might also be counterproductive if they are too complex. This raises the question on how interactive exhibits for museums can be optimized to attract and capture attention and interest of visitors, to invite them to discover new knowledge instead of overwhelming them with complexity. Gathering and analysing data regarding interactions of visitors with such exhibits therefore plays a vital role in optimising such exhibits (Serrell 2010).

The next section shows a brief overview of research regarding exhibit and exhibition design to achieve these goals. In the following sections we then present an automated approach for gathering data regarding the visitor-exhibit-interaction and analyse the role of time in the visitor-exhibit-interaction patterns.

2   State of the Art

Observing visitors on their path through an exhibition to learn what factors help in capturing visitors' attention and interest, and thus igniting their engagement, has a long history (Yalowitz and Bronnenkant 2009; Kirchberg and Tröndle 2012). According to Haywood and Cairns (2006) engagement is typically described regarding participation, narration and co-presence of other visitors, which is often detected by observation.

An early example of analysing the behavior of visitors in an exhibition are the studies of Melton (1935), who analysed the effect of an exhibit's distance from an exit on the

---

[1] Exploratorium San Francisco: https://www.exploratorium.edu/.
[2] Ontario Science Center: https://www.ontariosciencecentre.ca/.

time visitors spent with the exhibit. The closer an exhibit was placed to an exit, the less time visitors spent with the exhibit. Melton also identified a right turning bias of visitors when walking through a gallery (Melton 1935). However, the right turning bias could not be confirmed in studies reviewed by Bitgood (2006).

Bitgood also closely investigated visitor flow and defined a general value principle for predicting the choice behavior of visitors: the "ratio of perceived experience outcome (benefits) divided by perceived costs (time, effort, and so on)" (Bitgood 2006, p 463). Bitgood likened this measure to the prospect theory of Kahneman and Tversky (1979).

An important concept when it comes to optimising museum exhibits is museum fatigue, which describes a decrease of visitor interest towards exhibits during a visit (Davey 2005). In a literature review by Bitgood regarding museum fatigue he identified a disparity between self-reported und overt measures of fatigue. He describes museum fatigue as a difficult phenomenon to measure, as typically used measures like percentage of visitors stopping, or for how long visitors view an exhibit might be influenced by other factors too (Bitgood 2009). Davey suggests in his literature review, that to understand the causes of museum fatigue, it is best to take an integrational view, combining visitor attributes and environmental factors (Davey 2005). Typically, average visitors will experience fatigue after 30–45 min of a visit (Falk et al. 1985). Bitgood also described how exhibits should be designed to capture visitors' attention and counteract fatigue (Bitgood 2013).

Serrell investigated the viewing behavior for videos embedded into an exhibition regarding attracting power and holding power, where on average 32% of visitors were attracted to the videos. The typical watching time was found to be between one third to one half of the time of the video, 137 s on average. Serrell attributes this brief watching period to ongoing temptations by other exhibits. Serrell therefore recommends communicating important messages early on, before visitors move on to the next temptation (Serrell 2002).

Many studies in the context of visitor research, like the ones mentioned above, rely mostly on personal observations and questionnaires. Vom Lehm et al. have shown that video recordings of visitors' interactions with exhibits can reveal a much more detailed picture of the interaction processes and the whole museum experience. Their findings for example include the role of social interactions with friends and strangers during interactions with an exhibit (Vom Lehm et al. 2002, Vom Lehm 2006).

Turgay-Zıraman & Imamoğlu investigated the effect of exhibit order, relative size and proximity to larger objects regarding visitor attention and interest. They used a combination of live observations, video recordings, and visitor questionnaires. They confirmed the effect that early objects usually get higher attention than the ones placed at a later point in an exhibition, which was also observed and discussed by many previous studies and is partly attributed to exit attraction, object satiation, or simply fatigue (Melton 1935; Davey 2005; Bitgood 2006; Bitgood 2009). Regarding relative size they found that bigger exhibits not only attract more attention but are also able to capture it for a longer time. However, they also caution that big objects might have a suppressing effect on the overall attention level in an exhibition (Turgay-Zıraman and Imamoğlu 2020).

An obvious advantage of a video-based observation approach is that analysis of the recorded material can be done repeatedly and retrospectively, if new questions or hypothesis arise. Also, a little video camera might be less recognisable than an observer watching visitors. However, recording videos in public spaces is highly restricted regarding the later use of the captured videos and also bears heavy privacy concerns (they may vary depending on a country's laws, also see the General Data Protection Regulation[3] of the EU). Furthermore, analysis of video recordings can still be time consuming, especially if the observation spans a longer period of time.

Therefore, in this paper we present a privacy friendly and scalable approach to monitoring interactions of visitors with exhibits over a longer period of time. In the following sections we present a case study to analyse the benefits of continuous event logging and its implications on optimising the interaction experience of visitors.

3   Method

Today's interactive exhibits are often driven by some form of computers that take interaction events from visitors and trigger resulting actions accordingly. Often these computers are built into physical objects and are invisible for visitors (see Künz and Ritter 2015 for concrete examples). By mapping incoming interaction events to outgoing actions, they also offer the opportunity to log every interaction that occurs. This potentially enables a detailed analysis of all interactions with an exhibit without the need for an ongoing manual observation or time-consuming questioning of visitors. This is especially relevant as the time spent with an exhibit is considered an important measure for evaluating an exhibit (Sandifer 1997; Serrell 2002).

Our hypothesis is that interaction patterns vary among different situations and time during the run of an exhibition. Therefore, it might not be sufficient to only use brief observation periods spent in exhibitions to compare different variants for exhibit-optimization.

In a case study with automated logging of visitor interactions with an exhibit, we set up a simple audio-player with logging functionalities. As soon as the earpiece of the player is lifted, a time stamp is recorded. Another time stamp is recorded when the earpiece is put down again. This setup resembles a typical listening station, where visitors can get additional information regarding an exhibit.

We got the opportunity to use this logging audio-player for a special exhibition about the relationship between humans and animals called "Weiß der Geier" at the inatura museum[4] in Dornbirn, Austria. The inatura museum is famous for its philosophy that all exhibits should be touchable. They follow a hand's on approach to get visitors to learn new things by experimenting. Visitors of the museum cover a broad range of age: from children in pre-school age to elderly persons. Visitors enter the museum either individually or in groups.

Figure 1 shows the setup of the logging audio-player station with two earpieces. Both earpieces (left and right) can play the same audio material independently of each

---

[3] General Data Protection Regulation (GDPR): https://gdpr.eu.

[4] inatura museum: https://inatura.at.

other, so there can be one or two listeners at the same time. The audio material for this exhibit had a duration of 10 min.

Fig. 1. Audio station with two independent earpieces at the exhibition "Weiß der Geier" at the inatura museum Dornbirn, Austria

One common question for such listening stations is, for how long visitors will typically keep listening to the information presented. This is important to know for designing the audio material to make sure, important information is communicated before listeners hang up. In addition, not only the typical listening time is of interest, but also its change over time (e.g., within a day, between days, season or the phase of an exhibition). While the average listening time might be highly dependent on the audio stimulus and the setting of an exhibition, a change in listening time might reveal changes in underlying processes that might not be detectable in sporadic manual observations.

Within our previously described hypothesis, we focus mainly on the temporal aspect as an example of varying exhibition-situations and also check to see if the social setting has an influence on the listening time. For this, the following questions are meant to test our hypothesis:

1. What is the average/median listening time for the audio material?
2. Are there differences in listening time between weekdays and weekends (e.g., caused by a different visitor type or visitor alertness)?
3. Are there differences in listening time between different times of a day (e.g., caused by different visitor types or visitor alertness)?
4. Does the listening time change between the beginning and the ending phase of the exhibition (e.g., novelty of the exhibition, season)?
5. Does listening time change when the two earpieces are used at the same time (e.g., social effect)?

Data has been collected over a period of one year (the duration of the exhibition). In addition to the logs of the audio listening times, also the daily visitor count was recorded to estimate the percentage of visitors interacting with the audio-player exhibit.

4   Results

Between October 1st, 2019 and September 30th, 2020, a total of 40623 events have been recorded. This time span also includes a lockdown period from March 12th, 2020 to May 17th, 2020 when the museum had to be completely closed as a protective measure against the spread of COVID 19. To exclude brief functional tests before opening and after closing all events outside official opening hours have been removed and only events that lasted 2 s or longer have been considered. Therefore, a total of 37402 events haven been analysed.

Overall Listening Time (a). The median listening time was $Mdn = 13$ s, whereas the average was $M = 40.05$ s ($SD = 88.86$ s, $N = 37402$). Out of all listening events, 407 lasted for the whole length of the info-track (1.09%), 5003 lasted for more than one minute (13.38%) whereas 27578 already stopped within the first 30 s (73.73%). Figure 2 shows the histogram of listening times with a bin width of 10 s, a median line dashed in red and a mean line dotted in blue for the whole timeframe of the exhibition.

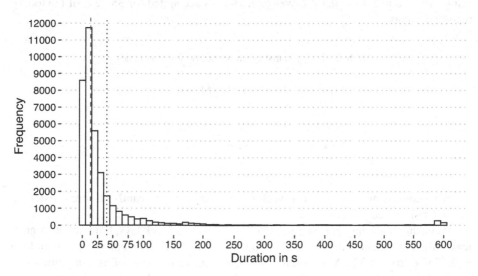

Fig. 2. Histogram of listening time with a bin-width of 10 s including the median (red dashed line, $Mdn = 13$ s) and mean (blue dotted line, $M = 40.05$ s, $SD = 88.86$ s, $N = 37402$). (Color figure online)

Relating the count of listening events to the daily visitor count shows that on average 53.2% of visitors were actually listening to the exhibit.

Listening characteristics between the independent left and right earpieces were nearly the same, with an equal median listening time of $Mdn = 13$ s and mean values of $M_{\text{left}} =$

39.52 s ($SD_{left} = 87.72$ s, $N_{left} = 20973$), and $M_{right} = 40.72$ s ($SD_{right} = 90.29$ s, $N_{right} = 16429$) (see Table 1). No significant differences were identified by a Mann-Whitney-U test performed in R ($p = 0.164$). The left earpiece was used 56% of the times, whereas the right one 44%.

Table 1. Usage statistics for left and right earpieces showing nearly the same use.

Earpiece location	Mdn (s)	M (s)	SD (s)	N
Left	13	39.52	87.72	20973
Right	13	40.72	90.29	16429

Day of Week Comparisons (b). Comparing listening characteristics between weekdays and weekends also revealed similar listening behavior, again with an equal median listening time of $Mdn = 13$ s and mean values of $M_{weekdays} = 40.61$ s ($SD_{weekdays} = 89.94$ s, $N_{weekdays} = 22920$), and $M_{weekend} = 39.16$ s ($SD_{weekend} = 87.12$ s, $N_{weekend} = 14482$) (see Table 2). No significant differences were identified by a Mann-Whitney-U test performed in R ($p = 0.436$). Weekend visitors accounted for 38.72% of the totally recorded events.

Table 2. Usage statistics on weekdays and weekends.

Day-type	Mdn (s)	M (s)	SD (s)	N
Weekdays	13	40.61	89.94	22920
Weekend	13	39.16	87.12	14482

Also comparing all days of a week did not show significantly different listening characteristics (see Table 3).

Weekends show higher user participations than other weekdays, however, no significant effect on listening durations could be detected using a Kruskal Wallis test in R ($p = 0.276$, $\chi^2(6) = 7.52$). Also visually comparing the distribution of listening times in a violin chart reveals no major differences in shapes (see Fig. 3).

Table 3. Usage statistics on different days of the week.

Day	Mdn (s)	M (s)	SD (s)	N
Monday	14	44.12	96.64	4390
Tuesday	13	42.36	95.08	4533
Wednesday	13	39.17	86.87	4616
Thursday	13	38.56	85.07	4349
Friday	13	39.07	85.77	5032
Saturday	13	42.14	94.04	6661
Sunday	13	36.62	80.68	7821

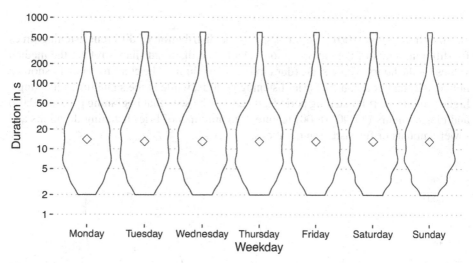

Fig. 3. Distribution of the different listening durations for different days of a week. The diamond shapes reflect the median listening durations. Note the log-scale for duration.

Hour of Day Comparisons (c). Comparing listening times for the different hours of a day reveals more variations (see Table 4).

Listening characteristics for the hour from 11:00 to 12:00 shows the highest listening durations ($Mdn_{11} = 15$ s, $M_{11} = 48.91$ s), but also the highest variations ($SD_{11} = 103.76$, $N_{11} = 5838$), while the hour from 10:00 to 11:00 ($N_{10} = 6911$, 18.48%) and 14:00 to 15:00 ($N_{14} = 6258$, 16.73%) accounted for the most listening cases.

A Kruskal-Wallis test in R reveals significant differences between listening durations for different hours of the day ($p < 0.001$, $\chi^2(8) = 186.31$). The $\eta^2(H) = 0.005$ shows a small effect size. To check, which hours differ significantly, pairwise comparisons were made using a Dunn-test in R using Holm-Bonferroni correction for multiple comparisons. Hereby, the hour from 11:00 to 12:00 shows significantly different results to

Table 4. Usage statistics on different hours of a day

Hour	Mdn (s)	M (s)	SD (s)	N
9	11	27.64	55.58	1133
10	14	38.62	82.67	6911
11	15	48.91	103.76	5838
12	13	43.80	97.23	4182
13	14	43.78	98.22	4658
14	13	34.69	76.67	6258
15	13	38.12	84.35	5750
16	11	34.00	82.31	2374
17	9	33.74	90.72	298

all other hours ($p < 0.001$). Figure 4 shows the distribution of different listening times for different hours of the day in a violin chart. The diamond shapes reflect the median values for the hours. The y-scale (duration) is logarithmic. The chart for hour 11 shows a noticeable smaller amount of brief listening periods, while at the same time reflecting a higher amount of full listening periods. It can also be seen that beginning (09:00–10:00) and closing hours (17:00–18:00) feature high amounts of brief listening durations and lower amounts of full listening durations.

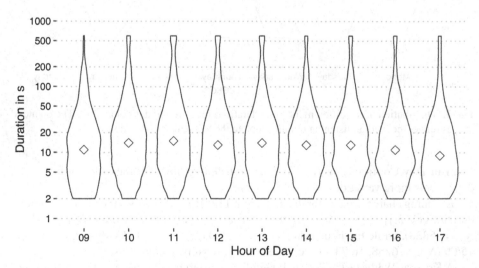

Fig. 4. Distribution of the different listening durations for different hours of the day. The diamond shapes reflect the median listening durations. Note the log-scale for duration.

Seasonal/Phase of Exhibition Comparison (d). To determine whether there are differences in listening characteristics between the starting phase of the exhibition and the ending phase, the time recordings were split into two groups: before and after the lockdown period, which was nearly half/half.

Table 5. Usage statistics from beginning/ending phase of the exhibition.

Phase	Mdn (s)	M (s)	SD (s)	N
Beginning	13	38.50	86.07	22821
Ending	14	42.48	93.00	14581

Listening durations at the beginning and end phase of the exhibition were slightly different, with a median listening time of $Mdn_{beginning} = 13$ s compared to $Mdn_{ending} = 14$ s. Also, the mean values were slightly different with $M_{beginning} = 38.50$ s ($SD_{beginning} = 86.07$ s, $N_{beginning} = 22821$), and $M_{ending} = 42.48$ s ($SD_{ending} = 90.29$ s, $N_{ending} = 14581$) (see Table 5). Significant differences are identified by a Mann-Whitney-U test performed in R ($p < 0.001$), however, analysis of the effect size by Cliff's Delta is reported as negligible ($cd = 0.037$).

Figure 5 shows the slightly changed listening behavior between beginning and ending phase of the exhibition, where the ending phase shows fewer brief listening periods, and slightly more long listening periods than the beginning phase.

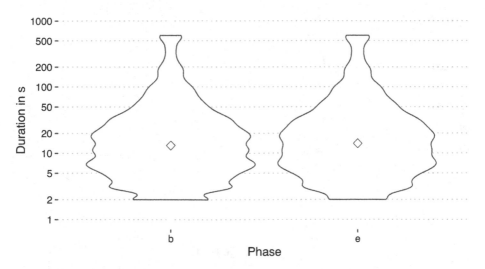

Fig. 5. Distribution of the different listening durations for the beginning (b) and ending (e) phase of the exhibition. The diamond shapes reflect the median listening durations. Note the log-scale for duration.

Single/Dual Listener Comparison (e). As an indicator for the influence of the social setting on the listening duration, events have been split into single use (only one earpiece have been in use), und dual use (both earpieces have been in use) during a listening event (Table 6).

Table 6. Usage statistics for single and dual listening cases.

Type	Mdn (s)	M (s)	SD (s)	N
Single	7	16.34	42.86	10243
Dual	18	48.99	99.44	27159

Listening behavior analysis between single and dual listening cases shows different median listening times. The median duration for single use was lower ($Mdn_{single} = 7$ s) than the median duration for dual use ($Mdn_{dual} = 18$ s). Also, the mean value for single use was lower ($M_{single} = 16.34$ s, $SD_{single} = 42.86$ s, $N_{single} = 10243$) compared to dual use ($M_{dual} = 48.99$ s, $SD_{dual} = 99.44$ s, $N_{dual} = 27159$). The majority of events occurred in a dual situation (72.61%).

Significant differences are identified by a Mann-Whitney-U test performed in R ($p < 0.001$). Analysis of effect size using Cliffs Delta shows a medium effect ($cd = 0.407$). Figure 6 shows the different usage behavior between single and dual use. Also, the boxplot shown in Fig. 7 reflects the different listening durations between dual und single usage mode.

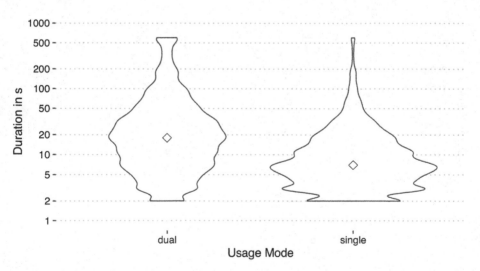

Fig. 6. Distribution of the different listening durations for the dual and single listening cases. The diamond shapes reflect the median listening durations. Note the log-scale for duration.

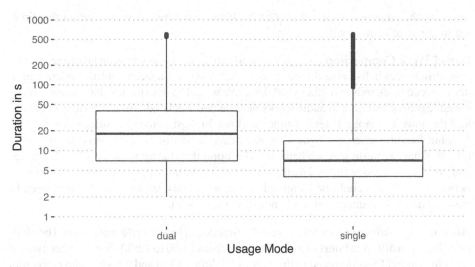

Fig. 7. Boxplot comparing listening durations between dual and single listening cases. Note the log-scale for duration.

5 Discussion

Overall Listening Time (a). When comparing the observed audio listening durations to the numbers reported by Serrell (2002) in her study regarding video watching behavior in exhibitions, the observed audio listening durations are far lower. Instead of 137 s average viewing time reported by Serrell, we observed an average listening time of 40 s. Serrell reported a holding power of one third to below one half of the video duration. In our case, the median listening duration of 13 s for the audio track equates to one fiftieth of the duration of the audio track – a much lower holding power. However, these different results aren't unexpected: First, it's not fair to compare audio to video, since video is perceived by multiple senses. Second, the attention time spent on media is highly dependent on the content and style of the media presented. Third, the context of the exhibit has a big influence on the attention item - an exhibit always faces competition from other exhibits and social interactions of visitors, like pointed out by Serrell (2002).

Our results are more in line with the typical time users spend on a website before they decide to move on. In their study regarding long-term web usage, Weinreich et al. found the median time spent on a page to be 12 s, on specific pages like search results this is reduced to only 8 s (Weinreich et al. 2008).

Another interesting observation regarding the listening behavior is that once listeners get over a certain point, they are more likely to keep listening to the whole track. 24.43% of listeners listening for at least 3 min listened to the whole 10 min track. Figure 1 illustrates this well. This also means, that average listening times are highly skewed, and a far better indicator regarding typical listening behavior is the median time, as it is insensitive to outliers.

As a conclusion regarding the observed listening times, really important content needs to be placed within the first few seconds of an audio-track. This observation is in line with the conclusions of Serrell (2002). If interest is not captured within this time, the majority of visitors will move on.

Day of Week Comparisons (b). In this study we could not confirm that there are significant differences in listening durations for different days of a week, and also interestingly not between weekends and other weekdays. We would have expected that visitors would spend less time listening to audio tracks on crowded weekends. While Sundays actually had the lowest average listening times and the highest activity, results were not significant. Sandifer also investigated the difference in visitor behavior between weekend and weekdays regarding group behavior. He found that during weekdays family groups and non-family groups showed a different behavior during weekdays, but no differences between the groups could be identified during weekends, which was also attributed to the crowded environments on weekends (Sandifer 1997).

Hour of Day Comparisons (c). A small difference in listening durations could be identified between different hours of a day. The hour from 11:00 to 12:00 shows longer median listening times (15 s compared to the overall median o 13 s) and a higher rate of visitors listening to the whole track. Figure 5 also reveals fewer brief listening periods than on other hours of the day. One possible explanation for this behavior could be that visitors might have to pass some time before getting lunch - which typically takes place at 12:00 in the region of the museum. Another possible explanation would be that at this time of the day another type of visitor is present in the museum, like e.g., people who combine the museum visit with having lunch at the restaurant afterwards.

One factor might also be the decline in activity from the hour before and the museum getting quieter. Our data shows that the hour from 10:00 to 11:00 is the most active of the day. However, the listening duration doesn't seem to be related to the absolute activity levels, as other hours have lower median listening times despite lower and higher activity levels.

Seasonal/Phase of Exhibition Comparison (d). Only negligible differences in listening durations could be observed regarding the starting and ending phase of the exhibition. A tendency can be seen towards longer listening durations in the second half of the exhibition period (a median listening duration of 13 s in the first half compared to 14 s in the second half).

As the beginning phase of the exhibition was mostly during the winter period and the ending phase during the summer period, effects of season or novelty of the exhibition cannot be differentiated in our case study. In addition to the seasonal/novelty aspect, the exhibition was interrupted by a lockdown due to COVID 19 protective measures in between the phases. The conscious savoring of a museum visit might have been somewhat higher after the lockdown. However, despite the only small differences observed, this might be an indicator that it could be relevant to consider longer term effects in exhibition design and optimization.

Single/Dual Listener Comparison (e). The comparison of single and dual listener scenarios revealed significant differences in listening duration and medium effect size between the two situations (median time of 7 s for the single scenario, 18 s for the dual scenario). The big difference in listening behavior between the two situations might be explainable by the social context. If two persons are listening at the same time, one might feel more resistance to hang up before the other person. This view might be supported by the observations made by Vom Lehm et al., who observed that the conduct of a visitor might be influenced by the conduct of others, even if there is some distance between them. As an example, they mention the phenomenon that visitors are attracted to an exhibit, if others are already looking at it (Vom Lehm et al. 2002, p 21). To actually confirm this theory, an observational study could complement the data gathered by automated logging.

Since we were only able to use the automatically logged data for our analysis, a basic limitation needs to be pointed out: based on this data it cannot be differentiated between one listener listening multiple times or multiple listeners. Based on the audio content, we highly suspect that the number of visitors listening repeatedly to the same content is negligible. However, some visitors might have expected that random audio content would play on another try or on the second earpiece. If this was the case, then our observed median listening time would be shifted towards the lower end. This demonstrates that automated log data cannot replace in-person observations at an exhibition but is a good complement to it.

6 Conclusion

In this paper we set out the hypothesis that interaction patterns with exhibits vary among different situations and time during the run of an exhibition. Therefore, it might not be sufficient to only use brief observation periods spent in exhibitions to compare different exhibit-variants for the optimization process, but rather it is also important to consider long-term effects.

In the study presented above, we automatically logged visitor-interactions with an audio-exhibit for one year and analysed changes in listening durations over different times and situations. We were able to identify changes in listening behavior between different times of a day, and between the beginning and ending phase of the exhibition. We were also able to reveal changes related to different listening situations (one or multiple concurrent listeners). These findings seem to confirm our hypothesis.

Therefore, long-term automated logging of visitor-exhibit-interactions can help to identify time and situation-based patterns in visitor behavior and thus might provide valuable insights for exhibit optimizations.

While data from one exhibit can already reveal interesting usage patterns as presented in this paper, combined data from many exhibits in an exhibition or even multiple exhibitions using big data analysis techniques might reveal even more interesting insights.

The presented automated long-term interaction logging system for interactive exhibits should in no way be seen as replacement of in-person observations at a museum. It should rather be seen as a valuable extension of the latter. Combining both observation methods will provide a solid foundation to base future exhibit-developments on. In a follow up study, the effect of different variants of interactive exhibits on visitor-interaction over time will be investigated.

References

Allen, S.: Designs for learning: studying science museum exhibits that do more than entertain. Sci. Ed. **88**, 17–33 (2004)

Aalst, I., Boogaarts, I.: From museum to mass entertainment: the evolution of the role of museums in cities. Eur. Urban Reg. Stud. **9**, 195–209 (2002)

Bitgood, S.: An analysis of visitor circulation: movement patterns and the general value principle. Curator: Museum J. **49**, 463–475 (2006)

Bitgood, S.: Museum fatigue: a critical review. Visitor Stud. (1064–5578), **12**(2), 93–111 (2009)

Bitgood, S.: Attention and Value: Keys to Understanding Museum Visitors. Left Coast Press Inc. (2013)

Davey, G.: What is museum fatigue? Visit. Stud. Today **8**(3), 17–21 (2005)

Economou, M.: A world of interactive exhibits. In: Marty, P., Jones, K. (eds.) Museum Informatics: People, Information, and Technology in Museums. Series: Routledge Studies in Library and Information Science, pp. 137–156. Taylor & Francis, New York (2007)

Falk, J., Koran, J., Dierking, L., Dreblow, L.: Predicting visitor behaviour. Curator **28**(4), 249–257 (1985)

Friedman, A.: The evolution of the science museum. Phys. Today **63**(10), 45 (2010)

Graf, B., Leinfelder, R., Trischler, H.: Museums as a site of knowledge production. In: Graf, B., Rodekamp, V. (eds.) Museums: Between Quality and Relevance - Denkschrift on the State of Museums, pp. 45–46. Berliner Schriften zur Museumsforschung, Berlin (2016)

Haywood, N., Cairns, P.: Engagement with an interactive museum exhibit. In: McEwan, T., Gulliksen, J., Benyon, D. (eds.) People and Computers XIX—The Bigger Picture, pp. 113–129. Springer, London (2006). https://doi.org/10.1007/1-84628-249-7_8

Hein, G.E.: The role of museums in society: education and social action. Curator: Museum J. **48**(4), 357–363 (2005)

Kahneman, D., Tversky, A.: Prospect theory: an analysis of decision under risk. Econometrica **47**(2), 263–292 (1979)

Kirchberg, V., Tröndle, M.: Experiencing exhibitions: a review of studies on visitor experiences in museums. Curator: Museum J. **55**, 435–452 (2012)

Künz, A., Ritter, W.: Alternative interfaces für museumsexponate. In: Kempter, G., Mayer, H.O., Weidmann, K.-H. (eds.) Empirische Designforschung zwischen Designer und Rezipient (Beiträge zur empirischen Designforschung, Bd. 4), pp. 145–160. Hohenems: Bucher (2015)

Melton, A.W.: Problems of Installation in Museums of Art. American Association of Museums Monograph New Series No. 14 (1935)

NEMO: Values 4 Museums. Network of European Museum Organisations: Berlin (2015). https://www.ne-mo.org/fileadmin/Dateien/public/NEMO_documents/NEMO_four_values_2015.pdf. Accessed 28 Jan 2021

Sandifer, C.: Time-based behaviors at an interactive science museum: exploring the differences between weekday/weekend and family/nonfamily visitors. Sci. Ed. **81**, 689–701 (1997)

Serrell, B.: Are they watching? Visitors and videos in exhibitions. Curator: Museum J. **45**, 50–64 (2002)

Serrell, B.: Paying More Attention to Paying Attention (2010). https://www.informalscience.org/sites/default/files/S&A.PA2.FinalDforCAISE2016.pdf. Accessed 28 Jan 2021

Turgay-Zıraman, A., Imamoğlu, Ç.: Visitor attention in exhibitions: the impact of exhibit objects' ordinal position, relative size, and proximity to larger objects. Environ. Behav. **52**(4), 343–370 (2020)

Vom Lehn, D., Heath, C., Hindmarsh, J.: Video based field studies in museums and galleries. Visit. Stud. Today **5**(3), 15–23 (2002)

Vom Lehn, D.: Embodying experience: a video-based examination of visitors' conduct and interaction in museums. Eur. J. Mark. **40**, 1340–1359 (2006)

Weinreich, H., Obendorf, H., Herder, E., Mayer, M.: Not quite the average: an empirical study of Web use. ACM Trans. Web **2**(1), 31 (2008). Article 5

Wilson-Barnao, C.: Museum or not? The changing face of curated science, tech, art and culture. In: The Conversation (2018). https://theconversation.com/museum-or-not-the-changing-face-of-curated-science-tech-art-and-culture-95507. Accessed 28 Jan 2021

Yalowitz, S.S., Bronnenkant, K.: Timing and tracking: unlocking visitor behavior. Visit. Stud. **12**(1), 47–64 (2009)

Zbuchea, A.: Museums as theme parks - a possible marketing approach? Manag. Dyn. Knowl. Econ. **3**, 483–507 (2015)

Engaging New Residents' City Exploration Using a Gamified Location-Based Information Interactive System

Yiyi Zhang[✉], Yujia Cao, and Tatsuo Nakajima

Department of Computer Science and Engineering, Waseda University, Tokyo, Japan
{zhangyiyi,mushishita,tatsuo}@dcl.cs.waseda.ac.jp

Abstract. This study aims to examine ways to assist new residents in exploring and acquiring location knowledge about their cities using gamified navigation systems. For residents who have just moved into a new city, the issue of how to better integrate themselves into the city and community and then establish connections and bonds with their surroundings is a challenge. Our goal is to help new residents who have moved into a new city know more about their urban environment and establish emotional connections with the surrounding places. We develop two systems for a case study to explore the demands and interaction during city exploration activities. We also conduct a user study to observe and evaluate user experiences using our systems. We hope our study provides some reflections for the further design of these types of services and systems that can engage residents in exploring cities and strengthen their connections with the cities.

Keywords: Augmented reality · Virtual reality · City exploration · Location-based service · Gamification

1 Introduction

Cities have very close connections with our lives. Some studies have indicated that a good relationship between residents and cities has an important impact on residents' sense of belonging and well-being. As for residents who have just moved to a new city, how to start exploring an unfamiliar environment and gain an in-depth understanding of a city is a major challenge.

With the continuous penetration of information and communications technology (ICT), location-based services provide effective assistance in a variety of scenarios, such as map navigation and wayfinding, popular recommendations based on points of interest, etc. Walking and exploring unfamiliar street blocks and discovering interesting new places will help residents better understand the unique atmosphere, multicultural nature, and landscape of a city, thus establishing a good connection between individuals and the city. A memorable city exploration experience requires some unexpected surprises. In addition, during city exploration activities, the motivation and demands of pedestrians are

© Springer Nature Switzerland AG 2021
M. Kurosu (Ed.): HCII 2021, LNCS 12762, pp. 412–428, 2021.
https://doi.org/10.1007/978-3-030-78462-1_32

dynamic. The method of city exploration support using digital technology has developed over time. In addition, smart mobile devices play an active role in these exploration processes by providing real-time information and changing how people interact with the real world. The solutions that an ordinary navigation system provides are less diverse. At present, the commonly used route planning and map systems focus on the shortest route recommendation and accurate navigation. Although accurate navigation can take pedestrians to a destination in the shortest amount of time, when roaming in city blocks, accurate navigation may lose the fun of exploration and even miss some points of interest that might be a surprise along the way. Therefore, the issue of how to provide interesting navigation to satisfy the needs of pedestrians and engage with pedestrians to explore city blocks is important.

To allow pedestrians to acquire better experience with smart mobile technologies while walking and exploring city streets, this research focuses on novel navigation systems rather than accurate navigation systems to support city exploration. Different from traditional map navigation, the novel navigation systems aim to provide more personal, interesting, and surprising explorations for pedestrians as they wander streets in a more comfortable and natural interactive way. To study the demands and interaction activities of residents who moved in a new city, we first designed a virtual reality (VR) city tour to simulate real-world walking and exploration and then designed a gamified augmented reality (AR) navigation system to enhance the resident user experience in city exploration. Through the user study experiment with our systems, we learn the demands and interaction design insight of these types of navigation for the future.

2 Related Work

2.1 Novel Navigation System

Exploring the city's neighborhoods through walking, both for tourists and for new and old residents living in the city, is a way to get to know a city better, feel the atmosphere of a city, discover communities of interest, and build emotional connections with a city and community. [15] presents the results from research that explored and set directions for computing's role in outdoor recreation. In addition, the study illustrated that spending time outdoors can positively impact mental and emotional well-being. In recent years, with the rapid development of mobile computing technology, ubiquitous computing devices and services have begun to penetrate our daily lives. Some researchers have focused on novel navigation rather than accurate navigation to support city exploration so as to promote pedestrian exploration experiences during these activities. Vaittinen and McGookin [12] proposed a navigation system based on foraging theory, which provides a means to assess the potential value one might gain from visiting an area. The starting point of the design was visualizing the locations of different types of venues in relation to pedestrians' positions, which provide a general directional navigation. Viswanathan et al. proposed an approach [13] to construct a visual aid on mobile devices that roughly supports navigation without demanding continuous user attention. The interesting neighborhoods of a city are represented as clouds on a mobile map. When the user finishes visiting a neighborhood, these clouds turn gray in the regions explored by the user. These studies pay more attention to designing an interesting navigation path for pedestrians to explore instead of following an accurate single map navigation route. This type of interest-based navigation provides us with insight into a method of engaging city exploration. However, some details that pedestrians use during interest-based navigation when exploring city blocks still need to be observed and studied using actual field experiments.

2.2 Virtual Reality and Augmented Reality

VR and AR are two technological breakthroughs that stimulate reality perception. Both have been applied in travel and tourism environments to enhance users' experience [17]. The application of VR in the field of tourism is mainly concentrated in digital displays, cultural heritage, digital museums, etc. while AR focuses on the expansion of the real world and some outdoor mobile interactions to improve users' travel experiences. Instead of creating a nonreal environment as in VR, AR enhances reality by amplifying it through information technologies [17]. There are more articles on mobile AR technology-related research [17]; however, compared with the popularity of VR in the tourism industry, the application of AR in the tourism industry needs to be broadened and deepened.

The popularity of Pokémon GO[1] has brought location-based games into the public's view and reached a mainstream status [8]. Mobile AR has greatly reduced the costs and threshold of the public to use AR technology, allowing people to go out and explore the outdoors [1]. Many HCI studies have found that interacting with destinations through location-based games is a good way to improve the user experience in exploration activities [3, 9]. These studies showed that game play satisfaction has a positive effect on destination satisfaction and that AR mobile games potentially influence tourism behavior.

There are many academics and industry practitioners studying and designing location-based augmented reality game experiences. [9] proposed constructing a behavior model for Pokémon GO users considering motivation, sport involvement, and tourism benefits; and the results illustrated that motivation has a significant influence on sport involvement and tourism benefits. The Tourism industry should attach importance to their attractions using Pokémon-related products and events to enhance the motivation of Pokémon GO users. Based on such research, we could combine location-based augmented reality technology with exploratory navigation to provide more attractive and interesting services. [10] proposed a novel pervasive mobile augmented reality location-based game. This game comprises a mobile client and an online authoring tool, which encourage visitors and locals to explore a city. In addition, [11] proposed a location-based game named City Explorer to find how transit commuters capture, share, and view community information based on locations. Research such as these papers provides insight into more possibilities for designing location-based augmented reality services for city exploration and digital community establishment.

Virtual reality provides a significant improvement in the freedom of traveling. For example, virtual traveling to a museum supports freedom of traveling in both space and time. Visitors have a wide range of choices from which to select their time to visit and the exhibition hall they prefer to visit, even at closing time or if they desire to visit exhibition halls in a totally confusing order. Weather and seasons [6] could also be adjusted in a

---

[1] https://www.pokemongo.com/en-us/.

virtual environment. With virtual reality devices, an immersive virtual environment with adjustable weather and seasons can improve the quality of travel experiences because travelers no longer need to be restricted to the current time, location and weather.

2.3 Gamification

Gamification is the theory of using game design elements in nongame contexts to motivate and increase user activity [4]. Gamification is commonly used to improve user engagement and organizational productivity, learning, crowdsourcing, employee recruitment, etc. In different situations, gamification elements and interactions are designed to improve user participation, motivation, loyalty, and fun. [18] design a mobile role-playing game (RPG) where the character evolves based on the exercises the user performs in reality, which can motivate and persuade a potentially large demographic of users to engage in physical activity for an extended period of time through the enjoyment of an engaging game. In [19], researchers investigate how different personalities respond to various persuasive strategies that are used in persuasive health games and gamified systems, which offer design guidelines for tailoring persuasive games and gamified designs to a particular group of personalities. Gamification promotes user engagement and creates higher intrinsic motivations. In addition, [20] applies gamification to employees' micro-learning and considers gamification as a method to increase user promote user engagement.

With the spread of mobile digital devices, ICT services bring many advantages to the travel and tourism industry to enhance user experiences [2, 7]. Among these advantages, gamification design influences tourists' satisfaction, tourism locations and the economy around tourist attractions [14]. Arkenson et al. [5] designed a location-based game by following tour guides to complete a variety of tasks that could lead a tourist through Tainan city in Taiwan. In [16], Pang et al. designed a location-based game with a storyline to engage the player (tourist) with the main urban sights following an augmented reality path while playing small games. Studies such as these papers provide insight into more possibilities for using gamification and casual games to design location-based services for city exploration. These studies focused on helping tourists to understand an entire city on the whole. In some multicultural cities, there are many street blocks with different characteristics and atmospheres, which may attract people with different interests and hobbies to explore and discover some fascinating surprises. Unfortunately, few studies pay attention to how to promote new resident user experiences in these activities using gamification systems and applications.

3 Preliminary User Study

To understand the demands of new residents for city exploration supported by mobile technologies, we conducted a questionnaire survey on 14 international students (13 males, average age $= 23$) from China who were going to live and study in Tokyo in the future. All of them had come to Tokyo for less than two months (1.8 months on average). We asked all the participants to answer a questionnaire and participate a short interview with some questions. As Fig. 1 shows, 71% of the participants liked to explore city streets by walking. In addition, all participants thought that map navigation was the most commonly used mobile technology in their exploration to help them know more about the new city they live in, as shown in Fig. 2.

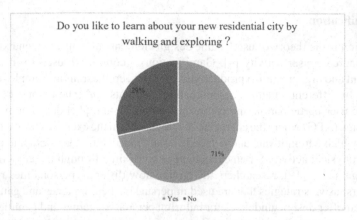

Fig. 1. Do you like to learn about your new residential city by walking and exploring?

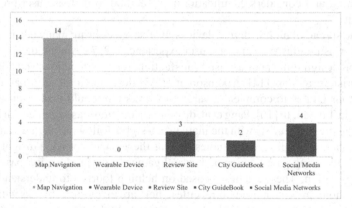

Fig. 2. What smart technology do you commonly use to learn more about the new city or new community in which you live? (choose 2 options).

In the survey, we learned that participants faced many challenges and difficulties while exploring the city, as shown in Fig. 3 and Fig. 4. For example, some participants said they paid too much attention to the navigation interface and neglected other information such as signs on a road.

One participant (P2) said that when using a traditional map to navigate, there was too much useless information or places that the user did not want overlaid, resulting in visual redundancy. Another participant (P4) reported that when he wandered in an area, he was unable to return to the previous location and route because he was exploring other paths or locations. Some participants also stated that the real-time information provided by the navigation systems or applications currently in use was sometimes inaccurate.

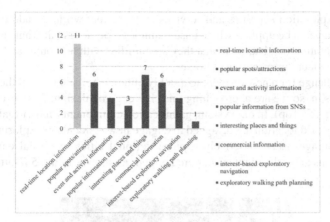

Fig. 3. What information or assistance do you want to acquire from smart mobile devices during city walking and exploring? (choose 3 options).

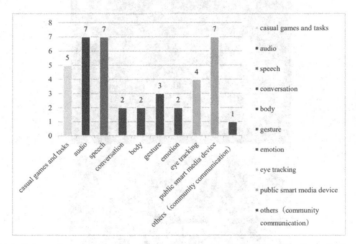

Fig. 4. Which interaction you prefer to support your city walking and exploring?(choose 3 options).

Based on the survey results, we summarized the ways in which new residents explore their basic needs in the city they live in and interact with mobile technologies. We developed two systems for a case study for observation and further study. We will introduce these two systems and describe the experimental details in later sections.

4   Case Study 1: Virtual City Tour

4.1   Overview

Virtual reality (VR) city exploration can simulate real city blocks while walking and break through the constraints of time and space; thus, we can use VR city exploration to test user exploration activities and services in the virtual world. In addition, VR city exploration can also be applied when a user cannot go outdoors but wants to simulate a roaming exploration in advance so that they are familiar with the routes and atmosphere and learn more local information at home.

It is a challenge for a new resident to quickly obtain a holistic view of the city blocks he or she lives in, so we are approaching this challenge by designing a virtual city tour, as shown in Fig. 5 (Top). In our system, gamification components and virtual interaction with the real-world location are designed to engage new residents in exploring the entire city. To encourage users to actively explore fictional cities in virtual environments, interactive icons and related interfaces are applied, as shown in Fig. 5 (Bottom).

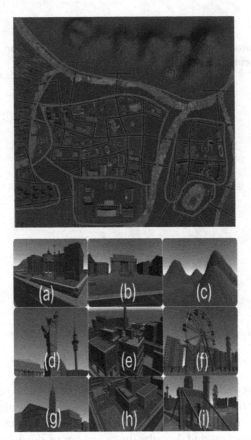

Fig. 5. **(Top)** Overview of the city distribution, and **(Bottom)** examples of buildings and spots (The typical spots and buildings in the city include the following: (a) a government building, (b) a museum, (c) surrounding mountains, (d) a statue at the city center, (e) a commercial area and a monument at the center, (f) an amusement park and residential area behind the center, (g) an art museum, (h) a school, and (i) a bridge over a river).

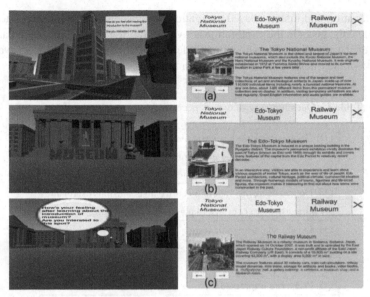

Fig. 6. **(Left)** Real-world location-based interaction and navigation in the process. **(Right)** The related interfaces of the museum. The related interfaces of the museum model include the following: (a) the Tokyo National Museum, (b) the Edo-Tokyo Museum, and (c) the Railway Museum. Each page includes four images of the introduced museum, which could be switched through the left/right arrows.

4.2 Implementation

To implement virtual exploration, a virtual environment is required. At the beginning, a mirrored scene according to reality is designed. To construct a virtual city scene, the Unity3D[2] platform is used. The virtual city consists of residential areas, commercial areas, centric areas, museums, an amusement park, a monument, a lake, rivers and surrounding mountains, as shown in Fig. 6 (Left). Buildings and infrastructure constructions, including roads, bridges, and flowerbeds, are prefabs available from the material library. A statue stands in the center of centric area. An art museum, a government building, and a school are located in a centric area. A TV station and signal tower are also included. Some detailed scenes and exploration interactions are illustrated in Fig. 6 (Right).

4.3 Experiment

To test the interaction between users and the real geographic location information in the virtual reality city during walking and exploration with our system, we invited 11 participants (7 males, average age = 23.9) to experience the virtual city exploration. Of the 11 participants, 63.6% of them had not used virtual reality systems or applications to explore the city. In the experiment, participants will explore an unfamiliar city block

---

[2] https://unity.com.

based on location and interest-based navigation in the scene, learn relevant knowledge, and complete the tasks in the exploration activity. After the experience, each participant will answer the questionnaire shown in Table 1 for experience satisfaction evaluation. The results of the questionnaire are shown in Fig. 7.

Table 1. Questionnaire of experience satisfaction evaluation for system.

Q1. Do you think the system is useful?
Q2. Do you like to explore and interact in the city streets using gamified interaction with a real destination?
Q3. Do you think this type of incentive mechanism is useful and encourages you to continue to play and explore more?
Q4. Do you like using this system?
Q5. Did you enjoy the experience?
Q6. Were you interested?
Q7. Were you impressed?
Q8. Do you think you were attracted?
Q9. Do you think these functions can meet your demands?
Q10. If it is perfect enough, would you like to use the system in the future?

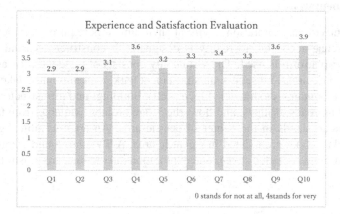

Fig. 7. The results of the experience satisfaction evaluation.

4.4   Discussion

Based on user study results, the majority of participants considered this exploration navigation to be useful (average value = 2.9), and they liked using it to learn more about the city streets (average value = 3.6). Most of them are willing to use it if it is perfect enough in practice (average value = 3.9).

Participant P3 stated that *"the system could actually do a classification in advance for different demands of people who come to a city, such as, to live, to travel, to study, or to see a doctor and so on. For example, you can do a preliminary classification at the beginning of the exploration, explore some options..."*. More than one participant suggested that if the roads and facilities of a virtual city were fully simulated in the real world, the system could be used by people who have difficulty getting out or who want to experience a route ahead of time. Participant P10 said that if he uses a VR city exploration system, he will prefer to interact with other players online, which inspired us to consider establishing a social network in the future.

People who are interested in exploring will want to use the system themselves. This group of people may use the system to see the cities they want to visit, plan their routes ahead of time, do their homework, and eventually actually experience the city. However, for those who prefer to stay at home rather than go out, using VR to explore cities offers more possibilities and perspectives on their lives. In other words, further experiments and discussions are needed on the classification of people using such systems.

The participants supposed that it is more important to combine the virtual world and information with the real-world location, which led us to consider how to add more interaction between the virtual world and reality. At the same time, in the questionnaire survey and interview, we learned that different people have different purposes for using virtual reality system to simulate real city tour, so they also have different demands for functions and user interface. For example, one participant suggested that, for specific roaming purpose, the location information could be simplified on the map display to highlight the target location information he needs.

After a user study test on VR city tours, we reviewed our navigation design and proposed a gamified AR navigation system to support user interaction during practical exploration.

5 Case Study 2: Gamified Navigation System: Enhancing Resident User Experience in City Exploration

5.1 Overview

In order to promote user experiences while city traveling, this research proposed an AR travel guide system based on a role-playing game (RPG), which combines an incentive mechanism of gamification and real-time geographic location services to provide users with appropriate travel information interaction without disturbing the user's own exploration and roaming. The system was designed to provide travelers with a more memorable, highly engaged, and satisfying travel experience. The functions of the system, which allow travel experiences to be more attractive and impressive so that the memory becomes clear, coherent and memorable, will be described in detail below.

Based on the analysis of the needs of travelers, the system designed in this research, based on ensuring that the user is provided with a real guide to attractions, adds role-playing gamified dialogue interaction and incentive mechanisms to improve the system's

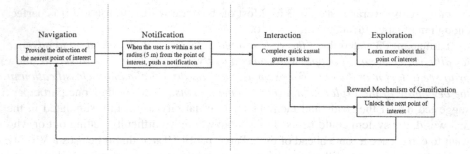

Fig. 8. The mechanism of the system is illustrated by a cycle consisting of four stages. They are the following: navigation, notification, interaction and exploration.

interest and immersion. The mechanism of the system, which aims to engage pedestrians in exploring points of interest one by one, is illustrated in Fig. 8. In terms of the navigation stage, we provide the direction of the nearest point of interest and display its distance from the pedestrian. We set a series of hotspots in destinations based on real geographical coordinates (using GPS). When the user is within a set radius (5 m) from the center of the point of interest, the system will send a notification, as shown in the figure. In order to encourage pedestrians to explore many more points of interest, we designed interactions and explorations with gamification reward mechanisms. In a manner similar to the conversation system of an RPG (role-playing game), users can complete some game tasks followed by conversation and interaction with virtual character assistants. A gamified reward mechanism would engage pedestrians to trigger navigation to another close point of interest. The screenshots of our system are illustrated in Fig. 9 and Fig. 10.

Fig. 9. A quick casual game for pedestrians to learn more information about this location.

Fig. 10. AR navigation and game conversation are activated by a virtual assistant (a virtual cat character).

5.2 Implementation

The system was developed using the Unity3D game engine. The augmented reality features are supported by Vuforia[3] SDK. The application is installed on an iPhone smart phone with the iOS12.1.4 system. The system UI interface is shown in Fig. 11.

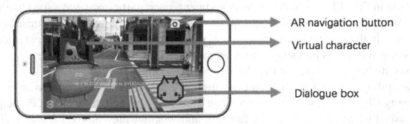

Fig. 11. Application UI interface.

5.3 Experiment

To evaluate user experiences (usability and engagement), we conduct a field experiment as a preliminary user study. We invited 5 participants (3 female and 2 male, average age = 23.8) to use our system to explore a real city block destination named Jiyūgaoka[4]. Jiyūgaoka is a residential area located in Setagaya City, Tokyo. It is surrounded by various shopping streets and residential districts. Various stores are hidden in the narrow streets that are popular with residents and visitors. In addition to colorful and interesting shops, there are also very famous places of interest, including the ancient Kumano Shrine, a miniature version of Venice and an old Japanese-style café Kosoan. We selected several popular locations located in Jiyūgaoka district and obtained their GPS coordinates (latitude and longitude) from Google Maps as hotspots for the experiments. The map of Jiyūgaoka is illustrated in Fig. 12 (left). It consists of coffee shops, bakeries, shopping malls, restaurants, beautiful architectures and other types of charming points of interest.

---

[3] https://developer.vuforia.com.

[4] https://www.jiyugaoka-abc.com.

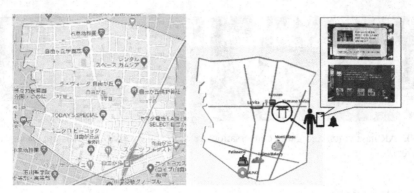

Fig. 12. Left: map capture of Jiyūgaoka from Google Map; right: location-based hotspot trigger function.

We asked participants to explore all the points of interest using our system. When the participant was close to a point of interest, a series of activities would be triggered, as shown in Fig. 12 (right). After the experiment, each participant was asked to answer a questionnaire. Then, all participants were invited to participate in a semistructured interview. In the interviews, all participants were asked to describe their experience and give some comments and suggestions on the functions of the system. The progress of the user study is illustrated in Fig. 13.

Regarding the system function evaluation, we asked the participants to answer the following 10 questions where answers range from 0 for not at all to 4 for very. Participants were asked whether they liked the function and whether they thought it was useful or not. The results are shown in Fig. 14.

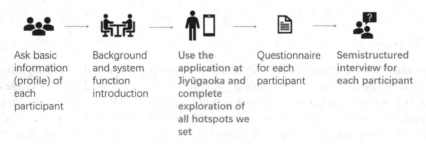

Fig. 13. The progress of user study.

Regarding the experience satisfaction evaluation of the system, we asked participants to complete the following 8 questions, as illustrated in Table 2, where answers range from 0 for not at all to 4 for very. Five participants were also invited to participate in a semistructured interview. The interview asked participants to describe their experience and provide some suggestions on the functions of the system. The results of the experience and satisfaction evaluation are shown in Fig. 15.

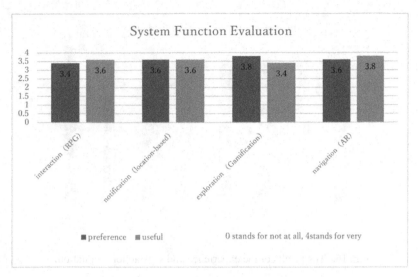

Fig. 14. The result of the system function evaluation.

Table 2. Questionnaire of experience satisfaction evaluation for system.

Q1. Do you think the system is useful?
Q2. Do you like using this system?
Q3. Did you enjoy the experience?
Q4. Were you interested?
Q5. Were you impressed?
Q6. Were you attracted to the system?
Q7. Do you think these functions can meet your demands?
Q8. If it is perfect enough, would you like to use the system in the future?

5.4 Discussion

From the results, we learned that most of the participants thought the functions of the system were useful (average value = 3.6) and liked to use this system to support their exploration demands (average value = 3.8). Most of the participants considered our system interesting, reaching an average value of 3.8. Some comments from the interview were as follows: *"I think this is a very interesting design. I was attracted by the gamification mechanism, which let me engage in exploring points of interests one by one..." (P1). "It is helpful for me to explore the interesting places by accident without the pre plan in advanced" (P5). "The proposal notification from the virtual character makes me feel accompanied even if I explore the city blocks alone..." (P2).*

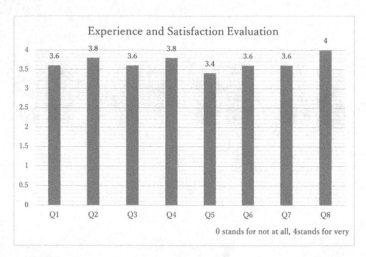

Fig. 15. The results of the experience and satisfaction evaluation.

According to these results, we learned that many of the participants thought this system enhanced interest in the entire exploration process. All the participants said that using this gamified navigation to explore destinations is more interesting than the traditional navigation or city guide applications they have used. Some participants believe that following the system's storyline to explore the attractions will help them generate complete and continuous memories. In addition, the interactive casual game tasks between the user and real environment made participants feel more connected with the destination. Furthermore, this type of interactive system based on location can not only help pedestrians have better experiences but can also drive the commercial prosperity of city blocks. For example, we can extend the interaction function to the reality business or with other residents and stores. We also found that the motivation and demands of participants were diverse. Some participants look forward to all kinds of navigation routes for them to choose.

We also found that some participants were unwilling to hold smart phones all the time during navigation and exploration. Therefore, providing diverse multimode interactions for exploration navigation is a valuable issue in the future. Based on our study results, we suggest some insights for location-based service and navigation design in city exploration. First, exploratory navigation routes should be diverse depending on different pedestrian preferences. Second, the exploratory navigation system needs to be more intelligent such as by possessing a context-aware ability, which could respond to changes in the environment. Then, multimode interaction should be considered to make navigation more comfortable and practical. Finally, more than one participant mentioned that they were concerned about safety and privacy when using this kind of system in city blocks, which are also challenges we need to solve in the future.

6 Conclusions and Future Work

In this study, we explored the needs and motivation of new residents in city exploration and how to encourage them to participate in retrieving, accessing, viewing and sharing the information of a specific location, making them better understand their living environment. We developed two systems and designed a case study to evaluate user experiences. Overall, our system encouraged participants to explore their city and learn more location-based information. We found that the motivation and demands of the participants were diverse. We expect to use gamified VR and AR interactive systems to improve residents' user experience of exploring their cities.

However, in the experiment, different people have obvious preferences due to their different purposes in using VR and AR systems. VR systems can simulate and test real-world location-based interactions and services, but for some people, they could not replace a wonderful real offline experience. On the other hand, the gamified AR interactive system could indeed increase the interest and interaction in the process of walking in the real city streets, but people will also worry that their attention will be occupied by too many digital devices and information, thus losing some fun of exploratory experience. Therefore, we suggest reflecting on location-based services and exploratory navigation design to help engage new residents in exploring and establishing connections with their cities.

First, exploratory navigation should be diverse depending on different interests and preferences, no matter in VR and AR systems. Second, the exploratory navigation system needs to be more intelligent such as possessing a context-aware ability, which could respond to changes in the environment and changes of people's demands. There also needs to be more discussion about how valuable information can be presented in the user interface for exploring navigation, providing users with more intelligent, comfortable and natural information interaction and visualization. In addition, regardless of virtual tours and the real world, it is important to consider multimode interactions to make exploration more interesting and practical.

In the future, we will continue to review the functions and interaction design, and recruit more real new residents to evaluate our systems. Based on the above results, we will continue to study how to design interactions and user interface in such navigation systems to help new residents explore their cities and establish emotional connections with their living environment.

References

1. Neal, J., Uysal, M., Sirgy, M.: The effect of tourism services on travelers' quality of life. J. Trav. Res. **46**, 154–163 (2007). https://doi.org/10.1177/0047287507303977
2. Buhalis, D., Amaranggana, A.: Smart tourism destinations enhancing tourism experience through personalisation of services. In: Tussyadiah, I., Inversini, A. (eds.) Information and Communication Technologies in Tourism 2015, pp. 377–389. Springer, Cham (2015). https://doi.org/10.1007/978-3-319-14343-9_28
3. Koo, C., Choi, K., Ham, J., Chung, N.: Empirical study about the PokémonGo game and destination engagement. In: Stangl, B., Pesonen, J. (eds.) Information and Communication Technologies in Tourism 2018, pp. 16–28. Springer, Cham (2018). https://doi.org/10.1007/978-3-319-72923-7_2

4. Deterding, S., Dixon, D., Khaled, R., Nacke, L.: From game design elements to gamefulness: defining "gamification". In: Proceedings of the 15th International Academic MindTrek Conference: Envisioning Future Media Environments (MindTrek 2011), pp. 9–15. Association for Computing Machinery, New York (2011)
5. Arkenson, C., Chou, Y.-Y., Huang, C.-Y., Lee, Y.-C.: Tag and seek: a location-based game in Tainan City. In: Proceedings of the first ACM SIGCHI Annual Symposium on Computer-Human Interaction in Play (CHI PLAY 2014), pp. 315–318. Association for Computing Machinery, New York (2014)
6. Ranasinghe, N., et al.: Season traveller: multisensory narration for enhancing the virtual reality experience. In: CHI 2018: Proceedings of the 2018 CHI Conference on Human Factors in Computing Systems, April 2018, Paper No. 577, pp. 1–13 (2018)
7. Koo, C., Gretzel, U., Hunter, W., Chung, N.: Editorial: the role of IT in tourism. Asia Pacific J. Inf. Syst. **25**, 99–104 (2015)
8. Paavilainen, J., Korhonen, H., Alha, K., Stenros, J., Koskinen, E., Mayra, F.: The Pokémon GO experience: a location-based augmented reality mobile game goes mainstream. In: Proceedings of the 2017 CHI Conference on Human Factors in Computing Systems (CHI 2017), pp. 2493–2498. Association for Computing Machinery, New York (2017)
9. Yang, C.C., Sia, W.Y., Tseng, Y.C., Chiu, J.C.: Gamification of learning in tourism industry: a case study of Pokémon Go. In: Proceedings of the 2018 2nd International Conference on Education and E-Learning (ICEEL 2018), pp. 191–195. Association for Computing Machinery, New York (2018)
10. Lochrie, M., Pucihar, K.C., Gradinar, A., Coulton, P.: Designing seamless mobile augmented reality location based game interfaces. In: ACM International Conference Proceeding Series (2013). https://doi.org/10.1145/2536853.2536914
11. Pang, C., Pan, R., Neustaedter, C., Hennessy, K.: City explorer: the design and evaluation of a location-based community information system (2019). https://doi.org/10.1145/3290605.3300571
12. Vaittinen, T., McGookin, D.: Uncover: supporting city exploration with egocentric visualizations of location-based content. Pers. Ubiquit. Comput. **22**(4), 807–824 (2018). https://doi.org/10.1007/s00779-018-1167-9
13. Viswanathan, S., Boulard, C., Grasso, A.M.: Ageing clouds: novel yet natural support for urban exploration. In: Companion Publication of the 2019 on Designing Interactive Systems Conference 2019 Companion (DIS 2019 Companion), pp. 313–317. Association for Computing Machinery, New York (2019)
14. Prakasa, F.B.P., Emanuel, A.: Review of benefit using gamification element for countryside tourism, pp. 196–200 (2019)
15. Anderson, Z., Jones, M.: Mobile computing and well-being in the outdoors, pp. 1154–1157 (2019). https://doi.org/10.1145/3341162.3344832.39
16. Pang, C., Pan, R., Neustaedter, C., Hennessy, K.: City explorer: the design and evaluation of a location-based community information system. In: Proceedings of the 2019 CHI Conference on Human Factors in Computing Systems (CHI 2019), Paper 341, pp. 1–15. Association for Computing Machinery, New York (2019)
17. Moro, S., Rita, P., Ramos, P., Esmerado, J.: Analysing recent augmented and virtual reality developments in tourism J. Hosp. Tour. Technol. (2019) https://doi.org/10.1108/JHTT07-2018-0059
18. Bartley, J., et al.: World of workout: a contextual mobile RPG to encourage long term fitness (2013)
19. Orji, R., Nacke, L., Di Marco, C.: Towards personality-driven persuasive health games and gamified systems, pp. 1015–1027 (2017). https://doi.org/10.1145/3025453.3025577
20. Göschlberger, B., Bruck, P.: Gamification in mobile and workplace integrated microlearning, pp. 545–552 (2017). https://doi.org/10.1145/3151759.3151795

The Impact of Facial Attractiveness and Affective Person Knowledge on Visual Awareness

Junchen Shang[1(✉)] and Hong Yang[2]

[1] Liaoning Normal University, Dalian, China
[2] School of Psychology, Inner Mongolia Normal University, Huhehaote, China

Abstract. Previous research reported face perception in binocular rivalry was influenced by facial attractiveness. Some studies reported that affective person knowledge may also impact face awareness in binocular rivalry. However, it is unclear whether the effect of facial attractiveness on visual awareness would be modulated by affective person knowledge. The present study investigated the impact of facial attractiveness and affective person knowledge on visual awareness in binocular rivalry. Using affective learning paradigm, faces were presented with positive or negative behavior. Participants learned face-behavior pairs. Then, in binocular rivalry task, participants viewed faces and houses simultaneously and report their percept continuously. The results showed that attractive faces dominated longer time and were more often seen as the first percept than unattractive faces. Moreover, faces which were paired with negative behaviors were more often seen as the first percept and were suppressed for shorter time than faces paired with positive behaviors. These findings suggested the processing advantage of attractive faces in initial perceptual selection and later consciousness. Furthermore, faces associated with negative information reached awareness more quickly and had an advantage in initial dominance.

Keywords: Facial attractiveness · Affective learning · Binocular rivalry · Awareness

1 Introduction

Facial attractiveness plays an important role in social interactions, such as mate choice and hiring. People prefer attractive faces may be adaptations for mate choice, since attractive faces signal mate quality, such as health [1]. Many studies suggested a processing advantage of attractive faces. For example, attractive faces automatically captures attention [2–4]. Attractive faces are better remembered than unattractive faces [5–7].

To examine whether facial attractiveness can be processed automatically or unconsciously, some researchers used binocular rivalry paradigm [8], in which a face was presented to one eye of the participant, while a house was presented to the other eye. In binocular rivalry, the images compete for visual awareness, with conscious perception alternating back and forth between the stimuli [9]. When the face was seen, the house

© Springer Nature Switzerland AG 2021
M. Kurosu (Ed.): HCII 2021, LNCS 12762, pp. 429–438, 2021.
https://doi.org/10.1007/978-3-030-78462-1_33

was suppressed in unconsciousness, vice versa. Mo et al. [8] showed that attractive faces dominated for longer time than average or unattractive faces, suggesting that facial attractiveness influence whether the face gains processing advantage in visual awareness. However, prolonged dominance may reflect increased conscious processing rather than purely unconscious processing. A more sensitive measure of the early unconscious perceptual selection is 'first percept' that records which stimulus is the first to gain dominance in each single trial [10, 11]. However, to our knowledge, no research report first percept analysis for facial attractiveness in binocular rivalry.

Affective person knowledge also influences neutral face perception via a paradigm called 'affective learning' [12–14], that is, when a neutral face is paired with a sentence which induces an affective response for sufficient times, the neutral face acquires affective value. Some research investigated the influence of affective learning on face perception in binocular rivalry and got mixed results. For example, Anderson et al. [15] asked participants to learn neutral faces paired with descriptions of negative, neutral, and positive behaviors. Next, participants completed a binocular rivalry task in which a previously learned or novel face was presented to one eye and a house was presented to the other eye. The results showed that faces previously associated with negative behaviors dominated visual awareness for longer time than faces of other conditions. Anderson et al. [15] did not find effect of affective learning on first percept. Mo et al. [8] replicated Anderson et al.'s findings [15] on dominance duration, while they did not report first percept. However, Stein et al. [10] used Anderson et al.'s paradigm [15], they failed to find effect of affective knowledge on dominance durations, suppression durations or first percept for faces. Thus, it is not clear whether affective knowledge influences visual awareness of faces.

Although previous research mainly shows that facial attractiveness and affective person knowledge influences face perception, it is unclear whether the two factors would interact in face perception in binocular rivalry. What will happen when people learn an attractive faces paired with negative behaviors? Will the face gain a priority to access awareness? The present study aimed to investigate the influence of facial attractiveness and affective knowledge on visual perception in binocular rivalry. We were interested in the conscious processing and unconscious processing of faces. For conscious processing, we measured dominance duration for faces. For unconscious processing, we measured first percept and suppression duration for faces.

2 Method

2.1 Participants

Twenty-two participants (17 females, M_{age}= 24.23, SD_{age} = 1.86) took part in the experiment. All participants reported normal or corrected to normal vision. They were naïve to the purpose of the experiment. They were paid for their participation after the experiment. This study was approved by the Institutional Review Board of Liaoning Normal University, China. Each participant provided informed consent before the experiment.

2.2 Design

This study employed a 2 (attractiveness: attractive vs. unattractive) $\times$ 2 (valence of behavior: negative vs. positive) within-subject design, with facial attractiveness and affective person knowledge as independent variables. The dependent variables were the mean dominance durations of the faces, the mean suppression durations of the faces, and the number of trials for which the face was the first percept.

2.3 Apparatus and Stimuli

244 frontal view faces (125 males and 119 females) were adopted from a prior study of our lab [16]. The faces all displayed neutral expressions and were grayscale. There were no famous persons and were unfamiliar to the participants. 48 participants who did not participate in the main experiment rated the attractiveness of the faces on a 7-point scale from 1 (not attractive at all) to 7 (very attractive). The average ratings of attractiveness of each face were calculated based on the data of the 48 participants. 16 faces (M = 5.53, SD = 0.38) were selected as attractive and 16 faces (M = 1.80, SD = 0.17) were selected as unattractive. In each face group, half faces were female. The attractive faces were rated as more attractive than the unattractive faces, $F(1,30) = 1289.83, p < 0.001$, $\eta_p^2 = 0.98$.

32 house images were adopted from Anderson et al. [15]. Each faces was paired with a house in the binocular rivalry task. The faces (excluding hair and ears) and houses were cropped to the same size using an oval window and were superimposed on a black background (80×103 pixels) using Photoshop CS (Adobe Systems Incorporated). To adjust the RMS contrast of faces and houses, we programed in Visual Basic and calculated the RMS contrast of all images, then set the RMS contrast of each image to this average value. To facilitate the stable fusion of the two images, a frame (90×110 pixels) which extended beyond the outer border of the stimuli was presented in binocular rivalry task.

Each face was paired with a behavior in the learning task. 32 descriptions of social behaviors were adopted from Bliss-Moreau et al. [12] and Shang et al. [17] (see the appendix for a full list). There were 16 sentences of positive behaviors, such as "gave up seat on the bus to a pregnant lady". There were 16 sentences of negative behaviors, such as "was arrested by a police officer". Half of attractive faces were paired with positive behaviors, the other half paired with negative behaviors. Also, half unattractive faces were paired with positive behaviors, the other half paired with negative behaviors. Thus, there were four conditions: attractive-positive, attractive-negative, unattractive-positive, and unattractive-negative.

Stimuli and instructions were presented using E-prime 2.0 on a 17-inch LCD monitor with a refresh rate of 60 Hz, and 1440 × 900 pixels resolution. The screen was black. The participants viewed the screen dichoptically through a mirror stereoscope (provided by Beijing Fistar Technology Co., Ltd.). The distance between the participants and the screen was 57 cm. The participants' heads were stabilized by a chin-and-head rest.

2.4 Procedure

There were three phases: affective learning phase, face-learning test and binocular task. In the affective learning phase, participants learned each face-behavior pair for 5 s. Participants were asked to image the person actually performing the behavior. 32 face-behavior pairs were presented in randomized order. Each pair was presented four times, for a total of 128 trials. The inter-trial interval was 0.3 s.

Afterwards, in the face-learning test, only the face was shown, participants were asked to recall the valence of behavior (negative or positive) paired with the face previously. Participants whose accuracy was greater than 80% correct proceeded to the binocular rivalry task. If their accuracy did not reach 80% correct, the learning phase and the face-learning test repeated until they reached 80% correct.

In the binocular rivalry task, in the beginning of each trial, a red fixation dot (0.09° × 0.09°) was presented to both eyes for 1 s. Then, a face was shown to one eye and a house was shown to the other eye for 10 s. Participants were asked to press A key when they saw mostly the face, the L key when they saw mostly the house, and the SPACE when they saw a mixed percept. They were instructed to continuously report their percept by pressing the corresponding key throughout a trial. Afterwards, a blank screen with the introduction "press any key to continue" was shown. The next trial began after the participants pressed a key. Participants completed 12 practice trials with stimuli which were not used in the formal experiment to understand the task. There were 64 trials, in randomized order. Each face was shown twice, one to the left eye and once to the right eye.

3   Results

Mean dominance durations, mean suppression durations, and the number of trials for which the face was the first percept in binocular rivalry task were calculated for faces in each condition. For calculation for dominance and suppression durations, percepts at the end of each trial were excluded because they were artificially shortened. The percepts which lasted less than 100ms were also excluded. Three 2 (attractiveness: attractive vs. unattractive) × 2 (valence of behavior: negative vs. positive) repeated measures ANOVA was conducted on dominance duration, suppression duration and first percept. The Descriptive Statistics in each condition were shown in Tables 1, 2 and 3.

Table 1. Summary of descriptive statistics of dominance duration (ms) (Mean ± Std.)

Valence of behavior	Attractive faces	Unattractive faces
Positive	3702.23(1224.39)	3301.80(1292.46)
Negative	3966.23(1130.81)	3425.66(1155.22)

Table 2. Summary of descriptive statistics of suppression duration (ms) (Mean ± Std.)

Valence of behavior	Attractive faces	Unattractive faces
Positive	3031.96(1228.87)	3230.30(1093.90)
Negative	2728.05(1205.89)	2838.81(1030.40)

Table 3. Summary of descriptive statistics of first percept (Mean ± Std.)

Valence of behavior	Attractive faces	Unattractive faces
Positive	7.09(3.57)	5.68(3.59)
Negative	8.32(3.54)	6.32(3.81)

For dominance durations of faces, the main effect of attractiveness was significant, $F(1,21) = 8.03, p = 0.01, \eta_p^2 = 0.28$, such that attractive faces dominated for significantly longer time than unattractive faces (see Fig. 1). The main effect of valence of behavior was not significant, $F(1,21) = 0.92, p = 0.35, \eta_p^2 = 0.04$. The interaction between attractiveness and valence was not significant, $F(1,21) = 0.15, p = 0.70, \eta_p^2 = 0.01$.

For suppression durations of faces, the main effect of valence was significant, $F(1,21) = 5.68, p = 0.027, \eta_p^2 = 0.21$, such that the faces paired with negative behaviors were suppressed significantly shorter time than those paired with positive behaviors (see Fig. 2). The main effect of attractiveness was not significant, $F(1,21) = 1.67, p = 0.21, \eta_p^2 = 0.07$. The interaction between attractiveness and valence was not significant, $F(1,21) = 0.06, p = 0.81, \eta_p^2 = 0.003$.

For the number of trials in which the face was seen as the first percept (see Fig. 3), the main effect of attractiveness was significant, $F(1,21) = 15.11, p = 0.001, \eta_p^2 = 0.42$, such that attractive faces were more often seen first than unattractive faces. The main effect of valence was also significant, such that the faces paired with negative behaviors were more often seen first than those paired with positive behaviors, $F(1,21) = 6.11, p =$

0.022, $\eta_p^2 = 0.23$. The interaction between attractiveness and valence was not significant, $F(1,21) = 0.60$, $p = 0.45$, $\eta_p^2 = 0.03$.

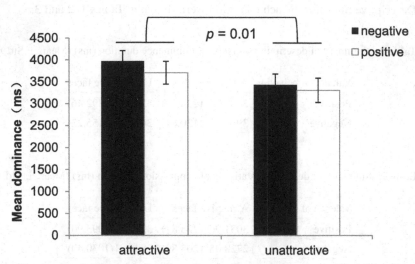

Fig. 1. Dominance duration as a function of attractiveness and valence of behavior. Error bars represent one standard error about the mean.

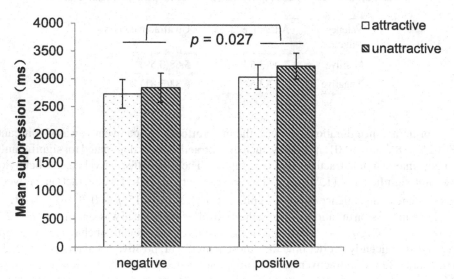

Fig. 2. Suppression duration as a function of attractiveness and valence of behavior. Error bars represent one standard error about the mean.

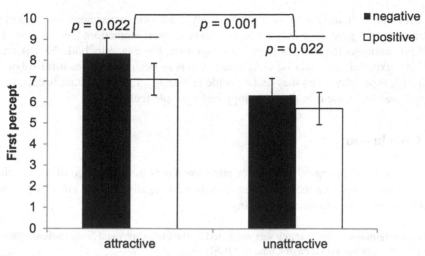

Fig. 3. The number of trials in which the face was seen as the first percept as a function of attractiveness and valence of behavior. Error bars represent one standard error about the mean.

4 Discussion

The present experiment examined how facial attractiveness and affective person knowledge influenced face processing in binocular rivalry. The findings of current study were similar with Mo et al. [8] that dominance durations of attractive faces was longer than unattractive faces, suggesting conscious prioritization for attractive faces. The results also showed that attractive faces were more often to be reported as the first percept than unattractive faces, suggesting that attractive faces also had an advantage in unconscious perceptual selection. However, facial attractiveness did not influence the suppression time for reaching awareness. This is not consistent with two studies using breaking continuous flash suppression (b-CFS) which is a variant of binocular rivalry. In those studies, attractive faces reached awareness more quickly than unattractive faces [18, 19]. The reason of inconsistence may be that b-CFS is more sensitive than binocular rivalry. In b-CFS, a face is presented to one eye and a flashing Mondrian-like pattern to the other eye. The contrast of the face is gradually increased to full contrast and is kept constant until the participant consciously see the face. In b-CFS, face may get more extensive processing [10]. Future research may investigate whether facial attractiveness and affective person information interact in face processing in b-CFS.

The results also showed effect of affective knowledge on suppression time and first percept of faces. Faces paired with negative information gained access to awareness more quickly than face paired with positive information. This may because that a neutral face associated with negative information may be a threat in the society. However, previous research [10, 15] failed to find these effects. The reason might be the different experimental design. There was only one factor in past research, while in the present study, there were two factors.

Furthermore, the results of the present study did not find interaction effect between facial attractiveness and affective information, which means that in face perception, these factors act individually. Though this study is a vision experiment, the finds of this experiment may give some insights on human computer interaction. Unconscious, low-level processing is the base for high-level cognition. For example, both the appearance and user experience should be considered in robots design. The beautiful robots are preferred, especially when they make people feel happy. Even if a robot is ugly, it may be preferred when the robot's technology make people feel good.

5   Conclusion

There was a processing advantage for attractive faces in early stage of unconscious-ness and later consciousness. Faces associated with negative person knowledge gained prioritization in unconscious processing.

Acknowledgments. This research was supported by the Philosophy and Social Science Planning Funding of Liaoning Province of China (L19BSH005).

Data Availability Statement. Inquiries about the data of this study can be directed to the corresponding author.

Appendix

Valence of behavior	Descriptive sentences of behavior
Positive	Celebrated a child's birthday
	Took a nice vacation with the family
	Helped an elderly woman with her groceries
	Gave up seat on the bus to a pregnant lady
	Complemented a coworker
	Cooked a fabulous dinner for spouse
	Celebrated a holiday with grandparents
	Bought ice cream for a young child on a sunny day
	Picked up friend at the airport after a long trip
	Tutored a struggling classmate for free
	Made donations to charities
	Gave coat to someone else when it was cold
	Help a child find his parents when he was lost in a store
	Answered a question with a smile on the face
	Rushed up regardless of personal danger when facing sudden danger
	Said hello to the elders, neighbors and colleagues voluntarily

(continued)

(continued)

Valence of behavior	Descriptive sentences of behavior
Negative	Provoked the man into a fistfight
	Cheated on a spouse
	Was arrested by a police officer
	Hit a small child
	Stole from a blind person
	Brandished a long knife at an unarmed crowd
	Deliberately killed a man with a car
	Broke into a school and killed five children
	Threw a chair at a classmate
	Spilled boiling water on friend
	Killed a child's pet
	Lost all of the company's money
	Lied to the investigator about the crime
	Crashed a friend's car
	Was jealous when a neighbor bought a fancy car, and then burst the tire in the middle of the night
	Was arrested on suspicion of hitting a child

References

1. Rhodes, G.: The evolutionary psychology of facial beauty. Annu. Rev. Psychol. **57**, 199–226 (2006)
2. Chen, W., Liu, C.H., Nakabayashi, K.: Beauty hinders attention switch in change detection: the role of facial attractiveness and distinctiveness. PLoS ONE **7**, e32897 (2012)
3. Liu, C.H., Chen, W.: Beauty is better pursued: effects of attractiveness in multiple-face tracking. Q. J. Exp. Psychol. **65**(3), 553–564 (2012)
4. Nakamura, K., Kawabata, H.: Attractive faces temporally modulate visual attention. Front. Psychol. **5**, 620 (2014)
5. Marzi, T., Viggiano, M.P.: When memory meets beauty: Insights from event-related potentials. Biol. Psychol. **84**(2), 192–205 (2010)
6. Zhang, Y., et al.: Identifying cognitive preferences for attractive female faces: An event-related potential experiment using a study-test paradigm. J. Neurosci. Res. **89**, 1887–1893 (2011)
7. Zhang, Y., Wei, B., Zhao, P., Zheng, M., Zhang, L.: Gender differences in memory processing of female facial attractiveness: evidence from event-related potentials. Neurocase **22**(3), 317–323 (2016)
8. Mo, C., Xia, T., Qin, K., Mo, L.: Natural Tendency towards Beauty in Humans: Evidence from Binocular Rivalry. PLoS ONE **11**(3), e0150147 (2016)
9. Tong, F., Meng, M., Blake, R.: Neural bases of binocular rivalry. Trends Cogn. Sci. **10**, 502–511 (2006)

10. Stein, T., Grubb, C., Bertrand, M., Suh, S.M., Verosky, S.C.: No impact of affective person knowledge on visual awareness: evidence from binocular rivalry and continuous flash suppression. Emotion **17**, 1199–1207 (2017)
11. Hedger, N., Gray, K.L.H., Garner, M., Adams, W.J.: Are visual threats prioritized without awareness? A critical review and meta-analysis involving 3 behavioral paradigms and 2696 observers. Psychol. Bull. **142**, 934–968 (2016)
12. Bliss-Moreau, E., Barrett, L.F., Wright, C.I.: Individual differences in learning the affective value of others under minimal conditions. Emotion **8**, 479–493 (2008)
13. Verosky, S.C., Todorov, A.: Generalization of affective learning about faces to perceptually similar faces. Psychol. Sci. **21**, 779–785 (2010)
14. Verosky, S.C., Todorov, A.: When physical similarity matters: mechanisms underlying affective learning generalization to the evaluation of novel faces. J. Exp. Soc. Psychol. **49**, 661–669 (2013)
15. Anderson, E., Siegel, E.H., Bliss-Moreau, E., Barrett, L.F.: The visual impact of gossip. Science **332**, 1446–1448 (2011)
16. Wang, H., Tong, S., Shang, J., Chen, W.: The role of gender in the preconscious processing of facial trustworthiness and dominance. Front. Psychol. **10**, 2565 (2019)
17. Shang, J., Jiang, H., Wang, C., Liu, Z., Wu, Y.: The influence of minimal affective learning on time perception of faces. J. Liaoning Norm. Univ. (Soc. Sci. Ed.) **39**(6), 37–42 (2016)
18. Hung, S.-M., Nieh, C.-H., Hsieh, P.-J.: Unconscious processing of facial attractiveness: invisible attractive faces orient visual attention. Sci. Rep. **6**, 37117 (2016)
19. Nakamura, K., Kawabata, H.: Preferential access to awareness of attractive faces in a breaking continuous flash suppression paradigm. Conscious. Cogn. **65**, 71–82 (2018)

Integrating SSTQUAL, Kano Model and Attractiveness Engineering to Analyze User's Emotional Needs in Self Check-in Service

Hsuan-Min Hsu and Hsi-Jen Chen[✉]

National Cheng Kung University, Tainan City 701, Taiwan
hsijen_chen@mail.ncku.edu.tw

Abstract. As "smart airport" serve as a final goal of every airport, self-service technology (SSTs) become widely used in every airport. However, in Taiwan's airport, only 20% of people use kiosks (automated self-service check-in machines).

From a perspective of design, human's perception of value has been changed due to market dynamics and challenges. The functionality and usability are no longer prominent success factors in product and service design. Instead, people are more expecting to perceive value, enjoyment, or experience while using products or services.

This paper aimed at (i) using SSTQUAL and kano model to identify and prioritize user's needs about airport kiosk, then (ii) build the relationship between emotional feeling and service attributes under the framework of attractiveness engineering, and using quantification theory type-I to quantify the correlation.

Research result indicates sense of relax, relieve, convenience and enjoyment are the most important feelings during using kiosks. Service providers can enhance these feelings by ameliorate some kiosks' function such as providing double-check system.

Keywords: Self-service technology · SSTQUAL · Emotional factor

1 Introduction

International Air Transport Association (IATA) revealed that present trends in air transport suggest passenger numbers could double to 8.2 billion in 2037, especially in the Asia-Pacific region. It will drive the biggest growth with more than half the total number of new passengers over the next 20 years coming from these markets. Under this circumstance, self-service technologies (SSTs) such as kiosk have been widely used.

1.1 Research Motivation

Compared to American and European, Taiwanese are much more satisfied with traditional ground handling service (Chang and Yang 2008; Lu et al. 2011), only 20% people used airport kiosk in 2015.

© Springer Nature Switzerland AG 2021
M. Kurosu (Ed.): HCII 2021, LNCS 12762, pp. 439–450, 2021.
https://doi.org/10.1007/978-3-030-78462-1_34

Referring to Taiwanese intention of using kiosk, most of the researchers follow the perspective of technology and functionality to explain this issue, indicated attributes such as perceived usefulness, perceived ease of use, and attitude toward using (Curran James 2005; Ku and Chen 2013; 呂錦隆、凌珮娟 2009; 林聖偉 and 蘇伃君 2016; 凌珮娟 2007; 陳俊宇 2014).

While the importance of design grows up, attributes which can influence people's intention are no longer limited in usability and ease of use. Experience, enjoyment, and sense are also included (宋同正 2014). Still, there are still few researches talking about service experience and emotional factors (Vakulenko 2018).

1.2   Research Purposes

Focusing on airport self-check-in service, this study planned to understand user's perceived feeling while using the service and figure out the cause of it. Suggestions for service provider to ameliorate the service will be conducted.

The study expected to (i) use SSTQUAL and kano model to identify and prioritize user's needs about airport kiosk, then (ii) hold a focus group to get qualitative date and build the relationship between emotional feeling and service attributes under the framework of attractiveness engineering, in the end, (iii) using quantification theory type-I to quantify the correlation.

2   Literature Review

In this chapter, two main topics will be reviewed. One is about SSTs, including airport kiosk. The other one is about the research tool used in this study.

2.1   Self-service Technologies

Self-service technology is a service tool that allows consumers (users) to complete the whole service without the participation of front-line staff. The physical machine and facility helps the entire service to proceed smoothly (Douglas Hoffman 2001).

Lots of advantages are conducted by the use of SSTs. It brings greater convenience, savings in time and money (Cunningham et al. 2008), and diversification of payment channels (Lee et al. 2013). Also, using SSTs transfers the role of consumer into co-producer, which can create additional value that affect satisfaction and customer loyalty (Chen and Wang 2016).

Kiosk

The application of kiosk in the airports does improve service efficiency. The average waiting time for those who used manual counters for check-in was 25.2 min, while the average waiting time for passengers who used KIOSK for self-check-in was 5.9 min (呂錦隆、凌珮娟 2009). It also keeps the cost down (Beatson et al. 2007; Lin and Hsieh 2007). IATA estimates that the use of SSTs technology for registration can save nearly $1 billion in costs for the global aviation industry each year, which can be described as a win-win situation for airlines and passengers.

Although self-service technologies can provide a "fast service", when companies introduce new technological services to the users, they will inevitably face some users who may feel anxious and pressured about the machine and its usage, how to solve operational errors, and how to prevent data leakage. These are all reasons why users are unwilling to use such services (Curran James 2005; Meuter et al. 2000; Rose et al. 2005). 呂錦隆、凌珮娟 (2009) also mentioned that "perceived risk" negatively affects the use intention, which means that when the user perceives the possible losses to the machine, such as information security, psychological pressure, and information interpretation, it will reduce the use intention.

2.2 Service Quality

Service quality has a beneficial effect on the use intention (Hung and Chang 2005; Shahid Iqbal et al. 2018; 呂錦隆、凌珮娟 2009). Its definition can be summarized as an attitude or feeling. It is not only an evaluation of service results, but also includes the feelings received and generated during the service process, which are closely related to personal experience and cognition. By deducing from the user's expectations of the service (Expected service, ES) and the actual perceived service performance (Perceived service, PS), the service gap can be counted (Parasuraman et al. 1985), and the service provider can optimize the service content according to the service gap.

Talking to how to measure service quality, Parasuraman et al. (1988) proposed a scale called SERVQUAL that divides services into five different dimensions, namely tangibles, reliability, responsiveness, assurance, and empathy. This method is widely used in the evaluation of different industries to capture service gaps and to improve service quality.

SSTQUAL

SST is different from traditional human services, so that the dimensions which affect service quality are also different. Lu et al. (2011) build a service quality scale named SSTQUAL for SSTs based on SERVQUAL.

The scale is divided into seven dimensions, with a total of 20 attributes (Table 1). The satisfaction of each attribute is positively correlated with service quality and the intention to use self-service technology. At the same time, the "design" dimension has the most powerful influence.

Kano Model

In SERVQUAL and other research related to service quality, it is assumed that relationship between service quality and satisfaction are linear, that is, the enhancement of service quality can increase satisfaction, and vice versa. While this relationship between quality performance and user satisfaction is not necessarily linear, different items and elements in different products/services have different effects on satisfaction (Tan and Pawitra 2001).

Table 1. SSTQUAL (Lin and Hsieh 2011)

Dimension	Label	Attribute
Functionality	FUN1	I can get my service done with the firm's SST in a short time
	FUN2	The service process of the firm's SST is clear
	FUN3	Using the firm's SST requires little effort
	FUN4	I can get my service done smoothly with the firm's SSTs
	FUN5	Each service item/function of the SST is error-free
Enjoyment	ENJ1	The operation of the firm's SST is interesting
	ENJ2	I feel good being able to use the SSTs
	ENJ3	The firm's SST has interesting additional Functions
	ENJ4	The firm's SST provides me with all relevant information
Security/Privacy	SEC1	I feel safe in my transactions with the firm's SST
	SEC2	A clear privacy policy is stated when I use the firm's SST
Assurance	ASU1	The firm providing the SST is well-known
	ASU2	The firm providing the SST has a good reputation
Design	DES1	The layout of the firm's SST is aesthetically appealing
	DES2	The firm's SST appears to use up-to-date technology
Convenience	CON1	The SST has operating hours convenient to customers
	CON2	It is easy and convenient to reach the firm's SST
Customization	CUS1	The firm's SST understands my specific needs
	CUS2	The firm's SST has my best interests at heart
	CUS3	The firm's SST has features that are personalized for me

Kano Model (Kano et al. 1984) mainly divides service quality into five types, each of which has different effects on satisfaction:

1. Must-be quality (M): also known as basic demand.
2. One-dimensional quality (O).
3. Attractive quality (A): or amazing demand.
4. Indifferent quality (I).
5. Reversal quality (R).

Kano model questionnaire consists of a set of forward and reverse questions, By combining the two answers in the following evaluation table, the product features can be classified (Fig. 1). And the order of improvement can be sorted according to the sequence of "required quality (M) → unary quality (O) → attractive quality (A) → indifference quality (I)" (Sauerwein et al. 1996).

Customer requirements → ↓		Dysfunctional (negative) question				
		1. like	2. must be	3. neutral	4. live with	5. dislike
Functional (positive) question	1. like	Q	A	A	A	O
	2. must-be	R	I	I	I	M
	3. neutral	R	I	I	I	M
	4. live with	R	I	I	I	M
	5. dislike	R	R	R	R	Q

Fig. 1. Kano evaluation table

2.3 Miryoku Engineering (Attractiveness Engineering)

"Attractiveness" can be regarded as a general term for conquering people's hearts, such as confusing, attractive, inducing, appealing, and emotional power (馬敏元, 洪嘉永 and 曾麗丹 2005). Many designers hope to extract the elements during the design process and apply them to product development, but "attractiveness" is an ambiguous concept, so it is difficult to make a specific evaluation (李學然 and 陳怡貞 2014).

In 1991, Ujigawa (2000) gathered several scholars to initiate the "miryoku engineering" research, with the goal of creating attractive products, space, technology and knowledge.

By doing in-depth qualitative interviews with highly involved target groups, user's glamorous feelings towards the product/service can be extracted.

Quantification Theory Type I
Quantification theory type I is a type of regression analysis that can find the linear relationship between a variable and other independent variable. In the statistical results of the quantitative theory type I, the larger the value of the partial correlation coefficient is shows the greater the influence of category items on the service attributes.

3 Methodology

The experiment of this research was carried out in three parts. In the first part, the priority improvement order of airport self-service quality was sorted out through the questionnaires of SSTQUAL and Kano Model.

In the second part, a focus group interview was conducted. The focus group will be consisted of five interviewees with design background, who have used airport self-check-in service.

The purpose of the interview is to find out the emotional factors of each service attributes and the specific evaluation items that constitute the service attributes (Fig. 2).

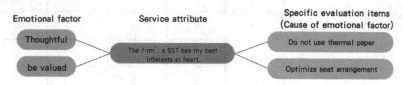

Fig. 2. Outcome of focus group (sample)

In the interview, the service attributes are used as a guide, interviews will first inquire about what the evaluation items are, and then comes to inventory emotional factors. The result of focus group will be organized into a hierarchical relationship diagram. Based on the diagram, the questionnaire for next part would be constructed (Fig. 3).

2. Talking about "sense of fashion" in airport self-check-in service, how important are the following attributes? (1 for totally unimportant, 5 for very important)

	1	2	3	4	5
The firm's SST appears to use up-to-date technology	○	○	○	○	○
The layout of the firm's SST is aesthetically appealing.	○	○	○	○	○

2.1 Talking about "sense of fashion" in attributes "The firm's SST appears to use up-to-date technology", which item is the most important?

○ Sensitive touch without delay	○ The appearance of the machine is novel and eye-catching

Fig. 3. Questionnaire (sample)

In the last part, the results collected from the questionnaire will be analyzed and discussed. Figure 4 describes the process of each stage in detail.

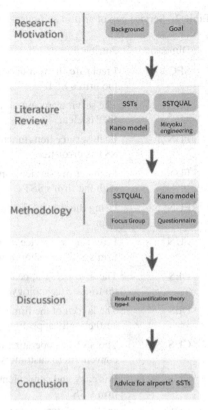

Fig. 4. Research process

4 Results

4.1 SSTQUAL and Kano Model

Questionnaire of SSTQUAL collected a total of 90 valid questionnaires, all the respondents have used airport kiosk before. Average of service gap is −0.199, with 14 attributes show negative value.

Questionnaire of kano model got a total of 174 valid answers. According to the rule classification of the quality attribute matrix in Fig. 1, among the 20 airport self-service attributes, 3 attributes are must-be quality (M), 2 attributes are one-dimension quality (O), 5 attributes belong to attractive quality attributes (A), and 10 attributes have indifferent quality (I).

Based on the fact that ENJ1, ENJ2, ENJ3, ASU1, and ASU2 have been satisfied in the existing services, and they are all classified as indifferent quality (I), this research does not discuss these five service factors. In addition, according to the user guides put forward by several airlines for KIOSK today, it is pointed out that this service is not applicable to "answering special requirement", so CUS1 and CUS3 was eliminated in this study. The final order of priority improvement of service attribute is as shown as Table 2.

Table 2. Service gap of airport self-check-in

Type of service quality	Dimension	Attribute	Ranking
Must-be Quality	SEC	I feel safe in my transactions with the firm's SST	1
	FUN	The service process of the firm's SST is clear	2
	FUN	Each service item/function of the SST is error-free	3
One-dimensional quality	FUN	I can get my service done smoothly with the firm's SSTs	4
	FUN	Using the firm's SST requires little effort	5
Attractive quality	FUN	I can get my service done with the firm's SST in a short time	6
	DES	The firm's SST appears to use up-to-date technology	7
	DES	The layout of the firm's SST is aesthetically appealing	8
Indifferent quality	CUS	The SST has operating hours convenient to customers	9
	CUS	It is easy and convenient to reach the firm's SST	10
	ENJ	The firm's SST provides me with all relevant information	11
	ASU1	The firm's SST has my best interests at heart	12
	SEC	A clear privacy policy is stated when I use the firm's SST	13

4.2 Focus Group

The result of focus group conducts 10 emotional factor of self-check-in service: relaxed, relieved, enjoyment, convenient, convenient, convenient, superior, achieved, thoughtful, fashionable, be valued, and comfortable.

4.3 Quantification Theory Type I

In this section, a total of 59 valid questionnaires were collected. The results of quantification theory type I shows that all 10 emotional factors are related to self-service check-in in different degree as shown in Table 3.

The one "relaxed" and self-service check-in has the strongest correlation. In this emotional factor, the most influential positive service item is "Important information can be double checked" under " I can get my service done smoothly with the firm's SSTs (FUN4)" At the same time, the sense of "relieved" indicates the second-highest correlation in quantification theory type I. In this emotional factor, the most influential positive service item is "finishing check-in by using passport only" under "each service item/function of the SST is error-free (FUN5)".

Table 3. Results of quantification theory type I

Correlation	r	Emotional factor	Attribute	Dimension	Item
High Correlation	0.901	Relaxed	I can get my service done smoothly with the firm's SSTs	Functionality	Important information can be double checked
	0.807	Relieved	Each service item/function of the SST is error-free	Functionality	Finishing check-in by using passport only
	0.743	Enjoyment	I can get my service done with the firm's SST in a short time	Functionality	Finishing check-in quicker than others
	0.739	Convenient	I can get my service done smoothly with the firm's SSTs	Functionality	Important information can be double check
Mid Correlation	0.640	Superior	I can get my service done with the firm's SST in a short time	Functionality	Using pictures as an ancillary information
	0.631	Achieved	Using the firm's SST requires little effort	Functionality	Understanding whether I can use this kiosk or not at one glance
	0.629	Thoughtful	A clear privacy policy is stated when I use the firm's SST	Security/Privacy	Providing mother language
	0.480	Fashionable	The layout of the firm's SST is aesthetically appealing	Design	The loading page design is not outdated
	0.463	Be valued	The layout of the firm's SST is aesthetically appealing	Design	Contents can be separated from background clearly
Low Correlation	0.358	Comfortable	The layout of the firm's SST is aesthetically appealing	Design	The loading page design is not outdated

5 Discussion

In this study, more than 90% of the questionnaire respondents are come from Taiwan, which means the experimental data might be limited and could not be inferred to a wider user population. Based on the experiment results, this study proposed 2 main insights.

5.1 Optimization Attributes in Dimension Functionality Can Highly Enhance user's Feeling Towards Self-check-In

Quantification theory type I shows that all 10 emotional factors are related to self-service check-in in different degree. The correlation coefficients of relaxed, relieved, convenient, and enjoyment are all greater than 0.7, which means high correlation. In these four factors with high correlation, the attributes with the highest partial correlation coefficient belongs to the functionality. Among them, the highest partial correlation coefficient in the sense of relieved is "Each service item/function of the SST is error-free." This attribute is also a "must quality", which shows that there are many opportunities for optimization in the dimension functionality.

According to the importance of functionality proved by quantification theory type I, building a double check system or allowing to finish check-in by using passport only can improve the function and enhance the user's sense of relieved and relaxed.

5.2 Optimization Attributes in Dimension Design Can Influence user's Satisfaction

In addition, if the service provider aims to improve user satisfaction and create amazing service quality for users, they can also try to start with the emotional factors related to design dimensions (such as fashion, be valued, and comfortable.) Although these three factors indicate medium or low-degree correlations, however, they belong to attractive quality, which means after optimization these attributes, the satisfaction will be highly raised.

5.3 Comprehensive Discussion

The initial positioning of self-service in the airport is to "save time for passengers." Therefore, convenience is not only the important feelings that users recognize, but also the main feelings that service providers expect to bring to users.

However, only providing faster and more convenient services cannot make all passengers intend to use self-service, because of the anxiety caused by unfamiliar to emerging technology products or the loss caused by the unsmooth operation process will produced great psychological pressure on users, thereby reducing the intention to use self-service. That is the reason why sense of "relax" is important.

Additionally, in SSTQUAL, enjoyment becomes an independent aspect, showing its importance to self-service service quality and satisfaction. Kim and Park (2019) pointed out that enjoyment has a high impact on usage intention of self-service and perceived satisfaction. Also, this conclusion explains the high correlation of enjoyment in quantification theory type I of this research.

6 Conclusion

This study first used SSTQUAL to sort out the current airport self-service gaps, then use kano model to prioritize the improvement of service attribute. Later, interviews and questionnaire surveys are used to figure out user's feelings of airport self-service and methods about how to enhance these feelings.

At last, this study found that sense of "relaxed", "convenience", "enjoyment" and "relieved" are highly correlated with self-service check-in. By ameliorating attributes in dimension functionality, these feelings can be raised.

References

Beatson, A., Lee, N., Coote, L.V.: Self-service technology and the service encounter. Serv. Ind. J. **27**(1), 75–89 (2007)

Chang, H.L., Yang, C.H.: Do airline self-service check-in kiosks meet the needs of passengers? Tour. Manag. **29**(5), 980–993 (2008)

Chen, C.F., Wang, J.P.: Customer participation, value co-creation and customer loyalty - a case of airline online check-in system. Comput. Hum. Behav. **62**, 346–352 (2016)

Cunningham, L.F., Young, C.E., Gerlach, J.H.: Consumer views of self-service technologies. Serv. Ind. J. **28**(6), 719–732 (2008)

Curran James, M.: Self-service technology adoption: comparing three technologies. J. Serv. Mark. **19**(2), 103–113 (2005)

Hung, S.-Y., Chang, C.-M.: User acceptance of WAP services: test of competing theories. Comput. Stand. Interf. **27**(4), 359–370 (2005). http://www.sciencedirect.com/science/article/pii/S09205 48904001266. https://doi.org/10.1016/j.csi.2004.10.004

Hoffman, K.D., Bateson, J.E.G.: Essentials of Services Marketing: Concepts, Strategies and Cases, 2nd edn.

Kano, N., Seraku, N., Takahashi, F., Shin-ichi, T.: Attractive quality and must-be quality. J. Jpn. Soc. Qual. Control **14**(2), 147–156 (1984). https://doi.org/10.20684/quality.14.2_147

Kim, J.-H., Park, J.-W.: The effect of airport self-service characteristics on passengers' perceived value, satisfaction, and behavioral intention: based on the SOR model. Sustainability **11**(19), 1–17 (2019)

Ku, E.C.S., Chen, C.D.: Fitting facilities to self-service technology usage: evidence from kiosks in Taiwan airport. J. Air Transp. Manag. **32**, 87–94 (2013). https://doi.org/10.1016/j.jairtraman. 2013.07.001

Lee, H.-J., Fairhurst, A., Cho, H.J.: Gender differences in consumer evaluations of service quality: self-service kiosks in retail. Serv. Ind. J. **33**(2), 248–265 (2013)

Lin, J.-S.C., Hsieh, P.-L.: The influence of technology readiness on satisfaction and behavioral intentions toward self-service technologies. Comput. Hum. Behav. **23**(3), 1597–1615 (2007)

Lin, J.-S.C., Hsieh, P.-L.: Assessing the self-service technology encounters: development and validation of SSTQUAL scale. J. Retail. **87**(2), 194–206 (2011)

Lu, J.-L., Choi, J.K., Tseng, W.-C.: Determinants of passengers' choice of airline check-in services: a case study of American, Australian, Korean, and Taiwanese passengers. J. Air Transp. Manag. **17**(4), 249–252 (2011). https://doi.org/10.1016/j.jairtraman.2010.12.011. http://www.sciencedi rect.com/science/article/pii/S0969699710001201

Meuter, M.L., Ostrom, A.L., Roundtree, R.I., Bitner, M.J.: Self-service technologies: understanding customer satisfaction with technology-based service encounters. J. Mark. **64**(3), 50–64 (2000)

Parasuraman, A., Zeithaml, V.A., Berry, L.L.: A conceptual model of service quality and its implications for future research. J. Mark. **49**(4), 41–50 (1985). https://doi.org/10.2307/125 1430

Parasuraman, A. P., Zeithaml, V., Berry, L.: SERVQUAL: a multiple- item scale for measuring consumer perceptions of service quality. J. Retail. (1988)

Rose, G.M., Meuter, M.L., Curran, J.M.: On-line waiting: the role of download time and other important predictors on attitude toward e-retailers. Psychol. Mark. **22**(2), 127–151 (2005)

Sauerwein, E., Bailom, F., Matzler, K., Hinterhuber, H.: The Kano model: how to delight your customers (1996)

Shahid Iqbal, M., Ul Hassan, M., Habibah, U.: Impact of self-service technology (SST) service quality on customer loyalty and behavioral intention: the mediating role of customer satisfaction. Cogent Bus. Manag. **5**(1) (2018). https://doi.org/10.1080/23311975.2018.1423770

Tan, K., Pawitra, T.: Integrating SERVQUAL and Kano's model into QFD for service excellence development. Manag. Serv. Qual. **11**, 418–430 (2001)

Ujigawa, M.: The evolution of preference-based design. Res. Dev. Inst. **46**, 10 (2000)

Vakulenko, Y.: Customer value in self-service kiosks: a systematic literature review. Int. J. Retail Distrib. Manag. **46**(5), 507–527 (2018). https://doi.org/10.1108/IJRDM-04-2017-0084

呂錕隆、凌珮娟: 國籍旅客對國際航線自助報到服務之使用意圖研究. *運輸學刊, 第二十一卷*(3), 299–328 (2009)

宋同正: 序-服務設計的本質內涵和流程工具. *設計學報 19*(2), 1–8 (2014)

李學然, 陳怡貞: 競速類行動裝置遊戲的魅力要素. *美育 199期*, 33–43 (2014)

林聖偉, 蘇伃君: 旅客採用自助服務科技行為模式之研究. [A study of tourists using self-service technology model]. *中原體育學報*(9), 69–78 (2016). https://doi.org/10.6646/CYPEJ.2016.9.69

凌珮娟: 航空旅客對自助報到服務之接受行為研究. *長榮大學航運管理研究所學位論文*, pp. 1–90 (2007)

馬敏元, 洪嘉永, 曾麗丹: 台灣地方文創意產業魅力評價研究---以觀光節產業為例. 行政院國家科學委員會補助專題研究計畫成果報告 (2005)

陳俊宇: *旅客對於機場自助報到機的接受度研究*. (碩士), 國立中山大學 (2014)

Technological Influence on Self-esteem: Towards a Research Agenda Through a Systematic Literature Review

Luã Marcelo Muriana$^{(\boxtimes)}$ and Maria Cecilia Calani Baranauskas

Institute of Computing, University of Campinas, Campinas, Brazil
1163144@dac.unicamp.br, cecilia@ic.unicamp.br

Abstract. Self-esteem is a concept developed from the personal experiences of a person in a society and refers to the assessment of a person about himself, so that it expresses an attitude of approval, or not, and indicates an extension in which a person believes to be capable, meaningful, dignified and successful in relation to his-her abilities, skills, social relationships and physical appearance, for example. Some studies indicate that technology has the potential to provide experiences that can alter the users' psychological states, including their self-esteem. This work contributes to a systematic literature review, with the objective of investigating technological solutions designed to influence self-esteem. Through automatic and manual search, we identified 3,668 papers, and we selected seven of them in the specific final selection and analyzed them based on inclusion and exclusion criteria. The results obtained helped us to understand what types of technology are used to affect/impact self-esteem, how technology has been used and the strategies for supporting this purpose, and the aspects of self-esteem the technology influences. Our results also indicate research challenges within this issue.

Keywords: Self-esteem · Technological influence · Systematic literature review

1 Introduction

Self-esteem refers to the evaluation of a person in relation to herself [13] and may be related to the success in the interaction of the person with other ones [12], such that it expresses an attitude of approval or not, and indicate an extent to which a person believes to be capable, meaningful, worth and successful [8]; it is related to their personal beliefs about skills, competencies, social relationships and future results [19].

In the last years, with technology and social media evolution, behavior patterns and social conventions have spread much more quickly, inducing great and others not so good effects on people. For instance, several studies have analyzed the interrelationship among technology usage and psychological well-being and self-esteem: Lee and Jang [18] and Marino et al. [20] focused on analyzing this relationship in social media; Apaolaza et al. [2], Park [26], and Pai and Arnott [25] studied how these technologies lead the user to become addicted to a specific technological medium; Muriana et al. [22], and Pai and

© Springer Nature Switzerland AG 2021
M. Kurosu (Ed.): HCII 2021, LNCS 12762, pp. 451–471, 2021.
https://doi.org/10.1007/978-3-030-78462-1_35

Arnott [25] expressed concerns about the relationship between technology, self-esteem, and affective states of people.

Based on the understanding that technology can affect self-esteem, we aimed to evaluate, synthesize, and present studies that have designed a technological solution for this purpose. Thus, our fundamental question in this systematic literature review was: *have technologies been developed to explicitly (positively) affect/impact self-esteem?* From this question, we raised other four (see Table 1) and considered them to analyze the selected studies. To answer these questions, we adopted the PRISMA protocol [21], and raised relevant studies through automatic and manual search. Based on inclusion and exclusion criteria, we held a paper eligible to be included if it explicitly relates technology and self-esteem, and if it describes how the former can affect the latter, from a design-focused perspective.

After automatically searching for relevant papers, we got 3,668 ones. From reading the papers' titles and abstracts, we selected 171 studies. Next, we conducted a full reading of these to find out if they addressed how and why the used technology would affect self-esteem. Then we selected 41 for careful reading. Finally, we got seven specific papers focused on our main issue. The final selection allowed us to analyze which technologies are being used to affect self-esteem, how technology can be used for this purpose, what types of support they provide, and what aspects of self-esteem they affect. Furthermore, we pointed out limitations and open challenges that researchers can further explore.

We organize the text as follows: on Sect. 2 we relate self-esteem and technology; on Sect. 3 we describe the SLR methodology; on Sect. 4, we present the general and specific results we got; on Sect. 5 we answer the research questions, and we list research challenges of the theme addressed, and point out research challenges in this issue.

2   Self-esteem and Technology

Self-esteem constitutes a product of the "self" insofar as the human being goes through good or bad experiences throughout life [1]. Such experiences can affect both the global and domain-specific self-esteem of a person. Global self-esteem refers to the general view that the person has about her/himself [24]. Domain-specific self-esteem relates to the point of view of the individual over some personal aspects, such as appearance or ability to do some task.

Self-esteem is an emotional response people experience, contemplate, and appraise regarding various aspects of themselves [11]. Social issues such as race, age, academic status, physical attraction, body image, and specific competence [11, 29] may also affect psychological aspects and, possibly, the self-esteem. Paay et al. [24] still say social issues can affect self-esteem such as race, age, economic status, educational level of the parents, among others. These aspects are related to self-concept, self-worth, and self-image, indicating the way people see, self-evaluate, and trust themselves. Although self-esteem is an individual concept built over a lifetime, it occurs based on the perceptions of the person from her/his particular backgrounds and social relationships. That occurs based on the perceptions of the person from his personal experiences and social relationships, and this may positively or negatively affect psychological aspects such as motivation, satisfaction, and self-confidence that will impact on global and/or domain self-esteem.

In this context, several studies have explored how technology can affect self-esteem, and how self-esteem can also be a determining factor in this relation. Some of them investigated what leads a person to use social networks: Pai and Arnott [25] say the major reasons are the pursuit of belonging to a group, hedonism, self-esteem, and pursuing reciprocity; Marino et al. [20] highlight the use of Facebook to reduce negative mood; Apaolaza et al. [2] and Hatchel et al. [10] argue social media can cause psychological well-being by increasing users' self-esteem. Boyd and Ellison [5] says young people, especially, use Facebook to establish friendships, connect with the world, share and gain knowledge, develop powerful personalities and start having a better social life. These studies argue social networks can impact self-esteem positively.

On the opposite direction, Chen and Lee [6] point out social networks have stimulated people to make comparisons thus increasing the mental stress level, and decreasing self-esteem. Zell and Moeller [33] and Scissors et al. [30] examined the relationship between "likes" and the number of comments on Facebook posts and the psychological well-being they cause on the users. They reported that the number of likes and comments, and depending on who does it, can impact self-esteem. Nie et al. [23] and Jang et al. [14] studied the relationship between the "real" and the "ideal" self, through self-presentation users make on Facebook as a mechanism to get more approvals from other members or to avoid negative judgments.

These studies, however, analyzed technological solutions that were not developed with the primary purpose of affecting self-esteem. If, on the one hand, social networks can cause great social and psychological impact on their users, on the other hand, the interface and the technological devices used also play a fundamental role in this context.

The technology usage at the same time that can yield a delightful and satisfying interaction for some users can also cause traumatic experiences for others. Bittencourt et al. [4] say the interface of the used device can provide different types of interaction to the user. In this context, Shank [31] states that technology can change how people feel while it realizes a way for people to express their emotions. Thüring and Mahlke [32] state the user experience when interacting with a particular technology is also a factor for the alteration of a person's affective state. Birks et al. [3], Park [26], and Muriana et al. [22] emphasize that the use of computer technologies can impact self-esteem and affective states of users.

Therefore, if the type and mode of use of the technologies can influence and affect the user's psychological well-being, including their self-esteem, this SLR aims to raise solutions that have been designed exclusively for this purpose so that, employing strategies for influencing the self-esteem, they can affect some of its aspects.

3 Systematic Literature Review Protocol

A systematic review is a literature study that uses specific and planned, justifiable, and explicit systematic methods to make critical and clear analysis for a research area defined from a question that guides this review [9]. As a result of identifying, interpreting, and evaluating the papers' data, one may gather evidences to draw conclusions and answer questions, and to raise challenges and limitations.

The Fig. 1 shows the SLR flow execution we followed and the number (n) of papers we got. In the coming subsections we describe each step we carried out, which were based

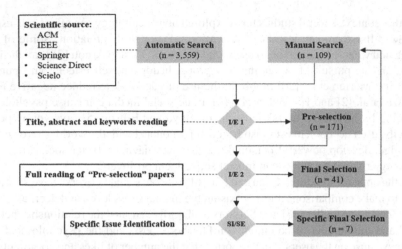

Fig. 1. Systematic literature review flow execution.

on and considered the PRISMA protocol (*Preferred, Reporting Items for Systematic Reviews and Meta-analyzes*) [21].

3.1 Research Questions

As presented in Sect. 1, the key question of this study is: *have technologies been designed to explicitly (positively) affect/impact self-esteem?* Based on this question, on Table 1 we raised four other specific questions and their motivations.

3.2 Search Bases and Search String

For raising relevant papers, we adopted two searching methods: automatic and manual. We carried out the automatic search according to a search string. In conformity to the research questions, we defined two main keywords to carry out the automatic searching: technology and self-esteem. We chose the term "technology" to not restrict the types of technologies in search; in this work, for "technology" we are considering everything that has some type of computational processing. The terms self-image, self-worth, and self-concept are often used as synonymous of self-esteem [27]. Therefore, we selected as keywords in this SLR the following terms: technology, self-esteem, self-concept, self-image, and self-worth. The search string was:

technology AND ("self-esteem" OR "self-concept" OR "self-image" OR "self-worth").

We carried out the automatic search on the main scientific bases followed by the computer academic community: ACM Digital Library, IEEE Xplore, SpringerLink, and Science Direct. We also considered Scielo because it indexes Brazilian journals. In SpringerLink we considered papers in the computer science area and that are classified as IHC subject. And in Science Direct we only examined papers from the "Computers in

Table 1. Research questions and their motivation.

Question	Motivation
P1. What types of technologies have been used to affect/impact self-esteem?	This question is important to raise the types of technologies that have been used to affect/impact user's self-esteem; in addition, to understand their limitations and prospect new ones to achieve this purpose
P2. How can technology be used to positively affect/impact self-esteem?	This question is essential to understand how technology is being used to positively affect/impact self-esteem and ascertain its limitations
P3. What aspects of self-esteem are affected through the technology usage?	This question raises the aspects of self-esteem that have been addressed in the literature. Besides, it helps to relate them to the characteristics of the technologies used
P4. What strategies have been adopted for influencing self-esteem through technological support?	This question is relevant to verify which possibilities and challenges exist in the process of influencing self-esteem through technologies usage

Human Behavior" and "Computers & Education" Journals, because, the first addresses the use of computers from a psychological perspective and self-esteem affects the human behavior, and the latter because digital technology can enhance education and self-esteem is an important factor for this context.

Although we selected scientific sources to cover this SLR multi-disciplinarity, we still considered manual search. We carried out the manual search through reading the final selected papers from automatic search (see "Final selection" on Fig. 1). Based on the text and its references, we raised other references that could be relevant to the scope of this work. We analyzed these new papers and considered the inclusion and exclusion criteria and the established steps to decide about incorporate the paper in the final selection or not.

3.3 Inclusion and Exclusion Criteria

As SLR examines existing papers, we decided what information we would consider to select a study or not. According to Kitchenham [17], inclusion and exclusion criteria definition helps to identify studies that provide evidence connected to research questions, in such a manner that the likelihood of bias is thus reduced. In this SLR, we held a paper eligible to be included if it presented a relationship between technology and self-esteem. We present all inclusion and exclusion criteria on Table 2.

We took the inclusion and exclusion criteria into account in two distinct moments (I/E 1, and I/E 2) to select the papers (see Fig. 1). We separated the inclusion and exclusion criteria into two groups to support us to refine the selection at each new screening step.

For each step, all the inclusion criteria were supposed to be reached; if we considered any of the exclusion criteria in any moment, we would not select the paper.

Table 2. Inclusion and exclusion criteria.

Inclusion criteria	
I1	Study that addresses the self-esteem issue
I1	Study published from 2009 to 2019
I1	Study from primary sources
I1	*Full paper* (conference articles), *journal* or book chapters
I2	Study that focuses on the relationship between technology and self-esteem
I2	Study that focuses on how technology affects/impacts self-esteem
SI	Study that supports to answer the research questions
SI	Study that explains the strategy used to influence self-esteem
SI	Study that focuses on technology design approaches to affect/impact self-esteem
Exclusion criteria	
E1	Study not related to the research context
E1	Study that does not address the use of technology and correlated areas
E1	Study from secondary source
E1	Study published before 2009
E1	Study that is not in English or Portuguese
E1	Duplicated Study
E1	*Short paper* (work with up to three pages)
E2	Study does not discuss "how" and/or "why" technology affect/impact self-esteem
SE	Study that does not present the design of a solution to influence self-esteem

Still, we considered some questions we were supposed to answer, besides criteria from Table 2.

Step I/E 1: the aim of this step was just to identify whether the paper was addressing self-esteem, the subject of this SLR. To support us with that, we asked the following question: *By the title, abstract and keywords, does the paper address the self-esteem issue in any way?* At this phase, we considered the I1 inclusion and E1 exclusion criteria. The selected papers are the "pre-selection" set (see Fig. 1).

Step I/E 2: after identifying studies that addressed the self-esteem issue ("pre-selection"), we read each one and analyzed whether we could answer the following questions (yes or no): *Does the paper address the correlation between technology and self-esteem? Does the paper address how and why technology affects self-esteem?* At this phase, we considered the I2 inclusion and E2 exclusion criteria and got the "final selection" (see Fig. 1).

From the "final selection" papers, we expected they could support us answer the questions presented in Table 1. But, as we discuss in Sect. 4.1, it was not possible because this SLR had specific questions about design and the process of influencing self-esteem, and if it described how the former can affect the latter from a design focused on influencing self-esteem. For this reason, we raised two questions to aid us to identify more relevant papers from those, after reading carefully the "final selection" studies: *Does the paper describe the design of some technological solution to affect self-esteem specifically? Does the paper describe any supporting strategy used to this purpose?* Thus, we defined more specific inclusion (SI) and exclusion (SE) criteria (see Table 2). After this stage, we got "specific final selection" studies (see Fig. 1).

3.4 Data Extraction

After reading in detail each one of the "final selection" studies, we extracted the following data to obtain metadata of the papers and other information regarding the objective of this SLR:

- *Paper information:* source; year; source type (journal or conference); authors list and their affiliation and nationality; and paper's title and context (industry or academia).
- *Type of research:* research method the paper carried out (*e.g.*, qualitative, quantitative, systematic review etc.).
- *User Interface category:* type of interface used for interaction with the proposed solution (*e.g.*, GUI, NUI, TUI, etc.).
- *Device category:* type of device used by the user to interact with the proposed solution. (*e.g.*, PC, TV, Mobile, etc.).
- *Interface design approach:* HCI approach used to develop the user interface (*e.g.*, participatory design, user-centered design, semio-participatory design, scenario-based etc.).

For the "specific final selection" papers, besides preview data, we also collected other information:

- *Name of the tool:* name of the developed tool.
- *Target audience:* the target audience for the developed solution (*e.g.*, children, adolescents, adults, elderly).
- *Users' location*: Where the user has to be to use the tool (*e.g.*, web, school, home).
- *Domain Application:* domain of the developed solution (*e.g.*, social network, education, games, etc.).
- *Evaluation category:* How the tool was evaluated (*e.g.*, end user participation, expert analysis, etc.).

- *Evaluation technique:* Which evaluation technique/method was used to evaluate the tool (*e.g.*, questionnaire, case study, controlled experiment, ethnography, think aloud, etc.).
- *Type of self-esteem:* Which type of self-esteem the developed solution supports. (*e.g.*, global or domain self-esteem).
- *Aspects of self-esteem:* Which aspects of self-esteem the solution direct or indirectly addresses (*e.g.*, self-confidence, self-image, social relationships, etc.).
- *Assessment tool of self-esteem:* method used to assessment of the users' self-esteem.

3.5 Quality Assessment

"Identifying the relevant research, checking that it is reliable and understanding how a set of research studies can help us in addressing a policy or practice concern is not a straightforward activity" [9, p. 7]. In this sense, assess the quality of the selected papers is relevant. The quality assessment supports us to trust the results we got to answer the research questions. We defined two type of assessment criteria metric to be used: independent and dependent variables.

In this way, based on [4], we defined the following questions for independent variables:

IV1. Is the **study objective** clearly mentioned?
IV2. Are the **study results** reported in a clear and unambiguous way?
IV3. Is the **design process** of the proposal described in detail?
IV4. Is there a clear **statement of findings**?
IV5. Is the **supporting strategy to influence self-esteem** reported in details?
IV6. Is there any **evaluation** of the proposed solution?
IV7. Are the **threats to the study validity** discussed?
IV8. How many **citations** does the paper have? (see Formulae 1)

$$IV8 = \frac{number\ of\ Citations\ of\ the\ paper}{maxNumber\ of\ Citations\ among\ all\ papers} \tag{1}$$

The final outcome of the independent variables is their arithmetic mean, as described in the following equation:

$$IVf = \frac{\sum_{i=1}^{n} IVi}{n} \tag{2}$$

Regarding dependent variables, we defined and applied the following questions:

DV1. How many **user interfaces** categories does the proposal cover?
DV2. How many **device categories** does the proposal cover?
DV3. How many **evaluation techniques** does the proposal use?
DV4. Is there any **user participation** during the evaluation?
DV5. How many **aspects of self-esteem** does the proposal cover?
DV6. How many **types of influences** does the proposal use?
DV7. Is the **user's self-esteem measured before** s/he used the proposal?

DV8. Is the **user's self-esteem measured after** s/he used the proposal?

The dependent variables DV1, DV2, DV3, DV5, and DV6, are related to the number of *answers* we got reading each paper. However, for the DV final calculation, we converted these answers in specific *values*. To do it, we used the *median* of each variable. Thus, if *answer = 0,* then *value = 0*; if *1 <=answer <= median* then *value = 0.5*; if *answer > median,* then *value = 1*. For variables DV4, DV7, and DV8, because of the type of the question, only two types of answers are possible (*yes* or *no*). Therefore, if the *answer = 1* (yes), the *value = 1*; otherwise, the *value = 0*.

Yet, we considered the importance of the variables considering the research questions of this SLR and gave *weight* to them. In this sense, the aspects of self-esteem (DV5), the supporting strategies (DV6), users participation (DV4), and their self-esteem assessment (DV7, and DV8) are the most important criteria in the context of this SLR and received *weigh 3*. The user interface category (DV1) and the devices category (DV2) received an intermediary value, *weigh 2*. And, the evaluation technique (DV1) received *weigh 1*.

Thus, the final outcome of the dependent variables is their weighted mean, as described in the following equation:

$$DVf = \frac{\sum_{j=1}^{m} wj \times DVj}{\sum_{j=1}^{m} wj} \tag{3}$$

Regarding the quality assessment of the "specific final selection" papers, we considered the scientific paper quality criteria (independent variables) and technological and self-esteem issue context of the solutions (dependent variables). For dependent variables, we considered important aspects to influence self-esteem through technology.

4 Results

From the automatic and manual searches, we got 3,668 papers (3,559 from the automatic process). Based on the papers' titles and abstracts reading, we selected 171 studies. In the sequence, we conducted a full reading of them to find out if they addressed how and why the used technology to affect self-esteem. Then, we selected 41 for careful reading, and investigated how they informed our research questions. Next, we present the results we got.

4.1 Overview of Findings

We performed the automatic and manual search from September 2019 to April 2020 considering the complete text, not just its *title* and *abstract*. It may help to justify the reason for the significant difference between the total number of papers and those of the final selection. Table 3 shows the number of papers we obtained in each of the chosen scientific bases and how many studies we selected.

From the 41 selected studies, only two of them have an author coming from the industry. Thus, studies of this nature seem to be mainly a concern of academic contexts.

From a temporal point of view, the graph in Fig. 2 shows the number of papers has increased considerably over the years. However, it should be mentioned that many of

Table 3. Total amount of papers.

	ACM	IEEE	Springer	Science D	Scielo	Manual	TOTAL
Total	1314	133	1160	940	12	109	3668
Pre-selection	26	30	13	57	3	42	171
Final selection	8	1	8	8	0	16	41

them identified automatically were not related to self-esteem in the way we intended to study; several works were more technically focused on artificial intelligence and sensors context, for example, or about social media use and addiction to technologies.

The year with the great number of papers in total was 2019. But, regarding "pre-selection" and the final selected papers, the graph in Fig. 2 shows 2018 was the year with the greatest number of studies correlating technology and self-esteem.

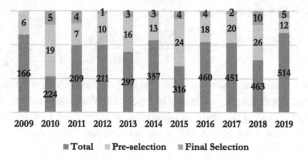

Fig. 2. Total amount of papers per year.

From the demographic point of view, there are contributions from 22 countries located across five continents: North America (17), South America (2), Europe (23), Asia (6), Africa (1), and Oceania (1). We based the country counting on the institution affiliation country of the researchers. The results may suggest that developed countries seem to be more concerned with the impact of technology on people's self-esteem.

About the type of research, 58.5% (24 studies) carried out quantitative research through surveys and controlled experiments, 29.3% (12 studies) conducted qualitative research and used prototyping, interviews, video analysis, and other HCI techniques, and 5 studies (12.2%) performed qualitative and quantitative research. One paper ran a literature review, but its focus differed from ours: a design for psychological well-being and regarded self-esteem as one of the study endpoints.

After reading the 3,668 papers' title and abstract, we select 171 ones. Afterward, we selected 41 which focused on some aspects of the relationship between technology and self-esteem. From the results of the analysis of the selected papers, we answered our key research question: *technological solutions have not been designed to affect self-esteem specifically*. Most of the papers' approach address self-esteem in existing social media context and analyzed, for example, how its mechanism such as Facebook 'like' can affect self-esteem, or how the user's self-esteem influences its usage. Some selected papers also analyzed how self-esteem influences social relationships through technological means such as chat, or analyzed, yet, how self-esteem may influence technology addiction or vice versa, for example. However, these types of approaches are not the focus of this SLR.

As we described in Sect. 3.3, we were concerned about papers that designed technological solution to influence the users' self-esteem specifically. Therefore, from the 41 select papers, seven studies ("specific final selection" – see Fig. 1) developed some solution with this purpose. We summarize the solution and its main user goal on Table 4. Next, we depict the specific results related to these seven papers.

4.2 Specific Results

The seven relevant studies identified in this systematic review allowed us to answer the fundamental question that led this research (*Have technologies been designed to explicitly (positively) affect/impact self-esteem?*). On Table 4, we briefly summarize each solution the included studies developed, as well as their target audience, domain, type of application, interface category, and technologies and devices they used for it.

The analysis of the seven selected studies shows the studies adopted three interface categories: GUI (P02, P03, P04, P07), TUI (P01), NUI (P06), and NUI + TUI (P05). GUI usage as the most used interface category was expected because it is the most common means by which people interact with the digital world. Yet, simple solutions seem to be preferred, such as a quiz (P03) and a shooting game (P04). Studies which adopted TUI and NUI, instead, seem to be aware of novel ways to interact with technology (*e.g.*, ubiquitous, pervasive), their relevance, and the possibilities these technologies raise. For instance, P05 uses the pressure and time the user types on the keyboard to give a feedback to him, and P06 considers the accuracy of the user's movement under a sensor with the information that is shown on the display to give a response to it.

With respect to the device categories, most of the papers (83.3%) made use of PC or TV as the main device for user interfaces. From those studies, P06 is the only one that used an interactive device that is not keyboard and mouse-based interaction: it is based on body movements on a carpet with sensors, or on a mobile controller to be adopted as a video game joystick. And P01 uses micro-controller, actuators, and button on a device placed on the wall; and a cell phone, its audio output, and its sensors, and a plush frog for the prototype of a second solution.

Although the focus of this systematic review is the design of solutions to positively influence self-esteem and we selected specific studies that address this issue, only P01 explained the (participatory) design process adopted and the techniques used (cultural study probe, interviews, prototyping, brainstorming and focus group) to build up the proposed solution. P02 reports they adopted user-centered design, looking at aspects of autism to design the final solution. The other papers do not mention the design approaches and techniques used.

Regarding to the proposed solutions evaluation, end-users used the tools. In P01 the participants used the solutions for four weeks in their homes, and the evaluation took place through usage logs, daily notes, emojis, and interviews. In P02 users used the tool for a few days at school, to self-assess their emotional state, and also made

Table 4. Solutions.

Solution	Target audience	Domain	Type of application	Interface category	Technology category
P01 - Happy Frog: comprises a stuffed frog with an LCD screen in its belly. When the user feels sad, he raises the frog which will say a motivational or encouraging message - the messages are editable via the internet. After the comment, the user must evaluate, on the LCD screen (mobile), how he felt when listening to the audio. Paay et al. (2018) [24]	Young adults	Psychology	Motivational	TUI	Mobile (cellphone)
P01 - Sun of Fortune: The user writes activities on paper and places each end of a sunbeam on the wall; at each end of the sun, there is a led. When feeling sad, the user presses the button in the center of the sun and one LED will light up randomly, showing which activity the user should perform. The goal is to make the person distract himself by avoiding negative thoughts. Paay et al. (2018) [24]	Young adults	Psychology	Motivational	TUI	Actuador (button, led), microprocessor
P02 - MindBook: consists of an online page designed to strengthen the self-esteem of children with depression through simulations of real situations that the child may face in their daily lives. The system resembles a social network and comprises videos, images, games, and a planner for children to plan their activities during the week. Schrammel et al. (2015) [29]	Children	Psychology	Informational/ therapeutic	GUI	Computer (display, keyboard, and mouse)
P03—Tutoring System: The system consists of a multiple-choice questionnaire related to logic with five questions in each of the three available contexts (geometric figures, numbers, and letters). The system aims to improve the user's self-esteem while answering the questions so that it supports his school performance. Jraidi and Frasson (2010) [15]	Young adults	Education	Informational/ educational	GUI	Computer (display, keyboard, and mouse), sensors
P05 - Batcave: Shooting game in which the player moves a car in a mine while he needs to dodge obstacles and shoot enemies to reach a treasure at the end of the cave. The game was developed to verify how self-esteem influences the player's motivation and to verify his post-game psychological state, checking, above all, his affective states. Birk et al. (2015) [3]	Not specified	Game	Leisure/ emotional	GUI	Computer (display, keyboard, and mouse)
P05 - ReacTickles: is a software used as a resource to support the relaxation and social encouragement of children with an autistic spectrum. The tool promotes curiosity through visual effects; the user interacting with the system through the keyboard and mouse will affect the interface depending on its frequency of interaction and pressure used to manipulate the objects. The system control is done by voice. Keay-Bright and Howart (2011) [16]	Children and young	Psychology	Therapeutic	GUI e NUI	Computer (display, keyboard, and mouse), microphone
P06—Dancing Game: consists of the user performing synchronous steps with the beat of the music being played. For this, the user must follow the indications of the steps represented by arrows that move on the screen. The game allows three types of interaction: by a carpet that detects the movements on the floor; by a control that has four buttons to be pressed with the hand; and by movements performed with a wheelchair. Gerling et al. (2014) [7]	Not specified	Game	Leisure/ motivational	NUI	TV, carpet with sensors, game pad control, notebook
P07 - eTutoring: consist in a platform for cross-age e-tutoring based on social networking tools, in which teenagers are tutors of other younger people. Through a video call and the functionalities made available, the tool supported the increase of the self-esteem of young people in the role of tutor and also of learning and social experiences by the younger ones. Le Roux and Loock (2015) [28]	Young	Education	Educational	GUI	Computer (display, keyboard, and mouse), webcam, microphone, mobile (cellphone)

Table 5. Self-esteem data.

	Self-esteem aspects	Self-esteem supporting		
		Focus	User's perspective	Strategy
P01	Self-confidence, self-image, self-reflection, motivation, satisfaction, social relationship, performance, affective state	Cognitive	Explicit	Motivational messages, activities to avoid negative thoughts
P02	Affective state, social relationship, self-reflection, behavior	Cognitive	Implicit	Demonstration of how positive self-expression is important, problem-solving and relaxation teaching, cognitive confrontation (behavioral training)
P03	Affective state, performance	Cognitive	Implicit	positive reflexive Association, change of affective states
P04	Competence, affective states, satisfaction, motivation	Action	Implicit	change of affective states, engagement/motivation and user (player) experience
P05	Social interaction, trustfulness, engagement/motivation, self-reflection, self-confidence	Action	Implicit	Encouragement/motivation
P06	Affective states, competence, autonomy, satisfaction, social relationship	Action	Implicit	Skills balancing strategies
P07	Motivation, satisfaction, social relationship	Action	Implicit	Cross-age e-tutoring

usability evaluation of the tool. In P03, the students were randomly assigned either to the experimental condition or to the control condition to use the system; during the experiment, physiological measures of users were recorded. P05 performed three experiments with children, but in the last one, only one child used the system for a few days and his teachers, through observation, noted his self-esteem had improved. P01, P03, P04, and P07 made assessments related to self-esteem after using the tools using specific questionnaires to measure it. P01, P04, and P07 also applied a self-esteem assessment questionnaire before the evaluation. And P06 carried out two controlled experiments before starting them, and at the end of each one, applied one questionary concerned to the user's psychological state and other related to the game interface.

Regarding the target audience of the solutions, the distribution was balanced between different age groups: young adults (P01, P03); and children and adolescents (P02, P05). P04, P06, and P07 do not mention the target audience, although they conducted experiments with young adults.

The seven studies have different solutions, domains, and proposals. About their domain, three studies are in the psychology field (P01, P02, P03), two are in the educational area (P03, P07), and the other two are entertaining games (P04, P06). Related to the types of solution, both solutions of P01 and P06 are motivational-based, P02 and P05 are therapeutic-based, and P03 and P07 are teaching/learning-based. Yet, P04 and P06, are leisure games, and there are some informational aspects in P02. Yet, we can note that the users do not seem to be self-aware of the fact these solutions should affect their self-esteem; just in P01 users know the solution's major aim was to affect their self-esteem.

All studies made use of self-esteem assessment tools to evaluate the effectiveness of the used strategies, except P05. P05 analyzed self-esteem through observation, because they performed the case study with just one child with spectrum of autism.

4.3 Quality Assessment

The quality assessment of the specific selected studies considered 8 independent variables related to scientific aspects of any research paper, and 8 dependents related to technology and self-esteem.

We defined the final quality assessment as follows:

$$QAf = \frac{IV + DV}{2} \tag{3}$$

Based on the results we got (see Fig. 3), we highlight all studies were rated over 0.61, which we consider it is very good quality regarding our aims. Based on the results and on the dependent variables, we can highlight: all studies present supporting strategy to influence self-esteem; the user participation is important in the evaluation process as well as the self-esteem assessment is fundamental to this type of context, but the number of evaluation technique and its type do not seem to be so relevant; it is important to embrace more aspects of self-esteem as much as possible. Yet, although the type of the technological device seems not to be such fundamental to influence self-esteem, we call attention to the greatest results (P01, and P06): both of them were the only two that used more contemporary technology and context, while P02, P03 and P07 made use of conventional computer usage. In this sense, although the total number of specific final selected papers were low, the quality assessment shows they supported us to answer our research questions with good quality.

5 Discussion

Although the solutions are distinct from each other and they have two primary target audience, their strategies have similar goals to affect/impact on self-esteem. Below we

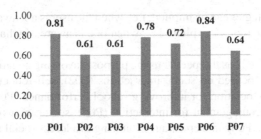

Fig. 3. Quality assessment result.

discuss in detail how technologies can be used to influence self-esteem, the strategies that were considered in the design of the solutions, and what aspects of self-esteem they may affect.

5.1 Technological Influence over Self-esteem

Table 4 supports us to answer question P1 (*What types of technologies have been used to affect/impact self-esteem?*). We observe that the technological devices are mostly the traditional ones, such as monitor, keyboard and mouse, in such a way that the communication interface with the user is the conventional one. Differently, P06 is based on a NUI-based system, and it uses a carpet with sensors to detect movements, and the study P01 moves towards pervasive and ubiquitous scenarios that have been increasingly present in society. Yet, we noticed, most of the solutions need an internet connection and services, or some specific software. Although nowadays to get internet connection is easier than some years ago, it may cause dependence and availability problems.

Regarding question P2 (*How may technology be used to positively affect/impact self-esteem?*), the seven works showed technology being used in several ways: motivational support, through messages for self-reflection (P01); intermediation, through suggested activities to help in forgetting negative thoughts (P01); everyday problem-solving simulation (P02); leisure, through games (P04, P06); question-and-answer system (P03); encouraging interaction and discovery (P05); and social experiences through learning (P07). Overall, the users' interactions with the tools are individual, except for solutions P06 and P07. As we can see, technology for affecting self-esteem is being used for leisure, motivation, scholar performing, information, therapy.

In this SLR, we sought studies that carried out the design of technological solutions with the primary objective of influencing the person's self-esteem, affecting some aspects. In Table 5 we present self-esteem data related to each one of the included studies. Based on Tables 4 and 5, we answered question P3 (*what aspects of self-esteem are affected through technology usage?*), and question P4 (*What strategies have been adopted for influencing self-esteem through technological supporting?*) together because they are correlated.

Based on the included papers, we realized the solutions can use either action-based supporting strategy, i.e., when the strategy used affects the user's psychological indirectly (P04, P05, P06, P07), or cognitive training-based supporting strategy, i.e., when the focus is to explicitly reach the psychological of the user through its cognitive aspect (P01, P02,

P03). Yet, these strategies can be implicit, i.e., when the user is not aware of the strategies and objectives of the tool, or explicit, i.e., when one is aware of what is happening and its pragmatic use.

Each tool identified has its specific usage purpose: avoiding negative thoughts (P01); behavioral training focused on social interactions (P02); self-reflection with the positive and affective association for improving school performance (P03); affective states changing (P04); encouragement for interaction (P05); social inclusion and not noting physical differences (P06); and cross-age e-tutoring to address social needs (P07). When we examined the intrinsic motives of these solutions, we concluded they intended to prevent users from negative self-assessments and feelings of lack of skill. Also, they expected to rouse the user's positive sense of capacity and confidence while they interact with the tools. For this reason, to influence the self-esteem, the solutions used several supporting strategies, for instance: motivation, by presenting positive messages (P01) and by using positive and affective words (P03); encouragement, by activating the user's curiosity in exploring technological artifacts (P05); behavioral training simulation of everyday situations to demonstrate how being positive is important to engage positive social relationships (P02); games as a means of affective states changes (P04 e P06); balancing the difficulty level and score system of a game so a wheelchair user, for example, does not feel less capable (P06); system interface similar to social networks so the user feels part of a group (P02); activity suggestion to avoid negative thoughts (P01); older student teaching youngers (P07); and online community formation (P07).

Through the strategies adopted, P02, P03, P04, P05, P06, and P07 promoted the user's competence and ability, increasing his/her self-confidence. P02 and P05 highlight self-confidence promotion when they consider real everyday situations and encourage children to cope with situations, even virtually; P01 also promotes the user's self-confidence using positive messages since it makes the user reflect on self-values, depending on the message content and the context in which the user hears it, affecting their self-image. The solution *sun of fortune* (P01) supports the user in avoiding negative thoughts, even if for a while. This strategy can also be seen in P03, which used positive and affective association with past experiences to help him face a situation that was not very good.

We figured out all strategies motivated users to perform tasks and experience some conditions such as social situations through simulation. Yet, they promoted positive feelings and affective states that are correlated to satisfaction, for good personal experiences.

5.2 Research Challenges

Although self-esteem is an individual concept, it is connected to how a person lives in society, sees her/himself, and self-assessments her/himself positively or negatively towards standards and behaviors s/he believes are society-defined. Despite the solutions P01, P02, P03, P04, P05 were developed for individual interaction, P06 and P07 made it explicit that the tool targets social interactions.

Although self-esteem is built from personal experiences in society, Paay et al. [24] (P01) argue affecting self-esteem through technology usage needs to be individual. However, Paay's results from the users' speeches make clear the opposite: the participants believe other family members and their friends should write the "happy frog" messages so they could feel more self-confident. In *sun of fortune* (P01), some participants said drawn activities sometimes involved talking to a family member. These also indicate social context is significant as an intervention strategy to affect/impact self-esteem.

Thus, one challenge is how to incorporate social aspects on the solutions to influence self-esteem. P02, although used a social-media-based interface to rouse the users to the sense of social belonging, the solution was to individual interaction and did not provide any means to allow any type of relationship. Social experiences promotion is challenging, because the context, the supporting and the users' needs are diverse. Another challenge is how to consider interactional aspects such as collaboration, conversation, and sharing to emerge social groups and relationship. It raises the challenge of how to avoid in users the feeling of not belonging socially.

In this social context, another challenge is to maintain the privacy of the user. In solution P04, the user's score at the end of the game session is exposed to everyone on a scoreboard along with his name and photo. This lack of privacy can affect him and harm his self-esteem even more, depending the information the system shows. In study P01 users argued it is important not to expose their situation to everyone. Therefore, we highlight maintaining the privacy of the user and protect him from situations that could cause him opposite psychological effect is important.

Still, it is important, and challenging to ponder about situations that cause users opposite psychological effects. In study P01, for instance, who writes the messages the "frog" shows is the user. In this case, some participants reported sometimes they had the sense they were "cheated". P02 used a similar social networking-based interface to arouse in the child the sense of social belonging. However, it can also have other negative effects on users, especially for those who suffer from depression, if this type of strategy also adopts other social media mechanisms such as "likes", and "comments". Thus, pondering about the consequences of strategies it is important for the effectiveness of the solution not to be compromised. This type of situation can affect the trust in the system, self-confidence, and the user's emotion.

In this perspective, no matter how the solutions adopt strategies to implicitly or explicitly affect self-esteem, they must concern about decisions they will take so that the desired solution does not have the opposite effect on that intended. In P01, the user knows since the beginning the main goal of the tool (explicit strategy by actions to deal with self-esteem). On the one hand, it is beneficial due to give him "freedom" to "menage" his moments of psychological discomfort. However, it is necessary to ponder the way of communication between technology and the user so that he does not have the sensation of having a problem or being one himself. Yet, it is worth caring about that in such a way the user does not feel incapable, for example, and not to expose his situation to everyone, as some participants reported in some studies. Also, there is the challenge of the solution being always available to the user and/or he has the necessary conditions to use it.

The tools that embraced implicit supporting strategy, even though it is action-based instead of using strategies aimed at cognitive training, need to be adaptable to as many users as possible. In paper P06, if the adjustment strategies for the wheelchair user to play are not "accurate" and "fair", for example, it can have reverse effects on both players. This can happen because one may have the sentiment of being wronged and/or the other, unable because of the system makes the game easier for the wheelchair one. In P03, on the other hand, if the questions that the user might answer are not under his knowledge level, there is no sense in the system making use of self-reflective and affective positive words. Similarly, if the game P04 is very challenging, the user may feel incapable, especially if other people are playing together.

Within this context, therefore, another existing challenge is that the strategy used tries as much as possible to make the user feel good, capable, motivated, and, above all, not feel judged. For this reason, the design could consider affective issues in real-time, in such a way that the system automatically adapts itself to what the user seems to be feeling and, thus, supports the user to overcome that sensation, which could affect, for example, his self-confidence and motivation.

The solutions we summarized in Table 4 adopted implicit-based or explicit-based supporting strategies through actions or cognitive training. Yet, they are for individual or collective use and have specific application domain and target audience. Their technological constraints are that the type of technology used imposes and the contexts they were developed to be used in. But all those concerns are reasonable for adjustment to be used at home or in other contexts, and by other target users, and also cover social aspects.

The proposals of the study P01 could be adapted for children and for parents and friends to collaborate with messages and activities. The study P03, on the other hand, could increase the difficulty of questions level to raise the user's confidence. Yet, other technological scenarios could use the implemented strategies pointed out in this SLR with other objectives. Paper P05 could expand the interactional objects and the social situations simulated, for example, in such a way the objects could communicate and interact among them through ubiquity and pervasiveness (IoT scenarios). Also, the system could consider corporal movements, like those used by study P06. Those new scenarios could also consider social interactions and physical changes in the environment where the solution would be placed. It would affect aspects of the user's self-esteem for providing him more realistic and natural experiences.

6   Conclusion

There are several studies in social media context about how technology may impact self-esteem and how it also biases the user experience. Besides social media applications, this systematic review aimed to raise studies that carried out the design of solutions to affect the self-esteem of people. Our major motivation in this study was to raise how technology can support self-esteem, what types of technologies have been used to do it, and the strategies they have relied on for this purpose. Besides, we wondered to find out which aspects of self-esteem these solutions impacted and the values they have achieved.

After the automatic selection of 3,668 papers and reading 41 ones, we noted not all addressed self-esteem in the way we intended. Seven papers developed solution with this purpose and were further analyzed in this work.

We noticed that new human-computer interaction approaches such as the use of voice, body movements, and objects embodiment to provide interactions more natural could have benefited the studies, like in P01 and P06. Results also showed most of the papers did not consider social aspects and social relationships in the solution's design. This highlight how challenging this self-esteem context is, especially because self-esteem is based on social life. We believe the solutions could consider the users' affective states in real-time, and turn solutions adaptable in real-time, avoiding negative effects on the user, for example.

In this sense, we argue it is relevant to explore new modes of interacting with technologies since they have evolved and altered the way people interact with them and with other people. Besides, in a society that is increasingly interconnected and dependent on computer technology, it is necessary to investigate social and interaction aspects, especially aspects that refer to self-esteem and affective states, since they have the potential to affect people's life.

Yet, alternative technological scenarios could use the implemented strategies pointed out in this SLR with diverse objectives. P05 could expand the interactional objects and the social situations simulated, for example, in such a manner the objects could communicate and interact among them through ubiquity and pervasiveness (IoT scenarios). Also, systems could consider body movements, like those used by study P06. Those new scenarios could also consider social interactions and physical changes in the environment where the solution would be placed. And, social awareness, social experiences, and human and technical values could enhance the design of these solutions. It might promote more meaningful, natural, and involving interactions.

Acknowledgments. This work is financially supported by National Council for Scientific and Technological Development (CNPq) through grants #140400/2020-6, #306272/2017-2, and #304708/2020-8, and by the São Paulo Research Foundation (FAPESP) through grants #2015/16528-0.

References

1. Altaf, J.G., Troccoli, I.R.: Essa Roupa é a Minha Cara: a contribuição do vestuário de luxo à construção da auto-imagem dos homossexuais masculinos. Organizações Sociedade **18**(58), 513–532 (2011)
2. Apaolaza, V., et al.: The relationship between socializing on the Spanish online networking site Tuenti and teenagers' subjective wellbeing: the roles of self-esteem and loneliness. Comput. Hum. Behav. **29**(4), 1282–1289 (2013)
3. Birk, M.V., et al.: How self-esteem shapes our interactions with play technologies. In: Proceedings of the 2015 Annual Symposium on Computer-Human Interaction in Play, pp. 35–45 (2015)
4. Bittencourt, I.I., Baranauskas, M.C., Pereira, R., Dermeval, D., Isotani, S., Jaques, P.: A systematic review on multi-device inclusive environments. Univ. Access Inf. Soc. **15**(4), 737–772 (2015). https://doi.org/10.1007/s10209-015-0422-3
5. Boyd, D.M., Ellison, N.B.: Social network sites: definition, history, and scholarship. J. Comput.-Mediat. Commun. **13**(1), 210–230 (2007)
6. Chen, W., Lee, K.-H.: Sharing, liking, commenting, and distressed? The pathway between Facebook interaction and psychological distress. Cyberpsychol. Behav. Soc. Network. **16**(10), 728–734 (2013)

7. Gerling, K.M., et al.: Effects of balancing for physical abilities on player performance, experience and self-esteem in exergames. In: Proceedings of the SIGCHI Conference on Human Factors in Computing Systems, pp. 2201–2210 (2014)
8. Gilbert, D.T., et al.: The Handbook of Social Psychology. Oxford University Press, Oxford (1998)
9. Gough, D., et al.: An Introduction to Systematic Reviews. Sage, Thousands Oak (2017)
10. Hatchel, T., et al.: The relation between media multitasking, intensity of use, and well-being in a sample of ethnically diverse emerging adults. Comput. Hum. Behav. **81**, 115–123 (2018)
11. Heatherton, T.F., Wyland, C.L.: Assessing self-esteem (2003)
12. Hutz, C.S., Zanon, C.: Revisão da apadtação, validação e normatização da escala de autoestima de Rosenberg. Avaliacao Psicológica: Interamerican J. Psychol. Assess. **10**(1), 41–49 (2011)
13. James, W.: As emoções (1890). Revista Latinoamericana de Psicopatologia Fundamental **11**(4), 669–674 (2008)
14. Jang, W.E., et al.: Self-esteem moderates the influence of self-presentation style on Facebook users' sense of subjective well-being. Comput. Hum. Behav. **85**, 190–199 (2018)
15. Jraidi, I., Frasson, C.: Subliminally enhancing self-esteem: impact on learner performance and affective state. In: Aleven, V., Kay, J., Mostow, J. (eds.) ITS 2010. LNCS, vol. 6095, pp. 11–20. Springer, Heidelberg (2010). https://doi.org/10.1007/978-3-642-13437-1_2
16. Keay-Bright, W., Howarth, I.: Is simplicity the key to engagement for children on the autism spectrum? Pers. Ubiquit. Comput. **16**(2), 129–141 (2012)
17. Kitchenham, B.: Procedures for Performing Systematic Reviews, vol. 33, pp. 1–26. Keele University, Keele (2004)
18. Lee, E.-J., Jang, J.: Profiling good Samaritans in online knowledge forums: effects of affiliative tendency, self-esteem, and public individuation on knowledge sharing. Comput. Hum. Behav. **26**(6), 1336–1344 (2010)
19. Lopez, S., Snyder, C.: Positive Psychological Assestment a Handbook of Models and Measure: The Measurement and Utility of Adult Subjective Well-Being. American Psychological Association, Washington, DC (2003)
20. Marino, C., et al.: A comprehensive meta-analysis on problematic Facebook use. Comput. Hum. Behav. **83**, 262–277 (2018)
21. Moher, D., et al.: Preferred reporting items for systematic reviews and meta-analyses: the PRISMA statement. PLoS Med. **6**(7), e1000097 (2009)
22. Muriana, L.M., et al.: Affective state, self-esteem and technology: an exploratory study with children in hospital context. In: Proceedings of the 18th Brazilian Symposium on Human Factors in Computing Systems, pp. 1–11 (2019)
23. Nie, J., Sundar, S.S.: Who would pay for Facebook? Self esteem as a predictor of user behavior, identity construction and valuation of virtual possessions. In: Kotzé, P., Marsden, G., Lindgaard, G., Wesson, J., Winckler, M. (eds.) INTERACT 2013. LNCS, vol. 8119, pp. 726–743. Springer, Heidelberg (2013). https://doi.org/10.1007/978-3-642-40477-1_50
24. Paay, J., et al.: Happy bits: interactive technologies helping young adults with low self-esteem. In: Proceedings of the 10th Nordic Conference on Human-Computer Interaction, pp. 584–596 (2018)
25. Pai, P., Arnott, D.C.: User adoption of social networking sites: eliciting uses and gratifications through a means–end approach. Comput. Hum. Behav. **29**(3), 1039–1053 (2013)
26. Park, J.: Emotional reactions to the 3D virtual body and future willingness: the effects of self-esteem and social physique anxiety. Virtual Real. **22**(1), 1–11 (2017). https://doi.org/10.1007/s10055-017-0314-3
27. Pereira Santos, C., et al.: Measuring self-esteem with games. In: Proceedings of the 22nd International Conference on Intelligent User Interfaces, pp. 95–105 (2017)

28. le Roux, P., Loock, M.: The impact and opportunities of e-tutoring in a challenged socio-economic environment. In: 2015 International Conference on Computing, Communication and Security (ICCCS), pp. 1–6. IEEE, Pointe aux Piments, Mauritius (2015). https://doi.org/10.1109/CCCS.2015.7374167

29. Schrammel, A., et al.: Mind book – a social network trainer for children with depression. In: De Gloria, A. (ed.) GALA 2014. LNCS, vol. 9221, pp. 152–162. Springer, Cham (2015). https://doi.org/10.1007/978-3-319-22960-7_15

30. Scissors, L., et al.: What's in a Like? Attitudes and behaviors around receiving likes on Facebook. In: Proceedings of the 19th ACM Conference on Computer-Supported Cooperative Work and Social Computing, pp. 1501–1510 (2016)

31. Shank, D.B.: Technology and emotions. In: Stets, J.E., Turner, J.H. (eds.) Handbook of the Sociology of Emotions: Volume II. HSSR, pp. 511–528. Springer, Dordrecht (2014). https://doi.org/10.1007/978-94-017-9130-4_24

32. Thüring, M., Mahlke, S.: Usability, aesthetics and emotions in human–technology interaction. Int. J. Psychol. **42**(4), 253–264 (2007)

33. Zell, A.L., Moeller, L.: Are you happy for me… on Facebook? The potential importance of "likes" and comments. Comput. Hum. Behav. **78**, 26–33 (2018)

Research on Emotional Design of Visual Interaction Based on Cognitive Psychology

Zhang Zhang and Yilian Hao[✉]

East China University of Science and Technology, Shanghai 200237, People's Republic of China
zhangzhang@ecust.edu.cn

Abstract. Based on Norman's three-level theory of emotion-instinct, behavior, and reflection, the article quantifies and analyzes the emotional elements in visual interaction design. Cognitive psychology provides a foundation for studying user behavior and habits for user design. "By comparing the emotional performance and function of visual design and the analysis of the emotional mechanism in interface design, it is concluded that the emotional expression of user interface has two functions: one is to shape and convey the emotional theme of the user interface, and the other is to satisfy the user's unique emotional appeal in different scenarios. The emotional stimulation in the interface can arouse the user's positive emotions and life state. Finally, through actual cases and design practices of sleep products with apps, the three aspects of Norman emotional design, instinct-behavior-reflection, were studied respectively.

The purpose of this article is to use the theoretical basis of cognitive psychology and emotional design to comb the concepts of emotional design and visual interaction design and establish their internal logic. Emotion is also a cognitive process based on the evaluation component, which has a significant impact on the overall quality of the interaction. Combining the emotional needs of users in cognitive psychology, it explores the elements of visual realization of emotional design in interactive interfaces and proposes specific methods to improve user emotions and optimize experience on the interface.

Keywords: Emotional design · Interactive app · Cognitive psychology · Visual design

1 Introduction

The development of Internet technology is followed by the popularization of Internet terminals. In the information age, interface has become an important interactive channel for consumers to obtain information. Visual design improves the efficiency of information transmission. However, the user's emotional needs are not paid attention to, and the user interface design can not replace the user's emotion and experience in real life. The interface simply meets the goal of obtaining information, and the low level of emotional experience provides users with low-quality interactive experience and reduce the frequency and stickiness of use.

© Springer Nature Switzerland AG 2021
M. Kurosu (Ed.): HCII 2021, LNCS 12762, pp. 472–481, 2021.
https://doi.org/10.1007/978-3-030-78462-1_36

In the last 20 years, the debate on the role of emotions in the field of industrial design has grown exponentially. Emotional Design emerged as the effort to promote positive emotions or pleasure in users by means of design properties of products and services [1]. According to Van Gorp and Adams (2012), design based on emotions can affect overall user experience deeply, since emotions influence decision making, affect attention, memory, and generate meaning [2]. There are currently two main methods for applying emotional design. The first method is based on the modification of the object's aesthetic appearance or interface, and the second one is dedicated to promoting smooth interaction [3].

Experience economy emphasizes the importance of life and scene, pursues the satisfaction degree of consumers in the process of experience, attaches importance to self-experience in the process of consumption, and also shows the direction of modern economy and design development. Emotion, as an oppressive and mandatory human experience, transforms the user's cognition, feeling, habits and values into a design language, improves the enthusiasm of the user, and has a higher degree of pleasure and repeated behavior in the interface use scene. Based on this, it is of high research value to explore the interface interactive design language to improve emotional experience and enhance user loyalty and identity.

2 An Overview of Cognitive Psychology and Emotional Design

In the 1970s, cognitive psychology, which focuses on studying the process of people's advanced activities, became one of the main research directions of western psychology. For the first time, cognitive psychology was defined in Nesser's book "Cognitive psychology" in 1967, which is summarized in the process of studying perception. Different from other subjects such as behaviorism, cognitive psychology focuses more on the process of transmitting objective information to the brain and processing than the appearance of human behavior. The research scope includes perception, cognition, thinking and so on.

As the mainstream theory of contemporary cognitive psychology, information processing theory regards people as an information processing system. Cognition is equivalent to the whole process of information processing, coding, storage and extraction. Perception under cognitive psychology contains two concepts, one is divided into three perceptual modes according to the characteristics of perception, the other is to divide perception into sensory systems such as vision, hearing and touch. Perception is the experience generated by external environment through sensory organs, including sound, taste, object, event and so on. Perception and feeling are not the same, feeling is based on visual touch and other information, perception is a higher psychological cognitive process, including the understanding of the object, as well as their own experience, memory and judgment. Perception is the result of the combination of various senses.

Cognitive psychology provides an important theoretical basis to meet the psychological, physiological and thinking needs of users in the early stage of interactive design, and the visual cognition in perception also supports the visual interaction design of emotional needs in this paper.

2.1 Emotion Design Level

Human emotion is a very complex and unique system. "People use the cognitive system to explain the world, and the emotional system to assess whether the environment affects the safety of life. It is a subconscious physiological reflex," Norman said in "Emotional Design" [4]. According to Norman's three-level theory of emotion - instinct, behavior, reflection, the emotional elements in visual interaction design are quantified and analyzed. The instinctive level refers to the reaction of instinct to the observation and understanding of appearance. The instinctive level is mainly based on the visual cognitive process of the viewer (Fig. 1).

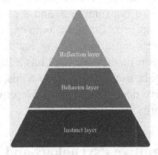

Fig. 1. A figure from 《Emotional Design》 by Donald Norman.

The behavior level is displayed through the interactive behavior between the user and the product, which mainly refers to the satisfaction and experience of the user in the process of using the product. User experience at this level is more rational, focusing on product comfort, operability, fluency and ease of understanding. Products must meet the functional needs of users in order to improve the experience.

Reflection level is the top level of emotion and cognitive psychology, which comes from the deeper emotion, consciousness, experience, cultural background and so on. It refers to the experience of the user after using the product. After the interaction process, the memory and good feeling of the interaction help to establish the long-term emotional bond between the product and the user.

The theory of emotional design guides the visual elements in the interface, so that the emotional elements are visualized into the interface design.

2.2 Interaction and User Interface Design

Interactive design is a new design field of the behavior for designers and systems. From the user's view, interactive design has the characteristics of easy operation and pleasant product. The concept of interactive design first appeared in the 1980s, when the progress of science and technology promoted the development of society, and computers gradually entered people's lives. Interactive design is also popular and rapidly transformed into digital product design. After a long exploration and development, the concept of interactive design is improved and updated, from the function-centered design process to the user-centered design goal. The interaction model also develops from the simple dialogue interface of the mobile phone to the free interface centered on the user experience [5].

Cognitive psychology provides design principles for interactive design, which includes mental models, perception/reality mapping principles, etc.

User interface is the medium of information interaction between system and user. In psychology, user interface is divided into two levels: feeling and emotion. User interface design includes the interaction between user and interface, and is also a cross field of cognitive psychology, design and other disciplines.

3 Research on Emotional Visual Interface in Cognitive Psychology

3.1 Copyright Form Cognitive Psychological Behavior and User Interface

User interface design is the process of information design. User browsing interface is the process of information cognition, good user interface can guide users and prepare to transmit information. In order to make users receive information more actively, user interface design needs designers to have a basic understanding of the psychological cognition and behavior of users. In the process of interface cognition, the user's experience evaluation of interface includes visual elements, layout, and operation. Cognitive psychology provides a basis for the study of user behavior and habits in user interface design. It can be considered that human-computer interaction input and coding storage share similar characteristics with the treating process of brain cognition" [6].

3.2 Emotional Expression and Function of Visual Design

Emotion covers all aspects of society, culture, background and other factors, but is also influenced by the individual's understanding of things and psychological response, and by the physiological and psychological mechanisms. Visual communication and emotion have a promoting relationship. Visual design shows different emotional tendencies through color text graphics and other elements. Emotional performance in visual communication design has the following functions:

1. The expression of emotion in visual design is pluralistic, that is, perceptual expressions along with rational logic. It can not only cause the direct emotional change of the viewer, but also cause the rational thinking of the social culture.
2. The relationship between visual design and emotional expression is not simply inter-available, but blending. Emotion is the communication between the designer and the viewer in the design process. In visual design, only under the premise of emotional communication, emotional works can be completed.
3. People's emotions are complex and changeable. Under the same visual presentation, in different experiences, backgrounds and cultures, the viewer's interpretation is also very different. The feelings conveyed vary from person to person.

3.3 Analysis of Emotional Mechanism in Interface Design

The main function of user interface is information transmission, and the main way is in the form of vision. Therefore, visual elements in interface design, as an important form of information exchange, are also important carriers of emotional expression [7].

Information visualization, as a way of information transmission, shows users a clear visual level and conveys emotion. Users obtain information more intuitively and quickly through visual elements and graphics other than words, and users focus their attention on the information they are more concerned about, thus deepening the memory of users and reducing the time of information screening, improving user access efficiency and making cognitive experience more pleasant.

The interactive experience with emotion not only needs the emotional design of interaction and vision, but also needs the emotional mechanism of user interface with more participation and substitution to realize good emotional experience. The design of emotion mechanism reshapes and optimizes the interaction flow and function of user interface. Moreover, it increases the contact of emotion expression.

The emotional expression of user interface has two functions: one is to shape and transmit the emotional theme of user interface, the other is to meet the emotional demands of users in different scenes. For example, in the bank user interface, users want the interface to have more secure and private emotional performance, thereby enhancing the user's sense of trust and utilization.

4   Study on the Elements of Emotional Design in Visual Interaction

4.1   Instinct Level - Color Language Elements

In the three levels of Norman emotional influence design, "Instinct level is above consciousness and thinking, which highlights the importance of shape, which forms the first impression of users. The design of instinct level is closely related to the initial effect, shape and texture of the product." Instinctive design is based on the user's instinctual response. The shape on the user interface is mainly composed of visual elements. Psychological research has found that the feeling produced by color accounts for 80% of the initial time of visual organs to observe objects, and after five minutes, the feeling of color and form accounts for half, and maintains this state. Color is the most direct and fast factor in visual elements. Rudolf Arnheim's "color conveys feelings" is irrefutable [8]. Color language elements play an important role in interface emotional design, especially in instinctive level.

Color is the basic element in visual design. Color perception, as the core element of aesthetics, directly affects the aesthetic sentiment of users. Color itself does not have emotion, the emotion produced by ornamental color comes from people's perception of color. People's physiological mechanism has caused changes in color such as warmth and coldness, light and shade, enthusiasm and cold. Color is the main element that affects color emotion. Different colors produce different psychological shocks relative to users and form different emotions. Goethe divides the color into positive and negative according to hue [9]. Positive colors (yellow, red and orange) have vitality and positive attitude. Negative colors (blue, purple) have gentle, uneasy color feelings. Secondly, the saturation and brightness of hue also affect color emotion. Different tone interface design also shows different emotions. High solid hue conveys vitality and passion. Mixed with white tone gives a clear, light feeling. The appropriate amount of gray hue has the characteristics of elegant and tranquil emotion. With a large number of black tones to show apathy, depression. The deployment of different hue and saturation has different emotional tendencies. For designers, the mastery of color and cognition is helpful to the design of emotional mechanism in interface design and to meet the emotional needs of users in different scenes.

In the U pillow application interface design, the interface color mainly takes a large number of negative colors blue and purple as the main tone, combined with the function of product assistant business travel users to obtain better sleep quality. The hue in the interface adds a proper amount of gray to convey a calm and peaceful psychological feeling. On "Spirit of Art", the inevitable connection between color and its form puts forward the influence of form on color" [10]. The app icon design combines rounded or circular design to enhance the overall interface to convey a soft and peaceful color emotion (Fig. 2).

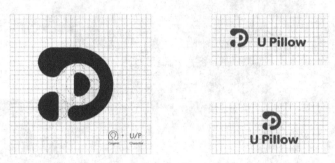

Fig. 2. The app icon designed by author. (Color figure online)

4.2 Instinct Level – Layout

The color and shape of interface design have certain emotional expressions. On the other hand, the arrangement and layout of visual elements will also produce different experiences. Typography in traditional visual systems includes four principles: intimacy, contrast, repetition, and alignment. In the interface design, the layout to produce pleasant emotional experience has three characteristics: balance, contrast and rhythm.

Balance refers to the static state of a contradictory element after the force is offset. In interface design, the position, proportion, color and texture of visual elements are the main design contents on the instinct level, and the balance relationship of interface on elements is the basic premise of visual aesthetic sense. A balanced symmetrical layout has a visual sense of stability and dignity. Asymmetric balance shows a more lively and dynamic emotional experience.

Contrast refers to the sharp difference of elements with different characteristics. And in the overall interface it presents harmony and unity. A reasonable contrast relationship is helpful to clarify the primary and secondary relationship of the interface, especially in the complex information interface, which can make the user obtain the desired content more efficiently, increase the activity of the interface, and avoid the dullness of a large amount of text information. At the heart rate interface of the U pillow sleep quality analysis, the text information about the user's sleep state can also be compared with the size and boldness, and the rest of the sleep state is also compared with the color, which is convenient for the user to distinguish and obtain the data quickly. In the recording interface, the effective sleep obtained by the user is compared with the sleep time of the day, and the efficiency and aesthetic experience of the user's information acquisition is also improved (Fig. 3).

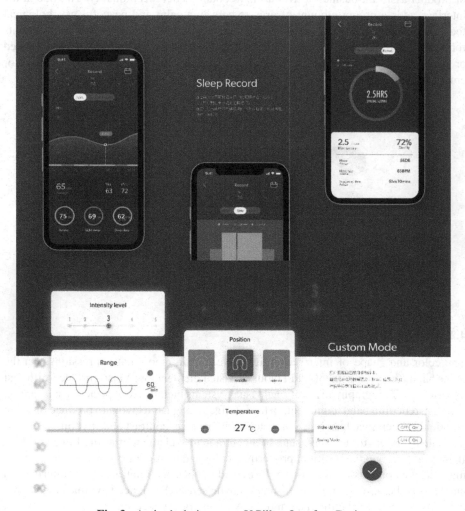

Fig. 3. Author's design case - U Pillow Interface Design.

The rhythm is meant to be repeated and changed in music, and the interface design refers to the sense of movement when the same visual elements are repeated continuously. The mechanical repetition of the same element will lead to dull boredom, while the visual effect of the rhythmic feeling formed by the change of element size and color enhances the identity and emotional experience of the use process.

4.3 Behavioral Dimensions - Intelligent Response Micro-interaction Elements

The behavior level emphasizes the utility value of the product, and the behavior level design which can produce good emotional experience is mainly manifested in the accessibility of interface information and the ease of interface design. The interaction in the interface design is to establish a more diversified communication mode with the user, at the same time, to establish a closer relationship between the user and the information, to meet the user's main participation in the information exchange and hands, thus producing a pleasant emotional experience.

The concept of micro-interaction first appeared in 2018, refers to the completion of a function in a specific scene, with a positive and pleasant user interaction. In the current interface design, it is also a very important trend. Micro-interaction settings can enable users to better understand the logic of the interface system, and help guide users to obtain a good experience. Micro-interaction includes a smooth effect design, which simplifies the cognitive process of users and reduces the negative emotions of delay and waiting. The gradual presentation of information through animation helps to sort out the hierarchical relationship of complex information.

Waiting is the most negative emotional reason that affects the user's product use experience. Data show that the interface does not get the user's expectation response in 140 ms time, the user will have the obvious delay feeling. Each delay of 1 s in the user interface jump process means 7% of the user conversion loss. The micro-interactive design of the waiting interface can effectively divert the user's waiting attention and anxiety. The micro-interactive design in the waiting process, the loading state and time of the interface can also alleviate the negative feelings of frustration.

4.4 Reflective Level - Narrative Dynamic Illustration

The reflection level emphasizes the user's experience of using the product, which involves the comprehensive role of many fields, including product information, product culture and significance value [11]. Research on product design based on reflection level in emotional design, making users realize emotional communication and impression in the process of product use is the key to realize visual reflection design in interface design.

The main point of the design of the reflective level lies in "touching the scene". In the Internet products, the users can arouse memories through the products or recall strong feelings of satisfaction and deep interest at the level of consciousness, and then realize the design of the reflective level. The introduction of storytelling in the visual design of the interface helps users understand the product more smoothly, and a good story can arouse the memory and thinking of the user. In this level of design, the plot should be conceived according to the emotional characteristics of the user in the scene.

The narrative illustrations are more plot in the interface design, and can stimulate the strong and lasting emotion of the user.

The dynamic illustrations of Alipay's annual bill in January are hot spots on social media platforms, and show that Alipay successfully evokes memories of the past year through illustrations of storytelling. The words and music deepen the resonance and brand identity of consumer groups. It is a successful case of reflective level design. Reflection level is the top level design idea of emotional design. At present, the research on interface emotional design is still in the exploration period. This paper briefly analyzes the role and significance of visual elements in the reflection level, to refer to make reference for future research (Fig. 4).

Fig. 4. Design of annual account interface for Alipay 2020.

The three levels of emotional design are not independent, but integrated. Emotional design can play a different role at the same time, in the instinct layer to attract the attention of users, in the behavior layer to enhance the satisfaction of the function, in the reflection layer to trigger recall and deeper emotion.

5   Summary

In line with the development of the new era and the changes of consumer demand, the functions of the previous design no longer meet the emotional needs of consumers. Emotional design to enhance users' positive feedback and happy experience has become an irresistible trend of the times. Visual element is the most intuitive carrier of emotional expression in interactive design. Users can resonate with the interface through visual interactive design and form positive interactive effect with the product to enhance the emotional experience of users. This paper mainly analyzes the influence and function of visual elements in interactive emotional design, and gives some guidance for the design of other areas and levels of emotion.

Acknowledgments. "Sponsored by Shanghai Pujiang Program".

References

1. Norman, D.A.: Emotional Design: Why We Love (or Hate) Everyday Things (2004)
2. Van Gorp, T., Adams, E.: Design for Emotions. Elsevier, Waltham (2012)
3. Triberti, S., Chirico, A., La Rocca, G., Riva, G.: Developing emotional design: emotions as cognitive processes and their role in the design of interactive technologies. Front. Psychol. **8**, 1773 (2017). https://doi.org/10.3389/fpsyg.2017.01773
4. Ding, H., Zhang, J.: Research on emotional visual elements design. Pack. Eng. **40**(10), 8–11+36 (2019)
5. Ma, J.: Application and research of cognitive psychology in interaction design. Qingdao University of technology (2018)
6. Xu, W.: User centered design: opportunities and challenges of ergonomics. Ergonomics **04**, 8–11 (2003)
7. Zhang, S., Ren, B.: Research on user interface design based on user emotional need. Grand View Fine Arts **2016**(06), 134–213 (2016)
8. Rudolf, A., Teng, S.: Art and visual perception. Contemp. Art. (04), 94 (2019)
9. Song, C.: Emotional design of web visual elements. Art Des. (Theory) (03), 52–54 (2014)
10. Kandinsky, W.: On the Spirit of Art, vol. 34. China Social Sciences Press, Beijing (1987)
11. Tang, J., Wang, R.: Research on product design based on reflection in emotional design. Electr. Tools **02**, 26–28 (2020)

Comparison of Kawaii Feelings for Magnets with Different Shapes Between 2007 and Present

Michiko Ohkura[✉] and Tipporn Laohakangvalvit

Shibaura Institute of Technology, 3-7-5, Toyosu, Koto-ku, Tokyo 1358548, Japan
ohkura@sic.shibaura-it.ac.jp, tipporn@shibaura-it.ac.jp

Abstract. In the 21st century, the Kansei/affective values of industrial products are considered very important. In this study, we focus our attention on "kawaii" as a Kansei value for future industrial products. We began our research to analyze kawaii attributes systematically with the aim of constructing kawaii products. "Kawaii" is a Japanese word that has positive meanings such as cute, loveable, and charming. From a survey of cultural studies, we form the following hypothesis: "Japanese men, especially middle-aged and older, tend to dismiss kawaii as an adjective only for living creatures and related figures and characters. On the other hand, Japanese women bestow feelings of kawaii not only on living creatures but also on industrial products." In order to test this hypothesis, we perform a simple experiment using four differently-shaped magnets: cat-shaped, puzzle-piece-shaped, whale-shaped, and heart-shaped. Twenty Japanese participants (10 males and 10 females) in their early 20s and twenty Japanese participants (10 males and 10 females) in their early 50s serve as volunteers. The kawaii scores for each magnet differ by age and gender, and we verify the above hypothesis. This observation suggests the strong potential of using kawaii in the future. In 2019 and 2020, we repeat this simple experiment employing Japanese males and females in their 20s. The differences and similarities of results between the two experiments show a reduction in gender difference and an increase in the diversity of evaluations by females.

Keywords: Kawaii · Kansei/affective value · Shape

1 Introduction

The rapid progress of science and technology in the twentieth century ushered in a materially affluent society. The striking development of information and communication technologies in its latter half of the century provided incredibly effective tools such as computers and network environments. Against this backdrop, people in the twenty-first century tend to place more importance on spiritual wealth than material wealth and have modified their value systems from physical-based to information-based ones (e.g., [1]). Moreover, to break through the stagnation that threatened Japanese manufacturing, the Japanese government selected Kansei (emotion or affection) as the fourth key product value, joining the values of function, reliability, and cost [2].

© Springer Nature Switzerland AG 2021
M. Kurosu (Ed.): HCII 2021, LNCS 12762, pp. 482–493, 2021.
https://doi.org/10.1007/978-3-030-78462-1_37

Hayao Miyazaki's animated films such as *Witch's Delivery Service*, *Totoro*, and *Spirited Away* are highly esteemed worldwide and have attracted audiences of millions of people. Such TV animations as Dragon Ball and Doraemon have also been aired in various countries, and Pikachu and other Pocket Monsters have been enthusiastically embraced by millions of children all over the world. Furthermore, in July 2016, Pokemon Go was unleashed worldwide and became a social phenomenon. One main reason for the success of those Japanese-born digital contents is the existence of kawaii characters and their highly sensitive techniques [3]. Even though "kawaii" is a Japanese word that denotes cute, lovable, or charming, we use it directly in English articles for the following reasons:

- Kawaii is not exactly the same as cute and/or lovable [4].
- Its use has gradually become internationally recognized and accepted [4, 5].
- It is defined as "(in the context of Japanese popular culture) cute" in the Oxford Dictionary [6].

For over 20 years, various Japanese characters, such as Hello Kitty and Pokemon, have spread worldwide. The word kawaii has become part of the international lexicon. However, until 2006, no research has focused on the kawaii attributes of industrial products themselves.

Therefore, we began to systematically analyze the intrinsic kawaii nature of industrial products, since kawaii is evoked by such attributes as shape, color, visual texture, and tactile texture [7, 8]. We aim to clarify a method for constructing kawaii products based on our results.

We surveyed cultural studies and confirmed the long history of "kawaii" as a Kansei value in Japan.

In addition, to support the potential of using "kawaii" as a Kansei value, we formed the following hypothesis:

"Japanese men, especially middle-aged and older, tend to dismiss kawaii as an adjective only for living creatures and related figures and characters. On the other hand, Japanese women bestow feelings of kawaii not only on living creatures but also on industrial products".

We tested this hypothesis by performing a simple experiment using four differently-shaped magnets with Japanese participants of different ages and genders. The kawaii scores for each magnet differed by age and gender, and we verified the above hypothesis.

These findings suggest that even if the short-term prospects of kawaii products might be disappointing, a strong possibility exists that they will spread in the future.

In 2019 and 2020, we repeated this simple experiment employing Japanese males and females in their 20s. We analyzed both the previous and the new experimental results in more detail than the analysis done for the previous experimental results. Furthermore, we compared the results of the two experiments and clarified the similarities and differences between them.

2 Experiment

2.1 Method

The method used in the more recent experiment was the same as that used in the previous experiment of 2007 [7]. We showed our participants four magnets made of the same materials (metal and rubber) but in different shapes (Fig. 1) and gave them the following questionnaire:

1. Rank these four magnets in order from the viewpoint of kawaii. If you cannot determine the order for some or all of the magnets, explain why.
2. Evaluate each magnet's degree of kawaii on a 10-point scale. If you cannot evaluate some or all of them, explain why.
3. Write down your scores and reasons for the above two judgements. If you do not have a particular reason, no comment is fine.

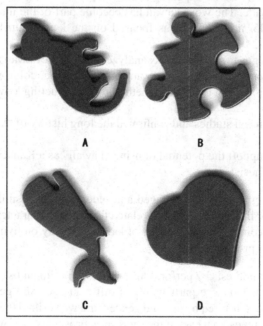

Fig. 1. Four kinds of magnets with identical materials but different shapes [7].

2.2 Results of Previous 2007 Experiment

Twenty Japanese participants (10 males and 10 females) in their early 20s and twenty Japanese participants (10 males and 10 females) in their early 50s served as volunteers. The numbers of participants who could not place the magnets in order or evaluate some of them are shown in Table 1; by assigning these evaluations a score of 0, we calculated the average scores for each magnet (Fig. 2) [7].

From the experiment's results and explanations by volunteers, we reached the following conclusions:

- Magnet A (cat-shaped) got high kawaii scores from all categories of participants. The following reasons for the high scores were common among the younger and the older and both genders:

  - Because I like cats.
  - Cats are kawaii.

- Magnet B (jigsaw-puzzle-piece-shaped) got the lowest kawaii scores of the four shapes, especially from the male participants in their early 50s. As for the men and women in their early 20s, the evaluations fell into high and low groups. Two reasons were given for the high scores:

  - It is good because it is orthodox.
  - It is rather exquisite.

  Just one reason was given for the low scores:

  - The puzzle piece is not kawaii.

- Magnet C (whale-shaped) got the second highest scores on average, especially from females in their early 50s. They gave the following two reasons:

  - Because it is an animal.
  - Because it is a whale.

- Magnet D (heart-shaped) got the most varied scores between males and females. The scores of the males were very low. The reason was the same for both the high and low scores:

  - Because it is a heart.

  A male in his early 50s complained that he could not tolerate the idea of looking at a heart shape at his age.

Recently, we performed a further analysis. A three-way mixed ANOVA (Between-subject: Gender, Generation; Within-subject: Magnet) was able to identify the significant main effects of Magnet ($p < 0.01$) and Gender ($p < 0.01$) as well as the interaction effect between Magnet and Generation ($p < 0.05$). The results of post-hoc tests show this order of the averaged scores of magnets:

$$A > C \geq D \geq B$$

where A > C (p < 0.01), A > D (p < 0.01), A > B (p < 0.01), and C > B (p < 0.01). The results of pairwise comparison are shown in Fig. 3.

Table 1. Numbers of participants who could not place in order or evaluate some magnets [7].

Magnet	Males in 50s	Females in 50s	Males in 20s	Females in 20s
A	0	0	0	0
B	3	2	2	2
C	0	0	0	1
D	2	0	2	0

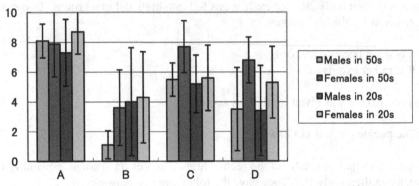

Fig. 2. Average magnet scores of first experiment (1) [7].

2.3   Results of 2019/2020 Experiment

A second experiment was performed from October to December 2019 and October to December 2020. However, this experiment had participants of only one generation: those in their 20s. Figure 4 shows the results of the mean values calculated in the same way as done in the first experiment. Table 2 shows the standard deviations of the first and second evaluations. The two-way mixed ANOVA (Between-subject: Gender; Within-subject: Magnet) identified significant main effects in Magnet (p < 0.01) and an interaction effect between Magnet and Gender (p < 0.05). The results of post-hoc tests show the order of averaged scores of magnets as follows:

$$A > C \geq D \geq B$$

where A > C (p < 0.10), A > D (p < 0.01), A > B (p < 0.01), and C > B (p < 0.01). The results of pairwise comparison are shown in Fig. 5.

In addition, Table 3 shows the number of participants who gave higher scores (more than 5) and lower scores (less than or equal to 5) for each magnet of the first and second

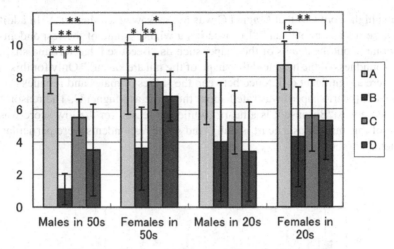

Fig. 3. Average magnet scores of first experiment (2).

evaluations. To summarize the comments of free description, we employed morphological analysis for Japanese using KH coder developed by Higuchi [9]. Figure 6 shows a histogram of the words appearing in the free description of the higher-score group of the cat-shaped magnet (66 participants), in which the original words are Japanese. Figure 7 shows a histogram for the lower-score group of cat-shaped (15 participants). Figures 8, 9, 10, 11, 12 and 13 show similar histograms for the other three magnets. From Figs. 4 and 5, Table 2, and the summaries of the free descriptions of the reasons for each group in Table 3, we obtained the following findings for each magnet:

- Magnet A (cat-shaped) got high kawaii scores from both categories of participants. The following reasons for the high scores were shared regardless of gender:

  - Because I like cats
  - Because cats are kawaii.

  However, as shown in Table 2, the standard deviation of the female participants' evaluations increased from the first experiment, and many of them gave reasons for their low evaluations, such as "the shape of the magnet is strange as a cat," and they were also concerned about the details of this shape.
- Magnet B (jigsaw-puzzle-piece-shaped) got the lowest kawaii scores among the four shape types. However, a total of 10 participants gave it the highest score, and the split was the same as in the first experiment. The reason for the high score was "The shape is fashionable," and the reason for the low score was "The puzzle pieces are not kawaii," which was also the same as the reason given in the first experiment. From Table 2, the standard deviations for both males and females became smaller than in the first experiment.
- Magnet C (whale-shaped) got the second highest mean kawaii score after Magnet A, but there was no significant difference between Magnet C and Magnet D. The reason

for this high score was that Magnet C was not as kawaii as Magnet A. In addition to "Because it's an animal" and "Because it's a whale," some of the respondents were particular about the details of the shape, such as "Because it has a round shape" and "The roundness of the head and the shape of the tail are kawaii." Only for this magnet was there a significant difference between the scores of males and females.

- Magnet D (heart-shaped) was rated about the same as Magnet C. The reason for the high score was "Because it is a heart," while the reason for the low score was "The shape of this magnet as a heart is dull," and some respondents were particular about the details of the shape.

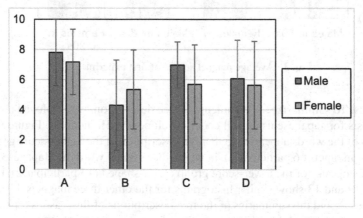

Fig. 4. Average magnet scores of second experiment (1).

Table 2. Standard deviation of kawaii scores from both experiments.

Magnet	2007		2019/2020	
	Males	Females	Males	Females
A	2.2	1.5	2.2	2.2
B	3.6	3.1	3.0	2.6
C	1.9	2.2	1.5	2.6
D	3.0	2.4	2.5	2.9

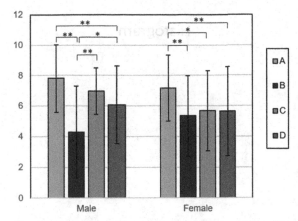

Fig. 5. Average magnet scores of second experiment (2).

Table 3. Numbers of participants who gave higher scores (more than 5) and lower scores (less than or equal to 5) for each magnet.

Magnet	2007		2019/2020	
	Higher score	Lower score	Higher score	Lower score
A	17	3	66	15
B	7	13	30	51
C	10	10	53	28
D	6	14	45	36

2.4   Comparison of the Two Experiments and Discussion

For males and females in their 20s, a three-way mixed ANOVA (Between-subject: Gender, Year, Within-subject: Magnet) identified significant main effects in Magnet ($p < 0.01$) and Year ($p < 0.05$) as well as an interaction effect between Year and Gender ($p < 0.05$), in which Year has the two elements of 2007 and 2019–2020. The results of "the significant interaction effect between Year and Gender" and "no significant gender difference in the two-way ANOVA for the second experiment" (described in Subsect. 2.3) suggest the reduction of gender difference between 2007 and 2019/2020.

As for the standard deviations of the evaluation scores shown in Table 2, they were smaller in the second than in the first experiment for males but larger for females except for Magnet B. These results indicate that individual differences in the evaluations of males became smaller and, conversely, that the evaluations of females became more diverse.

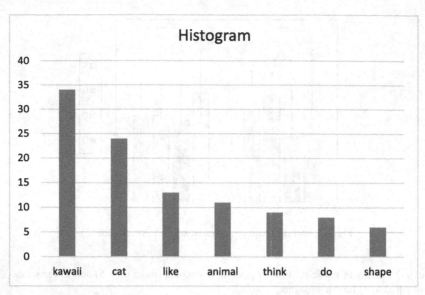

Fig. 6. Histogram of words appearing in free descriptions of higher-score group of cat-shaped magnet.

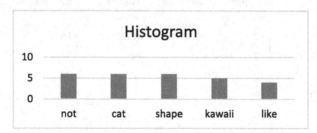

Fig. 7. Histogram of words appearing in free descriptions of lower-score group of cat-shaped magnet.

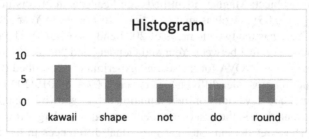

Fig. 8. Histogram of words appearing in free descriptions of higher-score group of jigsaw-puzzle-piece-shaped magnet.

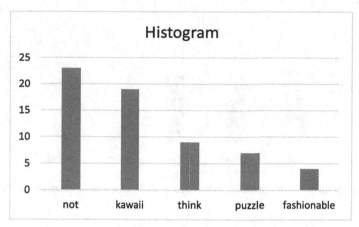

Fig. 9. Histogram of words appearing in free descriptions of lower-score group of jigsaw-puzzle-piece-shaped magnet.

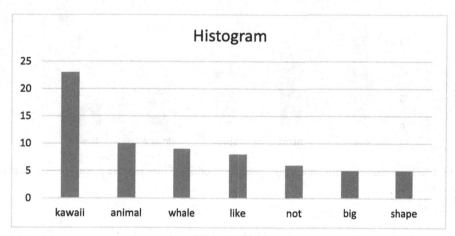

Fig. 10. Histogram of words appearing in free descriptions of higher-score group of whale-shaped magnet.

In the second experiment, detailed descriptions of the shapes were found for all shapes (described in Subsect. 2.3), which were not found in the first experiment, indicating that the participants tended to evaluate the degree of "kawaii" by giving more attention to detail in comparing the shapes of the magnets with their ideal shapes of abstract images such as cats and hearts. This is attributed to how the understanding of "kawaii" has evolved, and the evaluation of "kawaii" has come to include more detailed factors.

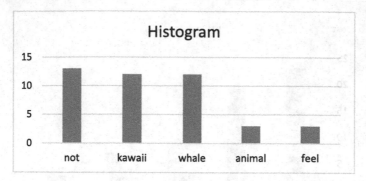

Fig. 11. Histogram of words appearing in free descriptions of lower-score group of whale-shaped magnet.

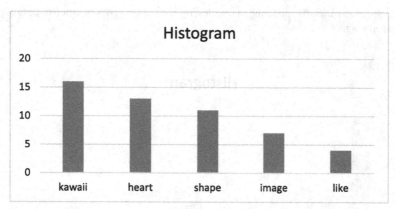

Fig. 12. Histogram of words appearing in free descriptions of higher-score group of heart-shaped magnet.

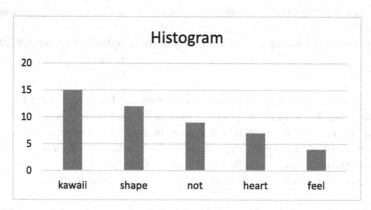

Fig. 13. Histogram of words appearing in free descriptions of lower-score group of heart-shaped magnet.

3   Conclusion

The questionnaire experiment on evaluating "kawaii," performed in 2007 using different shapes of magnets, was repeated in 2019 and 2020 for males and females in their 20s, and the results of the two experiments were compared. The analysis results suggest that the gender difference in evaluating "kawaii" was reduced between 2007 and 2019/2020. There is an interesting difference between males and females in the changes from 2007 to 2019/2020 regarding their standard deviations. The detailed descriptions of the shapes in the second experiment indicate a tendency of the participants to give greater attention to the details of the shapes in evaluating "kawaii."

Acknowledgement. The students of Chuo University and Shibaura Institute of Technology are thanked for their assistance in performing the experiments. This work was partially supported by a JSPS Grant-in-Aid for Scientific Research (20K12032).

References

1. Ohkura, M.: Interface for human-machine interaction. Trends Sci. **10**(8), 765–781 (2005). (in Japanese)
2. Ministry of Economy, Trade and Industry: Kansei Value Creation. https://www.meti.go.jp/pol icy/mono_info_service/mono/creative/kansei.html. Accessed 30 Jan 2021. (in Japanese)
3. Belson, K., Bremner, B.: Hello Kitty: The Remarkable Story of Sanrio and the Billion Dollar Feline Phenomenon. Wiley, Hoboken (2004)
4. The Asahi Shinbun: Kawaii (in the morning edition, 1 January 2006). (in Japanese)
5. Wikipedia: Kawaii. https://en.wikipedia.org/wiki/Kawaii. Accessed 30 Jan 2021
6. Oxford Dictionaries. https://en.oxforddictionaries.com/definition/kawaii. Accessed 30 Jan 2021
7. Ohkura, M., Aoto, T.: Systematic study for "Kawaii" products. In: Proceedings of the 1st International Conference on Kansei Engineering and Emotion Research 2007, Sapporo (2007)
8. Ohkura, M. (ed.): Kawaii Engineering. SSCC, Springer, Singapore (2019). https://doi.org/10. 1007/978-981-13-7964-2
9. Higuchi, K.: Quantitative Text Analysis for Social Research, 2nd edn. Nakanishiya Publishing, Kyoto (2020).(in Japanese)

Comparison of Color Features of Kawaii Fashion Styles in Japan

Peeraya Sripian[1]([✉]), Keiko Miyatake[2], Tipporn Laohakangvalvit[1],
and Michiko Ohkura[1]

[1] Shibaura Institute of Technology, 3-7-5 Toyosu Koto-ku, Tokyo 135-8548, Japan
peeraya@shibaura-it.ac.jp
[2] Kyoritsu Women's University, 2-2-1 Hitotsubashi Chiyoda-ku, Tokyo 101-8437, Japan

Abstract. In this work, we objectively compared various Kawaii fashion styles that can be observed in Japan. In addition to our previously collected Harajuku-type Kawaii fashion database, we collect three kinds of traditional and contemporary "Kawaii" fashion images: Classic, Orthodox, and Street. To clarify the positions of these styles objectively, we compare the saturation and Colorfulness of the collected fashion image. From the comparison of the saturation and Colorfulness, we found that Classic and Orthodox are the most similar, while Street is slightly different. Meanwhile, all three styles are significantly different from the Harajuku-Type Kawaii in terms of saturation and Colorfulness. This finding confirms the observation of fashion expert that Classic and Orthodox are somehow similar while Street can be different. Meanwhile, Harajuku-Type Kawaii is very distinct from other Kawaii styles, as investigated before in our previous works.

Keywords: Kawaii · Fashion · Feature analysis · Saturation · Colorfulness

1 Introduction

Kawaii has been officially recognized worldwide since Japan's Ministry of Foreign Affairs has appointed "Kawaii Ambassadors" in 2009 to promote the Japanese pop culture. Kawaii concept is adopted by many areas, not only aesthetic [1] or in entertainment but also in areas like system design and engineering [2], affective engineering [3], and so on. Although Kawaii research in various fields is propagating, not many focuses on fashion, which contradicts the recent fashion industry trend.

We have been investigated the transition of Kawaii fashion trends in Japan [4]. It could be suggested that the Kawaii fashion observed at Harajuku can be classified into Lolita fashion and otherwise [4]. The Lolita fashion often features clothing with frills and laces, decorated with many girly accessories [5]. Meanwhile, Harajuku-Type Kawaii fashion [6] is a kind of fashion that creates an impression of a disorganized Pop-style that does not comply with any fashion rules.

In our previous works [6–9], we collected fashion images that represent Harajuku-type Kawaii fashion and analyzed the image. We made the hypothesis that Harajuku-Type Kawaii fashion is somewhat high saturation and colorful, and objectively proved

© Springer Nature Switzerland AG 2021
M. Kurosu (Ed.): HCII 2021, LNCS 12762, pp. 494–504, 2021.
https://doi.org/10.1007/978-3-030-78462-1_38

the hypothesis by collecting fashion image data, data preprocessing, and then analyzed using saturation and Colorfulness. We successfully verified that Harajuku-Type Kawaii fashion contains statistically higher saturation and more Colorfulness than the street fashion observed at Harajuku and Shibuya [7, 9].

Table 1. The definition for each Kawaii fashion style.

Style	Definition
Classic Retro Doll	A doll-like and retro girlish style, with concepts of "classic", "vintage", and "antique style"
Orthodox Pretty and Cute	A style of the fashion brand that was once known as "Aka Moji Kei," fashion with concepts of "lovable," "attractive," "lady-like," or "beautiful". It is a style with beautiful, gentle feminine, and soft concept
Street Kawaii	A style with a street feeling based on sports and rock concepts, with sexy or more casual factors
Harajuku-type Kawaii	A mixed style created by multiple or unique colors, material, items, and impression. Colors or impressions that people would hesitate to use in general is adopted in this style, resulting in more creative and individually unique

To expand our research results, we employed three more Kawaii fashion styles based on the analysis on fashion styles in [10] in addition to Harajuku-Type Kawaii fashion style. The definition for each fashion style is shown in Table 1. We also show the definition of Harajuku-type Kawaii fashion in the table for better understanding.

Although "kawaii" is a very important affective value for Japanese fashion industries, especially in recent years, and Japanese kawaii fashion styles are rapidly spread all over the world, there are few studies for kawaii fashion styles employing an objective approach. The purpose of this work is to clarify objectively the positions of various kawaii fashion styles in Japan. The new findings of this work should be useful not only for the fashion research field but also for the fashion industries.

2 Method

To achieve the research purpose, we perform data collection, data preprocessing, and data analysis based on colors, which is basically the same method as our previous work [9].

2.1 Data Collection

We collect three kinds of traditional and contemporary "Kawaii" fashion images in Japan as follows:

– Classical Retro Doll
– Orthodox Pretty and Cute
– Street Kawaii

Various popular Japanese fashion brands represent these three fashion styles. For example, style 1: Classic Retro Doll (**Classic**) is represented by brands that have unique styles like *axes femme, fin.t, Liz Lisa*. Meanwhile, style 2: Orthodox Pretty and Cute (**Orthodox**) includes brands with styles like *Dazzlin, Jill by JILLSTUART,* or *Lodiospotto*. For style 3: Street Kawaii (**Street**), it represents brands with a design that catches the popular trend such as *Emoda, Ungrid* and *x-girl*.

Fashion images are selected from the brand's websites. All images are full-body photos with the brand's clothing combinations. Table 2 shows the full list of brands representing each style with numbers of images collected per brand.

2.2 Data Preprocessing

All images in each dataset contain background, which could interfere with the analysis. Therefore, we preprocessed the image to remove the background using Adobe Photoshop before proceeding to the data analysis. The preprocessed images from collected images of *axes femme* are shown in Fig. 1 with permission.

Table 2. List of brands with the number of images collected that representing each style.

Brand/number of images					
Classic Retro Doll		Orthodox Pretty and Cute		Street Kawaii	
Amavel	15	dazzlin	2	Candy stripper	15
Ank rouge	15	EATME	1	EMODA	5
axes femme	20	evelyn	11	HONEY MI HONEY	11
Favorite	5	FRAY ID	7	jouetie	15
fin.t	15	Heather	5	Little sunny bite	2
LEBECCA boutique	3	JILL by JILLSTUART	10	merry jenny	23
LIZ LISA	15	LAISSE PASSE	1	RNA	5
Secret Honey	13	Lily brown	12	SPINS	8
		LODIOSPOTTO	2	Ungrid	5
		MAJESTIC LEGON	10	wego	10
		MERCURYDUO	3	x-girl	1
		Noela	1		
		SNIDEL	10		
		SUPREME.LA.LA	1		
		titty&Co	19		
		who's who Chico	4		
		WILLSELECTION	1		
Total images	101		100		100

(a)   (b)   (c)

Fig. 1. Example of images preprocessed from images collected of axes femme.

Table 3. Top dominant color values (HSV) and the Colorfulness of images shown in Fig. 1.

Image	Hue (H)	Saturation (S)	Brightness (V)	Colorfulness
(a)	225	0.76	0.16	24.64
(b)	223	0.25	0.84	42.54
(c)	234	0.41	0.28	26.35

2.3 Data Analysis

In our previous work, we found that saturation of the dominant colors and Colorfulness were useful indicators to distinguish Harajuku-type Kawaii fashion from Harajuku street snap and Shibuya street snap [9]. Therefore, we also employ them in this work.

Saturation of the Top Dominant Color
Saturation defines the brilliance and intensity of a color. High saturation colors appear to be rich and full, while low saturation colors appear to be dull and grayish. We extract saturation of the top dominant color from each image based on the method in [11, 12]. To calculate the dominant colors, the following steps are performed:

(1) Convert the color space from RGB to HSV
(2) Perform color quantization by K-Means (N = 72)
(3) Create a histogram with 72 bins.
(4) Normalize the values of the histogram
(5) Sort the histogram in the decreasing order
(6) Obtain the HSV color values from the first bin as the top dominant color of that image

Table 3 shows the top dominant color values (HSV) of images shown in Fig. 1 that are obtained in process (6).

Colorfulness

Colorfulness is a holistic interpretation of color in an image. To quantify the variety of colors in an image, a Colorfulness metric is proposed by Hasler and Süsstrunk [13] in the context of image compression quality evaluation. The Colorfulness of an image can be calculated by defining the opponent color values using Eqs. 1 and 2 with R_p, G_p, and B_p are the values in the Red, Green, and Blue channels accordingly. For each image, we calculate Eqs. (1) and (2) of each pixel. The results of u and v for all pixels are stored in one-dimensional array accordingly.

$$u_p = R_p - G_p \tag{1}$$

$$v_p = \frac{1}{2}(R_p + G_p) - B_p \tag{2}$$

Then, μ_{uv} and σ_{uv} are computed using Eqs. (3) and (4). In the equations, μ_u and σ_u are the mean and the standard deviation of u_p, while, μ_v and σ_v are the mean and the standard deviation of v_p. Equation (5) shows the calculation of the final Colorfulness: C.

$$\mu_{uv} = \sqrt{\mu_u^2 + \mu_v^2} \tag{3}$$

$$\sigma_{uv} = \sqrt{\sigma_u^2 + \sigma_v^2} \tag{4}$$

$$C = \sigma_{uv} + \alpha \cdot \mu_{uv} \tag{5}$$

We use $\alpha = 0.3$ in our work, similar to Hasler and Süsstrunk [13]. The Colorfulness for images (a), (b), and (c) are shown in Table 3.

3 Result and Analysis

To objectively differentiate Kawaii fashion styles, we also add Harajuku-type Kawaii fashion (**HK**) style from our previous work in the comparison [9]. For the analysis, we compute saturation from the top dominant color of each image and Colorfulness of each image from all datasets.

3.1 Saturation of the Top Dominant Color

The boxplot comparison of saturation values for all styles are shown in Fig. 2. It can be seen from the figure that the median value of **HK's** saturation is higher than all of the other fashion styles, following by **Street** and **Orthodox**. From the observation, **Classic** is comparatively smaller than the other three styles, while **HK** is highest. The distribution of saturation, shown by the vertical length of the box, shows that the distribution of **HK's** saturation is the largest, while the distribution of **Classic's** saturation is the smallest. Also, although the median values of **Classic**, **Orthodox**, and **Street** are quite similar, their distribution is different.

A Kruskal-Wallis H test was run to determine if there were statistically significant differences in the saturation between the four fashion styles. Distributions of saturations were similar for all groups, as assessed by visual inspection of a boxplot. Median saturations were statistically significantly different between groups, $\chi2(3) = 105.307$, p < 0.0001. Pairwise comparisons were performed using Dunn's (1964) procedure with a Bonferroni correction for multiple comparisons. Adjusted p-values are presented. Post hoc analysis revealed statistically significant differences in median saturations between **HK** (0.51) and **Classic** (0.19) (p < 0.0001), **HK** and **Orthodox** (0.22) (p < 0.0001), and **HK** and **Street** (0.23) (p < 0.0001) fashion styles, but not between any other group combination.

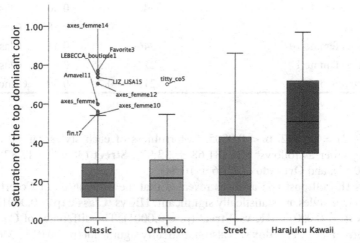

Fig. 2. Box plots for the saturation of the top dominant color for each fashion style. The points outside of the box are outliers of each style. (Color figure online)

From the boxplot, it can also be observed that there are many outliers in **Classic** and one outlier in **Orthodox**. We further analyze those outliers points by investigating each image's top dominant color. For all outliers from the boxplot, we show their colors and brand names with their corresponding HSV values in Table 4. These outliers show the differences of three fashion styles: **Classic**, **Orthodox**, and **Street**, even there are no significant differences between the medians of those fashion styles.

3.2 Colorfulness

The average Colorfulness of each data set with a standard deviation is shown in Fig. 3. From the figure, it can be seen that the Colorfulness of **HK** is extremely high compared to the other three styles. While **Street** is slightly higher than **Classic** and **Orthodox** with a bigger standard deviation, it can be seen that **Classic** and **Orthodox** are very similar.

Since the assumption of homogeneity of variance was rejected (p = 0.003), the Welch F-ratio should be employed. The result of a One-way Welch Analysis of Variance (ANOVA) shows the significant main effect of Colorfulness for fashion styles, Welch's

Table 4. The top dominant color for each image (leftmost of the table) and the HSV values. These values are outliers shown in Fig. 2. Most of **Classic's** outliers are reddish or brown.

Brand / Image No.	H	S	V	Style
Favorite 3	346	0.77	0.42	Classic
axes femme 14	225	0.76	0.16	Classic
LIZ LISA 15	354	0.74	0.37	Classic
LEBECCA boutique 1	355	0.74	0.65	Classic
Secret Honey 5	341	0.74	0.66	Classic
axes femme 12	346	0.70	0.47	Classic
Amavel 11	348	0.60	0.30	Classic
fin.t 7	20	0.55	0.58	Classic
axes femme 10	346	0.56	0.41	Classic
axes femme 1	214	0.55	0.36	Classic
titty&Co. 5	218	0.70	0.39	Orthodox

$F(3, 220.782) = 81.892$, $p < 0.0005$. Colorfulness of each styles can be ranked in descending order as follows: **HK** (81.68 ± 33.97), **Street** (35.97 ± 17.87), **Classic** (31.0 ± 10.85), and **Orthodox** (29.76 ± 10.54).

Games-Howell post hoc analysis revealed that the differences of Colorfulness of **HK** to all other styles are statistically significant: **HK** vs. **Classic** ($p < 0.0001$), **HK** vs. **Orthodox** ($p < 0.0001$), **HK** vs. **Street** ($p < 0.0001$). The difference of Colorfulness between **Street** and **Orthodox** was also statistically significant ($p = 0.017$). Meanwhile, the differences of Colorfulness between **Classic** and **Orthodox**, and **Classic** and **Street** were not statistically significant accordingly.

Figure 4 shows the density or violin plot of Colorfulness of each data set. The red dots in the middle of each plot shows the mean of Colorfulness. The width of the area at each level of Colorfulness indicates the data set's ratio of images. While the Colorfulness of **HK** is different from the other data set as seen from the figure, it is to be noted that the Colorfulness of **Classic** and **Orthodox** gathers around the mean more than the Colorfulness of **Street**. Also, the Colorfulness of **Street** is spreading in a little wider range than that of **Classic** and **Orthodox**. It can be implied from the figure that the distribution of Colorfulness in **HK** is different from the other styles, and **Street** is slightly different from **Classic** and **Orthodox**. At the same time, **Classic** and **Orthodox** are very similar.

4 Discussion

From the comparison of saturation described in Sect. 3.1, the medians of **Classic** and **Orthodox** are rather small compared to the other two styles. This is because the fashion seen in **Classic** and **Orthodox** are generally considered to be duller in color rather than bright color.

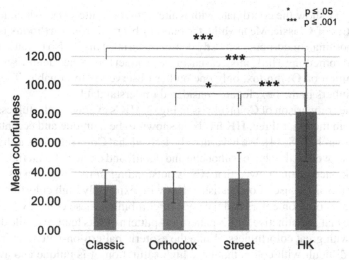

Fig. 3. Average colorfulness of each dataset, the bar indicates standard deviation

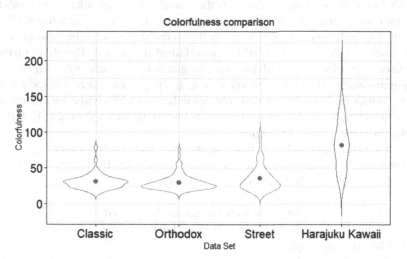

Fig. 4. The violin plot for each data set. The dots in the middle indicate mean of colorfulness

From the outliers seen from boxplot in Fig. 2, it can be seen that most of the colors (see Table 4) are vivid colors. The general understanding is that in **Classic** style, vivid colors are not often used. In other words, high saturation colors are not used. Similarly, highly saturated and sluggish colors are not adopted. However, the red color, which has been a trendy color for the past few years, is adopted to follow the fashion trend. From the coordination, even if red color is used, it is coordinated in tone with tone. For example, *Favorite* 3, although the image cannot be placed in this paper due to copyright, is composed of a light red blouse and a dark red flare skirt, with red hair accessory. Such a combination is the example of a tone in tone coordinate (light red and dark red). In addition, several images such as *LEBECCA boutique* 1, *Secret Honey* 5, and *Amavel* 11 show the coordinate with white item, or white yoke, which indicate the characteristics of **Classic**. Meanwhile, the outlier observed from **Orthodox** is *titty&Co.* 5, which coordinate incorporates mostly denim material. This is also because the creator wants to add something a little more casual in the product line. Since denim is not included in the definition of **Orthodox**, only one outlier observed is reasonable. Therefore, the observed outliers in the boxplot are considered understandable.

From the comparison of Colorfulness in Fig. 2, **HK's** average Colorfulness is greatly different from the other three. **HK** has been shown to be a unique and eccentric style in previous research [6, 8, 14]. We have already derived that Colorfulness is a characteristic of the color as well as the shape (silhouette and detail) and choice of material. The results of this work once again showed that **HK** is outstanding in its Colorfulness. One of the reasons for this is the use of outlandish colors with extremely high colorfulness that are different from common colors and the style of combining these colors, which creates a unique style that is distinctive. **HK's** pattern-on-pattern outfits feature textile designs that use colors with great colorfulness. While the esoteric pattern-on-pattern attire becomes even more difficult with colors that have high saturation, it is unique and avant-garde, which is a characteristic of Harajuku Kawaii. Therefore, the result that the average value of **HK's** Colorfulness is higher than the other three types is considered to be valid.

In the case of **Orthodox** and **Street**, **Street** has higher average **Colorfulness** (Fig. 2). From the creator's point of view, not only the shape and material but also the color is based on each style's definition, which is explained in Table 1. Therefore, **Orthodox** tends to choose colors that match the calm and gentle atmosphere and avoid colors with strong impressions. Meanwhile, **Street** tends to use pop colors for Sports and color with a strong impact for Rock. **Street** also proposes definition with vivid color or emphasized color as the accent color. Therefore, it is reasonable that the average value of Colorfulness is higher in **Street** than in **Orthodox**.

From the violin plot in Fig. 4, it can be observed that **HK** has a very large variance, but **Street** also has a larger variance than the other two. For **HK**, it is because the styles with high Colorfulness use strong colors as follows:

– unusual fluorescent colors, which are not generally adopted
– combination of items that are usually hesitated to combine
– use of highly colorful pattern.

Meanwhile, styles with low Colorfulness use items made of transparent materials that are usually difficult to use or adopt unique designs with extremely large shoulders that have an impact even if the Colorfulness is low. A strong impression can be expressed not only by color but also by material and shape. In **HK**, there are cases that an extraordinary conservative style would give Avant-guard impression. Since it is possible to express unique **HK** through design elements (color, material, and shape), whether Colorfulness is high or low, the result of **HK** with high variance is reasonable. Meanwhile, **Classic** and **Orthodox** styles tend to be limited to calm and gentler and do not incorporate accent colors or strong colors as described in Table 1. **Street**, on the other hand, also incorporates pop and intense colors that **Classic** and **Orthodox** do not. The variance of Colorfulness could be greater in **Street** than in **Classic** and **Orthodox** for this reason.

Except for **HK**, there are not many cases where Colorfulness is extremely low, while more cases are distributed toward higher Colorfulness (see Fig. 3). In particular, this tendency is greater for **Street** than for the other two styles. The reason why Colorfulness of **Classic**, **Orthodox**, and **Street** is not extremely small is that low Colorfulness would not only give a conservative impression but would also dissociate from the respective definitions (See Table 1) for the styles. Especially, **Street** is more distributed toward higher Colorfulness than **Classic** and **Orthodox** because the style use accent colors based on the style's definition in Table 1.

After all, these objective new findings are empirically known or explainable from the definitions of fashion styles. Because of the widespread of Japanese kawaii fashion styles all over the world, these are quite useful not only for the fashion research field but also fashion industries for their evidence-based development in the future.

5 Conclusion

In this work, we investigate the style of Kawaii fashion in Japan. We collected three additional datasets of Kawaii fashion: Classic Retro Doll (**Classic**), Orthodox Pretty and Cute (**Orthodox**), and Street Kawaii (**Street**). To clarify the difference of each category, saturation and Colorfulness is calculated and compared across all data sets with Harajuku-type Kawaii (**HK**). The comparison of saturation showed that **HK** was statistically significantly different from all of the other three styles and the saturation values were reasonable for each style. From the comparison of the Colorfulness, we found that **Classic** and **Orthodox** are similar with no significant difference, while **Street** is different from **Orthodox**. Also, all of the three styles are significantly different from the Harajuku-Type Kawaii, as investigated before in our previous works [7–9].

These positionings of kawaii fashion styles can be used for various purposes in fashion industries.

Acknowledgement. We thank IGA Co., Ltd for the permission to use the preprocessed images from the website of axes femme in this manuscript. This work was partially supported by JSPS KAKENHI Grant Number 20K12032.

References

1. Ngai, S.: Our Aesthetic Categories: Zany, Cute, Interesting. Harvard University Press Cambridge, MA (2012)
2. Cheok, A.D. : Kawaii/cute interactive media. In: Cheok, A.D. (ed.) Art and Technology of Entertainment Computing and Communication, pp. 223–254. Springer London, London (2010). https://doi.org/10.1007/978-1-84996-137-0_9
3. Ohkura, M. (ed.): Kawaii Engineering. SSCC, Springer, Singapore (2019). https://doi.org/10.1007/978-981-13-7964-2
4. Miyatake, K.: Japanese Kawaii Fashion-Historic changes in trends and styles. In: Spring Conference of Japan Society of Kansei Engineering, Nagoya (2018)
5. Yahata, M., Watanabe, A.: The Roots of Lolita Fashion - focus on street fashion after the 1980s. In: Annual Bulletin of Department of the Science and Living, Kyoritsu Woman University, vol. 56, pp. 11–31 (2013)

6. Miyatake, K., Sripian, P., Ohkura, M.: Study on style of Harajuku Kawaii fashion (1st Report) - design features. In: The 20th Annual Meeting of Japan Society of Kansei Engineering, Tokyo, Japan (2018)

7. Sripian, P., Miyatake, K., Ohkura, M.: Study on color feature of Harajuku Kawaii fashion. In: The 14th Spring Conference of Japan Society of Kansei Engineering (2019)

8. Sripian, P., Miyatake, K., Ohkura, M.: Study on style of Harajuku Kawaii fashion (2nd Report) - color features. In: The 20th Annual Meeting of Japan Society of Kansei Engineering, Tokyo, Japan (2018)

9. Sripian, P., Miyatake, K., Ohkura, M.: Study on the color feature of Harajuku-type kawaii fashion comparison with street snap images using colorfulness. TNI J. Eng. Technol. **8**(1), 63–72 (2020)

10. Yanagida, Y.: A Consideration of the fitness of fashion image terminology to fashion styles (2nd report) (in Japanese). J. Jpn. Soc. Kansei Eng. **16**(1), 9–18 (2017). https://doi.org/10.5057/jjske.TJSKE-D-16-00046

11. Yamada, A.: MPEG-7 Visual part of eXperimentation Model version 9.0. ISO/IEC JTC1/SC29/WG11/N3914 (2001)

12. Forczmański, P., Czapiewski, P., Frejlichowski, D., Okarma, K., Hofman, R.: Comparing clothing styles by means of computer vision methods. In: International Conference on Computer Vision and Graphics, pp. 203–211. Springer, Cham (2014). https://doi.org/10.1007/978-3-319-11331-9_25

13. Hasler, D., Suesstrunk, S.E.: Measuring colorfulness in natural images. In: Proceedings of SPIE (2003)

14. Sripian, P., Miyatake, K., Ohkura, M.: Study on Style of Harajuku Kawaii fashion (3rd report) - categorization by the difference of colorfulness. In: The 14th Spring Meeting of Japan Society of Kansei Engineering (2019)

Emotions and Cognition in HCI

Voice Switching in Voice-Enabled Digital Assistants (VDAs)

Dania Bilal[✉] and Jessica K. Barfield

University of Tennessee, Knoxville, TN 37996, USA
dania@utk.edu, jbarfiel@vols.utk.edu

Abstract. Voice-enabled digital assistants (VDAs) provide users with options to switch the "out-of-the-box" or default voice interface. Numerous studies have investigated digital assistants. However, no studies have examined factors influencing user decisions to switch the default voice interface in VDAs. Informed by the similarity-attraction behavioral theory, we investigated whether perceived age, accent, gendered voice, and personality of the voice interface influence user decisions to switch the voice in VDAs. Guided by the status quo behavioral theory, we examined factors influencing user decisions to keep the default voice unchanged (status quo). We recruited thirty-one participants who took an online survey consisting of 42 questions, including 27 closed and 15 open-ended, collecting participants' demographic information, experience in and knowledge of how to switch the voice, voice switching behavior, and preferences, among others. We employed the Big Five Personality Traits to assess the participants' personality traits and the perceived personality of the voice in VDAs. We found that nearly 39% of the participants switched the voice interface in VDAs. Another finding is that the majority of male participants and all female participants (switchers and non-switchers) had a female-gendered voice in the VDAs. We detected a high correlation between the participants' own personality traits and the perceived personality traits of their VDAs. Factors such as perceived age, accent, and gender did not influence the decision of the majority of the participants to switch the voice interface. The findings have implications for designing VDAs with personalities that leverage the user experience (UX).

Keywords: User experience (UX) · Voice-enabled digital assistants · Voice switching · Voice personality · Status quo theory · Similarity-attraction theory

1 Introduction

The use of voice-enabled digital assistants (VDAs) for accessing and searching for information on the internet is becoming the norm in people's everyday life. A recent study indicates that the number of voice assistant devices will reach 8.4 billion as early as 2024 and that voice-enabled devices led by smartphones will double in use in the same time period [1]. Digital Assistants can serve as memory aids as people increasingly delegate the task of memorization to their voice-enabled devices [2]. Considering the voice interface options provided by VDAs, the user may decide to converse with the default

© Springer Nature Switzerland AG 2021
M. Kurosu (Ed.): HCII 2021, LNCS 12762, pp. 507–520, 2021.
https://doi.org/10.1007/978-3-030-78462-1_39

voice provided (which represents the combination of a particular language, accent, and gendered voice); switch from the default voice to a different voice interface; or during initial device start-up, select a particular language, gender, and voice accent as the preferred interface. Despite the ubiquitous use of VDAs [3], and the different voice interface options currently available, we are yet to develop understanding of how these devices are used, specifically in relation to voice switching on digital devices. We lack knowledge of whether users prefer the default voice interface in their VDAs or switch to another one, and if so, for what reasons they do so. For example, do users choose a voice interface that matches their voice characteristics (gender, accent, language, etc.), or an interface that matches their personality traits, or both?

1.1 Rationale for the Study

VDAs represent a "social entity" with which users converse for a wide variety of purposes. As such, the voice interface offered by a VDA could influence a user's behavior across a range of tasks (see for example, [4–7]). Yet, voice switching behavior in VDAs has not been explored and understood.

Given that users attribute a personality to a computer, they most likely assign a personality to their voice-enabled digital assistants. This is especially true since the characteristics of a voice interface have been found to influence user attitude towards a device [8]. Additionally, the perceived gender of a synthesized voice has an impact on how users conceptualize a device such as a computer [9, 10].

Previous studies showed that the perceived personality of a computer influences a user's judgment of its appearance (e.g., attractiveness), and performance (e.g., credibility; informativeness) [7, 9]. Similarly, studies revealed that in using a recommendation system, users are able to perceive similarities between their personality and that of the system [11]. [12] note that building a personality in voice activated virtual assistants is a key aspect for generating user trust in this technology. [13] study of user perceived personality of voice-activated digital assistants in Google's Digital Assistant, Siri, Cortana, and Alexa showed that of the twenty-nine personality attributes mentioned in the survey, users associated five primary attributes to the personality of their digital assistant (Practical, Informed, Up-to-Date, Well-Mannered, and Logical and Helpful).

While several studies have explored user perception of computers and synthesized speech (voice), there is little we know about voice switching in VDAs. User voice switching in VDAs has implications for designing voice-enabled interfaces that automatically adapt to a user's voice characteristics and possibly personality traits, minimizing the cost (i.e., time), effort (physical), and cognitive load (i.e., mental effort), and negative affects while supporting the user's experience (i.e., cognitive and emotional).

2   Related Research

VDAs allow users to personalize the voice interface based on the user's own preferences. For example, in the US the default voice for Apple's Siri is gendered female with an American accent (see [14, 15]). This particular voice combination has created some controversy. [16] found that users stereotype the voice of a gendered female in a VDA as a subordinate; thus, sexualizing the technology based on its voice. Additionally, the English version of Siri can speak with a British, American, or Australian accent [17]. In languages other than English, Siri can speak in Arabic, French, and Dutch but its default voice is gendered male, unlike in the US [14]. Moreover, not all digital assistants provide a default voice, allowing the user to select a voice interface from various available options as part of the initial device set-up procedure. While supporting various voices, genders, accents, and languages to meet the needs of diverse users, VDAs can affect user perception of the device.

[18] examined user interactions with VDAs (including Google's Digital Assistant, Amazon's Alexa, Microsoft's Cortana, and Apple's Siri) to classify user reactions to humor. Analysis of the participants' online diaries and survey responses revealed that they frequently queried the VDA about its personality and opinions and made requests for jokes. [3] interviewed 19 VDA users and analyzed data logs from 82 Amazon Alexa devices (totaling 193,665 commands) and 88 Google Home Devices (totaling 65,499 commands). They found that music and locating information on the internet are among the most commonly used categories.

[19] compared the effectiveness of Google's Digital Assistant on a laptop and smartphone with Apple's Siri on smartphones in finding information on the topic of the cessation of smoking. Using 80 queries and analyzing responses from the digital assistants revealed that Google laptop voice-activated searches were ranked the highest in terms of quality and relevant information. Google's Digital Assistant on smartphones and laptop computers provided more relevant information on the topic than did the Apple's Siri.

Specific characteristics of a voice or speech may influence user perception and attitude toward a device. [20–23] investigated live help interfaces that used text-to-speech (TTS) voice. They found that TTS voice affected college students' cognitive and emotional trust in the device. In a similar vein, [24] examined the effect of the voice in an Embodied Conversational Agent on users' trust. They reported that voice pitch was inversely related to users' perceived trust. That is, the higher-pitched voice characteristics of a female-gendered voice was trusted less than the lower pitched male-gendered voice. [25] investigated the effect of a particular voice personality and gender on a patient's disclosure of health information. A male or female voice was designed to express an upbeat, professional, and sympathetic personality of a recorded script. Users were randomly assigned to one of the two voice personalities and completed a health survey using an interactive voice response system (IVR). [25] concluded that the voice did not significantly affect the patients' information disclosure. [26] focused on the effect of gender on user perception of agents embodied in a system. They developed a kiosk automated system that uses two embodied intelligent agents (i.e., SPECIES), one male and one female. They found that users perceived the agents embodied as males to be more powerful than their female counterparts, while female embodied agents were perceived as more likable than their male counterparts.

In sum, the reviewed literature showed a lack of empirical research on user voice switching in VDAs. Despite the prevalence of VDAs and their ubiquitous use in everyday life, we have many questions unanswered on how to design voice-based technology that communicates to a human in the most 'naturalistic' way [27], suggesting the need for additional research in user interaction with VDAs, including voice switching.

3 Theoretical Background

Behavioral theories, namely the *status quo theory* and *similarity-attraction theory* may provide explanations for user voice switching behavior in VDAs.

3.1 Status Quo Theory

The status quo is an emotional, cognitive bias theory that describes users' preferences for things to remain unchanged [28]. In the context of VDAs, users may decide to use the default voice option provided by their digital assistants (e.g., Siri's default voice is gendered female with an American accent) or select a new voice option and never revert to the default option. When users are faced with new options, they often stay with the status quo alternative [28–30]. More specifically, when users are reluctant to accept a new system or device or an interface, they may be concerned about the switching costs [31]. [32] and [33] explained this behavior as "loss aversion". That is, a person's tendency and preferences are to accept the status quo in order to avoid losing, compared to the cost of acquiring equivalent gains. Overall, people tend to be *loss averse*, meaning that they weigh losses more heavily than they do gains [34]. Losses can be a person's time, effort, and cognitive load invested in learning about the new device or system.

In the context of VDAs, changing the status quo requires that a user perform an action (e.g., select an option from a list of voice options), whereas, staying with the status quo alleviates the user from a voice switching act; thus, saving time and effort [35]. For example, to change Siri's voice interface on an iPhone, a user must open the iPhone's setting, scroll down and tap Siri, slide the Siri button to the "on" position, choose the accent, and choose a gender, and exit. In the realm of the status quo theory, users who are aware of the voice switching process, may decide not to switch due to a perceived potential cost (i.e., time, effort, and cognitive load). In fact, the higher the number of options in an interface, the stronger is the bias for the status quo [29]. From the human-computer interaction and use-centered design perspectives, and based on Hick's Law, the more choices (stimuli) a user is presented with in an interface, the higher is the level of confusion, and the longer it will take the user to interpret the choices and select a choice [36].

3.2 Similarity-Attraction Theory

[37] note that people tend to be attracted to others who are similar to themselves in certain respects, such as having a similar voice and personality [38–40], and recognize personality cues based on listening to computer synthesized speech [7, 41]. However, there are exceptions to this attraction behavior. For example, [42] found that women did not trust men with low-pitched voices to divide money equitably, but trusted men with feminized voices (i.e., higher frequency) to return their investment more than they did men with masculinized voices (i.e., lower frequency). [43] reported that women tend to be more sensitive than men to the dominance of cues present in female voices, and that they conform more to a male-voiced than a female-voiced computer in terms of accepting an opinion [9].

In relation to VDAs, it is possible that users who switch voice interfaces become attracted to the selected voice. Nonetheless, we lack understanding of the reasons for this attraction. Based on prior research (e.g., [7]), we speculate that this attraction may be attributed to a match between the users' personality traits and perceived personality of the voice interface.

3.3 Big Five Personality Traits

According to [44], personality is a psychological construct designed to capture stable individual characteristics that can explain and predict observable behavioral differences. In this study, we used the Big Five Personality Traits instrument to detect the relationship between users' self-reported personality traits and the perceived personality traits of the voice used frequently in their VDAs. This Big Five instrument provides a broad measure of basic personality traits, which has been validated across instruments and observers [45] and for its reliability [46]. The instrument has been applied in a number of studies (e.g., [45, 47, 48]). The Big Five instrument measures personality on five constructs, which are conceptualized as follows ([44], p. 363):

- *Extraversion*: Active, Assertive, Energetic, Outgoing, Talkative,
- *Neuroticism*: Anxious, Self-pitying, Tense, Touchy, Unstable, Worrying,
- *Conscientiousness*: Efficient, Organized, Planful, Reliable, Responsible, Thorough,
- *Agreeableness*: Appreciative, Kind, Generous, Forgiving, Sympathetic, Trusting, and
- *Openness*: Artistic, Curious, Imaginative, Insightful, Original, Wide interests.

3.4 Research Questions

We addressed two main questions to explore user voice switching in VDAs and detect whether the status quo and similarity-attraction theories can explain this switching behavior.

RQ1: What factors influence the likelihood of user voice interface switching in VDAs? The factors we considered include: a. perceived age of the voice interface, b. accent of the voice interface, c. gendered voice of the interface, and d. perceived personality of the VDA.

RQ2: What costs (time, effort, and cognitive load) are associated with user voice switching in VDAs, and to what extent do these costs influence the user's decision to switch the voice interface?

4 Method

This exploratory study employed quantitative and qualitative methods using a survey questionnaire.

4.1 Sample

We recruited thirty-one (n = 31) subjects to participate in this study. The participants were selected based on specific criteria, including owning a smart digital assistant as a stand-alone device (e.g., Alexa Home) or owning a device (e.g., smartphone, tablet, or computer) with an integrated digital assistant; and, in either case, setting the device on English as the default language; as well as being proficient in the English language. Sixteen males, fourteen females, and one participant who was identified as non-binary (mean age = 28.5 years) consented to participate in the survey.

4.2 Instrument

The survey was implemented in Qualtrics and consisted of 42 questions, including 27 closed and 15 open-ended questions. The survey collected participants' demographic information such as gender and age, evaluation of the VDA using Likert scale questions, and open-ended questions (e.g., asking participants to describe the personality of their digital assistant, and voice switching preferences), an assessment of user's own personality based on the Big 5 constructs (*Extraversion, Neuroticism, Conscientiousness, Agreeableness,* and *Openness),* and the participants' perceptions of the personality traits of the voice used most frequently in their VDA. Additionally, the survey included questions about the voice-based technologies owned by participants and their usage of such technologies. A particular focus of the survey instrument was to determine whether subjects switched to a voice interface (e.g., specific gender; accent), and whether that interface matched their own voice and personality characteristics.

4.3 Procedures

We collected data between January and February 2021. We contacted our personal networks, our colleges' and departments' listservs, social media (e.g., Facebook), and used word-of-mouth to identify participants. We sent an email invitation to those who expressed willingness to take the survey. The email described the purposes of the study and contained the survey URL. Once the URL is clicked, the survey questions were displayed one screen at a time. The average time the participants took to complete the survey was twelve minutes.

5 Results

We first report the results on the usage of VDAs to provide context for the findings. To offer a broad picture of VDA usage, we present the results for the entire sample (voice switchers and non-switchers combined).

VDA Usage. Eighteen of the 31 (58%) participants reported that they owned an Apple iPhone, 11 (35.4%) an Android phone, and one participant each owned a Google Pixel and Windows phone. In terms of which voice assistant was used the most, 11 (35.4%) used Apple's Siri, 12 (37.7%) Google's Digital Assistant, 7 (22.5%) Amazon's Alexa, and one Microsoft's Cortana. Considering the voice technology owned by the participants, 13 (41.9%) used Google's digital assistant and 18 (58%) used Apple's Siri the most.

In addition, all participants reported being either advanced or native English language speakers and all of them reported using English as the voice interface with their VDAs to perform tasks such as calling, playing music, checking the weather forecast, and as reminders and timers.

RQ1: Factors influencing user voice interface switching in VDAs?
Twelve (38.7%) of the participants reported switching the voice of their VDAs. Of the participants who reported switching the voice interface, they did so because it is *fun* to talk with the new voice or is *intriguing* (1–7 scale with 1 not so much and 7 a great amount; Mean = 5.92). Using the same scale, the mean *trustworthiness* of the new voice was 4.75. Other reasons for switching the voice interface are *curiosity*, the former voice sounded *robotic-like*; or that they *liked* the new *accent* of the voice interface.

Age. Of the 31 participants (switchers and non-switchers), 10 (32.2%) who switched the voice interface indicated that it is extremely important or very important that the age of their VDAs match their own age, 6 (19.3%) mentioned moderately important, and 15 (48.3%) noted slightly or not at all important.

Of those that did not switch the voice on their VDAs 5 (26.3%) mentioned that it was extremely important or very important that their VDAs match their age, 2 (10.5%) indicated moderately important, and 12 (63%) marked slightly or not at all important. Conversely, 5 (41.6%) of the switchers thought it was extremely or very important for the digital assistant to match their age, 4 (33.3%) moderately important, and 3 (25%) slightly or not at all important.

Gendered Voice. Participants were asked, "Thinking about your Digital Assistant, which gender is it?" Of the 16 male participants, 2 mentioned male gendered voice; 13 noted female, and 1 preferrred not to say. Of the 14 female participants, all indicated female. As for the non-binary participant, the gendered voice is female.

For the gendered voice match survey question, of the 31 participants, 6 (18.3%) believed it is extremely or very important that the gendered voice of their VDAs match their own, and 17 (54.8%) thought it is slightly important or not at all important (Fig. 1). As for all participants who switched voice interfaces, 4 (33%) indicated extremely or very important, and 5 (42%) noted that it is slightly or not at all important that their VDA's voice matched their gendered voice. Interestingly, among the twelve participants who switched voice interfaces, 6 (50%) mentioned that a gendered voice match is slightly or not important.

Accent. Of the 31 participants, 28 (90.3%) indicated that the voice in their VDA is American, and one each responded Australian, English, and Scottish. In relation to whether the accent should match that of the user, of the 31 participants, 8 (25.8%) indicated that it is extremely or very important that the voice accent of their VDAs match their own accent, and 14 (45.1%) thought it is slightly or not at all important. Interestingly, among the twelve participants who switched voice interfaces, 3 (25%) indicated that a match in accent is extremely important.

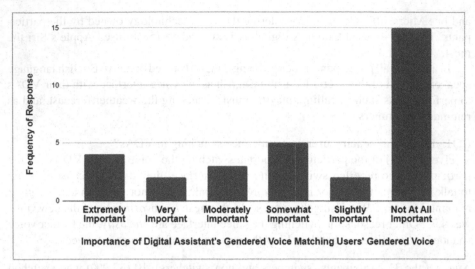

Fig. 1. Digital assistants' gendered voice match with users' gendered voice.

Personality. Nearly fifty percent of the participants (15; 48.3%) indicated that it is extremely or very important that the personality of their VDAs match their own personality traits, 4 (12.9%) marked moderately important, and 12 (38.7%) noted slightly or not important (Fig. 2). Of the 12 participants who switched the voice interface, 5 (41.6%) responded that it is extremely or very important, another 5 (41.6%) mentioned not at all important, one participant (8.3%) said somewhat important, and 2 participants (16.6%) noted slightly important.

In terms of all personality traits, the Pearson Product-Moment correlation revealed a strong correlation ($r = 0.90$) between the participants' self-reported personality traits and four of the five personality traits attributed to their VDAs in terms of being Open, Conscientious, Extroverted, and Agreeable (Fig. 2).

RQ2: Influence of participants' cognitive load and time on switching the voice interface in their VDAs.
The participants were asked to indicate whether switching or not switching the voice interface on their VDAs requires effort (in terms of steps or physical effort), cognitive load (in terms of mental effort), and time; as well as whether they knew how to switch the voice interface.

Cognitive Load. The majority of the participants (18; 58%) thought it takes little or no cognitive load to change the default voice interface in their VDAs and 2 (6%) reported it takes a lot of cognitive load (Fig. 3). Of the 12 switchers, 2 (17%) mentioned it takes a moderate amount of cognitive load, and 10 (83%) indicated that a little or no cognitive load is required to change the voice interface.

Effort. Seventeen (17; 65%) mentioned that it takes a little or no effort at all to change the voice interface, 6 (23%) said it takes a moderate amount, 3 (12%) indicated that it takes a great deal or a lot of effort, and 4 (13%) did not know how much effort it will

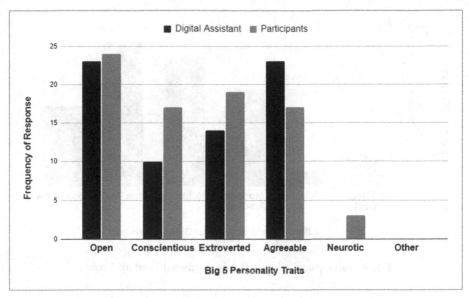

Fig. 2. Participants' self-reported personality traits and the personality traits attributed to their VDAs.

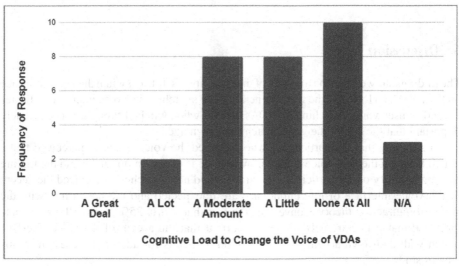

Fig. 3. Frequency of response for cognitive load required to change the voice interface of a digital assistant.

take to change the voice interface (Fig. 4). Those who knew how to switch the voice interface on their VDAs mentioned that it takes 2–7 steps to do this task.

Time. Nineteen (19; 61%) of the 31 participants indicated that it takes little or no time to switch the voice interface in their VDAs; 4 (13%) mentioned a great deal or a lot

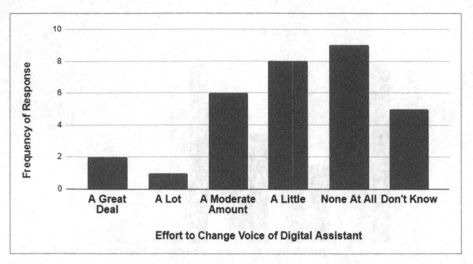

Fig. 4. Participants' effort to change the digital assistants' voice.

of time, 4 (13%) noted a moderate amount of time, and another 4 participants (13%) marked non-applicable. Of the twelve participants who switched the voice interface, 11 (92%) responded that it takes a little or "none at all" time to achieve this task.

6   Discussion

The findings showed that the majority of the participants did not switch the voice interface on their VDAs. However, the fact that nearly 39% switched the voice interface indicates a trend in user voice switching in VDAs. Those who switched thought it is extremely important that the age of the voice match their own age.

The finding that the participants who switched the voice interface perceived that a match between the new voice and their own voice is of low importance; and the finding that the majority of the participants (switchers and non-switchers) perceived the accent of the voice interface of low importance are unexpected and are not in line with the similarity-attraction theory. Conversely, the fact that nearly 25% across all participants indicated that it is extremely or very important that the accent of the voice interface match with their own accent suggests a trend and calls for additional research in this area of study.

Of note, the majority of male participants and all female participants (switchers and non-switchers) had a female-gendered voice in their VDAs. This finding concurs with the participants' responses to the survey question on perceived importance of voice match between the voice interface and their own voice. Although we do not know the reason for this preference, we speculate that since the "out-of-the-box" setting for the majority of digital assistants is gendered female [49], the participants have grown accustomed to the female-gendered voice on their VDAs. Another explanation is that the participants may find the female-gendered voice more likable than the male-gendered voice [26].

The high correlation we found between the participants' personality traits and the perceived personality of their VDAs indicates that a personality match is a more crucial aspect of the user's interaction than perceived age, gendered voice, and accent of the VDAs. This finding is not surprising, since the personality of digital assistants is a key aspect for generating user trust and engagement [13] and for providing a quality user experience. Being attracted to others who are similar to oneself in certain aspects, and in this case, to a similar perceived personality of one's VDA, is one of the central tenets of the similarity-attraction theory [37].

Our assumptions that the cost (time, cognitive load, and effort) required to switch the voice interface could influence user decision to switch or not switch the voice interface did not concur with the status quo theory. Additionally, knowledge of how to switch the voice interface did not influence the user's switching behavior. Given that this finding is based on the participants' self-reported data, we believe that by using observations and interviews and increasing the sample size in future research, we will be able to detect whether the cost factors have an effect on user voice switching behavior in VDAs.

7 Limitations

The limitations of this study lie in its small sample size. Nonetheless, the findings provided insights into the factors that users value the most in their VDAs, which will inform future studies. Another limitation pertains to using the survey approach as the sole method for data collection, which relies on self-reported data that might be prone to inaccuracy.

8 Conclusions

This pilot study provided insights into factors influencing user decisions to switch the voice interface in their VDAs, and whether these decisions are informed by the similarity-attraction and status quo theories. The strong correlation we found between the participants' perceived personality of the voice interface and their own personality traits has implications for designing VDAs that allow users to select not only the voice, accent, language, and gendered voice, but also the personality that best matches their personality traits. This is a challenging endeavor for UX designers, especially given that scarce studies have investigated the personality traits of VDAs from user perspectives. The successful deployment of personality in VDAs should elevate the user experience through balancing effectiveness and efficiency with trust and engagement, among others.

Future research should employ a mixed research method that combines surveys, interviews, and observations to gain deeper insights into user needs, requirements, and expectations, as well as the user interaction behavior in VDAs.

In this study, we used the Big Five Personality Traits instrument to detect the participants' personality traits and to elicit the perceived personality of their VDAs. Leveraging personality traits in other reliable instruments should be explored in future research to identify a wide spectrum of attributes users value in VDAs.

References

1. Juniper Research. https://www.juniperresearch.com/press/press-releases/number-of-voice-assistant-devices-in-use
2. Atkinson, P., Barker, R.: 'Hey alexa, what did i forget?': networked devices, internet search and the delegation of human memory. Convergence 21(1), 52–65 (2020)
3. Ammari, T., Kaye, J., Tsai, J.Y., Bentley, F.: Music, search, and IoT: how people (really) use voice assistants. ACM Trans. Hum. Comput. Interact. 26(3), 1–28 (2019)
4. Large, D.R., Clark, L., Quandt, A., Burnett, G., Skrypchuk, L.: Steering the conversation: a linguistic exploration of natural language interactions with a digital assistant during simulated driving. Appl. Ergon. 63, 53–61 (2017)
5. Lee, K., Nass, C.: Designing social presence of social actors in human-computer interaction. In: Chi 2003: Proceedings of the SIGCHI Conference on Human Factors in Computing Systems, pp. 289–296. Association for Computing Machinery, New York (2003)
6. Nass, C., Brave, S.: Wired for Speech: How Voice Activates and Advances the Human-Computer Relationship. MIT Press, Cambridge, MA (2005)
7. Nass, C., Lee, K.M.: Does computer-synthesized speech manifest personality? Experimental tests of recognition, similarity-attraction, and consistency-attraction. J. Exp. Psychol. Appl. 7, 171–181 (2001)
8. Aggarwal, P., McGill, A.L.: Is that car smiling at me? Schema congruity as a basis for evaluating anthropomorphized products. J. Consum. Res. 34(4), 468–479 (2007)
9. Lee, E.-J., Nass, C., Brave, S.: Can computer-generated speech have gender? An experimental test of gender stereotype. In: Chi 2000: Proceedings of the SIGCHI Conference on Human Factors in Computing Systems, pp. 289–290. Association for Computing Machinery, New York (2000)
10. Nass, C., Moon, Y., Green, N.: Are computers gender-neutral? Gender stereotypic responses to computers. J. Appl. Soc. Psychol. 27(10), 864–876 (1997)
11. Al-Natour, S., Benbasat, I., Cendetelli, R.T.: The role of design characteristics in shaping perceptions of similarity: the case of online shopping assistants. J. Assoc. Inf. Syst. 7(12), 821–861 (2006)
12. Perez Garcia, M., Saffon Lopez, S.: Building trust between users and telecommunications data driven virtual assistants. In: Iliadis, L., Maglogiannis, I., Plagianakos, V. (eds.) AIAI 2018. IAICT, vol. 519, pp. 628–637. Springer, Cham (2018). https://doi.org/10.1007/978-3-319-92007-8_53
13. Perez Garcia, M., Saffon Lopez, S., Donis, H.: Voice activated virtual assistants personality perceptions and desires: Comparing personality evaluation frameworks. In: HCI 2018: Proceedings of the 32nd International BCS Human Computer Interaction Conference (HCI), pp. 1–10. Association for Computing Machinery, New York (2018)
14. Lee, K.S., Kavya, P., Lasser, S.: Social interactions and relationships with an intelligent virtual agent. Int. J. Hum. Comput. Stud. 150, 102608 (2021)
15. Phan, T.: The materiality of the digital and the gendered voice of Siri. Transformations 29, 24–33 (2017)
16. Hwang, G., Lee. J., Oh, C.Y., Lee, J.: It sounds like a woman: exploring gender stereotypes in South Korean voice assistants. In: CHI EA 2019: Extended Abstracts of the 2019 CHI Conference on Human Factors in Computing Systems, pp. 1–6. Association for Computing Machinery, New York (2019)
17. Hoy, M.B.: Alexa, Siri, Cortana, and more: an introduction to voice assistants. Med. Ref. Serv. Q. 37(1), 81–88 (2018)
18. Lopatovska, I., Rink, K., Knight, I.: Talk to me: exploring user interactions with the Amazon Alexa. J. Librariansh. Inf. Sci. 51(4), 984–987 (2019)

19. Boyd, M., Wilson, N.: Just ask Siri? A pilot study comparing smartphone digital assistants and laptop Google searches for smoking cessation advice. PLoS ONE **13**(3), 1–6 (2018)
20. Qui, L., Benbasat, I.: The effects of text-to-speech voice and 3D avatars on consumer trust in the design of live help interface of electronic commerce. In: AMCIS 2004 Proceedings, pp. 3165–3173 (2004)
21. Qui, L., Benbasat, I.: Online consumer trust and live help interfaces: the effects of text-to-speech voice and three-dimensional avatars. Int. J. Hum. Comput. Interact. **19**(1), 75–94 (2005)
22. Qui, L., Benbasat, I.: Evaluating anthropomorphic product recommendation agents: a social relationship perspective to designing information systems. J. Manage. Inf. Syst. **25**(4), 145–181 (2009)
23. Qui, L., Benbasat, I.: A study of demographic embodiments of product recommendation agents in electronic commerce. Int. J. Hum Comput Stud. **68**, 669–688 (2010)
24. Elkins, A.C., Derrick, D.C.: The sound of trust: voice as a measurement of trust during integrations with embodied conversational agents. Group Decis. Negot. **22**, 897–913 (2013)
25. Evans, R.E., Kortum, P.: The impact of voice characteristics on user response in an interactive voice response system. Interact. Comput. **22**(6), 606–614 (2010)
26. Nunamaker, J.F., Derrick, D.C., Elkins, A.C., Burgoon, J.K., Patton, M.W.: Embodied conversational agent-based kiosk for automated interviewing. J. Manage. Inf. Syst. **28**(1), 17–48 (2011)
27. Chattaraman, V., Kwon, W.-S., Gilbert, J.E., Ross, K.: Should AI-based, conversational digital assistants employ social- or task-oriented interaction style? A task-competency and reciprocity perspective for older adults. Comput. Hum. Behav. **90**, 315–330 (2019)
28. Samuelson, W., Zeckhauser, R.: Status quo bias in decision making. J. Risk Uncertain. **1**, 7–59 (1988)
29. Kahneman, D., Knetsch, J.L., Thaler, R.H.: Anomalies: the endowment effect, loss aversion, and status quo bias. J. Econ. Perspect. **5**(1), 193–206 (1991)
30. Cheng, K.G., Ernesto, F., Ovalle-Bahamón, R.E., Truong, K.N.: Barriers to acceptance of personal digital assistants for HIV/AIDS data collection in Angola. Int. J. Med. Informatics **80**(8), 579–585 (2011)
31. Kim, H.-W., Kankanhalli, A.: Investigating user resistance to information systems implementation: a status quo bias perspective. MIS Q. **33**(3), 567–582 (2009)
32. Kahneman, D., Tversky, A.: Choices, values, and frames. Am. Psychol. **39**(4), 341–350 (1984)
33. Tversky, A., Kahneman, D.: Rational choice and the framing of decisions. J. Bus. **59**(4), 251–278 (1986)
34. Gal, D., Rucker, D.D.: The loss of loss aversion: will it loom larger than its gain? J. Consum. Psychol. **28**(3), 497–516 (2018)
35. Ritov, I., Baron, J.: Status-quo and omission bias. J. Risk Uncertain. **5**, 49–61 (1992)
36. Interaction Design Foundation. https://www.interaction-design.org/literature/article/hick-s-law-making-the-choice-easier-for-users
37. Berscheid, E., Dion, K., Walster, W., Walster, G.W.: Physical attractiveness and dating choice: a test of the matching hypothesis. J. Exp. Soc. Psychol. **7**, 173–189 (1971)
38. Byrne, D.: The Attraction Paradigm. Academic Press, New York (1971)
39. Ramadhar, S., Ho, S.Y.: Attitudes and attraction: a new test of the attraction, repulsion and similarity-dissimilarity asymmetry hypotheses. Br. J. Soc. Psychol. **39**(2), 197–211 (2000)
40. Rosenbaum, M.E.: The repulsion hypothesis: on the nondevelopment of relationships. J. Pers. Soc. Psychol. **51**(6), 1156–1166 (1986)
41. Blankenship, V., Hnat, T.G., Hess, T.G., Brown, D.R.: Similarity of personality attributes. J. Soc. Pers. Relat. **1**(4), 415–432 (1984)
42. Montano, K.J., Tigue, C.C., Isenstein, S.G.E., Barclay, P., Fienberg, D.R.: Men's voice pitch influences women's trusting behavior. Evol. Hum. Behav. **38**, 293–297 (2017)

43. Borkowska, B., Pawlowski, B.: Female voice frequency in the context of dominance and attractiveness perception. Anim. Behav. **82**, 55–59 (2011)
44. Aylett, M.P., Vinciarelli, A., Wester, M.: Speech synthesis for the generation of artificial personality. IEEE Trans. Affect. Comput. **11**(2), 361–372 (2020)
45. McCrae, R.R., Costa, P.T.: Validation of the five-factor model of personality across instruments and observers. J. Pers. Soc. Psychol. **52**(1), 81–90 (1987)
46. Mount, M.K., Barrick, M.R., Strauss, J.P.: Validity of observer ratings of the Big Five personality factors. J. Appl. Psychol. **79**(2), 272–280 (1994)
47. Gurven, M., von Rueden, C., Massenkoff, M., Kaplan, H., Vie, M.L.: How universal is the Big Five? Testing the five-factor model of personality variation among forager-farmers in the Bolivian Amazon. J. Pers. Soc. Psychol. **104**(2), 354–370 (2013)
48. Gosling, S.D., Rentfrow, P.J., Swann Jr., W.B.: A very brief measure of the Big-Five personality domains. J. Res. Pers. **37**(6), 504–528 (2003)
49. Fusion Hill. https://www.fusionhill.com/hey-siri-whered-you-get-your-personality-four-ways-to-make-a-digital-assistant-engaging

Facial Emotion Recognition in UX Evaluation: A Systematic Review

Erico de Souza Veriscimo$^{(\boxtimes)}$ ⓘ, João Luiz Bernardes Júnior ⓘ,
and Luciano Antonio Digiampietri ⓘ

School of Arts, Sciences and Humanities (EACH),
University of São Paulo, São Paulo, Brazil
{ericoveriscimo,jlbernardes,digiampietri}@usp.br

Abstract. In UX evaluation, pragmatic criteria still prevail over hedonic ones. However, emotion is an essential part of the user experience and has particular importance to system acceptance, thus it should be assigned more value in such assessments. Emotion recognition based on facial expressions is one of the tools that can be used to assess user emotion and it can be performed during the interaction and in a less intrusive way than with other sensors. In this context, this paper presents a systematic literature review about user experience evaluation using facial emotion recognition addressing the following research questions: which kinds of user studies take advantage of facial emotion recognition and to what purpose; how emotion recognition is implemented; how user experience is evaluated using this data and what strategies are used to validate these results. From 372 unique papers identified by the search string, 332 were initially discarded and, of the remaining 40 remaining papers that were read in full, only 14 were included in the final analysis. We identified that this area is still relatively novel, with few works published and all of them in the last eight years. Facial images were the most frequent type of data used and comparisons with self-reported emotions were the prevalent strategy to validate automatic emotion recognition, but just as often no such strategy was discussed.

Keywords: User experience · UX evaluation · Emotion recognition

1 Introduction

With the continuous growth of computing power and availability and the role it plays in a large and growing number of user lives, we now routinely interact with large amounts of data and many different applications using rather diverse hardware and software platforms. More complex ways of inference and data analysis have also become viable to assist in dealing with this large volume of varied, complex and multidimensional data, in applications such as knowledge discovery and decision making [14], among others. And an important way to

© Springer Nature Switzerland AG 2021
M. Kurosu (Ed.): HCII 2021, LNCS 12762, pp. 521–534, 2021.
https://doi.org/10.1007/978-3-030-78462-1_40

facilitate understanding and discovery within this context is the notoriously non-trivial task of exploring multiple dimensions in interaction, including the three spatial dimensions and the temporal one [7,12,17].

In view of this environment, a systematic review [22] focusing particularly in 3D interaction identified that, when evaluating the User Experience (UX) of interacting with these systems, pragmatic criteria (mostly related to user task performance) still prevail, and to a large degree, over hedonic criteria (more related to user emotions). Emotion is, however, an essential factor in UX [2] and of particular importance for system acceptance [21] and should therefore be given more attention in such evaluations. That systematic review also pointed out a lack of standardization in evaluation procedures and criteria, as well as, when emotion was analyzed at all, a very frequent reliance on its a posteriori self-reporting, very often as the only means of assessing it. Emotion recognition based on facial expressions is one of the tools that can aid in assessing user emotions, with the added advantage that it can be performed during interaction with the system, and is less intrusively than other sensor-based emotion recognition approaches.

This led to the work described in this present paper, a systematic literature review on the evaluation of user experience through facial emotion recognition, using the review methodology proposed by Kitchenham et al. [10] and addressing the following research questions: what types of studies take advantage of facial emotion recognition and for what purposes; how emotion recognition is implemented; how user experience is evaluated using this data and what strategies are used to validate these results. This review is not restricted to 3D interaction, unlike the work mentioned earlier.

Following this introduction, this paper is organized in four more sections. Section 2 describes how the methodology was applied in this study. Section 3 presents and discusses the results obtained, both in terms of statistical data about the reviewed papers and of discussing the research questions. Section 4 summarizes these results and, finally, Sect. 5 presents the main conclusions derived from this work.

2   Materials and Methods

This literature review is based on the guidelines proposed by Kitchenham et al. [10] involving a systematic search and analysis of previously published studies on a subject, in this case on the evaluation of UX through the recognition of facial emotion. Unlike traditional, more exploratory literature review processes, a systematic review is based on a defined search strategy, aimed at minimizing the various types of bias, identifying as much relevant literature as possible, and facilitating the reproducibility of the process. To apply this method, an exploratory research was initially carried out to identify common terms in papers in this area. A review protocol was then produced, which will be summarized in the next subsections. Papers where then retrieved from three digital libraries, filtered using previously decided inclusion and exclusion criteria and finally information was extracted from the selected papers and compiled here.

2.1   Research Questions

Three research questions were proposed for the present review:

- Q1: What types of studies take advantage of facial emotion recognition and for what purpose?
- Q2: How is emotion recognition implemented?
- Q3: How is the user experience evaluated using this data and what strategies are used to validate these results?

2.2   Data Sources and Search Strategies

Textual searches were conducted in three scientific digital libraries relevant to the field of computing: ACM Digital Library[1], IEEE Xplore[2] and Springer Link[3].

The following search string was used: ("emotion recognition" AND "facial expressions" AND ("User Experience" OR "UX") AND ("evaluation" OR "evaluate")).

2.3   Inclusion and Exclusion Criteria

Articles were considered adequate for inclusion when they met all inclusion criteria and no exclusion criteria. The criteria are:

Inclusion:

- A: Published works that are fully available in English in scientific digital libraries will be included.
- B: Only works that actually perform user evaluations will be included.

Exclusion:

- A: Papers that do not attempt to recognize emotions will be excluded.
- B: Works that do not assess UX or at least some of its aspects will be excluded.

2.4   References Management

Bibliographic reference information about the retrieved and selected papers was stored using StArt 3.3 [3]. Spreadsheets were also used to assist in managing the review process, information extraction and preparation of its results.

---

[1] ACM Digital Library dl.acm.org.
[2] IEEE Xplore ieeexplore.ieee.org.
[3] Springer Link https://link.springer.com/.

2.5   Data Extraction

For each selected paper, during information extraction from its full text, the following data was collected:

- Bibliographic information;
- What types of user evaluation were performed and how;
- How emotions were recognized automatically;
- How this automatic recognition was validated (or what was it compared to);
- Additional considerations;
- Abstract.

One piece of information that was purposefully not included in the present discussion is how well the automatic recognition systems were able to classify emotions. This paper's goal is to discuss how and to what ends facial emotion recognition is used in UX evaluation. A discussion of different sensors, image processing techniques and classification algorithms and how they affect the quality of emotion recognition is certainly interesting but should be the topic of another paper.

3   Results

This section presents the review results, including statistical data and information on user experience evaluation through facial emotion recognition.

3.1   General Information

In the search carried out, 372 unique references were found, 239 from Springer, 130 from ACM, and 3 from IEEE. After reading the title and abstract of these articles, 332 were initially discarded, according to the criteria defined in the methods described before. After reading the remaining 40 articles, 26 were discarded for not satisfying the inclusion and exclusion criteria. There were 14 remaining articles, which were read and from which data were collected. Table 1 shows the vehicles in which the articles were published and the number of publications in each one.

All selected articles were published in the last eight years, with publications starting in 2013. We surmise that, before this period, there was little availability or a technology deficit to carry out automatic emotion recognition in this sort of evaluation. Additionally, we can see the greatest growth in publications in 2015, a spike caused in part by a same group of researchers who published in that year and the next. We believe that, because technology is no longer such a limiting factor and the growing recognition of the importance of UX evaluation, including for user acceptance, there should be more growth in this area in the near future. Figure 1 shows the number of selected publications per year.

Brazil is home to the research group that published more papers in 2015 and 2016 and work from such diverse countries as Germany, Australia, Bangladesh, China, South Korea, Denmark, Greece, Mexico, Norway, Poland, the United Kingdom, Singapore, and Syria was also selected in this review, indicating that the interest in the subject is global.

Table 1. Articles per digital library

Digital library	Number of papers
ACM on Interactive, Mobile, Wearable and Ubiquitous Technologies	2
Ambient Intelligence for Health	1
Conference on Designing Interactive Systems	1
Design, User Experience, and Usability: Design Discourse	1
Informatics and Management Science V	1
International Conference of Design, User Experience, and Usability (DUXU)	1
International Conference on Electrical Information and Communication Technology (EICT)	1
International Conference on Human-Computer Interaction	1
International Conference on Human-Computer Interaction with Mobile Devices and Services Adjunct	2
International Conference on User Modeling, Adaptation, and Personalization	1
International Workshop on Emotion Awareness in Software Engineering (SEmotion)	1
Proceedings of the Multimedia, Interaction, Design and Innnovation	1

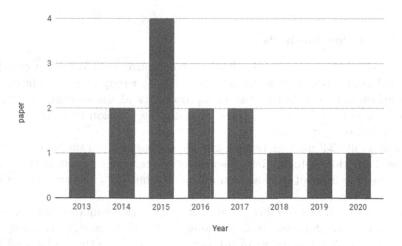

Fig. 1. Number of published articles per year

3.2   Evaluation Objective

Not all evaluations presented in these 14 papers necessarily focused on UX as a whole, instead many targeted some element or aspect of it. These evaluation targets, aside from UX itself, were: usability, engagement and cognitive performance. In terms of the number of articles per target, six dealt with UX as a whole, followed by five focusing on usability, two on engagement, and finally, only one exploring cognitive performance, as illustrated by Fig. 2, with percentage values.

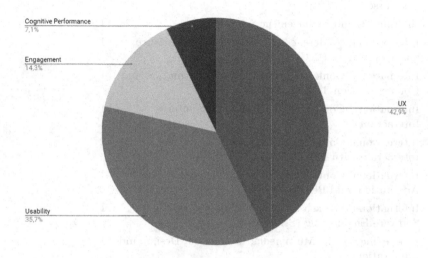

Fig. 2. Number of articles per target evaluated

3.3   Evaluation Methods

Menning et al. [15], create a timeline tracking sentiments. When an emotion is identified as negative, it is assumed something is "wrong" with the interaction. Some action is then taken to "fix this problem" and the emotion is extracted again. This is repeated several times creating the emotion timeline identifying how UX improves or worsens.

Xiang et al. [23] use the Tetris game for testing and a translation matrix for expressed emotions which where then used to increase or decrease the game's speed (and thus difficulty), in an example of dynamic difficulty adjustment based on facial expression.

In the research presented by Munim et al. [16], two human evaluators would identify one of five emotions in users along time (joy, surprise, fear, engagement, and anger) and create a report of this data. This report is then compared to the emotions extracted automatically by their system facial expression recognition. Their proposed tool brings together on the same interface recordings of user

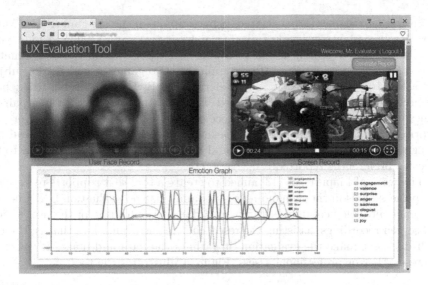

Fig. 3. Munim et al. [16] user interface

screens and user faces and produces graphs showing the extracted emotions. Figure 3 shows that system's interface.

In the work of Feijó-Filho et al. [4–6,8] an automated test is performed, which generates a graphic log report, with time-stamped positive and negative feedback. To induce negative feedback, users were asked to authenticate to a social network and post a text message, but the WLAN connection was turned off and on within 30 s while to induce positive feedback, users were asked to answer a questionnaire with funny questions and riddles.

Landowska [11] used a call center support application. Each participant had two recorded sessions of 6 min each. Several cameras were placed and participants received paper versions of instructions and questionnaires. As the objective of the study was to identify which emotion acquisition techniques would naturally integrate with the usability assessment context, usability assessment was not carried out, only the possibility of using emotion acquisition for such assessment was verified.

In the research developed by Carrillo et al. [1], 8 people (2 men and 6 women) aged between 60 and 83 years participated in an experiment which was explained to the participants individually. They were asked to sign the consent form and a mini-mental state examination was carried out. A set of photos was presented to the users, each image was exposed for 6 s and, immediately, the participant answered what was the impression when seeing the image, answering from 1 to 4 according to one of the following categories: pleasant, unpleasant, neutral and fear. The electrical activity of the brain was captured, stored and later used as input to the automatic recognition system.

Shaker and Shaker [18] evaluated 28 participants using the game Super Mario Bros. Each session consisted of playing at least two games followed by a post-experience game research design to collect self-reports using the 4-Alternative Forced Choice questionnaire. After completing two games A and B, the subject was asked to report whether: A is preferable to B; B is preferable to A; both are preferred equally; none is preferred. Each participant played three pairs of games, on average. 4 emotions were recognized (happiness, sadness, anger, and surprise) based on "visual reaction features", such as location of the head and changes in the properties of the eyes and mouth, and this was compared to the affective preferences reported.

The work of Liapis et al. [13] aimed to create a tool that supports researchers and professionals in the demanding task of analysis and evaluation UX. The tool combines physiological data, self-reported data, visualization of the user's video and screen recordings, assisting the researcher in the evaluation, that is, the tool itself does not make the evaluation, it gathers the data and makes it easier for the researcher or professional assess. Figure 4 illustrates the tool.

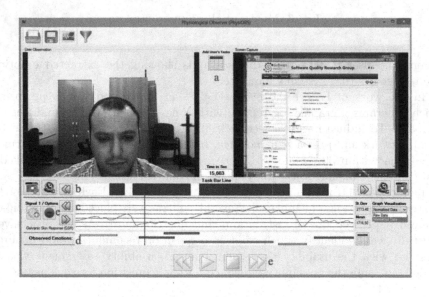

Fig. 4. Liapis et al. [13] user interface

In Soleimani and Law. [20], 46 volunteers participated in the study. An online shopping platform for Android was developed, which offered travel recommendations. An application was also created to record audio data captured by a microphone. At the beginning of each session, the experimenter describes the objectives of the study and procedures for the participant, including the thinking out loud protocol. Then, the session continues with a brief "think out loud" test phase, in which participants were instructed to verbalize thoughts and feelings. After completing the task, participants were asked to complete the final questionnaire. Then, a score was generated from the self-reported retrospective assessment of the dimensions of pleasure and excitement was obtained. The a posteriori self-evaluation and the automatic analysis of moment-to-moment think aloud data were then compared.

In the work of Huynh et al. [9], 54 mobile game players were recruited. For the test, six games were selected, one pair from each of three genres, one with a high user rating (>4.2 stars in the online store) and another with a low rating (<3.8 stars). At the beginning of each phase, each participant was shown a video with neutral content for three minutes to provoke a neutral emotional state in each participant, in order to eliminate, to the maximum, the confusion caused by the beginning of the study with different initial emotions. Then, participants were asked to play three different games (two sessions for each game) with the default setting for each game and provide a self-report on their levels of involvement after each play session using a simplified version of the Game Engagement Questionnaire; these reports were used the baseline "truth" for the study and compared with a multimodal emotion recognition approach employing data from three sensors: the touchscreen, a depth camera and a wristband sensing heartbeat and electrodermal activity.

In Sharma et al. [19], the cross-task reliability of physiological and facial responses was measured in order to assess cognitive performance. Four different experiments were used: using the Pac-Man game, an adaptive assessment task, a code debugging task and a gaze-based game. A score was produced for all experiments to assess cognitive performance. In studies involving games, scoring is related to the acquisition of skills and in educational studies, scoring is related to problem-solving abilities.

3.4   Validation

The strategies used to validate the automatic emotion recognition in the works selected in this review can be classified in three groups: manual comparison, self-report comparison and translation matrix. A fourth category includes those studies that did not explain which strategy was used, including some that simply classified user reactions as positive or negative and counted the number of positive reactions as a metric of quality without necessarily validating this classification. Figure 5 details the number of citations by validation strategy, with "no label" representing that fourth category.

Manual Comparison. Emotion is manually recognized and recorded by human observers (ideally with at least some training in how to classify the desired emotions), either during the experiment or later, watching recorded video and sometimes other data, and then these results are compared to those obtained from automatic recognition.

Self-report Comparison. Emotions recognized automatically are compared to those self-reported by the user, most often using some questionnaire applied

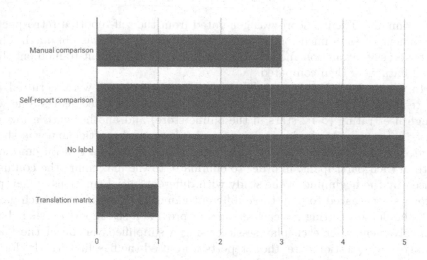

Fig. 5. Number of papers per validation strategy.

after task execution (which, unlike a more continuous record, notoriously tends to point out only modal emotions [20], i.e. those that were elicited most frequently during task execution).

Translation Matrix. A translation matrix is created combining performance metrics with recognized user emotions and thus facilitating the interpretation of obtained results. This may also allow real time adaptation of the interaction based on user responses.

3.5   Features

All selected papers classify emotions through the use of some artificial intelligence technique or use a library that makes use of it but, for this present review, what most significantly differentiates these works are the types of data or features are used in the recognition and how they are collected. Bearing in mind that this review also included works exploring multimodal emotion recognition, the features used can be classified as: facial images (even if later more features are extracted from it), tracking of only specific points on the face, facial muscle activity, data from electroencephalography or other sensors and voice data (in this particular case, understanding which emotion was being verbally self-reported, as opposed to detecting emotion from the voice directly). Figure 6 shows how many papers explored each type of data.

Other interesting information extracted in this review can be seen in Fig. 7, which shows which devices were used to capture this data and by how many of the selected papers.

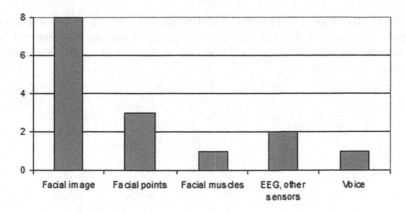

Fig. 6. Number of papers per type of data.

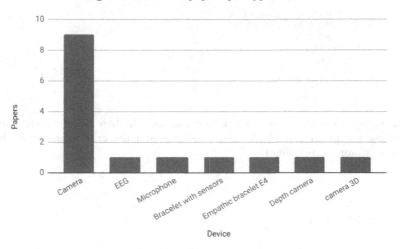

Fig. 7. Number of papers per device.

3.6 Emotions

Emotions discussed in the selected papers can be grouped in three categories: labeled emotions, unlabeled emotions, and emotional dimensions. Labeled emotions are those that can be described by a noun (the following were used: bored, relaxed, excited, frustrated, happy, engaged, surprised, angry, sad or neutral, meaning the absence of emotion). Unlabeled emotions are attempts to correlate the activity in different regions of the face (such as eyes, nose, mouth, and chin line) with variations in users internal emotional states (and with external events) without necessarily naming or classifying these states. Finally, emotional dimensions are given either by contrasting two opposing emotional responses (such as pleasant and unpleasant or positive and negative) of which one is reported, or by attempting to quantize the intensity of a labeled emotion, from instance with integers from 1 to 5. Figure 8 shows how many papers which emotions and in which way: blue bars indicate emotional dimensions, green bars labeled emotions and gray bars unlabeled emotions. Once again, the sum can be greater than the total number of articles since each one can make use of multiple emotions or categories of emotion.

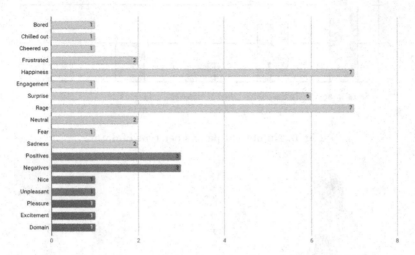

Fig. 8. Number of detected emotions in the articles. The blue bars indicate emotional dimensions, the green bars the labeled emotions, and the gray bars the non-labeled emotions. (Color figure online)

4   Conclusions

The initial goal for this review, motivated by the discussion in Veriscimo et al. [22], was confirmed by the results discussed above. There is indeed a gap regarding the evaluation of UX through automatic emotion recognition. This can be observed in the small number of papers found, both in total and by publication venue (Table 1), compared to the much larger number of other works about UX evaluation. The subject, however, appears to be a global concern with research from varied countries, and to be gaining growing importance in the last eight years, as shown by the evolution of the number of publications illustrated in Fig. 1. We also expected that, within the scope of this review at least, a larger percentage of works would evaluate UX as a whole, but we still found many who focused only on some aspects of it.

Three main strategies to validate automatic emotion recognition were identified. The most used was comparison with user self-reported emotions, but just as many works described no such strategy, reducing the reliability of their results. Among the detected emotions, labeled emotions were used most often, followed by unlabeled emotions, and among the labeled emotions, those most frequently employed were anger and happiness, followed by surprise.

Regarding the types of data used in emotion recognition, the large majority was facial images. Along with tracking facial points and the activity of facial muscles, even more papers explored facial expressions for emotion recognition. We believe that one of the reasons for the prevalence of this type of data is that it is often more simple to acquire and record with less intrusive sensors.

Thus, it is possible to conclude that the area of UX evaluation through emotion recognition is growing but still lacks in standardization and modernization of tools, procedures, and evaluation criteria, suggesting opportunities for relevant research in the area. It is expected that the present work will serve as a starting point to discuss these methods and strategies for interaction designers, developers and evaluators and for the development of new methods or assessment tools in the area.

References

1. Carrillo, I., Meza-Kubo, V., Morán, A.L., Galindo, G., García-Canseco, E.: Processing EEG signals towards the construction of a user experience assessment method. In: Bravo, J., Hervás, R., Villarreal, V. (eds.) AmIHEALTH 2015. LNCS, vol. 9456, pp. 281–292. Springer, Cham (2015). https://doi.org/10.1007/978-3-319-26508-7_28

2. Chang, H.-M., Díaz, M., Català, A., Chen, W., Rauterberg, M.: Mood boards as a universal tool for investigating emotional experience. In: Marcus, A. (ed.) DUXU 2014. LNCS, vol. 8520, pp. 220–231. Springer, Cham (2014). https://doi.org/10.1007/978-3-319-07638-6_22

3. Fabbri, S., Silva, C., Hernandes, E., Octaviano, F., Di Thommazo, A., Belgamo, A.: Improvements in the start tool to better support the systematic review process. In: Proceedings of the 20th International Conference on Evaluation and Assessment in Software Engineering, EASE 2016, New York, NY, USA. Association for Computing Machinery (2016). https://doi.org/10.1145/2915970.2916013

4. Filho, J.F., Prata, W., Oliveira, J.: Where-how-what am I feeling: user context logging in automated usability tests for mobile software. In: Marcus, A. (ed.) DUXU 2016. LNCS, vol. 9748, pp. 14–23. Springer, Cham (2016). https://doi.org/10.1007/978-3-319-40406-6_2

5. Filho, J.F., Prata, W., Valle, T.: Emotions logging in automated usability tests for mobile devices. In: Marcus, A. (ed.) DUXU 2015. LNCS, vol. 9186, pp. 428–435. Springer, Cham (2015). https://doi.org/10.1007/978-3-319-20886-2_40

6. Filho, J.F., Valle, T., Prata, W.: Automated usability tests for mobile devices through live emotions logging. In: Proceedings of the 17th International Conference on Human-Computer Interaction with Mobile Devices and Services Adjunct, pp. 636–643 (2015)

7. Ferreira, T.M., Costella, F.L., Zanetti, A.B., da Silva, S.E., Zanatta, A.L., De Marchi, A.C.B.: CrowdRec: a prototype recommendation system for crowdsourcing platforms using Google venture design: Google venture design sprint. In: Proceedings of the XV Brazilian Symposium on Information Systems, pp. 1–8 (2019)

8. Filho, J.F., Prata, W., Oliveira, J.: Affective-ready, contextual and automated usability test for mobile software. In: Proceedings of the 18th International Conference on Human-Computer Interaction with Mobile Devices and Services Adjunct, pp. 638–644 (2016)

9. Huynh, S., Kim, S., Ko, J., Balan, R.K., Lee, Y.: EngageMon: multi-modal engagement sensing for mobile games. Proc. ACM Interact. Mob. Wearable Ubiquit. Technol. **2**(1), 1–27 (2018)
10. Kitchenham, B., Brereton, O.P., Budgen, D., Turner, M., Bailey, J., Linkman, S.: Systematic literature reviews in software engineering - a systematic literature review. Inf. Softw. Technol. **51**(1), 7–15 (2009)
11. Landowska, A.: Towards emotion acquisition in it usability evaluation context. In: Proceedings of the Multimedia, Interaction, Design and Innovation, pp. 1–9. Association for Computing Machinery (2015)
12. LaViola Jr., J.J., Kruijff, E., McMahan, R.P., Bowman, D., Poupyrev, I.P.: 3D User Interfaces: Theory and Practice. Addison-Wesley Professional, Boston (2017)
13. Liapis, A., Karousos, N., Katsanos, C., Xenos, M.: Evaluating user's emotional experience in HCI: the PhysiOBS approach. In: Kurosu, M. (ed.) HCI 2014. LNCS, vol. 8511, pp. 758–767. Springer, Cham (2014). https://doi.org/10.1007/978-3-319-07230-2_72
14. Lyytinen, K., Grover, V.: Management misinformation systems: a time to revisit? J. Assoc. Inf. Syst. **18**(3), 2 (2017)
15. Mennig, P., Scherr, S.A., Elberzhager, F.: Supporting rapid product changes through emotional tracking. In: 2019 IEEE/ACM 4th International Workshop on Emotion Awareness in Software Engineering (SEmotion), pp. 8–12. IEEE (2019)
16. Munim, K.M., Islam, I., Khatun, M., Karim, M.M., Islam, M.N.: Towards developing a tool for UX evaluation using facial expression. In: 2017 3rd International Conference on Electrical Information and Communication Technology (EICT), pp. 1–6. IEEE (2017)
17. Schroeder, W.J., Lorensen, B., Martin, K.: The Visualization Toolkit: An Object-Oriented Approach to 3D Graphics. Kitware (2004)
18. Shaker, N., Shaker, M.: Towards understanding the nonverbal signatures of engagement in Super Mario Bros. In: Dimitrova, V., Kuflik, T., Chin, D., Ricci, F., Dolog, P., Houben, G.-J. (eds.) UMAP 2014. LNCS, vol. 8538, pp. 423–434. Springer, Cham (2014). https://doi.org/10.1007/978-3-319-08786-3_38
19. Sharma, K., Niforatos, E., Giannakos, M., Kostakos, V.: Assessing cognitive performance using physiological and facial features: generalizing across contexts. Proc. ACM Interact. Mob. Wearable Ubiquit. Technol. **4**(3), 1–41 (2020)
20. Soleimani, S., Law, E.L.C.: What can self-reports and acoustic data analyses on emotions tell us? In: Proceedings of the 2017 Conference on Designing Interactive Systems, pp. 489–501 (2017)
21. Szajna, B.: Empirical evaluation of the revised technology acceptance model. Manage. Sci. **42**(1), 85–92 (1996)
22. de Souza Veriscimo, E., Bernardes Junior, J.L., Digiampietri, L.A.: Evaluating user experience in 3D interaction: a systematic review. In: XVI Brazilian Symposium on Information Systems, pp. 1–8 (2020)
23. Xiang, N., Yang, L., Zhang, M.: Dynamic difficulty adjustment by facial expression. In: Du, W. (ed.) Informatics and Management Science V. Lecture Notes in Electrical Engineering, vol. 208, pp. 761–768. London, Springer (2013). https://doi.org/10.1007/978-1-4471-4796-1_97

Analysis of Emotion in Socioenactive Systems

Diego Addan Gonçalves[✉], Ricardo Edgard Caceffo,
and Maria Cecilia Calani Baranauskas

Institute of Computing, University of Campinas, Campinas, SP, Brazil
dagoncalves@inf.ufpr.br

Abstract. Facial expressions are important data to understand how systems in social environments impact people in it. The presence of new technologies and new coupled forms of interaction with the ubiquity of computing and social networks, present challenges that require the consideration of new factors as emotional. Socioenactive systems represent a complex scenario that requires the treatment of technological aspects in which the consideration of the social dynamic, enhanced by concepts such as affective computing and enactive systems. This work presents a proposal for facial recognition in the wild applied to outputs of socioenative systems. These results reinforce how the design of socioenactive systems can promote positive changes in the emotional state of children in an educational context and promote social interactions.

Keywords: Facial action units · Emotion recognition · Ubiquitous computing · Socioenactive system

1 Introduction

The presence of new technologies and new modes of interaction (tangible, wearable and natural interfaces), added to the ubiquity of computing and the way people interact in an environment in which this technology is disseminated, present challenges that require the consideration of new factors (emotional, physical and cultural) in the conception of computer-based systems. Enactive systems have been defined as computational systems made up of human and technological processes dynamically linked, i.e., constituting feedback cycles using sensors and data analysis, enabling a fluid interaction between human and computer [1, 6].

The concept of socioenactive systems has been characterized in a project [2], where the 'socio' highlights the explicit concern and focus on intersubjective aspects in enactive systems, which have not yet been addressed in the literature or scientific research, as far as it is of our knowledge. Intersubjective interaction involves directly perceiving intentions and emotions of others in the kinematics of their movements, in their postures, gestures, facial expressions, vocal intonations etc., as well as in their actions in situations which include physical environment, social roles, culture, etc. [3]. Socioenactive systems consider the actions that occur with the interaction between several people and systems integrated in a social-physical-digital environment. This type of environment, based on ubiquitous computing technologies, also uses physiological readings from people as data

M. Kurosu (Ed.): HCII 2021, LNCS 12762, pp. 535–544, 2021.
https://doi.org/10.1007/978-3-030-78462-1_41

input that can be used to define new system behaviors, leading to new human actions in the interaction cycle [7–9].

One of the results of socioenactive systems is the engagement built on experiences that can positively affect the emotional state of the participants. Since these systems are focused on people, understanding how emotions are changed in experiences in these environments and the impact of social and technological interactions in a socioenactive system are highly relevant especially within educational contexts.

The integration of the social element, which makes the environment more diverse and dynamic, with more data and information feeding back the system and generating new possibilities of action in the environment are challenges for the design and evaluation of this type of system.

Analyzing emotions automatically is an efficient way to identify emotional changes in children that may indicate interest in the group task, excitement, joy, among other positive demonstrations of children's interaction with the socioenactive system. This type of analysis applied to enactive scenarios is innovative and allows for deeper analyzes such as the relationship between the actions of a robot or other children in an individual's emotions in enactive environments.

This work presents a proposal for automatic recognition of emotions method applied to videos of a workshop designed and applied as a socioenactive system. The preliminary results presented help to understand whether the experience fosters social interactions and has a potential positive emotional impact on the involved people. The presented method intends to provide a technique for integrating the use of physiological data to make an analysis of emotional changes in a socioenactive environment. These results will help to better understand social interactions and the design of socioenactive systems, including those for educational contexts.

The next section presents the theoretical background and the methodology developed for the experiments that support our proposal (Sect. 2), followed by the main preliminary results on ... (Section 3) and discussion on highlighted aspects of results (Sect. 4). Finally, a conclusion is presented and suggestions for future works that extend the concepts are proposed (Sect. 5).

2   Theoretical Background and Study Methodology

This section presents the methodology applied in the construction of the automatic emotion recognition method applied to the outputs of an instance of a socioenactive system. Subsect. 2.1 presents related work concerning emotions recognition in the wild, and Subsect. 2.2 shows the applied context and methodology.

2.1   Emotions Recognition in Social Environments

The recognition of human emotions has been a challenging topic in the field of human-computer interaction. Automated facial expression recognition (FER) remains a challenging and worrisome problem [4, 10]. Although recent advances in deep learning have assumed a significant breakthrough in automatic FER, strong changes in pose, orientation, and point of view still lack practical models with high accuracy. Also, the acquisition of labeled datasets is costly.

Salunke and Patil [15] present an Automatic Face Emotion Recognition method which consists of three convolutional layers, each followed by maximum pooling, with massive training that solves the problem of images in an uncontrolled environment. The relevance of the final model presented by the authors is portrayed in a live video application that can instantly return the user's emotions based on their facial posture providing an important insight into the importance of using different data sets for training and validation. In this method, the training stage is still expensive despite the accuracy of the model.

Emotion Recognition algorithm gains accuracy in the classification process when it uses a detector of facial units that can perform parallel calculations of landmarks distances in the facial expressions recognition in the wild. Pons and Masip [16] propose a loss function that addresses the problem of learning multiple tasks with heterogeneously labeled data, improving previous multitask approaches using three datasets acquired in non-controlled environments, and an application to predict compound facial emotion expressions.

In general, these methods, even when using models with discriminative facial features or individual control points are costly [21, 22]. Applying them in uncontrolled and multi-sided environments becomes an unfeasible task for sequences of very long activities and involving many people. Socioenactives systems take place in environments where interactions are important and generating the recognition of several faces at the same time can indicate how the interactions affect the emotional relationship of its participants. That is why it is essential to use FER in the wild methods that are optimized and that provide an average accuracy in view of a low computational cost.

2.2 Study Methodology

The implementation of the proposed method is based on an adaptation of the Support Vector Machines pattern recognition method and sequential tracking of multiple tracked facial landmarks. The methodology followed the steps of: identification and extraction of facial landmarks in video from a socioenactive system workshop, selected as an example of the proposed experience; recognition of emotions of the children participants.

The proposed method was applied to videos recorded from a socioenactive system workshop situated in an educational context [5]. Children interactions were recorded in videos which were systematically analyzed by the researchers based on the Grounded Theory approach [5, 13, 14]. In this work, we aimed at observing the changes in children's emotions, acting within a mBot-based narrative scenario in a proposed group task, using the proposed method.

The input videos were recorded in a workshop [5], instance of a socioenactive system, where the children should try to recognize the facial expression that one of them reproduced in a telepathic box (artifact that isolated the child at the moment he performed his action, which could be one of the six basic emotions: joy, sadness, fear, surprise, disgust or anger) through pre-programmed actions of a robot.

The narrative encouraged children to dynamically understand mBot behaviors that lead them to build hypotheses to explain the behavioral patterns of the robot's actions. In this scenario, children's actions were developed so that the robot could express 6 basic emotions: joy, surprise, contempt, sadness, anger and disgust. First, for two weeks, the teachers organized storytelling activities displaying signs with emoticons related to each expression and the playful narrative was built and their actions were defined through the mBot robot.

The study environment for this work was composed of a video recorded with a "telepathic box" with a camera, isolated from the other parts; a stage for the robot to perform its actions; and a children's audience area. Eleven children were involved in the study.

The main objective of our study in this paper was to observe changes in the affective state of the participants when any robot action or social dynamics is initiated. For that, a basic facial expression recognition algorithm was trained that could identify multiple faces in a scene, considering the social aspects. The basic expressions consist of the six mentioned for the robot and any interpolation considered variations of one or more [12].

For the analysis of the classifications, the interactions proposed by the socioenative system were related to the labeled emotions of the children in order to identify positive changes in their facial expressions such as joy or surprise, indicating that the system fostered the interest of its participants.

3   Results

The automatic recognition of emotions in non-controlled environments sets physiological input interactions, as the facial expressions, an important element in socioenactive systems, and points out how these systems can positively impact the affective state of children.

The analysis process considered the tracked emotional changes observed together with the actions and behaviors that emerged from the interactions between the children and the robot. These categories of actions can suggest leadership, collaboration, engagement in solving group tasks, among other behaviors that emerge from this type of social experience in an educational environment.

The chosen excerpt of video input, named "00075.MTS" of 24:04 min, recorded from the workshop based on a socioenactive system [5] satisfactorily represents the interactions of the experiment since it is possible to observe the actions of the robots and the children's faces, allowing algorithms for recognizing facial expressions to be applied. For each part of the video where the robot performed an action (showing an expression on the display and a movement behavior), the children's facial reactions were analyzed in order to identify changes in facial expression and to relate them to the moments of interaction with the robot. Still, interactions between children were also classified as they can indicate changes in emotion due to these actions. There are two moments in the video where the action of the mBot robot happens in an expected way. In this excerpt, social interactions between children and changes in their facial expressions can be classified automatically using Machine Learning techniques such as convolutional neural networks or support vector machine., as shown in Table 1.

Automatic FER can be built and trained using machine learning and computational intelligence techniques. Although algorithms based on Convolutional Neural Network

Table 1. Excerpts from the analyzed video where the action of the mBot robot happens in an expected way triggering social interactions between children and changes in their facial expressions

Sample input video 00075.MTS	
Time	Sequence of action
09:21 - 09:38	mBot robot moves forward and displays a facial expression on the display
17:37 - 18:07	mBot robot makes a second diagonal walk action and displays a facial expression on the display

are usually computationally costly and focused on massive training to maintain generic and functional accuracy the same classification logic can be used by other machine learning algorithms such as Support Vector Machine (SVM), simplifying the training step [17, 18]. For this study, the videos and environments are internal and controlled, which allows for a less robust classifier training and, in turn, with a lighter computational cost.

Thus, the method used is based on the method presented by Kin et al. [11]. This method uses spatio-temporal features that assist in the identification of independent facial landmarks that are calculated through machine learning. In this study, the SVM algorithm was used to learn the spatial feature as well as its functions (Fig. 1).

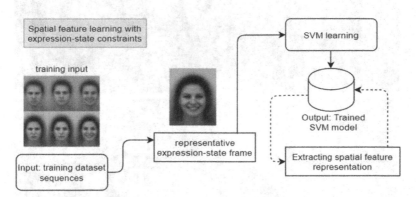

Fig. 1. Overall process of the used method for training and classifying base expressions using spatio-temporal features. This method is a simplification of the algorithm presented in [11].

The training stage was performed using 2D datasets. The CASME II dataset was used, which contains 246 expression sequences collected from 26 subjects with a temporal resolution of 200 fps [19] and the Averaged Karolinska Directed Emotional Faces (AKDEF) dataset that provide samples for the six base expressions interpreted by more than 20 subjects providing approximately 120 samples [20]. From the training with the bases that identifies the position of the face and from this tracking, the method calculates the position of the main facial landmarks; the data of spatial representation assist in the classification of the labels and updating of the training functions.

The SVM algorithm updates the recognition hypothesis with the spatial values of the landmarks, using spatial feature representation, which consists of a geometric estimate of the face position and from this recognizes the expression itself.

The classification process considered all faces recognizable in the scene, frame by frame, classifying based on the position of the main facial landmarks, estimating their positions and then calculating the distance from the points of interest of the facial regions. Figure 2 presents two excerpts from the video where the classifier labeled the emotions of each child. For reasons of occlusion or positioning in relation to the camera, some children do not have their emotions recognized in excerpts of the video, a problem that is solved by comparing the values classified in moments before and after the tracking is lost. In the figure it is possible to notice two moments of classification where facial expressions in the wild are labeled. These values, in relation to the interactions that occurred at each moment of the workshop, can indicate how the socioenactive system impacts children, generating surprise or joy, for example.

Fig. 2. Example of excerpts from the video where the classifier is able to label the facial expressions of children participating in the workshop.

Images were generated for each frame of the example video, with the faces already labeled, and the stretches where the interactions proposed by the socioenative system were initiated (robot actions or children's action instructions) were identified.

4 Discussion

Table 2 presents the sections where the robot interacted with the children besides the classification of the emotions of each child (C1, C2, ..., C9). The registered time stamp presented refers to the beginning and end of the robot's interaction. The children expressions presented are the most frequent in the interval from the previous section to the next, for each child.

Table 2. Example of the results of the analyzed video clip. The nine children present at the workshop had their expressions classified, being represented as C1 to C9 considering their position in the scenario.

Video excerpt (time stamp)	Labeled facial expression	Action description
09:21	Happy (C1, C4), neutral (C3, C9, C7), fear (C5, C8), sad (C2)	C1 interacts with C2, C4 interacts with teacher, C3 interacts with C1 and C2, robot shows emotion on display
09:39	Happy (C1, C3, C4, C7), neutral (C2, C5), fear (C8), surprise (C9)	The children argue among themselves in order to interpret the robot's expression; C1, C2, C3 and C4 interact with each other; C7 interacts with C8; robot moves and repeats the action
17:37	Happy (C1, C3), neutral (C4, C7, C8), sad (C2, C6), surprise (C5)	Researcher prepares the robot that initiates the movement action. Children do not interact with each other
18:08	Happy (C1, C2, C4, C5), neutral (C7), sad (C6), surprise (C3, C9)	Children watch the robot's action. C1 interacts with C2, C5 interacts with C6

The classified labels were calculated across the entire length of the video input, which alternates between the dynamics proposed for the workshop and excerpts for organization's and instructions. In the moments where interactions between the robot and the children occur, the feelings of surprise, happiness and fear appeared frequently, which can indicate excitement or curiosity about the activities involving the robot, as well as for the narrative and social interactions (Fig. 3). In moments of instruction, the feelings of happy, neutral and sad appeared, which reinforces that the interactions with the robot promoted feelings of curiosity and excitement in the children.

Although preliminary, the classification results indicate the relationship between the interactions proposed by the socioenactive system scenario and the emotional changes in the participants.

Fig. 3. Example of output from the automatic classification of emotions of a video excerpt from the workshop based on a socioenative system. We can perceive the feelings of joy and surprise identified after the interaction with the robot.

5   Conclusion

One of the main challenges in the construction of socioenactive systems involves inputs that enable the system to develop dynamic responses that foster social interactions applied to an educational environment. Facial expressions can indicate a child's emotional state during a social experience.

This work presented an analysis of affective expression changes within a scenario of children interacting with a robot within an educational context. For this analysis we based on automatic recognition of facial expressions in the wild, using some machine learning techniques. Although preliminary, the results indicate that the algorithm has a satisfactory accuracy of emotion recognition in the wild, pointing out emotional changes in non-controlled environments with low computational cost, using spatio-temporal characteristics. In addition, we can state at an early stage that the interactions of the robot with a group of children, positively influenced the emotional state of the participants, generating a fun learning experience.

Future work can deepen the analysis by comparing the changes in facial expressions with qualitative results made by researchers themselves using Ground Theory, to further investigate how the FER techniques could support the researchers analysis on data captured from children acting within a socioenactive scenario.

Acknowledgement. This work was financially supported by the São Paulo Research Foundation (FAPESP) (grants #2015/16528-0, #2015/24300-9 and #2019/12225-3), and CNPq (grant ##306272/2017-2). We thank the University of Campinas (UNICAMP) for making this research possible.

References

1. Kaipainen, M., et al.: Enactive systems and enactive media: embodied human-machine coupling beyond interfaces. Leonardo **44**(5), 433–438 (2011). https://doi.org/10.1162/LEONa00244
2. Baranauskas, M.C.C.: Socio-enactive systems: investigating new dimensions in the design of interaction mediated by information and communication technologies. FAPESP Thematic Research Project #2015/16528-0 (2015)
3. Gallagher, S.: Making enactivism even more embodied. Chapter 8 in Enactivist Interventions Rethinking the Mind. University Press, Oxford (2017)
4. Talipu, A., Generosi, A., Mengoni, M., Giraldi, L.: Evaluation of deep convolutional neural network architectures for emotion recognition in the wild. In: 2019 IEEE 23rd International Symposium on Consumer Technologies (ISCT), Ancona, Italy, 2019, pp. 25–27 (2019). https://doi.org/10.1109/isce.2019.8900994
5. Caceffo, R., et al.: Collaborative meaning construction in socioenactive systems: study with the *mBot*. In: Zaphiris, P., Ioannou, A. (eds.) HCII 2019. LNCS, vol. 11590, pp. 237–255. Springer, Cham (2019). https://doi.org/10.1007/978-3-030-21814-0_18
6. Rodríguez, A., González, P., Rossi, G.: Sketching for designing enactive interactions. In: Proceedings of the XV International Conference on Human Computer Interaction (Interacción '14). ACM, New York, NY, USA, Article 39, p. 2 (2014). https://doi.org/10.1145/2662253.2662292
7. Abascal, J., et al.: Personalizing the user interface for people with disabilities. In: Proceedings of the 23rd International Workshop on Personalization and Recommendation on the Web and Beyond (ABIS '19), p. 29. ACM, New York, NY, USA (2019). https://doi.org/10.1145/3345002.3349292
8. Namrata, S.: Using contactless sensors to estimate learning difficulty in digital learning environments. In: Adjunct Proceedings of the 2019 ACM International Joint Conference on Pervasive and Ubiquitous Computing and Proceedings of the 2019 ACM International Symposium on Wearable Computers (UbiComp/ISWC '19 Adjunct), pp. 399–403. ACM, New York, NY, USA (2019). https://doi.org/10.1145/3341162.3349312
9. Jansen, K.M.B.: How to shape the future of smart clothing. In: Adjunct Proceedings of the 2019 ACM International Joint Conference on Pervasive and Ubiquitous Computing and Proceedings of the 2019 ACM International Symposium on Wearable Computers (UbiComp/ISWC '19 Adjunct), pp. 1037–1039. ACM, New York, NY, USA (2019). https://doi.org/10.1145/3341162.3349571
10. Samira, E.K., et al.: Emonets: multimodal deep learning approaches for emotion recognition in video. J. Multimodal User Interfaces **10**(2), 99–111 (2016)
11. Kim, D.H., Baddar, W.J., Ro, Y.M.: Micro-expression recognition with expression-state constrained spatio-temporal feature representations. In: Proceedings of the 24th ACM international conference on Multimedia (MM '16), pp. 382–386. Association for Computing Machinery, New York, NY, USA (2016). https://doi.org/10.1145/2964284.2967247
12. Happy, S., Routray, A.: Automatic facial expression recognition using features of salient facial patches. IEEE Trans. Affect. Comput. **6**(1), 1–12 (2015)
13. Brennand, C.V.L.T., Brennand, C.A.R.L., Duarte, E.F., Baranauskas, M.C.C.: Evaluating the user experience in interactive installations: a case study. In: Proceedings of the 18th Brazilian Symposium on Human Factors in Computing Systems (IHC '19), pp. 1–10. Association for Computing Machinery, New York, NY, USA, Article 26 (2019). https://doi.org/10.1145/3357155.3358484

14. Luque Carbajal, M., Baranauskas, M.C.C.: Multimodal analysis of preschool children's embodied interaction with a tangible programming environment. In: Kurosu, M. (ed.) HCII 2020. LNCS, vol. 12182, pp. 443–462. Springer, Cham (2020). https://doi.org/10.1007/978-3-030-49062-1_30

15. Salunke, V.V., Patil, C.G.: A new approach for automatic face emotion recognition and classification based on deep networks. In: 2017 International Conference on Computing, Communication, Control and Automation (ICCUBEA), Pune 2017, pp. 1–5 (2017). https://doi.org/10.1109/iccubea.2017.8463785

16. Pons, G., Masip, D.: Multitask, multilabel, and multidomain learning with convolutional networks for emotion recognition. IEEE Trans. Cybern. https://doi.org/10.1109/tcyb.2020.3036935

17. Kabakus, A.T.: PyFER: a facial expression recognizer based on convolutional neural networks. IEEE Access **8**, 142243–142249 (2020). https://doi.org/10.1109/ACCESS.2020.3012703

18. Li, S., Deng, W.: Deep facial expression recognition: a survey. IEEE Trans. Affect. Comput. https://doi.org/10.1109/taffc.2020.2981446

19. Yan, W.-J., et al.: CASME II: an improved spontaneous micro-expression database and the baseline evaluation. PLoS ONE **9**(1), (2014)

20. Lundqvist, J.: The averaged Karolinska directed emotional faces - AKDEF. In: CD ROM from the Department of Clinical Neuroscience, Psychology Section (1998)

21. Liu, J., Wang, H., Feng, Y.: An end-to-end deep model with discriminative facial features for facial expression recognition. IEEE Access **9**, 12158–12166 (2021). https://doi.org/10.1109/ACCESS.2021.3051403

22. Elouariachi, I., Benouini, R., Zenkouar, K., Zarghili, A., El Fadili, H.: Explicit quaternion krawtchouk moment invariants for finger-spelling sign language recognition. In: 2020 28th European Signal Processing Conference (EUSIPCO), Amsterdam 2021, pp. 620–624 (2021). https://doi.org/10.23919/eusipco47968.2020.9287845

Affective Robot Learner: Implementation of Artificial Emotion System Inspired by Educational Psychology

Binnur Görer$^{(\boxtimes)}$ and H. Levent Akın

Department of Computer Engineering, Boğaziçi University, Istanbul, Turkey
{binnur.gorer,akin}@boun.edu.tr

Abstract. In this paper, we propose an affective robot learner system with artificial emotions. We define a generic teaching framework which has a planner for the phases of a regular teaching process. A single episode consists of interaction phase, teaching phase where the concepts are introduced to the robot by the human teacher, and testing phase where the learning performance of the robot is questioned by testing of the taught concepts. We frame the teaching process as a collaborative task between human and robot. In order to make the teaching process rewarding for the human teacher, we postulate to utilize academic emotions in our teaching framework. We base on educational psychology to generate education-related emotions in our computational emotion model. A simplified version of Control-Value Theory is implemented using fuzzy logic and presented within the framework. As an illustration of the framework, object teaching scenario is implemented on Nao robot, where a person can teach a number of daily used items to the robot.

Keywords: Teachable robots · Affective robotics · Robotic edutainment

1 Introduction

Robots have been used in the industry over for 20 years as powerful and fast machines. They can replace human power, indeed achieve much more. Although there are some ongoing studies to enhance the functional capabilities of such robots, the large part of the current interest is on developing robots which can operate with humans in home environments, in offices, and in factories. The idea of having a robot which operates nearby humans or with humans requires the researchers to investigate the problem of how humans accept the robots as an entity. Many studies in human-robot interaction focus on increasing the robot acceptability as a social being and enhancing the interaction between the subject and the robot. In the hardware part, this provided the generation of humanoid robots such as Asimo, Nao, and HOAP-2. However, the humanoid appearance has increased the expectation of users from the robot as to behave,

© Springer Nature Switzerland AG 2021
M. Kurosu (Ed.): HCII 2021, LNCS 12762, pp. 545–561, 2021.
https://doi.org/10.1007/978-3-030-78462-1_42

to respond and to operate like a human. Currently developed robotic systems perform well on rational tasks such as decision making and action selection in complex environments. On the other hand, they generally lack of enhanced social capabilities which have significant effects on cognitive processes of humans, which also affects how well humans accept the robots and collaborate with them.

Socially assistive robotics (SAR) mainly concerns the development of social robots which can teach, guide, or help their human interlocutors to achieve a task. Depending on the users' needs, the tasks may highly vary. Although the recent advances in machine learning improved accuracy in perception, we are still quite far away from a level of general artificial intelligence which can easily adapt to new tasks, new users, and new environments. Hence, socially assistive robots will need their human interlocutors to teach them a new ability while assisting them in other tasks which they can successfully perform. Although there is extensive literature which investigates the social aspects of assistive robots, there is relatively little work exploring the teachable robots, where the robot learns from human teachers, from human-robot interaction perspective.

The available studies show that the interaction aspects of teaching task between human (teacher) and robot (learner) play a significant role to improve the learning gain of the robot while keeping the human teacher willing and enjoyed for longer time periods. According to the literature in educational psychology, it is important to keep the teaching rewarding for the teacher to maximize the overall gain. One promising reward is that the efforts of the teacher really result in learning improvement of the learner. The teacher needs to recognize the improvement during the teaching interactions. However, congruence between the amount of provided teaching effort and the screened learning gain is also important. Neither the very fast learner nor very slow learner provide the desired reward for a teacher [15, 16]. In an artificially intelligent system, it is not always guaranteed that higher teaching effort will result in high learning performance. Hence we elaborate the teaching process itself from a different angle. We frame the "teaching" process as knowledge sharing between the human and the robot, for a domain where the user is expert and the robot is a newbie. We postulate that the robot may stimulate user to behave altruistically in order to get more help (to get more teaching efforts). In order to activate altruism in a person, one needs to explicitly express her situation with the ongoing task. We propose to utilize emotions to make the robot express its uneasiness or achievement in learning and to keep the human willing to help the robot with learning in order to alleviate the burden on the robot.

In this paper, we propose an affective robot learner system with artificial emotions. We define a generic teaching framework which consists of consecutive teaching and testing periods. We utilize educational psychology to generate education-related emotions in our computational emotion model. A simplified version of Control-Value Theory is implemented using fuzzy logic and presented within the framework. As an illustration of the framework, object teaching scenario is implemented on Nao robot, where a person can teach a number of daily used items to the robot.

In Sect. 2, the literature for teachable robots is discussed. Then, we present our methodology in Sect. 3.

2 Related Work

It is an important capability for social robots to ask and learn from naive users a new ability without putting too much cognitive and physical load on the user. Although there are many studies focused on learning a new task from humans following the emergence of learning from demonstration approach, analysis of this domain in terms of social interaction aspects is still relatively under-explored. Cakmak *et al.* have pioneer studies in teachable robots which investigate what kind of questions in which frequency should be asked by the robot in order to improve its learning process. They designed user experiments where each subject experienced each different condition and reported their preferences [2,3].

In [8], social and non social versions of a robot learner is tested with 38 participants where they are equally and randomly distributed between two conditions. The participant teaches animal classes through a tablet interface. In the social condition, the robot learner expresses its learning preference by fixating its gaze on a specific animal class shown on the tablet. This behavior increased the learning gain of the robot by mostly inducing the human teacher to shape its teaching according to the requests of the robot. In study of Pais *et al.*, the subjects are said to teach the robot manipulation of an object by directly controlling the hand of the robot [17]. The robot gives feedback to the subject about the situation of the demonstration success through three different feedback modalities; facial expression, verbal, and graphical user interface. In their between subject designed study, verbal feedback is preferred as the most intuitive modality for novice subjects. Their study also revealed that feedback provided by the robot removes the stress and burden on the human teacher as they can better predict the robot's learning state and shape their teaching accordingly.

In [4], the researchers investigate the impact of personalized interaction capabilities of a human companion robot on its social acceptance, perceived intelligence and likeability in a human-robot interaction scenario. The study uses an object teaching scenario where the user teaches different objects to the robot using natural language. The two systems, i.e. with and without the interaction module, are compared with respect to how different users rate the robot on its intelligence and sociability. The interaction module allows personalized conversation to engage the user before the teaching stage. Although the system equipped with personalized interaction capabilities is rated lower on social acceptance, it is perceived as more intelligent and likeable by the users.

Hayes *et al.* analyzed implicit human feedback to robot mistakes in a learning from demonstration scenario [9]. The subjects try to teach a number of dance movements to the robot by demonstration. After demonstration, the robot repeats the shown movements as much as it could learn in the face of the teacher subject. The researchers intentionally make the robot to perform incorrect movements in order to observe the subject's implicit feedback to the robot's mistakes.

They report valuable observations about nonverbal behaviors of the subjects during the experiments. They ask the subjects that "How do you perceive yourself as a good teacher?". Four participants said that they believe they are good teachers since they behave patiently during the interaction with the robot. Another four subjects responded negatively and stated that the failure of the robot was because of their own mistakes in demonstrations.

To the best of our knowledge, the only study which incorporates emotions in a teachable robot is [13]. They use a Keepon robot in their experiments where the task is teaching the robot a small set of very simple dance movements. At the end of each demonstration, the robot repeats the learned dance and receives a score. The given score is predetermined and independent of the robot's actual performance. According to the score, the robot says an utterance where the context is determined to convey the intended emotion. They utilized four different emotion groups, namely satisfaction, shame, happiness, and disappointment. The verbal utterances of the robot are prepared manually before the experiment. After the robot responds to its score, the user is asked to teach again or to continue with the next dance movement. The researchers tested the emotional robot versus non-emotional robot where the robot utterances do not convey any emotional content. In the emotional robot case, the subjects repeated the teaching demonstrations more compared to the non-emotional robot case. However, their study is not well grounded on educational psychology and the expressed emotions and the scenario itself are oversimplified. Our proposed framework is more complicated and generic with the emotional system inspired by educational psychology.

3   Methodology

3.1   Generic Teaching Framework

The process starts with the greetings of the robot. The robot briefly introduces itself and thanks for accepting to teach it. Then the robot approves it is ready for the teaching episode and requests the subject start teaching. The user is expected to teach the concepts one by one, in the given order. We denote this teaching period as *Phase 1*. During this time, the robot tracks the subject and performs a nodding gesture to communicate its interest. After teaching of all objects are completed, a supervised learning model is trained with the taught concepts. Once the training is completed, the subject is requested to start testing for if the robot has learned the concepts successfully. In the testing period, the subject presents a concept and waits for the prediction of the robot. Querying the previously trained supervised model, the robot notifies the prediction result to the subject. We denote this phase just before the outcome has occurred as *Phase 2_1*. The subject provides the truth value for the robot's prediction as true or false (and with the correct label). Then, the robot expresses its post-outcome emotional state. We denote this phase as *Phase 2_2*. Then, the robot prompts the subject to continue with the next concept to test. Once the testing period is completed, the robot asks the subject if s/he wants to continue teaching. If the subject approves, a new teaching episode starts. Otherwise, the robot thanks to the subject and the process ends up. The system flowchart is shown in Fig. 1.

3.2   Artificial Emotion System

In order to determine the emotion set to be used in the study, we utilized education psychology literature. According to the educational psychologists [12], the emotions emerged during a learning process belong to specific subset of emotions. Some basic emotions like fear and disgust are not very likely to occur during a learning process. In [6,11], the researchers observed students during a learning scenario, and analyzed the expressed affective states as well as their transition dynamics. They define the prominently observed emotions as boredom, engagement, confusion, frustration, delight, and surprise. Mello *et al.* trained a HMM (Hidden Markov Model) to find out the transition probabilities of affective states of the students in their experimental study [5]. In [18], a more complex model for achievement emotions, control-value theory, is presented. According to the control-value theory, the academic emotions arise from cognitive appraisals of control over the learning task and value in the learning activity. We select this theory to base the emotion model of the learner robot because of its following properties;

- situates the elicitation of emotion in education context and has empirical support in educational settings
- its inclusion of education related psychological processes like motivation, self-regulated learning

Control-value theory favors three dimensions; object focus, value, and control. Object focus differentiates between a learner's attention to an achievement outcome or learning activity itself. For the former, the emotion elicitation also depends whether the outcome has yet to happen (prospective outcome) or has already taken place (retrospective outcome). For example, a student can experience anxiety before the announcement of test results, while s/he can experience shame after a poor test score. The second dimension of control-value theory is how the learner values the objective. The third dimension, control stands for the learner's own control over the objective. A student who values learning activity positively may experience enjoyment if s/he feels control power over the activity. Similarly, s/he may experience frustration if s/he lost her/his control. The basic assumptions of control-value theory is shown in Table 1.

We used a simplified version of control-value theory for our learner robot's emotion model. The emotions of the robot to be expressed throughout the teaching process are determined according to this model. We hold the following assumptions for simplifications:

- Only pre and post outcome emotions are used.
- Learning activity is always positively valued. We assume that the robot learner has intrinsic motivation to learn, hence it values the learning activity positively. Affective states like anger and boredom are not experienced by our robot learner.

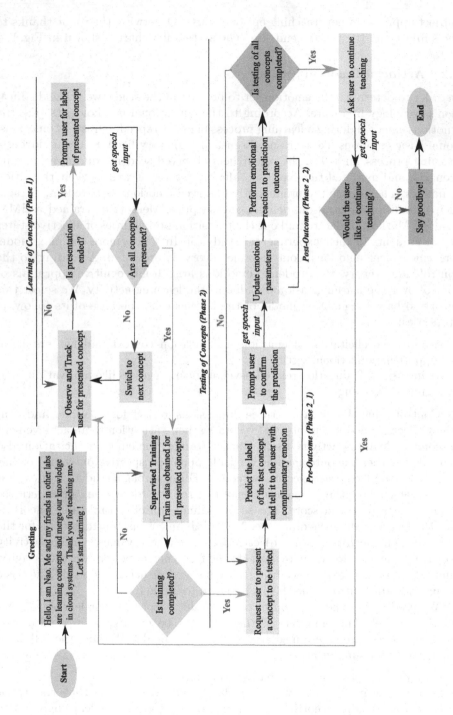

Fig. 1. Flowchart of the teaching framework.

Table 1. Basic assumptions on control, value, and emotions in control-value theory, adapted from [18]

Object focus	Appraisals		Emotion
	Value	Control	
Outcome/Prospective	Success	High	Anticipatory Joy
		Medium	Hope
		Low	Hopelessness
	Failure	High	Anticipatory Relief
		Medium	Anxiety
		Low	Hopelessness
Outcome/Retrospective	Success	Irrelevant	Joy
		Self	Pride
		Other	Gratitude
	Failure	Irrelevant	Sadness
		Self	Shame
		Other	Anger
Activity	Positive	High	Enjoyment
	Negative	High	Anger
	Positive/Negative	Low	Frustration
	None	High/Low	Boredom

- Although there is a shared control of learning activity between robot and human, we eliminate effect of other's control to determine robot's emotion as the robot's accusation of human for learning failures may be harmful for user's motivation.
- For the sake of simplicity, we decreased the control class into two as high and low.

Table 2 shows the simplified version of appraisal model.

Table 2. Simplified version of Control-Value Theory to determine our robot learner's affective state.

Object focus	Appraisals		
	Value	Control	Emotion
Outcome/Prospective	Success	High	Hope
		Low	Hopelessness
Outcome/Retrospective	Success	Irrelevant	Joy
	Failure	Irrelevant	Sadness

We represent joy and hope affective states in continuous domain, ranges from 0 to 1 (where hopeless is positioned at 0 and hopeful is at 1, similarly sad is positioned at 0 and joyful at 1). In order to determine the intensity level of hope and joy states, we used fuzzy logic inference. Fuzzy logic is based on the idea that the "trustiness" of something can be expressed over a continuous range. This is to say that something is not true or false but instead partially true or false. It differs from Boolean logic in the representation of inputs/outputs and application of inference rules.

We implemented two separate fuzzy models for hope and joy states. Hope is determined by the learning speed and overall learning performance of the robot. Overall learning performance at a time t is calculated as the mean of the prediction accuracy of each taught concept until this time. Learning speed is calculated as the difference in the last two prediction accuracy in order to capture immediate fluctuations in the learning performance. The membership functions for overall learning performance and learning speed are experimentally determined and shown in Fig. 2a. The output of the hope fuzzy model is shown in Fig. 2a. The inference rules of fuzzy model for hope are as follows:

- *Rule1:* If overall performance is low AND learning speed is low, THEN hope is low.
- *Rule2:* If overall performance is medium AND learning speed is low, THEN hope is medium.
- *Rule3:* If overall performance is medium AND learning speed is high, THEN hope is high.
- *Rule4:* If overall performance is high AND learning speed is high, THEN hope is high.

Similarly, joy level is determined with another fuzzy model that uses the last prediction accuracy and hope level as input. The last prediction accuracy is provided by the supervised model for the questioned concept in the testing phase. Output of the hope fuzzy model, which is the hope level, is given as input to the joy fuzzy system in order to satisfy coherence between hope and joy states. The same membership function for hope is used in the joy fuzzy system. The membership functions for the inputs, namely last prediction accuracy and hope level are shown in Fig. 2b. The inference rules of fuzzy model for joy are as follows:

- *Rule1:* If last prediction accuracy is highly not accurate AND hope is low or medium, THEN joy is low.
- *Rule2:* If last prediction accuracy is slightly not accurate AND hope is medium, THEN joy is medium.
- *Rule3:* If last prediction accuracy is highly accurate AND hope is low, THEN joy is medium.
- *Rule4:* If last prediction accuracy is highly accurate AND hope is medium, THEN joy is high.

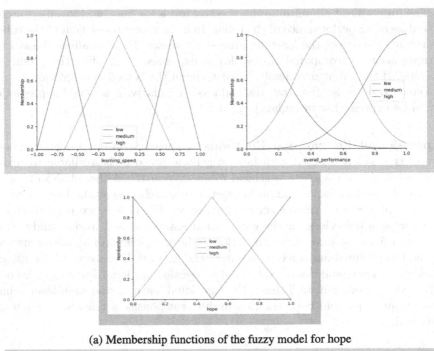

(a) Membership functions of the fuzzy model for hope

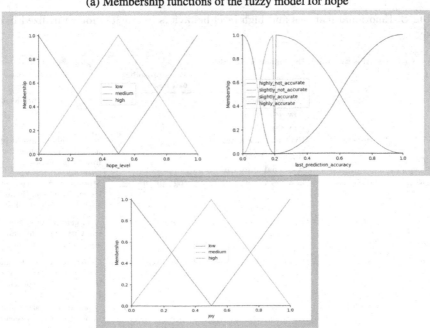

(b) Membership functions of the fuzzy model for joy

Fig. 2. Membership functions for fuzzy model inputs and outputs (inputs are shown in green frames and outputs are shown in orange frames) (Color figure online)

The fuzzy rules to determine the affective levels for hope and joy are centered around learning performance of the robot. In each wrong prediction of the robot, the robot's hope over the learning process decreases. Hope is affected less from learning accuracy compared to joy. Joy is expressed right after the prediction outcome. If the robot drastically failed to label the tested concept, joy level is expected to decrease (i.e. towards sadness). Similarly, a successful prediction should be expressed with higher joy.

Expression of Educational Emotions. Expression of emotions on robotic system is a widely studied area but no generic protocol is available to realize a given emotion on a given psychical robot system [1]. Although Nao robot is extensively used in social human-interaction research, the studied emotions are generally limited to Ekman's six basic emotions [7]. Hence, we need to configure expressive behaviors for the educational emotions used in our study. Since Nao robot does not have any actuator on its face, expression modalities are constrained to gestures and speech. We used the existing literature [10,14,20] and considered the capabilities of Nao robot to decide emotional features to be used in behavior generation. In Table 3, the emotional features and high level behaviors to express joy and hope emotion in different phases of teaching episode are described.

Table 3. Emotional features and high level behaviors for each emotion utilized in our study

Learning phase	Affective state	Expression modalities		High level behavior
		Gesture	Voice prosodic features	
Phase 1	Hopeless	Low movement activity Low acceleration Low spatial extensiveness	–	No special gesture head nodding open/close fingers no emotional speech
	Hopeful	High movement activity High acceleration High spatial extensiveness	–	No special gesture head nodding open/close fingers no emotional speech
Phase 2_1	Hopeless	Low movement activity Low acceleration Low spatial extensiveness	High pitch	Minimal arm movement gazing away emotional speech to indicate despair
	Hopeful	High movement activity High acceleration High spatial extensiveness	Low pitch	Arm gesture to side and front gazing to human, speech to indicate hope
Phase 2_2	Sad	Velocity, spatial extensiveness	Low pitch low speech rate	Close the face with hands close arm to the sides and lower the head speech to indicate sadness
	Joyful	Acceleration	High pitch high speech rate	Open arms to sides and upper the head speech to indicate joy

The robot tells its prediction for a tested concept with a nonverbal behavior configured for hope. As a pre-outcome emotion, hope expression is accompanied with a simple arm gesture shown in Fig. 3. The amplitude of the joints used in the gesture and the speed of the gesture are modulated regarding hope level.

Fig. 3. A sample gesture series for the expression of hope.

As the post-outcome emotion, joy is expressed after getting the true value of a tested concept. If the prediction of the robot aligns with the true value of the concept then joy level is positively affected. We discretize the joy level into five classes like sadness, slight-sadness, neutral, slight-joy, and extreme-joy with respective intervals $[0, 0.2]$, $[0.2, 0.4)$, $[0.4, 0.6)$, $[0.6, 0.8)$, $[0.8, 1]$. According to the joy level, the robot expresses one of the gestures of the corresponding class (see Fig. 4). Speech volume and pitch are also modulated as positively correlated with the level of joy. Higher blinking speed is employed for higher joy levels. The robot uses emotional speech with exclamation marks to notify learning outcome like "huh I predicted correctly!" or "super, that's correct" for joyful states and uses negative exclamation marks to emphasize sadness like "uf it is incorrect", "I can not learn it" etc.

Fig. 4. Hand crafted gestures for the expression of emotions in the joy dimension.

In phase 1, the emotion related features of the robot are modulated according to the hope level. There is no specific gesture or emotional speech in this phase.

However, regular gestures like open-close fingers and head nodding are performed in regulated movement speed and joint angle magnitudes by the level of hope.

4   Case Study

In this section we present a proof-of-concept application of our framework: teaching objects to the robot. We outline the implementation details and provide the results of simulated experiments.

4.1   Scenario

In order to illustrate the affective robot learner system, we selected object teaching as a case study. For SAR systems, it is vital to be adaptive to the continuously updated environments like a kitchen or a living room where the items can be replaced with their new ones or new items are added in. Supervised teaching of these items to the robot would be a more robust, fast, and convenient approach for a better human-robot collaboration.

The process starts with the greetings of the robot. The robot briefly introduces itself and thanks for accepting to teach it. Then the robot approves it is ready for the teaching episode and requests the subject start teaching. The user is expected to teach objects one by one, in the given order (see Fig. 5). During this time, the robot tracks the subject and performs a nodding gesture to communicate its interest. After teaching of all objects are completed, the subject is expected to start testing for if the robot has learned successfully. In the testing period, the subject shows an object and waits for the prediction of the robot. The user notifies the robot's prediction as true or false. The robot expresses its post-outcome emotional state. Then, the robot prompts the user to continue with the next object to be tested. Once the testing period is completed, the robot asks the subject if s/he wants to continue teaching. If the subject approves, a new teaching episode starts. Otherwise, the robot thanks to the subject and the process ends up.

A sample teaching process is recorded in https://youtu.be/bqg517hrYKI.

4.2   Implementation

Apparatus. A Kinect RGB-D sensor is used to track the participant. We do not use Nao's cameras as Nao needs to move its head (the cameras located in the head) during the interaction. This causes extra blur in the captured images in addition to the blur caused by the subject's movements. To record the subject's speech, we use a lapel microphone to get a clear and noise-free voice. Training process for supervised object learning task is executed on an Nvidia Jetson TX2 embedded AI computing device. It has an onboard GPU which allows deep neural networks operations for object learning. The devices communicate over ROS (Robot Operating System). The planner commands are sent to the Nao robot through its own Naoqi interface.

Fig. 5. Subject is teaching an object to the robot

System Components. The implementation of object teaching scenario in our generic teaching framework requires many different components to work in synchrony. They are depicted in Fig. 6. The modules drawn in blue are the modules run on Nao robot and the green ones run on a 2.6 GHz 8-core laptop and Nvidia Jetson.

– Eye blinking: In order to increase life-likeliness, we used LEDs on the eyes of Nao to create an eye blinking effect.
– Text to speech: The case study is prepared to be run in Turkish. Nao's builtin Turkish text to speech module is used to generate speech for the given text.
– Motion generator: For the stiffness and joint control, Nao's builtin motion proxy is used to control motor commands.
– Face tracking: Since the subject faces the robot, we used images captured through Nao's upper camera to decide if there is a face in the sight and where it is. We developed a smooth face tracking application which adjusts Nao's head angles to face the subject.

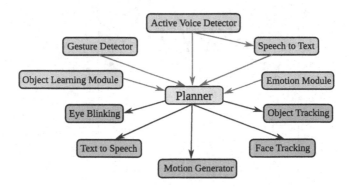

Fig. 6. System modules.

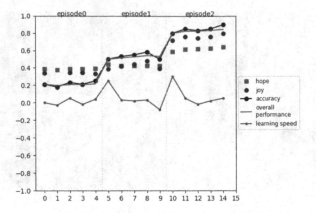

(a) Increasing learning accuracies across episodes.

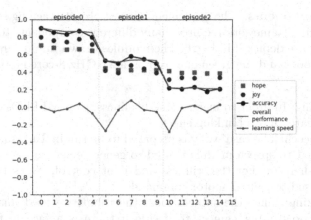

(b) Decreasing learning accuracies across episodes.

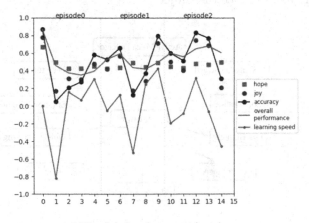

(c) Random learning accuracies.

Fig. 7. Fuzzy system simulations for different learning accuracy trends.

- Object tracking: The position of the object presented by the subject is determined by the gesture detector module. A tracking application, which is similar to face tracking, is developed to track the object in the scene of the robot. Intelligent switching between face and object tracking is controlled by the core planner.
- Voice Detector and Speech to Text: Turkish speech to text applications are very limited and not free. Among them, the state of the art is Google's speech to text[1] application. We use Google's speech to text API to get text from a given speech file. Since this is a paid service, we minimize the API request by filtering out the valid utterances only. For this operation, we use an open source active voice detector module[2] which detects when a speech starts and stops. The planner only processes speech inputs with Google's speech to text API when the robot requires the subject to speak, for example after asking the name of the presented object during the training phase.
- Object Learning Module: The object learning module is implemented on Nvidia Jetson board. We used inception v2 deep CNN [19] to extract features to be used for object learning. We used an optimized version of this network for Jetson architecture to decrease the execution time[3]. We take the values just before the logits layer of the network which constitutes 1024 dimensional feature vector for each given image. This feature vector is fed to SVM with RBF kernel and default penalty parameter.

4.3   Simulation Experiments

We simulated the fuzzy models for joy and hope with different learning performance patterns and visualized the results in Fig. 7. We take the number of objects to be taught as five (which shapes the membership function of learning accuracy around 0.2 as a random chance point). The simulation is performed for an experiment where three consecutive teaching episodes are performed. For the improved learning accuracies case across the episodes, both hope and joy level increases. However, joy level is more reactive to the last prediction accuracy, as defined with the inference rules. Similarly, if the robot's learning accuracies get worse, the elicited emotions by the robot converge to hopelessness and sadness. We also provide a case with random learning accuracies.

5   Conclusion

In this paper, we presented an affective robot learner system. We provided a generic teaching framework with an artificial emotion system which can be adjustable to any teaching scenario. Control value theory based academic emotions are employed in fuzzy logic based computational models. Although the

---

[1] https://cloud.google.com/speech-to-text/.

[2] https://github.com/amsehili/auditok.

[3] https://github.com/NVIDIA-AI-IOT/tf_trt_models.

parameters of the model are determined empirically, the proposed approach constitutes a novel design for human robot interaction in teachable robots domain.

To illustrate the system, we select object teaching scenario. We implemented the overall system on Nao robot with detailed component description. Simulated results are provided as well to give a basic idea about how emotional model responds to different learning patterns.

We can think of several improvements to our approach. We plan to perform a controlled human-robot interaction study (affective vs non-affective robot learner) to analyze the effect of academic emotions on human teacher's persistence in the teaching process. We would like to address two research questions by this study a)Does the emotional robot learner have an effect on the human teacher to increase the quantity and quality of the provided teaching data? b)Does the emotional robot keep the human teacher engaged and enjoyed over longer teaching periods?

The next step would be enhancing emotional models with larger set of inputs. Though the proposed system does not take human teacher related signals (like the emotional state of human teacher or quality of teaching effort) as an input to the emotional system, fuzzy logic based implementation allows to easily integrate any other inputs and thus making it adaptive to the human teacher. Teacher adaptive system may increase the rewarding impact of academic emotions represented by the robot.

References

1. Bethel, C.L., Murphy, R.R.: Survey of non-facial/non-verbal affective expressions for appearance-constrained robots. IEEE Trans. Syst. Man Cybern. Part C Appl. Rev. **38**(1), 83–92 (2007)
2. Cakmak, M., Chao, C., Thomaz, A.L.: Designing interactions for robot active learners. IEEE Trans. Auton. Ment. Dev. **2**(2), 108–118 (2010)
3. Cakmak, M., Thomaz, A.L.: Designing robot learners that ask good questions. In: Proceedings of the Seventh Annual ACM/IEEE International Conference on Human-Robot Interaction, pp. 17–24. ACM (2012)
4. Churamani, N., et al.: The impact of personalisation on human-robot interaction in learning scenarios. In: Proceedings of the 5th International Conference on Human Agent Interaction, pp. 171–180. ACM (2017)
5. D'Mello, S., Graesser, A.: Modeling cognitive-affective dynamics with Hidden Markov Models. In: Proceedings of the Annual Meeting of the Cognitive Science Society (2010)
6. D'Mello, S., Graesser, A.: Dynamics of affective states during complex learning. Learn. Instr. **22**(2), 145–157 (2012)
7. Ekman, P.: Expression and the nature of emotion. Approaches Emot. **3**(19), 344 (1984)
8. de Greeff, J., Belpaeme, T.: Why robots should be social: enhancing machine learning through social human-robot interaction. PLoS ONE **10**(9) (2015)
9. Hayes, C.J., Moosaei, M., Riek, L.D.: Exploring implicit human responses to robot mistakes in a learning from demonstration task. In: 2016 25th IEEE International Symposium on Robot and Human Interactive Communication (RO-MAN), pp. 246–252. IEEE (2016)

10. Juslin, P.N., Laukka, P.: Communication of emotions in vocal expression and music performance: different channels, same code? Psychol. Bull. **129**(5), 770 (2003)
11. Lehman, B., Matthews, M., D'Mello, S., Person, N.: What are you feeling? Investigating student affective states during expert human tutoring sessions. In: Woolf, B.P., Aïmeur, E., Nkambou, R., Lajoie, S. (eds.) ITS 2008. LNCS, vol. 5091, pp. 50–59. Springer, Heidelberg (2008). https://doi.org/10.1007/978-3-540-69132-7_10
12. Lehman, B.A., Zapata-Rivera, D.: Student emotions in conversation-based assessments. IEEE Trans. Learn. Technol. **11**(1), 41–53 (2018)
13. Leyzberg, D., Avrunin, E., Liu, J., Scassellati, B.: Robots that express emotion elicit better human teaching. In: Proceedings of the 6th International Conference on Human-Robot Interaction, pp. 347–354. ACM (2011)
14. Lim, A., Ogata, T., Okuno, H.G.: Converting emotional voice to motion for robot telepresence. In: 2011 11th IEEE-RAS International Conference on Humanoid Robots (Humanoids), pp. 472–479. IEEE (2011)
15. Lubold, N., Walker, E., Pon-Barry, H., Flores, Y., Ogan, A.: Using iterative design to create efficacy-building social experiences with a teachable robot. In: Proceedings of the International Conference for the Learning Sciences (ICLS 2018) (2018)
16. Matsuzoe, S., Tanaka, F.: How smartly should robots behave?: comparative investigation on the learning ability of a care-receiving robot. In: 2012 IEEE RO-MAN, pp. 339–344. IEEE (2012)
17. Pais, A.L., Argall, B.D., Billard, A.G.: Assessing interaction dynamics in the context of robot programming by demonstration. Int. J. Soc. Robot. **5**(4), 477–490 (2013)
18. Pekrun, R., Frenzel, A.C., Goetz, T., Perry, R.P.: The control-value theory of achievement emotions: an integrative approach to emotions in education. In: Emotion in Education, pp. 13–36. Elsevier (2007)
19. Szegedy, C., Vanhoucke, V., Ioffe, S., Shlens, J., Wojna, Z.: Rethinking the inception architecture for computer vision. In: Proceedings of the IEEE Conference on Computer Vision and Pattern Recognition, pp. 2818–2826 (2016)
20. Wallbott, H.G.: Bodily expression of emotion. Eur. J. Soc. Psychol. **28**(6), 879–896 (1998)

Effect of Shifting Own Hand Position in Virtual Space on Mental Body Model

Hikari Kobayashi[1(✉)], Miki Matsumuro[2], Fumihisa Shibata[2], and Asako Kimura[2]

[1] Graduate School of Information Science and Engineering, Ritsumeikan University, Kusatsu, Japan
kobayasi@rm2c.ise.ritsumei.ac.jp
[2] College of Information Science and Engineering, Ritsumeikan University, 1-1-1 Noji-Higashi, Kusatsu, Shiga 525-8577, Japan

Abstract. People have knowledge and images of their bodies called the mental body model. Several studies have revealed that the mental body model is changed based on visuo-tactile information, which changes behavior. Virtual reality (VR) and Augmented Reality (AR) technologies have attracted significant attention in various fields. Here, one may identify with a virtual avatar that has a different structure than one's actual body, or one's own body may be displayed differently from the actual position. Such visual changes in a body may affect the mental body model. This paper investigates whether and what extent we could change it by manipulating the visual position of the body parts in virtual space. We answered the following two research questions by analyzing the behavioral changes of the participants. One was whether visual or proprioceptive information was more weighted to determine the movement of the body. Another was whether the participant's movement in the target action changed after they completed a task by observing their bodies at different positions than at the actual position. The results showed that people relied on visual information more than proprioceptive information for determining body movement, and larger visual image of position changes led to a larger change in latter behaviors. This study revealed the possibility that the mental body model can be changed by controlling a visual image of the body.

Keywords: Mental body model · Virtual reality · Multimodality

1 Introduction

People have knowledge and image of their bodies called the mental body model, which includes information about one's body, such as where their limbs are, what the color of their bodies are, and how much their limbs weigh. With this model, we can recognize our body states, even though our eyes are closed. By integrating mainly visual and proprioceptive information, a mental body model is updated through action and even when we do nothing [1]. This process sometimes constructs a model that is different from the actual body. Rubber Hand Illusion is an example of such an incorrect update of the body model, where the synchronous visuo-tactile stimulation makes participants feel

© Springer Nature Switzerland AG 2021
M. Kurosu (Ed.): HCII 2021, LNCS 12762, pp. 562–570, 2021.
https://doi.org/10.1007/978-3-030-78462-1_43

the rubber hand as a part of their body [2]. The distorted body model would affect their behavior because people usually decide their actions based on the relationship between the external world and the mental body model [3]. In some cases, it leads to their limb hitting something and fail to grab something.

In some virtual environments, users must change their mental body model. For example, one may identify with a virtual avatar that has a different structure than one's actual body, or one's own body may be displayed differently from the actual position [4, 5]. In many cases, users use their bodies to operate such an avatar or own body in virtual reality (VR). Thus, it is essential to adapt the mental body model to the avatar or body in VR to move them quickly and accurately. Using the operator's mental body model for his/her actual body may cause unexpected problems. For example, when your arm is elongated in the virtual space, if you swing your arm as usual, your virtual arm will then hit the unintended objects in the virtual space.

In this study, we focused on the position of body parts in the mental body model and explored whether and to what extent we could change it by manipulating the displayed position of the body parts in virtual space. We answered the following two research questions by analyzing the participant's behavioral changes. One was whether visual or proprioceptive information was more weighted to determine the body movement. Another was whether the participant's movement in the target action changed after they completed a task by observing their bodies at different positions than at the actual position.

2 Experiment

2.1 Experimental Settings

Figure 1 shows an experimental setup. We used a head-mounted display (HMD; HM-A1, Canon, Tokyo, Japan) to present a visual stimulus to the participants.

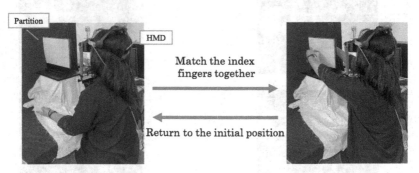

Fig. 1. Procedure of fingers touching task.

In the experiment, the participants touched their left and right fingers together at the front partition to stay at the same height (Fig. 1). Their right hand and left hand were displayed in the right half area and left half area of the participant's view from the camera on the HMD, respectively.

HMD consists of two cameras, each placed at the position of the left and right eyes. In this experiment, we used only the images acquired by one of the two cameras. The image to be used was randomly decided for each participant. We shifted the left half of the acquired image down and the right half up. We defined 0% of the shift amount as when we did not shift the image at all, and 100% as when the acquired image was displayed out of the HMD (Fig. 2). We used five levels of shift (0%, 5%, 10%, 15%, and 20%; Fig. 3).

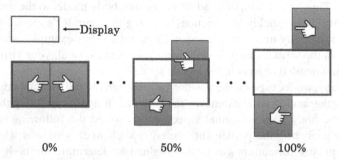

Fig. 2. Shift amount and display size.

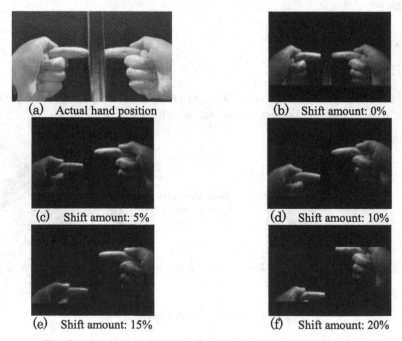

(a)   Actual hand position   (b)   Shift amount: 0%

(c)   Shift amount: 5%   (d)   Shift amount: 10%

(e)   Shift amount: 15%   (f)   Shift amount: 20%

Fig. 3. Fingers in real and displayed fingers in each shift amount.

2.2 Participants

Three males and nine females participated in this experiment. All participants had normal or corrected-to-normal vision ($M = 22$ years old, $SD = \pm0.426$). Nine participants were right-eye dominant and three participants were left-eye dominant.

2.3 Procedure

Each condition consists of three phases: pre-test, post-test, and training between them. In all phases, participants touched their left and right index fingers together at the front partition to stay at the same height as shown in Fig. 1. We recorded the positions of their left and right fingers when their fingers touched the partition.

Before the pre-test, the participants touched their left and right index fingers together at the front partition twice. In this phase, they did not wear the HMD and observed their hands carefully to align their index finger at the same height. This was conducted to cancel the effect of the preceding condition on the mental body model.

Then, the participants wore the HMD and touched their left and right index fingers together at the front partition with nothing displayed on the HMD. They were asked to move their hands based on their mental body model. This means the pre-test, measuring the baseline behavior before the training. The participants repeated this task three times.

After the pre-test, the participants touched their left and right index fingers together at the front partition while observing an image shifted with one of the shift amounts via the HMD as the training. They were not told that the images were shifted. We instructed them to move their fingers depending on their vision and proprioceptive information. We conducted this task five times.

Finally, the participants touched their left and right index fingers together at the front partition with nothing displayed on the HMD as in the pre-test. This indicates the post-test, measuring the behavioral change from the pre-test. The participants repeated this task three times.

The above procedure was conducted once for each shift amount. We randomized the order of five conditions for each participant. To reduce the effects of the preceding condition and physical fatigue, we gave five-minute rest between conditions. After completing all conditions, the participants commented on how accurately they could move their hands and whether they noticed the shifts in the images.

2.4 Evaluation

In this experiment, we analyzed the vertical difference between the left and right fingers calculated by subtracting the vertical position of the right finger from that of the left finger. The horizontal difference was not considered because we manipulated the image only in the vertical direction. The value of the vertical difference indicates how far the fingers are placed to each other. It was a negative value when the right hand was positioned higher than the left hand and a positive value when the left hand was positioned higher than the right hand. The vertical differences were averaged over in each pre-test, training, and post-test phase.

2.5 Results

The acquired data showed the same pattern regardless of the used camera and the dominant eye. Thus, we excluded those factors in the following analyses.

Training. Figure 4 shows the vertical difference in the training phase. In all conditions, the data distribution satisfied the normality assumption; all p-values in Shapiro-Wilk tests were larger than 0.200. ANOVA revealed a significant main effect of shift amount ($F_{(4,44)} = 222.387, p < .001$). Multiple comparisons with Bonferroni correction showed significant differences between all pairs (all $p < .010$). The vertical differences became larger as the shift amount increased.

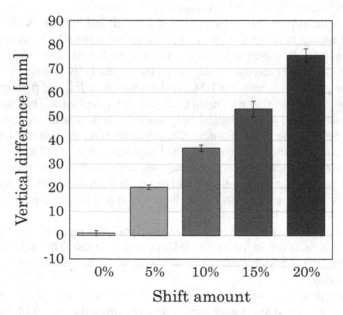

Fig. 4. Vertical difference in training phase.

Most participants moved their fingers to where their fingers matched each other in the manipulated image in the shift amounts. Only a few participants felt something strange in 15% and 20% conditions and tried moving their hands based on the proprioceptive. However, none of them could match their fingers at the same height in the shift amounts, except for the 0% condition. After the experiment, most participants answered that they did not notice the shifts in the images.

Change from Pre-test to Post-test. We calculated the change in the vertical difference from the pre-test to the post-test. Using this change, we analyzed how participant's behaviors changed through the task where they observed their bodies at different positions from the actual position. The change of the vertical difference was defined as the signed difference calculated by subtracting the vertical difference in the pre-test from that in the post-test.

Figure 5 shows the change of the vertical difference for each condition. In some conditions, the data distribution did not satisfy the normality assumption; Shapiro-Wilk tests showed almost significance ($p \leq .05$). We compared the change of the vertical difference among conditions using the Friedman test. There was a high significant effect of the shift amount (x^2 (4) $= 34.929, p < .001$). We performed multiple comparisons using the Wilcoxon signed-rank test with Holm's method to adjust the p-value. The change in 15% and 20% conditions was significantly larger than in 0% condition (both $p = .025$) and the change in 20% condition was significantly larger than that in 10% condition ($p = .031$). The differences between 0% and 5% conditions and between 0% and 10% conditions were marginally significant (both $p = .065$). There was a marginally significant difference between 5% and 20% conditions ($p = .053$), 15% and 20% conditions ($p = .076$), and 10% and 15% conditions ($p = .067$). In short, except for 5% and 10% condition, and 5% and 15% condition, the differences in all pairs were (marginally) significant.

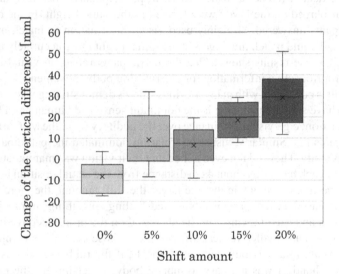

Fig. 5. Change of vertical difference from the pre-test to the post-test.

The vertical differences became bigger in the post-test in the shifted conditions (5%, 10%, 15%, and 20%) than in the baseline condition (0%), which was (marginally) significant. This result indicates that the participants started moving their hand higher through the training task where their hand had been displayed lower and vice versa. After the experiment, most participants answered that they could align their fingers at the same height more accurately in the post-test than in the pre-test.

3   Discussion

In this study, we investigated the effects of manipulating the body part's visual position on the mental body model based on behavioral changes. We had the following two research questions. One was whether visual or proprioceptive information was more weighted to determine the body movement. Another was whether the participant's movement changed after they completed the task by observing their bodies at different positions than the actual position.

3.1 Dominance of Visual Information

We analyzed the vertical difference in training to answer the first question: whether visual or proprioceptive information was more weighted to determine the body movement. If visual information is more weighted, the vertical difference would increase as the visual position of the hand shifted larger. However, if proprioceptive information is more weighted, the vertical difference would be constant regardless of the visual shift of the hand.

The experimental results showed that as the visual position of the hand was shifted largely, the vertical difference also increased. The participants moved their fingers so that the fingers displayed on the HMD were located at the same height. In the experiment, most participants answered, "I mainly used visual information to match my fingers." and "I felt that I could match my fingers at the same height more accurately using visual information." These results showed that the participants relied on visual information more than proprioceptive information for determining body movement.

This result is consistent with many previous studies demonstrating visual dominance. Researchers have shown that vision is the dominant sense and human has a bias toward visual information; e.g., visual dominance over the auditory (e.g., the McGurk effect [6]) and over haptics [7]. Similarly, visual information dominated the participants' performance in this study. They did not even notice that their vision was manipulated although the position of each hand was about 4 cm distance from the actual position in maximum.

In our experiment, we obtain that the larger the shift amount, the more the vertical difference increased. A few participants started feeling something strange in 15% and 20% conditions and tried moving their hands based on the proprioceptive information. As a result, they had smaller vertical differences in those conditions compared to the other participants. In a previous study on the RHI, if the rubber hand was placed too far from one's hand, it was not easy to induce body ownership for the rubber hand, resulting in that drift could have not occurred [8]. It means that the vertical difference could not increase or could decrease if the shift amount is greater than 20%; although we were not able to test more than 20% because of the limitation of our HMD. We need further investigations about when most participants realize the gap between the visual and proprioceptive information and rely on the proprioceptive information.

3.2 Change of Body Mental Model

By comparing the vertical difference in the post-test with that in the pre-test, we answered the second question: whether the participant's movement changed after they completed a task by observing their bodies at different positions than at the actual position. In the experiment, after they observed their hands in a higher (or lower) position than the actual, the participants started moving their fingers to a lower (or higher) position than they did before the observation. This result suggests that the hand position in the mental body model has been modified upward (or downward) by experiencing the task with visually manipulated hand position. The vertical difference could have increased because they used such a modified mental body model to estimate the hand position in the post-test where visual information was not available.

The effect of the training task with the distorted vision was strong, which could change the behavior in the dynamic task. Most previous studies used subjective position measurements of the manipulated body part without moving it after the task that corresponds to the training of this study [2, 9, 10]. When the body moved, we can acquire various and plenty proprioceptive information that might lead us to easily estimate the correct body posture. If the body mental model modification is not robust, it could not affect the post-test task behavior. The robust modification was also shown from that we observed the change in the vertical difference in all three trials in the post-test.

There were two possible reasons why such robust modification occurred. First, the participants moved both hands relatively comparing those positions, while most of the previous studies focused on a single body part. This task could permit the participants to modify their mental models by integrating relative positional information, which convinced them that the modified mental body model was correct.

The second reason was that the proposed method could keep the participants' body ownership sufficiently high. In previous studies, researchers used a fake or virtual body and only when the participants felt it was a part of their body, the drift occurred. This method was adopted because they were interested in the body ownership itself. However, inducing the body ownership was out of our interest, and we used the real-time video image of the participants' real hands (Fig. 3). Previous studies have emphasized that the reality and synchronized movement with the participants' hands were essential in increasing the body ownership of an object [4, 11, 12]. Thus, the participants had strong ownership toward the displayed hand from the beginning of the training phase and could change their mental body model robustly after five trials.

One limitation of the experiment was that our task was almost identical in all phases. It leads to the possibility that the participants learned the movement in the training phase and replicated it in the post-test. The comments after the experiment suggested that the participants did not replicate the movement in the training phase in the post-test but rather moved their fingers using their mental body model. If the participants replicated the movement in the training phase, the vertical difference in the post-test must be larger. In future work, we must use other tasks in the training phase or for the pre-tests and post-tests to confirm this point.

4 Conclusion

In this study, we focused on the position of body parts in the mental body model and explored whether and what extent we could change it by manipulating the displayed position of body parts. We answered the following two research questions by analyzing the participants' behavioral changes. One was whether visual or proprioceptive information was more weighted to determine the body movement. Another was whether the participant's movement in the target action changed after they completed a task by observing their bodies at different positions than at the actual position. We confirmed that participants relied on visual information more than proprioceptive information to determine body movement. After performing the task with hand movements, relying on distorted visual information, their behavior changed even without visual information. Such change increases as the distortion in the training task increases. This study showed that we can easily and robustly modify the mental body model through the dynamic task with both hands' movement under the distorted vision.

References

1. Carruthers, G.: Types of body representation and the sense of embodiment. Conscious. Cogn. **17**(4), 1302–1316 (2008)
2. Botvinick, M., Cohen, J.: Rubber hands 'feel' touch that eyes see. Nature **391**(6669), 756 (1998)
3. Warren, W.H.: Perceiving affordance: visual guidance of stair climbing. J. Exp. Psychol. Hum. Percept. Perform. **10**(5), 683–703 (1984)
4. Hoyet, L., Argelaguet, F., Nicole, C., Lecuyer, A.: Wow! I have six fingers!: Would you accept structural changes of your hand in VR? Front. Robot. AI **3**(27), 1–12 (2016)
5. Kasahara, S., et al.: Malleable embodiment: changing sense of embodiment by spatial-temporal deformation of virtual human body. In: CHI 2017 Proceeding of the 2017 CHI Conference on Human Factors in Computing Systems, pp. 6438–6448. Association for Computing Machinery, United States (2017)
6. McGurk, H., MacDonald, J.: Hearing lips and seeing voices. Nature **264**(5588), 746–748 (1976)
7. Ernst, M.O., Banks, M.S.: Humans integrate visual and haptic information in a statistically optimal fashion. Nature **415**(6870), 429–433 (2002)
8. Lloyd, D.M.: Spatial limits on referred touch to an alien limb may reflect boundaries of visuo-tactile peripersonal space surrounding the hand. Brain Cogn. **64**(1), 104–109 (2007)
9. Slater, M., Perez-Marcos, D., Ehrsson, H.H., Sanchez-Vives, M.V.: Towards a digital body: the virtual arm illusion. Front. Hum. Neurosci. **2**(6), 1–8 (2008)
10. Slater, M., Perez-Marcos, D., Ehrsson, H.H., Sanchez-Vives, M.V.: Inducing illusory ownership of a virtual body. Front. Neurosci. **3**(2), 214–220 (2009)
11. Ogawa, N., Narumi, T., Hirose, M.: Virtual hand realism affects object size perception in body-based scaling. In: 2019 IEEE Conference on Virtual Reality and 3D User Interfaces (VR), pp. 519–528. IEEE, Japan (2019)
12. Lin, L., Jörg, S.: Need a hand? How appearance affects the virtual hand illusion. In: Proceedings of the ACM Symposium on Applied Perception, pp. 69–76. Association for Computing Machinery, Anaheim California (2016)

Rehabilitation Aims and Assessed Brain Activity by Means of Brain-Computer Interfaces in People in a Vegetative State - Preliminary Results

Marian-Silviu Poboroniuc[1]([✉]), Dănuț-Constantin Irimia[1,2], and Gheorghe Popescu[3]

[1] Faculty of Electrical Engineering, "Gheorghe Asachi" Technical University of Iasi, Iași, Romania
mpobor@tuiasi.ro
[2] g.tec Medical Engineering GmbH, Schiedlberg, Austria
[3] Hyperbaric Medicine Clinic, Targu Mures, Romania

Abstract. Many patients who suffered a stroke, spinal cord injury, traumatic head injury etc. require long rehabilitative exercises to recover from their motor deficit. A special category of patients is the one that experience a vegetative state and need to be carefully monitored for changes or signs of improvement. In fact, there is no real treatment for this category of patients. The specialists from the Hyperbaric Medicine Clinic of Targu Mures, investigate an intensive rehabilitation method that might help to regain consciousness of a fraction number of persons in vegetative state. A tandem of hyperbaric oxygen therapy - intensive physiotherapy is under investigation. An EEG monitoring system has been used to detect any signs of consciousness in three patients diagnosed in vegetative state. Only one patient has shown some signs of consciousness while asked to perform motor imagery tasks.

Keywords: Vegetative state · Disorders of consciousness · Brain injury · Brain-computer interface · Aggressive rehabilitation

1 Introduction

1.1 Facts on Disorders of Consciousness

While, consciousness is defined as a state of being awake and aware of the surrounding environment, severe injuries to the brain are leading to so-called Disorders of Consciousness (DOC). In terms of brain injury, we may discuss about traumatic brain injury (e.g. fall from a high level building, a car accident), non-traumatic brain injury (e.g. related to a stroke) or a progressive brain damage (e.g. Alzheimer's disease). Intensive tests are required to assess the level of wakefulness and awareness in DOC people. Usually, the DOC patients falls in three categories: coma patients, patients in unresponsive wakefulness (UWS) and minimally conscious state (MCS) patients [1]. A coma patient shows no signs of being awake nor being aware. He/she lies with their eye closed and doesn't respond to any environmental stimulus, including pain. Patients in unresponsive

© Springer Nature Switzerland AG 2021
M. Kurosu (Ed.): HCII 2021, LNCS 12762, pp. 571–581, 2021.
https://doi.org/10.1007/978-3-030-78462-1_44

wakefulness state (UWS), sometimes called also vegetative state, open their eyes, regularly may wake up and fall asleep, present some basic reflexes (e.g. blinking the eyes), but doesn't show any meaningful responses. Finally, after being in a coma or UWS a patient may enter a minimally conscious state (MCS), meaning that he/she shows minimal or inconsistent awareness, and may have periods where he/she can respond to some commands (e.g. initiating a finger movement). Some behavioral tests to assess DOC patients are: Glasgow Coma Scale, Coma Recovery Scale-Revised, Rancho Los Amigos Revised Scale (RLAS-R) [2], but the correct diagnosis of DOC patients still remain a great challenge and misclassifications can often occur.

Among the methods to assess DOC patients one can find the neuroimaging methods: positron emission tomography (PET), functional magnetic resonance imaging (fMRI), electroencephalography (EEG), transcranial magnetic stimulation coupled with EEG (TMS-EEG), etc. [3, 4]. Each of them presents a number of advantages or disadvantages (e.g. cost, spatial or temporal resolution, accessibility). Newly, some new techniques aim to broaden the easiness in provide a diagnosis, with enhanced portability and performance. For example, a non-invasive technique of optical neuroimaging fNIRS (functional near-infrared spectroscopy) alone, or combined with EEG, provide moderate spatial and temporal resolution of brain data via a portable device [5]. The assessment and possible communication for people with DOC has been further investigated with equipment comprising brain-computer interfaces, audio and vibrotactile devices [1, 6]. The implemented paradigms mostly aim to deal with MCS patients to assess conscious awareness and even provide communication. The entire assessment might be performed with different paradigms (BCI-audio, BCI-vibrotactile) while there is a variability in performance among users experiencing one or another set-up. Other authors [7], propose a standardized approach, so-called perturbational complexity index (PCI), as a complementary evaluation. It is obtained from the electroencephalographic responses to transcranial magnetic stimulation, and it is claimed to allow a sensitivity of more than 94% in detecting MCS patients and subgroups of UWS patients with a clear option for consciousness not expressed in behavior.

An important issue related to comatose patients is their rehabilitation process which might be started early after the brain injury, and continued as long as they experience coma, vegetative state and of course during the time they might show wakefulness and awareness [8, 9]. It has to be adapted to each category of patients (coma, UWS, MCS). Supportive treatment (e.g. nutrition through a feeding tube, some exercises to their joints, cleaning the skin, regular change in position to not allow the development of pressure ulcers etc.) can't ensure recovery from a state of impaired consciousness but may contribute to improve chances of natural improvement. People experiencing a spinal cord injury and other neurological disorders are often involved in a so-called program of aggressive physical rehabilitation [10, 11]. Under specialized supervision it is of great interest to involve UWS and MCS patients in such a patient tailored aggressive rehabilitation programs. However, there are not so many investigation methods to show in real time if something is happening at the patient's brain level during the aggressive rehabilitative process.

This paper deals with the results of EEG monitoring of a limited number of patients, diagnosed to be in a vegetative state, while performing an aggressive rehabilitation program, expecting to find the seeds for a behavior which might move any of the monitored patients towards a minimal consciousness state classification.

2 Proposed Rehabilitation Program for Patients in a Vegetative State

The Hyperbaric Medicine Clinic (HMC) of Targu Mures currently deals with a number of classical procedures involved in neuromotor rehabilitation which are done in tandem with hyperbaric oxygen therapy (HBOT). HBOT encourage the formation of new connective tissue and new skin cells. It is well understood that a function (e.g. orthostatism, walking, grasping, speaking) cannot be recovered as long as the organic systems, which generate the respective functions, are severely affected (e.g. brain, spinal cord, nerves, muscles, skeleton). Therefore, first of all, there is the problem of improving their functioning. The central nervous system occupies a special place, of maximum importance, being also the most sensitive system to the lack of oxygen. Large populations of neurons that have not completely degraded but have lost their ability to manifest actively, can be restored to normal functioning through this tandem as hyperbaric oxygen therapy - intensive physiotherapy. The hyperbaric oxygen therapy is performed once a day for three hours, and entirely it counts from 15 to 20 days. The pressure chamber system is a Haus Starmed 2200 type (50 m diving depth/5.0 bar pressure) and accounts for a maximum number of 12 occupants plus a supervising person. In order to account for an aggressive rehabilitation program, the physiotherapy sessions last for two hours and are performed once or twice a day.

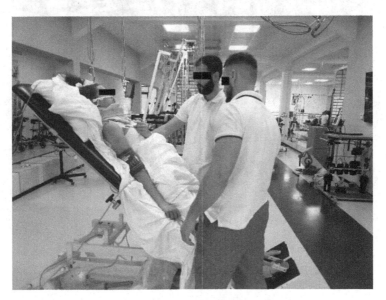

Fig. 1. A patient in vegetative state sitting on a tilt table in a 45° partially verticalized position.

The physiotherapy of a comatose patient involves complex measures considering that this type of patient is very fragile from a medical point of view. The main problems during the rehabilitative process may be related to: lack of communication, maladaptation to physical activity, often associated with polytrauma, fractures in the process of consolidation, patients being tracheostomized or gastrostomized, etc. Therefore, a careful monitoring throughout the patient's tailored rehabilitation program is mandatory, and the overall process requires special equipment and specialized personnel. It is a demonstrated fact that only the maximum functional stress triggers the rehabilitation mechanisms, as well as the recovery mechanisms. Some of the kinetic techniques that are used are presented as images. Figure 1 shows one of the applied physiotherapy procedures with a UWS patient sitting on a tilt table in partial verticalization at about 45°. A patient in vegetative state with complete verticalization is shown in Fig. 2.

Fig. 2. Patient in vegetative state with complete verticalization.

Figure 3 shows a patient in vegetative state which benefit from a body weight support to facilitate sitting mobilization from a partial vertical position.

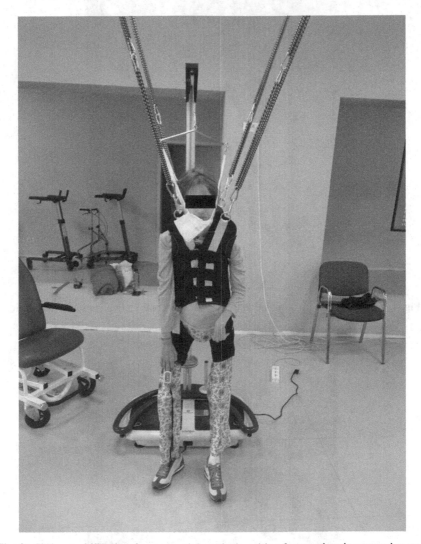

Fig. 3. Sitting mobilization from a partial vertical position for a patient in vegetative state

Apart from the physiotherapy procedures presented in Figs. 1, 2 and 3, the electrotherapy may be applied to elicit muscle contractions and to stimulate the proprioceptive system (see Fig. 4). Oral stimulation therapy is applied too, as presented in Fig. 5.

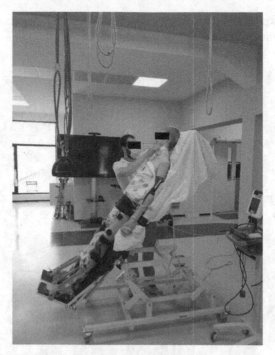

Fig. 4. Functional electrostimulation in a position of total verticalization in suspension

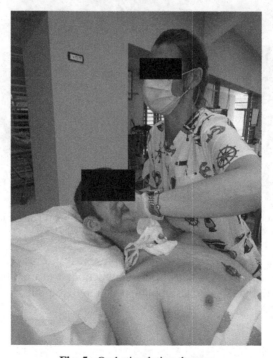

Fig. 5. Oral stimulation therapy

3   EEG Monitoring System

In order to perform the EEG recording a g.Nautilus (g.tec medical engineering GmbH) headset device was used to record the EEG data from 32 active electrodes sites (see Fig. 6). The electrode positions are selected at FP1, FP2, AF3, AF4, F7, F3, Fz, F4, F8, FC5, FC1, FC2, FC6, T7, C3, Cz, C4, T8, CP5, CP1, CP2, CP6, P7, P3, Pz, P4, P8, PO7, PO3, PO4, PO8, Oz according to the international 10/20 system. The sampling rate was 250 Hz and a bandpass filter with cutoff frequency at 0.5 and 30 Hz was applied.

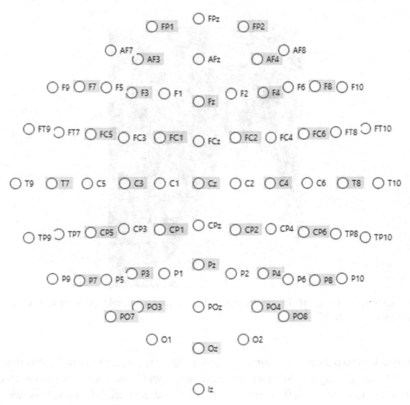

Fig. 6. The electrode placement used in this study, according to the 10–20 international system.

4   Results

The daily gym exercises of the patients in vegetative state, initially assessed by a clinical team, are provided by an experienced physiotherapist and usually include two-hour intensive patient tailored exercises. During the patient tailored rehabilitative exercises, the HMC's clinicians aim to investigate if somethings is also happening at the central nervous system level, in relation with some commands which are provided verbally by the trainers and/or by mechanically induced rehabilitative motions. Are there any resting cognitive abilities? In order to search for possible answers on that matter the above described brain-computer interface has been used and data have been recorded based on a proposed paradigm. Prior to any tests the patient's relatives provided their informed consent.

The patients were seated on a gym bed and depending on their condition the gym bed can be inclined towards an up-right position. Patients wore a EEG cap with 32 active electrodes (g. Nautilus, g.tec medical engineering GmbH, Austria; see Fig. 7). The impedance check has been performed prior any session and it was less than 30 kΩ, for each active electrode.

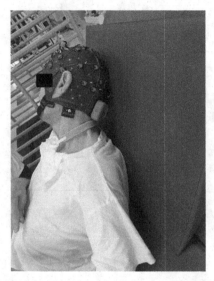

Fig. 7. An unresponsive wakefulness state patient sitting on a tilt table and wearing the g.Nautilus cap to easy record the EEG data.

Depending on patient condition (e.g. tiredness) we recorded 3–4 runs, each composed by 40–50 mental imagery (MI) tasks of hand movement which were communicated in a pseudo random order for left or right hand. In fact, at each trial the patient is few times verbally instructed which hand movement has to imagine and even to move. Sometimes, even a weak movement of the hand seems to be initiated, the therapist tries to help the correct hand (clue of the trial) initiated movement. The triggers are manually settled while recording the EEG data. The trial is organized as follow: at second 0 a 'start' verbal command is provided and in 1.5–2 s the verbal clue 'left' or 'right' is released; for 2–3 s the therapist tries few times to communicate the clue to the patient; then we consider a feedback phase for about 8 s; after that a 'relax' command is pronounced.

Three patients participated in this study, each of them performing the entire session in about one hour. All three patients were diagnosed as being in vegetative state when entering the aggressive rehabilitation program. The bellow described trials have been performed at the end of their treatment. The anonymized patient's data are the following:

P1: 38 years old, vegetative state (spastic tetraparesis) due to a work accident (electric shock, late resuscitation) that happened one year before.

P2: 60 years old, vegetative state (late resuscitated myocardial infarction, spastic tetraparesis); Carrier of tracheostomy and gastrostomy; 18 months old vegetative state condition.

P3: 50 years old, vegetative state (late resuscitated myocardial infarction, spastic tetraparesis); About 18 months old vegetative state condition.

Under investigation was the event-related desynchronization (ERD) for the data recorded at C3 and C4 sites in 8–13 Hz and 14–30 Hz frequency bands. We performed a "sign test" significance test between the baseline interval that was chosen to be the time segment of 1.5 s before the trigger, and the 5.0 s after the trigger, when the upper limbs of the patient were moved (and the patient was expected to perform correct MI) according to a randomized verbally communicated order. The triggers have been initiated manually in order to allow more flexibility in performing the experiment, while instructing the physiotherapist and trying to cooperate with the patient. Significant results were observed only in patient P1 data, C3 channel, alpha 8–13 Hz frequency band (see Figs. 8 and 9).

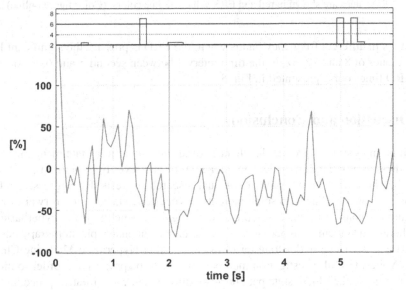

Fig. 8. Event-related desynchronization (ERD) averaged plot for patient P1, based on 8–13 Hz frequency bands of channel C3. (Color figure online)

Figure 8 presents the Event-Related Desynchronization (ERD) averaged plot for patient P1, based on 8–13 Hz frequency bands of channel C3. The red vertical line indicates the trigger and the red horizontal line reflects the reference interval for the ERD. The blue line on the top of the plot represent the moment where the difference between the reference and action interval is significant according to the sign test.

Figure 9 presents the ERD maps, calculated for C3 channel, between 8 to 30 Hz, with 2 Hz bandwidth of single bands and 2 Hz shift. Even though there are multiple time

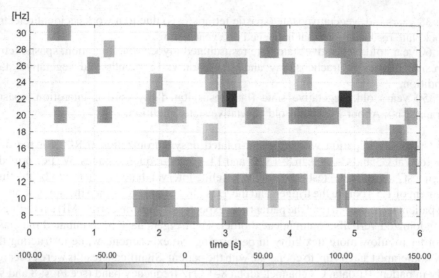

Fig. 9. Time-frequency plot of event related synchronization and event related desynchronization (ERS). ERD values are shown in red and ERS values in blue colors. (Color figure online)

segments in different frequency bands where the ERD is present, the significant ERDs are the ones of 8 and 12 Hz, in the time interval between second 5 and 6, according to the ERD time course presented in Fig. 8.

5 Discussion and Conclusions

Yet, it is impossible to predict the chances of an individual in a state of impaired consciousness improving. It may depend on: age, type and severity of brain injury, for how long they have been in that state etc. Actual research suggests that aggressive rehabilitation may offer a chance to some patients in vegetative state to step forward towards a minimally conscious state. Based on the recognized benefits of the hyperbaric oxygen therapy, a tandem of hyperbaric oxygen therapy - intensive physiotherapy has been started and is/will be under long term investigation at Hyperbaric Medicine Clinic in Targu Mures. Useful investigation methods still are to be proposed in order to monitor unresponsive wakefulness state patients even during their rehabilitative procedures.

An easy to don and doff EEG system has been used to monitor the unresponsive wakefulness state patients and a paradigm, based on motor imagery (MI), has been implemented, in order to try to investigate the level of consciousness in three unresponsive wakefulness state patients. All three of them have been diagnosed as being in vegetative state at the start of an aggressive rehabilitation process which includes both hyperbaric oxygen therapy and physiotherapy. During the MI-based paradigm to whom the patients were exposed at the end of their treatment, only one patient (P1) has shown significant ERD's, leading to the idea that he/she might be able to some extend to attend a minimally consciousness state. For the other two patients the results were inconclusive. Further trials have to be performed, on a large number of unresponsive wakefulness state patients in order to validate these preliminary results. On the other side, an easy in donning and doffing EEG system can be a valuable tool and may offer an important inside to the physiotherapists during the overall rehabilitative process in patients with disorders of consciousness.

Aknowledgement. This research was supported by a grant of the Romanian Ministry of Education and Research, CCCDI - UEFISCDI, project number PN-III-P2-2.1-PTE-2019-0136 (PNCDI III/25PTE-2020).

References

1. Murovec, N., et al.: Effects of a Vibro-Tactile P300 based brain-computer interface on the coma recovery scale-revised in patients with disorders of consciousness. Front. Neurosci. **14**, 294 (2020). https://doi.org/10.3389/fnins.2020.00294
2. Lucca, L.F., et al.: Predicting outcome of acquired brain injury by the evolution of paroxysmal sympathetic hyperactivity signs. J. Neurotrauma (2021). https://doi.org/10.1089/neu.2020.7302
3. Gosseries, O., Pistoia, F., Charland-Verville, V., Carolei, A., Sacco, S., Laureys, S.: The role of neuroimaging techniques in establishing diagnosis, prognosis and therapy in disorders of consciousness. Open Neuroimaging J. **10**(Suppl-1, M5), 52–68 (2016)
4. Bai, Y., Lin, Y., Ziemann, U.: Managing disorders of consciousness: the role of electroencephalography. J. Neurol. 1–33 (2020). https://doi.org/10.1007/s00415-020-10095-z
5. Rupawala, M., Dehghani, H., Lucas, S.J.E., Tino, P., Cruse, D.: Shining a light on awareness: a review of functional near-infrared spectroscopy for prolonged disorders of consciousness. Front. Neurol. **9**, 350 (2018). https://doi.org/10.3389/fneur.2018.00350
6. Ortner, R., Allison, B.Z., Pichler, G., Heilinger, A., Sabathiel, N., Guger, C.: Assessment and communication for people with disorders of consciousness. J. Vis. Exp. **126**, 1–8 (2017). https://doi.org/10.3791/53639
7. Sinitsyn, D.O., et al.: Detecting the potential for consciousness in unresponsive patients using the perturbational complexity index. Brain Sci. **10**(12), 917 (2020). https://doi.org/10.3390/brainsci10120917
8. Lippert-Gruner, M.: Early rehabilitation of comatose patients after traumatic brain injury. Neurol. Neurochir. Pol. **44**(5), 475–480 (2010). https://doi.org/10.1016/s0028-3843(14)60138-9
9. Oberholzer, M., Müri, R.M.: Neurorehabilitation of Traumatic Brain Injury (TBI): a clinical review. Med. Sci. (Basel, Switz.) **7**(3), 47 (2019). https://doi.org/10.3390/medsci7030047
10. Johnston, L., Aggressive physical rehabilitation. http://www.healingtherapies.info/Aggressive-Rehab.htm. Accessed 26 Feb 2021
11. Clark, J.F., Middendorf, A., Hasselfeld, K.A., Ellis, J.K., Divine, J.: Aggressive rehabilitation pathway targeting concussion symptoms: illustration with a case study. Brain Disord. Ther. **3**(4), 1–7 (2014). https://doi.org/10.4172/2168-975X.1000131

Online Classification of Cognitive Control Processes Using EEG and fNIRS: A Stroop Experiment

Leonhard Schreiner[1,3]([⊠]), Gerald Hirsch[1], Ren Xu[2], Patrick Reitner[1], Harald Pretl[3], and Christoph Guger[1,2]

[1] g.tec Medical Engineering GmbH, Sierningstraße 14, 4521 Schiedlberg, Austria
schreiner@gtec.at
[2] Guger Technologies OG, Herbersteinstraße 60, 8020 Graz, Austria
[3] Johannes Kepler University, Altenberger Straße 69, 4040 Linz, Austria

Abstract. *Introduction:* Brain-computer interfaces (BCIs) provide a broad range of applications for human-computer interactions. Exploring cognitive control and underlying neurophysiological mechanisms brings essential contributions to this research field. In this paper, neurophysiological findings connected to cognitive control processes using the Stroop experiment were investigated. Electroencephalography (EEG) and functional infrared spectroscopy (fNIRS) were employed for measuring brain activities. The Stroop-test was classified against resting-state activities.

Materials and Methods: The wireless g.Nautilus fNIRS system (g.tec medical engineering GmbH) with 16 channels of EEG, combined with 8 channels of fNIRS, was used for data acquisition. Six healthy subjects participated in the conducted Stroop experiment.

Results: A considerable hemodynamic response was present during the Stroop-test, as seen in the offline analysis. The EEG-based classification delay was considerably lower than those with oxygenated and deoxygenated hemoglobin-based classifiers. The online experiment analysis showed that the accuracy rose clearly within the first 2 s of the task. On average, a maximum accuracy of 81.0% was achieved at 6.2 s after the task onset.

Discussion: and Conclusion: In general, the hybrid approach seems superior by facilitating information from all three modalities. In conclusion, the capability of successfully determining frontal lobe activity is a promising indication to use hybrid BCIs for further research applications.

Keywords: BCI · EEG · fNIRS · Stroop · Prefrontal cortex

1 Introduction

Brain-computer interfaces (BCIs) represent an essential field in human-computer interactions. BCIs provide communication between a human brain and a computer or external device analyzing electrophysiological signals measured from the brain [1]. This technology has already proven its great potential in various assessment, communication,

© Springer Nature Switzerland AG 2021
M. Kurosu (Ed.): HCII 2021, LNCS 12762, pp. 582–591, 2021.
https://doi.org/10.1007/978-3-030-78462-1_45

and therapy methods [2–4]. Various approaches for measuring brain activities (brain signal acquisition technologies) can be applied to gather the desired information [5]. For non-invasive measurements, Electroencephalography (EEG) and functional near-infrared spectroscopy (fNIRS) are the state-of-the-art acquisition methods in BCIs [6–8]. EEG systems screen brain activities via measuring voltage potentials on the scalp resulting from the underlying neural activities. Due to its high temporal resolution, EEG systems come into use, especially for time crucial applications. Though, EEG has the limitation in its spatial resolution. The fNIRS uses optical densities to measure the oxygenated (HBO) and deoxygenated (HBR) hemoglobin concentrations. Active brain regions require more generous blood flow to fulfill increased energy demand, also known as neurovascular coupling. Based on this information, the cortical activity can indirectly be evaluated [9]. Using both approaches (EEG and fNIRS) as a hybrid method has enhanced performance in several BCIs [6–8, 10].

The identification and training in cognitive impairments (e.g., Alzheimer's disease, dementia) is an enormously increasing area of interest [11, 12]. The potential to process information and regulate actions and thoughts depending on the current task is called cognitive control or executive control (EC) [13]. Underlying cognitive adaption and filtering information on the importance and suppression of non-task-related and irrelevant content is vital for human decision-making [14]. EC processes and sub-processes are addressed while executing the Stroop-test. This experiment aims to trigger the Stroop effect, which reflects a mental conflict (unexpected mental load for a familiar task) [13]. Cognitive experiments, such as the Stroop-test, evoke brain activity in the frontal lobe area [15, 16].

The prefrontal cortex (PFC) plays a significant role when investigating memory and decision-making behaviors [17]. However, only a few studies have shown the influence of hemodynamic response in connection with EEG examining frontal lobe activities.

This study analyzed neurophysiological findings connected to cognitive control processes using Electroencephalography and functional infrared spectroscopy. As the basis for discussion, the results of prior published data from Motor-Imagery experiments using this hybrid EEG-fNIRS approach were exploited [18].

2   Material and Methods

The Stroop-test resulted in brain activation, which was measured by the *g.NAUTILUS fNIRS* (g.tec medical engineering GmbH) device and subsequently classified. The experiment is a binary classification problem and aims to differentiate between rest and shuffled Stroop-test (frontal lobe activation).

2.1   Data Acquisition

The *g.NAUTILUS fNIRS* system includes 8 transmitters and 2 receivers, resulting in 2×4 fNIRS channels for measuring the hemodynamic responses. The EEG signals were acquired using 16 independent electrodes of the hardware. A detailed optode and electrode setup is depicted in Fig. 1. Overall, 6 healthy subjects without known preconditions participated in the experiments.

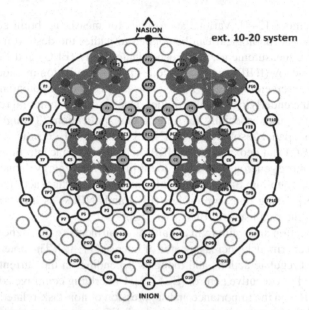

Fig. 1. The 16 EEG electrodes are placed over the frontal cortex. FPz, AFz, Fz, F1, F2, F3, F4, FCz, C1, C2, AF5h, AF6h, AFF7h, AFF8h, FFC1h and FFC2h. The 8 fNIRS transmitters are approximately placed at AFF4h, F6, AF8, AFp4, AFF3h, F5, AF7, and AFp3. The two fNIRS receivers at AF7 and AF8.

2.2 Paradigm

The paradigm's main sequence can be seen in Fig. 2 (pre-rest, instruction, task, rest, and post-rest). This sequence is the same for both the calibration and evaluation phase. Each phase consists of 40 trials. The two-folded experiment is training classifiers and common spatial pattern (CSP) filters in the calibration phase and subsequently performing online classification in the evaluation phase. The algorithm utilizes both EEG and fNIRS signals.

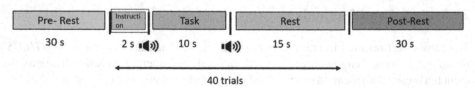

Fig. 2. The sequence of the experiment used in calibration as well as in the evaluation phase.

First, the Instruction window notified of the incoming task, which the subject then had to perform. The task itself was to read/imagine as many colors as possible within the 10 s task window. Overall a grid of 10x10 words was displayed. Instruction to relax was given as a control task. Control- and assorted Stroop-tests were sequenced in a stratified and randomized way.

2.3 EEG Processing

Signal processing was done in *MATLAB* (The Mathworks, Inc., Massachusetts, USA) and *g.HIsys High-Speed Online Processing for Simulink* (g.tec medical engineering GmbH). EEG processing involves pre-processing, CSP filtering, and feature extraction.

The EEG signals are bandpass filtered (6th order Butterworth filter, 8–30 Hz) and notch filtered (2nd order, 48–52 Hz) to set the focus on the α/μ and β band and remove interferences of the power line.

Further on, to maximize the weight of the channels that contain essential information, spatial filtering was performed adopting a CSP filter [18, 19]. The two first and last filters ($Z = [w_1, w_2, w_{15}, w_{16}]$) were applied to the pre-processed discrete EEG signal $x'[k] \in \mathbb{R}^4$:

$$x'[k] = Z^T x[k], x'[k] \in \mathbb{R}^4 \tag{1}$$

Finally, features were extracted by calculating the variance of the CSP filtered data. As this information is proportional to the band-power and the band-power is linked to cognitive activation, this is a suitable approach to gather information about the impact of the conducted Stroop-test [20]. From the four surrogate channels, the log variance was calculated and normalized over all channels:

$$y[k] = \log\left(\frac{var(x'_i[k])}{\sum_{i=1}^{4} var(x'_i[k])} \right) \tag{2}$$

2.4 fNIRS Processing

After removing artifacts based on the raw optical densities (ODs), the relative HBO and HBR concentrations from the acquired OD were determined. Signals were low pass filtered at 0.3 Hz with a 4th order Butterworth filter to remove pulsatile fluctuations. Power line noise was suppressed using a 2nd order notch filter. The concentration changes for HBO and HBR were calculated by applying a baseline correction that used the averaged signal (taken from the pre-rest phase) subtracted from the subsequent concentrations.

A rolling window $X' = \in \mathbb{R}^{N x T}$ was used for feature extraction, where N represents the number of channels and $T = 30$ the number of sampled points. Each sample $x'[k]$ was consequently represented by the feature vector $y'[k] \in \mathbb{R}^{(N7)}$. Two features, mean and slope, proved to be an optimal trade-off between accuracy and computational effort. The two chosen features were extracted from the pre-processed signals and passed to the classifier. The channel-wise mean is given as:

$$mean(X') = \frac{1}{T} \sum_{k=1}^{T} x[k]^T \tag{3}$$

The channel-wise slope is given as:

$$slope(X') = \frac{1}{T}\left(x[T]^T - x[1]^T \right). \tag{4}$$

2.5 Classification

Linear discriminant analysis (LDA) with Fischer's criteria was utilized to classify the EEG and fNIRS features, respectively [21]. The final prediction was performed by a meta-classifier using the scores of the individual classifiers.

2.6 Analysis

Performance analysis was done via trial-wise checking for correct classified samples. The classification accuracy was set to be the accumulated and averaged value for each time point. All three methods (EEG, HBO, and HBR) and the combination of the three classifiers (COMBINED) were analyzed this way. Classifiers with the best performance in the offline analysis were adopted for online classification in the evaluation phase.

3 Results

3.1 CSP Analysis

A weighting for channels in the frontal lobe, as suggested by w_{15} and w_{16}, can be extracted from the CSP analysis (see Fig. 3). With the available CSP weights, four surrogate channels could be calculated.

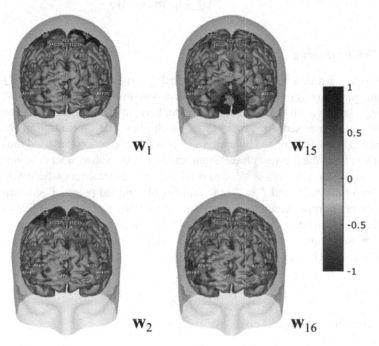

Fig. 3. Visualization of w_1, w_2, w_{15}, and w_{16} from the CSP analysis.

3.2 Offline Analysis

The time-variant 10 × 10 fold cross-validation (CV) was utilized for the offline classification performance analysis for calibration and, additionally, in retrospect, with the evaluation data. A considerable hemodynamic response (HR) was present during the Stroop-test, as seen in the offline analysis. The EEG-based classification delay was considerably lower than the one of HBO and HBR (Fig. 4). Results from the calibration and evaluation phase seemed to be comparable.

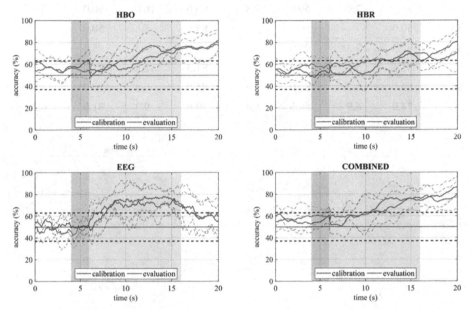

Fig. 4. Calibration and evaluation phase accuracies calculated from a 10x10 fold CV. Mean accuracy and standard deviation over all subjects and the real chance level (dashed line at $\alpha = 0.05$) are additionally plotted.

3.3 Online Analysis

The online performance results are the time-variant average online accuracies from the evaluation run. Table 1 shows the maximum achieved accuracies during the 10 s trial window with the relative appearance time. The maximum mean accuracy-based classification for the EEG was comparatively late with 9.3 s. As this is the global maximum, this might be misleading.

As seen in Fig. 5, the EEG accuracy rose clearly within the first 2 s of the task. On average, a maximum accuracy of 81.0% was achieved 6.2 s after the task onset. Further, the task window was divided into 10 slots, 1 s each. At 7–8 s after the task onset the following maximum accuracies (respective standard deviation) were achieved: Average = 83.6% (±12.3%), Class0 = 86.1% (±19.7%) and Class1 = 81.0% (±5.9%). Class1 in this case represents the Stroop activation and Class0 resting-state activity.

Table 1. The achieved maximum classification Accuracy (Acc) in percent with their relative timing (seconds) after the task onset from the Stroop-test. Suppose the accuracy did not exceed the chance level, the max. accuracy was considered to be 50%. Only maximum accuracies during the task window are shown.

Subject	HBO		HBR		EEG		META	
Nr	Acc(%)	Time(s)	Acc(%)	Time(s)	Acc(%)	Time(s)	Acc(%)	Time(s)
S1	78.5	7.0	87.5	5.2	82.5	2.2	90.0	6.2
S2	77.5	7.9	69.0	7.8	90.0	10.0	90.0	10.0
S3	50.0	-	50.0	-	84.0	8.8	50.0	-
S4	87.5	7.3	90.0	6.6	83.0	0.3	95.0	8.1
S5	81.5	5.7	50.0	-	81.5	2.8	81.0	6.5
S6	83.0	5.7	80.0	6.6	85.0	6.4	90.0	6.8
Mean	**74.0**	**6.9**	**66.5**	**6.4**	**79.0**	**9.3**	**81.0**	**6.2**

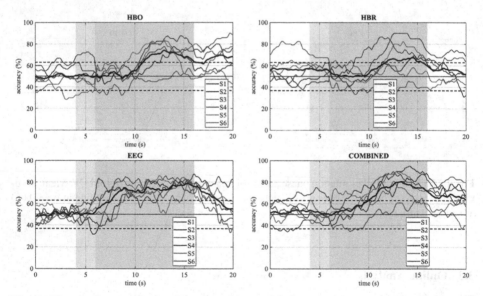

Fig. 5. Time variant accuracies from six subjects with the respective mean accuracy over all subjects and the real chance level (dashed line at $\alpha = 0.05$). The blue area represents the instruction window of 2 s (4 s–6 s). The red-marked field represents the 10 s task window (6 s–16 s) while performing the Stroop-test. (Color figure online)

4 Discussion and Conclusion

Prior research has already exploited the Stroop test's influence on an increased cortex activity, measured with fNIRS [23]. Hybrid EEG-fNIRS systems have also been employed to study brain activation during mental tasks [24, 25]. However, combining hybrid online-BCI systems using the Stroop task as a mental activation method has not been pointed out in the literature. The Stroop experiment's primary motivation was to investigate the frontal lobe activation, compared to the resting state, and to what extent this activity can be assessed via a hybrid EEG-fNIRS system. Equally, methods such as mental arithmetic or simple counting could be used to provoke frontal lobe activation.

The results of the CSP analysis emphasize the activation of the prefrontal- and motor cortex. One has to consider that eye movement artifacts during the word reading might also cause cortical activity. Compared to the one of the initially mentioned MI experiment [18], a distinct separation was less visible in the hereby present feature analysis. However, considering the temporal distribution, a similar onset was detectable. Overall, the results of both runs from the calibration and evaluation phases were comparable. The respective accuracy values' actual trajectories clearly showed that the EEG-based classifier had higher responsiveness than the HBO/HBR classifiers (see Fig. 4).

Using the 10×10 fold cross-validation for offline analysis turned out to be a suitable method for evaluating the signal quality and determining discrepancy from the different signal types (EEG, HBO and HBR). As the offline analysis has its limitations (e.g. overfitting), online analysis is crucial for the performance improvement and was seen as the assessment's final aim.

Despite many advantages, such as good usability, fNIRS has its limitations in a delayed response. As the temporal resolution is the major advantage of EEG systems, combining these systems shows to be superior to applying only one method. In this study, investigating cognitive control processes using these combined methods shows clear benefits.

Acknowledgments. This work was partially funded via the European Commission project RHUMBO – H2020-MSCA-ITN-2018-813234.

References

1. Wolpaw, J.R., Birbaumer, N., McFarland, D.J., et al.: Brain–computer interfaces for communication and control. Clin. Neurophysiol. **113**, 767–791 (2002). https://doi.org/10.1016/S1388-2457(02)00057-3
2. Wolpaw, J.R., Loeb, G.E., Allison, B.Z., et al.: BCI meeting 2005–workshop on signals and recording methods. IEEE Trans. Neural Syst. Rehabil. Eng. **14**, 138–141 (2006). https://doi.org/10.1109/TNSRE.2006.875583
3. Leuthardt, E.C., Schalk, G., Roland, J., et al.: Evolution of brain-computer interfaces: going beyond classic motor physiology. Neurosurg. Focus **27**, E4 (2009). https://doi.org/10.3171/2009.4.FOCUS0979
4. Lebedev, M.A., Nicolelis, M.A.L.: Brain–machine interfaces: past, present and future. Trends Neurosci. **29**, 536–546 (2006). https://doi.org/10.1016/j.tins.2006.07.004
5. Bandara, D.S.V., Kiguchi, K.: Brain signal acquisition methods in BCIs to estimate human motion intention – a survey. In: 2018 International Symposium on Micro-NanoMechatronics and Human Science (MHS), pp. 1–7. IEEE, Nagoya (2018). https://doi.org/10.1109/MHS.2018.8887072
6. Hong, K.-S., Naseer, N., Kim, Y.-H.: Classification of prefrontal and motor cortex signals for three-class fNIRS–BCI. Neurosci. Lett. **6** (2015). https://doi.org/10.1016/j.neulet.2014.12.029

7. Chiarelli, A.M., Croce, P., Merla, A., Zappasodi, F.: Deep learning for hybrid EEG-fNIRS brain-computer interface: application to motor imagery classification. J. Neural. Eng. **15**, 036028 (2018). https://doi.org/10.1088/1741-2552/aaaf82

8. Verma, P., Heilinger, A., Reitner, P., et al.: Performance investigation of brain-computer interfaces that combine EEG and fNIRS for motor imagery tasks. In: 2019 IEEE International Conference on Systems, Man and Cybernetics (SMC), pp. 259–263. IEEE, Bari (2019). https://doi.org/10.1109/SMC.2019.8914083

9. Midha, S., Maior, H.A., Wilson, M.L., Sharples, S.: Measuring mental workload variations in office work tasks using fNIRS. Int. J. Hum. Comput. Stud. **147**, 102580 (2021). https://doi.org/10.1016/j.ijhcs.2020.102580

10. Cicalese, P.A., Li, R., Ahmadi, M.B., et al.: An EEG-fNIRS hybridization technique in the four-class classification of alzheimer's disease. J. Neurosci. Methods **336**, 108618 (2020). https://doi.org/10.1016/j.jneumeth.2020.108618

11. Farina, F.R., Emek-Savaş, D.D., Rueda-Delgado, L., et al.: A comparison of resting state EEG and structural MRI for classifying Alzheimer's disease and mild cognitive impairment. Neuroimage **215**, 116795 (2020). https://doi.org/10.1016/j.neuroimage.2020.116795

12. Todri, J., Lena, O., Martínez Gil, J.L.: A single blind randomized controlled trial of global postural re-education: cognitive effects on Alzheimer disease patients. Eur. J. Psychiatry **33**, 83–90 (2019). https://doi.org/10.1016/j.ejpsy.2019.01.001

13. Heidlmayr, K., Kihlstedt, M., Isel, F.: A review on the electroencephalography markers of stroop executive control processes. Brain Cogn. **146**, 105637 (2020). https://doi.org/10.1016/j.bandc.2020.105637

14. Tafuro, A., Ambrosini, E., Puccioni, O., Vallesi, A.: Brain oscillations in cognitive control: a cross-sectional study with a spatial stroop task. Neuropsychologia **133**, 107190 (2019). https://doi.org/10.1016/j.neuropsychologia.2019.107190

15. Pijnenborg, G.H.M., Larabi, D.I., Xu, P., et al.: Brain areas associated with clinical and cognitive insight in psychotic disorders: a systematic review and meta-analysis. Neurosci. Biobehav. Rev. **116**, 301–336 (2020). https://doi.org/10.1016/j.neubiorev.2020.06.022

16. Yeung, M.K., Lee, T.L., Chan, A.S.: Neurocognitive development of flanker and Stroop interference control: a near-infrared spectroscopy study. Brain Cogn. **143**, 105585 (2020). https://doi.org/10.1016/j.bandc.2020.105585

17. De, A., Konar, A., Samanta, A., et al.: An fNIRs study to classify stages of learning from visual stimuli using prefrontal hemodynamics. In: 2017 Third International Conference on Biosignals, Images and Instrumentation (ICBSII), pp. 1–7. IEEE, Chennai (2017). https://doi.org/10.1109/ICBSII.2017.8082272

18. Hirsch, G., Dirodi, M., Xu, R., Reitner, P., Guger, C.: Online classification of motor imagery using EEG and fNIRS: a hybrid approach with real time human-computer interaction. In: Stephanidis, C., Antona, M. (eds.) HCII 2020. CCIS, vol. 1224, pp. 231–238. Springer, Cham (2020). https://doi.org/10.1007/978-3-030-50726-8_30

19. Blankertz, B., Tomioka, R., Lemm, S., et al.: Optimizing spatial filters for robust EEG single-trial analysis. IEEE Signal Process. Mag. **25**, 41–56 (2008). https://doi.org/10.1109/MSP.2008.4408441

20. Geraedts, V.J., Marinus, J., Gouw, A.A., et al.: Quantitative EEG reflects non-dopaminergic disease severity in Parkinson's disease. Clin. Neurophysiol. **8** (2018). https://doi.org/10.1016/j.clinph.2018.04.752

21. Bishop, C.M.: Pattern Recognition and Machine Learning. Springer, New York (2006)

22. Müller-Putz, G., Scherer, R., Brunner, C., et al.: Better than random: a closer look on BCI results. Int. J. Bioelectromagn. **10**, 52–55 (2008)

23. Schroeter, M.L., Zysset, S., Kupka, T., et al.: Near-infrared spectroscopy can detect brain activity during a color-word matching stroop task in an event-related design. Hum. Brain Mapp. **17**, 61–71 (2002). https://doi.org/10.1002/hbm.10052

24. Aghajani, H., Garbey, M., Omurtag, A.: Measuring mental workload with EEG+fNIRS. Front Hum. Neurosci. **11** (2017). https://doi.org/10.3389/fnhum.2017.00359
25. Al-Shargie, F., Kiguchi, M., Badruddin, N., et al.: Mental stress assessment using simultaneous measurement of EEG and fNIRS. Biomed. Opt. Express **7**, 3882 (2016). https://doi.org/10.1364/BOE.7.003882

A New Algorithm to Find Isometric Maps for Comparison and Exchange of Facial Expression Perceptions

Masashi Shinto and Jinhui Chao[✉]

Department of Information and System Engineering, Chuo University,
1-13-27 Kasuga, Bunkyo, Tokyo, Japan
jchao@ise.chuo-u.ac.jp

Abstract. Recently transformations between psychophysical spaces of different individuals found applications in various perceptional studies such as color science and facial expressions. These spaces are known to have structure of Riemann spaces of which the Riemann metric tensor is defined by the JND (Just-Noticeable-Difference) discrimination thresholds at every point. Therefore subjective differences between stimuli can be described by distances between the stimuli as points in the Riemann spaces. In particular, a map between these spaces preserving subjective differences is called an isometry or distance-preserving map in Riemann geometry. Until now, algorithms to compute such a map assumed information of the Riemann metric tensor or the hyperellipsoid of JND thresholds, therefore demand a large number of JND threshold data measurements. These methods solving a system of nonlinear equations can only obtain an isometry in a restricted form, but without uniqueness of the solution and are difficult to apply to high dimensional spaces.

In this paper, we propose a new algorithm to compute a local isometry in general form without restrictions between Riemann spaces and psychophysical spaces. We only need JND threshold data points more than the dimension of the space by solving a linear equation system which achieves uniqueness of the solution and statistical and numerical stability comparing with the known methods. We then apply the proposed algorithm to shown examples for comparison and exchange between facial expression perceptions of different observers.

Keywords: Facial expressions · Emotion · Psychophysical space · JND thresholds · Individual variations · Riemann geometry

1 Introduction

A psychophysical space is a space of physical stimuli in which psychological metric or the JND (Just-Noticeable-Difference) discrimination threshold at each point is available. This kind of spaces has therefore a natural structure of a

© Springer Nature Switzerland AG 2021
M. Kurosu (Ed.): HCII 2021, LNCS 12762, pp. 592–603, 2021.
https://doi.org/10.1007/978-3-030-78462-1_46

Riemann space in which the Riemann metric tensor at a point is defined by the hyperellipsoid of JND thresholds centered at the point. This structure turned out to be useful since subjective differences between different stimuli acquire a quantitative representation, or can be described by the distances in the Riemann space between the points of the stimuli. Important applications of these spaces have been found in various areas such as color science and expression recognition recently. In particular, a map between two Riemann spaces called an isometry or a distance-preserving map plays an essential role in these applications.

In fact, in the psychological space of facial expressions obtained in the dimension theory [1,2], a direct correspondence between physical stimuli or the expression images and expression perception was missing. Recently, a facial expression space was proposed as a psychophysical image space in which the JND discrimination threshold hyperellipsoids were measured [4]. This expression space is then studied further in [5,6].

In particular in [6] an new approach to compare and exchange expression perception between different observers was proposed by using an isometry or a distance preserving map between the expression spaces of two observers.

However, existing algorithms in [6,9] to compute such a map are based on matching of the Riemann metric tensors or the hyperellipsoids of JND thresholds, therefore require a solution of nonlinear equations, which demands a large number of JND threshold data. Other problems are they can only obtain an isometry in a restricted form, the solution is not unique and application to high dimensional spaces is not easy.

In this paper, we propose a new algorithm to compute a local isometry between Riemann spaces or psychophysical spaces to overcome these problems.

Without assumption of Riemann metric tensors or the hyperellipsoids of JND thresholds at points of two spaces, we only use JND threshold data points more than the dimension of the space. A unique isometry in general form can be obtained for arbitrary dimensional spaces by solving a linear equation system which can also achieve statistical and numerical stability comparing with the known methods.

We then apply the proposed algorithm to show examples for comparison and exchange between expression perceptions of different observers.

2   Riemann Geometry in a Psychophysical Space and Isometric Maps

Recall a Riemann space S is a space where a metric tensor $G(x)$ is defined smoothly for every point $x \in S$, and often denoted as $(S, G(x))$. (see e.g. [13,14]) The Riemann metric tensor $G(x)$ defines an inner product on the tangent space $T_x S$ at x:

$$\forall u, u' \in T_x S, \quad (u, u') := u^\mathsf{T} G(x) u'$$

In other words, a local geometry including distances and angles e.g. is defined around each point x of S by the metric tensor. If the dimension of the space S

is n, the metric tensor $G(x)$ is an n by n positive definite symmetric matrix. In a psychophysical space, G at the point x is defined by the set of points of the JND thresholds with the reference stimulus as x, or the subjective unit sphere

$$\forall u \in T_x S, \qquad u^{\mathsf{T}} G(x) u = 1$$

which is a hyper-ellipsoid centered at x.

Now assume f is a smooth map between Riemann spaces $(S_1, G_1(x))$ and $(S_2, G_2(y))$, $S_1 \ni x \longmapsto y = f(x) \in S_2$. If f preserves metrics between two spaces everywhere which is equivalent to

$$M^{\mathsf{T}} G_1(x) M = G_2(y) \qquad \forall x \in S_1, y = f(x) \in S_2 \qquad (1)$$

where $M := D_f$ denotes the Jacobian of f, then f is called a local isometry or an isometric map which preserves local geometry around x, e.g. distance and angle (Fig. 1).

In fact, a local isometry f preserves the inner product between the two Riemann spaces:

$$\forall u, u' \in T_x S_1, \text{ if } v = Mu, \ v' = Mu' \in T_y S_2$$
$$\text{then} \qquad (u, u') = (v, v').$$

Therefore, an isometry maps the unit sphere centered at $x \in S_1$ onto the unit sphere centered at $y = f(x) \in S_2$ and vice versa. In particular,

$$u^{\mathsf{T}} G_1(x) u = 1, \qquad \forall u \in T_x S_1$$

is mapped onto

$$v^{\mathsf{T}} G_2(y) v = 1, \qquad v = Mu \in T_y S_2.$$

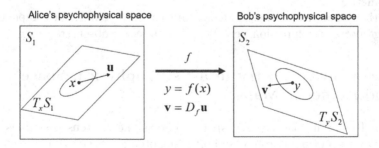

Fig. 1. A local Isometry preserves inner product and JND thresholds

Between psychophysical spaces S_1 of the observer 1 and S_2 of the observer 2, this simply means the Jacobian of an isometry f maps the JND threshold hyperellipsoid at any point $x \in S_1$ onto the JND threshold hyperellipsoid at

$y = f(x) \in S_2$. In other words, the isometry f maps stimuli in a neighborhood of x to a neighborhood of $y = f(x)$ in such a way that the subjective difference between the stimuli and x for the observer 1 is always the same as the subjective difference between the images of the stimuli and y for the observer 2. Therefore, an isometry is an interesting transformation between psychophysical spaces of different observers while preserving local subjective differences everywhere.

In fact, (1) is a local distance preserving condition around the point x, so the map f defined pointwisely by the local condition is called a local isometry. A global isometry is defined as a map which preserves the distance between any pair of points, even remotely separated ones. Here the global distance is defined by the geodesic or the shortest curve connecting the two points, which can be calculated as solutions of a nonlinear ODE defined by Riemann metric tensor. Such a global isometry can be built using a geodesic polar coordinate system and a multi-patch of the systems may be required to cover the whole space [10,11].

Fortunately the two definitions of isometries are equivalent or if one has a local isometry, it must be also a global isometry and vise versa [14].

Therefore an isometry between two psychophysical spaces of different individuals will transform stimuli while preserving subjective differences among the stimuli. Such a kind of maps is expected to play an important role in perceptional study in particular investigation of individual variance etc. e.g. it becomes possible to show to one observer what the other one percepts and vice versa. It can also be used to compare and even exchange subjective perceptions of the same stimulus between different observers. For example, the isometries between color spaces of normal and color-weak observers are used for compensation of color-weak visions and color reproduction [7], e.g. with local isometries in [8,9] and with global isometries in Oshima-CCIW09 [10,11]. A global isometry between low dimensional expression space and a Euclidean space is built in [5]. The transformations used in [6] for perceptional comparison and exchange were local isometries between expression spaces of different observers.

To build an isometry between two Riemann spaces, one has therefore two approaches either local or global isometries. A global isometry needs geodesic calculation which could be computationally complicated and costly comparing with the linear algebraic calculation for local isometries. Therefore, a reasonable choice is to build the computationally easier local isometries everywhere then paste the local coordinates to obtain a global coordinate system.

3   Construction of the Isometric Maps

In order to find such a local isometry f, it was proposed in [8,9] to use the Riemann metric $G_1(x), G_2(y)$ or the JND hyperellipsoids at $x \in S_1$ and $y \in S_2$ and solve the nonlinear equation (1) for the matrix M in 2D and 3D spaces.

Unfortunately, this matrix equation has an infinite number of solutions since the matrices $G_1(x), G_2(y)$ are symmetric, only $n(n+1)/2$ equations in (1) are independent where n is the dimension of the spaces. On the other hand, M has n^2 unknown entries. In other words, there are more variables than the equations so the solution space is not zero dimensional therefore the solution is not unique. The problem was solved by restricting M as a product of a rotation matrix and a diagonal matrix representing scaling along the principle axes of the ellipsoids. e.g. in the 2D, The matrix M is defined as

$$M = \begin{pmatrix} M_1 & M_2 \\ M_3 & M_4 \end{pmatrix} = \begin{pmatrix} \cos\theta & -\sin\theta \\ \sin\theta & \cos\theta \end{pmatrix} \begin{pmatrix} a & 0 \\ 0 & b \end{pmatrix}$$

Then the number of variables is three, equals the number of independent equations. Therefore, denote $G_1(x) = (g_{ij})$, $G_2(y) = (g'_{ij})$, the entries of M can be found by solving the following system of quadratic equations:

$$g_{11} = g'_{11}M_1^2 + 2g'_{12}M_1M_3 + g'_{22}M_3^2$$
$$g_{12} = g'_{11}M_1M_2 + g'_{12}(M_1M_4 + M_2M_3) + g'_{22}M_3M_4$$
$$g_{22} = g'_{11}M_2^2 + 2g'_{12}M_2M_4 + g'_{22}M_4^2$$
$$0 = M_1M_2 + M_3M_4$$

Indeed, this system of nonlinear equations has the same number of independent equations and unknown variables, therefore it has a solution space of zero dimension or a finite number of solutions, among which the true solution need to be selected under certain other conditions. As a high dimensional generalization shown in [6], in an n-dimensional space, the $n \times n$ matrix M is assumed to be a product of a matrix in $SO(n)$ or an n-dimensional rotation and a diagonal matrix. Then the number of variables equals the dimension of $SO(n)$ plus the dimension of the space $= n(n-1)/2 + n = n(n+1)/2$, which equals the number of independent equations. Therefore the solution space is zero-dimensional or a finite set. On the other hand, algorithmic procedure in high dimensions is not available yet.

Here a problem is that the method can only build isometries in a restricted form. The gap between the number of variables n^2 in a general form of M and $n(n+1)/2$ in the restricted form of M increases rapidly when the dimension grows higher.

Another problem is that the method assumes availability of the metric matrices $G_1(x)$, $G_2(y)$ or the JND hyperellipsoids at x and y. These metric tensors G_i have to be estimated from the JND threshold data points measured at x and y in S_1 and S_2. Since one point $\boldsymbol{u}$ of JND measurement at x creates an equation

$$\boldsymbol{u}^T G(x)\boldsymbol{u} = \sum_{i,j} u_i u_j g_{ij} = 1$$

which is linear in g_{ij}. The metric tensor $G(x)$ as an n by n symmetric matrix has $n(n+1)/2$ independent entries g_{ij}. Therefore, to obtain $n(n+1)/2$ entries of metric $G(x)$ at the point x, one needs more than $n(n+1)/2$ measurements of JND thresholds in S_1. According to [3], the dimension n of a facial expression space is about 50, to find $G(x)$ or the JND hyperellipsoid at one point x, one need more than 1275 measurements of the JND thresholds. This is the same for $G_2(y)$ at y in S_2 therefore one has to do the measurements for the whole space and for both observers. Such amount of experiments is obviously impractical.

4   Proposed Method

Our new algorithm to build an isometry does not assume the metric matrices and JND hyperellipsoids, but employ directly the measurement data points of JND thresholds.

Denote the psychophysical spaces of observers Alice and Bob are S_1 and S_2. To build an isometry M between the neighborhood around $x_0 \in S_1$ to the neighborhood around $x_0' \in S_2$, we use the measurement data points of the JND thresholds at the point x_0 and x_0'. Notice that usually a local isometry is used to map between the JND hyperellipsoids of two different observers at the same reference stimulus $x_0 = x_0'$. Hereafter we will also assume the reference points are the same $x_0 = x_0'$. Meanwhile in a more general formulation the method also works with different reference points $x_0 \neq x_0'$.

Assume a continuous variation such as a morphing sequence of stimuli $\mu_i, i = 1, 2, ..., m$ starting from x_0 towards different directions generated and shown to both observers,

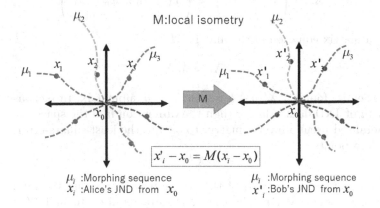

μ_i :Morphing sequence μ_i :Morphing sequence
x_i :Alice's JND from x_0 x_i' :Bob's JND from x_0

Fig. 2. Proposed method to build an isometry

Denote the JND threshold point from the reference stimulus x_0 along the morphing sequence μ_i as x_i for Alice and x_i' for Bob $i = 1, ..., m$, which are illustrated as in Fig. 2.

Thus the isometry M from Alice's space to Bob's around x_0

$$M : T_{x_0} S_1 \longrightarrow T_{x_0} S_2, \tag{2}$$
$$u \longmapsto v = Mu \tag{3}$$

should satisfy the following equations

$$v_i = Mu_i, \qquad u_i := x_i - x_0, \quad v_i := x_i' - x_0, \quad i = 1, 2, ..., m$$

or

$$x_i' - x_0 = M(x_i - x_0), \quad i = 1, 2, ..., m$$

The above system of linear equations can be rewritten in the form of matrices:

$$\begin{pmatrix} | & \cdots & | \\ \boldsymbol{v}_1 & \cdots & \boldsymbol{v}_m \\ | & \cdots & | \end{pmatrix} = M \begin{pmatrix} | & \cdots & | \\ \boldsymbol{u}_1 & \cdots & \boldsymbol{u}_m \\ | & \cdots & | \end{pmatrix}$$

or

$$\begin{pmatrix} | & \cdots & | \\ x'_1 - x_0 & \cdots & x'_m - x_0 \\ | & \cdots & | \end{pmatrix} = M \begin{pmatrix} | & \cdots & | \\ x_1 - x_0 & \cdots & x_m - x_0 \\ | & \cdots & | \end{pmatrix}$$

Denote the $n \times m$ data matrices as X' and X as follows,

$$X' := \begin{pmatrix} | & \cdots & | \\ \boldsymbol{v}_1 & \cdots & \boldsymbol{v}_m \\ | & \cdots & | \end{pmatrix} = \begin{pmatrix} | & \cdots & | \\ x'_1 - x_0 & \cdots & x'_m - x_0 \\ | & \cdots & | \end{pmatrix}$$

$$X := \begin{pmatrix} | & \cdots & | \\ \boldsymbol{u}_1 & \cdots & \boldsymbol{u}_m \\ | & \cdots & | \end{pmatrix} = \begin{pmatrix} | & \cdots & | \\ x_1 - x_0 & \cdots & x_m - x_0 \\ | & \cdots & | \end{pmatrix}$$

one has a matrix equation in the matrix M

$$X' = MX.$$

M can then be found if X' has a regular $n \times n$ submatrix. In fact, assume the number m of JND data is larger than the dimension n of the space, one can use the generalized pseudo-inverse matrix to obtain the least-square-error fitting to all the data points.

$$M = X'X^T(XX^T)^{-1}$$

One could increase robustness of the solution by increasing the number m of JND measurements. Meanwhile, the JND data required to find M is reduced from a quadratic order $O(n^2)$ to a linear order $O(n)$ of n.

Obviously, the proposed method estimate the isometry M in a general form without any restrictions assumed in the existing methods. Besides, the isometry is uniquely determined as the solution of a system of linear equations. Such a solution is also faster and numerically more stable than solutions of nonlinear equations in the known methods.

5   Experiments

The database 3D Scan Store Female01 [12] of facial expression images are used in the experiments. In order to create morphing sequences between the expression images, we build a mesh model for faces and choose 123 feature points for every images. They are used as the nodes in the mesh model of the face in Fig. 3, which then is used to produce morphing sequences between two target images. An example of morphing sequences is shown in Fig. 4.

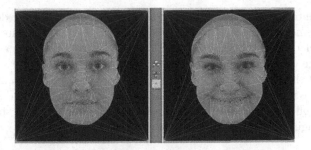

Fig. 3. Mesh model built from the 123 feature points

Fig. 4. An example of Morphing Images

In order to obtain the Riemann metric tensors, the JND discrimination thresholds of two observers were measured in an environment shown in Fig. 5. The screen is separated to the left and right parts. The left part is fixed to the image of the reference facial expression. The right part begins with the same images as the left, but then shows a morphing image sequence changing to another expression on requests.

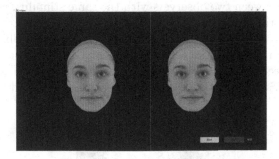

Fig. 5. Screen for JND threshold measurement

The objectives are asked to stop display of the morphing sequence as soon as the difference of expressions between the left and the right images are perceived. In order to prevent various bias in the measurements due to e.g. adaptation, prediction, learning and fatigue etc., the morphing sequences are chosen in a random order. A dark gray mode on the screen was shown as prelude before each

session and intermissions between two successive sessions. (For details see [5])
Along every morphing sequence the experiment is repeated three times in a
random order during the experiment. The JND threshold data are then taken
as the average of the three measurement values.

The JND threshold hyperellipsoids for two observers Alice and Bob at the
same reference image are obtained by the above experiments. The 2D sections of
them as two ellipses, the red for Alice and the blue for Bob are shown in Fig. 6
where the origin is the reference image.

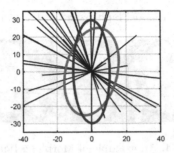

Fig. 6. Alice and Bob's JND thresholds (Color figure online)

We now build the local isometries between the expression spaces of Alice and
Bob, which map between the neighborhoods of the reference image in the spaces
of two observers. Therefore, an image in the neighborhood in Alice's space are
mapped to another image in the neighborhood in Bob's space, in such a way
that the JND hyperellipsoid and its 2D section ellipse of Alice are mapped onto
the JND hyperellipsoid and its 2D section ellipse of Bob.

To compare between two observers with the same stimulus, we use the image
in Fig. 7 as the original input.

The isometry from Alice's facial expression space to Bob's space (Fig. 8)
mapped the original image, the red point which lies inside Alice's JND hyperellipsoid to the green point in Bob's space which is outside of Bob's JND hyperellipsoid (although seemed lying inside the ellipse when projected to the 2D plane).

Fig. 7. Original input image

So Bob can compare his own view of the original with Alice's view shown to him as in Fig. 9. If he always looks at the right image instead of the left original input, his view is then exchanged with Alice's.

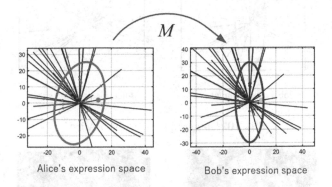

Alice's expression space   Bob's expression space

Fig. 8. Isometry from Alice to Bob

On the other hand, the isometry from Bob's facial expression space to Alice's space (Fig. 10) mapped the original image, the red point lying outside of Bob's JND hyperellipsoid to the green point in Alice's space which is inside her JND hyper-ellipsoid. Therefore Alice can compare her view of the original input with Bob's view shown to her as in Fig. 11. She can also always look at the right image instead of the left original input in order to exchange with Bob's perception.

Bob's view of the original   Alice's view shown to Bob

Fig. 9. Bob's view compared with Alice's view shown to him

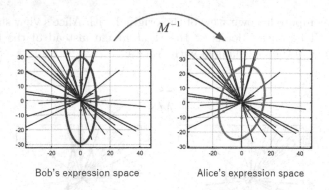

Fig. 10. Isometry from Bob to Alice

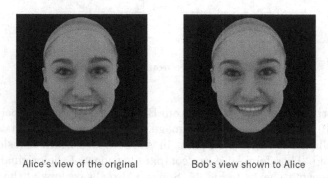

Alice's view of the original   Bob's view shown to Alice

Fig. 11. Alice's view compared with Bob's view shown to her

6   Conclusions

A novel algorithm to find local isometric maps between psychophysical spaces of different observers is proposed. Comparing the existing methods, the proposed method does not assume information of Riemann metric tensor or the hyperellipsoid of JND discrimination thresholds. It can estimate the isometry in a general form and provides the solution uniquely by solving a systems of linear equations. As a result, the amount of psychophysical experiments to measure JND thresholds is reduced from $O(n^2)$ to $O(n)$ in n-D spaces. Besides, the statistical and numerical stability of the solution is improved. Future works include construction of isometries between Riemann or psychophysical spaces by pasting local isometries of different neighborhoods to cover the whole space and comparison and exchange of perceptions between different individuals and groups.

Acknowledgment. This research is supported by the MIC/SCOPE #181603006.

References

1. Russell, J.A., Bullock, M.: Multidimensional scaling of emotional facial expressions: similarity from preschoolers to adults. J. Pers. Soc. Psychol. **48**(5), 1290–1298 (1985)
2. Young, A.W., Rowland, D., Calder, A.J.: Facial expression megamix: test of dimensional and category accounts of emotion recognition. Cognition **63**(3) (1997)
3. Calder, A.J., Burton, A.M., Miller, P., Young, A.W., Akamatsu, S.: A principal component analysis of facial expressions. Vis. Res. **41**(9), 1179–1208 (2001)
4. Sumiya, R., Lenz, R., Chao, J.: Measurement of JND thresholds and Riemannian geometry in facial expression space. In: Kurosu, M. (ed.) HCI 2018. LNCS, vol. 10901, pp. 453–464. Springer, Cham (2018). https://doi.org/10.1007/978-3-319-91238-7_37
5. Sumiya, R., Chao, J.: Transform facial expression space to Euclidean space using Riemann normal coordinates and its applications. In: Kurosu, M. (ed.) HCII 2019. LNCS, vol. 11567, pp. 168–178. Springer, Cham (2019). https://doi.org/10.1007/978-3-030-22643-5_13
6. Shinto, M., Chao, J.: How to compare and exchange facial expression perceptions between different individuals with Riemann geometry. In: Kurosu, M. (ed.) HCII 2019. LNCS, vol. 11567, pp. 155–167. Springer, Cham (2019). https://doi.org/10.1007/978-3-030-22643-5_12
7. Chao, J., Lenz, R., Matsumoto, D., Nakamura, T.: Riemann geometry for color characterization and mapping. In: Conference on Colour in Graphics, Imaging, and Vision, IS&T, pp. 277–282 (2008)
8. Mochizuki, R., Nakamura, T., Chao, J., Lenz, R.: Color-weak correction by discrimination threshold matching. In: Proceedings of CGIV 2008, pp. 208–213 (2008)
9. Mochizuki, R., Kojima, T., Lenz, R., Chao, J.: Color-weak compensation using local affine isometry based on discrimination threshold matching. JOSA **32**(11), 2093–2103 (2015)
10. Ohshima, S., Mochizuki, R., Chao, J., Lenz, R.: Color reproduction using Riemann normal coordinates. In: Trémeau, A., Schettini, R., Tominaga, S. (eds.) CCIW 2009. LNCS, vol. 5646, pp. 140–149. Springer, Heidelberg (2009). https://doi.org/10.1007/978-3-642-03265-3_15
11. Oshima, S., Mochizuki, R., Lenz, R., Chao, J.: Modeling, measuring, and compensating color weak vision. IEEE Trans. Image Process. **25**(6), 2587–2600 (2016)
12. 3DScanStore. https://www.3dscanstore.com/. Accessed 2 Feb 2020
13. Do Carmo, M.P.: Riemannian Geometry. Birkhäuser, Boston (2013)
14. Petersen, P.: Riemannian Geometry. GTM 3rd edn. Springer, Heidelberg (2006)

Definition and Estimation of Dimension in Facial Expression Space

Masashi Shinto[1], Reiner Lenz[2], and Jinhui Chao[1](✉)

[1] Department of Information and System Engineering, Chuo University,
1-13-27 Kasuga, Bunkyo, Tokyo, Japan
jchao@ise.chuo-u.ac.jp
[2] The Institute of Science and Engineering, Chuo University, 1-13-27 Kasuga,
Bunkyo, Tokyo, Japan

Abstract. It has recently been shown that the facial expression space as a psychophysical image space is a Riemann space where the metric tensor is defined by the JND (Just-Noticeable-Difference) discrimination thresholds at every point in the space. The major obstacle to understand this space is how to estimate the metric tensor in high dimensions which requires an inaccessible number of psychophysical experiments. In this paper we address two fundamental issues: methods to estimate the Riemann metric tensor in a high dimensional space and how to define and to determine the effective dimensions of Riemann spaces and psychophysical spaces. We introduce new definitions for these dimensions and novel algorithms for estimating the high dimensional Riemann metric tensor and for dimension reduction to low dimensional subspaces. We then apply these algorithms to the facial expressions space. The Riemann metric tensor of the high dimensional facial expression space is estimated from psychophysical measurements of JND data. We apply these methods to investigate the facial expression space. We describe our experiments to estimate the effective dimension (together with upper and lower bounds) of Riemann manifolds and psychophysical spaces.

Keywords: Facial expressions · Emotion · Dimension reduction · Psychophysical space · JND thresholds · Riemann geometry

1 Introduction

Current expression recognition methods mainly classify an arbitrary expression image into a discrete category of so-called basic expressions [9,13]. In the analysis and processing of complicated and subtle variations of expressions which are difficult to describe verbally it would, however, be desirable to work with continuous and quantitative representations. Until now, psychological expression spaces were provided in the framework of the dimensional theory [10]. These spaces are obtained from data in psychological experiments using the Affective-Grid or an SD (Semantic Differentiation) test. They are then reduced to low (2 or

© Springer Nature Switzerland AG 2021
M. Kurosu (Ed.): HCII 2021, LNCS 12762, pp. 604–621, 2021.
https://doi.org/10.1007/978-3-030-78462-1_47

3) dimensional spaces using MDS (Multi-Dimensional Scaling) [2]. These methods revealed e.g. a circular-like structure on the 2D principal MDS subspace, but a direct correspondence between the physical stimuli, or facial images, and the expression perception is missing. Due to discreteness of SD scores and the sensitivity of MDS to outliers, these psychological spaces are difficult to use as quantitative representations of facial expressions. In [15] a new facial expression space is proposed as a psychophysical space in which the Riemann metric tensor is defined by the JND (Just Noticeable Difference) discrimination thresholds of expressions. The authors measured the JND discrimination thresholds at 23 points and fitted 23 JND ellipsoids in the 3D and 2D subspaces of the facial image space with PCA (Principal Component Analysis) using a covariance matrix. These results showed that the expression space is not a Euclidean space but a Riemann space with a rich and interesting geometric structure.

The next step in constructing a theory of facial expression spaces requires, first of all, the estimation of the Riemann metric tensor in the full, high dimensional expression space.

The number of measurements of JND thresholds (number of psychophysical experiments) required in order to determine the Riemann metric tensor at one point (facial expression) is $n(n+1)/2$, where n is the dimension of the expression space. Very little was known about this dimension today, but in [11] it was shown that a morphing sequence connecting two expression images does not contain images of the expressions lying between them in the 2D plane. This is known as a paradox of the dimensional theory. This implies that the dimension of the space should be greater than two. It is believed that the dimension could be very high. If the dimension estimate 50 is used as in [12], the number of JND threshold measurements must be greater than 1275 at every point in the space. Since these repetitious psychophysical experiments require careful calibration and endurance of observers, measuring such a high number of data points is unfeasible in practice.

In a general framework this problem is rooted in two open questions shared by Riemann manifold learning and investigation of psychophysical spaces: how to estimate the Riemann metric tensor in very high dimensions efficiently, and how to determine the effective dimension of a Riemann or a psychophysical space.

One of the major goals of manifold learning is dimension reduction, i.e. the problem of representing sets of data points in very high dimensional spaces as data points on a sub-manifold of lower dimension [4,5]. Although the term "manifold learning" has often been used as a synonym of dimension reduction, we use it here to include the understanding of the geometric structure of the data set in terms of differential, topological or Riemann manifolds. In particular, Riemann manifold learning in this general sense should include the capture of both extrinsic and intrinsic geometric invariants such as metric tensor, curvature etc. It also includes the development of efficient computational algorithms for modeling and applications.

Dimension reduction's best-known example is PCA, which models the data set as a linear subspace in the Euclidean space, also called a linear variety or manifold. PCA can then be regarded as a linear manifold learning. It has been generalized to local PCA [1] and nonlinear PCA such as kernel PCA etc. The PCA dimension reduction may, however, not be meaningful for a psychophysical space since the correlation functions among physical stimuli are certainly different from subjective differences between perceptions of these stimuli.

MDS [2] and its variations such as ISOMAP [3] are other popular tools in perceptional studies for dimension reduction. Their goal is to map a high dimensional space onto a low dimensional space while preserving the Euclidean distances between data points (ISOMAP used Dijkstra graph distance). This should be an isometry, which is the most important map in Riemann geometry preserving global distances between all pair of points. It is known that there is no way to find such a global isometry in general even if it exists. In the current context one is less interested in physical differences between stimuli, instead subjective distances are more relevant. However they are usually difficult to define and measure e.g. for two remote stimuli. Another difficulty is the fact that distances in a Riemann manifold are the lengths of the shortest paths called geodesics defined by Riemann metric tensor and, as mentioned above, the estimation of the metric tensor demands a large number of psychophysical experiments.

The MDS solution may also not be meaningful even in a sense of approximation if the algorithm is applied to data whose topology is not trivial (as for example in the popular Swissroll example) since such a global isometry as a single map does not exist in general [27]. Besides, these Dijkstra distances may cause jitter or numerical instability due to the discontinuity of lengths of the shortest paths on the data point graph.

In many investigations of Riemann manifold learning and applications [6–8], an essential assumption is that a Riemann metric is available or can be easily calculated. As mentioned above, the metric is inaccessible for psychophysical spaces even when procedures for JND threshold measurement are well established. Besides, it seems that the intrinsic geometry of Riemann manifolds has never played a substantial role in the dimension reduction methods until now.

In this paper, we first introduce definitions of effective dimensions for Riemann manifolds and psychophysical spaces in terms of Riemann metric tensor and the reciprocal lengths of the principal axes of the JND threshold hyperellipsoids.

We then use a divide-and-conquer strategy to estimate the high dimensional metric tensor from ellipses/ellipsoids fitting in 2D, 3D or low dimensional subspaces. At the same time, a partial dimension reduction is also possible. It makes use of a degeneration phenomenon of the ellipses/ellipsoid fitting in the 2D and 3D subspaces. These algorithms reduce the number of psychophysical experiments required for determination of n-dimensional Riemann metric tensor from $O(n^2)$ to a constant independent of n. This is an essential step which frees the Riemann geometric approach from the necessity of laborious psychophysical experiments and makes it suitable for practical applications.

We apply these algorithms to JND measurement data obtained from psychophysical investigations of facial expression recognition. We mainly investigate properties around the Neutral which is originally not included in the basic six expressions but believed to be an important expression itself lying in the center of the expression space. Upper and lower bounds for the effective dimension of the expression space are also obtained.

2   Riemann Spaces and Psychophysical Spaces

Recall that a Riemann space is a space S which has a Riemann metric tensor $G(p) = (g_{ij})$ defined smoothly at any point $p \in S$, which establishes a local geometry around a point p or in the tangent space T_pS in the terms of an inner product [28, 29]. In particular, an inner product between two tangent vectors $\boldsymbol{x}, \boldsymbol{y} \in T_pS$ is defined as

$$(\boldsymbol{x}, \boldsymbol{y}) := \boldsymbol{x}^T G(p) \boldsymbol{y} = \sum_{i,j} g_{ij} x_i y_j \tag{1}$$

which determines the angles and lengths, e.g.

$$\|\boldsymbol{x}\|^2 = \boldsymbol{x}^T G(p) \boldsymbol{x} = \sum_{i,j} g_{ij} x_i x_j \tag{2}$$

G is an $n \times n$ positive-definite symmetric matrix where n is the dimension of S.

A psychophysical space is a space of physical stimuli with the JND discrimination threshold data available at every point. In other words, a psychophysical space is a Riemann space where the Riemann metric tensor is defined by the JND discrimination thresholds for every stimulus.

The totality of vectors with unit distance from the point p or the subjective unit circle centered at p is defined as

$$\boldsymbol{x}^T G(p) \boldsymbol{x} = \sum_{i,j} g_{ij} x_i x_j = 1 \tag{3}$$

which is a hyper-ellipsoid in the space of physical stimuli that represents the JND discrimination thresholds from the point p.

It is known that the color space is a Riemann space whose metric tensor is defined by the JND color discrimination thresholds known as the MacAdam ellipses/ellipsoids [18, 19]. The Riemann metric of a color space is used in color reproduction and uniform color space construction [20–23]. JND thresholds for normal and color-weak vision observers are used to simulate and compensate color-weak vision so that e.g. each color-weak observer can share the same color perception with normal observers [24] and [25].

3   Psychophysical Expression Space

In [15], a new facial expression space was introduced as a psychophysical space. The JND discrimination thresholds measured in the expression image space turned out to be not circles of the same size everywhere, as the subjective unit circles are expected if the space is Euclidean. Instead ellipsoids/ellipses with different sizes and shapes were found. They form a smooth distribution in the space and therefore define the Riemann metric tensor for the expression space (Fig. 1).

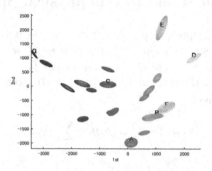

Fig. 1. 23 JND threshold ellipses in 1st–2nd PCA subspace [15]

The Riemann geometric structure was then used to produce a "uniform" expression space by building a global isometry mapping from the expression space to a Euclidean space [16]. Other applications such as the comparison and the mapping between the expression perceptions of different observers were reported in [17].

The metric tensor $G = (g_{ij})$ is an $n \times n$ positive-definite symmetric matrix defined at every point with $n(n+1)/2$ independent entries. To estimate the $G(p)$, measurements of JND threshold $\boldsymbol{x}_k, k = 1, ...,$ around the center p were used, each $\boldsymbol{x}_k$ by (3) defines a linear equation $\boldsymbol{x}_k^T G \boldsymbol{x}_k = 1$ in g_{ij}. So to obtain a unique estimate of G, one needs at least $n(n+1)/2$ points of JND threshold to obtain a system of independent linear equations of the same number. Thus, to obtain G from the JND threshold data is trivial if the dimension n is low such as in the case of color spaces. In a high dimensional space, a large number $n(n+1)/2$ of JND discrimination thresholds at every point are required in order to estimate the metric tensor.

4   Effective Dimension of Riemann and Psychophysical Spaces

4.1   Definition of Effective Dimension for a Riemann Space

First we introduce a definition of the effective dimension for a Riemann manifold in terms of the local geometry defined by the metric tensor G.

The dimension is a local attribute as discussed in [26] and [27], e.g. the local dimension at a point p is the dimension of the tangent space T_pS, which is the same everywhere in a manifold and therefore equals the global dimension. The effective dimension is therefore also the effective dimension at every tangent space.

Assume the expression space forms an e dimensional submanifold S in the data space or the embedding space $\mathbb{R}^n$, then every tangent space of the expression space will be an e dimensional affine subspace of $\mathbb{R}^n$. The Riemann metric tensor $G(p)$ defined in $\mathbb{R}^n$ will be an $n \times n$ rank e matrix at every point $p \in S$.

Assume the eigenvalues of $G(p)$ at the point $p \in S$ are in a descending order $\lambda_i, i = 1, ..., n$ with the eigenvectors e_i. Then, even if noise or observation error exist, the inner product can be approximated by the sum up to the first e dominant eigenvalues $\lambda_i, i \leq e$ or for all $x, y \in T_pS$,

$$(x, y) = \lambda_1 u_1 v_1 + \ ... \ ... + \lambda_n u_n v_n \approx \lambda_1 u_1 v_1 + ... + \lambda_e u_e v_e$$

with $\{u_i\}, \{v_i\}$ as the eigen-coordinates of x, y. The distance can also be approximated as

$$\|x\|^2 = \lambda_1 u_1^2 + ... + \lambda_n u_n^2 \approx \lambda_1 u_1^2 + ... + \lambda_e u_e^2.$$

Definition 1. The effective dimension e of a Riemann space S at a point p is defined as the dimension of the subspace of the tangent space T_pS on which the metric tensor $G(p)$ is positive-definite. This is the effective rank of the metric tensor $G(p)$. A statistical equivalent of e can be defined as the number of the first dominant eigen-values λ_i of $G(p)$.

4.2   Definition of Effective Dimension for Psychophysical Spaces

The estimation of the dimension of the expression space remained an open and difficult task in the expression theory. Psychological spaces in dimensional theory used low dimensional principal MDS subspaces without a discussion on the upper bound of the dimensions. The principal PCA subspaces of the image space used in engineering applications is not a good choice since they contain information irrelevant to expression perception.

From the point of view of psychophysics, the JND discrimination thresholds at an expression are reciprocals of the perceptual sensitivity around the expression. The directions with minimal JND thresholds are the most significant dimensions in perception, while the directions with large JND are insensitive and therefore less important in perception or could be ignored.

Here we define the dimension of a psychophysical space as the number of the principal directions which are the most significant in perception or the most perceptually sensitive.

Definition 2. The effective dimension e of a psychophysical space S at a point p is the number of the perceptional-significant directions in the tangent space T_pS of p. In particular, these directions are those along which the principal axes of the JND threshold hyper-ellipsoid have shortest lengths.

In other words, these directions are given by those eigenvectors of the Riemann metric tensor $G(p)$ at the point p with dominant eigenvalues, which are reciprocal square lengths of the principal axes of the JND threshold hyperellipsoid.

Denote the JND discrimination threshold at the point p as

$$x^T G(p) x = \sum_{i=1}^{n} \frac{u_i^2}{a_i^2} = 1$$

a hyper-ellipsoid with the i-th principal axis of the length a_i along the i-th eigenvector e_i of the matrix $G(p)$, the eigenvalue $\lambda_i = 1/a_i^2$, $\{u_i\}$ the eigencoordinates of x.

Let $\tau > 0$ be the upper bound of JND threshold, or a highest tolerable insensitivity, we define

$$e := \#\{a_i \leq \tau, i = 1, ..., n\}.$$

Obviously Definitions 1 and 2 are equivalent for a psychophysical space such as the expression space.

5   High Dimensional Riemann Metric Tensor from Low Dimensional Subspaces

We will now describe a method to determine the Riemann metric tensor $G(p)$ of the expression manifold S in the high dimensional space $\mathbb{R}^n$ from a number of low dimensional subspaces.

The Riemann metric tensor at the point p

$$G = (g_{ij}),\ 1 \leq i, j \leq n,\ g_{ij} = g_{ji}$$

as an $n \times n$ semi-positive-definite symmetric matrix has $n(n+1)/2$ independent entries g_{ij}.

Now we consider the projection of the JND threshold hyper-ellipsoids in the embedding space $\mathbb{R}^n$ to a low dimensional subspace. E.g. 2D and 3D subspace. The projection of $T_p\mathbb{R}^n = \mathbb{R}^n$ onto the 2D subspace $[X_i, X_j]$

$$I_{ij}:\quad x = (x_1, ..., x_n)^T \longmapsto x_{ij} := (0, .., x_i, .., x_j, ..., 0)^T$$

is defined by the diagonal matrix

$$I_{ij} := diag(0, .., \overset{i}{1}, ...\overset{j}{1}, ...0), \qquad x_{ij} = I_{ij} x$$

Under this projection onto $[X_i, X_j]$, the JND threshold hyper-ellipsoid in $T_p\mathbb{R}^n = \mathbb{R}^n$ centered at p

$$x^T G x = \sum_{i,j} g_{ij} x_i x_j = 1$$

is projected onto an ellipse in the 2D subspace:

$$x_{ij}^T G x_{ij} = x^T I_{ij}^T G I_{ij} x = 1 \quad \text{or} \quad (x_i, x_j) G_{ij} \begin{pmatrix} x_i \\ x_j \end{pmatrix} = 1$$

The matrix G_{ij} turns out to be a 2×2 submatrix of G.

$$G_{ij} := \begin{pmatrix} g_{ii} & g_{ij} \\ g_{ji} & g_{jj} \end{pmatrix}, \qquad g_{ij} = g_{ji}$$

G_{ij} can be obtained by ellipse fitting of the JND points also projected onto $[X_i, X_j]$. If one repeats on other 2D subspaces $[X_i, X_j], i, j = 1, ..., n$ to obtain G_{ij} using projections of the same data points onto $[X_i, X_j]$, the high dimensional metric tensor $G = (g_{ij})$ can be eventually uniquely determined.

Example: Assume $n = 3$. Then G is a 3×3 matrix whose estimate requires at least 6 points or measurements of JND data. We now show how to estimate G with only 3 data points. If we project the point $x = (x_1, x_2, x_3)^T$ to $x_{13} = I_{13} x = (x_1, 0, x_3)^T$ in $[X_1, X_3]$ plane, the JND ellipsoid $x^T G x = 1$ is projected to

$$x_{13}^T G x_{13} = (x_1, 0, x_3)^T G \begin{pmatrix} x_1 \\ 0 \\ x_3 \end{pmatrix} = x^T I_{13} G I_{13} x = 1, \text{ or } (x_1, x_3) G_{13} \begin{pmatrix} x_1 \\ x_3 \end{pmatrix} = 1$$

which is an ellipse in x_1, x_3 defined by the matrix

$$I_{13} G I_{13} = \begin{pmatrix} 1 & 0 & 0 \\ 0 & 0 & 0 \\ 0 & 0 & 1 \end{pmatrix} \begin{pmatrix} g_{11} & g_{12} & g_{13} \\ g_{21} & g_{22} & g_{23} \\ g_{31} & g_{32} & g_{33} \end{pmatrix} \begin{pmatrix} 1 & 0 & 0 \\ 0 & 0 & 0 \\ 0 & 0 & 1 \end{pmatrix} = \begin{pmatrix} g_{11} & 0 & g_{13} \\ 0 & 0 & 0 \\ g_{31} & 0 & g_{33} \end{pmatrix}, \text{ or } G_{13} = \begin{pmatrix} g_{11} & g_{13} \\ g_{31} & g_{33} \end{pmatrix}.$$

The submatrix G_{13} of G can be estimated by ellipse fitting with only 3 JND points projected onto $[X_1, X_3]$. All g_{ij} can be found using projections onto and ellipses fitting in $[X_1, X_2], [X_2, X_3]$ planes, using projections of the same 3 data points. Notice that only 3 not 6 points (obtained from experiments by human observers) in 3D space of general position are sufficient to estimate the whole G.

We also show this procedure for the 3D case. The projection of $\mathbb{R}^n = T_p \mathbb{R}^n$ onto a 3D subspace $[X_i, X_j, X_k]$

$$I_{ijk}: \quad x = (x_1, ..., x_n)^T \longmapsto x_{ijk} := (0, .., x_i, .., x_j, ..., x_k, ..0)^T$$

is defined by the diagonal matrix

$$I_{ij} := diag(0, .., \overset{i}{1}, ...\overset{j}{1}, ..., \overset{k}{1}, ..., 0), \qquad x_{ijk} = I_{ijk} x$$

The JND threshold hyper-ellipsoid in $T_p \mathbb{R}^n = \mathbb{R}^n$ is projected onto the 3D subspace as an ellipsoid

$$x_{ijk}^T G x_{ijk} = x^T I_{ijk}^T G I_{ijk} x = 1 \quad \text{or} \quad (x_i, x_j, x_k) G_{ijk} \begin{pmatrix} x_i \\ x_j \\ x_k \end{pmatrix} = 1$$

where G_{ijk} is a 3×3 submatrix of G

$$G_{ijk} := \begin{pmatrix} g_{ii} & g_{ij} & g_{ik} \\ g_{ji} & g_{jj} & g_{jk} \\ g_{ki} & g_{kj} & g_{kk} \end{pmatrix} \qquad g_{ij} = g_{ji}$$

The G_{ijk} can be obtained from ellipsoid fitting using at least 6 JND data points projected onto the 3D subspace $[X_i, X_j, X_k]$. The whole matrix G is obtained by the same procedure in all 3D subspaces using the same 6 data points.

One should notice that the geometry in the high dimensional space is different from those in the subspaces, e.g. the principal axes of the JND threshold ellipses or ellipsoids in subspaces do not coincide with the principal axes of the JND threshold hyper-ellipsoids in the high dimensional space $\mathbb{R}^n$. Nevertheless, this divide-and-conquer strategy breaks down the estimation of the Riemann metric tensor in the high dimensional space to estimations of the metric tensors in various 2D and 3D subspaces. The number $n(n+1)/2$ of the JND data required for the hyperellipsoid fitting is then reduced to 3 for 2D ellipses fitting and 6 for 3D ellipsoids fitting. Therefore, the number of psychophysical measurements of the JND thresholds is reduced from $O(n^2)$ to a constant. Meanwhile, one still needs to repeat about $O(n^2)$ times of projections and ellipse/ellipsoid fitting in low dimensional subspaces. In practice, a reasonable number of uniformly distributed JND points remains desirable so that JND points of general position can be expected after being projected onto low dimensional subspaces. This strategy is also applicable to subspaces of dimensions higher than 3.

One can observe a repetition of estimates for the same entry g_{ij} of G in different subspaces. These different estimates can be used to obtain an average to increase the statistical stability of the estimate value of G. In particular, when 2D subspaces are used, n different estimate values of the diagonal entries g_{ii} can be obtained from all subspaces $[X_i, X_j], j = 1, ..., n$. 3D subspaces could be advantageous in this sense since all entries g_{ij} can be averaged among the n different estimate values from subspaces $[X_i, X_j, X_k], k = 1, ..., n$. Besides, this approach can be implemented in parallel.

6   Dimension Reduction in Low Dimensional Subspaces

First we discuss a phenomenon in the low dimensional fitting of ellipses and ellipsoids i.e. degeneration of the JND ellipses/ellipsoids in the low dimensional subspaces, often observed when the dimension of the manifold in $\mathbb{R}^n$ is low.

A natural assumption in these fittings in low dimensions is that the data points of JND thresholds projected from $\mathbb{R}^n$ will be in a general position e.g. fill the subspace. As a result, the ellipse or ellipsoid fitting in 2D or 3D subspace will be a well-conditioned problem.

However, it is possible that in certain choices of the 2D or 3D subspaces, there is a perceptionally insensitive direction along which the principal axis of the JND threshold ellipse or ellipsoid is very long. It means the data set has a smaller degree of freedom. E.g. lies on a proper submanifold inside a subspace of the 2D or 3D subspace or as its parallel shift along the direction. In these cases, the metric tensor G_{ij} or G_{ijk} has an eigenvalue near to zero or could have a negative value due to numerical errors.

For example, consider a 3D subspace $[U, V, W]$ with coordinates u, v, w where the JND threshold data projections are fitted by an ellipsoid

$$\lambda_1 u^2 + \lambda_2 v^2 + \lambda_3 w^2 = \frac{u^2}{a^2} + \frac{v^2}{b^2} + \frac{w^2}{c^2} = 1.$$

If the JND threshold data points projected from the high dimensional psychophysical space are not in a general position. E.g. in the case where the JND hyperellipsoids is of a dimension lower that n, and w-axis is not included in the dimensions defining the JND hyperellipsoids. Then the data will not fill the space but distribute inside along the $[U, V]$ plane, so the JND threshold is actually a planar curve i.e. an ellipse.

$$F(x, y) = 0, \qquad \lambda_1 u^2 + \lambda_2 v^2 = \frac{u^2}{a^2} + \frac{v^2}{b^2} = 1 \tag{4}$$

then the fitting ellipsoid will become a degenerated surface

$$\lambda_1 u^2 + \lambda_2 v^2 = \frac{u^2}{a^2} + \frac{v^2}{b^2} = 1, \; \forall w. \quad \text{i.e.} \quad c = \infty, \; or \; \lambda_3 = 0$$

which is a parallel shift of the ellipse (4) along the w-axis on which the principal axis of the ellipsoid is infinitely long.

We will then remove all these perceptually insensitive directions whenever such a degeneration occurs. Dimension reduction of the data space will be achieved by applying this procedure to all low dimensional subspaces.

7 Experiments

7.1 Image Preprocessing, Feature Points and Morphing

In the experiments the database 3D Scan Store Female01 [14] with 38 facial expression images is used. Two of them are shown in Fig. 2. For each image 123 feature points are selected as shown in Fig. 3. They are used as the nodes in the 3D mesh model of the face, which is then used to produce morphing sequences between two target images. The set of feature points alone can be regarded as a compressed representation of the facial expressions. To reduce computational cost, two kinds of inputs are used: the gray-valued or density images of the expressions obtained from the color images, and the feature points of the same images.

7.2 JND Discrimination Threshold Measurement

The JND discrimination thresholds at the Neutral expression were measured using the screen in Fig. 4. In the beginning both the left and right images are

Fig. 2. Examples of two expression images used in the experiments

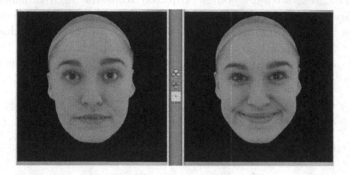

Fig. 3. 123 feature points

the same, the left image is fixed and the right one shows the morphing image sequences changing to another expression. The objectives of two male students are asked to stop the morphing as soon as he percepts the difference of expressions between the left and the right images. Care is taken to prevent bias due to adaptation, prediction, learning and fatigue. Therefore, the morphing sequences are randomly ordered, with dark mode prelude and intermissions between two experiments. (For details see [16]). Each experiment along a morphing sequence is repeated three times, then the JND thresholds are determined by an average of the three measurement values.

8   30D Subspaces of PCA and Non-metric MDS

The facial expression image spaces used in the experiments have the follow dimensions.

- Color images: 7.8×10^5 dimensions.
- Gray-valued images: 2.6×10^5 dimensions.
- Feature point images: 246 dimensions.

To evaluate and to compare with the proposed definitions and algorithms, we need a subspace of moderate dimension. Here, we choose the 30D principal subspaces of PCA and non-metric MDS in the expression space. As references for

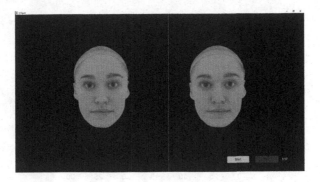

Fig. 4. Screen for JND threshold measurement

later comparison to the proposed method for dimension estimation, we also calculated and show the eigenvalues distribution of PCA and the Stress of the non-metric MDS from which we obtain estimates of dimensions in the conventional sense as below. On the other hand, computations in the feature point image space of full dimension 246 are feasible as will be shown in the next section.

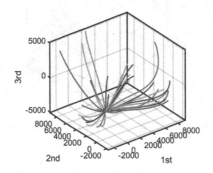

Fig. 5. Morphings in the 1st, 2nd, 3rd PCA subspace of gray-valued images

The 37 morphing sequences in the first 3D PCA subspace are shown in Fig. 5. The eigenvalue distribution normalized by the sum of all eigenvalues in the 30D PCA subspace is shown in Fig. 6. Using the 5% threshold or elbow rule the dimension estimate is around six.

The morphing sequences in the first 3D MDS space are shown in Fig. 7. The graph of the stress in the 30D subspace of non-metric MDS is shown in Fig. 8. The dimension estimate based on the 5% rule is approximately four.

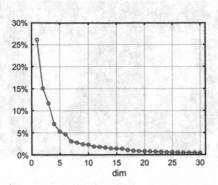

Fig. 6. Eigenvalue distribution of PCA of gray-valued images

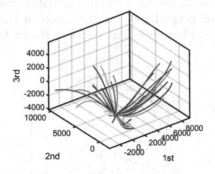

Fig. 7. Morphings in the first 3D non-metric MDS subspace of gray-valued images

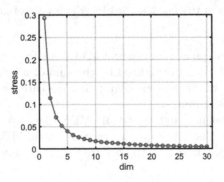

Fig. 8. Stress of non-metric MDS of gray-valued images

9 Dimension Reduction of 30D PCA, MDS Subspaces and Feature Point Space in Low Dimensional Subspaces

The dimension reduction by ellipse and ellipsoid fitting in lower dimensional subspaces is applied to the JND threshold data of the two observers we call them Observer A and B.

First, the results of the dimension reduction in the first 30D subspaces of both PCA and non-metric MDS spaces are shown in Table 1. The 246 dimensional space of feature points is also reduced with ellipse fitting and ellipsoid fitting in all 2D and 3D subspaces respectively. The results are shown in Table 2.

Table 1. Dimension reduction in 30D subspaces of PCA and non-metric MDS

Objective	Space	Reduction method	Original dim	Reduced dim
A	PCA	2D ellipse fitting	30	29
B	PCA	2D ellipse fitting	30	18
A	PCA	3D ellipsoid fitting	30	6
B	PCA	3D ellipsoid fitting	30	9
A	Non-metric MDS	2D ellipse fitting	30	27
B	Non-metric MDS	2D ellipse fitting	30	25
A	Non-metric MDS	3D ellipsoid fitting	30	7
B	Non-metric MDS	3D ellipsoid fitting	30	9

Table 2. Dimension reduction in 246D and 30D subspace of feature points

Objective	Reduction method	Original dim	Reduced dim
A	2D ellipse fitting	246	125
B	2D ellipse fitting	246	62
A	3D ellipsoid fitting	246	12
B	3D ellipsoid fitting	246	7

10 Reciprocal Square Lengths of Principal Axes of JND Threshold Hyper-ellipsoid

The Riemann metric tensor and reciprocal square lengths of the principal axes of the JND hyper-ellipsoid are calculated for PCA and non-metric MDS subspaces and the subspaces of feature point images obtained in the previous section.

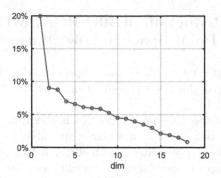

Fig. 9. Reciprocal square lengths of JND hyper-ellipsoid axes in PCA space

The 18D PCA subspace of gray-valued images obtained by 2D ellipses fitting dimension reduction is used here. The reciprocal square lengths of the principal axes of JND hyper-ellipsoid normalized by the sum of all axis lengths is shown in Fig. 9. The Riemann metric tensor is obtained with 3D ellipsoid fitting. The effective dimension of the PCA space by reciprocal axis lengths is approximately nine. The 25D non-metric MDS subspace of gray-valued images obtained by 2D ellipses fitting dimension reduction is also used here. The normalized reciprocal square lengths of the principal axes of JND hyper-ellipsoid is shown in Fig. 10. The Riemann metric tensor is obtained with 3D ellipsoid fitting. The effective dimension of this space by the reciprocal axis lengths is approximately eight.

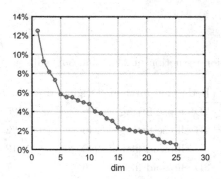

Fig. 10. Reciprocal square lengths of JND hyper-ellipsoid axes in non-metric MDS space

Using 2D ellipse fitting in dimension reduction and 3D ellipsoid fitting in estimation of the Riemann metric tensor G, the reciprocal squared lengths of the principal axes of the JND hyper-ellipsoids or the eigenvalues of G in the space of the feature point images are shown in Fig. 11. The effective dimension of the feature point space by the axis length distribution is approximately four. When using 3D ellipsoid fitting in both dimension reduction and estimation of

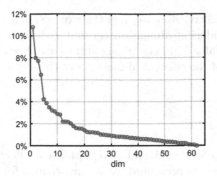

Fig. 11. Reciprocal square lengths of JND hyperellipsoid axes in feature point space, 2D ellipse fitting for dimension reduction and 3D ellipsoid fitting for metric estimate

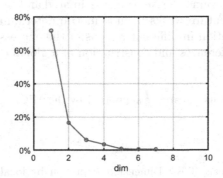

Fig. 12. Reciprocal square lengths of JND hyperellipsoid axes in feature point space, 3D ellipsoid fitting for dimension reduction and metric estimate

the metric tensor G, the reciprocal square lengths of the principal axes of the JND hyper-ellipsoids or the eigenvalues of G in the 246D space of the feature point images are shown in Fig. 12. The effective dimension of the feature point space from this distribution is approximately three.

11   Discussion

It can be observed that the non-metric MDS dimensions are lower than the PCA dimensions which suggests that PCA extracts more information irrelevant to facial expressions.

The dimension estimates for feature point images are lower than those for gray-valued images. This indicates that the feature point images contain less information for expression perception than the gray-valued images. Therefore the dimensions estimated from feature point images and from the gray-valued images serve as a lower bound and an upper bound for the true effective dimension of the expression space.

As a result, the effective dimension of the expression space should be between four and eight. Considering dimension estimates derived using PCA and non-metric MDS of gray-valued images are six and four in Sect. 8, we conclude that a reasonable estimate of the effective dimension of the expression space is between four to six.

12 Conclusion

Definitions of both geometrical and psychophysical effective dimensions for a facial expression space are presented. Novel algorithms for Riemann metric tensor estimation and dimension reduction in subspaces are proposed and evaluated with JND discrimination threshold data. As a result, the effective dimension of the expression space around the Neutral is estimated and shown in terms of lower and upper bounds. Future works include metric determination and dimension reduction and estimation in different regions of the expression space, investigation of individual differences and construction of a global coordinate system for the space.

Acknowledgment. This research is supported by the MIC/SCOPE #181603006.

References

1. Kambhatla, N., Leen, T.K.: Dimension reduction by local principal component analysis. Neural Comput. **9**(7), 1493–1516 (1997)
2. Richardson, M.W.: Multidimensional psychophysics. Psychol. Bull. **35**(9), 659–660 (1938)
3. Tenenbaum, J.B., De Silva, V., Langford, J.C.: A global geometric framework for nonlinear dimensionality reduction. Science **290**(5500), 2319–2323 (2000)
4. Gorban, A.: Principal Manifolds for Data Visualization and Dimension Reduction. Springer, Heidelberg (2007). https://doi.org/10.1007/978-3-540-73750-6
5. Ma, Y., Fu, Y.: Manifold Learning Theory and Applications. CRC Press, Boca Raton (2011)
6. Goh, A.: Riemann manifold clustering and dimension reduction for vision-based analysis. In: Wang, L., Zhao, G., Cheng, L., Pietikäinen, M. (eds.) Machine Learning for Vision-Based Motion Analysis, pp. 27–53. Springer, London (2011). https://doi.org/10.1007/978-0-85729-057-1_2
7. Brun, A., Westin, C.-F., Herberthson, M., Knutsson, H.: Fast manifold learning based on Riemannian normal coordinates. In: Kalviainen, H., Parkkinen, J., Kaarna, A. (eds.) SCIA 2005. LNCS, vol. 3540, pp. 920–929. Springer, Heidelberg (2005). https://doi.org/10.1007/11499145_93
8. Lin, T., Zha, H.: Riemannian manifold learning. IEEE Trans. Pattern Anal. Mach. Intell. **30**(5), 796–809 (2008)
9. Ekman, P., Friesen, W.V.: Facial Action Coding System: A Technique for the Measurement of Facial Movement. Consulting Psychologists Press, Palo Alto (1978)
10. Russell, J.A., Bullock, M.: Multidimensional scaling of emotional facial expressions: similarity from preschoolers to adults. J. Pers. Soc. Psychol. **48**(5), 1290–1298 (1985)

11. Young, A.W., Rowland, D., Calder, A.J., et al.: Facial expression megamix: test of dimensional and category accounts of emotion recognition. Cognition **63**(3), 271–313 (1997)
12. Calder, A.J., Burton, A.M., Miller, P., Young, A.W., Akamatsu, S.: A principal component analysis of facial expressions. Vision Res. **41**(9), 1179–1208 (2001)
13. Benitez-Quiroz, C., Srinivasan, R., Martinez, A.M.: EmotioNet: an accurate, real-time algorithm for the automatic annotation of a million facial expressions in the wild. In: Proceedings of IEEE-CVPR (2016)
14. 3DScanStore. https://www.3dscanstore.com/. Accessed 2 Feb 2020
15. Sumiya, R., Lenz, R., Chao, J.: Measurement of JND thresholds and Riemannian geometry in facial expression space. In: Kurosu, M. (ed.) HCI 2018. LNCS, vol. 10901, pp. 453–464. Springer, Cham (2018). https://doi.org/10.1007/978-3-319-91238-7_37
16. Sumiya, R., Chao, J.: Transform facial expression space to Euclidean space using Riemann normal coordinates and its applications. In: Kurosu, M. (ed.) HCII 2019. LNCS, vol. 11567, pp. 168–178. Springer, Cham (2019). https://doi.org/10.1007/978-3-030-22643-5_13
17. Shinto, M., Chao, J.: How to compare and exchange facial expression perceptions between different individuals with Riemann geometry. In: Kurosu, M. (ed.) HCII 2019. LNCS, vol. 11567, pp. 155–167. Springer, Cham (2019). https://doi.org/10.1007/978-3-030-22643-5_12
18. MacAdam, D.L.: Visual sensitivities to color differences in daylight. JOSA **32**, 247–273 (1942)
19. Brown, W., MacAdam, D.: Visual sensitivities to combined chromaticity and luminance differences. JOSA **39**, 808–823 (1949)
20. Chao, J., Lenz, R., Matsumoto, D., Nakamura, T.: Riemann geometry for color characterization and mapping. In: Conference on Colour in Graphics, Imaging, and Vision, IS&T, pp. 277–282 (2008)
21. Chao, J., Osugi, I., Suzuki, M.: On definitions and construction of uniform color space. In: CGIV, IS&T, pp. 55–60 (2004)
22. Suzuki, M., Chao, J.: On construction of uniform color spaces. IEICE Trans. Fundam. **E85-A**(9), 2097–2106 (2002)
23. Ohshima, S., Mochizuki, R., Chao, J., Lenz, R.: Color reproduction using Riemann normal coordinates. In: Trémeau, A., Schettini, R., Tominaga, S. (eds.) CCIW 2009. LNCS, vol. 5646, pp. 140–149. Springer, Heidelberg (2009). https://doi.org/10.1007/978-3-642-03265-3_15
24. Mochizuki, R., Kojima, T., Lenz, R., Chao, J.: Color-weak compensation using local affine isometry based on discrimination threshold matching. JOSA **32**(11), 2093–2103 (2015)
25. Oshima, S., Mochizuki, R., Lenz, R., Chao, J.: Modeling, measuring, and compensating color weak vision. IEEE Trans. Image Process. **25**(6), 2587–2600 (2016)
26. Tasaki, H., Lenz, R., Chao, J.: Simplex-based dimension estimation of topological manifolds. In: Proceedings of ICPR, pp. 3598–3603. IEEE (2016)
27. Tasaki, H., Lenz, R., Chao, J.: Dimension estimation and topological manifold learning. In: Proceedings of IJCNN, Budapest, 14–19 July 2019. IEEE (2019)
28. Do Carmo, M.P.: Riemannian Geometry. GTM, vol. 171. Springer, Cham (2016). https://doi.org/10.1007/978-3-319-26654-1_9
29. Petersen, P.: Riemannian Geometry. GTM, 3rd edn. Springer, New York (2006). https://doi.org/10.1007/978-3-319-26654-1

Mobile Multitasking in Urban Contexts: Habituation and Countermeasures

Zoubeir Tkiouat[✉], Pierre-Majorique Léger, and Ryad Titah

HEC Montréal, Montréal, QC, Canada
{zoubeir.tkiouat,pierre-majorique.leger,ryad.titah}@hec.ca

Abstract. With the increase in adoption of mobile electronic devices such as smartphones, it becomes more and more important to address the risks associated with their use. As such, this research paper addresses the behavior and habit formation of mobile multitasking, i.e., *the use of a mobile IT device while performing a motor task such as walking*, and its negative impacts on the individual's performance and safety. To have a better understanding on how different countermeasures impact the behavior of mobile multitasking in the short term as well as the habit of mobile multitasking in the long term, the present research paper introduces a classification of the different countermeasures that are put in place to curb the risks of mobile IT multitasking in an urban context. Then, it proposes a conceptual framework that explains the mechanisms and the impacts of the deterrent countermeasures as well as the preventive countermeasures on both the behavior of mobile multitasking and the habit formation of mobile multitasking.

Keywords: Mobile multitasking · Mobile IT distraction · IT distraction countermeasures

1 Introduction

The adoption of mobile electronic devices such as smartphones has rapidly increased during the last ten years to reach entire populations in some cases, e.g., young adults' adoption of smartphones in the US reached 96% of this population in 2019 [1]. While the use of mobile devices has produced several important benefits in our everyday lives, important risks are associated with their use. The mobile multitasking; i.e., the use of a mobile IT device while performing a motor task such as walking; can have important negative impacts on an individual's performance and safety due to the cognitive load associated with switching between different tasks [2, 3].

Although there is considerable research on the negative impact of mobile multitasking on individuals' attention and associated risks [4–7], very few studies investigated the effects of countermeasures on the risks associated to this behavior. More importantly, our review of information systems and pedestrian safety literatures, shows that there have been very little theoretical and empirical studies that investigated these countermeasures, or their efficacy and efficiency in altering the behavior and breaking the habit of mobile multitasking.

© Springer Nature Switzerland AG 2021
M. Kurosu (Ed.): HCII 2021, LNCS 12762, pp. 622–632, 2021.
https://doi.org/10.1007/978-3-030-78462-1_48

In this context, the objective of the present research is to develop a conceptual framework with theoretical propositions that allows us to better understand *"how do different countermeasures impact the behavior of mobile multitasking in the short term as well as the habit of mobile multitasking (MM habit) in the long term?"*. The paper starts with a review of the mobile IT multitasking and pedestrian distraction literatures. Then, we introduce a classification of the different countermeasures that are put in place to curb the risks of mobile IT multitasking in an urban context. Finally, we develop the conceptual model that explains the effects of the different countermeasures on the risky behavior of *"mobile IT multitasking"* and its habit formation.

2   Mobile IT Multitasking and Countermeasures for Pedestrian Distraction

The phenomenon of interest in this paper is mobile IT multitasking that we define as *the concurrent performance of one or more information technology tasks with small electronic devices such as a smartphone, a smart watch, or a gaming device while performing a movement such as walking* [8]. While we acknowledge past research on the impact of electronic mobile devices on the cognitive and attentional capacity of individuals, in this paper, we specifically focus on mobile users performing a motor task.

We use the term "countermeasures" to refer to the controls and interventions that are put in place to curb the safety risks associated with the behavior of mobile IT multitasking. These controls or interventions can be targeted at the behavior itself or at other risk factors within the environment. We also focus on countermeasures in an organizational context (i.e., implemented by organizations). This section is devised in two parts. The first part addresses the phenomenon of mobile IT multitasking among pedestrians as well as the issue of distraction caused by electronic devices. In the second part, we review the literature on countermeasures and conceptualize these countermeasures based on the deterrence framework in IS.

2.1   Mobile IT Multitasking and Pedestrian Distraction

The use of mobile technology devices is pervasive in our societies and more so amongst the younger generations. As shown in a recent survey, the proportion of US teenagers (12 to 17) owning a smartphone was already at 47% in 2012 with one out of four teenagers accessing internet primarily using a mobile device [9]. With the increase of the variety of technology in mobile devices and the replacement of older cellphones with smartphones, the adoption of smartphone amongst young adults (18 to 29) in the US has reached 96% in 2019 [1].

With the many advantages that mobile devices bring to individuals there are different costs associated with this adoption. For example, the distracting effect of cellphone use makes pedestrians less attentive to traffic, leaving them less time to cross streets safely and exposing them to more collisions and "close calls" (i.e., very small gaps between incoming vehicles and pedestrians) [4–6]. In their observational study, Thompson and colleagues found that one third of pedestrians engaged in a distracting activity including talking, texting, and listening to music on a mobile IT device, which provides further evidence for the pervasiveness of this issue [10].

In their review on how media multitasking affects the performance of tasks such as driving, walking, working, and performing academic activities, Levine et al. (2012) concluded that based on the attentional switching cost from one task to the other, the sharing of attentional resources between those two tasks lead to a decrease in performance when compared to doing only one task [11]. In the context of pedestrians, this drop in performance leads to lower chances for distracted pedestrians to correctly identify and process cues from their environment [7] making them more prone to take risks and more vulnerable to dangers that may occur while walking. Mobile IT multitasking also affects the speed of pedestrians while walking [12] and their ability to find opportunities to cross streets safely [5, 13].

While the performance of two tasks can be improved with practice, it is only possible in specific contexts. Given that automatic detection develops as a result of consistent mapping of stimuli to responses over time [14] a necessary condition for one of the two tasks, i.e., walking and using the mobile IT device, to become automatic is consistency in the environment [15]. Similar to mobile IT multitasking while driving [15], pedestrians using a mobile device while walking must react to unanticipated stimuli that occur in their environments, e.g., flow of traffic or walking in new routes, which makes the activity of walking difficult to become automatic. On the other hand, a multitude of functionalities and usages can be performed on a mobile IT device. Even under the assumption that an individual would use the device for only one specific task such as a text conversation, this one highly varies from one text conversation to the other. This lack of consistency in the environment of both tasks makes it highly unlikely for individuals to automate one of them in order to raise their performance in multitasking.

In their meta-analysis that included fourteen experimental studies, Simmons et al. [16] found that when comparing specific tasks done on mobile phone by pedestrians, namely, texting, conversing on the phone and listening to music, both conversing on the phone and texting increased the rate of close calls and actual hits. In some cases, the use of mobile devices prohibits its user from perceiving warnings used by other actors involved. In their study that analyzed reports of pedestrians' injuries and deaths published between 2004 and 2011, Lichenstein and colleagues found that 74% of cases had pedestrians wearing headphones at the moment of the crash, and that in 29% of the cases, a sound warning had happened before the crash [17].

An important factor that hinders the risk assessment of distracted walking in general, and particularly mobile IT distractions, is the lack of data about the phenomenon [18]. According to their review, Mwakalonge and colleagues [18] found that most of studies are experiments and simulations. The results of these studies are difficult to generalize and without data on pedestrian-auto accidents it is difficult to make the case for the use of mobile IT devices as an important causal factor in accident risks.

2.2 Mobile IT Multitasking Countermeasures

Due to the undesirability of using an IT mobile device while walking, we will look at the countermeasures that can potentially be implemented to mitigate this behavior based on a deterrence theory framework.

Deterrence theory has its root in criminology [19] and has been adapted to other types of undesirable behaviors in the management fields including the IS field in the case of behaviors such as employee policy violations [20] and employee computer abuse [21]. According to this theory, individuals weigh the costs and benefits of committing a crime, i.e., an undesirable behavior, and if the costs of committing the behavior outweigh their benefits, they will not engage in it. The main element contributing to the evaluation of these costs are the risks of getting caught and the severity of the penalty (sanctions). The main types of sanctions that individuals consider in their evaluation are formal sanctions, informal sanctions and shame [22]. Formal sanctions are the punishment that is explicitly put in place by organizations in the form of policies and laws in case of individuals breaching these regulations. The Informal sanction are a social type of punishment such as the loss of reputation, and social censure from colleagues, friends, and family. Shame on the other hand is self-imposed which means that it is a deterrent stemming from the feeling of guilt or embarrassment if others knew of one's socially undesirable actions.

To reduce systems' risk, and information systems' risk in particular, Straub and Welke introduced three more types of countermeasures in addition to the deterrent countermeasures [23]. The four types of countermeasures are: deterrent countermeasures, preventive countermeasures, countermeasures for detection, and countermeasures for remedy or recovery. As we are looking at countermeasures that minimize the safety risks associated with the mobile IT multitasking, we choose to look at the preventive and deterrent countermeasures with the other countermeasures, i.e., "detection" and "remedy" being outside the scope of this paper.

According to Straub and Welke several potential system abuses are controlled by deterrent measures [23]. In the context of system abuses, these include policies and guidelines concerning proper usage of a system as well as awareness and educational programs that are aimed at the user. The deterrent countermeasures are passive as they do not inherently provide enforcement. Education (or awareness training) represent one important type of deterrent countermeasure in the sense that it emphasizes two important components of the general deterrence theory. The certainty of the sanction and its severity as perceived by the individuals potentially engaging in the behavior [24].

In the IS context, a study looking into the impact of sanction perceptions on the intention to misuse an IS and the impact of security countermeasures on the sanction perception found that the perceived severity of sanction have a more significant impact when compared to the perceived certainty of the sanctions [25]. The countermeasures that were hypothesized by D'Arcy and colleagues [25] increasing the perceptions of sanctions are 1) security policies; 2) security, education, training, and awareness programs, as well as 3) computer monitoring. All of these were found to have a significant impact in increasing the perceived sanctions. Since their focus was on the user awareness they have only focused on the deterrent countermeasures.

Preventive countermeasures are controls put in place to inhibit individuals from engaging in an undesirable activity even if they want to by making them deplete their resources in pursuing such activity [26]. In other words, they are active measures that make it difficult for individuals who ignore the deterrents to engage in the behavior [23]. Examples of such preventive measures in the case of software piracy are physical locks on computer rooms, as well as other software-based solutions that include encryption and password protection [26, 27]. In the context of pedestrian's distraction by mobile IT devices, we define preventive countermeasures in relation to the consequences of the behavior (i.e., injury, or death that might be the result of distracted pedestrians). Thus, these encompass controls that makes it difficult for the individual to engage in such a behavior as well as controls that act on the other sources of risks to reduce the negative consequences that might result from a mobile IT device distraction of a pedestrian. One example of this type of preventive countermeasure is the physical separation between pedestrians and traffic. So, even if individuals are distracted due to mobile multitasking, the risks of them being involved in an accident is reduced since they do not share the same space as vehicles.

When we look at the literature on the countermeasures to pedestrians' safety, we find three main types of countermeasures that prevent and control safety risks. These are also known as the three Es, i.e., Education & awareness, Enforcement, and Engineering [28]. Education type of countermeasures aim to increase the knowledge of road users around one or multiple issues [29]. Enforcement countermeasures are the development and application of regulation in place to deter an undesirable behavior by road users [29]. Engineering countermeasures are the design, construction and alteration of physical systems. These systems include the infrastructure of transportation as well as systems implemented in users' vehicles such as airbags, and driver's assistance [29].

As shown in Table 1, we classify these countermeasures as either preventive or deterrent countermeasures. Following the literature on road safety, we separate deterrent countermeasures into enforcement and education. For the preventive countermeasures, we differentiate between general engineering and design countermeasures and specific engineering and design countermeasures. The general engineering and design countermeasures are controls that were designed without consideration of the problem of Mobile IT distraction and are still effective in reducing the risks associated with this issue as they effect external elements such as the speed of traffic surrounding the pedestrians and the visibility of the pedestrians by drivers. The specific engineering and design countermeasures on the other hand are designed in response to the issue of mobile IT multitasking. Such countermeasures are not exclusive to mobile IT multitasking and could be informed by similar issues in other fields such as inattentional deafness to unexpected salient sounds under attention-demanding conditions (e.g., [30, 31]) and attentional funneling when individuals invest most of their attentional resources to a specific task to the point that they neglect important visual and auditory signals [32]. A growing number of countermeasures to such issues in aeronautics revolve around the user's interface. An example of such countermeasure is the use of part of the screen on which the user is focused to display the signal (i.e., the warning) [32]. The two principles driving these countermeasures are a) *"the subtle modification of information presentation"* that the user is focusing on and *"its replacement by an accurate visual stimulus"* that will change the focus of the user [33].

3   Conceptual Model

After classifying the different countermeasures for mobile IT multitasking, in this section we develop a conceptual framework (Fig. 1) that describes the various links between the

Table 1. Mobile IT multitasking countermeasures

	Countermeasures	Key characteristics	Examples of mechanisms
Preventive	General engineering and design	Controlling for risk factors unrelated to mobile IT multitasking	– Speed limits at signalized and unsignalized intersections [34], – Improving lighting on urban corridors [34], – Standardizing crosswalks at unsignalized intersections [34]
	Specific engineering and design	Targeted to the behavior of mobile IT multitasking	– In-ground flashing lights at level crossings [35], – Vehicle-to-pedestrians alerts using cell phone apps [36, 37]
Deterrent	Regulation and enforcement	Establish sanctions for risky mobile IT multitasking	– Prohibition of distraction including IT mobile devices while crossing rail tracks [18]
	Awareness and education	Have long-term goals, Educate individuals about the risks associated with mobile IT multitasking	– Awareness campaigns highlighting pedestrian facilities in new infrastructures [34] – Education of pedestrians about the dangers of distracted walking [38] – Education programs, especially towards children advising them not to use electronic devices while crossing roads [38] – Visual messages about distracted cell phone use [39]

deterrent and preventive countermeasures and the behavior of mobile multitasking as well as how is translates in the long term in the formation of mobile multitasking habit. These links are reflected in the propositions presented below.

Several researchers [24, 40] consider that deterrence theory can be applied to other types of conduct than crime as "there is no theoretical reason why the notion of deterrence cannot be extended to other types of sanctions and other types of conduct, but the research literature has generally ignored them" [40]. As such, even though mobile IT multitasking is not considered a criminal behavior, we argue that its characteristics make it eligible for an investigation through the lens of deterrence theory. As such, we have developed a deterrence theory-based framework to classify the different countermeasures for the risky behavior of mobile IT multitasking.

Deterrent countermeasures impact the behavior of mobile multitasking because of the certainty and severity of the sanctions that result if individuals engage in such behavior [24]. These sanctions can be formal (i.e., resulting from regulation and policy violations), informal (i.e., of social nature such as the loss of reputation and social censure), or self-imposed such as guilt or embarrassment [22]. Therefore, the higher the perceived certainty and severity of the sanctions of mobile multitasking in a specific context, the less likely individuals will engage in it. In other words, deterrent countermeasures that establish sanctions against risky mobile-multitasking behaviors, such as prohibiting the use of mobile phones in dangerous spaces, increase individuals' perception of the potential sanction which hence reduces the likelihood of their engagement in such behavior.

Another important mechanism by which these countermeasures impact the behavior of individuals can be captured through the lens of protection motivation theory (PMT) [41]. The basic assumption of protection motivation theory is that individuals respond to a fear appeal. According to PMT, appraised severity, expectancy of exposure and efficacy of the response are the main drivers of the adoption of a specific response by individuals. The deterrent countermeasures are designed to positively impact some or all of these three drivers. Awareness and education campaigns, as well as the regulation and enforcement countermeasures, increase the individuals' awareness of the different risks associated with the behaviors of mobile multitasking [38] and aim at showcasing proper and safe behavior regarding mobile-multitasking, e.g., avoiding dangerous spaces where individuals are most vulnerable [34]. Since the source of the threat relating to mobile multitasking is the individual's behavior itself, the efficacy of the response is within the control of the individual.

As mobile-multitasking habit is an automaticity characterized by a rigid contextual cuing of mobile multitasking that does not depend on the individual's goals and intentions. Deterrent countermeasures will affect mobile-multitasking habit through an intentional effort from the individuals to change their behavior. This change in behavior e.g., a pedestrian that intentionally reduces his mobile device usage in risky areas such as crossing, reduces the frequency of behavioral repetition in this specific context [42]. The reduction of the frequency of repetition weakens the habit formation of mobile multitasking [43]. As such we propose:

P1: Deterrent countermeasures will negatively impact the mobile-multitasking habit mediated by the mobile multitasking behavior.

Preventive countermeasures impact the behavior of mobile multitasking because they make it difficult for the users of mobile devices to engage in such a behavior even if the deterrent countermeasures are ineffective or ignored. For example, in-grounds flashing lights at level crossings [35] signal to the individuals that they are in a dangerous zone and provides them with cues that are more easily perceived (as in-grounds flashing lights are in line of sight of a IT mobile device user). Another example can be found in alerts sent to individuals using cell phone apps [36]. These countermeasures make it difficult for individuals to engage in mobile multitasking. They also disrupt the behavior of individuals who are engaged in mobile multitasking.

In the long term, the effect of preventive countermeasures on mobile-multitasking habit is different than that of deterrent countermeasures. Preventive countermeasures alter the context by introducing other cues (e.g., in-ground flashing lights, warnings displayed on the mobile device) that will be associated with a different behavior in that context. Altering the environment is effective in breaking established habits as it discontinues the exposure to habitual cues, thus disrupting the habitual behavior [43, 44]. Preventive countermeasures also act as a reminder for the individuals to perform a different behavior, i.e., paying attention to the individual's surroundings, which is an effective intervention to disrupt the performance of the established habit [43]. Therefore, we propose:

P2: Preventive countermeasures will negatively impact the mobile-multitasking habit mediated by the mobile multitasking behavior.

The distracting effect of Mobile multitasking [4–6] is explained by the attentional switching cost from one task to the other. When individuals share their attentional resources between two tasks, their performance of these tasks decreases when compared to doing only one task [11]. In the case of mobile multitasking, individuals become less attentive and have lower chances of correctly identifying and processing cues from their environment [7]. This, of course, entails several safety risks (e.g., pedestrians engaging in mobile multitasking become less attentive to traffic, which leaves them less time to cross safely and exposes them to collisions). This state of distraction is also reflected in a slower walking speed of the distracted individuals [12].

Preventive countermeasures impact the relationship between mobile multitasking behavior and the state of distraction. Preventive countermeasures including visual and auditory solutions [35] act in a way that alerts individuals to the surrounding risks. Other preventive countermeasures that can be implemented directly into mobile devices,

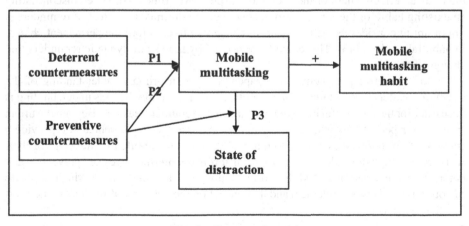

Fig. 1. Conceptual model

(e.g., an application that shows warnings on the user's smartphone) provide cues to reorient the attention of individuals from the mobile devices to important elements in their environment (e.g., traffic in the case of pedestrians). As such we propose that the preventive countermeasures reduce the effect of mobile multitasking behavior on the state of distraction:

P3: Preventive countermeasures negatively moderate the relationship between mobile multitasking behavior and the state of distraction.

4 Conclusion

This study contributes to the literatures on multitasking in IT as well as IT distraction in HCI by providing a better understanding of the impact of different countermeasures on mobile multitasking, as well as their effect on breaking mobile multitasking habit in the long term. We first proposed a classification of the different countermeasures that are geared toward the behavior of mobile multitasking based on how they are designed and the mechanism that drives their impacts. Through this classification we were able to clearly define both preventive and deterrent countermeasures and map these to the different existing countermeasures that are used for distracted pedestrians. We then explain the mechanisms through which the deterrent as well as the preventive countermeasures operate to impact the behavior of mobile multitasking and how these impacts translate in the longer term in the mobile multitasking habit.

While both deterrent and preventive countermeasures negatively impact the behavior of mobile multitasking and ultimately the habit of mobile multitasking, they do so differently. The impact of deterrent countermeasures is salient in formation stage of the habit. On the other hand, preventive countermeasures help breaking an already established mobile multitasking habit. Therefore, they can be seen as complementary when the targeted population is containing individuals with varying degrees of mobile multitasking habit.

When implementing and designing these countermeasures, it is important to consider the reduced effectiveness of their reminder aspect over time [45]. When discontinuing an existing habit, or the formation of a new one, the diminishing effect of reminders is important to consider as the reminder may lose its effect before the permanent change in habit takes place [43]. This could be remedied by the use of dynamic reminders that change over time.

From a practice perspective, this paper provides a primary understanding of the effect of countermeasures for mobile multitasking on individuals. This understanding is necessary for the successful implementation of these countermeasures. Beyond the urban contexts for pedestrians where these countermeasures are implemented, we provide a framework for companies aiming to mitigate the risks of mobile multitasking for their workers. Through the understanding of the different countermeasures i.e., preventive and deterrent countermeasures, and their roles; managers can better select which portfolio of countermeasures to implement and their effect on the behavior of workers in the short and the long term.

References:

1. Pew Research Center. Mobile Fact Sheet (2019)
2. Haga, S., et al.: Effects of using a smart phone on pedestrians' attention and walking. Procedia Manufact. **3**, 2574–2580 (2015)
3. Mourra, G.N., et al.: Using a smartphone while walking: The cost of smartphone-addiction proneness. Addict. Behav. **106**, 106346 (2020)
4. Neider, M.B., et al.: Pedestrians, vehicles, and cell phones. Accid. Anal. Prev. **42**(2), 589–594 (2010)
5. Schwebel, D.C., et al.: Distraction and pedestrian safety: how talking on the phone, texting, and listening to music impact crossing the street. Accid. Anal. Prev. **45**, 266–271 (2012)
6. Stavrinos, D., Byington, K.W., Schwebel, D.C.: Effect of cell phone distraction on pediatric pedestrian injury risk. Pediatrics **123**(2), e179–e185 (2009)
7. Courtemanche, F., et al.: Texting while walking: an expensive switch cost. Accid. Anal. Prev. **127**, 1–8 (2019)
8. Léger, P.-M., et al.: Task switching and visual discrimination in pedestrian mobile multi-tasking: influence of IT mobile task type. In: Davis, F.D., Riedl, R., vom Brocke, J., Léger, P.-M., Randolph, A., Fischer, T. (eds.) Information Systems and Neuroscience. LNISO, vol. 32, pp. 245–251. Springer, Cham (2020). https://doi.org/10.1007/978-3-030-28144-1_27
9. Madden, M., et al.: Teens and technology 2013. Retrieved 1 Dec 2013
10. Thompson, L.L., et al.: Impact of social and technological distraction on pedestrian crossing behaviour: an observational study. Inj. Prev. **19**(4), 232–237 (2013)
11. Levine, L.E., Waite, B.M., Bowman, L.L.: Mobile media use, multitasking and distractibility. Int. J. Cyber Behav. Psychol. Learn. (IJCBPL) **2**(3), 15–29 (2012)
12. Ferraro, F.R., Holte, A.J., Giesen, D.: Does texting make you slower? Curr. Psychol. (2020). https://doi.org/10.1007/s12144-020-00821-1
13. Byington, K.W., Schwebel, D.C.: Effects of mobile Internet use on college student pedestrian injury risk. Accid. Anal. Prev. **51**, 78–83 (2013)
14. Schneider, W., Shiffrin, R.M.: Controlled and automatic human information processing: I. Detection, search, and attention. Psychol. Rev. **84**(1), 1 (1977)
15. Strayer, D.L., Watson, J.M., Drews, F.A.: Cognitive distraction while multitasking in the automobile. In: Psychology of Learning and Motivation, pp. 29–58. Elsevier (2011)
16. Simmons, S.M., et al.: Plight of the distracted pedestrian: a research synthesis and meta-analysis of mobile phone use on crossing behaviour. Inj. Prev. **26**(2), 170–176 (2020)
17. Lichenstein, R., et al.: Headphone use and pedestrian injury and death in the United States: 2004–2011. Inj. Prev. **18**(5), 287–290 (2012)
18. Mwakalonge, J., Siuhi, S., White, J.: Distracted walking: examining the extent to pedestrian safety problems. J. Traffic Transp. Eng. (Engl. Edn.) **2**(5), 327–337 (2015)
19. Beccaria, C.: On Crimes and Punishments and Other Writings. Bobbs-Merrill, Indianapolis (1963).Paolucci, H. (Trans.), Original work published 1764
20. Siponen, M., Vance, A.: Neutralization: new insights into the problem of employee information systems security policy violations. MIS Q. **34**, 487–502 (2010)
21. Willison, R., Warkentin, M.: Beyond deterrence: an expanded view of employee computer abuse. MIS Q. **37**, 1–20 (2013)
22. Paternoster, R., Simpson, S.: Sanction threats and appeals to morality: testing a rational choice model of corporate crime. Law Soc. Rev. **30**, 549–583 (1996)
23. Straub, D.W., Welke, R.J.: Coping with systems risk: security planning models for management decision making. MIS Q. **22**, 441–469 (1998)
24. Williams, K.R., Hawkins, R.: Perceptual research on general deterrence: a critical review. Law Soc. Rev. **20**, 545–572 (1986)

25. D'Arcy, J., Hovav, A., Galletta, D.: User awareness of security countermeasures and its impact on information systems misuse: a deterrence approach. Inf. Syst. Res. **20**(1), 79–98 (2009)
26. Gopal, R.D., Sanders, G.L.: Preventive and deterrent controls for software piracy. J. Manag. Inf. Syst. **13**(4), 29–47 (1997)
27. Morgan, M.J., Ruskell, D.J.: Software piracy—the problems. Ind. Manag. Data Syst. **87**, 8–12 (1987)
28. Zegeer, C.V., Bushell, M.: Pedestrian crash trends and potential countermeasures from around the world. Accid. Anal. Prev. **44**(1), 3–11 (2012)
29. De Winter, J.C., Kovácsová, N.: How science informs engineering, education, and enforcement: a message for driving instructors. In: Handbook of Teen and Novice Drivers (2016)
30. Dehais, F., et al.: Failure to detect critical auditory alerts in the cockpit: evidence for inattentional deafness. Hum. Factors **56**(4), 631–644 (2014)
31. Fenn, K.M., et al.: When less is heard than meets the ear: change deafness in a telephone conversation. Q. J. Exp. Psychol. **64**(7), 1442–1456 (2011)
32. Dehais, F., Causse, M., Tremblay, S.: Mitigation of conflicts with automation: use of cognitive countermeasures. Hum. Factors **53**(5), 448–460 (2011)
33. Dehais, F., Tessier, C., Christophe, L., Reuzeau, F.: The perseveration syndrome in the pilot's activity: guidelines and cognitive countermeasures. In: Palanque, P., Vanderdonckt, J., Winckler, M. (eds.) HESSD 2009. LNCS, vol. 5962, pp. 68–80. Springer, Heidelberg (2010). https://doi.org/10.1007/978-3-642-11750-3_6
34. Haleem, K., Alluri, P., Gan, A.: Analyzing pedestrian crash injury severity at signalized and non-signalized locations. Accid. Anal. Prev. **81**, 14–23 (2015)
35. Larue, G.S., et al.: Pedestrians distracted by their smartphone: are in-ground flashing lights catching their attention? A laboratory study. Accid. Anal. Prev. **134**, 105346 (2020)
36. Liu, Z., et al.: POFS: a novel pedestrian-oriented forewarning system for vulnerable pedestrian safety. In: 2015 International Conference on Connected Vehicles and Expo (ICCVE). IEEE (2015)
37. Rahimian, P., et al.: Using a virtual environment to study the impact of sending traffic alerts to texting pedestrians. In: 2016 IEEE Virtual Reality (VR). IEEE (2016)
38. Arason, N.B., et al.: Countermeasures to Improve Pedestrian Safety in Canada. Canadian Council of Motor Transport Administrators, Ottawa (2013)
39. Barin, E.N., et al.: Heads up, phones down: a pedestrian safety intervention on distracted crosswalk behavior. J. Community Health **43**(4), 810–815 (2018)
40. Meier, R.F., Burkett, S.R., Hickman, C.A.: Sanctions peers, and deviance: preliminary models of a social control process. Sociol. Q. **25**(1), 67–82 (1984)
41. Rogers, R.W.: A protection motivation theory of fear appeals and attitude change1. J. Psychol. **91**(1), 93–114 (1975)
42. Lally, P., et al.: How are habits formed: modelling habit formation in the real world. Eur. J. Soc. Psychol. **40**(6), 998–1009 (2010)
43. Lally, P., Gardner, B.: Promoting habit formation. Health Psychol. Rev. **7**(sup1), S137–S158 (2013)
44. Verplanken, B., et al.: Context change and travel mode choice: combining the habit discontinuity and self-activation hypotheses. J. Environ. Psychol. **28**(2), 121–127 (2008)
45. Tobias, R.: Changing behavior by memory aids: a social psychological model of prospective memory and habit development tested with dynamic field data. Psychol. Rev. **116**(2), 408 (2009)

Automatic Recognition of Experienced Emotional State from Body Movement

Jan-Niklas Voigt-Antons[1,2]([✉]) [iD], Petr Devaikin[1], and Tanja Kojić[1] [iD]

[1] Quality and Usability Lab, Technische Universität Berlin, Berlin, Germany
jan-niklas.voigt-antons@tu-berlin.de
[2] German Research Center for Artificial Intelligence (DFKI), Berlin, Germany

Abstract. Although body movement carries information about a person's emotional state, this modality is not widely used in automatic emotion measurement systems. With this paper, we address the question of the automatic recognition of a person's affective state by analyzing the way a person moves. We present the approach which was used to build a classifier of experienced, non-acted emotions. To collect the data to train and validate the classifier, a controlled laboratory study was conducted. During the study, the music mood induction procedure was used to evoke different emotions in the participants. The participant's movement was recorded using a depth sensor, two accelerometers, and two electromyography sensors. An accuracy of 43% was achieved to recognize four emotion classes, corresponding to four quadrants of the valence-arousal space. For the participants with lower dance or movement proficiency, recognition was more accurate. The same was discovered for the participants with higher comfort levels of moving in front of a camera. The findings show the potential for the automatic analysis of a person's body movements to gather information about an affective state.

Keywords: Automatic emotion recognition · Affective computing · Movement-based interaction · User interfaces · Input devices and strategies · Interaction styles

1 Introduction

Our emotional state and the way we move influence one another [24,33]. From movement dynamics, we can decode the emotional state of a person. This ability was observed in children starting at age five [6]. Along with the voice and facial expression, the whole-body expression is a means to communicate emotions [36].

Information about a user's emotional state can be used in Human-Computer Interaction in order to reduce user frustration or enable communication of user emotions [28], to make interfaces *"more natural, effective, entertaining and healthy"* [21].

Researchers have proposed different computational models and frameworks to sense and analyze full-body movement and recognize users' emotions. However,

© Springer Nature Switzerland AG 2021
M. Kurosu (Ed.): HCII 2021, LNCS 12762, pp. 633–652, 2021.
https://doi.org/10.1007/978-3-030-78462-1_49

the research has been mostly focused on identifying acted emotions when the participants were asked to show a particular emotion with a gesture or perform being in a specific emotional state.

Our research aimed to determine if it is possible to build a computational model that recognizes real, experienced emotions based on movement characteristics. To achieve this goal, we conducted a controlled laboratory study. During the study, we used the Music Mood Induction Procedure (MMIP) to alter the participants' emotional state and measured the participants' movements using three types of sensors, namely Microsoft Kinect One, accelerometers, and Electromyography (EMG) sensors. Subsequently, a self-report technique was applied to measure the emotional response to various music snippets. The data was used to cross-validate a classifier of four classes defined on the valence(pleasure)-arousal space and two levels of valence and arousal separately.

This paper describes the approach we used to build and validate an emotion classifier and report the classifier evaluation results. We defined five questions to answer by interpreting the evaluation results.

1. Is the recognition accuracy higher than a chance level?
2. Does the recognition accuracy differ when just one arm is fitted with sensors, namely accelerometer and EMG-sensor, versus both?
3. Is the recognition accuracy different for the classifiers trained on the data from; different sensors exclusively, all the sensors and only the wearable sensors, i.e., accelerometers, and EMG-sensors.
4. Does the recognition accuracy differ for various selections of participants based on their level of movement or dance proficiency?
5. Does the recognition accuracy differ for various selections of participants based on the level of comfort of moving in front of a camera?

2   Background

Our research is related to three domains, namely (1) automatic movement analysis, (2) emotion recognition, and (3) emotion induction.

2.1   Automatic Movement Analysis

Movements can be described on different levels of abstraction, using different notations. Laban Movement Analysis (LMA), *"a theoretical and experiential system for the observation, description, prescription, performance, and interpretation of human movement"*, is often used for automatic movement analysis and synthesis, including movement segmentation [7], dance expressivity recognition [9] and motion rendering [23].

Each movement has its trajectory and dynamic characteristics. In dance-related fields, movement dynamics are often described using a notion of movement qualities. Movement qualities can be defined as *"the distinctly observable attributes or characteristics produced by dynamics and made manifest in movement"* [5]. In LMA movement dynamics can be conceptualized using four Effort

Motion Factors, namely *Flow, Weight, Time* and *Space*. Each Factor is a continuum with two polarities. For example, the *Weight* Factor has the *Light* and *Strong* polarities.

The use of movement qualities as a modality in Human-Computer Interaction has its advantages over simple trajectory tracking, providing a richer user experience *"favoring explorative and expressive usage"* [1]. Knowing that an affective state can be decoded from movement dynamics [29], analysis of movement qualities can be used for automatic emotion recognition. Camurri et al. [10] proposed a four-layer conceptual framework for automatic movement expressivity analysis, starting from the first level, which corresponds to physical signals measured with a variety of sensors, and ending with the fourth level, which relates to information about nonverbal emotions. The framework was created in order to model an observer of a dance performance and was used in the context of emotion recognition [27].

There are a variety of sensors that allow us to retrieve positioning (coordinates of body parts), dynamic (acceleration of body parts), and physiological (electrical activity of muscles) information about body movement, as was shown in the task of automatic Laban Effort Factor recognition [15], A better recognition rate can be achieved using a combination of multiple sensor data.

2.2 Emotion Recognition

Kleinginna et al. [17] defined emotion as a *"complex set of interactions among subjective and objective factors, mediated by neural-hormonal systems, which can (a) give rise to affective experiences such as feelings of arousal, pleasure/displeasure; (b) generate cognitive processes such as emotionally relevant perceptual effects, appraisals, labeling processes; (c) activate widespread physiological adjustments to the arousing conditions; and (d) lead to behavior that is often, but not always, expressive, goal-directed, and adaptive."*.

Ekman et al. [13], there are seven basic emotions, namely anger, fear, surprise, sadness, disgust, contempt and happiness. As opposed to a categorical approach, Russel [31] proposed using a dimensional model, in which emotions are represented as a linear combination of valence or pleasure-displeasure continuum and arousal. Such emotional states as *"delighted"* and *"happy"* belong to the first quadrant of the valence-arousal space (positive valence, high arousal), *"upset"* – to the second quadrant (negative valence, high arousal), *"depressed"* – to the third (negative valence, low arousal) and *"relaxed"* – to the fourth quadrant (positive valence, high arousal).

Emotions of a person can be measured or automatically recognized from physiological and behavioral reactions or self-report techniques.

One way to measure an emotional response is to ask a person to describe it. Self-Assessment Manikin (SAM) is a non-verbal technique, which utilizes the dimensional model of emotions and measures an effect on three scales, namely valence (pleasure), arousal, and dominance [8]. Each scale is presented by pictograms, making this technique usable regardless of the subject's age and cultural background. One of the disadvantages of the self-report technique, according to

Robinson et al. [30], is that a subject is asked about experienced emotions after the event, meaning that the person could report what they believe to be experienced emotions, rather than what they actually felt.

Another approach to collect information about an affective state of a person is to measure and analyze bio-signals. Changes in heart, respiratory and sweat rates can indicate a change of an emotional state, [14]. Computational models, which recognize emotions from the skin conductance response [25] or heart rate variability [2,18] has been proposed by different researchers. Measuring the electrical activity of the brain could also be used for automatic emotion recognition [19].

Observing a person's behavior, we can also recognize experienced emotions. Researchers presented different emotion classifiers based on analysis of voice intonations [26] and facial expressions [20].

Body posture and movement, being a behavior characteristic, can also be analyzed to recognize emotions. Castellano et al. [11] reached an accuracy of 67.59% in recognizing four emotions: joy, pleasure, anger, and sadness, from recorded movements. Piana et al. [27] achieved recognition of 82% and 68.5% for four (joy, fear, sadness, anger) and six (joy, fear, sadness, anger, disgust, and surprise) emotion classes, respectively. In these two articles, the task for a classifier was to recognize emotions explicitly acted by actors, whereas Bernhardt et al. [4] proposed a model for recognizing emotions from every day, or so-called "non-stylized" movements, such as walking and knocking. A recognition sensitivity, or recall, of 81% was reached. Although the movements were non-stylized, they were acted according to a task describing a particular emotional state.

2.3   Emotion Induction

Music can alter a person's affective state [37] through such mechanisms as Musical Expectancy, Arousal Potential, Mood Contagion, Associations, and Mental Imaginary [16]. The so-called Music Mood Induction Procedure (MMIP) can be used to induce the desired effect with a 75% accuracy [37].

The selection of tracks for MMIP can be based on music databases. Soleymani et al. [35] collected a database of 1000 songs from different genres with corresponding perceived emotion labels. Emotions are presented using two dimensions, valence and arousal. At least ten people performed the annotation of each track during the experiment. Although it is essential to distinguish induced (evoked) from expressed music emotions [16], There is a correlation between them. For example, as shown in [22], happy music "generated more happiness" and sad music created the opposite effect.

3   Building an Emotion Classifier

We built an emotion classifier, which was then cross-validated with the data recorded during the laboratory study.

3.1 Input and Output

The classifier's input is an excerpt of recordings of the participant's skeleton position in the 3D space, acceleration of participant's wrists and EMG-signals measured on biceps, sampled with a frequency 60 Hz. A skeleton should include 13 points, namely *Head*, *Left* and *Right Shoulders*, *Elbows*, *Hands*, *Hips*, *Knees* and *Feet*. Acceleration was represented by the *X*, *Y* and *Z* components for both hands. EMG-signal was represented as a signal envelope. The length of one excerpt can vary.

In the case of recognition of both valence and arousal levels, the output of the classifier is one of four emotion classes. The numbers of classes correspond to the numbers of quadrants on the valence-arousal space. In the case of recognition of only valence or only arousal levels, the output is one of two classes. Class 1 – positive valence or high arousal, Class 2 – negative valence or low arousal.

3.2 Data Processing

The data recording excerpts were filtered. For each fragment, a series of movement features were calculated. The series was used to calculate the input vector for the Support Vector Machine (SVM).

Filtering. The software, which was used to track a skeleton (see the Equipment and Software section), sometimes mistakenly recognized a position of one to a few joints. In case of a mistake, the Z-component of joint coordinates was set to a value close to 0. A threshold filter was applied to exclude samples with wrongly recognized joint coordinates, which replaced all the samples with Z-value less than 1.6 with the preceding sample. The threshold value was chosen as a minimum distance in meters between the Kinect sensor and a participant according to the study setup, which is described in the section Equipment and Software.

After the threshold filter, a Blackman window-based low-pass filter with 10 HZ cut-off frequency was applied to remove the frequencies exceeding the human movement capacities [34]. The same Blackman filter was applied to the signals from the accelerometers and EMG-sensors.

Movement Feature Calculation. For each record excerpt, a set of 28 movement feature series was calculated (see Table 1). The features to be calculated from the Kinect data were selected similar to the ones presented in [27]. For the data from the accelerometers and EMG-sensors, the corresponding smoothness, spectral centroid, and impulsiveness features were calculated for both hands. In addition, the same features were calculated for the body mass center velocity.

The smoothness of a signal was calculated using the metric proposed by Balasubramanian et al. [3]. Fourier transform of a signal was performed using a window size and a shifting step equal to 256 samples (about 4 s) and 15 samples (0.25 s), respectively. The spectral centroid of a signal was calculated according to the definition. The impulsiveness of a signal was calculated as an average magnitude of the Fourier transform of a signal in a frequency range from 2,08 Hz 10 Hz, i.e., between the frequency that corresponds to the beat rate of the music snippets (see the next section) and the maximum frequency of human movement [34].

Table 1. Movement features, calculated from the sensors data.

Sensor	Movement feature
Kinect	Kinetic energy
Kinect	Contraction index, static
Kinect	Contraction index, dynamic
Kinect	Leaning coefficient, static
Kinect	Leaning coefficient, dynamic
Kinect	Posture symmetry
Kinect	Distance between hands
Kinect	Distance between hands and a head
Kinect	Distance between feet
Kinect	Body mass centre velocity smoothness
Kinect	Body mass centre velocity spectral centroid
Kinect	Body mass centre velocity impulsiveness
Accelerometers	Wrist acceleration magnitude
Accelerometers	Wrist acceleration smoothness
Accelerometers	Wrist acceleration spectral centroid
Accelerometers	Wrist acceleration impulsiveness
EMG-sensors	EMG-envelope magnitude
EMG-sensors	EMG-envelope smoothness
EMG-sensors	EMG-envelope spectral centroid
EMG-sensors	EMG-envelope impulsiveness

Movement Feature Representation Following the approach presented in [27], each feature series was used to calculate a "histogram". We tried two methods of choosing the range of values to calculate histograms. First, the range was calculated for the data from all the participants. Second, the range was calculated individually for each participant, i.e., the movement feature values were normalized per participant. The histograms with various numbers of bins (5, 10, 20, and 40), each representing one movement feature, were concatenated into an input vector. Also, we tried to add mean and standard deviation values for each feature.

Thus, to calculate the input vector, the following variables should be defined:

- Whether a histogram is calibrated per participant or not.
- Number of histogram bins (5, 10, 20, 40).
- Whether mean and standard deviation values are included or not.

3.3 Training the Classifier

A Support Vector Machine with the linear kernel was used as a classifier. In order to reduce the length of the input vector, recursive feature elimination was performed [12]. However, in contrast to the standard feature elimination algorithm, the features were excluded not by one but as a group of values that correspond to the same movement feature (histogram bins, mean, and standard deviation values). Accuracy, defined as a number of correctly recognized samples over a total number of samples, was chosen as a scoring measure.

The stratified random split was performed during the feature selection procedure, dividing the data set into two equal parts, the training and testing subsets. To adjust a sample per class distribution of the training set, random oversampling was used. Then the classifier was trained and the recognition accuracy was calculated. The procedure was repeated 50 times. The average accuracy value was chosen as a scoring measure to eliminate the features.

The set of the movement features resulting in the highest accuracy was chosen for the classifier's final training. The eliminated features were not used in the input vector.

4   Evaluation

A controlled laboratory study was conducted to collect the data for classifier cross-validation.

4.1   Participants

Twenty people (eleven male, nine female) were recruited to participate in the study. The age range was 19–37 (M = 28.52, SD = 4.51). The participants were asked to estimate their dance/movement proficiency on a scale from 1 to 5, where 1 – no proficiency, 5 – professional. The reported proficiency level was 2.45 (SD = 1.36). The participants were also asked to estimate how comfortable they feel about dancing or moving in front of a camera on a scale from 1 to 5, where 1 – absolutely uncomfortable, 5 – totally comfortable. The reported comfort level was 3.21 ($SD = 1.18$).

One participant reported some health problems which could affect their movement. Two other participants reported that one of the EMG-sensors disconnected during the recording session. Visual examination of the signal line-charts showed that for one more participant, the EMG sensor was not placed properly and the signal never went lower than a level of 1 V. Therefore, the recordings from these four participants were not used for classifier evaluation.

4.2 Equipment and Software

Two software applications were built to conduct the study. The first for movement recording and automatic playback of the music snippets. The second for the emotion self-report.

The application for movement recording and playback of music snippets was built using the openFrameworks toolkit and ran on a laptop. Two audio speakers were connected to the computer. Participants' movement was captured using Microsoft Kinect One, two accelerometers SparkFun ADXL335 placed on wrists and two EMG sensors MyoWare Muscle Sensor placed on biceps. The accelerometers and EMG-sensors measurements were made using the Arduino Nano module and sent to the computer via Bluetooth (see Fig. 1). A skeleton was tracked using Microsoft Kinect One and the OSCeleton tool [32]. A skeleton position, accelerometers raw data, and EMG envelopes were recorded with a sampling frequency 60 Hz.

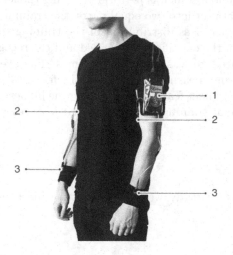

Fig. 1. Placement of the sensors. 1 – Arduino, Bluetooth module and battery, 2 – EMG-sensors, 3 – accelerometers

Sixteen music snippets were played to the participants. Playing order was generated randomly for each participant. The track snippets were overlapped with linear fade-in and fade-out effects in order to make a transition smooth. The delay before the first snippet, the duration of each snippet and the in-between transition could be set up in the application.

To measure the participants' emotional response to the music snippets, a web application was built. It played the music snippets in the same, previously defined order and allowed the participants to report their experienced emotions on the valence and arousal scales from 1 to 9, represented using the SAM-pictograms.

For building a classifier, the scikit-learn library was used.

The experiment setup is shown in Fig. 2.

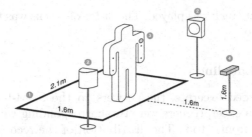

Fig. 2. Experiment setup. 1 – designated dancing area, 2 – speakers, 3 – Arduino with two accelerometers and two EMG sensors connected, 4 – Kinect

4.3   Music Selection

Knowing that evoked emotions could be linked with the emotions expressed by music [22], we decided to use the "Emotion in Music Database" [35] for music selection. The database collects 1000 tracks labeled with corresponding perceived valence and arousal levels. Eight tracks with different combinations of the valence and arousal levels were chosen from that database. In addition, eight tracks were chosen by ourselves in order to increase the chances to cover all the valence-arousal combinations. The tempo of the selected tracks was adjusted to the same value of 125 BPM (beats per minute).

4.4   Study Procedure

At the beginning of the experiment, the participants were asked to read the study introduction and sign the consent form. Subsequently, they completed a questionnaire regarding their age and gender, dance or movement proficiency, the comfort of moving in front of a camera and health issues that could affect movement.

The participants were then asked to stand in the center of the designated dance area (see Fig. 2), facing the Kinect. The sensors were placed on the participant, as it is shown in Fig. 1. The participants were instructed to dance or freely move when the music starts playing. When the participant was ready to start, 16 music snippets were played automatically after a 15 s delay. During the recording session, the participants were left alone in the room.

The length of each snippet, excluding the in-between transition, was 30 s. The track snippets were overlapped with linear fade-in and fade-out effects, making the 1.92 s transition between the tracks. After the playlist ended, the sensors were removed from the participant.

In the final stage of the study, the participants were asked to report the experienced emotions using the software described in the previous section. The software played each music snipped back. The participants were asked to evaluate the emotions evoked by the snipped using two scales, valence and arousal, from 1 (negative valence or low arousal) to 9 (positive valence or high arousal), represented by the SAM-pictograms. When the valence and arousal levels were submitted, the next track was played. The order of tracks was the same as during the recording session.

4.5 Fragment Labeling

To label the recorded excerpts, the answers to the SAM-based questionnaire were used. For each excerpt, there were two corresponding values on the valence and arousal scales from 1 to 9. The distribution of the record excerpts answers of the participants is shown in Fig. 3. The valence-arousal space was divided into four classes by the mean values.

Class 1 – positive valence and high arousal. *Class 2* – negative valence and high arousal. *Class 3* – negative valence and low arousal. *Class 4* – positive valence and low arousal.

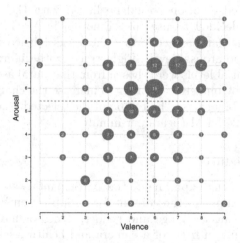

Fig. 3. Distribution of the recording fragments on the valence-arousal space according to the answers to the SAM-based questionnaire.

4.6 Calculation of Performance Metrics

Performance metrics, such as accuracy, precision, recall, and F1 score, were calculated during classifier cross-validation. The procedure was repeated 50 times to check the statistical significance of the obtained results with a Wilcoxon Signed-rank test.

Cross-validation of the classifier was repeated for different approaches of input vector calculation, namely.

– With the different number of histogram bins: 5, 10, 20, or 40.
– Including or excluding mean and standard deviation values.

- With or without normalization of each movement feature values per participant.
- Using the data from all the sensors, from Kinect, accelerometers and EMG-sensors separately or from only the wearable sensors (accelerometers and EMG).
- Using the data from the sensors placed on both hands or only on the left hand.

In addition to the variety of classifier parameters, different participant selection conditions were applied, namely.

- All the participants.
- Participants with the proficiency level higher than the average (*Pro*) and lower than or equal to the average value (*Nonpro*).
- Participants with the comfort level higher than the average (*Comf*) and lower than or equal to the average value (*Uncomf*).

5 Results

5.1 Highest Recognition Accuracy

The highest recognition accuracy of four classes on the valence-arousal space, using the data from all the sensors, was equal to 42.73% (SD = 3.49%). It was reached by using the 10-bin histograms and mean and standard deviation values as an input vector for SVM. Movement feature values were not normalized per participant. The confusion matrix and performance measurements (Accuracy, Precision, Recall and F1 Score) for four classes are shown in Table 2 and Table 3 respectively.

Table 2. Confusion matrix for recognition of four classes on the valence-arousal space for the case of the highest achieved overall accuracy. *Class 1* – positive valence and high arousal. *Class 2* – negative valence and high arousal. *Class 3* – negative valence and low arousal. *Class 4* – positive valence, low arousal.

Actual class	Recognized class			
	Class 1	*Class 2*	*Class 3*	*Class 4*
Class 1	**900**	410	415	325
Class 2	313	**418**	136	83
Class 3	313	108	**668**	261
Class 4	362	209	186	**343**

In the case of recognizing two classes of the valence and arousal levels separately using the data from all the sensors, the accuracy level of 66.20% (SD = 3.30%) and 71.54% (SD = 4.22%) was reached respectively. The movement features were represented by 10-bin histograms, normalized per participant, and mean and standard deviation values in both cases.

Table 3. Performance measurements for recognition of four classes on the valence-arousal space for the case of the highest achieved overall accuracy. *Class 1* – positive valence and high arousal. *Class 2* – negative valence and high arousal. *Class 3* – negative valence and low arousal. *Class 4* – positive valence, low arousal.

	Accuracy	Precision	Recall	F1 Score
Class 1	0.61	0.48	0.44	0.46
Class 2	0.77	0.37	0.44	0.49
Class 3	0.74	0.48	0.50	0.49
Class 4	0.74	0.34	0.31	0.32

5.2   Measuring Signals from One or Both Hands

To achieve the highest recognition accuracy the sensors placed on both hands were used. To check if it is possible to achieve the same accuracy using Kinect and the sensors placed only on a left hand, the classifier was cross-validated with the corresponding input vectors.

The recognition accuracy of four classes on the valence-arousal space for the "one-hand" case was equal to 41.49% ($SD = 3.33\%$). The recognition accuracy of valence was at a level of 66.29% ($SD = 3.71\%$). A Wilcoxon Signed-rank test did not indicate a significant difference between the "one-hand" and "both-hands" cases.

However, a Wilcoxon Signed-rank test indicated a statistically significant decrease in recognition accuracy of arousal from 71.54% (SD = 4.22%) for the "both-hands" case to 70.46% ($SD = 3.16$) in the "one-hand" case, $Z = -6.15$, $p < .05$. For the recognition of valence or valence-arousal levels a significant difference was not indicated.

5.3   Impact of Sensors

To find out how the use of different sensors affects the recognition accuracy, the classifier was cross-validated on the data retrieved from Kinect (case *Kinect*), accelerometers (case *Acc*) and EMG-sensors (case *EMG*) separately. Additionally, the classifier was cross-validated using the data from only the wearable sensors, the accelerometers and EMG-sensors, excluding Kinect (case *Acc+EMG*). The results were compared to ones achieved using all the sensors (case *All*).

A recognition accuracy of four classes on the valence-arousal space dropped from 42.73% ($SD = 3.49\%$) for the *All* case to 38.50% ($SD = 2.68\%$) for the *Kinect* case. A decrease in accuracy was also observed for the *Acc* case ($M = 40.75\%$, $SD = 4.14\%$) and for the *EMG* case (36.44%, $SD = 4.48\%$). A Wilcoxon Signed-rank indicated a significant difference between the cases *All* and *Kinect* ($Z = -5.14$, $p < .05$), *All* and *Acc* ($Z = -2.36$, $p < .05$), *All* and *EMG* ($Z = -5.59$, $p < .05$).

The accuracy for the *Acc+EMG* case was equal to 41.89% ($SD = 3.85\%$). A significant difference between *All* and *Acc+EMG* was not indicated.

The recognition accuracy of four classes on the valence-arousal space for different sets of sensors is shown in Fig. 4.

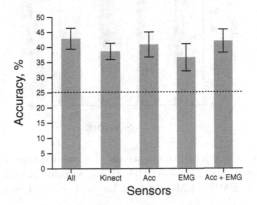

Fig. 4. Recognition accuracy of four classes on the valence-arousal space using different sets of sensors for different sets of sensors. All – all the sensors, Kinect – Microsoft Kinect, Acc – accelerometers, EMG – EMG-sensors. Dashed line – chance level.

In case of the recognition of two classes of valence, the accuracy dropped from 66.20% ($SD = 3.30\%$) for *All* to 58.62% ($SD = 2.60\%$) for the *Kinect* case and to 61.94% ($SD = 4.72\%$) for the *EMG* case. A Wilcoxon Signed-rank test indicated a significant difference between the cases *All* and *Kinect* ($Z = -6.07$, $p < .05$) and *All* and *EMG* ($Z = -4.20$, $p < .05$).

A recognition accuracy for the cases *Acc* and *Acc+EMG* was equal to 66.88% ($SD = 3.10\%$) and 66.20 ($SD = 3.30$) correspondingly. A significant different was not indicated.

For the recognition of two classes of the arousal level, the accuracy dropped from 71.54% ($SD = 4.22\%$) for the *All* case to 63.57% ($SD = 2.55\%$) for *Kinect*, to 69.25% ($SD = 3.16\%$) for *Acc*, to 61.76% ($SD = 4.13\%$) for *EMG* and to 68.61% ($SD = 3.78\%$) for *Acc+EMG*. A significant difference in accuracy was indicated by Wilcoxon Signed-rank test for the pairs *All* and *Kinect* ($Z = -6.15$, $p < .05$), *All* and *Acc* ($Z = -6.65$, $p < .05$), *All* and *EMG* ($Z = -6.16$, $p < .05$), *All* and *Acc+EMG* ($Z = -6.15$, $p < .05$).

The recognition accuracy of two classes of valence and arousal levels separately for different sets of sensors is shown in Fig. 5.

5.4 Proficiency

Cross-validation of the classifier was performed with a different selection of the participants based on their proficiency level according to their answers to the initial questionnaire. The results were also compared to the case when all the participants were selected.

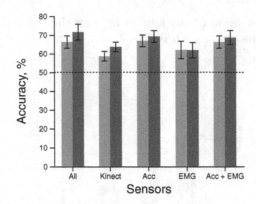

Fig. 5. Recognition accuracy of two classes on the valence (green) and arousal (blue) dimensions for different sets of sensors. All – all the sensors, Kinect – Microsoft Kinect, Acc – accelerometers, EMG – EMG-sensors. Dashed line – chance level. (Color figure online)

The recognition accuracy of four classes on the valence-arousal space for the group of participants whose movement or dance proficiency was higher than the average (*Pro*) was at the level of 44.34% (SD = 6.15%). A Wilcoxon Signed-rank test did not indicate a significant difference with the case when all the participants were selected ($M = 42.73\%$, $SD = 3.49\%$). However, for the participants with the level of movement or dance proficiency lower than or equal to the average (*Nonpro*) a significant increase in accuracy ($M = 48.18\%$, SD = 4.99%) was indicated in comparison to both, *All* ($Z = -4.52, p < .05$) and *Pro* ($Z = -3.35$, $p < .05$) cases.

The recognition accuracy of four classes on the valence-arousal space for different groups of participants, selected based on their proficiency level, is shown in Fig. 6.

In the case of the valence recognition, the participants' selection by their proficiency level increased the accuracy up to 68.87% (SD = 4.94%) for the *Pro* group and to 69.75% (SD = 4.43%) for *Nonpro* group. In comparison, the accuracy for the *All* group was equal to 66.20% ($SD = 3.30\%$). Significance of a difference between the *All* and *Pro* groups ($Z = -2.83, p < .05$), *All* and *Nonpro* groups ($Z = -6.65, p < .05$) was indicated by a Wilcoxon Signed-rank test. The difference between *Pro* and *Nonpro* was not indicated.

The recognition of arousal level was less accurate for the *Pro* group ($M = 70.69\%$, $SD = 5.90\%$) than for the *All* group ($M = 71.54\%$, $SD = 4.22\%$). However, it increased to a level of 73.46% ($SD = 4.23\%$) for the *Nonpro* group. A Wilcoxon Signed-rank test indicated a significant difference between all the groups, *All* and *Pro* ($Z = -6.15, p < .05$), *All* and *Nonpro* ($Z = -6.15, p < .05$), *Pro* and *Nonpro* ($Z = -2.43, p < .05$).

The recognition accuracy of two classes of valence and arousal separately for different groups of participants, selected based on their proficiency level, is shown in Fig. 7.

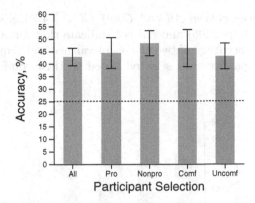

Fig. 6. Recognition accuracy of four classes on the valence-arousal space for different groups of participants, selected based on their proficiency or comfort level. All – all the participants, Pro – participants with dance or movement proficiency higher than the average, Nonpro – with dance or movement proficiency lower than or equal to the average, Comf – participants with the level of comfort of moving in front of a camera higher than the average, Uncomf – with comfort level lower than or equal to the average. Dashed line – chance level.

5.5 Comfort Level

The performance metrics were calculated with the selection of participants, who estimated their level of comfort of moving in front of a camera higher than the average (*Comf*), versus the participants with the level of comfort lower than or equal to the average value (*Uncomf*).

The recognition accuracy of four classes on the valence-arousal space raised from 42.73% (SD = 3.49%) for the *All* group to a level of 46.22% (SD = 7.42%) for the *Comf* group and stayed at a level of 42.92% (SD = 5.15%) for *Uncomf*. A Wilcoxon Signed-rank test indicated a significant difference between *All* and *Comf* ($Z = -2.57$, $p < .05$), *Comf* and *Uncomf* ($Z = -2.63$, $p < .05$) and did not indicate a difference between *All* and *Uncomf*.

The recognition accuracy of four classes on the valence-arousal space for different groups of participants, selected based on their comfort, level is shown in Fig. 6.

The recognition of valence was also more accurate for the *Comf* group ($M = 71.69\%$, $SD = 5.68\%$) than for *All* ($M = 66.20\%$, $SD = 3.30\%$) or *Uncomf* ($M = 66.61\%$, $SD = 4.88\%$). A significant difference was indicated by a Wilcoxon Signed-rank test for the pairs *All* and *Comf* ($Z = -4.47$, $p < .05$), *Comf* and *Uncomf* ($Z = -4.00$, $p < .05$) and was not indicated for *All* and *Uncomf*.

In case of the arousal recognition, an increase in accuracy was also observed for the *Comf* group ($M = 76.43\%$, $SD = 5.29\%$) in comparison to the *All* ($M = 71.54\%$, $SD = 4.22\%$) and the *Uncomf* ($M = 71.39\%$, $SD = 4.10\%$) groups. Similar to the previous cases, a Wilcoxon Signed-rank test indicated a significant difference between *All* and *Comf* ($Z = -4.79$, $p < .05$), *Comf* and *Uncomf* ($Z = -4.40$, $p < .05$) and did not indicate that for *All* and *Uncomf*.

The recognition accuracy of two classes of valence and arousal separately for different groups of participants, selected based on their comfort level, is shown in Fig. 6.

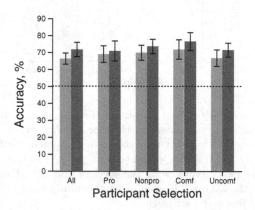

Fig. 7. Recognition accuracy of two classes on the valence (green) and arousal (blue) dimensions for different groups of participants, selected based on their proficiency or comfort level. All – all the participants, Pro – participants with dance or movement proficiency higher than the average, Nonpro – with dance or movement proficiency lower than or equal to the average, Comf – participants with the level of comfort of moving in front of a camera higher than the average, Uncomf – with comfort level lower than or equal to the average. Dashed line – chance level.

6   Discussion

The results of the experiment show that the recognition accuracy of four classes of emotions, defined on the valence-arousal space, is higher (M = 42.73%, SD = 3.49%) than the chance level, which is equal to 25% for four classes. It shows that there are motion cues, which can be measured by various motion sensors in order to detect an emotional state of a person. Therefore, the corresponding computational model could be built.

The recognition of two classes of valence and arousal is also higher than the chance level, which equals to 50% for two classes. The recognition of arousal level (M = 71.54%, SD = 4.22%), is more precise than that of valence (M = 66.20%, SD = 3.30%).

The relatively big deviation of the accuracy can probably be explained by the small size of the training dataset. To get more precise results, a bigger number of recordings could be required.

The average sensitivity (recall) of recognition of four classes (42%), is lower than 50% – the average sensitivity of a computational model using biased features, presented by Bernhardt et al. in their article [4]. It is important to note, that Bernhardt et al., in their work used the recordings of the movements performed by actors playing according to a defined emotional state. In contrast, in our research we attempted to recognize an experienced, non-acted emotional state of a person. It seems reasonable to assume that it is easier to recognize affect from a movement performed to communicate a specific emotion wittingly.

The precision and recall values of recognition of *Class 4* ("positive valence and low arousal") are much lower than those for the other Classes. It means that the classifier is more sensitive to such emotional states as, for example, delight, boredom and anger as opposed to calmness.

In our experiment, we used the sensors placed on both hands. When the data from only a left hand was used, recognition accuracy of arousal level slightly dropped by 1.08%. As for the recognition of valence or both, valence and arousal, using the data from one or both hands, there was no significant difference indicated. It shows that the cost of the device could be reduced by using only one accelerometer and one EMG sensor, which is important for practical applications.

A better recognition rate of emotions was achieved using multiple sensors versus one type of sensor. The same conclusion, but in the context of Laban Effort Factors recognition, was made by Alaoui et al. in their article [15]. An exception in our study was the recognition of valence, when the results achieved using all the sensors, only the accelerometers and only the wearable sensors, were not significantly different.

Assuming that in some situations, the use of Kinect is not possible, the classifier was cross-validated using the data retrieved only with wearable devices (accelerometers and EMG-sensors). The recognition accuracy of arousal dropped by 2.93% in comparison to the case of use of all the sensors. However, in the case of the valence or valence-arousal recognition, the difference was not statistically significant.

The study shows that the recognition accuracy varies for the participants with the different dance proficiency and comfort of moving in front of a camera levels. The recognition of the emotional state (valence, arousal or valence-arousal) of persons with a low proficiency level was more accurate. A similar increase of accuracy was observed for the group of participants with a high comfort level.

7 Conclusion and Prospective

In this article we presented the approach which we used to build and validate a classifier of the emotional state of a person from the way a person moves. The results of classifier cross-validation show that it is possible to automatically gather information about the emotional state of a person by measuring his or her body movement characteristics. The research also revealed how various selections of participants, based on their proficiency and comfort level, and the use of different sensors influenced the recognition accuracy.

The highest recognition rate was achieved using the data from all the sensors, namely Microsoft Kinect, accelerometers placed on wrists and EMG-sensors placed on biceps. The accuracy of arousal recognition was higher than that for the valence level. A noticeable increase in accuracy was observed for a selection of the participants with a low proficiency level. An emotional state was also recognized more accurately for the participants who felt more comfortable moving in front of a camera.

The novelty of this work is in the attempt to recognize a real emotional state, whereas the previous work has been mostly focused on the recognition of acted emotions. To evoke various emotions, the Music Mood Induction Procedure was applied.

The conclusions drawn in our research are preliminary. Using a larger amount of data to train and validate a classifier could give more precise results. Further investigation could also be focused on building a real-time classifier of emotions. The use of a classifier of emotional state derived from movement dynamics in combination with other approaches, for example, facial expression recognition, is also a topic to be explored.

Acknowledgement. We are grateful for Martin Burghart and Sonia Sobol's help to finalize the manuscript.

References

1. Alaoui, S.F., Caramiaux, B., Serrano, M., Bevilacqua, F.: Movement qualities as interaction modality. In: Proceedings of the Designing Interactive Systems Conference, pp. 761–769. ACM (2012)
2. Appelhans, B.M., Luecken, L.J.: Heart rate variability as an index of regulated emotional responding. Rev. Gen. Psychol. **10**(3), 229 (2006)
3. Balasubramanian, S., Melendez-Calderon, A., Burdet, E.: A robust and sensitive metric for quantifying movement smoothness. IEEE Trans. Biomed. Eng. **59**(8), 2126–2136 (2012)
4. Bernhardt, D., Robinson, P.: Detecting emotions from everyday body movements. Presenccia PhD Sym., Barcelona (2007)
5. Blom, L.A., Chaplin, L.T.: The Intimate act of Choreography. University of Pittsburgh Pre (1982)
6. Boone, R.T., Cunningham, J.G.: Children's decoding of emotion in expressive body movement: the development of cue attunement. Dev. Psychol. **34**(5), 1007 (1998)
7. Bouchard, D., Badler, N.: Semantic segmentation of motion capture using Laban movement analysis. In: Pelachaud, C., Martin, J.-C., André, E., Chollet, G., Karpouzis, K., Pelé, D. (eds.) IVA 2007. LNCS (LNAI), vol. 4722, pp. 37–44. Springer, Heidelberg (2007). https://doi.org/10.1007/978-3-540-74997-4_4
8. Bradley, M.M., Lang, P.J.: Measuring emotion: the self-assessment manikin and the semantic differential. J. Behav. Ther. Exp. Psychiatry **25**(1), 49–59 (1994)
9. Camurri, A., Lagerlöf, I., Volpe, G.: Recognizing emotion from dance movement: comparison of spectator recognition and automated techniques. Int. J. Hum. Comput. Stud. **59**(1), 213–225 (2003)

10. Camurri, A., et al.: The dancer in the eye: towards a multi-layered computational framework of qualities in movement. In: Proceedings of the 3rd International Symposium on Movement and Computing, p. 6. ACM (2016)

11. Castellano, G., Villalba, S.D., Camurri, A.: Recognising human emotions from body movement and gesture dynamics. In: Paiva, A.C.R., Prada, R., Picard, R.W. (eds.) ACII 2007. LNCS, vol. 4738, pp. 71–82. Springer, Heidelberg (2007). https://doi.org/10.1007/978-3-540-74889-2_7

12. Chandrashekar, G., Sahin, F.: A survey on feature selection methods. Comput. Electr. Eng. **40**(1), 16–28 (2014)

13. Ekman, P., Cordaro, D.: What is meant by calling emotions basic. Emot. Rev. **3**(4), 364–370 (2011)

14. Ekman, P., Levenson, R.W., Friesen, W.V.: Autonomic nervous system activity distinguishes among emotions. American Association for the Advancement of Science (1983)

15. Fdili Alaoui, S., Françoise, J., Schiphorst, T., Studd, K., Bevilacqua, F.: Seeing, sensing and recognizing Laban movement qualities. In: Proceedings of the 2017 CHI Conference on Human Factors in Computing Systems, pp. 4009–4020. ACM (2017)

16. Juslin, P.N., Laukka, P.: Expression, perception, and induction of musical emotions: a review and a questionnaire study of everyday listening. J. New Music Res. **33**(3), 217–238 (2004)

17. Kleinginna, P.R., Kleinginna, A.M.: A categorized list of emotion definitions, with suggestions for a consensual definition. Motiv. Emot. **5**(4), 345–379 (1981)

18. Lane, R.D., McRae, K., Reiman, E.M., Chen, K., Ahern, G.L., Thayer, J.F.: Neural correlates of heart rate variability during emotion. Neuroimage **44**(1), 213–222 (2009)

19. Li, M., Chai, Q., Kaixiang, T., Wahab, A., Abut, H.: EEG emotion recognition system. In: Takeda, K., Erdogan, H., Hansen, J.H.L., Abut, H. (eds.) In-Vehicle Corpus and Signal Processing for Driver Behavior, pp. 125–135. Springer, Boston (2009). https://doi.org/10.1007/978-0-387-79582-9_10

20. Lien, J.J., Kanade, T., Cohn, J.F., Li, C.C.: Automated facial expression recognition based on FACS action units. In: Proceedings of the Third IEEE International Conference on Automatic Face and Gesture Recognition, pp. 390–395. IEEE (1998)

21. Lisetti, C.: Affective computing (1998)

22. Lundqvist, L.O., Carlsson, F., Hilmersson, P., Juslin, P.N.: Emotional responses to music: experience, expression, and physiology. Psychol. Music **37**(1), 61–90 (2009)

23. Masuda, M., Kato, S.: Motion rendering system for emotion expression of human form robots based on Laban movement analysis. In: 2010 IEEE RO-MAN, pp. 324–329. IEEE (2010)

24. Mogenson, G.J., Jones, D.L., Yim, C.Y.: From motivation to action: functional interface between the limbic system and the motor system. Prog. Neurobiol. **14**(2), 69–97 (1980)

25. Nakasone, A., Prendinger, H., Ishizuka, M.: Emotion recognition from electromyography and skin conductance. In: Proceedings of the 5th International Workshop on Biosignal Interpretation, pp. 219–222 (2005)

26. Nwe, T.L., Foo, S.W., De Silva, L.C.: Speech emotion recognition using Hidden Markov Models. Speech Commun. **41**(4), 603–623 (2003)

27. Piana, S., Staglianò, A., Odone, F., Camurri, A.: Adaptive body gesture representation for automatic emotion recognition. ACM Trans. Interact. Intell. Syst. (TiiS) **6**(1), 6 (2016)

28. Picard, R.W.: Affective computing for HCI. In: HCI (1), pp. 829–833 (1999)
29. Pollick, F.E., Paterson, H.M., Bruderlin, A., Sanford, A.J.: Perceiving affect from arm movement. Cognition **82**(2), B51–B61 (2001)
30. Robinson, M.D., Clore, G.L.: Belief and feeling: evidence for an accessibility model of emotional self-report. Psychol. Bull. **128**(6), 934 (2002)
31. Russell, J.A.: A circumplex model of affect. J. Pers. Soc. Psychol. **39**(6), 1161 (1980)
32. Serra, T.: Osceleton vol 1.2.1 [software], July 2011. https://github.com/ Sensebloom/OSCeleton
33. Sheets-Johnstone, M.: Emotion and movement. A beginning empirical-phenomenological analysis of their relationship. J. Conscious. Stud. **6**(11–12), 259–277 (1999)
34. Sinclair, J., Taylor, P.J., Hobbs, S.J.: Digital filtering of three-dimensional lower extremity kinematics: an assessment. J. Hum. Kinet. **39**(1), 25–36 (2013)
35. Soleymani, M., Caro, M.N., Schmidt, E.M., Sha, C.Y., Yang, Y.H.: 1000 songs for emotional analysis of music. In: Proceedings of the 2nd ACM International Workshop on Crowdsourcing for Multimedia, pp. 1–6. ACM (2013)
36. Van den Stock, J., Righart, R., De Gelder, B.: Body expressions influence recognition of emotions in the face and voice. Emotion **7**(3), 487 (2007)
37. Västfjäll, D.: Emotion induction through music: a review of the musical mood induction procedure. Musicae Scientiae **5**(1_Suppl.), 173–211 (2001)

Author Index